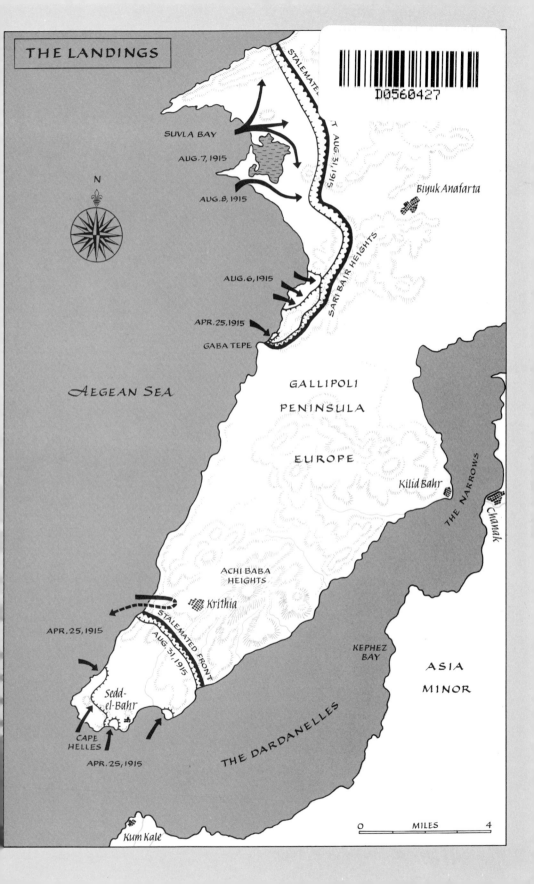

THE LANDINGS

SUVLA BAY

AUG. 7, 1915

N

AUG. 8, 1915

STALEMATEO

AUG. 31, 1915

Biyuk Anafarta

SARI BAIR HEIGHTS

AUG. 6, 1915

APR. 25, 1915

GABA TEPE

AEGEAN SEA

GALLIPOLI

PENINSULA

EUROPE

Kilid Bahr

THE NARROWS

Chanak

ACHI BABA
HEIGHTS

Krithia

STALEMATED FRONT

APR. 25, 1915

AUG. 31, 1915

KEPHEZ
BAY

ASIA

MINOR

Sedd-
el-Bahr

CAPE
HELLES

APR. 25, 1915

THE DARDANELLES

Kum Kale

0   MILES   4

CHURCHILL

Young Man in a Hurry
1874–1915

TED MORGAN

SIMON AND SCHUSTER
New York

DESIGNED BY EVE METZ

MANUFACTURED IN THE UNITED STATES OF AMERICA

1 3 5 7 9 10 8 6 4 2

LIBRARY OF CONGRESS CATALOGING IN PUBLICATION DATA
MORGAN, TED, [DATE]
CHURCHILL: THE RISE TO FAILURE, 1874–1915.
INCLUDES BIBLIOGRAPHICAL REFERENCES AND INDEX.
1. CHURCHILL, WINSTON, SIR, 1874–1965.   2. GREAT
BRITAIN—POLITICS AND GOVERNMENT—1901–1936.   3. PRIME
MINISTERS—GREAT BRITAIN—BIOGRAPHY.   I. TITLE.
DA566.9.C5M675   941.082′092′4 [B]   81–23331
ISBN 0–671–25303–4   AACR2

Acknowledgments

The principal source for all books on Churchill is the official biography. This multivolume work, which in its present state goes up to the start of World War II, September 1939, was begun by Randolph Churchill, who had access to the Churchill papers in the Chartwell Trust, and the first volume was published in 1966. Since then, the official biography has grown to five volumes totaling 4,494 pages for the biography proper, and twelve volumes totaling 10,207 pages for the companion volumes, a collection of documents relating to Churchill's life. These documents volumes constitute the most exhaustive data bank ever compiled about a single human being. They contain not only nearly every letter Churchill wrote from the age of seven on, but the correspondence of every other important figure in his life. They include Churchill's school report cards, bills from his wine merchant, the terms of a loan arranged by his mother, the size of his chest when he was measured for a uniform at Sandhurst, and every other conceivable scrap of information that was committed to paper. They also include much of the official correspondence in the various Cabinet posts that Churchill occupied, the minutes of War Council meetings, and the correspondence of other Cabinet ministers. They are the bricks of any Churchill biography.

Randolph Churchill died in June 1968, after having completed the first two volumes, which took Churchill up to the age of forty. The work was carried on by Martin Gilbert, a young historian who was then a Fellow at Merton College, Oxford, and who had been involved in the project as a researcher for just over five years.

When Martin Gilbert took over, the official biography improved in two ways. First, he opted for chronological order in the companion volumes, which Randolph Churchill had preferred to arrange by topic. Second, he departed from Randolph Churchill's stated theme of "he shall be his own biographer," which all too often meant that in the biography volumes, long extracts were printed from the documents volumes (or other documents not to be found in the documents volumes) with sparse connective tissue. Rather than proceed with this "cut and paste" method, Martin Gilbert brought to the great undertaking his historian's gift of narrative skill, a sense of period, and a depth of analysis derived from unequaled knowledge.

In addition to the material in the official biography, the present work is the result of research in every available collection of papers that could throw light upon Churchill between his birth and 1915. For their help, I would like to thank the librarians at the Bodleian Library and Nuffield College Library in Oxford, at the British Library, and at the House of Lords Record Office; thanks to Mr. A. E. B. Owen, Senior Under Librarian, Cambridge University Library, and to Mr. Rod Phillips of the New York Public Library; particular thanks to Marion M. Stewart, archivist at the Churchill College Library, Cambridge, which has collected one of the richest single Churchill archives.

For permission to quote, thanks to Lord Fisher (Fisher papers), Mr. David McKenna (McKenna papers), Lord Hankey (Hankey papers), Mr. M. R. Bonham Carter (Asquith papers), Walters Fladgate, solicitors (Churchill letters not in Chartwell Trust), the Warden and Scholars of New College, Oxford (Milner papers), and Lord Esher (Esher papers).

Thanks to William Heinemann and Houghton Mifflin for permission to quote from the official biography and companion volumes by Randolph S. Churchill and Martin Gilbert, to Her Majesty's Stationery Office for permission to quote from Hansard, to St. Martin's Press for permission to quote from Elgin and Churchill at the Colonial Office by Ronald Hyam, to Cassell, Ltd., for permission to quote from Journalism and Politics by J. A. Spender and Politics from the Inside by Austen Chamberlain, to Hutchinson for permission to quote from the Memoirs of Almeric Fitzroy and Tempestuous Journey by Frank Owen, to Harcourt Brace Jovanovich for permission to quote from Winston Churchill, an Intimate Portrait by Violet Bonham Carter, to Eyre Methuen for permission to quote from My Early Life by Winston S. Churchill, and to Longmans for permission to quote from Edward Marsh—Patron of the Arts by Christopher Hassell.

In addition, I would like to thank Cameron Hazlehurst and Christine Woodland for compiling their useful work A Guide to the Papers of British Cabinet Ministers 1900–1951 (London, 1974); Sir John Colville, who served as Churchill's secretary, for his interesting appraisal of his former employer; Trumbull Higgins, the distinguished military historian, for his helpful advice on the 1914–1915 period; my researchers, Mary Donald and Jacqueline

ACKNOWLEDGMENTS

Williams; my copy editor, Patricia Miller, sharp-eyed and indefatigable, who saved me from many traps and precipices; and my editors, Nan Talese, whose sound advice was crucial to the early chapters, Tom Wallace, who shepherded the manuscript into its present form, and Michael Korda, who saw it through the final stages.

THIS BOOK IS DEDICATED TO
GABRIEL MORGAN

Contents

CHURCHILL

Young Man in a Hurry
1874–1915

I

CHILDHOOD

SPANKED INTO LIFE like the rest of us, Winston Leonard Spencer-Churchill was born on Monday, November 30, 1874, in Blenheim Palace. That vast dwelling, three hundred rooms that gave off the unventilated aroma of stored history, had been built by his ancestor John Churchill, the 1st Duke of Marlborough, and named after a Bavarian town where in 1704 he had routed the Sun King's armies. Its present occupants were the seventh Duke and Duchess, Winston's grandparents.

His parents, twenty-year-old Jennie and twenty-five-year-old Randolph, wed that April, had come to Blenheim for the hunting. An outstanding horsewoman, Jennie was determined not to let childbearing interfere with her activities—in any case, she was only a little more than seven months pregnant. She fell while walking with a party of shooters, and a rough ride back to the palace in a pony-drawn carriage brought the pains on Saturday night.[1]

Jennie continued in labor all through Sunday, refusing the relief of chloroform as she lay heaving in the brass bed in the small ground-floor room where she had been carried after her fall. Blenheim was only eight miles from Oxford, but their Oxford physician would not come on a Sunday.[2] Randolph wired Jennie's London obstetrician, William Hope, but there were no trains on Sunday evening. At 6 P.M. the pains began in earnest, and it was clear that the event would not be long delayed. Randolph had to settle for a local country doctor, Frederic Taylor, the coroner for the adjacent village of Woodstock. At one-thirty on Monday morning, he delivered Jennie of a male child, wonderfully pretty, with dark eyes and hair, small though healthy, considering his early arrival. Dr. Taylor was paid twenty-five guineas, and by the time Jennie's London doctor showed up at nine that morning, mumbling apologies, the baby was washed and dressed.[3]

Winston had arrived upon this earth so unexpectedly that cradle and baby linen were not at hand. The Churchills borrowed what they needed from the Woodstock solicitor's helpful wife, Elizabeth Ann Brown, who was herself expecting.[4] It was immediately arranged that a wet nurse and a nurse would come to Blenheim. Women of the upper classes did not in those days nurse their children, for nursing interfered with their social life. Women of lesser means, whose own children were often stillborn, could always be found to feed the offspring of the well-to-do. Social reformers disapproved of wet-nursing: how could a rich mother not feel some compunction in purchasing for her own child what was taken from another mother? But the practice was widespread, and thus it was that the infant son of an English aristocrat and an American heiress, who might have preferred to nurse her son herself, was suckled at the breast of an anonymous commoner.

On December 3, Jennie was still in bed, doing well, her milk subsiding. Randolph, the proud and attentive father, was pleased to see that all the little troubles with her milk were disappearing.[5] Soon she could go for a carriage ride. The birth in Blenheim had been a blessing, it was so much nicer for her there than in London. Telegrams of congratulation had begun to arrive, but Randolph was irritated that the one he had sent to Jennie's father had not been answered. It was so unsatisfactory when important news went unappreciated.[6] After all, Leonard Jerome *was* the boy's godfather and namesake, as well as his grandfather.

Jerome was a stockbroker who had come to Wall Street when it was still the unregulated Eden of quick fortunes. It would later be said that Winston, by temperament, was far closer to his adventurous American grandfather than to his English one, the priggish Marlborough duke. Leonard Jerome married Clara Hall, a cultivated woman who had some Iroquois blood, her great-grandmother on her mother's side having been an Indian maiden named Meribah.[7] This Indian heritage, so pronounced in Clara that she became known as "Sitting Bull," did not show up in Winston, whose complexion ranged from fair to rubicund.

Clara gave her husband four daughters, one of whom died at the age of seven. Jennie, the second, was born in Brooklyn in 1854, but the family moved in 1859 to fashionable Madison Square, at a time when most of Manhattan was farmland. Growing up the daughter of a millionaire sportsman, Jennie's life was made up of piano lessons, matinees at the Opera, summers at Newport, and visits to the race track with her father, a noted improver of the breed and an admirer of lady singers, who told her that "the greatest sin for a woman is to sing a false note or jerk a good horse in the mouth."[8] When she was eleven, Lincoln was assassinated, and the house in Madison Square was draped in black.

On the other side of the Atlantic, sixteen-year-old Randolph Churchill was at Eton, following family custom. The second son of the 7th Duke of Marlborough distinguished himself neither in games nor in studies. His Eton contemporary Lord Rosebery, who would one day become Prime Minister, called Randolph a "scug."[9] In a narrow sense, a scug was someone who did not get his "colors," that is, who did not qualify for any athletic team. In a larger sense, being a scug meant that you had mismanaged your years at Eton. Only imbecility or hereditary degeneracy, it was said only half in jest, could account for the natural viciousness of a scug.

Failing in his first attempt to get into Oxford, Randolph had to be privately tutored. Still unruly, he was fined for smoking in his cap and gown (he confessed that he smoked cigarettes "until his tongue hurt"), and on one occasion he was arrested and fined ten shillings for assaulting a policeman after a drunken brawl in Oxford's famous Randolph Hotel, during which he broke some of the hotel's windows. One of the waiters, who testified that Randolph had threatened him with a wine-cooler, later lost his job—because, it was said, of pressure from Randolph. After a time, he decided to work seriously for his degree in history and law, and narrowly missed a first. He did well in the *viva voce*, but poorly in constitutional law.[10]

Aside from having four daughters, Leonard Jerome sired several illegitimate children, and was so flagrantly unfaithful that in 1867, when Jennie was thirteen, Clara took her and her two sisters to live in France, giving Leonard visiting rights. A woman of determined social aims, Clara took it for granted that she would join the elite of any country where she chose to alight, and was duly introduced to the court of Napoleon III and Empress Eugénie. Jennie became fluent in French, flirted with counts and barons, and was invited to the Emperor's court, walking between the Cent-Gardes up the grand staircase of the Tuileries palace in her first low-cut gown.[11]

But the pleasures of the Second Empire were short-lived, for in 1870 Prussia invaded France, and Clara took her three girls to England, with the Parisians' cries still ringing in her ears: *"Tout est perdu—les Prussiens sont à nos portes* (All is lost—the Prussians are at our gates)." The arrival in

England was a sad time for Jennie, with her friends dispersed or fighting at the front.[12]

By the time Randolph left Oxford for the mandatory Grand Tour, he was a slim and self-possessed young man with bulging eyes (his nickname at Eton was "Gooseberry"), a mustache, and a harsh, jaylike laugh.[13] He never forgot that he was the son of a duke: his manner was easily contemptuous and often insulting. He was, in the phrase of the day, an inequalitarian, a six-syllable word for snob.

But there was another side to Randolph, a romantic and impressionable side, which he would demonstrate shortly after the end of his Grand Tour, in August 1873. When the London season ended in July, the season began at Cowes, a tiny village on the Isle of Wight, where the Royal Yacht Squadron had its headquarters. Cowes was the Prince of Wales's favorite summer spot, and everyone who counted followed in his wake to watch the regattas, take picnics to Shanklin Bay, and attend the balls. On August 12 the officers of the cruiser *Ariadne*, on duty at Cowes as a guard ship, gave a ball in honor of the visiting Czarevitch and his wife.[14]

As sleek yachts skimmed over the water, their great sails cutting and tacking, officers in starched uniforms helped the guests aboard the *Ariadne*, and beautiful bare-shouldered women waltzed to the music of the Marine Band. Among the dancers was nineteen-year-old Jennie Jerome, whose mother was firmly entrenched as a member of society in London and Cowes.

It was in this operetta setting, elegantly nautical, that Randolph was introduced to Jennie, whom he found so beautiful that he was at first struck dumb. Jennie would always remember the night at Cowes, with the lights of the *Ariadne* glimmering on the water, the immediateness of the attraction, and the certainty that this was the man with whom she would spend her life. Randolph found ways to see her again. "I keep turning up like a bad shilling," he wrote her, unwilling to be associated, even in a colloquialism, with the common penny.[15] On the third night after they met, he proposed.

Anglo-American marriages were rare in those days—as experimental as mating with Martians, one of Jennie's nephews said. The English regarded American women as somewhere between a Red Indian and a Gaiety Girl. The highest compliment for good behavior, which Jennie would hear often, was: "I should never have thought *you* were an American."[16]

What sort of family were the Jeromes? the Duke snorted when he heard of his son's marital plans. This Leonard Jerome was a vulgar man, the sort of sporting type who drove six or eight horses in New York. He was a Wall Street stockbroker, and everyone knew the kind they were; one had only to look at that financial buccaneer James Fisk, murdered by a business associate.[17] And now the daughter of this interloper presumed to marry into one of the great English ducal families, a family founded by the greatest general England had known, John Churchill, who had fought ten campaigns as captain general of Queen Anne's armies in the War of the Spanish Succession. What did it matter that he had made a fortune in kickbacks from contractors and prolonged the war for his own advantage? Four times he defeated the armies of Louis XIV, at Blenheim in 1704, at Ramillies in 1706, at Oudenarde in 1708, at Malplaquet in 1709. His power, his dukedom, his wealth, the great heap of Taynton stone unfinished at his death in 1722, were the fruit of those four victories.

Simply by lasting and holding on to its estates, a family like the Churchills contributed in ways recurrent and unforeseen to the destiny of the nation. Not that a ducal title and a palace were a guarantee of greatness in each generation. Sometimes it seemed quite the reverse—a succession of dabblers and caretakers without drive or ambition, combining a sense of superiority with a hobbyist approach to life, certain that their dues were paid by attending Eton and Oxford, marrying lady this or lady that, and producing a son.

John Churchill produced a son who died and four daughters, and the title reverted first to the oldest, Henrietta, and then to the next in line, Anne, who had married a Spencer. For nearly a century, the Dukes of Marlborough were Spencers. The fifth Duke, George, retrieved the Churchill when he succeeded in 1817, two years after Waterloo, with military glory back in fashion. But the illustrious name was resumed at a low point in the family fortunes. George was so debt-ridden that he could barely pay his sons' tuition at Eton. To make ends meet, he rented the hunting and fishing at Blenheim at so much an hour, and melted and sold the gold plate the Elector of Bavaria had given the first Duke, substituting ormolu to deceive the trustees. He was about to cut down and sell the trees in the park when a Court of Chancery ruling intervened.[18]

Winston's grandfather, John Winston Spencer-Churchill, who became seventh Duke in 1857, was impoverished by the extravagance of his predecessors. In ducal terms, impoverishment meant that he had an annual income from his lands of forty thousand pounds a year, barely enough to keep the roof fixed, the rooms dusted, the Meissen cleaned, the silver polished, and the hedges pruned. All of the family income went toward the maintenance of this vast estate. John Winston was compelled to sell the famous Marlborough gems and the prestigious Sunderland Library. With each generation, Blenheim was emptied of more treasures.[19]

Active in politics, John Winston reached Cabinet rank as Lord President of the Council in the third Derby government. His wife, Frances, a daughter of the Marquess of Londonderry, had six daughters and five sons, but only two of the sons survived, of whom Randolph was the younger. Had the accident of birth made Randolph the elder, he and Winston would have succeeded to the ducal title. Trapped in the House of Lords, Winston would subsequently have been kept from the highest office. As a son of the second son, he was freed from the care of Blenheim, and able to stand for the House of Commons.

This then was the family these upstart Americans boldly sought to join, a family linked to great events in British history (even though there had been no Churchill of national importance since the death of the first Duke in 1722), a family landed and prestigious, connected by marriage to the proudest names in England, the Trevors, the Bedfords, the Galloways, the Londonderrys, the Abercorns. An American connection would be a dreadful break in the Churchill tradition.

On August 31, the alarmed Duke wrote Randolph that his feelings were uncontrolled, his proceedings were unwise, and his judgment was paralyzed. Truly love was blind, for he was blind to the troubles he was heaping on his parents. The Duke was making inquiries about the Jeromes, and in the meantime, whatever the young lady's attractions, no man in his senses could call the connection respectable.[20]

Randolph's brother, Lord Blandford, also wrote, not because he disapproved of Jennie, but to warn Randolph against marrying at all. Blandford was unhappily wed to the Duke of Abercorn's daughter, a brisk woman who liked practical jokes of the inkpot-over-the-door variety. Marriage was a delusion and a snare, he said, and worse than other snares in that it was irrevocable.[21]

There was not at first an overwhelming enthusiasm for the match on the Jerome side either. As an owner and breeder of horses, Leonard Jerome did not think much of the overbred English aristocracy. His sleek and sound Jennie was much too good for the thin-blooded and supercilious son of a Marlborough duke. He was piqued that while Randolph waited to consult his snobbish parents, his own acceptance was taken for granted. He knew that Jennie was a deep one, not meant to love lightly, and that if she married the wrong man she would suffer untold misery. But he would not object to anyone she chose of whom her mother approved, as long as he was not a Frenchman or any other of those "Continental cusses."[22]

Jennie wrote her father that Randolph was young, ambitious, and uncorrupted, and that, best of all, he loved her. Mr. Jerome pronounced himself "delighted," and promised to give her two thousand pounds a year. It would take "heaps of love" to overcome the British prejudice against " 'those horrid Americans.' "[23]

Randolph approached the problem of his parents' opposition as a strategist. "I can plot and intrigue like a second Machiavelli," he told Jennie.[24] The first thing he did was enlist the help of the Prince of Wales. The Prince was a friend, one who admired female beauty and understood the reasons of the heart. The Prince's secretary, Sir Francis Knollys, was a close friend, and would be Randolph's best man. The Prince wrote Lord Blandford, approving of the marriage, and sent a copy of the letter to Randolph, who informed his parents of its contents. The Prince was sure that his letter had done the trick. Many years later, when he was King Edward VII and Winston Churchill was a member of the Asquith government, he told his confidant Viscount Esher: "If it had not been for me, that young man would not have been in existence." "How is that, sir?" asked Esher, much startled. "The Duke and Duchess both objected to Randolph's marriage," Edward explained. "It was owing to us that they gave way."[25]

In case royal support was not enough, Randolph had another strategy. Lord Blandford, five years Randolph's senior, was a disappointment to his parents. He had been expelled from Eton, was erratic and willful, and treated his wife badly. The Duke and Duchess had their hopes set on Randolph, expecting him to run for the tiny constituency of Woodstock, a Blenheim fiefdom whose voters were kept loyal with cash gifts. Randolph confided to Jennie that he was quite prepared to blackmail his father by refusing to stand for Woodstock, or, what would be even more Machiavellian and deep, to stand but at the last moment to withdraw, leaving the Liberal candidate to win the seat.[26] That a Liberal should stand for Woodstock, which had for more than a century returned to Parliament Churchills with more acres than brains, was more than his father could bear. Randolph held him in his power, and would not hesitate to thwart his own political career at the outset and deal a cruel blow to his father if his marriage plans were obstructed. The blackmail scheme, however, did not have to be carried out, for parental consent was obtained.

The negotiations with his parents had taken months. Jennie had gone back to Paris to stay with her mother, and the separation was cruel. In January 1874, Gladstone's Liberal government, in power since 1868, lost a series of by-elections, and the Prime Minister, old and ill, dissolved Parliament. Randolph began his campaign for Woodstock against an Oxford don named George Brodrick,[27] who had accused the Duke, in a prior election, of bribing the voters.

Randolph complained to Jennie that he was visiting too many dirty cottages and shaking too many unwashed hands. When he arrived in the village, he heard one of the "lower orders" standing in the crowd say, "There's a rum specimen." He was so angry he wished he were an Ashanti king so that he could have the fellow summarily executed. But Woodstock was a family borough, and Randolph had his father's money and influence behind him. On February 3, he won by 569 votes to 404, in an election that returned the Conservatives to power under the leadership of Disraeli.

While lovers pined, lawyers haggled over the marriage contract, reaching a record of pettiness over who should pay for the sixty-one dollars in telegrams and postage. The Duke settled one thousand pounds a year on Randolph, and Leonard Jerome gave two thousand pounds a year to Jennie, half paid to Randolph and half to her.[28]

On April 15, Randolph and Jennie were married in the chapel of the British Embassy in Paris. The Duke and Duchess did not attend, even though Randolph was their favorite son and they had given the match their blessing. The caste reflex proved stronger than their feelings for their son, and they avoided meeting the vulgar Americans of whom they disapproved. The Duke also felt that Mr. Jerome had behaved disgracefully in insisting that Jennie keep control of part of her dowry. The family was represented by Randolph's brother and three of his six sisters. Leonard Jerome was proud of his daughter. This was the greatest match any American had made since Louisa Caton, the daughter of a Baltimore merchant, had married the Duke of Leeds.[29]

As the wife of a promising young Tory with a famous name, Jennie was thrust into London society, where she was scrutinized by ladies who resented her capture of Randolph and by men who were curious to see if she had the social ease to match her looks. Randolph gave his maiden speech in the House of Commons on May 22. The issue was less than momentous: Should a small garrison be built two miles from Oxford? Alexander Hall, the new Conservative member for Oxford City, supported the plan. When Hall sat down amid cheers, Randolph rose and opposed it, arguing that it would turn the university city into a garrison town, and that students and learned professors would have to mingle with "roystering soldiers and licentious camp followers." Watching the debate with amusement, Disraeli thought Randolph had made an impressive debut. He had said many imprudent things, but his energy and manner had captivated the House.[30]

Jennie bore the rigors of the London season, dinners and balls from May to July, the writing of notes, the leaving of cards, the thousand little efforts and courtesies that had to be made toward social acceptance. She was taken up by the Prince of Wales, who thought American women brought a little fresh air into society. The Prince, it was said, helped himself to his friends' wives as easily as to a second helping of trifle.

In August, the London season was over, Jennie was pregnant, and she and Randolph moved into the house the Duke had found for them at 48 Charles Street, near Berkeley Square. With her confinement approaching, Jennie could not travel, but they often went to Blenheim for a change of scene. Jennie dreaded those visits, feeling that her mother-in-law hated her because she was prettier than Randolph's sisters. The Duchess found fault with everything she did, said, or wore. Jennie disliked the cold formality of Blenheim, the Duchess's dictatorial manner, the solemn meals, and the inflexible daily routine—it was like being back in school. It was a trying situation for a twenty-year-old girl accustomed to the easy companionship of her mother and sisters.[31]

On November 30, seven and a half months to the day after the wedding, Winston was born. Babies born that early usually weigh three and a half to four pounds and are prone to illness. There is no clue in the Churchill papers concerning Winston's premature birth, except that he was born "small." No weight was recorded, and there were no postnatal complications. He was a robust and healthy baby. The possibility arises that Winston was conceived before the wedding. Randolph was often in Paris in February and March, although Jennie was under the supervision of her mother. The romantic Randolph could have been overcome by passion, or the Machiavellian Randolph could have decided to put an end to the legal bickering by forcing the issue.

The baby was healthy, but the father was not. In January 1875, only a month after Winston's birth, Randolph made repeated visits to the family doctor, Oscar Clayton, for an undisclosed ailment. According to Frank Harris, the editor of *Fortnightly Magazine*, who published the revelation in his scandalous autobiography, *My Life and Loves*, Randolph caught syphilis while at Oxford, waking up in bed with an ancient prostitute after a drunken night. Harris claimed to have heard the story from Louis Jennings, a follower and devoted friend of Randolph's, who published a book of his collected speeches. The treatment of syphilis in those days was primitive, consisting of mercury and potassium iodide, and often ineffective. The disease went on for years, going through three distinct stages, with periods of remission that made the victim think he was cured. In the second stage, sores appeared on the mouth, the groin became swollen, and there were pimples on the genitals. In the third and fatal stage, the mind became affected. Moreover, syphilis was highly contagious and could be passed on to an unborn child.

It seems unlikely that having contracted syphilis, Randolph would have taken the risk of transmitting it to his bride and begetting a diseased child. A more probable account was given by Shane Leslie, the son of Jennie's sister Leonie and self-appointed family historian, who said that Randolph's syphilis was contracted from a Blenheim housemaid shortly after Winston's birth in 1874. Once the disease was diagnosed, he could no longer sleep with his wife. At about that time, Jennie and Randolph became estranged. Jennie often went to parties alone, or with her sister Clara, and was always attended by a troop of men, among whom the Prince of Wales had precedence.

Surrounded by friends, and invited everywhere, Jennie seemed to her infant son as radiant as the evening star, and as distant. Winston wanted but could not have the exclusive attention of his mother. At the age of two he delivered his first ultimatum: "I can't have my Mama go—and if she does I will run after the train and jump in."[32] But it did no good. His claims, however valid, were not recognized. The hours of a beautiful woman in society were distributed like Biblical loaves and fishes.

Only in his nanny, Elizabeth Everest, did Winston have a loving presence he did not have to share. As an infant, he called her "Woom" or "Woomany," using the term later as a nickname, for she represented womanhood far more than his mother did. She was near while his mother was remote, earthly while his mother was godlike, a comforting and loving presence while his mother was an object of worship. Winston spent the entire day with Nurse Everest, while seeing his mother was a privilege.

Elizabeth Everest was forty-one when she was hired to care for the newborn Winston, yet she was referred to by the Duchess of Marlborough as "Old Everest." She came from Kent, the "garden of England," and told Winston stories of the strawberries, cherries, and plums that grew there.[33] Before joining the Churchill household, she had worked twelve years for the

Cumberland clergyman Thompson Phillips, taking care of his daughter Ella. Elizabeth Everest never married, but was called "Mrs.," having attained that state of unwed motherhood conferred on nannies when parents left the care of their children to total strangers. When a nanny said, as Mrs. Everest could, "I had him from the month," it meant, quite simply, "This is my child."

By the nature of her duties, Mrs. Everest developed a physical closeness to Winston that his mother did not have. She toilet-trained him, with the nanny's vested interest that the sooner he learned to use the potty the sooner she would not have to wash diapers. She held his penis while he urinated, and washed it for him afterward. She fed him, and cleaned up the mess when he heaved, and gave him baths, and wiped his bottom, and hugged him, and held him while he learned to walk. Hers was a presence Winston depended upon on an hour-by-hour basis.

Mrs. Everest was a caring but also a powerful figure. She was responsible for Winston's health; she chose his food, his clothes, his activities and playmates. She was his advocate, defending his interests against those of his neglectful parents. Jennie complained in a letter to Randolph that Everest had been bothering her, saying that it was disgraceful how few and shabby Winston's clothes were.[34] When her charge's clear-cut interests were at stake, Mrs. Everest spoke up with considerable moral authority.

Jennie saw her son at designated times, and took him out on nanny's day off. Randolph saw even less of him, for aside from attending the House of Commons, he had become embroiled in a quarrel with the royal family. There was a side of Randolph that sought quarrels and controversy. He was a throwback to feudal times, when a duke thought himself the equal of the king.

In October 1875, the Prince of Wales went on a tour of India, and took with him Lord Aylesford, a diverting young man known as "Sporting Joe," for his love of boxing, horse racing, and brothels. Randolph's brother was in love with Lady Aylesford, and in her husband's absence they resolved to go away together, precipitating one of those Victorian scandals that seem asinine by today's standards but that managed to perturb the royal family and the Disraeli government. Divorce was a serious matter in a society based not on the cultivation of virtue but on the prevention of scandal.

One can imagine what a shock it must have been for the priggish Duke of Marlborough. First Randolph had married the daughter of a parvenu New York speculator, and now Blandford had run off with the wife of one of the Prince of Wales's closest friends. It was more than a man could bear.

Aylesford at once returned to England and said he would seek a divorce. At this point, Randolph entered the picture, as the defender of family honor. Randolph was convinced that his brother was the victim of a plot. In Randolph's view, the Prince of Wales had taken Aylesford to India although Lady Aylesford had begged him not to. There was, Randolph believed, collusion between the Prince and Lord Aylesford to throw Lady Aylesford into his brother's arms.[35]

Upon this misconception Randolph acted. He did not approve of his brother's behavior, but felt that royal influence had been wrongly used. He saw himself as a righter of wrongs, and determined that the Prince should now use his influence to stop the divorce. He was angered that Lord Aylesford was going around London quoting the Prince as saying that Blandford was "the greatest blackguard alive."

The Prince of Wales, another of Lady Aylesford's admirers, had written her letters containing improper proposals. The letters were the weapon Randolph needed to blackmail the Prince, who only recently had befriended him by approving of his American fiancée, into stopping the divorce action. For if Aylesford went into divorce court, the Prince would be dragged into the witness box. And if the Prince was a witness, the letters would become a matter of public record, and if that happened, the Prince of Wales would never sit on the throne of England.

Randolph bragged that he held the crown of England in his pocket.[36] He did not stop to think that he was doing grave injury to the Prince, and by extension to Queen Victoria, that by resorting to blackmail he was violating the code of honor he pretended to uphold, that his premise of collusion was unfounded, that his good offices had not been sought, or that his brother might be to blame for wanting to elope with another man's wife.

In early March, Randolph called upon the Princess of Wales, who had not accompanied her husband to India, and urged her to bring pressure on the Prince to stop the divorce. At the same time, he told a number of people that he held the Prince's compromising letters. A reaction from Queen Victoria was not long in coming. On March 10 she wrote the Prince that the whole business was dreadful and disgraceful, and that it had been unpardonable to draw the young and inexperienced Princess into it. Foreseeing a major scandal, she sought the counsel of her Prime Minister, Disraeli. "Blandford I always thought was a scoundrel," Disraeli commented, "but this brother beats him."[37] This was an attack on the throne, as troublesome as a Balkan crisis.

The scandal was averted when Aylesford agreed not to seek a divorce. His own past was far from unblemished, and he did not want to drag in the Prince, who returned to England on May 11, to a scolding from the Queen. She asked him to give up the fast society he frequented, and hoped that he would no longer get mixed up in the private affairs of dubious persons.

There now remained the matter of Randolph's apology, which was accepted that summer. But the Prince let it be known that neither he nor the Princess would attend any social function at which the Churchills were present, effectively banishing them from London society. Perhaps, Disraeli advised Randolph's mother, it would be better if they all left London for a time. "My dear Lady," he said, "there's but one way: make your husband take the Lord Lieutenancy of Ireland and take Lord Randolph with him. It will put an end to it all."[38]

Because of Randolph's meddling, his father was forced to take an unwanted government appointment in Ireland. The Queen, receiving the Duke and Duchess at Windsor before their departure, found them looking wretched and anxious. In January 1877, with Randolph and Jennie and the two-year-old Winston, they left for Dublin, where they would remain in exile for three years. Randolph acted as his father's secretary and continued to represent Woodstock in the House of Commons.

Winston's earliest memories were of a long, low white building with green shutters and verandas, the Little Lodge, in Dublin's Phoenix Park, where Jennie and Randolph had set up house, a stone's throw from the Viceregal Lodge. Mrs. Everest took him for morning walks in the park, where he could see black-coated soldiers firing at targets. She warned him that there were wicked men about called Fenians, who might try to harm the Lord Lieutenant's grandson. The Pope was behind them, and they had murdered a man who had given Winston a drum.[39]

Winston knew that his father was important—he often went to London and made speeches that were reported in the newspapers. His grandfather was even more important—he received delegations and presided at ceremonial functions. Winston watched him unveil the statue of a famous soldier, Lord Gough. It was a scene he would never forget: the great crowd stirring in the Dublin square, the scarlet soldiers on horseback, ropes pulling away a shiny brown sheet, and the formidable old Duke saying: "And with a withering volley he shattered the enemy's line."[40]

He often saw his mother in a skintight riding habit spotted with mud. Jennie rode with nearly every pack of hounds in Ireland, over the "trappy" fences of Kildare County, and the banks and narrow doubles of Meath. Once she fell into a ditch, and Randolph was so relieved to see her unhurt that he took her flask and emptied it. It became a standing joke between them that she had had the fall and he had had the whiskey. Sometimes Winston was frightened because his father or his mother did not come back for many hours after they were expected.[41]

Riding gave Jennie a reason to escape from the watchful eyes of her mother-in-law at a time when her marriage had become dutiful rather than passionate. She gathered about her a devoted circle of male admirers, one of whom, Edgar Vincent, later Lord D'Abernon, said she had more of the panther than of the woman in her look. Another was John Strange Jocelyn, dark-haired and handsome, a dashing colonel in the Scots Fusilier Guards. "The delightful Strange," as Jennie once called him, was whispered to be a man of many affairs.

In the summer of 1879, Jennie was pregnant once again. Randolph was away much of the time, sitting in Parliament, and on February 4, 1880, she gave birth to a healthy, dark-haired boy. She named him John Strange Churchill—an indication that Randolph was not his father.[42] His paternity was the subject of wry comment within the family, particularly on the part of Shane Leslie, who made it his business to know which skeleton was in which closet. Jack, as he became known, did not have the characteristic Churchill looks, and grew up to be a placid young man, totally unlike Randolph or Winston.

In April 1880, there was a General Election, and Disraeli's government went down, to be replaced, with the inevitability of two partners on a seesaw, by Gladstone. Randolph saved his seat in Woodstock by sixty votes, but his father was ousted as Lord Lieutenant of Ireland. The five-year-old Winston saw Gladstone as a very dangerous man who had turned his grandfather out of his job, and who went about rousing people up, lashing them into a fury so that they voted against the Conservatives.

Randolph and Jennie returned to London soon after the election, to a house at 29 St. James's Place. At the age of thirty-one, Randolph was an obscure backbencher, still snubbed by the Prince of Wales; he had made four or five speeches in the House in as many years, and his main achievement had been to antagonize his queen and a future king. But in the next five and a half years, with his party in opposition, Randolph made his reputation. The years of isolation from court had made him ambitious. Without the crisis, he would have subsided into a placid trustee for a family borough.

Randolph's rise to Parliamentary fame came about in a characteristic manner. He formed a tiny splinter group that divided its efforts between attacking the Opposition and the leadership of his own party. Randolph was a natural schismatic, who saw himself at the center of orthodoxy. He represented the real Tory Party; everyone else offered a diluted version. Around him he grouped Sir Henry Drummond Wolff, a shrewd Parliamentarian who was nineteen years his senior; Sir John Gorst, a prominent lawyer and astute politician; and Arthur James Balfour, Lord Salisbury's languid nephew, who toyed with philosophy and knew a great deal about music.

These four men (who were really three, for Balfour wavered in his loyalty) called themselves the Fourth Party (the other three being Conservative, Liberal, and Irish), and made up in noise what they lacked in numbers. Randolph's group broke party discipline and announced that it would pursue an independent course. It found discreet backing from some Tories, including Disraeli, who thought the Fourth Party might be a serviceable burr under the Conservative saddle. In fact, it was never more than "a body of skirmishers, altogether *en l'air*," as Randolph himself described it.[43]

The Fourth Party's main target was the old and distinguished leader of the Tory Opposition, Sir Stafford Northcote, who was hounded and harassed because he was not considered forceful enough. Randolph called him "the goat," because of his beard, and attacked him relentlessly. Northcote protested mildly in March 1883: "What I must object to is the apparent maintenance of a distinctive organization within the Party. It produces infinite soreness and difficulty."[44] Northcote thought that by its constant carping the Fourth Party put the Tories at a disadvantage in the eyes of the rest of the country. But Randolph insisted on his right to go his own way.

The Fourth Party operated in an atmosphere of schoolboy mischief, petty vendettas, and backstairs intrigue, but Randolph was tolerated, for he was thought to represent some of the younger Tory elements, and he spoke well. Newspapers began to report his mordant speeches verbatim, and his bulging eyes and cocky stance lent themselves to the cartoonist's pen. He was witty, unpredictable . . . "Randolphian!" There were, however, Tory leaders like Lord Salisbury who viewed his antics with deep misgivings. In May 1884, during General Gordon's Sudan expedition against the Mahdi, Salisbury wrote: "Randolph and the Mahdi have occupied my thoughts about equally. The Mahdi pretends to be half mad, and is very sane in reality; Randolph occupies exactly the converse position."[45]

Although Randolph was most comfortable in the role of faultfinder, he did make one positive contribution to his party with the launching of Tory Democracy. To try to rally the working classes at a time of the extension of the franchise was a shrewd idea. Randolph had a genuine though paternalistic concern for the laboring man. He wanted him to be properly fed, clothed, and sheltered, but to remain what he was. Thus, he was against free higher education, which made tax rates go up, but for improved housing, which would keep workers out of pubs, and for the Eight Hours' Bill. Tory Democracy was an alliance of the aristocracy and the workingman against the middle class, based on the lord's contempt for the shopkeeper. But the Tory Party was already middle-class, and the squires and great landholders were being joined by a new breed of businessman-leader.

There was something cynical in Randolph's attempt to appropriate the working class. It takes no great sacrifice for someone at the top of the class system to tell those at the bottom that if they stay quietly in their place they will be thrown a bone from time to time. As Winston would put it twenty-five years later: "The Tories love the working man. They love to see him work."

Randolph's goal was to maintain a docile working class that voted Tory in exchange for an improvement in their standard of living. Aside from a few isolated expressions of support, Tory Democracy remained little more than a catchword, and in another quarter of a century the working class formed its own party and a union leader reached Cabinet rank.

As Randolph rose to prominence in the House of Commons, and Jennie worked at being readmitted by London society after a long absence, Winston spent his days near the welcoming arms of Mrs. Everest. He was part of a family of five: a busy father who did not like children and who treated him with calculated coldness; a pleasure-loving mother who admitted that Winston was a difficult child to manage; a baby brother toward whom he showed no sibling rivalry; a loving nurse who asked for nothing in return and knew that in time she must relinquish him; and a small boy, with the imperious demands of the very young, whom Mrs. Everest saved from deprivation.

Jennie often sent her sons to stay with their grandparents at Blenheim. It was from there, on January 4, 1882, that the seven-year-old Winston wrote his first letter, to thank his mother for the toy soldiers, flags, and castle he had been given for Christmas.[46] Winston's interests at that time combined the military and the pastoral. One day found him pretending to pitch a tent with a borrowed umbrella, while the next he gathered primroses and wild hyacinths. He liked Blenheim, the gardens were so much nicer than Hyde

Park. Every morning he did lessons with Grandmama. One day near the cascade he saw a snake crawling in the grass and wanted to kill it, but Mrs. Everest would not let him.[47] In dutiful letters, he expressed the hope that his father, seriously ill with an inflammation of the mucous membrane, was better.

That spring and summer, the children went to the seaside with Mrs. Everest, to Ventnor, a resort on the Isle of Wight, built in terraces on the side of a cliff. Mrs. Everest had a sister there whose husband was a prison warden. Winston made friends with the old warden, and they discussed convict mutinies and the war with the Zulus in South Africa. Winston was very angry with the Zulus, and glad to hear that they were being killed.

Winston and the warden took long walks on the cliff overlooking the sea. One day they saw a great ship with all her sails set, only a mile or two offshore. It was a troopship bringing men back from the war. Winston later learned that the ship had capsized in a squall, going to the bottom with its three hundred soldiers. The divers who went down to find the corpses fainted when they saw the fish nibbling away at the bodies.[48] The story left a scar on his mind.

That November, when he was not quite eight, Winston was snatched from the security of his home, the benevolent presence of Mrs. Everest, and his thousand-strong army of toy soldiers. On a dark November afternoon, a small, frail boy with freckles and hair the color of marmalade took the train to Ascot with his mother. At the top of the hill near the station stood a red-brick building, St. George's, a school that modeled itself on Eton.

The headmaster and his wife offered tea. Winston worried about spilling his cup and making a bad start, and stared at the odd-looking headmaster, the Reverend H. W. Sneyd-Kynnersley, a tall, thin, loose-limbed man with angular features and red whiskers that floated like a bat's wings on his cheeks.

Winston's schooldays were the only truly unhappy period of his life. Even by Victorian standards, the neglect shown by his parents was unusual. His pathetic requests for visits went unanswered. He hated St. George's and did poorly. In his first report, covering the month of November, he was eleventh out of fourteen boys, and the headmaster called him "a regular 'pickle,'" who had not yet fallen into school ways.[49] In the June and July term in 1883 he was thirteenth out of thirteen. His spelling was terrible, and the divisional master wrote that he "does not quite understand the meaning of hard work."[50]

When his form master told him to memorize a Latin declension, Winston was emboldened to ask why *mensa* meant both a table and O table. "O table," the form master said: "you would use that in addressing a table, in invoking a table. You would use it in speaking to a table." "But I never do," Winston blurted out in honest amazement. "If you are impertinent," the form master warned, "you will be punished, let me tell you, very severely."[51]

His general conduct for the spring term in 1884 was "very bad—is a constant trouble to everybody and is always in some scrape or other." Among the scrapes was kicking to pieces the headmaster's sacred straw hat.[52] Punishment for such infractions was a flogging, for the Reverend Mr. Sneyd-Kynnersley was a sadist who derived intense excitement from applying the birch to the bare bottoms of his young charges. On the first morning of the term he explained to the students with solemn gusto that he reserved for himself the right to administer a good sound flogging with a birch rod. The ritual for this was precise and solemn. Every Monday morning, the whole school assembled in the Hall and each boy's report was read aloud. When the headmaster came to a bad report, he would pause and, after a moment's awful silence, would invite the culprit to "come up to my study afterwards." In the middle of the study was a large box draped in black cloth. In austere tones, the offending boy was told to take down his trousers and kneel before the block while being held down by two other boys. The flogging was given with the Reverend Mr. Sneyd-Kynnersley's full strength, and it took only two or three strokes before droplets of blood began to form. By the time the fifteen or twenty strokes were done, the boy's bottom was a mass of blood. Generally, the boys bore it with courage, but sometimes there were scenes of howling and struggling that made the other boys sick with disgust. "There was a wild red-haired Irish boy," wrote the painter and art critic Roger Fry, who had been at St. George's a few terms before Winston, "himself rather a cruel brute, who whether deliberately or as a result of pain or whether he had diarrhoea, let fly. The irate clergyman instead of stopping at once went on with increased fury until the whole ceiling and walls of his study were spattered with filth. I suppose he was afterwards somewhat ashamed of this for he did not call in the servants to clean up but spent hours doing it himself with the assistance of a boy who was his special favorite."[53] Winston remembered that the floggings "exceeded in severity anything that would be tolerated in any of the Reformatories under the Home Office."[54]

At the end of the summer term of 1884, he was removed from St. George's, perhaps after Mrs. Everest had seen the welts from his birching and told his mother. The school and its headmaster, who would have made an interesting case study for the author of *Psychopathia Sexualis*, are best remembered for a single comment in Winston's mid-term report of 1884: "He has no ambition."[55]

That September, when he was not quite ten, he was sent to a little school in Brighton, at 29 and 30 Brunswick Road, run by two elderly spinsters, Kate and Charlotte Thomson. The school may have been recommended by Robson Roose, who was treating Randolph for his syphilis and had become the Churchill family doctor. A specialist in the treatment of gout and neurasthenic diseases, Roose divided his practice between London and Brighton, and sent his son Bertie to the Thomsons' school. Within three months, Winston was in another scrape. At work in a drawing examination, he fought with his seatmate over a penknife the tutor had lent them. The other boy grabbed the knife and stabbed Winston in the chest. Summoned, Dr. Roose saw that the knife had done only minor damage, penetrating to a quarter of an inch. The knife wielder was expelled—it was not his first offense.[56] But Jennie was sure it was all Winston's fault; he must have teased the other boy dreadfully. Instead of coming to her son's defense, as any mother might have done, she assumed that he was in the wrong. His record of poor conduct weighed against him. A short time later, she was able to write Randolph, who was touring India, that it was just as she thought; Winston had started it by pulling the other boy's ear. This would be a lesson to him.[57] Randolph, busy with tigers and maharajas, was not much concerned, and commented only: what adventures Winston does have.

What seemed like rebelliousness was in fact Winston's determination not to be bullied, or ordered about, or made to do anything he objected to. But he liked Brighton, for the Misses Thomson handled him with ingenuity rather than the birch. When they attended services in Brighton's Chapel Royal, the boys were placed in pews that ran north and south. But when the Apostles' Creed was recited, everyone turned east. Certain that Mrs. Everest would have considered this practice popish, Winston refused to turn, expecting martyrdom, but nothing happened. The next time the students went to chapel, the pews faced east, so that no turning was called for when the Creed was said. Winston, who would at another time in his life oppose the policies of Mahatma Gandhi, learned the difference between active and passive resistance. It was one thing not to turn when others did, quite another to turn away when no one else did. That was one inning the Misses Thomson won. Not being resisted or ill-treated, Winston yielded to a broad-minded orthodoxy.[58]

Moral courage he seemed to have aplenty, physical courage had to be acquired. One day, frightened by boys throwing cricket balls at him, he took refuge behind some trees. This remained a shameful memory, the very embodiment of what he must never do: back down.[59] Puny for his age, he resolved to overcome his physical drawbacks. He learned to swim. He rode three times a week, making his pony canter, and asked Jennie to send him a nice riding suit, as his trousers rucked up to his knees. He practiced cricket until he made the team as the extra man on the first eleven,[60] and proudly reported to his father that in one match he had hit a "twoer."

Winston was becoming aware of what it meant to be the son of a famous man. Randolph was a successful politician, a nationally known figure, whose words worked magic, whose plans were great. Winston saw people in the street remove their hats when Randolph passed and workmen grin when they saw his big curly mustache. At school, he read issues of *Punch* in which his father was caricatured. There he was, with goggle eyes and bristling mustache, alone in a rowboat, blocking the passage of the team sculls, with the caption: "Athwart the course: Randolph Churchill (an aggravating boy): 'In the way again!' 'Ooray!'" Everyone wanted Randolph's autograph, and Winston was delighted when he was sent half a dozen to pass around. He picked up political information that he eagerly passed on: he had been riding with a gentleman who thought that Gladstone was a brute and that "the one with the curly mustache ought to be Premier . . ."[61] But Randolph did not thank him for his efforts, and wrote infrequently. What loneliness and heartache there was behind this twelve-word plea from a ten-year-old in April 1885: "I should be very proud if you would write to me, Papa."[62] Later that year, in October, Randolph came to Brighton to campaign and did not even visit his son.[63] Winston's disappointment was acute. He wanted to show off his father, to be seen in his company, to bask in his aura.

By 1885, Randolph's pugnacious tactics had won him a position in his party. He had a following that applauded the pithy phrases with which he skewered the Liberal Opposition—Gladstone was "the Moloch of Midlothian," and Joseph Chamberlain was "the pinchbeck Robespierre." Randolph was seen as the man who had revivified the party. When the Tories came to power again, he would have to be given a Cabinet post, for with his talent for invective, he would be more dangerous outside the government than in it.

Gladstone fell in June 1885, and Lord Salisbury formed a caretaker government until a General Election could be held that November. Salisbury disliked Randolph and was disturbed by his mood swings and shrillness. He told a friend that Randolph's temperament was essentially feminine, "and I have never been able to get on with women."[64]

But Randolph's position in the party was too strong to ignore, and Salisbury asked him to be Secretary of State for India, a post where it was felt he could do little mischief. In those days, the India Office was second only to the Foreign Office in importance, and Randolph should have been grateful that it had been offered to a man of thirty-six with no Cabinet experience. But instead of accepting, he dictated terms: his old foe Sir Stafford Northcote must be replaced as Leader of the House of Commons, and his Fourth Party loyalists must be given their due.

Increasingly enfeebled by the syphilis that was destroying his health and judgment, Randolph fell into a fit of despondency as he waited to see if his bluff had worked. "I am very near the end of my tether," he told a friend at the Turf Club. "In the last five years I have lived twenty. I have fought society. I have fought Mr. Gladstone at the head of a great majority. I have fought the Front Opposition Bench. Now I am fighting Lord Salisbury. I have said I will not join the government unless Northcote leaves the House of Commons. Lord Salisbury will never give way. I'm done."[65]

But Lord Salisbury did give way, kicking his old and respected friend upstairs by giving him a peerage with the title of Earl of Iddesleigh, and making John Gorst Solicitor General and Henry Drummond Wolff a Privy Councillor. As for Arthur James Balfour, who had lately disassociated himself from the Fourth Party, but who was the Prime Minister's nephew, he was made President of the Local Government Board.

Randolph arrived at the India Office at a time when it was still possible to share in the drama of Empire by annexing new territories for the Crown. There were men who could say "I added Nigeria," or "I added South Africa." There was the British general who, in defiance of orders, invaded the Indian province of Sind and cabled back a single word of explanation: *Peccavi* (I have sinned). While Randolph was at the India Office, and largely through his efforts, Burma was annexed. This was the one lasting achievement of his political career. But his disparagement of Indian spokesmen as "Bengali Baboos" anticipated Winston's sneering remarks about Gandhi.

Only a month after attaining Cabinet rank, Randolph was mired in another quarrel with the royal family, again resisting what he felt to be an abuse of the Crown's influence. Queen Victoria wanted her son the Duke of Connaught to be named commander in chief in Bombay, one of India's two major military commands. Randolph objected, and this time he had better grounds

35

than in the Aylesford affair, for the command would give the Duke a seat on the India Council, where he would be making political decisions. There was, however, a strong current in favor of the appointment. Lord Salisbury wanted to see the Queen's wishes carried out. Lord Dufferin, the Viceroy of India, thought it would be a very good idea if one of the Queen's sons served in India. Only Randolph barred the way, and at once set about provoking a crisis.

Through Lord Salisbury, the Queen had privately asked Lord Dufferin about her son's fitness for the job. Randolph saw this as deepest treachery. The Queen and Lord Dufferin were conspiring behind his back, with Lord Salisbury's complicity. If so important a matter was being taken out of his hands, and if he had lost the confidence of the Queen and the Prime Minister, there was only one thing to do: resign. Alarmed that one of his Cabinet ministers wanted to resign only two months after taking office, Lord Salisbury was as accommodating as possible. The Queen had always written private letters to the Viceroy, he explained. If it made Randolph feel better, Salisbury would give up his own right to communicate with Lord Dufferin. On August 15, Randolph repeated his threat to resign, since "a first-class question of Indian administration has been taken out of my hands."[66] Patiently, Lord Salisbury reasoned with Randolph, worked out a compromise, and persuaded him to remain. Randolph was brought around, Lord Salisbury informed the Queen, "after taking calomel."[67] This reference to medication was well chosen, for Randolph's condition was so alarming that he thought of resigning for reasons of health. "I have no longer any energy or ideas," he wrote a friend, "and am no more good except to make disturbance,"[68] which was a fairly clear-sighted appraisal. Randolph won the battle over the Duke of Connaught, however, for on October 9 the Cabinet decided that it was undesirable to appoint him to Bombay. But he did not endear himself to Victoria and her sons. Nothing was less accurate than the formal phrase with which he began his messages to the Queen: "Lord Randolph Churchill presents his humble duty to Your Majesty . . ." In addition, Randolph's promptness to use resignation as a weapon was not lost on Lord Salisbury.

By the time the General Election came around in November 1885, Randolph had lost his family borough, Woodstock, which was attached to another constituency as the result of an election reform bill. Bravely, he stormed the Liberal stronghold of Birmingham. How Winston hoped his father would win! If he did, they would have a special victory supper at school.[69] Defeated, Randolph was given a safe Conservative seat in South

Paddington (in those days, elections were staggered over a period of weeks, and a candidate beaten in one place could run in another). The Liberals were in again. It was Gladstone's next-to-last government. The Grand Old Man, now seventy-six, would govern only four months before he went down on the Irish question. Randolph was out of the Cabinet, having served at the India Office only a few months.

In March 1886, Winston came down with double pneumonia. His constitution was fragile, and he regularly visited Dr. Roose, with Randolph complaining about the bills. This time it was a battle of life and death, with Winston running a temperature of 105°. Dr. Roose gave up his London work and moved into the room next to Winston's at school. Jennie came to stay at the Bedford Hotel, and Randolph showed up briefly, bringing sandwiches and sherry. They spent some anxious nights, but Winston put up a wonderful fight and was out of danger by March 17.[70] His bout with an illness that could be fatal taught him that good health was an inestimable treasure.

Another election in July 1886 brought back the Conservatives, again under Lord Salisbury. Randolph was a mosquito buzzing around his head, but a mosquito that could draw blood. Once again, he had to be brought into the government. Since he was the most aggressive Tory figure in the House of Commons, it was natural that he be made Leader of the House; he took the job recently held by the man he had so mercilessly ridiculed, Sir Stafford Northcote. Despite his misgivings, Lord Salisbury also made Randolph Chancellor of the Exchequer. He hoped that Randolph would grow in the office, and knew that if he did not, a break would follow. On July 25, he confided his concern to the Queen, and she agreed, "for he is so mad and odd, and also in bad health."[71]

When Randolph became Chancellor of the Exchequer and Leader of the House of Commons in August 1886, he was only thirty-seven years old. As Winston would later write in his life of his father: "With a swiftness which in modern Parliamentary history had been excelled only by the younger Pitt, he had risen by no man's leave or monarch's favor from the station of a private gentleman to almost the first position under the Crown." If he had come this far at thirty-seven, where would he be at fifty? Surely, here was another Prime Minister in the making.

Proud of his father, Winston hoped that as Leader of the House he would cut the ground from under the feet of the Liberals. He too wanted to become a good speaker, and was learning *Paradise Lost* for elocution. He required another half-dozen autographs.[72]

But for a man as ill as Randolph to combine the leadership of the House with the Treasury was an intolerable burden. The irony was that as he reached high office, his illness grew worse and made him less fit for it. At thirty-seven, he was like an enfeebled old man. That August he ran a high fever and had to take to his bed. Jennie found him so distant and bizarre that she suspected he had a mistress.

Jennie had a life of her own, surrounded by admirers. The Irish novelist George Moore once affirmed that her lovers had numbered two hundred.[73] Foremost among these was the Austro-Hungarian gentleman rider Charles Kinsky, who in 1883 had gained a measure of fame by winning the Grand National on his own horse. At that time, Kinsky was twenty-five, four years younger than Jennie, who seemed to prefer younger men, and would, after Randolph's death, marry a man Winston's age. Jennie and Count Kinsky became lovers, which Randolph did not seem to mind, for Kinsky came from time to time to the Treasury to discuss politics.[74] The affair was jestingly referred to as "The Austrian Alliance."

Randolph remained in office less than five months, becoming the only Chancellor of the Exchequer of his time who did not keep the job long enough to introduce a budget. Once again, his behavior followed the pattern of unreasonable demands and threats of resignation. This time it was over military spending. Randolph knew precious little about economic matters, felt like a schoolboy in the presence of Treasury officials, and complained, when shown some decimals, about "those damned dots." He decided to concentrate on something he could understand, paring the budgets of the Army and the Navy. Although extravagant and unbusinesslike in his private life, he became a demon for economy, assailing the War Office and Admiralty expenses like a husband trying to make his wife stick to her household budget. Some of this rubbed off on Winston, who complained to his mother that the Brighton seawall was being enlarged at a cost of nineteen thousand pounds, which was a great waste of money.[75]

All Chancellors, as they prepare their budgets, try to trim the estimates of various departments, but they go about it in a spirit of open-minded negotiation. If they cannot agree with the department heads, they ask the Prime Minister to arbitrate. In extreme cases, they might threaten to resign, while not intending to. But this was not Randolph's way. His opening position, as he wrote Lord Salisbury on December 15, was "an absolute and unalterable inability to consent to any Army Estimates which do not show a marked and considerable reduction."[76] He told the head of the War Office, W. H. Smith, that he would resign if his demands were not met. Randolph did not have a good case, for the combined estimates of the War Office and the Admiralty, thirty-one million pounds, were lower than those of the year before. It would be a serious responsibility, Lord Salisbury warned him, to refuse the demands of a War Minister with as little imagination as W. H. Smith. From other high officials, Lord Salisbury was hearing indignant denunciations that the Army was not spending enough. As for Lord George Hamilton, the First Lord of the Admiralty, the Prime Minister was surprised to hear that he had agreed to cut his estimates by seven hundred thousand pounds.

On December 16, Lord Salisbury saw the Queen and said, of the Cabinet: "We are not a happy family." The Queen urged her Prime Minister not to give in to Randolph. W. H. Smith agreed, telling Lord Salisbury: "It comes to this: is he to be the Government? If you are willing that he should be, I shall be delighted, but I could not go on on such conditions."[77]

It was not just the estimates. Randolph's quarrel was with the entire government program, foreign and domestic. As he had planned to blackmail his father by not running for Woodstock, as he had blackmailed the Prince of Wales with his love letters to Lady Aylesford, he would blackmail Lord Salisbury, who could not run the risk of letting him resign, for if he did, the government might fall, and in the reshuffle, who knew what might happen? Having bluffed Lord Salisbury before, Randolph did not stop to think that in politics the cemeteries are full of indispensable men.

On Monday, December 20, he was invited to dine and spend the night at Windsor. At the Queen's table that evening, he spoke of the Parliamentary session about to begin, and the new rules of procedure. Then, upon retiring, he took a sheet of Windsor Castle notepaper and wrote Lord Salisbury: "I do not want to be wrangling and quarreling in Cabinet, and therefore must request to be allowed to give up my office and retire from the Government. I am pledged up to the eyes to large reductions of expenditure, and I cannot change my mind on this matter."[78]

Lord Salisbury's answer was not long in coming. There was a chance of war on the Continent, and it was not advisable to cut military estimates. Although Randolph's withdrawal from the government would be injurious to the public interest, Lord Salisbury had no alternative but to accept his resignation. Privately, the Prime Minister told the Queen that Randolph was a most selfish statesman, who did not care for the good of the country so long as he got his way. In months to come, when the possibility of Randolph's return to office came up, Lord Salisbury said: "Did you ever know of a man who, having got rid of a boil on the back of his neck, wants another?"[79]

By not informing the Queen of his decision while under her roof, Randolph had once again offended the monarchy. With great astonishment, Victoria learned of Randolph's resignation in the newspaper. What a want of respect he had shown her, she thought; what a strange and improper way of going about things. It was unprecedented![80]

The Prime Minister found a replacement in the Liberal Unionist George Goschen, less mercurial than Randolph, who remained Chancellor of the Exchequer for five years. Randolph, who was sure Lord Salisbury would turn down his resignation, was reputed to have commented: "I forgot Goschen!"[81] But he could not have forgotten Goschen, who had figured in every coalition hypothesis for years. If it had not been Goschen, Salisbury was prepared to give the Exchequer to W. H. Smith. Anything to get rid of Randolph.

It was not Goschen, but his own rashness. In one stroke, and by his own hand, Randolph had wrecked his political career. The man who was believed to have the succession to the premiership in his pocket would never hold Cabinet rank again. During the rest of his public life he would encounter nothing but disappointment and failure. His political influence lost, his friends unable to help, his oratorical powers gone, he spent the last eight years of his life "dying by inches," as his lifelong friend Lord Rosebery put it, in the grip of the fatal illness that was the origin of his pathological conduct. Jennie was saddened. It was such a splendid position he had thrown away. His head had been quite turned; he had felt he could do anything.[82]

Not long after his resignation, Randolph was sitting at dinner next to an outspoken young woman named Margot Tennant, who would later marry Herbert Asquith. "I am afraid you resigned more out of temper than conviction, Lord Randolph," she said. "Confound your cheek!" Randolph replied. "What do you know about me and my convictions? I hate Salisbury! He jumped at my resignation like a dog at a bone."[83] All of Randolph's bitterness focused on the man who had let him resign. What a pig he was, he wrote his mother in 1890. And a year later, he wrote his old friend Francis Knollys: "When shall we get rid of that ineffable humbug, Lord S? I would not mind reading his obituary notice."[84]

While his father destroyed himself, Winston was developing the character trait that would make him famous: tenacity. In the spring of 1887 he decided that he must attend Queen Victoria's Golden Jubilee. A jubilee came only once in a schoolboy's life. Jennie had promised, and if she changed her mind, he would never trust her promises again. Needing the permission of the Misses Thomson, he sent his mother a draft of the letter she should write.[85] Here, at the age of twelve, forcing the issue by writing his mother's letter for her, his stubbornness apparently prevailed.

Winston was doing better at school, particularly in geometry; his weak point was Greek. He was in the first eleven in soccer and sang Robin Hood to Bertie Roose's Marian in an operetta called *The Merry Men of Sherwood Forest*. In imitation of his father, who had played with grand masters, he was learning chess. His grandmother the Duchess, with whom he spent holidays at Blenheim, feared that he was too clever for the Brighton school, where it was too easy for him to be the boss. Although he was not seriously naughty, he needed a firm hand, for he used bad language and wanted his way.[86]

In August 1887, Randolph joined Jennie and the children at Cowes. Randolph's ear was attuned to all sounds of grumbling about the Salisbury government, and he was possessed by dreams of returning to the Cabinet, seizing on straws in the wind—someone had told him he should have the War Office. He was once again on good terms with the Prince of Wales, who asked the family on a day's voyage aboard his yacht, the *Osborne*. Randolph protested that the outing would spoil Winston and make him too excitable, but the Prince insisted and was much taken with the twelve-year-old boy, telling his father that he had better retire altogether, for Winston was much cleverer than he had ever been. He gave Winston and his brother Jack pins, and when Winston lost his, the Prince gave him another. Randolph was furious. He did not think Winston should be rewarded for his carelessness. Why on earth was the Prince of Wales so pandering?[87]

Randolph found a cure for his despondency in travel, often with one of his male friends instead of Jennie. But in December 1887, he took her to Russia, Germany, and France, where he met "the man on horseback," General Boulanger, who planned to return the French monarchy to power. Randolph was much impressed by the ambitious general, seeing perhaps a mirror image of his own quixotic behavior, and invited him to London, where he introduced him to influential people. When someone suggested that Boulanger would fail, Randolph said: "Failure! I shall be his guest at the Elysée next November."[88] But Boulanger, about to be prosecuted for treason, fled to Belgium and committed suicide.

Winston was due to finish at Brighton, and Randolph wondered where to send him next. The Churchills had always gone to Eton, but Winston's health was so delicate, it seemed that the doctor was never out of the house. Harrow might be healthier. It was on a hill, so the air would be better, and it was close to London, so Dr. Roose could keep an eye on him. For a man of Randolph's prominence, getting Winston admitted to one of England's two most exclusive public schools, where the sons of the Establishment were often signed up at birth, was not a problem. Randolph's brother-in-law Edward

Marjoribanks, who had a son at Harrow, simply wrote the young headmaster, the Reverend J. E. C. Welldon, and a place was found.[89]

Winston had thought he would be going to Winchester, and was worried about the Greek. In September, he was told that Harrow had been chosen. He had not been consulted, being given no voice in any important decision affecting him, but he was glad, because the entrance examination for Harrow was easier than the one for Winchester, and because it was so near London, half an hour by train, that his parents could visit him often. Had Randolph gone to Harrow, Winston asked?[90] It was a measure of the lack of communication between them that he did not know his father was an Etonian.

Winston spent his last months at Brighton studying for his entrance examination, which he went to Harrow to pass on March 14, 1888, chaperoned by Charlotte Thomson. He suffered from such nervous excitement that he was unable to answer a single question on his Latin test. He wrote his name at the top of the page, wrote the number of the question, I, and after much reflection put a bracket around it. He gazed for two whole hours at the blank page, until merciful ushers collected his paper with the others. He was so upset after the exam that he insisted to Miss Thomson that he had never before translated Latin into English. Although she knew that he had been translating Virgil for a year and Caesar for more than a year, she did not contradict him, for he had worked himself up into such a state that he was sick to his stomach, delaying their departure.[91] But miracles happen, particularly to the sons of prominent men, and Winston scraped through, being placed in the school's bottom class, the Third Remove of the Fourth Form, the form for stupid boys, who were beneath Greek and Latin.

After spending three and a half years at Brighton, Winston remained nearly five years at Harrow, which had in 1871 celebrated the three hundredth anniversary of its foundation. Harrow was a church school, which meant that its governors had to be members of the Church of England, and that its headmaster was a clergyman. Study was based on the ancient tongues of Greece and Rome, although a course in natural science had recently been introduced. Other innovations were the "Modern" side, where mathematics and modern languages were stressed, and the Army Class, which prepared the boys for military academies. These latter two were considered second-rate. The classics were the proper pursuit for Harrovians, among whom could be counted two Prime Ministers, Lord Palmerston and Spencer Perceval, and a lyric poet, Lord Byron.

Harrow had been in decline in the first half of the nineteenth century.

When C. J. Vaughan arrived as headmaster in 1844, there were only sixty boys. He revived the school, although he had to resign in 1859 after having an affair with a student to whom he wrote passionate love letters. When he left, there were five hundred boys, the number enshrined in song:

Five hundred faces and all so strange!
Life in front of me, Home behind—
I felt like a waif before the wind
Tossed on an ocean of shock and change.

One of those faces, arriving at the school in April 1888, was that of thirteen-year-old Winston Leonard Spencer-Churchill (as he appeared in the register), who moved into a small house of fifteen boys run by H. O. D. Davidson. It was at Harrow that he dropped the Spencer, having taken a dislike to it when he was almost last in a line of boys arranged alphabetically.[92]

When boys are separated from their parents and thrust into a highly regulated environment, they become dependent on one another and on the institution. The public-school bond is formed, based on the concept of being a "Harrovian," or an "Etonian," or a "Wykehamist" (as the students of Winchester were known after its founder, Bishop William of Wykeham), which means having assimilated a multitude of odd practices grouped under the heading of custom and tradition. The story is still told of the British pilot shot down over Belgium who was interrogated by the resistance to make sure he was not a German agent. "What is a Wykehamist?" he was asked. "*I am a Wykehamist*," he replied.

The old school tie is a badge of membership that compensates for the loss of home life and parental love. The badge is acquired through learning the special Harrow way of doing things, and the special Harrow vocabulary, impenetrable to outsiders. At Harrow, there was, for instance, the time-honored practice by which the head boy addressed the governors in a Latin speech, which must contain six jokes, discuss national events, and record the achievements and failures of Harrovians. There was the Harrow way of calling the roll, different from that of Eton. At Eton the boys stood in a cluster and lifted their hats when their names were called. At Harrow they filed past a master in the schoolyard and answered one by one.

Winston had to learn the language by which Harrovians communicated: roll call was "bill," a day's holiday was an "absit," being confined to the school was being "on lines," getting on the cricket team was "getting your flannels," and an athlete was a "blood." Although he got through Harrow without any major crisis, Winston never shone in such a managed environment. The great public schools were stunningly successful experiments in behavior modification, which he intuitively resisted. School did not seem real to him. He would rather have been apprenticed to a bricklayer or helped his father to dress the front window of a grocer's shop.[93]

In later years, he developed a fondness for the place, and came regularly to address the boys and to sing Harrow songs. He may have come to realize that Harrow had provided his first real immersion in English political life, for it was there that boys established connections that continued in Parliament and Cabinet rooms. Some of the faces he saw in the House of Commons, like those of Jack Seely and Leo Amery, he had known since Harrow. In 1922, he bought his country house, Chartwell, from an old Harrovian, Captain Archibald Campbell-Colquhouse, with whom, in the Third Fourth, he had disputed the honor of being last in class. It was reassuring that so many of the men who mattered in England had known one another since they were schoolboys.

There was an unpleasant underside to public-school life, which left no scars on Winston. He seems to have avoided the homosexual attachments that boys at Harrow often formed, and the humiliation and inculcation of servility that derived from fagging, the practice by which younger boys were made to be the servants of older ones. Some boys had the power to inflict punishment. No Prime Minister, no Field Marshal, Winston later reflected, had the personal power available to a prefect or a captain of school. He had direct experience of this, having been the fag of an eminent upperclassman named Nugent Hicks (later Bishop of Lincoln), who "whopped" him for some offense. "I shall be a greater man than you," the impertinent boy announced, to which Hicks replied, "You can take two more for that," and gave them.[94]

Winston's mainstay was the example of his father, to whom he constantly referred. One day, Leo Amery, a Sixth Former who was head of his house and had won his football colors, was standing on the edge of Ducker, Harrow's open-air swimming pool. He felt himself propelled into the water by a foot in the small of his back, while unseen hands took his towel, and he emerged spluttering to see which of his friends had committed this indignity, only to meet the gleeful grin of a small, freckled, red-haired boy he had never seen before. Next day at bill, Winston approached him and said, with disarming frankness: "I am very sorry. I mistook you for a Fourth Form boy. You are so small." This did not seem to help matters, so Winston added: "My father, who is a great man, is also small." (Actually, Randolph was five feet nine, above average height.) Amery laughed and told Winston he had enough "cheek."[95]

Academically, Winston did not flourish. On July 12, 1888, after he had been at Harrow about three months, his housemaster, H. O. D. Davidson, wrote his mother an alarming letter. Winston was not

> in any way *willfully* troublesome; but his forgetfulness, carelessness, unpunctuality, and irregularity in every way, have really been so serious, that I write to ask you, when he is at home to speak very gravely to him on the subject.
>
> When a boy first comes to a public school, one always expects a certain amount of helplessness, owing to being left to himself so much more in regard to preparation of work &c. But a week or two is generally enough for a boy to get used to the ways of the place. Winston, I am sorry to say, has, if anything, got worse as the term passed. Constantly late for school, losing his books and papers and various other things into which I need not enter—he is so regular in his irregularity that I really don't know what to do; and sometimes think he cannot help it. But if he is unable to conquer this slovenliness (for I think all the complaints I have to make of him can be grouped under this head, though it takes various forms), he will never make a success of a public school. . . . As far as ability goes he ought to be at the top of his form, whereas he is at the bottom. . . . I have written very plainly to you, as I do think it very serious that he should have acquired such phenomenal slovenliness. . . .[96]

Lady Randolph, as was her habit, showed the letter to her husband, and one can imagine him throwing up his arms and groaning that his worst fears were confirmed. Winston's sloth may have been a way of saying that since his parents did not seem to care for him, there was no reason for him to care about school. In fact, he demonstrated an odd mixture of sloth and competitiveness. He would not study, but won a prize that year in the Speech Room for declaiming twelve hundred lines of Macaulay's *The Lays of Ancient Rome*. His name in the school register was followed thereafter by an italic *P*. Having discovered that he could learn anything by heart almost effortlessly, he competed for a Shakespeare prize, and was very "put-off-ified"[97] when an upper-form boy got 127 marks to his 100.

As the son of a famous man, always in some sort of hot water, Winston had become a well-known figure at Harrow, pointed out to visitors. One July morning in 1889, Jack Seely, who had left Harrow just before Winston's arrival, was back on a visit, standing on the little bridge at the narrow end of Ducker, munching buns with two Sixth Formers and watching the boys scrambling onto logs in the water. "You see that little redheaded fellow having a row with the log," said one of the Sixth Formers, pointing to a boy trying to push a heavy log onto the bank, "that's young Winston Churchill." "Hi, Churchill," the Sixth Former called out, "I bet you two buns to one you don't get it out." Winston looked up at his challenger, bent his head deep in thought, and said: "No, I won't bet, because I have been told never to bet if I am likely to lose."[98]

That summer there was further evidence that Winston would not study. Ever eager to believe the bad news about his son, Randolph gave up on his going to Oxford or Cambridge and transferred him to the Harrow Army Class, which would prepare him for Sandhurst. This decision was taken because Winston showed a great affinity for all things military. At Harrow he had joined the Rifle Corps. They fired full-sized Martini-Henry rifles, the same ones the Army used. They kicked a good deal, but it was "awfully jolly."[99] When he went out on maneuvers, he sent his mother the sketches of battle plans. Also, at the age of fourteen, he still had a passion for toy soldiers. He had fifteen hundred, all one size, all British, organized as an infantry division with a cavalry brigade, while his brother, Jack, commanded a ragtag army of colored troops that was not allowed to have artillery. One day, when his son was home from school, Randolph came to inspect the troops, which Winston had arranged in the correct formation of attack. After studying the scene, and reflecting perhaps that the blood of a great soldier flowed in his veins, he asked Winston if he would like to go into the Army. The boy replied "Yes" at once, seeing himself at the head of a real rather than a toy army.[100]

Winston soon regretted so rashly accepting his father's offer, for he did not like the Army Class, which meant extra lessons in the evening and on half-holidays. He complained that he was being distracted from the work of his form, which he professed for the first time to have found interesting, and that his term was spoiled. Harrow might be a charming place, but Harrow and the Army Class did not agree. Soon he was put on report, which meant that he had to obtain weekly reports on his work and show them to the headmaster. An added aggravation was that because he had opted for the Army Class he was still in the Fourth Form. Harrow was a "hell of a place," he wrote his mother in November 1889 (then crossed out the impertinence); it was all very well for monitors and cricket captains but quite a different thing for Fourth Form boys. Only Jennie could stick up for him, no one else would, and she must speak to the headmaster and get him off report.[101]

Things improved a bit that month when his father came to see him after repeated pleas, and Winston proudly showed him the Vaughan Library, the gym, the racquet courts, and Hance's tuck shop, where he went for deviled kidneys or fried plaice and chips whenever he had a little money in his pocket.

Money was a sore point. There were constant requests: the exchequer was low; a remittance would not be altogether misplaced. When his mother did not comply, he asked Mrs. Everest, or borrowed from schoolmates, but always came back at Jennie with further demands. She was horrified by his extravagance. What did he do with it? Perhaps he only wanted something from his mother, and sought it in terms of material gain. Although Harrow's proximity to London did not increase the frequency of her visits, and money could not satisfy his need, it was a tolerable substitute.

In the summer of 1890, Winston was supposed to take the preliminary exam for Sandhurst. But because his geometrical drawings were weak, the Reverend Mr. Welldon decided to put it off until December. This delay, added to a bad report, led to an outburst from Jennie, who had become a go-between, voicing Randolph's discontent. She and Randolph were terribly disappointed and unhappy. She had built up such hopes and felt so proud, and now it was all gone. Really, his work was an insult to his intelligence. Randolph was threatening to send him off with a tutor for the holidays, and it would take a great deal to pacify him. He had just sent Winston five pounds. Was this the way to thank him? In the meantime, Jack was at the head of his class in Brighton every week, in spite of his poor eyesight. A good pull was needed, before it was too late.[102] On top of everything, he had taken up smoking and looked ridiculous. Jennie promised to give him a gun and a pony if he gave it up and passed his Prelim.[103]

On December 10, 1890, Winston took the Prelim. He was taking Latin in the Army Class, but he was fortunate that this was the last Prelim in which the hated subject was optional. Among the other subjects there was geography, and the night before, with a gambler's instinct, he had listed on little scraps of paper the names of the twenty-five maps he was supposed to know, picking one which he learned by heart. Lo and behold, the one he had picked, New Zealand, was the first question on the exam paper. Surely a special providence was looking out for him.[104] Of the three essay subjects, Rowing versus Riding, Advertisements—Their Use and Abuse, and the American Civil War, he chose the third. On December 11 came the second part of the exam, algebra, geometry, and French. All in all, Winston thought he had done well. The results, announced in the middle of January 1891, confirmed his optimism. Of twenty-nine candidates from Harrow, twelve, including Winston, had passed in all subjects.[105] The Reverend Mr. Welldon was encouraged enough to tell him that if he was quiet, sensible, and industrious, he would get into Sandhurst. A large, broad-shouldered man with a full face, the headmaster from that time on gave Winston special attention, tutoring him for a quarter of an hour before evening prayer three times a week.

Winston had proved that when he wanted to, he could do well. Only his parents took a dim view of his ability. Others who met him were impressed. There was something about him that left an imprint. At about the same time he passed the Prelim, Winston went to see the distinguished throat specialist Sir Felix Semon, who was one of the Prince of Wales's doctors. Winston had a slight lisp and wanted Dr. Semon to correct the impediment. "But that can't matter so very much," Semon said. "It won't interfere with you in the Army." Semon did not understand, Winston replied. Of course he intended to go to Sandhurst, and afterward to join a regiment of hussars in India. But it was not his intention to become a professional soldier. He only wanted to gain some experience. One day he would be a statesman as his father was before him. When that day came, and he had to give an important speech, he did not want to be haunted by the idea that he must avoid every word beginning with the letter *s*. When his consulting hours were over that day, Semon told his wife: "I have just seen the most extraordinary young man I have ever met."[106] Such certainty about the future was unusual in a boy of sixteen.

His parents saw his future somewhat differently, particularly after an incident in May 1891. Winston and four other boys had climbed into the ruins of a large abandoned factory. Some windows remained unbroken, and the boys facilitated the ravages of time, with the result that the watchman complained to the Reverend Mr. Welldon. Winston, one of the boys caught, was "swished" by the headmaster. For once the hand of providence was absent. Whether from candor or ingenuity, he did not wait for his parents to hear about the vandalism from the school, but immediately wrote his father what he had done.[107]

Randolph, who had broken windows while at Oxford, was by this time in South Africa, where he had gone to improve his health and to visit gold mines. He left a trail of rudeness everywhere. In articles written for the *Daily Graphic*, he called the Boer farmers dirty, lazy, and barbarous. To the Boers, he embodied the high-handed British imperialism they had come to hate and would in a few years rebel against.

That September, while still in South Africa, Randolph read in a newspaper that the British ambassador to Paris had died. Why, this post would be perfect for him, he thought, completely oblivious to the fact that his friendship with the renegade General Boulanger would make him persona non grata to the French government. The time had come to trade on his old friendship with Balfour. In the Fourth Party days, Randolph had tolerated Balfour as a disciple. He seemed so utterly devoid of energy or ambition that Randolph had nicknamed him "Postlethwaite." In those days, Balfour had fetched and carried for Randolph, and felt rewarded by a nod of approval.

As Randolph's fortunes had fallen, Balfour's had risen. In 1887 he had been sent to Ireland as Chief Secretary, and this graveyard of great reputations made him. Who would have thought that the easygoing Member of a family borough, who called Lord Salisbury Uncle Robert, would be able to control the unruly Irish? But the esthete's languid frame had a spine of steel, and his ruthlessness in Ireland earned him the sobriquet of "Bloody Balfour."

Randolph wired Balfour to try to get him Paris, and receiving no reply, thought he had been snubbed. So much for old friends; Balfour was like all the rest, he would not move a finger to help him. In fact, Balfour had done all he could. He had taken Randolph's request to Lord Salisbury, who had found it impossible to comply, because of Randolph's well-known sympathies for General Boulanger. "I should be much grieved to think that you conceived yourself to have any grounds of complaint against me," Balfour wrote Randolph in January 1892, when he was back in England, "especially as I have done *everything* in my power to further your request."[108] But there was no reassuring Randolph, whose disordered mind was now obsessed by failed opportunities and imagined slights.

While Randolph was in South Africa, Jack came down with the mumps, and Winston copied out by hand a long letter from his father and sent it to his brother. Jack was the favored son, but there was never a trace of jealousy or envy in Winston. He was open and generous in his affections. Although his parents repeatedly disappointed him when he asked for visits, not even turning up on Speech Day, when all the other parents came, he never resented it, but kept hoping. Much has been made of Churchill's streak of melancholy, which he called "Black Dog," a term he learned from Mrs. Everest, but as a boy he was optimistic and ebullient. His glaring faults were his erratic study habits and his extravagance. His mother complained that his letters always had the same refrain: "Please send money." He did go through it in the most rapid manner. Even the loyal Mrs. Everest, for once, did not take his part.[109] He had spent fifteen shillings in a week, while there were families of six and seven persons who had to live on twelve shillings a week. This time she would keep him short and teach him the inconvenience of being penniless.

The year 1891 ended with more bad luck. The Reverend Mr. Welldon wanted Winston to spend the Christmas holidays in France with a tutor. The Sandhurst exam was coming up, and his French needed improving. Winston, who had not seen his father in months, and who blamed Welldon for wanting to ruin his holiday, announced that he would not go. Annoyed by his obstinacy, Welldon lost his composure and said: "Very well then, you must give up the Army."[110]

His parents agreed with the headmaster, leading to the worst test of wills thus far between Winston and Jennie. He wrote her that she and his father were treating him like a machine, moving him about against his will. Had his father been asked to give up his holiday while at Eton? Jennie was so angry she sent him back his letter after reading only one page, complaining that he was making everything disagreeable for himself and everyone around him. Winston was wretched. How could his mother be so unkind, the one person he thought he could count on, cutting the ground from under him. But combined with the unhappiness of a boy rejected by his parents there was a retaliatory note. Winston replied that he knew why she had not read his letter—it was because she was too busy with her parties and arrangements for Christmas. This reference to Jennie's neglect of her son in favor of her social life was meant to sting. So was the phrase "I too can forget."[111] They were now equals, Winston was telling his mother, and he would give as good as he got.

Losing the battle, Winston left for Versailles on December 21 with one of the French masters at Harrow, Bernard Minssen. He was to stay a month, but argued with Minssen that a lunar and not a calendar month was meant. Again he lost, but could not be faulted for lack of combativeness. Two things in Paris impressed him, for he loved all things military, and was not squeamish about the dead: the toy soldiers at the Bon Marché, particularly the artillerymen in the position of loading and firing three black cannon, and the morgue, a bizarre but popular tourist attraction, to which Randolph's friend Baron Hirsch, a wealthy Jewish industrialist, took him. Winston was disappointed, for there were only three bodies; it was not a good bag.[112]

In January 1892, he returned to Harrow to prepare for his Sandhurst exam. His father urged him to work like a little dray horse; he would have plenty of time in the Army for amusement and idleness. But Winston had other things on his mind, such as testing his literary abilities by writing articles for the *Harrovian*. The articles, which appeared sometimes as letters to the editor and sometimes as School Topics, had a reformist bent. Winston wanted to put right what was wrong with Harrow, and complained that the drafty Speech Room tower was used as a classroom, that organ music was played all day long, distracting the students, and that there were not enough towels in the gymnasium dressing room. Signed with pseudonyms such as Junius Junior, the articles came to the attention of the Reverend Mr. Welldon, who summoned Winston and told him: "My boy, I have observed certain articles which have recently appeared in the *Harrovian*, of a character not calculated to increase the respect of the boys for the constituted authorities of the school. As the *Harrovian* is anonymous I shall not dream of inquiring who wrote those articles, but if any more of the same sort appear, it might become my painful duty to swish you."[113]

Buried in these blithe teen-age efforts were a few Churchillian nuggets, such as: "Gas has two duties to perform—to light and to warm. Harrow gas does neither—it only smells."[114]

Another field where Winston tested himself was fencing. Too slight to excel at football or cricket, he wisely chose a sport where his small frame and light weight were advantages. He became a first-rate fencer, at Harrow far and away the best, in fencing terms a *monsieur à outrance*. On March 24, 1892, he won the Harrow fencing cup. It was the first time he had been best in a sport, and he had his photograph taken in his fencing attire with one hand on the cup. On April 8, he won the Public Schools competition at Aldershot, which had gone to a Harrovian only once before. The school newspaper reported that he did not fence in the orthodox manner, and that his success was due to quick and dashing thrusts that took his opponent by surprise. Randolph sent him two pounds to buy a present for his instructor, Sergeant Queese, but Winston spent one pound on a clock for the Sergeant, paying off debts with the other pound. His furious father warned him that a millionaire could not be more extravagant,[115] and that if he was not careful, he would be in bankruptcy court six months after going into the Army.

These extracurricular activities distracted Winston from his studies. The Reverend Mr. Welldon was not sanguine about his chances at the July exam, which, after the Prelim, was called the Further. Winston failed the exam, ranking 390th out of 693, with 5,100 points. He needed 6,457 on the sliding scale to enter Sandhurst. His parents were upset. Jennie felt that it was her fault; she had made too much of a fuss over him, had made him out to be some sort of paragon. Randolph pointed out that he was fifteen hundred marks from the last successful candidate and had obtained seven hundred marks less than his cousin and fellow Harrovian Dudley Marjoribanks, who had not done nearly so well as Winston in the Prelim. What was Randolph to do with him? The boy was some sort of incompetent, not only could he not get into Oxford or Cambridge, he could not even get into the Army, the dunce's refuge. Randolph would have to find a clerk's job in the City for him through his connection with bankers like Nathaniel Rothschild and Ernest Cassel.[116]

It was a time of strain for Randolph. In the last stage of his illness, he was deteriorating fast. He knew now that his political career was over. He had money worries and suffered the humiliation of having to give up his country house in Banstead and his London house at 2 Connaught Place and move into 50 Grosvenor Square with his mother (his father had died in 1883). In October, Jennie fell seriously ill with pelvic peritonitis. She took morphine to dull the pain, and the "pelvic storm," as the doctors called it, passed. On November 9, Randolph's brother, Lord Blandford, died, at the age of forty-eight. He had not amounted to much, having lived for years in France with his paramour, Lady Aylesford. But in 1888 he had left her to marry a wealthy New York woman, Lilian Warren Hammersley. He and Randolph quarreled and became estranged, but the death of his only brother was nonetheless a shock.

It was at this time, just before his care-beset father gave up the house at Banstead, that Winston, home on holiday, fired a double-barreled rifle at a rabbit right under his father's window. Randolph blew up. But seeing Winston's distress, he tried to reassure him. Winston then had one of the three or four long, intimate conversations with him that were all he would be allotted in his father's lifetime. He listened spellbound to this sudden departure from Randolph's usual reserve, amazed at his father's grasp of all his affairs, amazed that he was at all understood. Then, for the one and only time in Winston's life, Randolph asked for his son's indulgence. "Do remember things do not always go right with me," he said. "My every action is misjudged and every word distorted. . . . So make some allowances."[117]

In November 1892, Winston took the Further for the second time. He had been working hard, and the Reverend Mr. Welldon thought he was well up to the Sandhurst level. He had to take math, Latin, and English, and his electives were French and chemistry. The results were not announced until January 20, and Winston spent an anxious month and a half waiting. Once again he was "ploughed," coming out 203rd out of 664, with 6,106 points. He had improved his performance by more than a thousand points, but the standards this time were more severe. Winston was dejected at having failed a second time, just as his father knew he would. Randolph wrote Lieutenant General Reginald Gipps, a Military Secretary at the War Office, to see if there was any way to get him into Sandhurst without the exam, and was told that he might have a chance if he joined the militia.[118]

When Winston heard the bad news in January 1893, he was recovering from an accident that had almost killed him. One of his aunts, Lady Wimborne, had lent the family her estate at Bournemouth, about fifty acres of pine forest going down to the smooth beach of the Channel. Through the middle of the forest there ran a deep ravine, crossed by a fifty-yard rustic bridge. Winston, then eighteen, was being chased by his twelve-year-old brother and a fourteen-year-old cousin. They caught him on the bridge, one at each end. To escape capture he jumped off, hoping to grab the top of a fir tree. Instead, he fell twenty-nine feet to the ground. Jack and the cousin went back to Jennie and said: "He jumped over the bridge and he won't speak to us." With a ruptured kidney, Winston was on the mend for about six weeks.[119] His father arrived from Dublin, where he had been spending Christmas without Jennie, with one of London's greatest surgeons in tow. Winston was gratified to see that his parents spared no expense for his well-being. Baron Hirsch, Randolph's Paris friend, who had shown Winston the morgue, wrote that to have survived such a fall, he must have several lives, like a cat.[120]

With two failures behind Winston, the Reverend Mr. Welldon recommended Captain James's, the blue ribbon of Sandhurst "crammers." No one who was not a congenital idiot, it was said, could fail to pass into the Army from there. Captain Walter Henry James, formerly of the Royal Engineers, knew with almost papal infallibility the sort of questions that would be asked. In March 1893, Winston, still shaky from his fall, started attending the crammer at 18 Lexham Gardens. He did not make a favorable impression. Captain James urged Randolph to speak to his son about his casual manner. He meant well, but was inclined to be inattentive and to think too highly of his own abilities. He was disposed to teach his instructors rather than learn from them. They in turn complained that he did not apply himself. He was prone to take the bit between his teeth and go his own course. One day, he announced loftily that his knowledge of history was such that he needed no further instruction in it.[121]

Winston's assessment of his abilities was not far off the mark. When he took the exam for the third time that June, he had the highest mark in English history, 1,278 points out of 2,000, and also scored high marks in French and math. In Latin, there was the usual slump, 362 points out of 2,000. But Winston was no dunce; he did well when his mind was absorbed, poorly when his interest lagged. This time he scraped by, coming in 95th out of 389, with 6,309 points, four places too low to win an infantry cadet-ship but enough for the cavalry. He was in Switzerland on a walking tour when he heard from his Aunt Lily, Lord Blandford's widow, who had promised him a charger if he passed: "So pleased and glad you have passed. Must look out for good horse for you when you return. . . ."[122]

Winston was so glad to send his father the good news. At last he had come up to the standards expected of him; he had worked hard and succeeded. But Randolph was going mad. There were reports of his strange behavior in the House of Commons, where he was observed "foaming and inarticulate." His decline was so noticeable that in July, as Winston was waiting for his exam results, Jennie consulted Dr. Thomas Buzzard, a specialist in nervous diseases. Randolph fumed about the people who were spreading absurd rumors about his health, but agreed to see Buzzard,[123] who diagnosed general paralysis, the medical term for tertiary syphilis. Randolph's condition was a textbook description of the symptoms: slurring of tongue, jerky gait, fits of depression alternating with high spirits, the hatching of grandiose schemes, and a creeping physical and mental paralysis.

Winston's success was cause for rejoicing. But Randolph, in the grip of paralysis, was angrier with his son than he had ever been. Why, the boy had missed the last place in the infantry by about eighteen marks, which proved his great slovenliness of work. He had gone and got himself into the cavalry, those second-rate performers, and it would cost him two hundred pounds a year more because of the horses. It only showed what little claim Winston had to cleverness, knowledge, or any capacity for settled work. His great talent was for "show-off," exaggeration, and make-believe. In all his exams, he had bragged about results that never came. He was in the Army, but that was a very wretched pitiable consolation. Both at Harrow and Eton, Randolph wrote the Duchess, Winston had proved his total worthlessness as a scholar or a conscientious worker.[124] Randolph was by then so deluded that he was under the impression that Winston had attended both schools.

As far as he was concerned, Randolph wrote Winston on August 9, he had failed again. His sloppy, happy-go-lucky, harum-scarum style of work had kept him from getting into the infantry. He had never received a good report from any of Winston's masters or tutors, but only incessant complaints of total want of application. Winston had boasted that he was sure to obtain seven thousand marks, but Alas! that estimate was some seven hundred marks deficient. Perhaps he would find consolation in having failed to get into the 60th Rifles, one of the finest regiments in the Army. Not that Randolph would let him stay in the cavalry. As soon as possible he would have Winston transferred to an infantry regiment of the line.

Randolph wanted to throw in the sponge. He was certain that if Winston did not prevent himself from leading the idle, useless, unprofitable life of his schooldays, he would become a social wastrel, one of the hundreds of public-school failures who degenerated into a shabby, unhappy, and futile existence.[125]

Shaken by this prophecy of a dim future, and dependent on his father's approval, so eager for the praise that never came, Winston replied without a trace of resentment, and without pausing to consider that these were the ravings of a madman: I "will try to modify your opinion of me by my work and conduct at Sandhurst . . . My . . . low place in passing in will have no effect whatever on my chance there."[126]

Nothing Winston did could satisfy his father, but he had the good sense not to be unduly disheartened. The main thing was that he was going to Sandhurst. As it turned out, he learned at the end of August, three months short of his nineteenth birthday, that he had got an infantry cadetship after all, for other applicants had dropped out. He would join the 60th Rifles, even though, with his short stature and ability as a horseman, he was better suited to the cavalry—anything to please his father. Randolph was mollified. At least he would save two hundred pounds a year. But he still resented his son. He even resented those who were kind to Winston, like his brother's widow, Duchess Lily, whom Randolph considered silly and gushing. Horrified at the idea that Winston might borrow money from her, Randolph gave him an allowance of ten pounds a month.[127]

Winston's childhood was at an end. Soon he would be wearing the uniform of a Sandhurst officer cadet. During his formative years, he had been shaped by two crucial influences, one life-enhancing, the other life-diminishing, Mrs. Everest and his father. Jennie was always a little in the background, adored but just out of reach, or arbitrating between father and son.

Mrs. Everest remained close to Winston after he had gone away to school, writing long letters to her "darling Winny," full of affectionate admonitions from his "loving old Woom"; he must wear his coat in wet weather, not eat too many nasty pickles, not board the train when it was moving, as he habitually stood at the bookstall reading until it started pulling out of the station, not go to sleep and forget his candle burning at his bedside; such practical advice concerning his safety and health was conspicuously absent from the letters of his parents. Mrs. Everest was still able to do all sorts of small favors for Winston: she sent him money, cakes, chicken pies, and heroin syrup (a widely used pain-killer in Victorian times) for his toothache; she made dentists' appointments for him, and saw to it that his bicycle was fixed when he came home on vacation; she prayed for him to be kept from all evil and temptation. In short, this kind and loving woman filled a vacuum left by his self-absorbed parents.

Winston's tribute to Mrs. Everest came some years later, when he was a young officer in India and wrote an adventure novel called *Savrola*, in which he introduced the character of an old housekeeper:

> She had nursed him from his birth up with a devotion and care which knew no break. It is a strange thing, the love of these women. Perhaps it is the only disinterested affection in the world. The mother loves her child; that is maternal nature. The youth loves his sweetheart; that too may be explained. The dog loves his master; he feeds him; a man loves his friend; he has stood by him perhaps at doubtful moments. In all these are reasons; but the love of a foster-mother for her charge appears absolutely irrational. It is one of the few proofs, not to be explained even by the association of ideas, that the nature of mankind is superior to mere utilitarianism, and that his destinies are high.[128]

Jennie's love was episodic, unreliable. She was fickle, and took the side of his father and the Reverend Mr. Welldon. She broke promises, and did not come to visit when she said she would. She could not be entirely trusted; she had too many other interests. But Mrs. Everest was entirely devoted to her charges. Winston discovered a constant love that was not based on any biological tie or mutual interest. It was baffling that such a feeling could exist. Things should have a reason. What was Mrs. Everest's? It could only be that he was worthy of love. His earliest feelings of his own worth came not from his parents but from his nanny. She loved him *unconditionally*, no matter how many windows he broke or how many exams he failed. Mrs. Everest validated him, she provided the encouragement of a mothering figure to the fragile developing self of the child.

Through some mysterious nongenetic transmission, some of Winston's character traits seemed to have been inherited from Mrs. Everest rather than his parents. Humbly born, Mrs. Everest brought Winston into contact with the views of the population at large. Some of her anti-Catholicism rubbed off on him. As he later wrote his cousin Ivor Guest, "Catholicism—all religions if you like—but particularly Catholicism—is a delicious narcotic. It may soothe our pains and chase our worries, but it checks our growth and saps our strength."

Winston had the common touch. He did not inherit Randolph's cutting manner with social inferiors. One of his more endearing traits was his ability to meet everyone as an equal. Never pretentious or pompous, he was gifted with an easy sense of humor that made it hard for him to keep an enemy. At the same time, the faith in himself that he derived from Mrs. Everest's nurturing promoted some of his more disagreeable traits, his obstinacy, his bragging, his dogged sense of always being in the right. Mrs. Everest seems to have communicated to him that he had a sacred leave to have his way.

But there was something else at the core of Churchill's character that he did not get from Mrs. Everest, something not self-made but self-created. Somehow, he found the resources to accommodate his personality to that of his father, in ways that made him stronger instead of destroying him. Winston got a distorted response from his father. Randolph did not view him with pride as a chip off the old block, and did not allow him access to his world of adult greatness, which is the usual way a father can help his son achieve self-integration. He was unable or unwilling to establish empathic contact with his son, whom he saw as a mischievous idler who would never amount to much, and was fit only to go into the Army. Winston was the scapegoat who could do no right, even when he passed the Sandhurst exam, while Jack was the favorite son who could do no wrong. But instead of resenting his father's disapproval, Winston strove to live up to expectations he could never meet, his admiration undimmed. When he was twelve, he was taken to a pantomime where there was a sketch on Randolph. He burst into tears, turned furiously on a man applauding in the seat behind him, and blurted out: "Stop that row, you snub-nosed Radical!" Pleased for once with his son, Randolph sent him a sovereign.[129]

To maintain this spirit of reverence for a father with whose disapproval he had to contend, Winston achieved an amazing feat. We all perpetuate our parents, or the idea we have formed of them. As one of Ibsen's characters says, "It's not only what we've inherited from our fathers and mothers that exists again in us, but all sorts of old ideas and opinions. They aren't actually alive in us; but they hang on all the same, and we can never rid ourselves of them." But Winston went much further: he created a fantasy father he could worship and emulate. Not the ravaged syphilitic of unsound mind whose political career was a shambles, and who was regarded as a madman by Lord Salisbury and Queen Victoria, but a man of consistency and idealism, a statesman who possessed the key alike to popular oratory and political action.

Winston took his politics unquestioningly from his father, read industriously every word he had spoken, and learned by heart large portions of his speeches. Randolph was the greatest and most powerful influence in his early life. Not the real Randolph, who seldom condescended to speak to him, and then usually to scold him for some petty breach of behavior, but a Randolph who was thoughtful and caring, and had a strong and masterly character. Young Winston invented an ideal father, complete with a sense of mission that he could in time make his own. He invented what he himself wanted to be and eventually became, convincing himself that he was only imitating his father. This fantasy, carried over into adulthood, was enshrined in the two-volume biography he wrote about Randolph.

In fact, Randolph never had the slightest sense of mission. Once, asked what he meant by Tory Democracy, he replied, "Mostly opportunism, I think." He was never more than an Opposition demagogue, with a bitterness against his own class and against the royal family that went back to his exile after the Aylesford affair. This, and the irrationality brought on by syphilis, were the springs of his action.

But in the biography he became "a great elemental force in British politics," a leader who "warmed the heart of England and strangely stirred the imagination of her people." Tory Democracy was not opportunism but an idea that "grew vital and true at his touch." The Fourth Party was not a knot of troublemakers, but the rejuvenation of the Conservative Party. "He accomplished no mean or temporary achievement," Winston wrote, "insofar as he restored the healthy balance of parties, and caused the ancient institutions of the British realm once again to be esteemed among the masses of the British people."[130] One might have thought the Tory Party was in mortal danger, whereas in fact it was in power almost without interruption between 1885 and 1906, showing under Lord Salisbury's leadership remarkable health.

Even the petty economizing that spurred Randolph's resignation Winston saw as a statesmanlike act, a reduction in military spending that would be the first step in a policy of noninterference in the affairs of Europe. At his first slip, the "Old Gang" of Tories who owed their long reign to his courageous struggle had thrown him out, showing themselves utterly destitute of generosity or gratitude. This was how Winston interpreted his father's mad conduct.

For a young boy to create a fantasy father and to sustain that fantasy for many years was remarkable indeed. It showed an ability to forge the required conditions of his development. He had built the model he wanted to follow. It showed an unusual capacity to integrate illusion and reality, to tolerate different perspectives. In later years, he would pursue schemes, no matter how farfetched, with obstinate energy. He would integrate different elements of his nature, the humane and the ruthless, the dreamer and the man of action, in a way that most people cannot. Most people cannot tolerate so many different facets and the tensions they create. They are baffled and upset by inconsistency. They break down, or their behavior becomes pathological. But Churchill was able to adopt contradictory points of view with equal brilliance and insight, and an equal sense of conviction about the rightness of his position, investing it with a deeply felt moral authority. He had done it as a child, when he invented his own version of his father, and he would do it again, at every step of his political ascent.

II

SOLDIERING

O N September 1, 1893, eighteen-year-old Gentleman Cadet Winston S. Churchill took the main Portsmouth road to Sandhurst, thirty miles from London. His cab, crowded with luggage, reached a narrower road that wound through a forest of larch, birch, and pine, with a glimpse of a lake seen through the trees. At the edge of a large clearing there were cricket and football grounds, tennis courts, golf links, and parade grounds, and farther on, low, white stone buildings. It was here, at the Royal Military Training College, founded in 1802, that he would spend the next sixteen months, as one of 120 new and ardor-filled cadets, who would hopefully be transformed into officers and gentlemen.

Winston was measured for his uniforms of blue serge, and scarlet and gold for full dress. His height, and he would grow no taller, was five feet six and a half inches. His chest measurement of thirty-one inches, with an expansion of two and a half inches, was deemed so sparrowlike that he was told he would not get his commission unless he increased it.[1] Puny and unmuscular, he was hardly a warriorlike figure, with no hair on his chest and a slight lisp in his voice. His body was his curse, particularly at a place like Sandhurst, where he had to keep up with the Spartan routine in competition with stronger cadets.

Winston was posted to E Company, commanded by Major Oswald Ball of the Welsh Regiment, a peppery martinet who started out by telling his cadets: "I like to know the boys whom their parents can trust." This placed Winston at a disadvantage, for he was not among them. His father refused to grant him a "no restriction" leave. He knew it was no use trying to explain matters, and that he would go on being treated as "that boy" until he was in his dotage.[2]

He settled into the Sandhurst routine, determined to do well. His room, which he shared with two other cadets, was divided into cubicles like stalls in a stable. There was no carpet or curtain, no ornament of any kind, no hot water, and the food was terrible, even though the names of the dishes at dinner were written in French upon the menu. Reveille was at six-thirty, and discipline was strict—a cadet had been put under arrest for talking after being told to keep silent.

The day was taken up with studies, riding, and drill. Winston, who was not much good at drill, was put in the "awkward squad." He liked the studies, they seemed real to him, not like Greek and Latin. He was learning his trade: tactics, fortification, topography, military law, everything from keeping regimental accounts to inspecting meat. There was something exhilarating in this military routine in which everything was done according to the rules. For the first time in his life, he was punctual.

It seemed to the young cadet a pity that the age of wars between civilized nations had come to an end forever. He would have liked to be nineteen in 1793, with twenty years of war against Napoleon ahead of him. All that was over. The British Army had not fired at white troops since the Crimea. The world was peaceful; the great days would not come again.[3]

Another drawback was that polo and fox hunting were banned, since they were beyond the reach of most cadets. This equalitarian prohibition did not appeal to Winston, who had been given a horse by his aunt, and whose upper-class instincts viewed the measure as pure Socialism.

But all in all, Sandhurst was a revelation. For the first time in his life, he accepted discipline willingly. The insubordination he had displayed at Harrow and his other schools was gone. Sandhurst was strict, but fair. There was no flogging or fagging. He had not taken school seriously, but this was the Army, and his career depended on his performance. All the games he had played as a child, such as building fortifications and parapets, he was now doing in earnest, pushing himself to the point of collapse. On October 13, after a three-quarter-mile run with rifle and pack, he had to be helped off the parade ground by two sergeants, who took him to the infirmary, where the doctor told him he had a weak heart.[4]

Another reason for liking Sandhurst was that he was now considered fit company for his father, who felt that the college was doing wonders for him. His appearance had smartened up, he held himself straight, and his manners were quiet and polite. Randolph took him to parties at Lord Rothschild's house at Tring, where he met political leaders and the rising young men of the Conservative Party. To Winston, his father seemed to own the key to almost everything worth having. But when he tried to turn these friendly relations into true comradeship, he was rebuffed. Once, when he suggested that he might help the private secretary write some of his letters, Randolph froze him into stone. Winston hoped this was only a passing phase, and that the day would come when they would be friends.

That October, Winston's grandmother, Duchess Fanny, decided to dismiss Mrs. Everest. Randolph and Jennie were doubling up with her at Grosvenor Square, money was tight, and they were crowded. The Duchess, whose blind adoration of Randolph left no room for affectionate or even humane feelings toward the servants, said she had no further use for the faithful nanny. With Winston at Sandhurst and Jack at Harrow, she must go as an economy measure. This was done in a particularly underhanded and cruel way. She was told that she was going away on a holiday. Duchess Fanny planned to cut off her wages when she left, and to dismiss her by letter.

Winston was shocked at this shabby treatment of his beloved nurse. Jennie told him it was none of his business, but he knew that it was. He could not allow her to be cut adrift without protest, and besides, he did not want her to leave Grosvenor Square, because the loving companion of his early years was, more than anything else, associated with the idea of *home*. She was old and penniless and had been Jennie's devoted servant for twenty years. To pack her off as Duchess Fanny suggested, so that she would not know where to go or what to do, would be the end of her.[5]

He could not bear to see her gotten rid of in such a manner and wanted Jennie to tell the Duchess that she could not be sent away until she had found a good place. After that, she must be given a pension that would last the rest of her life and keep her from want. But Winston's loyal impulse did no good, and despite his anguish, he did not attempt a direct confrontation with his grandmother.

Mrs. Everest was turned out of the family whose children she had raised and went back to her former employer, Thompson Phillips, now archdeacon of Barrow-in-Furness, a kinder person than Duchess Fanny, who took her in, having less reason to. Although always short of funds or in debt, Winston regularly sent her a few pounds.

He turned nineteen that November 30 and began to be considered an eligible bachelor. Over the Christmas holiday he went to stay with Lord and

Lady Hindlip, where the chief attraction was their beautiful niece, Adela Hacket, known as Polly or Molly. All his life Winston had gone to boys' schools, sequestered from girls his own age, although he had in his mother a much-admired standard of female beauty. Now he had reached manhood, one of whose benefits was consorting with that exotic novelty, the opposite sex. He and Polly carried on a flirtation that lasted about a year. Winston gave her some sugar plums, and they corresponded, but it was all quite proper, for Lady Hindlip knew about it. Polly, a young woman dismayingly given to baby talk, asked for amusing "letterkins" and by March was calling Winston "best love."[6] He had promised a snapshot, which she wanted so much, and she hoped he would come and see her when she came to London. For a while he saw a good deal of Polly, but a year later, when she married his friend Kenneth Wilson, he showed no trace of sorrow. Polly was in a hurry to find a husband, whereas he had a great deal to accomplish before he could look for a wife.

Randolph told him that it was time to substitute "Father" for "Papa" in his letters. Winston tried, but kept lapsing, which Randolph thought was stupid and idiotic. Winston did not seem to notice that anything was wrong with his father, but the family doctor, Robson Roose, urged him to give up public life. Randolph insisted on attending Parliament, where his shambling gait and blank expression moved his worst enemies to pity. On March 19, 1894, when his old friend Lord Rosebery was Liberal Prime Minister, Randolph moved a motion that Rosebery had infringed the laws and liberties of the House of Commons over a procedural point. H. W. Lucy, the Parliamentary correspondent for *Punch*, saw a sad wreck of a man standing at the table attempting to read a prepared text in a voice so jangled that it was almost impossible to catch the meaning of consecutive sentences. As soon as Randolph rose to speak, members began to move toward the door, and when he sat down he had talked the place half empty. And this was the man whose speeches had once been reported verbatim, who had filled the House to capacity with the power and brilliance of his words.[7]

Randolph insisted that he was all right, but those who happened to run into him on social occasions knew otherwise. Lord Carnarvon sat next to him at dinner and reported that his conversation was "as mad a one as I ever listened to from mortal lips." Frank Harris, at another dinner, witnessed a scene both sad and comical. As the grouse was going around, the footman saw that it was not properly cut and bypassed Randolph to get it carved at the sideboard. "E-e-e-e-e!" squealed Randolph, as if in pain, pointing with outstretched hand. "What is it, Lord Randolph?" asked the host. "E-e-e-e-!" Randolph repeated, pointing after the footman. "I want that—e-e-e-! Some of that!" "It shall be brought back," said the host. "I'm very glad you like it."[8]

Randolph's one remaining satisfaction was to vent his spleen on Winston. When he was at Captain James's, Randolph had given him an expensive gold watch made by the exclusive London watchmaker Messrs. M. F. Dent. Winston cherished the watch, as he did anything that came from his father, and had a leather case made to protect it. In March 1894, as he was putting the watch in its case, a cadet running past him knocked it out of his hand and it fell to the pavement and broke. The repair bill from Messrs. Dent came to three pounds and seventeen shillings. A month later, on a Sunday, Winston placed the watch in his breast pocket, not having as part of his uniform a waistcoat pocket to hold it. Strolling on the Sandhurst grounds, along the Wish Stream, he stopped to pick up a stick, and the watch fell out of his pocket into the stream's only deep place for miles. Winston at once threw off his clothes and dove in, but the water was so cold and the bottom was so uneven that he had to give up.[9]

He was determined to retrieve the watch, however, and the way he went about it revealed his resourcefulness and instinct for command. The next day he had the pool dredged, but still no watch. On Tuesday, he obtained permission from the Sandhurst Governor to do anything he wanted, provided he paid the expenses. He borrowed twenty-three men from the infantry detachment and had them dig a new course for the stream. He then commandeered the Sandhurst fire engine, which pumped the pool dry. The rescue operation cost him more than three pounds, but he recovered the watch. The story became famous at Sandhurst, and grew with each telling: Winston Churchill had persuaded an entire Sandhurst company to help him pump the pond dry.

Back the watch went to old Mr. Dent, who was shocked at the way one of his best timepieces had been treated. The works were in a horrible state of rust and had to be completely dismantled. It was Winston's bad luck that while his watch was being repaired, his father came to inquire about his own watch and was shown the remains of his son's. Randolph hit the roof. It was as though Winston had to bear the blame for everything that went wrong in his father's life. There were, after all, worse examples of carelessness than breaking a watch, contracting syphilis being one of them. Once again, Randolph vented his wrath. How could Winston be such a young stupid? Clearly, he was not to be trusted with a valuable watch. When it was returned from

Messrs. Dent, Winston would not get it back. He had better get a two-pound watch, which was cheap to replace when it was broken. Look at Jack, who had kept the watch Randolph had given him longer than Winston had, without breaking it. But in all qualities of steadiness, taking care of his things, and never doing stupid things, Jack was vastly his superior.[10]

As usual, Jennie took her husband's side. She rarely came to Winston's defense. Kept informed by Dr. Roose and Dr. Buzzard, she knew the condition of Randolph's mind and did her best to calm his jangled nerves. What a harum-scarum fellow he was, she wrote Winston, and when would he stop being so childish? She sent him two pounds to help meet his expenses in recovering the watch.

Winston did not object to his father's unfair reprimands, or the endless comparisons favoring Jack. It was as if, sensing that Randolph was a dying man, he had decided to treat him with infinite patience. He apologized about the watch, and asked not to be judged on the strength of a single incident. He valued the watch and had done his best to get it back. Everything else his father had given him was in a good state of repair.[11]

That June, Randolph decided to take Jennie on a trip around the world. He wanted, among other things, to visit Burma, the land he had annexed. The doctors argued that a long and arduous journey to places where the heat was extreme was the worst thing for him, but he insisted. They hoped Jennie would return him at once to England should he show any further disturbance of his mental faculties.

Before leaving, he had another outburst for Winston, who had asked his father to open a bank account in his name and deposit fifteen pounds that he could draw on for special expenses. Randolph replied that Jack would have cut off his fingers rather than write such a free-spoken letter to his father. He was returning Winston's letter so that he could review its pedantic and overgrown schoolboy style. Perhaps it was due to his stupid typewriter, an objectionable machine designed to spoil his handwriting.[12]

There was also the matter of Winston's regiment. Randolph had put his name down for the 60th Rifles, the regiment of the Duke of Cambridge, who was a cousin of Queen Victoria's, and commander in chief of the British Army. Winston wished he was going into the 4th Hussars, a cavalry regiment that was leaving for India in three years and was just right for him. He hated the infantry, where his physical weakness was a disadvantage and where his only good sport—riding—was of no use. Randolph told him to put that idea out of his head, at any rate during *his* lifetime.[13]

On June 26, Winston was making a road map of Chobham Common when a cyclist messenger brought him an order from the college adjutant to go to London and see his father on his last day in England. An ordinary application for special leave having been refused, Randolph had telephoned the Secretary of State for War, Sir Henry Campbell-Bannerman, whom he had recently insulted in the House of Commons by accusing him of sleeping through a debate, and obtained his intercession. One thing Winston learned from his father was to do business, whenever possible, with the man at the top. They drove to the station the next morning—Randolph, Jennie, Winston, and Jack. Despite the bushy beard he had grown on his trip to South Africa, Randolph's face was haggard and worn with mental pain. He patted Winston on the knee in a simple gesture that seemed to the young man sadly eloquent, and was gone.[14]

Jennie at this time was forty. Still very beautiful, still sought after by a multitude of men, she had been married to Randolph for twenty years and had seen her hopes shattered as he sank into lunacy. She still loved Count Kinsky, although she had treated him badly, giving him up for another lover, Lord Wolverton, a member of the Prince of Wales's circle. Randolph complained that Jennie was practically living with Freddy Wolverton. She dreaded the idea of a trip that might take six months to a year, away from her lovers, her children, and the London society she had made her own. But her affection for Randolph and her sense of loyalty overcame her misgivings. They sailed aboard the S.S. *Majestic* with a young doctor who had been hired for the trip, George Keith, and Randolph's devoted personal servant, Thomas Walden. Somewhere during their bizarre six-month odyssey, they acquired a macabre piece of luggage, a lead-lined casket. The trip was a nightmare for Jennie, who dreaded each new place they arrived at. She dreaded the casual friendships formed with strangers while traveling, never knowing whether Randolph would be pleasant or launch into an irrational tirade. He changed by the hour. One moment he would be quiet and good-tempered, and the next he would attack his servant or sack his doctor. Once, aboard ship, he drew a loaded revolver and threatened her with it, but she snatched it away, pushed him back on his berth, and locked his cabin.

On every lap of the trip, there was a new crisis. In August, in California, Randolph flew into violent rages. In September, in Japan, his left hand went numb and became almost useless. In October, in Malacca, his speech was jumbled, and he had delusions. In November, in Singapore, his gait was staggering and uncertain, and his lower lip and chin were paralyzed, giving his face a cretinous expression. Dr. Keith warned him that it was folly to go to Burma, but Randolph insisted that he must see the land he had annexed. Keith felt then that he had lost all control over Randolph, and knew that he would not last more than a few months.[15]

Sometimes, when he was calm, Jennie watched him and thought of the brilliant man he had been, a man of such bright promise, and of what he was now.[16] In Madras, they saw another doctor who confirmed what Keith suspected—Randolph had about six months. It was cruel to let strangers see him this way, Keith thought. With the help of telegrams from Randolph's other doctors in London, he was prevailed upon to cut short the trip, and they sailed from Bombay at the end of November.

In his father's absence, Winston did a bit of maneuvering to get into the cavalry regiment he wanted, the 4th Hussars, and went to see its commander, Colonel John Brabazon. That September, Winston ran into the Duke of Cambridge, whose regiment his father wanted him to join, and Colonel Brabazon. "You're at Sandhurst, aren't you?" the Duke asked. "Do you like it?" Winston said he did, and Colonel Brabazon chimed in: "Going into my regiment, eh?" "Oh, I am very glad," the Duke of Cambridge said.[17] Winston thought the Duke must have forgotten all about his father's request. But what else could he say? He knew Winston's name was down for the 60th Rifles, but he was not about to enter into a tug-of-war with Colonel Brabazon.

Far from his father's condemning eye, Winston ran up debts, borrowed money, and stopped short of accepting an offer from a moneylender, the first step to ruin. He had two pairs of field glasses and thought of pawning one. His Aunt Sarah (Randolph's sister, and "such a cat") spread the gossip of "Winston's thievish practices" through the family, who believed her. Although not by nature vindictive, Winston would never forget her meddling. What a liar that woman was![18] In fact, Winston seemed incapable of committing a dishonest act. When his grandmother mistakenly began sending him twenty pounds a month for his allowance, he was quick to remind her that his father sent him only ten. Often, when he got into scrapes, it was because instead of hiding his actions, he proclaimed them.

During their twice-a-month leave from Saturday noon until Sunday midnight, Winston and his friends sometimes visited the Empire Theater, a music hall where young women not averse to the attentions of officer cadets could be found strolling in a broad open area behind the dress circle, which was lined with bars.

This mingling of Venus and Bacchus, with its attendant merrymaking, horrified Victorian reformers. Mrs. Ormiston Chant, a onetime assistant manager of a lunatic asylum who had taken up the cause of good morals, launched a campaign to cloister the Empire bars from the adjoining promenade. The issue was widely discussed in the London press, and the *Daily Telegraph* published a series headed "Prudes on the Prowl."

As a result of Mrs. Ormiston Chant's campaign, canvas screens were erected to separate the bars from the area where the ladies of the evening ambled. Winston was incensed. He saw the issue as one of freedom against coercion. England had too long obeyed the voice of the prudes. They and the weak-minded creatures who listened to them were extremely detestable. In trying to be original they had lapsed into the aboriginal. The "new woman," as exemplified by Mrs. Ormiston Chant, was merely the old Eve in a divided skirt.

In the Empire Theater controversy, Winston committed his first political act, in defense of the rights of the individual. Alive to the lessons of history, he saw himself resisting tyranny, like John Hampden, who had died on the battlefield in 1643 fighting the injustices of Charles I, and Algernon Sidney, who had plotted against Charles II to establish a republican government and been sentenced to death in 1683 after an unfair trial.

On November 3, the first Saturday after the partitions had gone up, Winston and some of his Sandhurst cronies arrived at the Empire and found a large number of university students there, already protesting. Someone poked his cane through the canvas, and soon Winston found himself leading a mob of about two hundred rioters that proceeded to tear down the offending obstructions. Climbing on the debris, the nineteen-year-old Sandhurst cadet gave his first public speech, which repeated a theme he had already aired in a letter to the *Westminster Gazette* on October 18: "The only method of reforming human nature and of obtaining a higher standard of morality is by educating the mind of the individual and improving the social conditions under which he lives." It was an abiding theme of his political life, although in this case its thrust may have been blunted by the "schoolboy prank" nature of the incident. But as the students and cadets sallied into Leicester square brandishing fragments of wood and canvas, Winston could not help thinking of the storming of the Bastille. He truly felt that he had resisted tyranny.

Winston wrote his father, hoping that he disapproved of the campaign against the Empire, but Randolph in his deteriorated state was past caring. Up until now, Winston had not realized that there was anything seriously wrong with his father. But the tone of his mother's letters made him ask Dr. Roose to tell him the truth. The trip was a disaster, Roose admitted, and

Randolph had only months to live. Winston was shocked and unhappy. It must be awful for his mother, but at least she was there near him. He was thousands of miles away, not knowing how much time his father had left, or whether he would see him again. Anxiously, he waited for his parents' return, and thought of meeting them in India.[19]

But he had to finish Sandhurst, where he was doing well, and might come out with honors. For once, there would be nothing for Randolph to criticize. On December 7, having just turned twenty, he competed for the riding prize with fourteen other cadets, which was considered a great honor. They jumped with and without stirrups, without reins, and with their hands behind their backs. Five were weeded out, and the remaining ten rode over fences. Six more were dismissed. Wild with excitement at being one of the four finalists, Winston rode as he never had before, but missed the prize by one point, coming in second with 199 out of 200. He sent an account of the event to his dying father, hoping he would be pleased. It was far easier to pick a regiment when the colonel knew you could ride.[20]

The Sandhurst exams were over on December 15. Winston did well in all subjects except drill (ninety-five out of two hundred points) and passed twentieth out of 130. Lo and behold, his conduct was listed as "Good."

As she sailed homeward with Randolph, Jennie pondered her future. She had received news that had shaken her as badly as her husband's madness. The faithful, lovable Kinsky, the one man she could count on, who was a friend to her husband and a companion to her sons, was marrying a young and lovely Austrian countess. If only he could have waited a bit longer. She knew Randolph was dying. Now she would lose not only Randolph, but Kinsky as well. She was being paid back for having mistreated him. Why had she listened to Wolverton, who had urged her to give Kinsky up, even though he did not intend to stick to her. If only Kinsky would wait, and she could have one more chance, she would make everything all right. The girl would be willing to give him up; she must know of his attachment to her. Her love for him was a form of addiction, it was like opium or drink, she could not help herself.[21]

By the time of Kinsky's wedding, on January 17, 1895, Jennie was back in London, with a cadaverous Randolph. What a dreadful homecoming, she thought; there was not a glimpse of hope. The doctors said he might die at any moment. When one thought of his brilliant abilities and vigorous mind, and all he might still have done, it was too tragic. Lord Salisbury had much to answer for. There was a time when a generous hand held out might have saved Randolph, but Lord Salisbury and the others were too jealous of him . . . one of these days it would all be known.

Randolph was past caring about Winston's results at Sandhurst. Alternately raving and comatose, he could barely recognize him. The scene at 50 Grosvenor Square was lugubrious, with masses of Churchills sitting with the old Duchess and filing one by one into Randolph's room.

In the predawn darkness of January 24, Winston, who had been farmed out to neighbors, was summoned, and ran across snow-lapped Grosvenor Square. The end was painless. Randolph had been in a stupor for days. As Winston gazed at the becalmed face on the pillow, his fondest hope was destroyed. It was a hope born when he was a child and saw his father under attack in and out of Parliament. Someday he would be elected to the House of Commons and come to his father's aid. There were other father-and-son teams. There was Gladstone's son Herbert, who helped his father cut down oak trees and accompanied him everywhere, and Joseph Chamberlain's son Austen, fighting at his father's side. Winston had attended the House on the day in 1892 when Austen Chamberlain made his maiden speech. Gladstone rose and called it "a speech which must have been dear and refreshing to a father's heart." It was a moving moment, with Chamberlain pink with emotion, half rising and making a little bow. Winston had often imagined the day when he would give his maiden speech, in defense of his father's principles. They would be allies, laboring together for the good cause. He would win his father's esteem, and they would talk as equals.[22]

Now he felt cheated, for they would never share the great world of Gladstone and Chamberlain, a world where high rules reigned and every trifle in public conduct counted, a dueling ground where, although the weapons might be loaded with ball, there was ceremonious personal courtesy and mutual respect. He would never be able to prove that he was not idle, not stupid, not what his father said he was. There remained only for him to pursue his father's aims and vindicate his memory. Many years later, when he had far outdistanced his father, he would grow maudlin and say: "Why could *he* not see what I have done?"[23]

On January 28, Randolph was buried in the churchyard of Bladon, a village near Blenheim, where his wife and sons would also be buried. On the same day, a memorial service was held at Westminster Abbey. Winston stood next to his mother, who was pale but perhaps relieved that Randolph's suffering was ended. In arctic cold, they listened to the "Dead March" from *Saul*. When it was over, Jennie and her sons received condolences from Randolph's political colleagues: Lord Rosebery, Randolph's friend since Eton, pink-cheeked from the cold, who had risen to become Prime Minister the year before, as Randolph descended into madness; Arthur Balfour, tall and distinguished, Randolph's disciple in the Fourth Party days, whose political fortunes had blossomed as quickly as Randolph's had faded; and Lord Salisbury, bearded and myopic, looking like an Old Testament prophet, who would return to the premiership for the third time that June.[24] These were the men who governed England. Randolph might have had his rightful place among them. But fate had decided otherwise.

He could not allow himself to think so, but his father's death was a blessing for Winston. First off, it solved the problem of his regiment. Randolph had told him that so long as he was alive, he would not go into the cavalry. Now he could join the 4th Hussars. Had he followed his father's instructions and gone into the 60th Rifles, he would never have been sent to India or taken part in the frontier war that launched his reputation as a writer.

Randolph alive would have been a continuing obstacle, reduced to a spluttering rage by the most venial of Winston's sins, keeping him on a short leash financially, insisting that he stay in the Army and out of politics, and persisting in favoring Jack at his expense, even though Jack, if any meaning could be attached to Jennie's naming him after her lover, John Strange Jocelyn, was not his son. Now, Winston could recast his father into the ideal-statesman mold, and explain his own overpowering ambition as a need to vindicate his memory.

Also, Winston could now form a true partnership with his mother. She had too often had to act as a buffer between father and son, placating the one and excusing the other. The way was clear for Jennie to become Winston's mainstay, helping him in his plans and confiding her own problems. She was a beautiful and youthful woman of forty-one, who knew everyone in London, and whose twenty-year-old son was about to launch a promising military career. They were natural allies. Winston was no longer a boy begging for money. He would soon contribute to her exchequer, as she dissipated her private income. Randolph had died in debt, owing the sum of £66,902 to the Rothschild Bank. With his father and both his grandfathers dead, he had become the man of the family. His father's death had freed him to grow at his own pace. "Solitary trees," he would write some years later, "if they grow at all, grow strong; and a boy deprived of a father's care often develops, if he escapes the perils of youth, an independence and vigor of thought which may restore in after life the heavy loss of early days."[25]

Thanks to Colonel Brabazon, a friend of Jennie's, a vacancy was found for

Winston in the 4th Hussars, a fashionable cavalry regiment stationed in Aldershot, site of the largest military training center in England, eight miles from Sandhurst and thirty-five miles from London. Brabazon, the dandified son of an impoverished Irish landlord, had impeccable social credentials; he had been aide-de-camp to the Queen and was a friend of the Prince of Wales. His aristocratic lisp and elegance of dress and manner had earned him the nickname "Bwab." Many stories were told about him. "And what chemist do you get this champagne fwom?" he had once asked the mess president. Another time, he was posted to an infantry regiment, and a friend asked which one. "I can never wemember," he said, "but they have gween facings and you get 'em fwom Waterloo."[26]

On February 19, 1895, Winston arrived at Aldershot, as a second lieutenant on pay of 120 pounds a year, with his own room and a servant. Sergeant Hallaway, a veteran 4th Hussar who had been in the charge at Balaclava, saw him walking over the squadron parade ground toward his stable, in his new uniform, and thought how odd he looked, his hair and his gold lace forage cap were the same color.[27]

The 4th Hussars subalterns were a lighthearted group, with their studies behind them, in the first flush of adult life, and much given to carousing and practical jokes. They had put their regimental riding master, a tyrant called "Jocko," in a terrible temper by placing an ad in the Aldershot *Times* that had made him the butt of much ridicule: "Major Jocko, Professor of Equitation, East Cavalry Barracks. Hunting taught in 12 lessons and steeple-chasing in 18."[28]

Aldershot was rolling country, good for cavalrymen, but Winston found the training arduous. After mounting and dismounting from a bareback horse at a trot or canter, and jumping a high bar without stirrups or saddle, he ended the day stiff and swollen and in pain. But barracks life had its pleasant aspects, for Winston had known many of these lively young officers at Sandhurst, and there was also a strong Harrow contingent. There was polo, steeplechasing, and five months' leave a year, which the officers were encouraged to spend fox hunting. Winston developed a passion for polo and went into debt buying ponies. His tailor had to wait six years to get paid. He also liked steeplechasing, although he had never tried it. But in March, a month after his arrival, he was invited to ride in the Cavalry Brigade's annual Aldershot races. One of his new friends, Lieutenant Albert Savory, had two horses entered in the 4th Hussars Subalterns' Challenge Cup, run over two miles and five furlongs, and worth twenty-eight pounds to the winner. Savory would ride one horse himself, but could not find a rider for the second, and asked Winston, who agreed, thinking that it would establish him as a good sport in the eyes of his peers. It was his first steeplechase, and the danger was real, for he had never jumped regulation fences. When his mother heard of his plan, she told him that steeplechasing was idiotic and dangerous, and Mrs. Everest reminded him that Count Kinsky had broken his nose at it.[29]

Five horses were entered in the Challenge Cup. Winston rode Savory's horse Traveler, and the four others were ridden by their owners, Lieutenant Reggie Barnes on Tartina, Second Lieutenant Henry Watkins on Dolly-do-Little, Lieutenant Alan Francis on an outsider named Surefoot, and Savory on Lady Margaret, a 5 to 4 favorite that had already won the Regimental Cup.[30]

On March 20, an apprehensive Winston arrived at the Aldershot track and mounted Traveler. Off they went, over the high fences. Dolly-do-Little fell, Tartina was out of the money, and the horse that Winston was riding came in third, a good showing for a first effort. The 6 to 1 outsider Surefoot came in first, followed by Lady Margaret. But when the official results were announced, Lady Margaret was declared the winner, and her name, with Albert Savory's, was engraved on the cup.

What had happened? It took a year for the stewards of the National Hunt Committee to publish their report. Because of a grave irregularity, the 1895 Challenge Cup race was declared null and void. The five horses that had taken part in the race were disqualified for all future races under National Hunt Rules.[31]

The announcement, published on February 20, 1896, in the *Racing Calendar*, gave no further explanation. Apparently another horse had been entered in the place of Surefoot. The replacement was discovered, and those who had backed the ringer lost their money. This was a serious matter in a land that holds sacred anything to do with the turf. Lord Salisbury did not call Cabinet meetings when there was racing at Newmarket, and the House of Commons adjourned for the Derby. And here was Winston caught up in a scheme to run a race with a ringer. This was no schoolboy prank, like breaking windows in an abandoned factory, but a full-fledged racing scandal.

The scandal broke in the pages of *Truth*, a muckraking periodical run by the politician and journalist Henry Labouchère, who made a specialty of exposing fraud. Labouchère expressed shock that the War Office had taken no action in the case, having come to the conclusion that the five gentleman riders had merely erred through ignorance of the laws of racing, and not with any dishonorable intention. But Labouchère saw something more serious, a rigged race. Surefoot was regarded as not having a chance. A much better horse was substituted and won. What of all the people who had bet on the favorite, Lady Margaret? If the substitution had not been discovered, they would have been cheated. And how could cavalry subalterns in a crack regiment, who owned, rode, and backed their own horses, and regularly attended races, be ignorant of the rules, and not see the impropriety of what they had done?[32]

The War Office maintained its position in spite of Labouchère's prodding. It seemed clear, however, that Winston had taken part in a discreditable affair, for he could not have ridden in the race without knowing about the substitution. He no longer had his father monitoring his behavior. Moreover, having been something of an outsider at Harrow and his other schools, he welcomed the chance to be popular in his regiment.

After the Challenge Cup, he was taken up by a trio of older and senior officers, all participants in the race, Albert Savory, Reggie Barnes, and Alan Francis. They made him feel that he belonged, that he was a regular fellow, who could, in regimental jargon, "go the pace." What a contrast this was from the criticism he had suffered all his life from his father and his teachers. Winston basked in the approval of this band of brothers. His need for acceptance was reflected in his letters to his mother. When he saw how some fellows who were disliked were treated, he wrote on April 27, he was very thankful that he had made his own friends and found his footing. In another letter, he referred to how short a time those who did not get along stayed; if you weren't liked, you had to go, and that meant going through life with a very unpleasant stigma.

Winston was so determined to be liked that he did things that went against his basic nature in order to win the approval of his peers. He became a ringleader in a gang that boycotted and forced out of the regiment an unpopular officer. Winston had been bullied as a child, hiding behind a tree from boys throwing cricket balls at him, and knew what it meant to be the victim of gang action. He might have been expected to come to the help of the underdog. But this time he was on the side of the bullies.

The 4th Hussars had a reputation for persecuting officers whom the inner circle of "bloods," men like Barnes and Savory, deemed undesirable. Among the undesirables were officers who did not have enough money to keep their own horses, or who displayed cowardice, poor horsemanship, or effeminacy. In January 1894, a year before Winston's arrival, a young man named

George C. Hodge had been gazetted to the 4th Hussars, with an allowance of three hundred pounds a year. At the mess, he was asked where his hunters and racehorses were kept, and he said he could not afford to keep either. "Then what the hell did you join this regiment for?" a captain demanded. Hodge said he had been appointed to it by the War Office.

Hodge was unsuited to the cavalry. In training he refused to jump the bar, held on to the saddle and cried, and finally would not mount his horse. Several times he reported himself sick but the doctor found nothing wrong with him. Hodge was hazed mercilessly by his brother officers. They forced the locks of his drawers and tore up and burned his clothes. Four subalterns, including Barnes and Savory, broke open his door at two in the morning, dragged him into the yard, and forced him into a horse trough, pushing him under the bars until he was bruised and bleeding. A mixture of salt and cayenne pepper was forced down his throat. He was made the butt of a remorseless boycott, harder to bear than the hazing. A small group of officers, who felt they represented the best traditions of the regiment, turned, with a tribal, almost cannibalistic instinct, against those who they decided did not belong. Hodge gave up. He went on sick leave, a complete wreck, sent in his papers, and left for the colonies. Winston probably had Hodge in mind when he wrote his mother about the stigma of being expelled from the regiment.[33]

The Hodge affair took place before Winston came to Aldershot, but he was involved in a similar incident, which must stand as the most shameful episode of his early life. In April 1895, Second Lieutenant Alan Bruce was gazetted to the 4th Hussars as a replacement for Hodge. A good horseman, a good shot, and a good enough fencer to have been in a sword display before the Duke of Cambridge, Bruce had been at Sandhurst with Winston, where they had apparently been rivals.

Before joining the regiment, Bruce was invited to dinner at the Nimrod Club in London by six subalterns, including Winston and three of the four other riders in the rigged Challenge Cup. At the conclusion of the dinner, Winston, acting as spokesman for the junior officers, told Bruce he was not wanted in the regiment. On his allowance he could not keep up. Bruce, who had an allowance of five hundred pounds, whereas Winston's was about three hundred pounds, found his behavior offensive and insulting. The diners then told him that they had gotten rid of Hodge and would get rid of him too. He could make a graceful exit now or a disgraceful one later. Bruce told his hosts that he had no intention of giving up his military career. After what had passed he was not that eager to join the 4th Hussars, but unless he could get another regiment, he would.

Bruce then went to Aldershot to report the threats to Colonel Brabazon, who was away. He saw the adjutant, Captain De Moleyns, who dismissed the matter, and shortly thereafter Bruce joined the regiment. He soon found that his dinner hosts had organized a boycott against him. Bruce was not like Hodge; he could hold his own. Indeed, he seems to have been a bit of a ruffian, using violent language to noncoms and soldiers serving under him. He coached a regimental team for a shooting meet at Bisley, site of the ranges of the National Rifle Association. The 4th Hussars won the Duke of Cambridge's Shield. But for this he received no thanks, from the Colonel or anyone else. At Bisley, Bruce had lost his temper with the sergeant of another cavalry regiment who Bruce thought had addressed him improperly. Colonel Brabazon was placed in the humiliating position of having to apologize for Bruce to the officer in command of the other regiment. Small wonder that the Colonel sympathized with the officers who wanted to get rid of Bruce. Winston was a favorite of the Colonel's, while Bruce, with his rough ways, was not the sort of man to keep up a high level of gentlemanlike feeling and conduct.

On Boxing Day, the first weekday after Christmas, Bruce was Orderly Officer in the barracks. That evening, he was told that there was a veteran of Balaclava in the noncoms' mess. Wanting to meet a survivor of that great event, he went there, although strictly speaking the noncoms' mess was off limits for officers. The regimental sergeant major asked Bruce, since it was Christmas, to drink the health of the mess, which he did, returning to his quarters half an hour later.

Three days later, on December 29, he was placed under arrest, remaining in his room until January 7, without knowing the charges against him. The Colonel then told him that either he or Bruce would leave the regiment. Bruce asked what the charges were and was told that he was under arrest for "improperly associating with noncommissioned officers." It was clear to Bruce that he had been framed with the collusion of Colonel Brabazon and the sergeant major, who had testified against him. He had been lured into the noncoms' mess and invited to drink with the sergeants, then was arrested on a trumped-up charge. Three days later, Bruce was brought before Lord Methuen, the major general commanding the Home District, who told him that if he did not send in his papers, his services would be dispensed with. Bruce had no choice. He left the Army.

Again, it was Labouchère's *Truth* that brought the Bruce case before the public, and there were questions in Parliament, but again, no action was taken. Who, asked Labouchère in the House of Commons, were the ungentlemanly officers, Bruce or the men who had told him they would turn him out because he had only five hundred pounds a year? As for himself, Labouchère said, he did not believe a more disreputable set of young men existed in the whole Army.[34]

The Bruce case did not end with his expulsion from the regiment. He left Aldershot in January 1896 and was replaced by Second Lieutenant Ian Hogg (a brother of Douglas Hogg, later 1st Viscount Hailsham). Bruce's father, Alan Cameron Bruce-Pryce, was a respectable sixty-year-old barrister, a graduate of Oxford. Twice married, he was the father of a remarkable number of children, ten sons and seven daughters. Incensed over the treatment of his son, Bruce-Pryce was sure that Winston had instigated the whole thing. At Sandhurst, Winston and his son had been bitter rivals in shooting, fencing, and riding. He alleged that his son knew too much about Winston, particularly about the case of a Sandhurst cadet who had been publicly flogged for committing acts of gross immorality of the Oscar Wilde type with Churchill. Bruce-Pryce was looking into the matter and would make a statement to the War Office.

Bruce-Pryce included these defamatory accusations in a letter dated February 11, 1896, to Ian Hogg, who was buying some of his son's things. He was accusing Winston of committing homosexual acts while at Sandhurst, and such acts were a criminal offense under the law of 1885, the same law under which Oscar Wilde had been found guilty and sentenced. Winston lost no time in suing Bruce-Pryce for criminal libel, asking for twenty thousand pounds in damages.[35] Colonel Brabazon approved of his prompt action in the courts. Even though he was guiltless, one could not touch pitch without soiling one's hands. Malignant and preposterous as the charge was, it could not remain unchallenged; people would hem and haw and wink about it.[36]

On March 12, Bruce-Pryce withdrew the charges and Winston won five hundred pounds in damages. After paying his legal fees, he had four hundred pounds left, which he wanted to give to charity, but his lawyer told him the money was just as much his as if a jury had brought in a verdict in his favor.[37]

Even in anger, it was thoughtless of a man trained at the bar to make accusations based on hearsay, of which he had no personal knowledge. Unable to prove the slander, Bruce-Pryce had to settle by paying damages. But in one respect, that of seeing Winston as the instigator of the conspiracy against his son, Bruce-Pryce was closer to the mark.

Lord Wolseley, who had replaced the Duke of Cambridge as commander in chief of the British Army in 1895, conducted a personal inquiry into the Bruce case, which was in effect a whitewashing of the officers involved. But one paragraph in Lord Wolseley's report, referring to the dinner at the Nimrod Club, was of particular interest:

"Such action on the part of Mr. Bruce's brother officers was certainly reprehensible, but it seems to have been really occasioned by a prejudice against him arising from reports which had reached the regiment as to his previous career, the alleged insufficiency of his means being put forward merely as a pretext."[38]

Here was the nub of the matter: How had reports about Bruce reached the regiment? No one there had any interest in the man except Winston, his rival at Sandhurst. It was Winston who had spread stories about him, with Bruce unable to defend himself, and who had convinced the Savory-Barnes clan that he should be drummed out of the regiment. To malign a young officer before he has had a chance, and prejudge his fellow officers against him, was a slander as grave as Bruce-Pryce's. The injury to Bruce, with the collusion of Colonel Brabazon and the cover-up of the War Office and Lord Wolseley, was considerable. He was forced out of his chosen career, after a long and expensive period of training, and his prospects in life were impaired. As Lord Wolseley's report said, such action was "reprehensible."

In the spring of 1895, shortly after Bruce's arrival, Winston wrote his mother that he had made a great many friends in the regiment, and knew his ground, in marked contrast to the unfortunate fellows who did not know how to get on. He was quite ashamed of enjoying himself so much while others were miserable. Although he had hurt his leg racing, he had ridden in a point to point with forty-nine fences and was one of five finishers in a field of thirteen. He was also playing polo, the finest game in the world; he would almost be content to give up any ambition to play it well and often. His social life was flourishing. He had so many invitations he could have gone to a ball every night had it not been for the exhausting drills and field days. One of the young ladies he was seeing was Muriel Wilson, the youngest daughter of a prosperous shipping line owner, Arthur Wilson, who owned an Italianate mansion called Tranby Croft. He later proposed to Miss Wilson, who turned him down (she did not marry until she was forty-three years old), and he resolved after that never to marry for money. She remembered him at Tranby

Croft, walking up and down the drive and repeating sentences with lots of s's in them, to correct his lisp, such as "The Spanish ships I cannot see, for they have not yet sailed in sight."

That June, Winston was staying at Blenheim and went to Bladon to visit his father's grave. The church service was going on and the children's voices rose in song. The sun had dried the grass a bit, but the rosebushes were in bloom, and Winston was struck by the quiet and the old-world air of the place, and knew that this was the spot his father would have chosen.[39]

That visit to Bladon was the prelude to another melancholy event. On July 3, Mrs. Everest died of peritonitis at the age of sixty-two, severing Winston's strongest link with his childhood. He went to London, arriving for the end, and engaging a nurse. It was shocking to see the poor woman drift off, but Winston was sure that his coming had made her die happy. Of one thing he was certain: he would not know such a friend again. He had never stopped to think how much poor old Woom had meant to him, and felt very low. On July 5, he went to her funeral, and as he watched her wreath-covered coffin being lowered into the ground, he thought of the days at Connaught Place when his father was a rising young politician and fortune still smiled. He was very despondent. It was the third funeral he had attended in five months.[40] There had been Randolph's in January, and Jennie's mother, Mrs. Jerome, had died in April. All that one could learn was the insignificance of human grief. Who was left? Only his mother. He could not imagine what he would do without her.

Winston was restless. His life was pleasant enough, and he liked the Army, but one thing was missing: there was no fighting. He felt the want of active service, and worried that pacifist governments would make wars obsolete. Officers scrambled for tidbits of battle in the Sudan or on the Indian frontier. Scarcely a subaltern could be found in Her Majesty's forces who had even seen the smallest kind of war.

Winston pondered this unhappy situation. His winter season of five months' leave was coming up, and there was one corner of the globe where the general peace in which mankind languished had been broken. An insurrection had erupted in Cuba, with the return from exile of two rebel leaders, Máximo Gómez and José Martí. The Pearl of the Antilles, under Spanish occupation since the sixteenth century, was in an actual state of war. The great Spanish general, Martínez de Campos, had occupied the principal towns to confine the rebellion to the outlands, but guerrillas engaged the Spanish troops as soon as they ventured from their barracks.

This would be as good as fox hunting, Winston thought, and convinced his friend Reggie Barnes to go with him. He planned to bring back a quantity of Havana cigars, which could be laid down in the cellar of his mother's house at 35 Great Cumberland Place. The first step was an introduction to the Spanish commander. His father's old friend Sir Henry Drummond Wolff was British ambassador to Spain. Would he give Winston a letter to Martínez de Campos? He would. The next step was army permission to visit the battle scene. Going right to the top, he went to see Lord Wolseley, who said all right, but hinted that it would have been better to go without asking.

Winston also called on General Edward Chapman, the head of Military Intelligence, who gave him maps and information, and asked him informally to find out what he could about a new bullet the Spanish were using. Imbued with a sense of mission, he went to the *Daily Graphic*, the newspaper that had printed his father's letters from South Africa, and obtained a commission to write reports on Cuba at five guineas each, which would help cover his expenses.[41] Not the least of his motives was a passion to emulate and outdo Randolph, whose South African journey had created a storm of controversy. All this having been done, Winston felt that everything was "Sir Garnet" (an expression of the time meaning "shipshape," after Sir Garnet Wolseley, who was sent to trouble spots in the Empire to set matters right). He was displaying unusual enterprise for a youth of twenty, and an uncanny instinct for knowing what button to push to get things done.

Winston and Reggie sailed from Liverpool on November 2, 1895, arriving in New York on the tenth. It was his first visit to the land and city of his mother's birth. The two subalterns were met at the dock by one of Jennie's recent lovers, a former New York congressman and Tammany Hall politician named Bourke Cockran, then a forty-one-year-old widower. Cockran, an Irishman of the silver tongue and golden heart variety, made a strong impression on Winston. He later said that he modeled his speaking style on Cockran's. "In point, in pith, in rotundity, in antithesis and in comprehension," he wrote, "Bourke Cockran's conversation exceeded anything I have ever heard."

Cockran put them up at his apartment at 763 Fifth Avenue and took them to visit points of interest. Winston sat in on the trial of a man who had killed his sister's lover after she had died of an abortion. He visited West Point and was surprised at how strict it was; the cadets could not smoke or keep money and got hardly any leave. He gave America mixed reviews. American hospitality was a revelation; he could not get over the fuss that was made over them. The country was great and utilitarian, but completely without reverence and tradition. In the courtroom there had been no robes or wigs or uniformed ushers, but they managed to hang a man all the same. The newspapers struck him as vulgar; the best ones were written for housemaids and footmen. They had been odious about his cousin "Sunny," the 9th Duke of Marlborough, who had just married an heiress, Consuelo Vanderbilt. He reserved his deepest contempt for paper currency. Accustomed to gold sovereigns, he viewed the paper dollar as the most disreputable "coin" the world had ever seen. And yet there was a remarkable strength and energy to American society; the capitalist system seemed to work. Benefits had been secured for the people not by confiscating the property of the rich or by arbitrary taxation, but simply by business enterprise—out of which the promoters themselves had made colossal fortunes. Small wonder that the first-class men were in the countinghouses while the less brilliant ones were in government. All in all, Winston felt, America was a great lusty youth moving about his affairs with a good-hearted freshness that might well be the envy of older nations of the earth.[42]

After a week in New York, Winston and Reggie took a train to Key West and embarked on the steamer *Olivette*, which docked in Havana on November 20. Winston was worried that he would have trouble getting his pistols through customs in wartime, but his letters of introduction did the trick. He checked into the Grand Hotel Inglaterra and at once began setting up contacts. Alexander Gollan, the British consul, took him to see General Arderins, the military commander of Havana, who wired Marshal Martínez de Campos that two young British officers were on their way to the front.

Martínez de Campos received them in Santa Clara, a hundred and fifty miles east of Havana, and sent them to his chief of staff, General Valdez, at Sancti Spiritus, forty miles farther on. Valdez gave them horses and servants, and they stayed with his unit in the field for eight days, advancing with the picturesquely clad Spanish troops, who wore cotton uniforms and broad-brimmed straw Panama hats. They slept in hammocks and ate at the General's mess, which was quite good until the cook got shot. The troops covered about eighteen miles a day, with time out for a siesta.

Winston was too eager for the smell of battle to give much thought to the merits of the war. General Valdez was in pursuit of a rebel band under Máximo Gómez, whose abandoned camps they kept finding. On November 30, his twenty-first birthday, Winston got the finest present he could have hoped for—he came under fire. The column had stopped for breakfast in a small clearing, and as he stood chewing on the remains of a scrawny chicken, some rebels armed with American rifles opened fire from behind the trees.

The next morning, the march continued through thick forests, and on December 2, in open country, General Valdez attacked the rebels' rear guard. Winston, staying close to the General, watched the Spanish infantry move across the plain toward a low grass hill, firing its Mausers. The General, on a gray horse, resplendent in a white-and-gold uniform, drew a great deal of fire, and the casualties on his staff were out of all proportion. The firing, Winston thought, was like the buzz of an offended hornet. He was impressed at how many bullets it took to kill a man.

The enemy retreated, and Winston was surprised that General Valdez did not attempt pursuit. Two thousand of the best troops on the island, under a General of Division, had been quite content to kill thirty or forty rebels and take an insignificant hill. Such tactics would make the war interminable. Winston's assessment was shrewd, for a month after his visit, Marshal Martínez de Campos was replaced by the more dogged and ruthless General Weyler.

A great lover of battles and medals, Winston had taken part in his first action, which became known as the Battle of La Reforma, and won his first decoration, the Rioja Cruz, for gallantry.[43] Although gallantry implied active participation, he did not boast about what he had done to win it, for his position was delicate. As a guest of the Spanish Army, he was not supposed to take part in hostilities. Indeed, he told the press on his return to America that he had not even fired his revolver. The decoration was just a courtesy.

Winston had finally succeeded in imitating his father. The press rebuked him as it had Randolph after his insulting remarks about the Boers. American newspapers sympathetic to the rebel cause (the United States would go to war with Spain over Cuba in 1898) said he was a British agent sent to give military advice to the Spaniards. On December 7, the *Newcastle Leader* wrote: "Sensible people will wonder what motive could possibly impel a British officer to mix himself up in a dispute with the merits of which he had absolutely nothing to do. Mr. Churchill was supposed to have gone to the West Indies for a holiday . . . Spending a holiday in fighting other people's battles is rather an extraordinary proceeding even for a Churchill." The *Eastern Morning News* on the same day said: "Difficulties are certain to arise and Lord Wolseley will probably order him to return at once and report himself."[44] But Lord Wolseley and the War Office preferred to ignore the subaltern's adventures, which brought him more notoriety than glory.

In his articles for the *Daily Graphic*, Winston saw a case for the Cubans. They were overtaxed, and the administration was corrupt, with all the offices reserved for Spaniards. This was the first direct experience of imperialism and colonial abuse for the future Colonial Under-Secretary, who felt that a national and justifiable revolt was the only possible result of such a system. But although he sympathized with the principle of rebellion, he did not approve of the rebels, an undisciplined band of sham heroes who burned cane fields and fired into sleeping camps. He also foresaw that in the event of a rebel victory, racial strife would break out between the Hispanic and Negro elements.

Winston later wondered whether his reporting had been honest, whether he had lived up to the principle of "this above all: to thine own self be true." Perhaps, he reflected, in not wanting to run down his hosts, he had been unfair to the insurgents and had made a case for Spain. But Ambassador Sir Henry Drummond Wolff, who had used his influence on Winston's behalf, wrote him in February 1896, after the articles had appeared in Spain: "Please read the enclosed which is attributed to you. I should be very glad if you could avoid saying things unpalatable to the Spaniards; having obtained the letters on your behalf which secured your good treatment I am reproached for the unfavorable commentaries you make. I am sure you will be careful as this kind of thing places me here in a painful dilemma."[45]

The start of the new year, 1896, saw Winston back in England. His regiment, on the eve of being stationed in India, had moved from Aldershot to Hounslow, a suburb ten miles southwest of London, once the site of a Roman camp. Through friends of his father, Winston had access to the principal political figures of his time. On January 26, he went to Tring to see "Natty" Rothschild. Perfectly at ease, the twenty-one-year-old subaltern chatted about current events with two future Prime Ministers, Arthur Balfour and Herbert Asquith. Hubert Howard, the *Times* reporter who had covered the Cuban war on the other side, tried to lure Balfour into recognizing the rebels, and Winston was glad to see that he refused to be caught. The big news was the invasion of the Boer Republic of Transvaal by Cecil Rhodes's right-hand man, Leander Jameson, with a force of six hundred. The Jameson raid was ostensibly in support of the mainly British non-Boer population, called *Uitlanders*, to whom the Boers denied political rights. Hoping to capture Johannesburg with *Uitlander* help from inside the city, Jameson had been caught and handed over to British authorities. Believing that Jameson and his men deserved exemplary punishment, Balfour said: "It is a case for the jury." Winston thought that South African opinion, which would bitterly resent a severe sentence, should not be altogether disregarded.[46] In May, he was invited to dinner by Mrs. Adair, a noted London hostess, with his commander in chief, Lord Wolseley, and Joseph Chamberlain, then Colonial Secretary, with whom he discussed South Africa. At his Aunt Lily's, he met Sir Bindon Blood, a respected general on the Indian frontier, and made him promise that if he ever again held command in India, he would appoint Winston to his staff. Once, taking a late train for a weekend, he kept the Prince of Wales waiting. "Don't they teach you to be punctual in your regiment?" the Prince asked, glaring.[47]

All this hobnobbing with the famous seems to have turned Winston's head. He now looked upon going to India with his regiment as useless and unprofitable exile. He wanted to go to South Africa, where the Jameson raid anticipated the Boer War. He was sure he could win some medals and return with enough fame to beat his sword into an iron dispatch box—for he had decided to go into politics. His mother preached the gospel of patience, but Winston would not listen. It was intolerable to be going to India when so much was going on in South Africa.

In favor of a political career, Winston had his father's example, easy access to Conservative circles, powerful contacts in both parties, and unlimited drive and intelligence. But he had no money, and in those days Members of Parliament received no salary. The usual doors of entry were closed, for he did not have a university education, and could not subsidize politics with a law practice. The Army would have to be his platform. If he won fame as a soldier, he could make the transition. He remembered his father's words: "The Army is the finest profession in the world if you work at it and the worst if you loaf at it." He also thought that a career in journalism might provide the funds other young men already had to enter politics. His uncle Moreton Frewen, who had given him his first typewriter in 1893, praised his articles and advised him to write more crisply. Winston replied that the only great prose writer he had read was Gibbon, who could not be accused of crispness. Winston felt that composition was an artificial science. To make a short sentence tell, it should be sandwiched in between lengthy and sonorous periods. The contrast was effective.

Winston made a halfhearted effort to get transferred to South Africa, but at that time he was under a cloud, for the Labouchère articles on the Bruce scandal had begun to appear in *Truth*. The Reverend Mr. Welldon had been following his fortunes with a strong feeling of affection, but wrote him that "it is impossible that I should not hear of your follies and impertinences if you are guilty of them and you will recognize that you put a severe strain upon my friendship if you ask me to treat you as a friend when other people speak of you with indignation or contempt."[48] Stung, Winston thought that Welldon's letter did not do him credit. If he believed the tales and reports of his enemies, his friendship was valueless. As for Labouchère, he was an unprincipled scoundrel, and one day Winston would make him smart for his impudence. But if Labouchère's accusations went unchallenged, his chances of a public life would be ruined. He did not, however, challenge them, although he had been quick to sue Bruce-Pryce.

On September 11, 1896, the 4th Hussars sailed from Southampton for Bombay aboard the hired transport *Britannia*, after a farewell speech in which Colonel Brabazon, who was giving up the regiment, referred to "India, that famous appanage of the Bwitish Cwown." The trip, across the Mediterranean and through the Suez Canal, took twenty-one days. A fervent advocate of free trade, Winston was furious at having to declare a long list of objects for duty, even his regimental saddle. This was his first direct experience of protectionism. (Later, in the House of Commons, he would sponsor a bill to exempt from Indian duty the musical instruments of regimental bands.) It was disgraceful that public servants going to India on government service should be taxed this way. To impose a tax on a saddle used only in military employment was a monstrous act of injustice, the detestable fault of bureaucracy, a pitiful act of parsimony on the part of the Indian government.[49]

When they landed at Bombay on October 2, they took skiffs into the harbor. As Winston disembarked, grabbing iron rings attached to a stone wall for handholds, his skiff, rising and falling with the swell, swung away, and he slipped on the dripping stone steps, dislocating his right shoulder. It was an injury that crippled him for the rest of his life. He could not play tennis, and when he played polo, his right arm had to be strapped to his body with a leather belt so that it did not swing too freely. The shoulder would come out at the most unexpected moments; once it almost went as a result of a too-expansive gesture in the House of Commons.[50]

From Bombay, the 4th Hussars took a train to their garrison in Bangalore, about six hundred miles to the south, in the tip of the Indian subcontinent, due west of Madras. The climate was pleasant, for Bangalore was three thousand feet above sea level, and garrison life was quiet. The only action was at the other end of India, on the North-West Frontier, policing hostile tribes. Winston shared a palatial bungalow with Reggie Barnes and Hugo Baring, complete with a rose garden, a butler, a houseboy, and a groom. The garden had seventy kinds of roses, and every morning Winston cut enough to fill three basins. Another pastime was catching butterflies, for all about the garden flew purple emperors, white admirals, and swallowtails. Winston sent for boxes, boards, and pins, and caught butterflies as he did everything, intensely, until his bunkmates complained that the place was turning into a taxidermist's shop. He had collected sixty-five different species when they were destroyed by a marauding rat.[51]

There was not much to do in the way of duty; sometimes a little office work, or an inspection of kit or saddlery. By lunchtime the day's work was done, and the officers could devote themselves to polo in the cool hours of the afternoon and evening. Winston was in every chukka, for to him, polo was not a game but a serious purpose in life. He borrowed rupees from fat and rapacious Madras moneylenders to keep up his string of ponies (which he used as collateral). His pay by now was about three hundred pounds a year, and his mother's allowance was five hundred, but it was never enough.

Winston and his teammates trained for the Inter-Regimental Cup, which had never been won by a cavalry regiment from southern India. They thought nothing of traveling a thousand miles on a train, a thirty-six-hour ride, for a polo match with another regiment. On one occasion, they went to Ambala, north of Dehli, to play the Royal Scots Fusiliers. A young fusilier nicknamed "the Camel," because he carried a small head on a tall frame, found himself playing against Winston, who banged his polo stick across the neck of his adversary's pony. "Play to the rules," the young fusilier shouted, "and take that stick out of my eye." But Winston leaned across all the harder, and they galloped along until sheer deadlock brought them to a standstill. The squarely built, sandy-haired Winston, who even with a bad shoulder was a formidable opponent, said: "Who the devil were you talking to? If you've a complaint, speak to the umpire." Furious, the young fusilier knocked the stick out of Winston's hand and galloped off. His name was Hugh Trenchard, and he would become known as the father of the R.A.F. The two young polo players would meet again under friendlier circumstances, when Churchill was Secretary for War and Air in 1919 and Trenchard became his Chief of Air Staff.[52]

In November, Winston went to Hyderabad, a mere three hundred miles north of Bangalore, to compete for the Golconda Cup. At the garrison parade, he watched elephants dragging large cannons in tandem, and saluting with their trunks as they passed. The best team were the Golcondas, the bodyguards of the Nizam of Hyderabad. The 4th Hussars defeated these turbaned warriors by 9 to 3, setting a record of winning a first-class tournament within fifty days of landing in India.

At another tournament in Secunderabad, ten miles from Hyderabad, Winston met the most beautiful girl he had ever seen, "bar none," Pamela Plowden, the daughter of the Hyderabad Resident, Trevor Chichele-Plowden. Seven months older than Winston, Pamela was a blonde with a soulful expression, big blue eyes, and a Cupid-bow mouth. In the drawings done of Winston and Pamela by Lady Granby, they look like mirror images. Winston was smitten, and took her on an elephant ride through the city of Hyderabad. He was glad for her company, infrequent though it was, for nice people in India were like oases in the desert. He had no fondness for the Anglo-Indian community; they were nasty, vulgar creatures, and the women thought themselves great beauties.[53] Lord and Lady Elgin, the Viceroy and his wife, were stiff and pompous and unpopular.

Winston went through fits of depression when he saw himself as an insignificant subaltern condemned to wait in a garrison town that was like a third-rate watering place out of season. The life in India was stupid and dull and uninteresting. He would have learned more about the country as a young MP in three months than as a soldier in five years.[54] Jennie, who was ambitious for her son in a pragmatic American way, tended to agree. How little one heard of generals in time of peace, she wrote him; there was very little glory and honor to be gotten out of the Army, a moderately good MP got better known and had more chance of success than a really clever man in the Army.

But it was one of Winston's strengths that he never allowed circumstances to overwhelm him. His was a self-created personality that instinctively found ways to complete its missing parts. He lacked the well-rounded education of a university man. At Sandhurst, the studies were martial. He resolved to exercise his "empty, hungry mind" by reading works of history and philosophy, of which he remembered every word, for his memory was phenomenal. He used the idle midday hours, when his fellow officers napped or played cards, to do his serious reading. From November to May, he read four or five hours a day, twenty-five pages of Gibbon and fifty of Macaulay, and other equally serious tomes. He "rode triumphantly through Gibbon," scribbling his opinions in the margins. "First we shape our dwellings," he would say fifty years later, "and then our dwellings shape us." He also read all the old volumes of the *Annual Register* that mentioned his father, adding his comments. In the *Annual Register* for 1876, next to an account of a debate on female suffrage, he wrote: "I shall unswervingly oppose this ridiculous movement. If you give women votes you must ultimately allow women to sit as members of Parliament. True the Civil Servants and Clergymen have votes & don't sit. But they are few & their votes cannot coerce the community. Once you give votes to the vast number of women who form the majority of the community, all power passes to their hands."[55] In the light of Churchill's subsequent quarrels with the suffragettes, it is interesting to find this early opposition to female suffrage.

Sergeant Hallaway, who was Winston's troop sergeant in Bangalore, recalled that "Mr. Churchill was a real live one. The great thing about him was the way he worked. He was busier than half the others put together. I never saw him without pencils sticking out all over him. And once when I went into his bungalow I could scarcely get in what with all the books and papers and foolscap all over the place."

Winston's reading did not interfere with his military duties, far from it. After a field day, he would arrive at the stables with paper and pencil and question Sergeant Hallaway about the movements they had done at the exercises. Short of stable hands, Hallaway was too busy to discuss tactics just when he was unsaddling and grooming and feeding the horses. Winston was a major annoyance. If Hallaway ignored his questions, Winston would say: "All right, you are bad-tempered today."[56]

Usually, officers stationed in India did not return to England for three years, but in May 1897, Winston somehow wangled three months' leave after only eight months' service. It was the year of Queen Victoria's Diamond Jubilee, celebrating her sixty years on the throne. He had seen the Golden Jubilee while at the Misses Thomson's school and wanted to see its sequel. How many Diamond Jubilees would a young officer see in his lifetime? On the boat back to England, he met a tall, thin colonel named Ian Hamilton, then in charge of musketry training in India. Winston liked him at once; he was a good storyteller, and had an interesting mind. He formed a friendship with the higher-ranking officer, who was twenty years his senior, and who would, in later years, command the troops in the Gallipoli expedition. Hamilton at once saw that Winston was one of destiny's tots; but his wife, Jean, the hardheaded daughter of a Glasgow businessman, had no use for his new friend. Several years later, when Winston was an MP, she wrote in her diary that she had gone to the terrace of the House of Commons for tea and that "Winston Churchill did not come, thank goodness. I can't bear him, which is rather a pity as Ian thinks such a lot of him and says he is bound to be a commander-in-chief or a Prime Minister—whichever line he cares to cultivate."

On July 2, Winston took his mother to the great ball given by the Duchess of Devonshire at Devonshire House in Piccadilly, which would be converted, in a more commercial age, into an automobile showroom. He was glad to have seen this glittering spectacle of a vanishing world, where the guests were costumed as great figures from the past: Joseph Chamberlain as Louis XIV, the Duchess of Sunderland as Charlotte Corday, Lord Rosebery as Horace Walpole, and Jennie as Theodora, the dancing girl turned Empress of Byzantium through her marriage with Justinian.

Winston's aim during his stay was to nudge open the door of the Conservative Party. In July he went to St. Stephen's Chambers to see Captain Fitzroy Stewart, the secretary of the Conservative Central Office. Was there any chance for a young officer on leave to speak at a political meeting before rejoining his regiment? It appeared that there were hundreds of meetings, indoors and outdoors, fetes, bazaars, and rallies, all clamoring for speakers. Bath was selected as the site of his maiden effort. Winston would speak on July 26 at the meeting of the Primrose League on Claverton Down, a park belonging to an elderly gentleman named H. D. Skrine, who headed the league in Bath.

On the appointed day, Mr. Skrine fastened the Primrose League badge on Winston's lapel and launched him on his career as a public speaker. The topic was a compensation program for injured workmen, which would have been dear to the Tory Democrat heart of his father. The Radicals had called it an Employers' Liability Bill, Winston pointed out, while the Tories called it a Workmen's Compensation Bill. Radical methods were slapdash, reminding him of the man who, on being told that ventilation was an excellent thing, broke all the windows in his house and died of rheumatic fever. Conservative policy was a look-before-you-leap policy, slow and constant, and this bill showed that the Tories were willing to help the workingman.[57] Winston was cheered loudly, and several newspapers commented favorably on his delivery, mental agility, and striking resemblance to his father in features and coloring. But the *Eastern Morning News* of August 3 warned of the danger of being spoiled by flattery and public notice. The House was full of sons of famous men who had become political nonentities.[58]

Winston was at the Goodwood races a day or two after his Bath speech when a newspaper headline caught his eye: the Pathan tribesmen had revolted on the northwest border of India and Afghanistan, and a field force of three brigades had been formed in Malakand, under the command of Sir Bindon Blood. These frontier wars were a by-product of Britain's "Forward Policy" of pushing up to the borders of Afghanistan. Into the medieval lives of mountain tribesmen the troops brought British administration and the breech-loading rifle. Irked by the imperial presence, the tribesmen frequently fought the former with the latter. Winston telegraphed at once to remind Blood of his promise to take him on his staff, cut short his leave, and took the train to Brindisi, where he caught the S.S. *Rome* to Bombay. But in Bombay there was no word from Sir Bindon. Winston went to Bangalore to obtain leave from his colonel, just in case Blood could make room for him, but when he had not heard by August 17, he began to think that someone at Army headquarters had put a spoke in his wheel. Winston was disgusted. The frontier was ablaze, fifty thousand men had been concentrated in the area, but his chances of joining in the action seemed to be evaporating. Every day his hopes dimmed. This was a lesson as to what his chance of success in the Army was worth. About a week later, however, he heard from Sir Bindon, who had filled up his personal staff, but advised Winston to come as a press correspondent, for it was not unusual in those days for officers on active duty to double as journalists. As soon as there was a vacancy, that is, a casualty, Blood would do a little intervening on Winston's account.[59]

With great difficulty, and thanks to the efforts of his old friend Reggie Barnes, who was now the regimental adjutant, Winston obtained a month's leave from his colonel, who did not like to see his subalterns wandering about India and attaching themselves to other units. He also managed to get ac-creditation to the *Pioneer*, a newspaper in Allahabad that had published some of Kipling's early work. His mother in the meantime succeeded in getting him a contract with the *Daily Telegraph*, whose proprietor, Edward Levy Lawson, specified that he wanted "picturesque forcible letters."

Winston was in the Malakand camp on September 5 when he heard the good news, having traveled about fifteen hundred miles by train, in an August heat so oppressive that he could almost lift it with his hands, to reach the front near the Khyber Pass, close to India's northernmost point. He wanted to sign his letters, for they might help him politically, but on the advice of Lord Minto, a former correspondent in the Afghan and Egyptian wars, who would become Governor-General of Canada in 1898, Jennie had them signed "by a young officer," to Winston's intense annoyance, compounded because he had asked for ten pounds a letter and was paid half that. Jennie would have to make up her mind to his doing unusual things, and to the ensuing publicity.

But these were minor annoyances. The main thing was that Winston had fulfilled his dream: to command British troops in a real war. "I have faith in my star," he wrote his mother, "that is that I am intended to do something in the world."[60] This was his first explicit disclosure of a new fantasy that had been grafted onto the childhood vision of an ideal father. He was developing an irrational conviction that he was on earth for a special purpose. This was why the hand of providence protected him in battle. Such grandiose thinking seemed like an aspect of infantile omnipotence; the child saw himself as the center of the universe. But in Winston's case, instead of being an empty dream, the sense of destiny propelled him to act in order to make it valid. It was more than a need to compensate for childhood deprivation by gaining fame. It was a mystical certainty that he was marked for greatness, which nothing in his life thus far warranted.

Winston spent six weeks with the Malakand Field Force and sent fifteen dispatches to the *Daily Telegraph*. It was a strange war, he thought, as he went reconnoitering in the villages along the Afghan border, one moment the people were your friends and the next moment they were shooting at you. At first he was attached to the brigade of Brigadier General P. D. Jeffreys, whom he thought of as a nice man but a bad general. On September 16, the brigade went on a punitive expedition to the Mamund Valley, driving off the tribesmen's cattle, cutting their crops, destroying their water tanks, and burning their villages. The brigade was attacked by a large body of tribesmen, and Winston took part in his first battle as a combatant, the biggest battle in India since the Afghan war. It turned out to be a rout for the British, who left their wounded behind to be savagely mutilated.[61] Out of 1,300 men, they lost 150 killed and wounded.

Winston was with the 35th Sikhs and saw their adjutant, Lieutenant Victor Hughes, fall. Four of his men lifted him, but he was heavy, and when they were rushed by half a dozen Pathan swordsmen, they dropped him and fled. The leading tribesman slashed at Hughes's prostrate figure, and Winston, watching thirty yards away, forgot everything else except an urgent desire to kill the man. He fired several times but was not sure he had hit him. He then carried a wounded sepoy (Indian soldier) back to the lines, staining his pants with the man's blood. He was disappointed that no one had seen him perform this gallant action. Given an audience, no act was too daring. At any rate, no one could say that he lacked physical courage. He had been under fire from 7:30 A.M. to 8:30 P.M., and had ridden his gray pony all along the skirmish line when everyone else was taking cover. He expected to get a medal or a couple of clasps. Winston was a shameless glory hound and medal hunter, for the whole purpose of his joining the field force was to gain a reputation that he could translate to the political arena. He was quite candid about it, and constantly referred to the medals he hoped to win.

After the costly reverse of September 16, he was attached to the 31st

Punjab Infantry Regiment as a matter of "extreme urgency," for they had only three white officers left. Even this took some doing, for there was a marked hostility toward him on the part of the authorities in Simla, the summer capital of the Indian government. Winston wondered why high-ranking military men spent so much time harrying an insignificant subaltern, simply because he had not paid his obeisance to the higher-ups, while every tame cat and lapdog was hurried into the best place that could be found. They were childish in their malice, and one day he would find out to whom he owed all the attention and settle scores, although his enemies were so much older than he was that they might be in the grave before his chance for vengeance came.[62] He did not stop to think that he was acting in an unorthodox manner calculated to annoy his superiors, using his own and his mother's contacts in London and throughout the Army to pick and choose where he wanted to be and what he wanted to do. No army could approve of such independent behavior. Who was this Churchill who would not stay put, who was always asking for leaves and transfers, who never went through proper channels, and who seemed to think that the military hierarchy would part for him like the waves of the Red Sea?

Winston had a language problem in the Punjab Infantry, but found that he could get by with three words, *maro* (kill), *chalo* (get on), and tallyho! On September 30 there was a battle at Agrah. It was the fiercest fighting on the frontier in forty years. In command of one hundred men and hoping for some *action d'éclat* that would win him a medal, Winston was under fire for five hours. In a force of twelve hundred, there were sixty killed and wounded. The tribesmen, firing Martini-Henry rifles, were crack shots, and could run up hills twice as fast as the British, who were using Lee-Metford rifles with dumdum bullets. Winston wanted his mother to talk to the Prince of Wales about the heavy losses in the Mamund Valley, so that a special clasp might be given to those who had fought there. He did not win any medals or clasps, however, but was mentioned in a dispatch that praised "the courage and resolution of Lieutenant W. L. S. Churchill, 4th Hussars, the correspondent of the *Pioneer* newspaper with the force who made himself useful at a critical moment."[63]

In mid-October, after a fortnight's extension of his month's leave, Winston was ordered to leave the Malakand Field Force and return to the 4th Hussars in Bangalore. What a "dirty tale of petty childish malice" on the part of the Simla authorities, he thought.[64] His mood improved when he learned on December 2, a few days after his twenty-third birthday, that he had been mentioned in dispatches. Since he thought of himself as in many ways a coward, particularly during his schooldays, there was no ambition he cherished so keenly as gaining a reputation of personal courage. Those six weeks had been the best of his life. A smiling providence had looked after his welfare, for no bullet had come close. And now he was back in his sleepy garrison town, going to target practice instead of firing at Pathan rebels.

To amend for the anonymity of his letters, Winston decided that November to expand them into a book, *The Story of the Malakand Field Force*. But he had a rival; Alexander Fincastle, the *Times* correspondent, who had won the Victoria Cross, was also putting his dispatches between hard covers. Winston worried that the subject was so small there was not room for two books. Everything depended on who finished first. Working at a breakneck pace, and astonishing himself with his industry and application, he wrote the book in seven weeks. Jennie took the manuscript to A. P. Watt, one of the first literary agents, who negotiated a contract with Longmans. Winston thought the terms were fair and hoped to make three hundred pounds. He asked his uncle Moreton Frewen, who had encouraged his writing and had a literary reputation in the family on the strength of a pamphlet on bimetallism, to edit the book and go over the proofs. He could not do the job himself because of the long delay in transmitting the material back and forth to India. This was his one mistake, for Frewen, a dreamer whose financial schemes invariably collapsed, and whose nickname was "Mortal Ruin," did a sloppy job. The review in *The Athenaeum* said that Winston's book "suggests in style a volume by Disraeli revised by a mad printer's reader . . . one word is printed for another, words are defaced by shameful blunders, and sentence after sentence ruined by the punctuation of an idiot or of a school-boy in the lowest form."[65]

Winston was furious. Having given Moreton the job was like asking a butterfly to carry his bags. The glittering prize of literary appreciation had been snatched away.[66] But someday he would write something that would take its place in permanent literature.

Aside from this blunder, however, the book was well received and came out ahead of his rival's. Between March 1898 and January 1899, 8,500 copies were published. It was a solid little octavo volume of three hundred pages. On the jacket was a pensive young man with thinning hair who, dressed in a morning coat with silk lapels, did not look in the least like the officer on active duty whose experiences the book recounted.

In January 1898, Winston asked his mother to tell him what parts of the book she liked best. "I love the praise," he said. "It is delicious." Through his life until then he had heard a long list of uncomplimentary comments, "Indifferent," "Untidy," "Slovenly," "Bad," and "Very Bad." Now, he was told that he had a wisdom and comprehension far beyond his years.

He had in fact cleverly deflected any critique that focused on his age by writing that "there will not be wanting those who will remind me that in this matter my opinion finds no support in age or experience. To such I will reply that if what is written is false or foolish, neither age nor experience should fortify it; and if it is true it needs no such support. The propositions of a Euclid would be no less indisputable were they propounded by an infant or an idiot."

Winston was not timid about criticizing British policy. What was the point of extending the British presence into the inaccessible North-West Frontier? he asked. The tribesmen were best left alone. He wrote with a natural authority that was astonishing in a self-taught twenty-three-year-old subaltern. The only sign of immaturity was an unconcealed admiration for what he called "the great game of war," but this he kept all his life. To hear him tell it, war was an ideal occupation, full of wonderful opportunities: "The healthy open-air life, the vivid incidents, the excitement, the generous and cheery friendships, the chances of distinction which are open to all, invest life with keener interests and rarer pleasures. The uncertainty and importance of the present, reduce the past and future to comparative insignificance, and clear the mind of minor worries. And when all is over, memories remain, which few men do not hold precious."

He also showed a fondness for describing the gore of battle, which may partly have accounted for the book's success, for in Winston's words, "the English are essentially a warlike, though not a military people; that is to say, they are always ready to fight, though not always prepared to do so." He lingered lovingly on the wounded, their faces drawn by pain and anxiety, looking ghastly in the pale light of the early morning; officers with hands and legs smashed; a doctor holding between his finger and thumb the artery of a man who had fainted from loss of blood. Such scenes recur so frequently that the reader begins to wonder about Winston's appetite for blood, which he freely admitted when he wrote: "Yet the reader will forgive me if he has ever seen the lance point covered with blood and glittering redly in the sunlight. It will recall a vivid impression." Partly it was the exuberance of a young man who, having survived combat, was fascinated by those who had not, as in this passage: "Riding back to camp, I observed a gruesome sight.

At the head of the column of coolies and stretchers were the bodies of the killed, each roped on to a mule. Their heads hung down on one side, their legs on the other. There was no other way, and it was better than leaving their remains to be insulted and defiled by the savages . . ." Partly, it was a genuine feeling that war was a pinnacle of human activity, in that it provided an outlet for disinterested behavior. It was a proving ground for the noble and heroic. Winston echoed Kipling's sense of the stoicism of the soldier of Empire, as in:

> *When you're wounded and left out on Afghanistan's plains,*
> *And the women come out to cut up what remains,*
> *Jest roll to your rifle and blow out your brains*
> *An' go to your Gawd like a soldier.*

Winston was making a name for himself. Letters of praise came from George Curzon, then Under-Secretary of State for Foreign Affairs and soon to be Viceroy of India, and from the Prince of Wales, who had spotted his cleverness early on, and who now wrote: "I cannot resist writing a few lines to congratulate you on the success of your book! I have read it with the greatest possible interest and I think the descriptions and the language generally excellent. Everybody is reading it, and I only hear it spoken of with praise. . . ."[67]

Family matters took Winston's attention away from his book. Jack, now eighteen, wanted to go to Oxford. With Randolph dead, Winston provided paternal advice. He approved of Oxford, for Jack's mind was reflective rather than inventive, and he should have a university education, even though he believed that Oxford was the home of more bigotry and intolerance, and had defended more damnable errors and wicked notions, than any institution under the sun except the Catholic Church. Jack felt he was made for the Army, but Jennie would not hear of it, she already had one son in the Army, and it was a poor career, removing him to distant places, away from his mother. Jack toyed with the idea of the bar, or the Foreign Office, or the City, lacking Winston's resoluteness. Winston told him to make up his mind and do what he wanted.[68]

Unpleasant papers arrived at the start of 1898 from Jennie's solicitors, Lumley & Lumley. She had taken out a seventeen-thousand-pound loan. The collateral consisted of life insurance policies in her name and Winston's. In the event of Jennie's death, Winston would have to pay the premiums, amounting to seven hundred pounds a year. Winston and Jack would each get about eighteen hundred pounds a year when their mother died, and seven hundred pounds was almost half of that. Winston was annoyed that such an important matter had been presented to him in a sketchy letter from a solicitor. It was like Harrow: decisions were made without consulting him. His own extravagance was nothing compared with his mother's. In the three years since his father's death she had spent a quarter of their entire fortune, and now had to stoop to borrowing. This insurance scheme left a dirty taste in his mouth. He would sign the papers out of pure affection, but only on two conditions: that his mother continue his allowance of five hundred pounds a year for the rest of her life and that Jack agree to split the premium when he came of age.[69] Winston did not let his love for his mother stand in the way of his interests. She was still his "dearest Mama," but the role of victim was one he never learned.

In late February of 1898 Winston went to Meerut, about forty miles northeast of Delhi, with the 4th Hussars polo team for the Inter-Regimental Cup match. His team was second best, beaten only by the Durham Light Infantry, the only infantry regiment ever to win the Cavalry Cup. That night, there was a festive dinner to celebrate the event, and a great many toasts were drunk to the health of all the teams. Spurred by the libations, Winston rose and said: "Now, gentlemen, you would probably like me to address you on the subject of polo." Ignoring the cries of "No, we don't" and "Sit down," he discoursed on the subject with a genial smile, silencing the audience with an easy flow of words. Polo, he said, was not only the finest game in the world, but the most noble and soul-inspiring contest in the whole universe. He wound up with a peroration that brought his fellow players cheering to their feet. Then someone rose and said, "Well, that is enough of Winston for this evening." Several husky subalterns grabbed him and wedged him under an overturned sofa upon which two sentries remained seated with orders not to allow him out for the rest of the evening. Winston soon popped up from beneath the angle of the arm and took his place at the table, saying: "It's no use sitting upon me, for I'm India rubber."[70]

From Meerut, Winston went to Peshawar, only six hundred miles away, the railhead for another punitive expedition on the North-West Frontier. The Afridi tribesmen, traditional keepers of the Khyber Pass, had revolted in October 1897, capturing the surrounding army posts in the Tirah area and attacking the forts near Peshawar. Winston hoped to get appointed to the Tirah Field Force, see more action, and perhaps win a medal.

Winston reached Peshawar, the chief military station of the North-West Frontier Province, on March 5, and found his way to the headquarters of the Tirah Field Force commander, General Sir William Lockhart. The General's aide-de-camp, Captain Aylmer Haldane, was in his office when a short, sandy-haired young man with the steel chains of a cavalry officer on his shoulders burst in. He said he had been given a few days leave from his regiment, the 4th Hussars, and was anxious to be employed. Winston had by now gained enough notoriety so that his reputation preceded him. Haldane, a tall and solemn-faced Scotsman, knew that Winston was regarded as superprecocious but insufferably bumptious. But he liked the young man's enthusiasm and took him across the road to meet Sir William, suggesting that Winston could replace an orderly officer who was leaving. Busy with his paper work, Lockhart looked up and said, "All right, take him if you like."[71]

The Captain and the Second Lieutenant quickly became friends. When one got to know him, Haldane thought, Winston was not all that assertive. Undoubtedly, he was a prodigy, cut from a vastly different pattern than any officer of his years Haldane had ever met, and not born to blush unseen. They took long walks along the dusty roads outside the city, and Winston quoted from his father's speeches and vowed to follow in his footsteps.

Winston thought Haldane was overbearing, irritating, and indiscreet, but in many ways remarkable. Undoubtedly, he was one of the best wire-pullers in the Army. Haldane confided the dark secret that was ruining his life. Although a member of a famous Scottish family, and a cousin of Richard Burdon Haldane, who would later gain renown as a great Secretary of State for War, Aylmer Haldane had been tricked into marrying a barmaid who told him she was pregnant. He could not stand the sight of her and offered her half of everything he owned in exchange for a divorce, but she was bent on being a lady. His career would be ruined by his private life.

Winston's response was properly Victorian. The girl was not a virgin when she had married Haldane. Therefore she was to blame. Such a thing would never happen to him; he would be more careful. What was her health like? Winston asked. Excellent, Haldane replied. In that case, Winston facetiously suggested, murder was the only solution.[72]

He had hoped for a fight, but the fighting was over. The Afridis sued for peace, and the operations languished. His stay in Peshawar had not been a total loss, however, for he had made new friends in high places. In any case, there was a much bigger war on, which he decided he must join. Since 1896, Sir Herbert Kitchener, Sirdar, or commander, of the Egyptian Army, had been moving southward up the Nile, reconquering the Sudan in short stages, building a railway as he advanced with his Egyptian troops stiffened by British units. Winston had three months' leave coming for having been in the Malakand campaign and planned to take it from June 15 to September 15 and join Kitchener's army.

At once, he put his mother to work pulling strings. She wrote Kitchener, whom she knew slightly, mentioning Winston. By coincidence, she was traveling to Egypt on a winter holiday, but Winston thought she was making a special trip on his behalf and wrote her that it was an action that would certainly be admired if he ever had a biographer.[73] How many twenty-three-year-olds have there been, one wonders, who numbered among their preoccupations whether they would have a biographer? There was no limit to Winston's self-confidence, as he was the first to admit. In a moment of self-analysis, he saw himself as not caring so much for the principles he advanced as for the impression his words produced and the reputation they won for him. He could rarely detect genuine emotion in himself. In most matters his head or wits directed. When Ian Hamilton wrote him, "You have in you the raw material for several successful careers," he realized that he had to be careful, for the Admirable Crichton many-sided sort of career led to dispersion of effort, indefiniteness of aim, and ultimate disappointment and defeat. It would be nice to achieve the combined careers of Marlborough, Napier, and Pitt, but it was unrealistic.[74]

On April 8, Kitchener fought and won a major battle at the town of Atbara, on the Nile, about two hundred miles north of Khartoum, routing sixteen thousand Dervishes. Winston was bitter that he had missed the fighting, and told Jennie not to relax one volt of her energy, for there would be more battles ahead. In the meantime, he was back with his regiment in Bangalore. It was hot and the polo ground was deep in dust. He was working on a novel, a political romance temporarily titled *Affairs of State*. Spurred by the good notices of his first book, he contemplated a steady output of literary production, including a life of Garibaldi, a short history of the American Civil War, and a volume of short stories.[75]

Winston sailed from Bombay on June 18, 1898, with two thoughts uppermost in his mind: to get himself assigned to the Sudan expedition and to address some more political meetings. But on arriving in London, he found that the efforts of the petticoat brigade, consisting of Jennie and her friend Lady Jeune, who was prodding Sir Evelyn Wood, the Adjutant General, had miscarried. Too many high-ranking officers were asking questions about

Winston. Who the devil was this fellow? How had he managed to get to these different campaigns? Why should he write for the papers and serve as an officer at the same time? Why should a subaltern praise or criticize his senior officers? Why should generals show him favor? How did he get so much leave from his regiment? Why, he was nothing but a medal hunter and a self-advertiser. These murmurs must have reached Kitchener's tent, for the Sirdar did not want him, although he was willing to have his rival officer-correspondent, Lord Fincastle. Sir Evelyn Wood wrote again to Kitchener, and Lady Jeune sent him a telegram making a rash promise in her eagerness to help: "Hope you will take Churchill. Guarantee he won't write."[76]

But Kitchener was not noted for responding to appeals from society women, and Winston was wondering what to do next when rescue arrived in the form of an invitation from Lord Salisbury, then Prime Minister and Foreign Secretary, who wanted to meet the young author of the book on the Malakand Field Force. In mid-July Winston went to call on the man who was the master of the British world, three times Prime Minister, and unchallenged leader of his party. In the spacious room overlooking the Horse Guards Parade, the stout and patriarchal figure greeted him and led him to a seat on a small sofa. There had been bitter debates on the frontier policy in Parliament, Lord Salisbury told his young guest, adding that "I myself have been able to form a truer picture of the kind of fighting that has been going on in these frontier valleys from your writings than from any other documents which it has been my duty to read." Salisbury kept him for half an hour and said as he left, "If there is anything at any time that I can do which would be of assistance to you, pray do not fail to let me know." The man who had destroyed his father's career, whom Randolph had hated and wanted to see dead, was holding out a helping hand. Winston seized it eagerly and wrote Lord Salisbury on July 18, asking him to put in a word with Lord Cromer in support of his appointment. Lord Cromer, the British consul general in Cairo, was in fact the political master of Egypt, and presumably carried some weight with Kitchener. Lord Salisbury saw Lord Cromer on the following day, but as it turned out, his intervention was not necessary.[77]

Lady Jeune, that determined woman, had told Sir Evelyn Wood that she had heard someone at a dinner party grumble that Kitchener was going too far in picking and choosing among the officers recommended by the War Office. Indignant at the Sirdar's high-handed conduct, Sir Evelyn expressed himself with considerable feeling on this subject. But although Kitchener had absolute control over the Egyptian Army, the British contingent was part of the Expeditionary Force, under the authority of the War Office. When Lady Jeune told Winston about her conversation, he said: "Have you told him that the Prime Minister has telegraphed personally on my behalf?" She said she had not. "Do so," Winston said, "and let us see whether he will stand up for his prerogatives."[78]

Two days later he received the following message from the War Office: "You have been attached as a supernumerary Lieutenant to the 21st Lancers for the Sudan Campaign. You are to report at once at the Abbasiya Barracks, Cairo, to the Regimental Headquarters. It is understood that you will proceed at your own expense and that in the event of your being killed or wounded in the impending operations, or for any other reason, no charge of any kind will fall on British Army Funds." The death of a young officer in the 21st Lancers, P. Chapman, had created the vacancy that sent Winston to Egypt. Now he had to get an extension of his leave from the military authorities in India.[79]

Winston had not been idle while waiting for his appointment to come through. On July 14, he spoke at a Conservative meeting in Bradford, a center of the worsted industry near Leeds, and his father's old stamping ground. The hall was packed, and he was received with enthusiasm. When he announced that he had spoken for an hour, they shouted, "Go on for another hour" and "Coom back, lad." At the supper afterward at the Midland Hotel, broad hints were made that the local party leaders would like to have Winston back in "another capacity."[80] This, his second speech, was a crucial test. He saw that his lisp was not a hindrance, that his voice was strong enough, and that he had the ability to rouse and amuse his audience. With practice, he knew, he would achieve great power. He was sure that the moment was not far off when he would resign his commission.

Winston left England at the end of July, without knowing whether his new assignment had been cleared with his regiment in India, and took the paquebot *Sindh*, "a filthy tramp—manned by these detestable French sailors," from Marseilles to Egypt, reaching Cairo on the evening of August 2 and going straight to the 21st Lancers' barracks. Since no telegrams of recall awaited him, he concluded that " 'silence has given consent.' " His squadron started south the next day, aboard a slow steamer that carried men and horses on the rising river against a six-knot current. How strange it was, after the busy streets of London and the elegant dinner parties, to be floating on the muddy Nile and looking at groves of palm trees and the sails of the dahabiahs. Winston no longer thought of speeches and constituencies, but of swords, lances, pistols, and soft-nosed bullets.[81]

There was also the chance to write another book. He had contracted with the *Morning Post* to write articles at fifteen pounds each and finished the first two during the long boat ride to Wadi Halfa, on the border of Egypt and Sudan. He did not feel bound by his promise to Lady Jeune not to write anything, for the promise was contingent on Kitchener's accepting him in the Egyptian cavalry. But he asked his mother to put the case before her, not wanting her to think he had broken his word.

Winston reached Atbara on August 14, 1898, and reported to his regiment, the 21st Lancers, known as the "Saucy Devils." The Lancers hated attached officers, whom they regarded as meddlesome intruders, and made no attempt to conceal their dislike of the new arrival. Instead of being given a troop to lead, he was put in charge of the mess stores. Winston's self-assurance astounded his fellow officers. He was always sounding off. For instance, he announced that Thomas Gray's "Elegy Written in a Country Churchyard" was a beautiful poem, and that there was not a word in it *he* would care to alter. He told everyone that he did not intend to stay in the Army, not caring to spend the rest of his life "in the company of intelligent animals." He asked one of the Lancer officers, Lieutenant R. N. Smyth, how he could be content to remain a troop leader of cavalry at the age of thirty. Smyth found that in spite of Winston's faults, he could not help liking him. He was very young, but if he survived the River War he would be a big man someday.[82]

Churchill's presence nagged at Kitchener like a backache. He knew Winston was not going to stay in the Army, and was there only to make his reputation. He disapproved of his coming out in the place of others whose careers were at stake, and thought that Sir Evelyn Wood had acted wrongly by sending him. He had come up the hard way, and had no fondness for young patricians who obtained appointments through favoritism, and even less did he like those who combined the jobs of officer and war correspondent.

Winston did not much like Kitchener either. With the class blinkers of his time, he divided the world into those who were gentlemen and those who were not. Kitchener might be a good general, but he would never be a gentleman.

Made aware of Kitchener's resentment by a fellow correspondent, Colonel Frank Rhodes of the *Times*, Winston was nagged by anxiety. Every day he expected Kitchener to say, "Send him back to the base; let him come on with the remounts after the battle." Whenever he saw a staff officer, he imagined it was Kitchener's emissary coming after him.[83]

Then forty-eight, Horatio Herbert Kitchener, the grandson of a tea merchant and the son of a professional soldier, had graduated from the School of

Military Engineering at Chatham, and his great gift was for organization. Commander in chief of the Egyptian Army since 1892, he was a man of striking appearance, tall, with a mustache that completely covered his mouth, and strange eyes, the upper lids a straight line, giving a tigerish cast to his face. The burden of command made him morose and surly, and he gained a reputation for ruthlessness and pathological thriftiness. The conquest of the Sudan, which he had begun two years earlier, was a crusade to avenge the disastrous Nile expedition of 1884–1885, in which General Gordon had been killed.

In 1882, an ascetic Moslem holy man who called himself the Mahdi, meaning "he who is chosen," had led an uprising of Arab tribes in the Sudan, forcing out the Egyptians. The Mahdi wanted to detach the Sudan from Egypt and establish an independent Moslem state. The British, who had occupied Egypt, sent General Gordon to defeat this dangerous religious reformer, but after being surrounded and blockaded for ten months in Khartoum, the General was killed in 1885, two days before the arrival of a rescue column. Across the White Nile from Khartoum, the Mahdi built a new capital called Omdurman, with a mosque in which he was buried when he died of typhus soon after his victory. But his movement lived on, under the leadership of a Khalifa, who now awaited Kitchener in Omdurman with sixty thousand Dervish troops.

Kitchener's 8,200 British and 17,600 Egyptian troops were moving slowly up the Nile with their artillery, Maxim guns, horses and mules, past villages with unfamiliar names, Wad Habeshi, Shabluka, Um Teref. This last place they reached on August 28, some thirty miles from Omdurman. Winston, whose regiment had caught up with the main force, rested in the shade of palm trees, and protested with the others when fatigue parties chopped them down for wood for the gunboats. The next morning, while the horses were being watered, he climbed to the top of a hill twenty miles from Omdurman and observed through his field glasses the great army spread out below, the brown masses of infantry and artillery, the fringe of cavalry dotting the plain, the chocolate-colored men of the Camel Corps on their cream-colored mounts, the white gunboats stealing up the Nile, and, far in front, the enemy's patrols. A long account awaited settlement. . . .

On September 1, from the top of another hill, he could see both armies, separated by only five miles. The Khalifa's army, dark smears and smudges on the brown of the plain, was on the move. Kitchener's force had grouped in a crescent formation, with its back to the Nile, covered by gunboats. It was 1

P.M., and if the Khalifa's movement continued, he would reach Kitchener's army before dark. Winston's regimental commander, Colonel Rowland Hill Martin, chose him to convey this information to the Sirdar. As he rode toward Kitchener's *zeriba*, or encampment, Winston wondered, would he be angry, would he say, "What the devil are you doing here? I thought I told you not to come," would he be disdainfully indifferent, or would he simply receive the report without troubling to ask the name of the officer who brought it?

Winston found Kitchener riding a few hundred yards from the *zeriba*, followed by a dozen staff officers. He drew his horse alongside and slightly to the rear and saluted. It was the first time he had seen that remarkable countenance, the heavy mustache, the queer rolling look of the eyes, the sunburned and almost purple cheeks and jowl. "Sir," he said, "I have come from the 21st Lancers with a report." Kitchener listened in absolute silence as Winston told him that the enemy was advancing in large numbers between the British position and the city of Omdurman. "You say the Dervish army is advancing," Kitchener said. "How long do you think I have got?" The commander in chief was asking a subaltern's advice, which Winston did not hesitate to give. "You have got at least an hour—probably an hour and a half, sir, even if they come on at their present rate," he said. Kitchener tossed his head in a noncommital manner and with a slight bow indicated that the meeting was over. Winston saluted, reined his horse in, and let the Sirdar's retinue flow past. In search of lunch, he rode back to the *zeriba* and went into a mess tent where he found himself with the German military attaché, Baron von Tiedmann, who had come along as an observer, and who said: "This is the first of September. Our great day, and now your great day; Sedan and Sudan."[84] Winston laughed at his ponderous wit, and wondered about the outcome of the battle. If he was killed, he had written his mother, she must reflect on the insignificance of all human beings. And if he survived, he would come back wiser and stronger and find a wider sphere of action.[85]

Later in the day, when it had become apparent that the Dervishes had stopped advancing, Winston was strolling along the bank of the Nile with a friend when a naval officer called out from one of the gunboats in the river, "How are you off for drinks? We have got everything in the world on board here. Can you catch?" A bottle of champagne was flung toward the shore, landing in the water. Winston nipped in up to his knees and seized the precious cargo, which he carried triumphantly back to the mess.[86] The officer in command of the gunboat was a twenty-seven-year-old naval lieutenant named David Beatty, who was destined for high commands.

There was some concern over Kitchener's position. The Khalifa had sixty thousand men to his twenty-six thousand. What if he used his overwhelming superiority in numbers in a night attack, when British firepower would be ineffective. He could stampede the horses and mules and break into the *zeriba*. All night long, the gunboats swept no-man's-land with their search-lights, and the British dug trenches and reinforced the enclosure of thorn-bushes, but the Dervishes did not attack.

As soon as it was light enough on September 2, between 5 and 6 A.M., cavalry patrols were sent out to report on the Khalifa's position. The Dervishes were in the plain, great masses of men on a front nearly five miles long, with the first rays of dawn glancing off their spearpoints. To Winston, out on a patrol, they looked like the armies in the Bayeux tapestry, with rows of white and yellow banners held upright. He was close enough to hear a tremendous roar come up as the horsemen began their charge.

Kitchener and his staff could hardly believe the news. The Khalifa was in a vast open plain, without an inch of cover, moving into the range of the combined British firepower of twenty thousand rifles and Maxim guns. They could not have picked a better place. It would be a unique encounter between a medieval army of Moslem fanatics, basically unchanged since the days of the Prophet, armed with spears and antiquated muskets, and the late-nine-teenth-century army of a highly industrialized Western nation armed with the most advanced weapons. As Hilaire Belloc put it:

> *Whatever happens we have got*
> *The Maxim Gun and they have not.*

Nothing like it would ever be seen again, Winston thought as he saw the Dervishes fall through dense clouds of smoke, for there would never be such fools in the world again. The Khalifa's warriors were cut down with "undis-turbed efficiency." In the meantime, the gunboats, assisted by a howitzer firing fifty-pound shells, bombarded Omdurman and its forts, breaching the city walls and silencing enemy fire.

The impetus of the Dervish attack carried them across the British front. Seizing the chance, Kitchener re-formed his brigades for an attack on Omdurman. Flashes of light from a heliograph ordered the 21st Lancers to cut off enemy stragglers and prevent them from re-entering the city. Off rode the 310 officers and men of Winston's regiment, advancing at first at a walk toward what looked like a group of Dervish spearmen, who turned out to have rifles and who opened fire at close range. Only two courses were open, left wheel into line and gallop off, leaving the wounded behind, or right wheel into line and charge, the order that Colonel Martin gave.

The trumpet played, the horses swung around and locked into a long galloping line, and Winston took part in the British Army's last great cavalry charge, into the gravelly bed of a dried-up stream. Men in dark blue fired in a thin film of smoke, and the bullets sent the hard gravel flying. The Lancers bowed their helmets forward to shield their faces from the stinging dust, like cuirassiers at Waterloo. The Dervishes stood fast, four deep, and the Lancers had to knock them over, "arse over tip," as Winston put it, as they tried to hamstring the Lancers' horses and to cut their bridles and reins. After the initial collision, a chaotic melee ensued, with Winston firing his Mauser pistol at point-blank range. He was sure he killed at least three. The main thing was to stay on your horse, for if you were dragged off, the Dervishes would cut you to pieces. The Lancers drew out of the Dervish mass and gathered two hundred yards away for a second charge. But as they regrouped, and saw riderless horses galloping across the plain and blood-soaked men clinging to their saddles, they realized the gravity of their losses. The Lancers dismounted and opened fire with their carbines, sending the Dervishes scattering. Winston was disappointed. He wanted a second charge, feeling that the British cavalry should aim at the magnificent rather than the practical.[87]

To David Beatty, watching from his gunboat in the Nile, the Lancers' charge looked like plum duff—brown currants scattered about in a great deal of suet.[88] The charge had taken two minutes, for Winston the most dangerous two minutes he would ever live to see, and for Kitchener, worrying about "the butcher's bill," the costliest two minutes. Kitchener's losses for the day were 48 dead and 428 wounded, both British and Egyptian. Out of that number, the Lancers accounted for 21 dead and 49 wounded, all British, for a *"beau geste"* charge that did not affect the battle's outcome.

Winston was glad to have added the experience of a cavalry charge to his military repertoire. He knew there were no medals in it, even though he had fought in the day's most gallant action. As an attached officer, disliked by Kitchener, there was only one section of the dispatches where he might have been mentioned, the casualty list. Too many of his friends *were* mentioned. Lieutenant Robert Grenfell was dead, as was the *Times* correspondent Hubert Howard, who had covered the Cuban war from the rebel side, killed by a British shell. Colonel Frank Rhodes, the other *Times* correspondent, was wounded, and Lieutenant Richard Molyneux had a bad sword cut.

Winston was pleased to confirm the fantasy of his invulnerability, which was not that different from the superstition of the Dervishes that magic amulets would protect them. He had been under fire all the way, and not only was he untouched, he was the only officer whose clothes, saddlery, and horse were untouched.[89]

The battle was over by midmorning, and in the afternoon Kitchener's troops occupied Omdurman. Winston toured the battlefield, which stank from ten thousand Dervish corpses, hunting for trophies. The horrifying scene remained in his mind long after he had left the field. When he thought of vengeance and the paying of a debt, he reminded himself that he must not drain that particular cup to the bottom, for the dregs were filthy-tasting. He believed, to paraphrase Burke, that magnanimity in war was not seldom the surest wisdom.

The Sudan campaign would continue for a year, but the words Khalifa and Khartoum could now be handed over to the historian. Frugal Kitchener was pleased with the victory, but so furious with the Lancers that they were barely mentioned in dispatches. The charge had been a costly and unnecessary mistake. Since they had suffered so heavily, they were sent home. Winston was detained in Omdurman for a week on a transport detail, which he saw as an instance of petty spite on the Sirdar's part.

Omdurman made Kitchener a national hero. He won a peerage, the thanks of both houses of Parliament, and a grant of thirty thousand pounds. He boasted that he had conquered a country of one million square miles at a cost of two pounds, six shillings, and sixpence a square mile. But there was another side of the story that tarnished his noble image when it began to come out in newspaper reports and in Winston's book *The River War*. Winston knew that the book would not bring him many friends. But friends of the cheap and worthless everyday variety were of no importance to him. On September 6, when he was still in Omdurman, Kitchener had ordered that the Mahdi's tomb be razed to the ground and that his bones be thrown into the Nile. This posthumous act of vengeance for the death of General Gordon was entrusted to his nephew, Major W. S. Gordon, and the Mahdi's skull was presented to Kitchener as a trophy. He planned to send it to the College of Surgeons in London, where it could be exhibited alongside Napoleon's intestines, which he erroneously believed were kept there.

This caused a great scandal when it became known. Queen Victoria found the whole matter extremely distasteful. Opening graves smacked of the Middle Ages. On February 27, 1899, Lord Salisbury wired Lord Cromer in Cairo that "the Queen is shocked by the treatment the Mahdi's body has received, and thinks the head ought to be buried. Putting it in a museum, she thinks, will do great harm." Lord Cromer retrieved the skull and had it buried in a Moslem cemetery.[90]

Winston, who had not previously expressed strong feelings in religious matters, but who may have seen his pen as mightier than Kitchener's sword, denounced the desecration in his book as a wicked act that could only be viewed with abhorrence. Was this the chivalry of the conquerors to the memory of a man who had been a priest and a patriot? He also blamed Kitchener for not insisting before the battle that the wounded should be spared, estimating that no less than one hundred wounded Dervishes, who had thrown down their arms and appealed for mercy, had been killed. "The mind turns with disgust from the spectacle of unequal slaughter," he wrote.[91]

In his summing up, Winston tried to give a balanced portrait of the man who would become his Cabinet colleague in the first year of World War I. He had a breadth and strength of intellect that transcended the limitations of experts, but with his industry, his patience, his perseverance, came corresponding defects. He treated all men like machines, he neglected the care of the sick and injured, his stern and unpitying spirit was communicated to his troops, and his victories were accompanied by acts of barbarity. And yet, a great and splendid figure remained.[92]

On his way back to England in mid-September, Winston went to see his wounded friend and messmate Dick Molyneux in Cairo. A great rawboned Irish doctor was dressing Molyneux's wound, a deep sword cut above the right wrist, and he needed a patch of skin for a graft. "Oi'll have to take it off you," he told Winston, who rolled up his sleeve. He cut a piece of skin about the size of a shilling from the inside of Winston's forearm with a razor, saying: "Ye've heard of a man being flayed aloive? Well, this is what it feels loike."[93]

Winston's articles in the *Morning Post* appeared between September 23 and October 8. One of his readers was the Prince of Wales, until now an admirer, but who on this occasion wrote him a disapproving letter: "I must say that I think that an officer serving in a campaign should not write letters for the newspapers or express strong opinions of how the operations are carried out."[94]

The Prince's letter was mild compared to the broadsides that began appearing in the *Army and Navy Gazette*. On December 17, an anonymous general wrote that according to the Army List, Winston Churchill was a junior subaltern in the 4th Hussars, but this young officer, with less than four years' service, was here and there and everywhere as a special correspondent. Could it be for the good of the service that subalterns criticized their superior officers? Something had to be done to put a stop to this fad of subaltern correspondents, which Churchill had carried to the limits of absurdity.[95]

On December 24, an equally anonymous field officer seconded the motion in the service weekly. Something was radically wrong in a system that allowed young officers to leave their regiments and run off to all parts of the world. At first it was comical, but now it was becoming serious, and was likely to do incalculable mischief. It was something all soldiers should object to.[96]

Winston by this time was back with his regiment in Bangalore, after spending about two months in England seeing his mother and brother, and giving several political speeches. He was not about to let the charges in the *Army and Navy Gazette* go unanswered. Early in his life he made it a rule to fight back when attacked. Anyone who took him on found that out. In addition, here was a rare chance for a subaltern to cross swords with a general. In a letter on January 8, 1899, Winston argued that an army organization existed to reprimand young officers who behaved improperly. Since he had not been reprimanded, how could he have acted improperly? There was something of the Jesuit in him, even though he had inherited Mrs. Everest's anti-Catholicism. He did not address himself to the substance of the general's remarks, but relied on rhetoric, adopting a tone of wounded dignity: ". . . to make personal attacks on individuals, however insignificant they may be, in the publicity of print, and from out of the darkness of anonymity, is conduct equally unworthy of a brave soldier and an honorable man."[97] There was, however, so much indignation in the Army over the split personality of the officer/correspondent that the practice was discontinued after the Battle of Omdurman.

When Pamela Plowden wrote him that he was making unnecessary enemies, Winston replied by quoting from General Gordon's journal: "We may be quite certain that Jones cares more for where he is going to dine, or what he has got for dinner, than he does for what Smith has done, so we need not fret ourselves for what the world says." Pamela, who had not seen much of Winston as he trotted around the globe, accused him of being incapable of affection. "Perish the thought," Winston replied. "I love one above all others. And I shall be constant. I am no fickle gallant capriciously following the fancy of the hour. My love is deep and strong. Nothing will ever change it. I might it is true divide it. But the greater part would remain true—will remain true till death." Who was it that Winston loved with such single-minded devotion? The answer, he said, was over the page—it was . . . *himself*, Winston S. Churchill.[98]

In this lighthearted letter, Winston mocked the conventions of romantic love and humorously confessed his own self-absorption, for he had too many other matters on his mind to think seriously of Pamela, uppermost among them the Inter-Regimental Cup tournament in Meerut that February.

The 4th Hussars had never won it, and this was Winston's last chance, for he had decided to leave the Army. The team embarked with its thirty ponies for practice in Jodhpur on February 2. Aside from Winston, it consisted of Albert Savory, whose horse he had ridden in the rigged race at Aldershot; Reggie Barnes, his companion in Cuba; and Major Reginald Hoare. In Jodhpur, Winston fell down some stairs, spraining both ankles and dislocating his bad shoulder. He was very low and unhappy at the bad luck, which shook his belief in his invulnerability. At any rate, it was better to have bad luck in the little things of life than in the big undertakings. But how could he play, being such a shocking cripple? His teammates insisted on keeping him, even though his upper arm had to be strapped tightly to his side, restricting the arc of his swing. He could play the No. 1 position, keeping after the opposing back and hampering him.

Just before leaving Jodhpur, Winston wrote Sir Algernon West, a Privy Councillor and onetime political adviser of Gladstone. West had published an appreciation of Randolph, and Winston had struck up a correspondence with him. The letter, which mentioned a plague epidemic that was sweeping India, showed a strain of flippant cynicism that Winston would, as he matured, outgrow, or at least conceal. The plague, he wrote, "has killed 70,000 persons in Bombay and Southern India, and is now just beginning to get a good hold. If I may continue to ramble, Nature applies her own checks to populations, and a philosopher may watch unmoved the destruction of some of those superfluous millions, whose life must of necessity be destitute of pleasure."[99]

The tournament opened on February 20 and started well. In the first round, the 4th Hussars beat the 5th Dragoon Guards by 16 to 2, and in the second round, they beat the 9th Lancers 2 to 1 in a hard-fought match. The final of what was probably the biggest sporting event in India, against the 4th Dragoon Guards, took place on February 24 in fine weather before a large crowd. The 4th Hussars won 4 to 3, and Winston wrote his mother that he had scored three of his team's goals. But according to the account in the

Pioneer Mail, he scored only one goal.[100] Either he was bragging or the newspaper's experienced polo correspondent twice mistook the identity of the scorer. This sometimes happened when a long shot reached the goal mouth and was popped in by another player. In any case, the bell that ended the match allowed the 4th Hussars to say: "We have won the Inter-Regimental Tournament of 1899."

It should be noted in passing that Winston had a highly unorthodox method of dismounting from his polo ponies. Swinging the right leg behind the saddle, with the left foot in the stirrup and the left hand on the pommel of the saddle—the usual way—was too slow for him. Instead, he dismounted on the off side, throwing his left leg over the pony's neck and slipping to the ground. His fellow players warned him that it was careless, but he said he had done it a thousand times. Finally, in 1922, the day came when a pony threw him as his leg was going over its neck, and he took a bad fall that left him bedridden for five days.

A day or two later, Winston attended a meeting of the Indian Polo Association to oppose a measure to limit the height of polo ponies, which had been suggested by the respected polo umpire Major John Sherston. An extract of the discussion, reported by the *Pioneer Mail,* gives an idea of the presence of mind that would serve Winston so well in Parliament:

CHURCHILL: "This system will subject polo ponies to the same rigorous preparations that the poor racing ponies are suffering from at present, and the wretched polo ponies will have to be walked about with sacks on their backs and be drugged like the racing ponies. Far from increasing the evil we should try to reduce it."

SHERSTON: "The Calcutta Turf Club is at present taking steps to prevent these practices."

CHURCHILL: "What guarantee have we of this? Besides in some cases the polo clubs are far from the railway."

SHERSTON: "There will be two official measurers paid to go to all such places."

CHURCHILL: "Will two official measurers be sufficient to go all over India? However much you pay a man he cannot possibly be in two places at once." (*Laughter.*)[101]

The end of Winston's army career was approaching. He believed he could earn enough money with his pen to run for the House of Commons. By March 26 he had sent his papers in and was preparing to leave for England.

It was a farewell to his youth, to the adventurous life of a subaltern, to expeditions and battles and the comradeship of arms. It was a great wrench to put on his uniform and medals for the last time and to leave companions he had known since the days at Aldershot, with whom he had shared escapades like the rigged race and drumming that ruffian Bruce out of the regiment. Moreover, this was the profession chosen by his father, whose memory remained sacred. And yet he had to do it. The Army was too confining, too many petty minds blocked his way; he was meant for higher things.

He stopped off in Cairo for ten days to collect information for his book. Lord Cromer took him under his wing and was a valuable source, giving him a revisionist view of a British hero, General Gordon. Cromer was bitter about Gordon and begged Winston not to pander to the popular view, for he was erratic, unreliable, bad-tempered, and frequently drunk; and yet he had great abilities and a great sense of honor. Winston worried that he would have to cut all the fine phrases and pleasing paragraphs he had already written about Gordon.[102] Another difficult figure to describe was Kitchener. Winston thought of him as a vulgar, common, brutal man, but having overcome his feelings of resentment, he decided to tone down his most severe criticisms.[103] Through his writing, he was discovering the complexity of great men.

III

FAME

In London that April of 1899, a former cavalry officer was in search of a constituency. When he had visited the Central Offices of the Conservative Party the year before, Winston had been introduced to the party manager, Richard Middleton, known as "the Skipper," who had been most cordial, affirming that the party would find him a seat. How much could he afford to give to the constituency? Winston said he could pay no more than his personal expenses. Ah, said the Skipper, but the best constituencies liked large contributions from their members; there were cases where members paid a thousand pounds a year in subscriptions and charities in return for the honor of holding the seat. No doubt this was an exceptional case on account of his father, and his war experience, which would make him popular with the Tory workingman; he would do what he could.[1]

Winston was put in touch with Robert Ascroft, a Tory member for Oldham, a cotton-spinning center in Lancashire, which, because of its size, was a two-member constituency where the Tories held both seats. Ascroft told him: "Young people very often do not have as much money as older ones." There was nothing Winston could say to contradict this painful fact.

Now that Winston was back, Ascroft wanted him to run for Oldham in the place of the second member, James F. Oswald, who was ailing. Overtures also came from a constituency in Birmingham. Winston was wondering what to do next when Robert Ascroft died on June 19, and the ailing Oswald resigned his seat. This left two openings in Oldham, where a by-election would have to be held. The Skipper advised Winston to wait for a General

Election. By-elections were tricky. The Opposition would criticize without putting forth a program. Oldham was a fickle constituency, where the Tories were unpopular at the moment, owing to the Clerical Tithes Bill introduced by Lord Salisbury to benefit Church of England clergymen. There was a strong Methodist element in Oldham that hated the bill.

Winston decided to plunge in and went to Oldham on June 20 to start his meetings. His fellow candidate, James Mawdsley, was, oddly enough, a Socialist running on the Conservative ticket. As secretary of the Amalgamated Association of Cotton Spinners, he was running as a "Tory Socialist," for there was then no Labour Party. Mawdsley said he was proud to stand on the same platform with a scion of the ancient British aristocracy.

The two Liberal candidates were Walter Runciman, the son of a Newcastle shipowner, and Alfred Emmott, whose family were local millowners. They both had strong ties to the community and knew the largely working-class electorate. Winston knew nothing about Oldham or the British workingman, and repeated the slogans of Tory Democracy inherited from his father, who had given a free trade speech there in 1881.

The *Manchester Evening News* said that Winston, barely out of his political swaddling clothes, might be carried into Parliament by his running mate, who would bring in the working-class vote. His Liberal opponent, Walter Runciman, reminded the Oldham voters that he had not been "a swash-buckler round the world." Winston replied, "And I do not belong to a Party composed of prigs, prudes, and faddists."

Feeling the tide running against him, Winston asked his mother and Pamela Plowden to come to Oldham and help out. His mother came, but Pamela stayed home. Winston wore her charm and thought of her often. He wrote her on July 2, four days before the election, that he was delivering eight speeches a day and had made a very good impression. But there were too many crosscurrents. George Whiteley, the Tory member in nearby Stockport, had crossed the floor (gone over to the Liberal Party) over the Clerical Tithes Bill, declaring it to be "a bare-faced and cynical revival of the dole system, by which the clergy were to profit." Winston felt that this breaking of ranks would do him a great deal of harm and vowed that he would make Whiteley regret his treachery one of these days.[2] But the very next day, Winston himself repudiated the Clerical Tithes measure, announcing at a meeting that he would have voted against it. He later realized that he had made a bad mistake—it was no use standing for a party unless you could defend the weakest plank in the platform.

The election took place on July 6, and the Liberal candidates carried both seats. Winston, not yet twenty-five years old, had run in his first election and lost. He had not matched his father, who had won *his* first election handily in the family borough of Woodstock. In the words of Dr. Thompson, the Master of Trinity College: "We are none of us infallible, not even the youngest among us." It was a defeat but not a disgrace. He had polled 11,477 votes, trailing after the two Liberals, Emmott (12,976) and Runciman (12,770), but slightly ahead of Mawdsley (11,449), his fellow Tory.[3]

There was considerable resentment in the Conservative Party over the loss of two seats, and Winston was blamed for his clumsy reversal on the Clerical Tithes issue. Arthur Balfour, now Leader of the House of Commons, said: "I thought he was a young man of promise, but it appears he is a young man of promises."[4]

On July 8, Winston wrote Balfour an apologetic letter that blamed his defeat on other factors than his campaign: "I am very sorry I could do us no better at Oldham . . . Bad registration and organization accounted for a good deal . . . Altogether I return with less admiration for democracy than when I went. The great size of the constituency added to the difficulties . . . There were several districts in which I could not even hold a meeting although we averaged four a night."[5] Balfour replied that by-elections were unpropitious, conditions in Oldham had not been promising, and the clergy had resented his repudiation of the bill. But this small reverse would have no permanent ill effect on his political fortunes.

Chastened, Winston went to Blenheim in August to work on the proofs of his book, glad to be back in the strange but controllable world bounded on the north by the preface and on the south by the appendix, where the constituents were words that could be lined up into sentences. He was concerned about his mother, who wanted to marry a young Guards officer almost half her age named George Cornwallis-West. There were spiteful press notices about the match, and Winston received several letters from the young man's father. Winston did not think Jennie would go through with it. George would be crushed by family pressure.[6]

In any case, Winston had his own love affair to think about. He was in love with Pamela, who returned his love, and came to see him at Blenheim. No one understood her as he did. He was always seeing new sides to her character, some good and some less good, but he liked them all. Jennie tried to make trouble between them by repeating gossip that Pamela had ruined the career of an officer named Everard Baring by leading him on and then spurning him. Winston replied that quite the contrary, Baring was doing very well in the service (he would be promoted to brigadier general in 1916); Pamela had been Baring's guiding star, and they might have married if she had not fallen in love with him.[7] But in September, Pamela went on a trip to Germany, and Winston was lonely without her.

In the meantime, wondering at his own industry, he put the finishing touches to his book, which he dedicated to Lord Salisbury. He was also, as if sensing his next important move, cultivating the Colonial Secretary, Joseph Chamberlain, the most powerful man in the Salisbury government. The Birmingham screw manufacturer and former Liberal had fought with Gladstone over Home Rule, left his party, and gone into the political wilderness for nine years. He then came into the Salisbury government as a Liberal Unionist, a Liberal splinter group that voted with the Conservatives, becoming the most forceful advocate of British power in South Africa, where the focus of events was about to shift.

South Africa consisted of two British self-governing colonies, Cape Colony and Natal, and two Boer republics, Transvaal and Orange Free State. England had annexed Transvaal in 1877, but four years later the Boers won back their independence by defeating the English at Majuba Hill. When gold was discovered there in 1886, Transvaal quickly became the richest country in Africa, strengthening its armed forces and taking a hostile stance toward Britain. At the same time Transvaal was overrun by outsiders seeking their fortune, whom the Boers called *Uitlanders*. The Transvaal President, Paul Kruger, refused to give them the vote or the right to settle. The Salisbury government championed their cause, not only because most of them were British, but to further the aims of Empire in South Africa. After the Jameson raid, Transvaal formed a military alliance with the Orange Free State. A unified Boer front challenged British imperialism, exemplified by Joseph Chamberlain in London and Sir Alfred Milner, the Cape Colony High Commissioner, in Capetown.

Matters came to a head early in 1899, when the *Uitlanders* petitioned the Queen for their rights, aggressively backed by Milner, who wrote in a famous dispatch: "The spectacle of thousands of British subjects permanently in a position of helots, constantly chafing under undoubted grievances and calling vainly to Her Majesty's Government for redress does steadily undermine the influence and reputation of Great Britain and the respect for the British Government within the Queen's dominions." On May 31, Milner met Kruger in Bloemfontein, the capital of the Orange Free State, to negotiate the

Uitlander problem, but the talks broke down and the two sides moved to the brink of war. It was at this point, with Chamberlain trying to get the Boers to agree to some form of enfranchisement of the *Uitlanders*, that Winston came to see him. He felt that a strong line should be taken, but Chamberlain said that was premature, it was "no use blowing the trumpet for the charge and then looking around to find nobody following."[8]

When another, more conciliatory offer on behalf of the *Uitlanders* was rejected by the Boers in September, Winston was convinced there would be war. So was Alfred Harmsworth, owner of the *Daily Mail*, who wanted to hire him as a war correspondent. Winston used the *Daily Mail* offer to get a better deal from Oliver Borthwick of the *Morning Post*, who had published his River War dispatches. His contract was so lucrative that it helped raise the scale of other journalists' salaries: 250 pounds a month for a minimum of four months, 200 pounds a month thereafter, expenses, and copyright of his work.

On October 9, the Boers presented an ultimatum calling for the withdrawal of British troops. When the ultimatum expired on October 11, the war began, and the first shots were fired on the twelfth. Winston thought it was very sporting of the Boers to take on the whole British Empire. Wanting introductions, he again went to see Chamberlain, who was sanguine about the outcome. General Sir Redvers Buller, a veteran of the Ashanti and Zulu wars, had been named to command the British force and would soon be on his way. "Buller may well be too late," Chamberlain opined. "He would have been wiser to have gone out earlier. Now, if the Boers invade Natal, Sir George White with his sixteen thousand men may easily settle the whole thing." Winston asked about Mafeking, right on the border of Transvaal, which was held by five hundred irregulars under Colonel Baden-Powell. "Ah, Mafeking, that may be besieged," Chamberlain said. "But if they cannot hold out for a few weeks, what is one to expect?"[9]

Chamberlain could not give Winston an official letter, but did write Milner in the following terms: "I am sending a line to anticipate a probable visit from Winston Churchill, the son of Lord Randolph Churchill, who is going out as a correspondent for the *Morning Post* . . . He is a very clever young fellow with many of his father's qualifications. He has the reputation of being bumptious, but I have not myself found him so, and time will no doubt get rid of the defect if he has it . . . He is a good writer and full of energy. He hopes to be in Parliament but want of means stands in the way . . ."[10]

Busying himself with preparations prior to sailing, Winston made sure that he would not go thirsty in the dry South African veld, and took along thirty-six bottles of wine, eighteen bottles of ten-year-old Scotch, and six bottles of Very Old brandy.[11] On Saturday, October 14, he sailed from Southampton aboard the *Dunottar Castle*, along with General Buller, the General's two horses, Ironmonger and Biffin, and his entire staff. Red-faced and jowly at fifty-nine, Buller strode up the gangplank in a long dark overcoat and a felt hat. As the foghorn sounded and the ship heaved away from the wharf, on-lookers shouted cheerful slogans like "Bring back a piece of Kruger's whis-kers."[12] Winston was pleased to hear from those in the know that the Boers would put up a good fight, for he did not want it to be over before he got there.

He would not be in England for the publication of *The River War* in the first week of November. It was quite a coup to have turned six weeks of service in the Sudan campaign into a two-volume, thousand-page opus. His personal observations were padded with historical background. This was the weightiest work on the Sudan's conquest. The initial printing of two thousand copies sold out, and another one thousand copies went to press. It was generally seen as an excellent but flawed book, too long, with a sonorous style too much like Gibbon's, used to describe events that did not call for organ music. A grouchy notice in the *Saturday Review* on November 18 said that "only this astonishing young man could have written these two ponder-ous and pretentious volumes. . . . The airs of infallibility he assumes are irritating. . . . He is perpetually finding fault . . ."[13]

Actually, aside from his sniping at Kitchener, Winston made himself the bard of British courage, British arms, and British stoicism under stress—Lord Tullibardine extracting a bullet from a wounded man's right kneecap with a buttonhook was one example. Again he seemed drawn to gory scenes, as in this description of Sergeant Freeman collecting his troops after the charge: "His face was cut to pieces, and as he called on his men to rally, the whole of his nose, cheeks, and lips flapped amid red bubbles." Most remark-able was an early example of the resistance-at-all-costs tone he would adopt as Prime Minister in 1940. Reflecting on the courage of the outgunned Der-vishes, he wrote: "I hope that if evil days should come upon our country, and the last army which a collapsing Empire could interpose between London and the invader was dissolving in rout and ruin, that there would be some—even in these modern days—who would not care to accustom themselves to the new order of things and tamely survive the disaster." That there were lessons to be learned from an enemy was a theme he would sound again in the Boer War.

On board the *Dunottar Castle*, Winston thought eagerly about his book and the reception it would receive. He wanted his mother to send Pamela one of the first copies, with a line in it. He was also busy making contacts, for it might be wise to regain military status so that he could take part in the fighting. A civilian in a war was like a land animal in the ocean. He asked General Buller's aide-de-camp, Lord Gerard, to find him a commission as a Yeomanry officer.[14]

Among Winston's shipmates was John Black Atkins, a correspondent for the *Manchester Guardian* who had covered the Turco-Greek and Spanish-American wars. Atkins noticed a slim, red-haired young man plunging along the deck "with neck thrust out," as Browning had described Napoleon, folding and unfolding his hands as if trying to untie mental knots. Shy he was not—he spoke to his seniors as if they were his own age or younger. But the ability to laugh at himself leavened his self-importance. He told Atkins of visiting the *Morning Post* to look at the proofs of a report on one of his speeches. The editor was surprised at his modesty when he struck out "Cheers" at the end of a rousing passage, but recovered when he substituted "hard and prolonged applause."[15] As he got to know Winston, Atkins reflected that he had never seen such open and unabashed ambition, so removed from the public-school stereotype of cultivated diffidence.

When the *Dunottar Castle* reached Capetown on October 31, the news was not good. The Boers had invaded Natal and surrounded General Sir George White's army at Ladysmith, a town on the railway line 150 miles northwest of Natal's principal seaport, Durban. General Buller and his staff continued to Durban on the same ship, but Winston and Atkins and another correspondent, eager to get to the heart of the action, found that by taking a train to East London, halfway between Capetown and Durban, they could catch a steamer to Durban, getting several days' head start. Before leaving Capetown, Winston paid a call on Sir Alfred Milner, whose pessimism was disturbing. The Boers, said Milner, had come out in far greater numbers than were expected. The two British colonies were contaminated by the uprising, and the whole of Cape Colony was "trembling on the verge of rebellion."[16]

In Durban harbor, Winston visited the hospital ship *Sumatra* and was shocked to find his closest friend from the 4th Hussars days, Reggie Barnes, badly shot through the groin, with his right leg paralyzed. Barnes had been wounded in the battle of Elandslaagte, a town ten miles northeast of Ladysmith, on October 21. It had been a victory for the British, but a costly one. These Boers knew how to fight; they were good with horse and rifle, even though they were volunteers who did not wear uniforms. Winston realized that they had been greatly underrated. In less than a month of war, a bunch of wild irregulars had beaten the cream of the British Army. This would be a long and fierce struggle in which many lives would be lost.

The correspondents did not get to Ladysmith, for the railway line was cut. On November 10, they stopped at Estcourt, about thirty miles south of Ladysmith, and pitched their tents in the railway yard. In Estcourt, which was held by two thousand British troops, Winston ran into two old acquaintances, Captain Aylmer Haldane, the officer who had befriended him on the North-West Frontier, who had also been wounded at Elandslaagte; and Leo Amery, the boy Winston had thrown into the pool at Harrow, who was now chief of the *Times*'s war correspondent service. They had a jolly time, drinking Winston's St. Emilion and inviting to dinner the officers commanding the Estcourt force. One evening, as they dined, the clang of field guns being loaded into wagons could be heard. Colonel C. J. Long, the Estcourt commander (who had been in charge of the artillery at Omdurman), explained that the Estcourt position could not be held and that they were pulling back to the Natal capital of Pietermaritzburg, about sixty miles south along the railway line. With an assurance that his fellow correspondents half admired and half deplored, Winston argued that Piet Joubert, the Boer commander, was too cautious to advance in force beyond the protection of the Tugela River; it would be a pity to show him the way to 'Maritzburg. A little later, the sound of field guns being unloaded could be heard, and Winston said, with visible self-satisfaction: "I did that." Adding as an afterthought: "We did that."[17]

Winston was wrong. A force of two thousand mounted Boers, led by Joubert and his brilliant young aide, Louis Botha, crossed the Tugela on November 14 and laid dynamite under the bridge at Colenso, in case they needed to destroy it in the future. They rode on across the veld, along the railway line to Durban, and stopped that evening on the outskirts of Chieveley, twenty miles north of Estcourt. Joubert had no intention of attacking Estcourt, where he knew the British were out in strength. This was a reconnoitering mission, to study enemy positions.[18] Joubert left Botha in charge at Chieveley with five hundred Commandos.

At Estcourt on the evening of the fourteenth, Captain Haldane was detailed for another reconnoitering mission. Colonel Long, having heard that Boers were about, told him to take two companies of men in an armored train the next morning and patrol the line in the direction of Colenso. Haldane was unhappy about the mission. The armored train, clamped to the rigid line and advertising its arrival with loud puffs from its engine, made too good a target. It could be immobilized by damage to the track. It was a flimsy military machine, known to the men as "Wilson's deathtrap," apparently after its designer. What a very foolish idea to send three hundred men out in a train to obtain information that a few horsemen could get. As Haldane came out of the Colonel's office, he noticed Winston hanging about with some of the other correspondents. Haldane asked him to come along, and Winston grudgingly agreed. He had been out in the armored train before and had vowed not to go again, for you could see practically nothing. Haldane went to sleep that night wondering what he would do if the Boers ambushed the train.[19]

Winston was sharing a tent with Leo Amery, who said he would go too. At four-thirty on the morning of November 15, Winston's Indian servant woke him up. Amery looked out and saw that it was pouring rain. He turned over and went back to sleep.[20]

Winston and Haldane clambered over the loopholed sides to get into the leading wagon, which carried a seven-pound naval gun and was followed by an armored wagon, the engine, the tender, two more armored wagons, and a repair wagon. Troops from the Dublin Fusiliers and the Durban Light Infantry climbed in, as did a telegraphist and a breakdown gang, and the train puffed northward out of Estcourt at 5:10 A.M. on a rainy, chilly morning. They reached the next station, Frere, at 6:20, having spotted no Boers, and proceeded to Chieveley over the iron bridge that spanned the Blaauw Krantz River. Headquarters in Estcourt telephoned Haldane that the Boers had occupied Chieveley station the night before, and that he should go back to Frere.

To Botha, hiding in the hills with his Boer column of five hundred Commandos, the armored train he saw chugging into Chieveley was a godsend, one of those unexpected prizes that suddenly appear in war, which is at best a contest of blunders. The trap was soon sprung, just outside Frere, where the line swung to the right at the bottom of a hill.[21]

The train steamed back southward from Chieveley. Botha's Commandos, on either side of the line, waited until it had crossed the iron bridge and then opened up at six hundred yards with their field guns, hitting the leading wagon. As expected, the engineer put on full steam, and the train ran down the gradient of the hill at high speed, whipping around the bend, where it crashed into boulders blocking the tracks.

The first wagon, carrying the tools of the breakdown gang, was flung in the air and lay upside down on the embankment. The next, an armored car, was derailed and thrown on its side. The third, another armored car, lay half on and half off the rails. The rest of the train, including the engine, was still on the tracks. As the Boers poured shells and bullets into the stranded train, some of the soldiers scattered across the veld and hid in the riverbed. The engineer, Charles Wagner, whose scalp, cut open by shrapnel, streamed with blood, sprang out of his cab and ran to the shelter of an overturned wagon. Winston, who had been in the rear wagon observing the action through his field glasses, asked Captain Haldane if he could clear the line. While Haldane ordered his men to return the enemy fire, Winston found the engineer, who complained bitterly that he was a civilian—what did they think he was paid for? Winston told him that no man was hit twice on the same day. He rallied a gang of volunteers, and for more than an hour, under heavy fire, he worked at clearing the partly derailed wagon from the tracks, using the engine to push it. He left his Mauser pistol and his field glasses in the cab as he directed the operation.

The tracks were finally cleared, and the engine was uncoupled from the rear cars. About fifty men, most of them wounded, piled into the cab, and the engine departed for Estcourt. Haldane tried to gather his men and make a run for some houses eight hundred yards away, where he hoped to continue the battle. But the men were spread out, and to his disgust, he saw two Tommies[22] at the bridge hold up white handkerchiefs. The Boers stopped firing and called upon the British to surrender. It was out of the question for Haldane to fire when the white flag had been accepted.

In the meantime, Winston had been helping to carry the wounded into the cab. When the engine started up, he stayed aboard for about half a mile, then hopped off and walked back to help the others. Looking around for Haldane, he saw instead two Boers firing their rifles at him less than a hundred yards away. "Two soft kisses sucked in the air," as Winston put it, adapting the vocabulary of love to warfare. He ran for cover, but a horseman carrying a rifle in his right hand caught up with him and shouted a command. Winston was unarmed, and there was no chance of escape. He held up his hands, surrendering to an enemy for the first and last time in his life. As he was led through the tall grass he tried to get rid of the two Mauser clips of dumdum bullets he had in his pockets. He dropped one and had the other in his hand when the Boer asked, "What have you got there?" The Boer took the clip, examined it, and threw it away.

Winston later convinced himself that the mounted rifleman who had captured him was Louis Botha, leader of the Commandos, and later to become the first Prime Minister of the Transvaal Colony and the first Prime Minister of the Union of South Africa. There was a pleasing symmetry in one great man being captured by another. It is far more likely that he was captured by an obscure field-cornet named Oosthuizen, who was killed later in the war. This was stated unequivocally by Captain Danie Theron, the leader of the Boer Scout Corps, in a letter on November 28, 1899, to Francis Reitz, the State Secretary of Transvaal. "Churchill called for volunteers," Theron wrote, "and led them at a time when the officers were in confusion. According to *Volkstem* and *Standard & Digger News* [two Natal newspapers], he now claims that he took no part in the battle. That is all lies. He also refused to stand still until Field-Cornet Oosthuizen warned him to surrender. He surrendered only when he aimed his gun at him. In my view Churchill is one of the most dangerous prisoners in our hands. The Natal papers are making a big hero out of him."[23]

It was, however, Botha who had planned the ambush and who cabled jubilantly to Pretoria: "Our guns were ready and quickly punctured the armored trucks. The engine broke loose and returned badly damaged. Loss of the enemy 4 dead, 14 wounded and 58 taken prisoner, also a mountain gun [the ship's cannon]. . . . Our loss 4 slightly wounded. . . . Blood visible everywhere. Much rain. Am in good health. Publish. Greetings."[24]

Despite the indignity of capture, Winston was in a cheerful mood when the prisoners were rounded up and marched sixty miles through the rain to the Boer railhead at Elandslaagte. The clearing of the line, he confided to Haldane, in full view of the soldiers and the railway personnel, who would spread the tale when they got back to Estcourt, had brought him into prominence.[25]

The train ride to Pretoria took almost twenty-four hours, and upon arrival at the Boer capital on November 18, the officers and Winston were taken to a State Model School while the other ranks were imprisoned on a race course. The school, adapted to wartime use as a detention center, was a single-story brick building with a gravel-covered back yard, surrounded by a six-and-a-half-foot-high corrugated iron paling. The Zarps (South African Republic Police guards) were easygoing army rejects, and the treatment was good— the prisoners were allowed to write and receive letters, read Boer newspapers, full of the most amazing lies, Winston thought, and borrow books from the state library.

Trying to get released through channels, Winston took the position that he was an unarmed correspondent, who had not fought, but only cleared the line of debris. Captain Haldane perjured himself in a statement supporting Winston's contention that he had been unarmed. "I certify on my honor," he wrote on November 19, "that Mr. Winston Churchill, Correspondent of the *Morning Post*, accompanied the armored train on the 15 November as a noncombatant, unarmed and took no part in the defense of the train."

Winston peppered Boer officials with letters, insisting on his noncombatant status. But General Joubert was not impressed. Without him, the General said, not a single Englishman would have escaped. He was dangerous, and must not be released.[26] Upon hearing a rumor that the Boers might be willing to exchange prisoners, Winston tried another tack. On November 26, he wrote Sir Alfred Milner, asking to be remembered in the event of an exchange: "Of course you will have learned that I am a prisoner with the British officers in Pretoria. I do not want to cause any trouble, but I trust that if any exchange of prisoners is arranged you will do your best to have my name included in the list. My *status* as a press correspondent and a noncombatant has not protected me, it being alleged—I can only deny it—that I was taken with arms . . . I make no complaints against the humanity of the Republican authorities."[27] But the exchange did not materialize, and he spent his twenty-fifth birthday in prison, in anguish at the thought of how little time remained.

Winston continued to clamor for release, promising to give his parole not to serve against the Boers or disclose any military information. This fresh request was forwarded to General Joubert, who had a change of heart, perhaps impressed by the young man's persistence. On December 12, Joubert wrote Francis Reitz that if he accepted Winston's version of events, "then my objections to his release cease. Seeing that a parole was promised him and that he suggested leaving Africa to return to Europe where he would report and speak only the truth of his experiences—and if the Government accepts this and he does so—then I have no further objections to his being set free, without our accepting somebody else in exchange." Joubert added a postscript, remembering Randolph's ill-natured treatment of the Boers: "Will he tell the truth? He will also be a chip off the old block."[28] Winston had succeeded in obtaining his release, but the matter had become irrelevant, for on the same day that General Joubert offered to let him go, he escaped.

The escape plan had been hatched by Captain Haldane and A. Brockie, a colorful character who was a regimental sergeant major in the Imperial Light Horse. He had posed as a lieutenant when captured so as to be sent to the officers' camp. A native of Johannesburg, Brockie spoke Afrikaans and one of the native dialects, a decided advantage in any escape attempt. The plan was to hide in a circular latrine in a badly lit corner of the back yard, from the roof of which the iron fence could be climbed, landing them in the garden of an adjoining house. They intended to walk by night and hide by day until they reached a friendly border. Haldane had collected money, food, and information on trains, and had a small map of Pretoria that he had cut out of a library book.

Haldane disclosed the plan to Winston, who asked to go along, since his request for release had been turned down. Haldane was not keen to have him, for his presence would increase the risk of capture. He was the most conspicuous prisoner, one of the sights of Pretoria, who had been visited by reporters and officials, and whose absence would be noticed at once. Brockie too was strongly opposed to the idea. Haldane said that in the face of Brockie's opposition he could not ask him to come, but Winston insisted. Haldane gave in, because Winston could have escaped aboard the armored train but had chosen not to. This gave him a valid claim. Winston specified that they must not blame him if they were caught by virtue of his presence. Haldane made it clear that he was the leader of the group and that Winston must conform to orders. Winston's joining them caused Haldane great anxiety. With Brockie he could manage, but Winston had not been keeping fit, and had a bad shoulder. Could he climb the fence without a "leg up"? Could he keep up? Haldane doubted it.[29]

On December 11, they decided to try that night. Winston was in a great state of excitement, telling everyone he was escaping, even though Haldane had asked him to keep it quiet, for some officers felt that if anyone escaped they would be treated more severely. Just before 7 P.M., Haldane and Winston went over to the latrine. Sentries strolled along a double line of trees, chatting when they met. Bad luck—a sentry stood on duty in the corner and would not budge.

On December 12, bursting with impatience, Winston said: "We must go tonight." "There are three of us to go," Haldane replied, "and we will certainly do so if the chance is favorable." At seven o'clock they were back at the latrine, but the sentry was there again, and they returned to the veranda. "You're afraid!" Brockie jeered. "I could get away any night."

"Very well," Haldane said, "go and see for yourself." Brockie went toward the latrine, followed by Winston, who said, "I am going over again, don't follow immediately." Brockie came back and told Haldane, "That damned fool Churchill wanted to stop and talk within earshot of the sentry. I told him that it was useless to try to escape then." Winston having vanished into the latrine, Haldane and Brockie went in to dinner.[30]

Winston felt strongly that they would waste the whole night in hesitation unless someone did something. When he saw the sentry turn to light his pipe, he jumped to the ledge of the wall, and in a few seconds he was safely on the other side, in the garden. When the chance came, he could not resist the temptation, and did not stop to consider that in acting alone, he might compromise the escape of his companions. Now, he crouched behind a few leafless bushes and waited for the others to come. People kept passing, and the lights of the house behind him were burning. By tapping gently, he managed to attract the attention of an officer who was in the latrine answering the call of nature, and told him to pass the word to Haldane that he was over. Haldane arrived, and pulled himself up to the wall, but when his shoulders were about level with the top, the moon shone full on his face, and the sentry spotted him, raising his rifle and calling out, "Go back, you damned fool!" The sentries now became more alert. Haldane went to the fence and told Winston he could not get away. Winston said: "Tell Brockie to come." With his knowledge of Kaffir and Dutch, Brockie was his only chance of buying food without being detected.[31]

Haldane was furious that Winston thought only of Brockie, whom he needed, while totally disregarding him. He said neither of them could go. What was Winston to do? His situation seemed hopeless. He could not climb back in because there was no ledge on the outside, and he would have made a terrible racket. But how could he go alone, without any local knowledge, without even a compass or a map, or any fixed plan except to walk by night and hide by day? And yet he must go, for he could not retrace his steps.

Winston disappeared into the night, and Haldane felt disgusted at being left behind. Winston had snatched the bread right out of his mouth. The escape plan had been his and Brockie's, and Winston had insisted on tagging along, against their better judgment, and then had gone without them. He had not played fair. When Brockie heard the news, Winston came in for a full dose of the epithets of which he had a liberal command. "Your trusted friend," Brockie kept repeating, "a nice kind of gentleman." Many of the other prisoners, complaining that Winston was not even an officer, and had now spoiled the chance for them, joined in the chorus of abuse that went on for some days.[32]

Winston did not for a moment think he had betrayed his friends. He had taken the lead, and they had been unable to follow, placing him in a situation where he felt his chances were practically nil. As he recalled the incident in later years, there had been no agreement to go over the fence together. It never occurred to him that he was not free to get over it as best he could.

Also, he was piqued by Brockie's jeer and wanted to show Haldane that he did not need a "leg up."

Whatever the merits of the case, and one can sympathize with the officers who were left behind without blaming Winston's impulsive departure too harshly, the stigma of having behaved badly toward his fellow prisoners followed him for years, in versions more or less accurate. About a year after Winston's escape, Lord Rosslyn, one of the officers at the State Model School, published a book on his Boer War experiences called *Twice Captured*, in which he wrote: "There was a general impression that Churchill had behaved in an unfair way to the other fellows—taking their plan of escape and leaving them behind him. At any rate he seems to have followed the plan of '*sauve qui peut*' instead of 'shoulder to shoulder.'" Furious, Winston ranted about the enormous number of liars in the world and threatened to sue the publisher, William Blackwood, who deleted the offending paragraph in subsequent editions.

Twelve years later, when he was First Lord of the Admiralty, he was still being subjected to the same accusations. This time he did sue *Blackwood's Magazine* for saying that he had broken his parole when a prisoner in 1899. This was clearly false, for he had never been asked to give it, although he had offered it in exchange for his release. Haldane, by then a brigadier general in command of an infantry brigade, was summoned to the Admiralty, and Winston asked him to go into the witness-box and testify that he had behaved properly.[33]

Haldane offered to make a qualified statement, to the effect that Winston had not realized his escape was unfair to Brockie and himself. According to Haldane, Winston assumed a browbeating air, and said that if Haldane did not support him, he would state in court that he and Brockie had funked going, which had clinched the matter. Haldane replied that he could state what he liked, but the truth was that he had been thinking of three individuals, while Winston had been thinking of only one man, himself.

As an officer on active service, Haldane did not wish to make a declared enemy of Winston, a powerful minister running one of the service departments. Nor did he wish to be slandered. Haldane knew what a creature of impatience Winston was, and how, bitterly regretting that he had acted on the spur of the moment in Pretoria, he might adopt the precept of "I hate whom I have wronged."

He went to see his solicitor, who advised him that if Winston said one word against him in court, he should write to the *Times*, pointing out that

Winston had threatened to call him a coward unless he agreed to whitewash him. Despite further requests, Haldane did not testify in the libel hearing on May 20, 1912, which in any case was undefended. After their meeting, Haldane felt nothing but regret that a man of such splendid ability and brilliant parts, whom he had once regarded as a friend, but could never trust again, had allowed himself to commit an action that he had then lied about.[34] Winston in this case had been, as General Joubert put it, a "chip off the old block," resorting to threats and blackmail in a fit of temper toward an officer who had befriended him on more than one occasion, like his father in the Aylesford affair. Though quick to lose his temper when his reputation was at stake, Churchill harbored no grudge against Haldane, for in 1920, when he was Secretary of State for War, he appointed Haldane to the highest military command he would ever hold, Commander in Chief of British forces in Mesopotamia, and worked with him through critical times on the best of terms.

In spite of their letdown, which increased with the years, Haldane and Brockie did what they could to make good Winston's escape. They arranged a dummy in his bed that looked so lifelike that a soldier servant invited it to take its customary cup of coffee on the morning of December 13. There being no reply, the coffee was left on a chair. It was only when a roll was called at nine-thirty that Winston's absence was noticed. The Boers were not pleased at losing their most famous prisoner, about to be released. What a scoundrel he was, Joubert said. At the State Model School, there was a tightening up of the rules, roll call twice a day, petty annoyances, newspapers and the beer ration stopped.

The warrant for Winston's arrest described him as an "Englishman 25 years old, about 5 ft 8 in tall, average build, walks with a slight stoop, pale appearance, red brown hair, almost invisible small moustache, speaks through the nose, cannot pronounce the letter 'S,' cannot speak Dutch, has last been seen in a brown suit of clothes." By the time the warrant was issued, on December 18, the dangerous character it described was some distance from Pretoria. He knew there were trains to Portuguese East Africa, about 280 miles away. He found the railway line and boarded an eastbound train two hundred yards from the station, on an uphill gradient that slowed it down and on an outward curve where he would be concealed from the engineer and the guard. He spent the night in a wagon full of empty coal bags, and got off at dawn, waiting in the veld during the day. Hungry and exhausted, he decided when night fell to take the risk of approaching the only house he could see. Luck was with him; it was the home of an English colliery manager. He was seventy-five miles east of Pretoria and still some two hundred miles away from the border. The colliery manager, John Howard, hid him for six days, arranging the next step of his escape. On December 19, he gave Winston a pistol and some food and smuggled him aboard a train bound for Lourenço Marques with some bales of wool. Winston had memorized the names of the stations, and when he saw through the slits in the freight wagon that he had reached Ressano Garcia and freedom, he was so carried away with delight that he fired his gun in the air.[35]

At the British Consulate in Lourenço Marques, he took a bath, put on clean clothes, and read the newspapers. The war was not going well. Sir Redvers Buller had plodded from one disaster to the next. He had suffered a staggering defeat at Colenso, a few miles south of Ladysmith, with casualties on a scale unheard of in England since the Crimean War. Winston was eager to rejoin the fray. Some of the best fighting still lay ahead. Perhaps his commission had come through. The consul was no less eager to get rid of him, fearing that Boer sympathizers might try to kidnap him in neutral territory. The steamer *Induna* was sailing that night for Durban, and a group of armed Englishmen saw him safely on board. The *Induna* docked at Durban on December 23, and Winston landed to a hero's welcome. His exploit, a solitary example of gallantry and success amid a series of crushing defeats, had made him famous. His name was in headlines, he was deluged with congratulatory telegrams, and well-wishers wrote to say they were naming their children after him. Sir Redvers Buller said he wished Winston were leading irregular troops instead of writing for a rotten paper. One telegram, which he only saw later, had been sent to Jennie, and said: "Thank God— Pamela."[36]

Having made a stirring address from the steps of the Durban town hall, received with an ovation by the crowd, Winston set out for Buller's headquarters at Chieveley, where he had been captured forty days before. He found the General with his forward groups about to attack the Boers near Colenso and asked for a commission. "What about poor old Borthwick?" Buller asked, referring to the publisher of the *Morning Post*. Winston said he was still under contract, which raised the question of the dual role. Officers were no longer allowed to be correspondents. It was most awkward. Buller paced the room and finally said: "All right. You can have a commission in Bungo's regiment. You will have to do as much as you can for both jobs. But you will get no pay for ours."[37] "Bungo" was Colonel Julian Byng, commander of the South African Light Horse. With a commission from Buller himself, no one complained about this "curse of modern armies," as Lord Wolseley had described the war correspondent.

The nineteenth century was ending, and in the first months of the new year, Winston would take part in some of the worst fighting of the war. What a change had taken place since the generals at the War Office had boasted that fifteen thousand men could conquer the Transvaal. There had been nothing but defeats, plaguing the last years of the old Queen. In her speech dismissing Parliament on October 27, 1899, the term "victories won" was replaced by "the splendid qualities displayed by our soldiers." Was this the collapse of the British Empire? Many thought so. The mightiest empire could only be taken seriously if it had the best army. The British Army could crush ragged tribesmen on the Afghan border and Dervishes armed with spears, but when it had to fight well-armed white men for the first time since the Crimean War, it did not do so well. There was too much tradition-bound complacency in soldiers accustomed to lording it over Indians and Kaffirs. When an order came that officers must not wear their medal ribbons into battle, as they made colorful targets for Boer marksmen, Colonel Paget, who had seven, refused, saying: "I never heard of such damned rot."

In South Africa, Sir Redvers Buller was fighting the first twentieth-century war with a nineteenth-century army. Gone was the one-day battle like Balaclava or Omdurman, where two great armies clashed in a decisive moment. The Boer War was a series of interlocking actions spread out over days or weeks, and requiring new infantry tactics and a new use of artillery, not merely for the initial barrage before the infantry attack but for hour-by-hour support of the troops. This was a fluid war against an innovative enemy whose tactics ranged from guerrilla to trench warfare.

Buller's task in January 1900 was to cross the Tugela River, rout the Boers entrenched in the hills, and come to the rescue of General Sir George White and his sixteen thousand men trapped inside Ladysmith. Each time he tried, he was beaten back. He crossed the Tugela so many times he was nicknamed "the Ferryman." At Ladysmith, the men were dying of typhoid and dysentery. They would have starved had they not killed and eaten the cavalry horses, another shocking departure from army tradition.

On January 25, there was the nightmare of Spion Kop, where the British were butchered trying to hold a hill. Winston saw carnage more shocking than the Mamund Valley or the Lancer charge, hundreds of corpses mutilated by shell fragments, men crawling on their hands and knees, men fallen in a stupor, or seeming drunk, although there was no alcohol. It was a terrible disappointment for the besieged garrison, one of whose officers wondered how on earth men who called themselves Englishmen could have been turned off a hill by a pack of Dutch peasants. Buller was called "Sir Reverse" by his own men.

At the end of January, during a lull in the fighting, Winston went to Durban for a family reunion. Jennie had arrived aboard the *Maine*, a hospital ship equipped and maintained with forty-one thousand pounds in American donations she had raised. Jack was there too, having been commissioned in the South African Light Horse. "And so we three met all together again, about 7,000 miles from where we expected each other to be," Jack wrote. Jennie had arrived in time to take the wounded from Spion Kop, and Jack went to the front with Winston, who was concerned about his younger brother,[38] for he had no combat experience. But it was a great joy to have him along and do him the honors.

On February 12, Winston's unit made a reconnaissance six or seven miles to the east of the railway line, occupying a wooded rise known as Hussar Hill. Riding slowly homeward up a smooth grass slope, Winston looked back over his shoulder and said, "We are still much too near those fellows." No sooner had he spoken than bullets started whizzing by in dozens. They leaped off their horses, threw themselves on the grass, and returned the fire. Jack, lying by Winston's side, suddenly jumped and wriggled. He had been shot in the calf in his very first skirmish and was sent back to Durban, where he was attended by his mother and her doctors aboard the *Maine*.[39] J. B. Atkins, the *Manchester Guardian* correspondent who had sailed from England with Winston, commented: "It seemed as though he had paid his brother's debts." Winston continued to believe that he was preserved by a strange luck, or the favor of heaven, perhaps because he was to be of use someday.

In February, the military situation improved. The British made good use of their artillery, with fifty guns to the Boers' eight. The guns were in constant use as the British extended their hold like a gigantic right arm reaching toward Ladysmith. There was some fierce fighting when they crossed the Tugela for the fourth time on February 25 on wood-and-canvas pontoon bridges. The men of the South African Light Horse, known as the "Cockyoli-birds," wore a distinctive feather in their hats. Winston wrote Pamela that his feather had been cleft by a bullet. Casualties were high, and as the troops approached Ladysmith, he saw a continuous stream of wounded flow by to the hospitals, a thousand in two days.

By February 27, they had taken the hills that circled the town. Winston saw forty-eight Boer prisoners brought back, a rare sight until now. What ordinary men, he thought, what a puzzling contrast between these men chattering and grinning like loafers outside a pub and the terrible enemy they had fought in the trenches an hour earlier.

On February 28, the 118th day of the siege, the men in the garrison saw through their field glasses the billowing white shapes of Boer wagons leaving on dusty roads. At 5 P.M. the relief column was in sight. An hour later, the first British troops entered the city, to be met by soldiers and townfolk cheering and yelling like lunatics. Sir George White appeared, and the meeting of rescuer and rescued was sealed in a handshake.

Winston gave an eyewitness account of this memorable occasion in his autobiographical *My Early Life*: ". . . two squadrons of the S.A.L.H. were allowed to brush through the crumbling rearguards and ride into Ladysmith. I rode with these two squadrons, and galloped across the scrub-dotted plain, fired at only by a couple of Boer guns. Suddenly from the brushwood up rose gaunt figures waving hands of welcome. On we pressed, and at the head of a battered street of tin-roofed houses met Sir George White on horseback, faultlessly attired. Then we all rode together into the long beleaguered, almost starved-out, Ladysmith. It was a thrilling moment." In fact, Winston was nowhere near the scene he described so well. He was miles to the rear, with the commander of the 2nd Mounted Brigade, Lord Dundonald, who did not arrive until after dark, when the public celebrations were over.[40] When Winston did arrive, it did not take him long to make himself noticed. A group of officers was standing around chatting with Sir George White when a young subaltern made his way through the group. Without ceremony, he engaged the General in conversation in a loud voice, as though they were equals, and then strode off. "Who on earth is that?" an older officer asked Sir George. "That's Randolph Churchill's son Winston," the General said. "I don't like the fellow, but he'll be Prime Minister of England one day."[41]

It was extraordinary that this should be said about a young man of twenty-five who had never held political office, and yet it was not an isolated example. Captain Percy Scott, commander of the cruiser *Terrible*, who had invented a carriage that enabled heavy naval guns to be used on land, was acting military commandant of Durban when Winston met him after his escape. Scott wrote Winston: "I feel certain that I shall someday shake hands with you as Prime Minister of England, you possess the two necessary qualifications, genius and plod . . ."[42] The man marked for greatness at an early age is a cliché of the heroic biography, like Napoleon being recognized as a great strategist after a snowball fight in a schoolyard. And yet in Winston's case it was documented, rather than due to the biographer's hindsight.

But if Winston had genius, where was the plod? It was in the relentless way he pursued his goals. He never gave up. He would hear from three different directions that Kitchener did not want him, and he would try a fourth. His research on *The River War* was an example of plod. Absorbing himself in the subject, he read all the Parliamentary Blue Books, as well as works of history and travel. Then he went to Cairo to interview the participants, including a leading Egyptian nationalist, for he wanted data from all sides. Churchill had the quality that Talleyrand saw in Napoleon, *l'art de fixer sur les objets longtemps sans être fatigué* (the art of concentrating for a long time without becoming tired).

Winston's feelings about the Boers had gone through a number of changes. After the armored-train disaster he admired their military skill. Soon after being captured, he heard a sound more awesome than the sound of shells— the sound of Boers singing psalms. What sort of men were they fighting? he wondered. They were sure they had the better cause, and in a war the cause was everything. But in his conversations with his captors, he reached the conclusion that the real reason for Dutch aversion to British rule was fear and hatred of the movement that sought to place the native on a level with the white man. A Boer farmer told him: "We know how to treat Kaffirs in this country. Fancy letting the black filth walk on the pavement." Winston had second thoughts about the Boers' nobility, the citizen soldiers fighting for the soil their fathers had won through suffering and peril. Scratch a farmer and you found a racist. But after the relief of Ladysmith, he was one of the first to see that peace might be negotiated and cabled the *Morning Post* "that a generous and forgiving policy be followed . . . the wise and right course is to beat down all who resist, even the last man, but not to withhold forgiveness or friendship from any who wish to surrender."

Winston stayed in Ladysmith for several weeks attending to business. There were offers from magazines and a lecture agent, and he was already thinking of his next book, *London to Ladysmith*, which should be worth at least two thousand pounds. He also heard that the novel he had started as a subaltern in India, but had set aside to finish his more topical books, had been published in February in New York and London. The original title, *Affairs of State*, had been changed to *Savrola*, the name of the hero, a philosophical rebel who leads the people of an imaginary state called Laurania in the overthrow of a dictator. The dictator, Antonio Molara, is killed, and Savrola falls in love with his wife, Lucile, "the most beautiful woman in Europe."

Presented as a romantic adventure, *Savrola* was in fact a fantasy in which Winston worked out his Oedipal problem in a purely intuitive manner, for there is no indication that he had ever heard of Freud, whose *Three Essays on the Theory of Sexuality*, in which it was first suggested that children had sexual urges involving their parents, was published in 1905, five years after *Savrola*. The novel depicted the classical Oedipal situation of the son's instinctive need to slay the father and win the mother, but in the style of a chaste Victorian romance, full of notions of chivalric honor. Savrola was Winston as he would have liked to be. "All of my philosophy is put into the mouth of the hero," he told his mother. The dictator was a stern and unforgiving authority figure, like his father. Lucile was beautiful and witty and sought after, like his mother, and Winston asked Jennie for help in understanding the character, for, as his grandmother Duchess Fanny had told him when she read the manuscript, it was clear that he had no knowledge of women or experience of love.

When the uprising led by Savrola succeeds, the dictator is shot by the mob as he defends his palace. Savrola, expressing the ambiguity of the son's Oedipal drive, is wounded trying to save Molara. Lucile does not mourn her husband. When Savrola comes to get her, he says, " 'I would not marry a goddess.' " " 'Nor I a philosopher,' " she replies. "Then they kissed each other, and thenceforth their relationship was simple." In Winston's fantasy, the character representing his idealized self won the mother away from the father. Savrola and his beautiful consort lived happily ever after.

Savrola is another example, like the earlier creation of the fantasy father, of Winston's ability to integrate his character through the use of myth and analogy. On another, and equally astonishing level, Savrola was a fairly accurate portrait of what he would become, a leader of men who could electrify a public meeting and whose very presence inspires confidence in his followers, an administrator scribbling pithy comments on official papers, whose talent was not for political thought but for articulating the feelings of the masses. " 'Do you think I am what I am,' " Savrola asks, " 'because I have changed all those minds, or because I best express their views? Am I their master or their slave? Believe me, I have no illusions.' " As a novel, *Savrola* was like an album of cardboard cutouts, even though at least one reviewer compared it with the novels of Disraeli, but as the expression of Winston's secret longings, it was eloquent.

After Ladysmith, the unlucky Sir Redvers Buller was replaced as commander in chief by Lord Roberts, who brought with him as chief of staff none other than the conqueror of the Sudan, Lord Kitchener. Roberts, a little gray terrier of a man, planned a push through the Orange Free State to the Boer capital of Pretoria. Winston applied for accreditation to Roberts' army and languished in Capetown's Mount Nelson Hotel while awaiting a reply. Once again, the military authorities blocked the way. Roberts did not want him, for Kitchener had been offended by passages in *The River War*. But Winston had friends in Roberts' entourage, primarily Ian Hamilton, whose pleas prevailed. On April 11, Roberts agreed to let Winston come—for his father's sake. He joined the British column near Dewetsdorp, in the Orange Free State, and later joined a unit led by his 4th Hussars commander, Colonel Brabazon.

Two days later, on April 13, 1900, in the heart of Wales, the thirty-seven-year-old Member of Parliament for Carnarvon Boroughs addressed an antiwar rally. The young Welshman, Lloyd George, was the most outspoken critic of the war in the House of Commons, risking his political career to back an unpopular cause. The rally on April 13 is the first recorded mention of Winston by Lloyd George, and it is worth noting, for the pacifist and the soldier became the towering figures of twentieth-century British politics and would soon establish a long-term love-hate relationship. Wales was a center of antiwar feeling, for in many Welshmen there was a natural sympathy for separatist movements. At the Penrhyn Hall in Bangor that night, someone who tried to sing "Soldiers of the Queen" was drowned out by the audience singing the Welsh anthem "Hen Wlad Fy Nhadau." Lloyd George said the Boers were being butchered; there were only forty thousand of them, and ten thousand had been wiped out, and the British were using dumdum bullets. Mr. Winston Churchill had written that the only way to conquer the Boers was to grind them down, to kill them one by one, dozen by dozen, Commando by Commando. There were cries of "Shame!" at Lloyd George's mention of Winston's dispatch. At this point, rocks came heaving through windows, and the police had to keep the crowd outside from rushing the building. Lloyd George was pummeled as he left, taking refuge in a café in High Street.[43] It was a close call. The life of an antiwar activist was almost as perilous as life at the front.

In late April, Winston had a close call. He wrote his mother that he had never been so near destruction. On a sortie near Dewetsdorp with a unit of scouts, he had dismounted at the foot of a hill when from behind some rocks at the top appeared the grim and hirsute heads of a dozen Boers. Frightened by the firing, his horse bolted when he tried to remount. Winston was alone, with no cover, one hundred yards from the enemy, and on foot. As he ran to dodge bullets, providence arrived in the shape of a scout named Clement Roberts, who took Winston on his horse and rode out of range of Boer fire.[44]

In May, he joined Ian Hamilton's column of fifteen thousand men, which was marching to Pretoria. The main British force under Lord Roberts advanced in the same direction. In all, two hundred thousand men were massed for the capture of the Boer capital. Hamilton's job was to smooth the advance of the main column. He rode across the veld, his shattered wrist flapping at the saddle, a memento of the Boer victory at Majuba, and a score to settle. Near him were Winston and his cousin Sunny Marlborough, the ninth Duke, who was serving as Hamilton's aide-de-camp. Outside Johannesburg, they met resistance near the Rand mine. Hamilton ordered a frontal attack up a heavily defended hill, Doornkop, the very spot where Jameson and his raiders had surrendered four and a half years before: a second score to settle.

The Gordon Highlanders charged up the hillside, their kilts swinging, with the same drill-book tactics that had been used at Balaclava. They took the hill, but lost one hundred dead and wounded in ten minutes. When Winston saw the bodies of eighteen Highlanders waiting for burial, he was seized with rage. Was this nothing more than a war for the control of mineral wealth? The dead men lay only a few feet from the mountain of gold. He found himself scowling at the tall chimneys of the Rand.[45]

On June 5, having covered four hundred miles in forty-five days, the British Army entered Pretoria. Lord Roberts thought the war was nearly over. Returning after six months to the site of his imprisonment, Winston and his cousin Sunny liberated the new prisoner-of-war camp, a long wooden building with a tin roof. Prisoners washing their clothes that morning saw two horsemen gallop into the compound, tear down the Boer flag, and hoist a homemade Union Jack amid cheers. Weapons were handed over, and the Boer guards changed places with the prisoners.[46]

The war would drag on for two more years, but for Winston it was over. He was eager to be back in England, where various things were hanging fire, politics, Pamela, his next book, his lecture tour, all needing attention. On July 4, he sailed for home on the same ship that had brought him out nine months before, the *Dunottar Castle*.

The military period of Winston's life was coming to an end. In his five years as a second lieutenant he had seen more action than any other officer his age, or than most senior officers. He had observed one war, in Cuba, and fought in three others, in India, the Sudan, and South Africa. It was natural for a young Army officer to seek action, and in Winston's case, the hunger for experience was combined with professional assignments to report on what he saw. This he did with a relish for the blood of battle that sometimes seemed extreme, but also with a sense of compassion for the suffering of the wounded and the humiliation of the vanquished. In *The River War* he made the point that the enemy of today was not the enemy of tomorrow, and that the moment of triumph was the moment of the greatest test.

As he was chasing wars, Winston displayed a curious need to expose himself to danger, partly to prove that he was not a coward and partly to test his feelings of invulnerability. Others fell, but Winston remained standing. His brother was shot beside him, Reggie Barnes was badly wounded, Albert Savory was shot and killed by a Boer sniper, and his fellow correspondent Hubert Howard was killed at Omdurman—it was, as J. B. Atkins had said, as if others paid Winston's debts.

Freed by his father's death, he had done what he had set out to do, to use the Army as a platform for a political career and to find a way to finance that career. His father had annexed Burma, but he had fought for the Empire in places thousands of miles apart and made a name for himself. It seemed that history had conspired to help him by breaking the Pax Britannica in two continents. Now he intended to cash in on that experience. In deliberately seeking medals and glory as a way of gaining fame, he antagonized some of his superiors and his fellow prisoner, Captain Haldane, who saw him as untrustworthy and selfish. The word most often used about Winston was "bumptious," and there can be no doubt that at this stage of his life he was self-assertive, self-absorbed, and supremely self-confident. It was un-British to be so manifestly ambitious, to want honors so badly, to push and insist and find shortcuts. There was something vaguely distasteful to the ceremonious Victorian mind about excessive drive. But even those who disliked Winston could not deny his pluck and tenacity. The word "genius" did not seem out of place next to his name. He was a phenomenon, not one of Kitchener's men but a whirling Dervish, always in motion, with a Mauser in one hand and a pen in the other. He had not done it alone, for since Randolph's death his mother had become his chief aide, conniving to advance his military career, campaigning for him at Oldham, and arranging for the publication of his articles and books.

Already, a few months short of his twenty-sixth birthday, Winston had done enough "to astonish cold posterity." But whatever he accomplished, it was never enough, for the deepest spring of his ambition was the need to correct his father's negative assessment. Thus he had to enlarge upon reality, bragging to his mother that he had killed five men at Omdurman, whereas to Ian Hamilton he gave the more realistic figure of three, and telling her he had scored three goals in the polo tournament, whereas the newspaper account credited him with one. Thus, in *My Early Life*, a book published thirty years after the event (though not in his dispatches or in the book published at the time, *London to Ladysmith*, where he might have been caught out), he presented as eyewitness reports material he had gathered secondhand, so deep was his need to be always at the heart of the action. Impatient to succeed, he worried that the years were slipping by, and that he had not even begun. At twenty-six, Napoleon was a general, and Pitt had become Prime Minister at twenty-four.

IV

PARLIAMENT

WINSTON LANDED in Southampton on July 20, 1900, in time for his mother's wedding to George Cornwallis-West, who had not given in to family pressure. Said to be the handsomest man in England, George was twenty-five, sixteen days older than Winston and twenty years younger than Jennie. A lieutenant in the Scots Guards, he had been invalided out of the Boer War with enteric fever. Their engagement shocked London society. The Prince of Wales told Jennie that he did not approve and did not want his name on the list of gift givers. Informed that he was not wanted in his regiment, George went on half-pay. Lady Dorothy Nevill, the octogenarian matriarch of Mayfair, when asked what she was doing in Hyde Park, strolling among the children, replied: "Well, if you want to know, my dear, I am searching in the perambulators for *my* future husband."[1]

Winston was losing his greatest ally. Married, his mother would no longer devote herself to his career. Whatever his private thoughts, he was loyal and supportive, more so than Jack, who remained sulking in South Africa. On the day of the wedding, July 28, at St. Paul's Church in Knightsbridge, not a single member of the Cornwallis-West family turned up, but there was a solid phalanx of Churchills, who by their presence ratified the match. Winston gave his mother a tremendous hug, and his new stepfather was grateful for his sympathy and understanding, and promised never to come between them.[2] The marriage lasted thirteen years, until George left Jennie for Mrs. Patrick Campbell, the actress, who described marriage as "the deep, deep bliss of the double bed after the hurly-burly of the *chaise longue*."

While Jennie and George went honeymooning in Scotland, Winston moved into handsome rooms at 105 Mount Street, picking up the lease from his cousin Sunny. Practical arrangements such as furnishing flats irritated him, for he was indifferent to his surroundings. So long as a table was clear and there was plenty of paper he was happy. There was a busy time ahead, for a General Election was due in October and Oldham wanted him again. He would be running against the two Liberals who had beaten him in the 1899 by-election, Emmott and Runciman, but with a new Conservative running mate, Charles Birch Crisp, a journalist turned stockbroker. Winston felt that he had greatly improved his position. When he visited the House of Commons two days after his mother's wedding, he was treated with great civility by all sorts of members, from Joseph Chamberlain on down.[3] Even his opponent, Walter Runciman, sent him a cordial note, expressing the hope that since Oldham was a double seat, they might both be elected and become colleagues.

The Conservatives had called for an election to exploit the successes of the Boer War, the fall of Pretoria and the relief of Mafeking in May after a siege of 216 days. It was the first "khaki" election in British history. The Liberals were in disarray, split into pro- and antiwar factions. Conservative strategy turned the election into a referendum on the war. A poster showed Lord Roberts and Lord Kitchener alongside the text: "Our Brave Soldiers in South Africa Expect That Every Voter This Day Will Do His Duty . . . Remember! To Vote for a Liberal Is a Vote to the Boer."

This was a crude but effective approach, and Winston's poster for Oldham may have reached a record for crudeness: "Be it known that every vote given to the Radicals means 2 pats on the back for Kruger and 2 smacks in the face for our country." His private opinion of the war was more thoughtful. As he wrote Milner on September 8, he was concerned about some of the harsh punitive measures the British were carrying out, such as farm burning. People were worried about the prolongation of the conflict and doubt was creeping into many hearts. Winston offered to act as Milner's mouthpiece in England: "I have neither influence nor power, but I can reach a wide public and if there be anything you want said—without saying it yourself—and my political conscience approves it, I would be proud to be your servant. At the present time I can command an audience of 4,000 people in any big town."[4]

Parliament was dissolved on September 17, and Winston had less than two weeks to campaign, for Oldham voted on October 1. The situation was complicated by a depression in the cotton trade. Winston had admired capitalism when he had passed through New York on his way to Cuba in 1895, but now he hoped the Lancashire manufacturers would "break the necks of those odious Americans" who were trying to corner the market by dumping inferior cotton.

Pleading with Balfour for a visit, Winston wrote: "We want the weight that comes from authority and experience badly. More arguments from one so young as me does not convince waverers."[5] Balfour was too busy, and Winston settled for a telegram of support that he could use as a placard. But he drew a trump in Joseph Chamberlain, then perhaps the most admired political figure in England, who came to Oldham from Birmingham, at considerable inconvenience,[6] to speak in behalf of a candidate "who I think has inherited some of his father's great qualities, his originality, and his courage." With a gleam in his eye, Chamberlain told Winston: "The first time I came here was to sell them screws."

The election was close, with all four candidates polling between 12,500 and 13,000 votes. Winston came in second behind Emmott, with 12,931, beating Runciman by 222 votes. It was a great moment, the start of a political career that would last for more than sixty years. He had attained what Curzon, in congratulating him, called "the first object of a politician's ambition"—a seat in the House of Commons. At last, he could take his father's place, as he had vowed to do at his deathbed, and mingle with men who had been Randolph's colleagues and Jennie's admirers. Only personal popularity, Winston was sure, had carried him, for there were still more Liberals than Conservatives in Oldham. This was no safe seat, and it would be hard to hold, but for the moment it was his.

With staggered polling, early results had a bearing on elections still to be fought. Winston became the "star turn" of his party, and spoke for Balfour, who had been too busy to speak for him. When the Tories won with a majority of 134 seats, he felt that he had a share in the victory.

Parliament would convene in February 1901, and in the meantime Winston went on a lecture tour to make money, the missing ingredient in his plans. It was partly because of money that he had decided not to marry Pamela. Jennie had written Winston while he was still in South Africa that it was only a question of time before the two of them were wed. But Winston had second thoughts. Was this the time to take a wife, when he was just starting out in politics, and had no guaranteed income? And was Pamela the right woman? She was spoiled, and would be better off marrying a rich man.

Mr. Christie's lecture bureau booked him for twenty-nine lectures between October 30 and November 30, and Winston toured England with his magic-lantern slides, talking about "The War As I Saw It." In East Fife, he stayed with a prominent Liberal, Herbert Asquith, whom he had met at "Natty" Rothschild's. Asquith's daughter, Violet, a precocious child suffering from polio, asked her father if Winston was like Randolph. "No—not really," Asquith said. "He is like no one else. He derives from no one. He is an original and most extraordinary phenomenon." From the bow window of her bedroom the next morning she watched him leave, his head jutting from a slightly hunched back.[7]

On December 1, having just turned twenty-six, Winston sailed for New York aboard the *Lucania*, a tour having been arranged by Major James B. Pond of the Lyceum Lecture Bureau, who had also organized the speaking engagements of Arthur Conan Doyle. ". . . you must not drag me about too much," Winston had specified, "and I don't want to wear myself out by talking to two-penny-half-penny meetings in out of the way places. In all my social engagements I shall exercise my entire discretion. . . . I don't want to be dragged about to any social functions of any kind nor shall I think of talking about my experiences to anybody except when I am paid for so doing."[8] On his second trip to America, as he wrote Bourke Cockran, Winston was pursuing profits, not pleasure.

At quarantine on December 8, the New York ships' reporters were on hand to interview the young lecturer in the square-topped derby and the astrakhan-trimmed coat. The Duke of Manchester had just married Helena Zimmerman, a Cincinnati heiress, and Winston assured the press that "I am not here to marry anybody. I am not going to get married, and I would like to have that stated positively." Referring to the Duke, Winston said: "He did a pretty thing for himself, didn't he?" "I understand the Duchess's father is not so wealthy as was at first thought," a reporter said. "Dear me!" Winston said, laughing. "Is that so? Dear, dear! It's too bad!"[9]

Pond's advance work left Winston so angry that he threatened to call off the tour. Posters hailed him as "the hero of five wars," at least one too many. A reception committee of local dignitaries featured so many Dutch names that it might have been made up of Boers. There was Van Ness, Van Dyke, Van Brunt, and the mayor of New York, Van Wyck. Some of these gentlemen had not been consulted, and wrote letters to the editors of various newspapers repudiating any connection with the event.

Things were not off to a good start. At his first appearance, as a dinner guest of the New York Press Club, Winston made some jocular remarks about Anglo-American friendship: "The chief characteristic of the English-speaking people as compared with other 'white' people is that they wash, and wash at regular periods. England and America are divided by a great ocean of salt water, but united by an eternal bathtub of soap and water." When he repeated his observations on hygiene three days later, *The New York Times* commented that "the amiable Lieutenant ran on at great length about the superior cleanliness of Englishmen and Americans as compared with all the rest of the world, and pictured them as advancing hand in hand from land to land, introducing the bath tub wherever they go and so elevating reluctant nations to unwonted heights of civilization . . . Fortunately all this was very funny, for it was also rather outrageous, and just a little disgusting . . ."[10]

On December 10, Winston went to Albany to meet the Governor of New York and Vice-President-elect, Theodore Roosevelt, who had charged up San Juan Hill two months before Winston's charge with the Lancers. Here were two soldier-politicians fired in the same furnace: both had been frail as children, had combat experience, and would change parties, reach the highest office of their respective countries, and win the Nobel Prize. But Roosevelt took an immediate dislike to Winston, which he kept all his life. Perhaps, as a "Rough Rider" who had fought the Spaniards in Cuba, he resented Church-ill's youthful foray there as an observer with the Spanish Army. The feeling was so intense that when he visited England in 1910 he saw every other public man of note but refused to meet Churchill. After the Albany visit, Roosevelt wrote a friend: "I saw the Englishman Winston Churchill here, and . . . he is not an attractive fellow . . ."[11]

Winston had to deal with the strong pro-Boer sentiments that existed among many Americans. In his first talk, in Philadelphia, he presented the war as a conflict between two right-minded adversaries who had to resort to arms. When an audience defiantly applauded the magic-lantern slide of a Boer cavalryman, Winston said: "You are quite right to applaud him; he is the most formidable fighting man in the world."[12]

In New York on December 12, the anniversary of his escape from Pretoria, in the Grand Ballroom of the Waldorf Astoria, Mark Twain introduced him. White-maned at sixty-five, he said of Winston:

"Although he and I do not agree as to the righteousness of the South African war, that's not of the least consequence, for people who are worth anything never do agree . . . Mr. Churchill will tell you his personal experiences. I have an inkling of what they are like, and they are very interesting to those who like that kind of thing. I don't like that kind of thing myself. I saw a battlefield—once. It was raining, and you know they won't let you carry an umbrella, and when shells are added to the rain it becomes uncomfortable. I think that England sinned when she got herself into a war in South Africa which she could have avoided, just as we have sinned in getting into a similar war in the Philippines. Mr. Churchill by his father is an Englishman, by his mother he is an American, no doubt a blend that makes the perfect man. England and America; we are kin. And now that we are also kin in sin, there is nothing more to be desired."

A Mark Twain introduction was a hard act to follow, but Winston was delighted, and asked him to inscribe a twenty-five-volume set of his works, which Twain did with this remark: "To do good is noble; to teach others to do good is nobler, and no trouble."[13]

In Washington, Senator Chauncey Depew of New York introduced Winston to President McKinley, whom he liked, and in Boston he met the American novelist Winston Churchill, author of *Richard Carvel*. A headline in the *Boston Herald* said: "Namesakes Meet, Winston Churchills Fast Friends." After lunch, as they strolled across one of the bridges spanning the Charles, Winston said to Winston: "Why don't you go into politics? I mean to be Prime Minister of England: it would be a great lark if you were President of the United States at the same time."[14] The American Winston may have taken the advice, for two years later he was elected to the New Hampshire legislature.

Winston spent Christmas in Ottawa with the Governor-General, Lord Minto, who had advised his mother not to put his name on his Malakand dispatches. A pleasant surprise awaited him, for Pamela was one of the guests. He found her as pretty as ever and quite happy. They had no painful discussions. There was still no doubt in his mind that she was the only woman he could ever live with. Jennie, who was catty about Pamela, wrote Winston that perhaps she had been sent to Canada to get her away from an officer she was seeing in London, Captain Graham.[15]

Another guest at Lord Minto's was George R. Parkin, a teacher at Upper Canada College, and a friend of Sir Alfred Milner's, who wrote Milner this interesting appraisal: "Winston Churchill was there furnishing us with a curious study. If he had some mentor to direct his force into normal channels there would be great promise in him: as it is I should think his future was what the wisest could not forecast with any approach to certainty. It is odd that Harrow and Sandhurst and the Indian Army should not have licked off angularities which will be sure to prove a hindrance to him. Still he has force and endless energy and courage."[16]

Pursuing his tour, Winston fought with Pond—he was nothing but a vulgar Yankee impresario, who was taking 30 percent of the fees and subcontracting some of the lectures to local agents for a fixed guarantee. He sold Toronto for 100 pounds, and Winston got only 70, even though the takings at the door amounted to 450. In one town, instead of speaking in a hall, he was hired out for 40 pounds to perform at a party in a private home, like a magician.[17] According to *The New York Times* of December 29, "Disagreement leads to the correspondent refusing the lecture at Brantford Ontario last night." But Winston was no quitter; he was glad that he had a cynical vein that helped him go on. At Ann Arbor on January 9, 1901, he met with boos and hisses when he said: "When we have won this war—as we surely shall . . ."[18] and in Chicago, "this strange place of pigs,"[19] they applauded the Boers.

On January 21, he spoke in Winnipeg. Twenty years ago, there had been only mud huts, and now men in evening dress and women in décolletés filled the opera house, and he took in 230 pounds. The next day, the news reached him that Queen Victoria had died. She had reigned for sixty-four years. As H. G. Wells remarked, her death removed a great paperweight that had sat on men's minds for half a century. Winston had spent five years in the Queen's service and had fought in the Queen's wars. A part of him would remain forever Victorian. He looked back upon the period as a pinnacle of English life.

> This was the British Antonine Age [he later wrote], . . . Englishmen felt sure that they had reached satisfactory solutions upon the material problems of life. Their political principles had stood every test . . . There were plenty of topics to quarrel about, but none that need affect the life or foundations of the State. A sense of safety, a pride in the rapidly opening avenues of progress, a confidence that boundless blessings would reward political wisdom and civic virtue, was the accepted basis upon which the eminent Victorians lived and moved.[20]

Winston wondered about the new king, from whom he had received signs of friendship. Would the crown revolutionize his way of life? Would he sell his horses and drop his Jewish friends, or would the Sassoons be enshrined among the crown jewels? Would he become desperately serious? Would his mistress, Alice Keppel, be appointed First Lady of the Bedchamber? At least he had got his innings at last, for he was sixty, and several times a grandfather. It would be interesting to see how he played it.[21]

Homeward bound aboard the *Etruria* on February 2, Winston was pleased with himself. He had amassed a capital of 10,000 pounds in less than two years. His English lectures had earned him 3,782 pounds, his American lectures accounted for another 1,600, and the rest came from his books. Not one person of his age in a million could have done it. Financially independent at last, he entrusted his fortune to his father's banker friend Sir Ernest Cassel, hoping to see it grow.

The first Parliament of the century and of King Edward's reign opened on February 14. Winston took a backbencher's seat and waited with the others for the knock of the Black Rod on the door of the Chamber announcing that the King awaited them in the House of Lords to read his first address. He had entered a world where he would remain until he was decrepit with age, serving in the House of Commons from 1901 until 1964, with an interruption of two years, between 1922 and 1924, when he had no seat. Those years he considered the only truly useless ones in his life, for he was without the ability to legislate or speak in the House. He was a writer, a Cabinet minister, the leader of his nation, but above all, he was a Member of Parliament. This was his profession, his battleground, his forum and true home. He liked to refer to himself as "a child of the House of Commons." Over the years, he would represent Oldham, North-West Manchester, Dundee (a safe Liberal seat), and the Epping Division of Essex (a safe Conservative seat), which later became Woodford.

New members were usually in a state of bewilderment at the strange practices, but Winston knew the protocol and language of the House by heart, from studying his father's career. The Mace on the table was the symbol of the King in Parliament. When money matters were discussed, it went under the table, to emphasize the power of the Commons over the purse. It was all so paradoxical. When bills were debated, that was called a reading, but the bills were not read. When the House moved adjournment, it settled down to debate. The method of voting, known as a division, was the most cumbersome possible. Bells rang, and members had nine minutes to assemble in the lobbies situated at the ends of the halls flanking the Chamber. As they divided into the Aye and No lobbies, their names were ticked off on lists by four tellers.

He knew the routine of the House in session, how it met at two-thirty and could go on until midnight, how the Speaker entered the Chamber, its two sides separated by a few square feet of baize carpet, and the Speaker's Chaplain said prayers, and the Speaker took the chair, and the House started its business for the day, conveyed by the Notice Paper of Public Business, known as the Order Paper. He knew that questions for Cabinet ministers had to be left in advance in writing, but that a straightforward written question might be a Trojan horse for a nasty supplementary sprung on the floor. He knew the vocabulary, as foreign to outsiders as that of Harrow—"another place" was the House of Lords, and "out of doors" were speeches away from the House. He knew the forms of address—"The Right Honorable" for Privy Councillors, "My Right Honorable Friend" for leaders of his own party, "The Right Honorable Gentleman" for Opposition leaders, "My Right Honorable and Gallant Friend" for a leader of the armed forces, and "My Learned Friend" for a solicitor. He knew the correct tone of the House, which it might have taken another years to learn: speeches must not be read and must be addressed to the Speaker; members could attack each other violently without damaging friendships or cordial relations. The rule was to give no quarter and bear no malice. The convention, usually observed, was to inform the target of one's attack before it took place in a note along the following lines: "I beg to give you notice that if I am called in the debate on Wednesday, I shall make certain observations which may be regarded as a personal attack upon you." Even when the attack was personal, the delivery was not, for the name of the person attacked was not used. When Winston went after Balfour, the butt of his remarks was "My Right Honorable Friend from East Manchester." It was not the man who was attacked, but the representative of a constituency. And although harsh things were said, they had to be in order. In the House, one was either in order or not in order, depending upon nuances of phrasing as subtle as the Latin declensions Winston had never been able to learn. "Willful falsehood" was in order; "deliberate lie" was not. Certain phrases often in use he already knew by heart: "The honorable member has been in the House long enough to know . . ." "Had the honorable member been present while I was speaking . . ." All of these things Winston knew as well as he knew the lines in his hand.

Now that he was in the House, he was no longer Winston; he became Churchill, or Churchill in the making, for he settled into his life's work of helping to shape his country's policies. When Edward VII made his first speech from the throne that day, much of it was devoted to the Boer War, where hopes of an early victory had dimmed. Lord Roberts had handed over

his command to Kitchener, who was fighting a war of attrition against guerrilla bands. Lord Milner still believed that complete military victory must
precede any negotiations. It was in this climate of South African deadlock
that the Parliamentary session opened. Within an hour of the King's speech,
Churchill had subscribed to the oath and taken his seat. An hour later, he
voted in his first division against the leaders of his own party. Balfour had
moved to pass an order forbidding peers from taking part in Parliamentary
elections. Churchill opposed the motion and ended up in the lobby with the
Irish and the Liberals, a sign of things to come.

The Liberal leader Sir Henry Campbell-Bannerman said of the new government: "The stable remains the same, the horses are the same, but every
horse is in a new stall." Lord Salisbury was still Prime Minister, since God
knew when, and would remain in office until July 1902. His ministry was
known as "the Hotel Cecil," for he had packed the Cabinet with relatives—
his son Viscount Cranborne was Under-Secretary of State for Foreign Affairs;
his nephews, Arthur and Gerald Balfour, were respectively Leader of
the House of Commons and First Lord of the Treasury, and President of the
Board of Trade; and his son-in-law, Lord Selborne, was First Lord of the
Admiralty. It was very much a family-run business, except for the Boer War,
which Salisbury called "Joe's war."

"Joe's war" was the topic under discussion in the House of Commons
debate in answer to the King's speech. Should Churchill try his fortunes at
once? Some said to wait a few months until he knew the House. He had
fought in the war, others argued, it was his subject; he must not miss the
chance. He decided to plunge in. A rising young Welshman named Lloyd
George, a pro-Boer, one of the bugbears of the Tories, was speaking on
February 18, and he would follow.

The House was filled to overflowing that night, for Lloyd George had a
following, and many wanted to see whether the young member making his
maiden speech was the equal of his father. Jennie and four of his father's
sisters pressed their faces against the grille of the Ladies' Gallery, and the
Peers' Gallery was crowded with lords and bishops.

Lloyd George spoke on the evening of the eighteenth, bitterly attacking the
new policy of herding Boer families into concentration camps. "All those
who surrendered voluntarily were given full rations," he said. "All the families whose husbands were on commando were put on a reduced scale. It
would be increased to the full allowance if the husbands surrendered. . . .
[Cheers from the Conservative benches] Members who cheer that would

cheer anything. It means that unless the fathers came in their children would be half-starved. It means that the remnant of the Boer army who are sacrificing everything for their idea of independence are to be tortured by the spectacle of their starving children into betraying their cause."[22]

This was more than Chamberlain could stand. He walked out of the House, to cries of "There he goes!" and "Come back!" "The author of this is ashamed of his misdeeds," Lloyd George taunted, and an Irish member, William Redmond, added: "He flies the white flag."[23]

It was in an excited House that Churchill spoke at ten-thirty, from the corner seat above the gangway, behind the government front bench, the seat from which Lord Randolph had made his resignation speech. Lloyd George was supposed to move an amendment, but did not. This was a reversal for Churchill, who had carefully prepared his reply to the move. Thomas Gibson Bowles, onetime owner of *Vanity Fair*, who was sitting next to him, whispered to the beginner that he might say, "Instead of making his violent speech without moving his moderate amendment, he had better have moved his moderate amendment without making his violent speech."[24]

The moment he rose to speak, the word went out that "Churchill's up," and every inch of the Chamber was occupied; even the side galleries and the bar were thronged. He got off to a good start with the borrowed quip. Speaking with authority, from personal experience, Churchill said that the Boers would attach no importance to the words of Lloyd George. "No people in the world received so much verbal sympathy and so little practical support as the Boers," he said. "If I were a Boer fighting in the field—and if I were a Boer I hope I should be fighting in the field—" At this admission the pro-Boer Irish members whooped, and Joseph Chamberlain, who had returned to listen, turned to a neighbor and complained: "That's the way to throw away seats." Churchill continued, "I would not allow myself to be taken in by any message of sympathy, not even if it were signed by a hundred honorable members."[25] Tory benches chuckled over this sly allusion to a telegram sent by one hundred Radical MP's four years before to the King of Greece, a week or two before he was forced to sue for peace with the Turks.

Churchill reminded his audience that the South African question was not unfamiliar to him when he said: "From what I saw of the war—and I sometimes saw something of it—I believe that as compared with other wars, especially those in which a civil population took part, this war in South Africa has been on the whole carried on with unusual humanity and generosity." And again, in a reference to his capture and escape: "I have traveled a good deal about South Africa during the last ten months under varying circumstances . . ."

He also took a swipe at the man who had exposed his escapades as a subaltern, Henry Labouchère, editor of *Truth* and a member for Northampton: "Some honorable members have seen fit, either in this place or elsewhere, to stigmatize this as a war of greed. . . . If, as the honorable member for Northampton has several times suggested, certain capitalists spent money in bringing on this war in the hope that it would increase the value of their mining properties, they know now that they made an uncommonly bad bargain. With the mass of the nation, with the whole people of the country, this war from beginning to end has only been a war of duty."[26]

In essence, this maiden effort was a conventional endorsement of the government's war policies, of no great originality or impact. Its true importance was in its last lines, when Churchill announced that by his presence in the House, he was inheriting his father's legacy: "I cannot sit down without saying how very grateful I am for the kindness and patience with which the House has heard me, and which have been extended to me, I well know, not on my own account, but because of a certain splendid memory which many honorable members still preserve."[27]

When Churchill had finished, Sir Robert Reid, the Liberal member for Dumfries Burghs, said: "I am sure the House is glad to recognize that the honorable member who has just sat down possesses the same courage which so distinguished Lord Randolph Churchill during his short and brilliant career in this House." The comparison was hard to avoid.

After the debate, when Churchill was applying what he called "the usual restoratives," he was introduced to Lloyd George in the bar. "Judging from your sentiments," Lloyd George said, "you are standing against the light." "You take a singularly detached view of the British Empire," Churchill replied.[28] They would have many more conversations about the war. "We do not always agree," Lloyd George said, "but at the same time we do not black each other's eyes." Churchill at first disliked the Welshman, and wrote a leading member of the Birmingham Conservative Association on December 23 that "personally, I think Lloyd George a vulgar, chattering little cad."[29]

Compliments abounded on the maiden speech, and the *Times* gave him more than a column, but the Liberal *Daily Chronicle* described him as "a medium-sized, undistinguished-looking young man, with an unfortunate lisp in his voice . . . and he lacks force." Few commentators passed up the chance to match the son against the father.

Churchill at first tried to be a loyal party man. On March 12, he helped get his front bench out of a tight spot over the dismissal of Major General Sir Henry Colville, accused of being too timorous a warrior in South Africa. Colville had appealed his resignation in a letter to the press, and an inquiry was called for in the House. Churchill argued that the right to promote and dismiss must be left with the military authorities, and the amendment asking for an inquiry was defeated. Sure that his speech had led to cross-voting, he was highly pleased with himself.[30]

He had never been so busy, and felt hunted to death. There were one hundred unanswered letters on his desk at Mount Street, before which he sat in a large chair of carved oak that had been presented to his father by the city of Manchester. He could not go on without a secretary, unless he got one he would be pressed into his grave with all sorts of ridiculous requests and obligations.[31]

In March, having been in the House about a month, a change came over him. He grew critical of the government. There was a good deal of dissatisfaction in the party, and a shocking lack of cohesion. The Treasury Bench was sleepy and exhausted and played out. He had begun to realize that the role of dutiful party hack was not going to lead to the Parliamentary equivalent of medals and clasps. As he would write in his life of his father, "Even in a period of political activity there is small scope for the supporter of a Government. The Whips do not want speeches, but votes. The Ministers regard an oration in their praise or defense as only one degree less tiresome than an attack. The earnest party man becomes a silent drudge, tramping at intervals through lobbies to record his vote and wondering why he came to Westminster at all." Would it not be better to follow Dr. Johnson's advice: "When I was beginning the world and was nobody and nothing, the joy of my life was to fire at all the established wits, and then everybody loved to hallow me on."

There was also the example of his father, who had made his reputation against his party. In the next three years, Churchill would be possessed by the spirit of his father as though by a dybbuk. In an uncanny manner, he re-created Randolph's career, storming against his leaders, forming a splinter group, quixotically crusading for economy in the Army. The cast of characters was the same, for Lord Salisbury was Prime Minister, as he had been when Randolph resigned, and the issue was the same, the army budget.

The Secretary of State for War, St. John Brodrick, who had been Under-Secretary to W. H. Smith when Randolph assailed the army estimates in

1886, wanted to create six army corps at a cost of three million pounds. This was the issue Churchill seized on, even though he had been a soldier, knew the need for a strong army, and had the previous August urged, in a speech at Plymouth, that the armed forces be provided with expensive modern weapons. When he spoke on May 13, it was to vindicate his father and adopt his cause. There was a Shakespearean sense of drama to the evening, reminiscent of Mark Antony vindicating the murdered Caesar. Asking if he might be allowed to revive a half-forgotten episode, Churchill described his father's resignation and quoted from his letter to Lord Salisbury, closing the book he was reading it from when he was halfway through, to show that he knew it by heart.

"Wise words, Sir, stand the test of time," he said when he had finished quoting, "and I am very glad the House has allowed me, after an interval of fifteen years, to lift again the tattered flag of retrenchment and economy." In case anyone doubted his intention, he repeated it: "I stand here to plead the cause of economy. I think it is about time that a voice . . . should stand forward and say what he can to protest against the policy of daily increasing the public burden. . . . I say it humbly, but with I hope becoming pride, no one has a better right than I have, for this is a cause I have inherited, and a cause for which the late Lord Randolph Churchill made the greatest sacrifice of any Minister of modern times."[32]

The *Times* the next morning said: "Mr. Churchill repeats again the most disastrous mistake of his father's career." The Liberal Opposition cheered the speech, but his own party leaders were less pleased. Mocking Churchill, Brodrick said a few days later that Parliament "will not sleep the less soundly because of the financial heroics of my honorable friend the member for Oldham. Those of us who disagree with him can only hope that the time will come when his judgment will grow up to his ability, when he will look back with regret to the day when he came down to the House to preach Imperialism, without being willing to bear the burdens of Imperialism, and when the hereditary qualities he possesses of eloquence and courage may be tempered also by discarding the hereditary desire to run Imperialism on the cheap."[33]

It was easy to show up this new boy in a hurry, who after only three months in the House had the gall to attack the leaders of his party. Sensing perhaps that he sounded too big for his britches, Churchill made an atypically self-effacing remark: "I am, I know, a very young man . . ."

The next step in his imitation of his father was to form a latter-day Fourth Party with a few dissident and wellborn young Tories—Arthur Stanley, a younger son of the Earl of Derby; Lord Percy, son of the Duke of Northumberland; and Ian Malcolm, a friend of the Churchill family. Grouping themselves around Hugh Cecil, the Marquess of Salisbury's fifth son, they became known as the Hughligans or Hooligans. Churchill was drawn to Hugh Cecil's overbred Oxford-trained intelligence, although the two men were a study in contrasts. Tall and cadaverously thin, pale-faced and burning-eyed, Hugh Cecil was known as "Linky," because of a supposed resemblance to the Missing Link. Five years Churchill's senior, he was a defender of religious and party orthodoxy, a purist of maddening obstinacy and misdirected brilliance, a cranky and pedantic young man who never married and pursued marginal causes.

The Hooligans proclaimed their independence of mind, but their main activity was to invite prominent politicians to dinner. They cultivated the right wing of the Liberal Party, men like Rosebery, Haldane, Asquith, and Sir Edward Grey.

After a summer visit to Scotland, Churchill renewed his attacks on the government's South African policy, placing the blame at the feet of Balfour and Chamberlain, who had befriended him by arranging a meeting with Milner in Capetown, and stumping for him in the Oldham election. In October, Chamberlain sent Churchill a warning letter, a little like the warnings about the dangers of forming a party within the party that Sir Stafford Northcote had sometimes sent to Randolph. Chamberlain did not think that Churchill's criticism of the government and the military authorities was profitable. ". . . you must see yourself," he added, "that its first result is to encourage the enemy to blaspheme, both at home and abroad."[34]

But Churchill continued to criticize, feeling that the government was making one mistake after the other. He was disgusted in October when General Sir Redvers Buller, after being recalled to England, was dismissed. The poor old man, who had done him the kindness of giving him a commission in the South African Light Horse—how tactless and cowardly the government had been. Churchill was cultivating the Liberal Imperialists, Haldane and Grey and Asquith. If he were of their forces, he wrote Lord Rosebery, he would be all for vigorous action. Already, he was contemplating a change of party. In September, he had been invited to Cecil Rhodes's Scottish estate, Loch Rannoch, for a shooting party. Unburdening himself to Rhodes, he said that he was inclined to leave the Tory leadership to Balfour and proclaim himself a Liberal. He wanted power, and the road was blocked by the Cecils and other young Conservatives, whereas the Liberal path was open. Rhodes was all in favor of the change.[35]

Now that he was launched and busy, Churchill adopted a different tone in his letters to his mother. No longer waiting for her visits, no longer needing her help, he became almost patronizing: "No, my dear, I do not forget you. But we are both of us busy people, absorbed in our own affairs, and at present independent. Naturally we see little of each other. Naturally that makes no difference to our feelings."[36]

The year ended with a significant event: Churchill discovered the poor, and his social conscience was born. That November, responding to a fan letter, H. G. Wells had written him, stressing the difference in their backgrounds: "You belong to a class that has scarcely altered internally in a hundred years. If you could be transported by some magic into the Household of your ancestors of 1800, a week would make you at home with them. In that time the tailor, hairdresser & the atmosphere of different manners only have done all that was needed. But of the four grandparents who represented me in 1800 it's highly probable two could not read & that any of them would find me and that I should find them as alien as contemporary Chinese. I really do not think that your people who gather in great country houses realize the pace of things."[37]

That may have been true, but in December Churchill read a book by Seebohm Rowntree called *Poverty: A Study of Town Life,* and was shaken by its account of the poor in the city of York. It was terrible and shocking that one-fifth of the population did not have enough to eat. What glory could there be in an Empire that ruled the waves and was unable to flush its sewers? The government, looking abroad, paid no attention to domestic matters. Imperial development should be coordinated with the progress of social comfort and health.[38] Churchill's own experience was that of a duke's grandson and a far-flung soldier of Empire, but thanks to the chance reading of a book he was made aware of new political realities, and seeds were planted that would be harvested when he was President of the Board of Trade seven years later.

The start of 1902 found Churchill more reluctant than ever to follow the party line. He could work up no enthusiasm for speeches on the government's behalf, and yet audiences seemed eager for party claptrap. He was toying with the idea of a Middle Party in conjunction with the Liberal Imperialists, but that was premature. How could he respond to their invitations when they had no house to entertain in, when all they had was a share in a dilapidated umbrella? It was wiser to keep both feet firmly planted on Tory terra firma until there was equally firma land, Middle or other, to step on to.

He kept sniping at Brodrick's army reforms and at the war policy in South

Africa. The war dragged on, and the Boers still held out for independence, despite Kitchener's strategy of blockhouses and concentration camps. "Jumped into the peerage," Lord Milner had moved to Pretoria, and wrote Chamberlain that the concentration-camp policy was a disaster: "The black spot—the one very black spot—in the picture is the frightful mortality in the concentration camps . . . The whole thing I think now has been a mistake."[39] But Milner still wanted total surrender.

Churchill's membership in the Hooligans led him to adopt some rather dubious causes, such as his opposition to the Deceased Wife's Sister Bill, a measure that would allow a widower to marry his sister-in-law. Churchill thought this was a reasonable arrangement, for a man with young children needed help to bring up his family. Many happy homes had been constructed on this basis. But to Hugh Cecil, such unions were immoral because they had been declared "incestuous and unlawful" by the canons of the Anglican Church in 1604. In the Prime Minister's youngest son, Churchill had found a true Tory, right out of the seventeenth century. Cecil was scandalized at Churchill's approval of the bill. How could he completely ignore ecclesiastical law? Once one's moral and intellectual feet slipped upon the slope of plausible indulgence, there could be no stop short of general paganism and hedonism.[40] Burning with the flame of true belief, Lord Hugh recruited Churchill in a prolonged and successful obstruction of the bill, which gave the Hooligans a bad name because of their tactics.

The plot to kill the bill was acted out on February 5. A division on the Second Reading was called for shortly after 5 P.M., after which the bill would go to committee. Under the rules of that time, an opposed bill could not be dealt with after 5:30 P.M. The Hooligans loitered in the No lobby until time ran out. When a clear majority in favor of the bill was announced, it was too late to send it to committee. No more time could be found for the bill in the current session, and it lapsed.

Many members were offended by these tactics, all too reminiscent of Fourth Party obstruction of Gladstone's government. On February 6, Henry Campbell-Bannerman, leader of the Liberal Opposition, asked Balfour, the Leader of the House: "Is the right honorable Gentleman aware that the House was ready to proceed with the next stage of the Bill, that the large majority in favor of the Bill showed what the feeling of the House was, and that it was prevented from having the opportunity desired by the deliberate action—["No, no"]—yes, of certain members who not only in that particular division delayed in the lobby, but also in previous divisions did the same thing with the direct purpose of frustrating the intentions and wish of the majority of the House?"[41]

Churchill, who had no real objection to the bill, but who had gone along with Cecil out of loyalty, and because it was a chance to copy his father's tactics, weakly argued: "Is it not the case that what happened was owing, not to undue delay on the part of the minority, but to undue haste on the part of the majority?"[42] Thanks to the intercession of the Speaker, the Hooligans escaped a charge of misconduct.

In April, they again banded together against their party in the case of Mr. Cartwright, the editor of a newspaper called the *South African News*. Found guilty of libeling Kitchener, Cartwright was sentenced to a year in jail. Having served his sentence, he was forbidden to travel to England, under the existing martial law. When John Morley, a leading anti-Imperialist Liberal, raised the issue by moving the adjournment of the House, the explanation given by the War Office spokesman was that "it seemed inexpedient to increase the number of persons in this country who disseminated anti-British propaganda." Morley called this the most outrageous and indefensible statement ever given to the House.

The issue was debated along party lines. The Liberals argued that Cartwright was a British subject, and that denying his freedom of movement was an attack on the liberties of every Englishman. The Tories held that under martial law, Kitchener had every right to take whatever measures he felt were necessary to prevent someone from coming to England and spreading dissent against the war.

Breaking with his party, Churchill noted that Cartwright had not been tried by a court-martial, but by a judge and jury, and that no power could hold a man who had served all that the law had a right to require of him. Further, there was a constitutional principle of freedom of opinion involved. "There are some of us on this side of the House," he said, "who are not prepared to see a great constitutional principle violated, not, I think, with any deliberate intent, but simply because those who administer the law have got used to an over exercise of power, and, having overstepped themselves on this occasion, should be made by the due authority of this House to withdraw within the limits of the law."[43] When Morley's motion came to a vote, Churchill and the Hooligans sided with the Liberals, but the motion was defeated by 279 to 182. That night, April 24, the Hooligans gave Chamberlain a dinner. He chided them, saying: "I am dining in very bad company. What is the use of supporting your own Government only when it is right? It is just when it is in this sort of pickle that you ought to have come to our aid."[44] But Churchill did not accept the principle of "my party right or wrong." Indeed, still guided by his father's example, he sometimes voted against his party when he knew it to be right.

The Cartwright debate was the last time Churchill would differ from his party on any matter connected with the Boer War, for the war ended that June. Short of horses and food, their families in concentration camps, their control over the African population dwindling, the Boers' situation had become hopeless, and they signed a surrender in Pretoria. South Africa would be a British Dominion, not a Boer Republic. From the bottom of his heart, Churchill rejoiced in the settlement that had ended the dragging, draining, dangerous war. He could now concentrate on his pet project, economy. Balfour had given in to his repeated urgings and appointed a House committee on spending, upon which Churchill sat. In his father's shadow, he tried to play the thrifty retrencher, fretting about the leap of expenditures by seven million pounds a year, but it was not a role for which he was suited.

In July, Lord Salisbury resigned (he would die thirteen months later), and Balfour inherited his uncle's office. The Prime Minister was back in the House of Commons and would remain there. Would Balfour reconstruct the government and bring Churchill in, as his uncle had brought in Randolph, if only to silence a heckler? Balfour made a few changes, but history did not repeat itself, although one of the Hooligans, Lord Percy, was made Under-Secretary of State for India.

The man who had been Randolph's disciple in the Fourth Party days had finally reached the highest office. He would keep it for three and a half years, leading his party to ruin, from which it would take seventeen years and one world war to recover. Although Balfour and Churchill both came from great landed families, no two more dissimilar men ever led England. Everything Balfour did seemed effortless and unstudied. He had every advantage from birth, wealth, brains, good looks, elegance, and one of those safe Cecil seats that came with the monogrammed silver. He had a stately home in Scotland and a mansion in Carlton House Terrace. He could afford to indulge his passions for Handel and philosophy. A lifelong bachelor, he never had to raise a family. The "Balfourian manner" was one of well-bred detachment. He seemed devoid of ambition, reluctantly accepting public office when it was thrust upon him, in the tradition of the brilliant amateur with an interest in public life. The worst offense of a civilized Englishman, his bearing seemed to say, was to express desire. He had made of aloofness such a virtue that

Churchill lamented, "There was no way of getting at him." And yet Balfour was not a weak man; he had that singularly English mix of lethargy and vigor.

Everything Churchill did seemed hard-fought. Nothing came easily, whether it was mastering the letter *s* or winning a seat in the House. He worked, he worried, he pulled strings, he enlisted and insisted, and, more often than not, he got what he wanted. Where Balfour was detached, he was pugnacious; where Balfour pretended (or actually felt) indifference to power, he was openly ambitious. Churchill, who labored for days learning his speeches by heart, asked Balfour whether he prepared his. "No," he replied, "I say what occurs to me, and sit down at the end of the first grammatical sentence." Churchill, with a great need to feed his ego, subscribed to a press-cutting service. Considering such services vulgar, Balfour said: "I have never put myself to the trouble of rummaging an immense rubbish-heap on the problematical chance of discovering a cigar-end." Here were two polar opposites, emblematic of the contrasts between two ages, the Age of Certainty and the Age of Doubt, the Age of Privilege and the Age of Merit, the Age of British Supremacy and the Age of British Decline.

With Balfour Prime Minister and with Churchill moving toward systematic opposition to his party, they would come into open conflict on more than one occasion. The first occurred that July, when Churchill and the Hooligans took up the case of administrative injustice at Sandhurst. Five fires had broken out, the latest in the C Company building, clearly the work of an arsonist. On June 25, Lord Roberts, now commander in chief of the Army, ordered all the cadets who could not prove they were absent at the time of the most recent fire to be suspended unless the guilty came forth. No one came forth and twenty-nine cadets were suspended. It seemed unfair to Churchill that the innocent should be punished along with the guilty, for suspension meant a loss of six months' seniority and an extra term of school to be paid by the parents. He and Hugh Cecil publicized the case in the *Times*, and on July 10, they brought the matter up on the floor of the House at question time:

> CHURCHILL: "I beg to ask the Secretary of State for War whether he will state how many of the twenty-nine cadets who have been rusticated from Sandhurst in consequence of the recent incendiary fires had been previously punished on the occasion of the Camberley Fair?"
>
> [Seven of the twenty-nine, St. John Brodrick replied.]

CECIL: "Is there any reason to suppose that the whole twenty-nine were guilty?"

BRODRICK: "I cannot say the exact number."

CECIL: "Has the smallest inquiry been made as to their guilt?"

BRODRICK: "It is impossible to state the exact numbers or the names of those who were engaged in the disturbance . . . the general state of indiscipline at Sandhurst has been such during the last few weeks that it was necessary for the Commander in Chief to take serious action."[45]

Churchill then tried to move the adjournment of the House, which would have allowed a debate on the matter, but Balfour said: "I could not, as at present advised, with the small remaining time at our disposal before the adjournment for the holidays, give special facilities for discussing it." The matter was raised in the House of Lords, however, and Lord Roberts eventually reinstated all but two of the cadets and had the commandant of Sandhurst replaced. In the Sandhurst and Cartwright incidents, Churchill showed his concern for protecting the individual against an all-powerful and unjust bureaucracy.

But these were mere pigeon shoots, and Churchill was hunting bigger game. His thoughts returned to the idea of a third party, which would be equally free from the sordid selfishness and callousness of the Tories and the blind appetites of the Liberal masses. It was an ideal, but it might be worth working for—some sort of central coalition of like-minded Liberals and Tories. Of course, everyone would say that he was moved only by restless ambition. That difficulty would disappear only if some issue arose that he could seize upon, a crucial issue, like protectionism against free trade.[46]

As if responding to Churchill's need, Chamberlain on May 15, 1903, dropped a bombshell in his political stronghold of Birmingham: he came out in favor of tariff reform and Imperial preference. There had been free trade in England since the repeal of the Corn Laws in 1846. In the Tory Party it was an article of faith that free trade had brought cheap food and prosperity. To doubt it was like doubting the existence of God at an Ecumenical Congress. But to Chamberlain the Empire builder, a colonial customs union was a way of cementing the Empire after the humiliation of the Boer War, at a time of doubt and confusion about Britain's place in the world. And to Chamberlain the Birmingham businessman, tariffs were a way of protecting British manufacturers against the foreign goods that were flooding England.

Having divided the Liberal Party in his opposition to Home Rule, Cham-

berlain now proceeded to split the Tory Party in his espousal of protectionism. The whole country was agog. No one talked of anything else. The Tories
were split between free traders and tariff reformers. With new elections approaching, what a gift this was to the Liberals, divided by the Boer War.
They buried their differences and rallied behind Campbell-Bannerman to
exploit the Tory split and champion the cause of free trade.

What was Balfour to do? It would have been better to choose at once
between Chamberlain and his free trade Chancellor of the Exchequer,
Charles Ritchie. But such a clear-cut decision was not in the nature of the
author of *A Defense of Philosophic Doubt*. He preferred to pretend that no
problem existed. Where did he stand? When asked in the House, he said: "I
should consider that I was ill performing my duty, I will not say to my Party,
but to the House and to the country, if I were to profess a settled conviction
where no settled conviction exists." A Prime Minister without convictions on
the glaring issue of the day? He was, said one of his critics, like the British
ambassador who wrote in a dispatch: "Some say the Pretender is dead and
some say he is alive. For my part I believe neither." Where was the government heading? There were opportunities galore for Tadpole and Taper,
Disraeli's fictitious MP's, who liked to indulge in gossip and speculation.

It was in this atmosphere of rudderless Tory drift that Churchill seized on
the free trade issue and made it his own. He had finished with army reform,
harassing into surrender "poor old Brodrick," who would soon be transferred
to the India Office. Churchill's first reaction to Chamberlain's speech was
astonishment. How ill considered and premature and unsound it was to raise
this controversy. Why, it would tear the Unionist (Tory) Party from one end
to the other.[47] Churchill was a free trader by conviction and because he
believed that his father had been one. On May 25 he wrote Balfour to tell
him where he stood, and added: "I should like to tell you that an attempt on
your part to preserve the Free Trade policy & character of the Tory Party
would command my absolute loyalty . . . But if on the other hand you have
made up your mind & there is no going back, I must reconsider my position
in politics. . . ." Balfour's reply was evasive; it was his impression, he said,
that Chamberlain wanted a duty only on foodstuffs.[48]

In the House on May 28, two prominent Liberals, Sir Charles Dilke and
Lloyd George, asked whether Chamberlain's views were endorsed by the
government. Balfour, making subtle distinctions between what was and was
not free trade, said that fiscal opinions were not a test of party loyalty.
Churchill disagreed. "What is the cause of this change?" he asked. "Never

was the wealth of the country greater, or the trade returns higher, or the loyalty of the colonies more pronounced. It is that we are tired of these good days? There is no popular demand for this departure. I do not know what popular demand or popular movement the Colonial Secretary with his great popularity and persuasive manners may not be able to excite, but at the present moment there is no demand whatever, and not for the last one hundred years has a more surprising departure been suggested."[49]

And so the lines were drawn, and Churchill became a leader of the free trade movement, even though he suspected that Balfour, for all his waffling, was committed to Chamberlain. He felt that he was taking the true Tory line. The taxation of food would frighten the workingman with the prospect of the "little loaf" and would estrange the masses from the Imperial ideal.

On July 8, Churchill had a chance to question Beatrice Webb, the well-known Fabian Socialist, about working-class feeling. She met him at a dinner and formed this first impression:

> Restless—almost intolerably so, without capacity for sustained and unexciting labor—egotistical, bumptious, shallow-minded and reactionary, but with a certain personal magnetism, great pluck and some originality—not of intellect but of character. More of the American speculator than the English aristocrat. Talked exclusively about himself and his electioneering plans—wanted me to tell him of someone who would get up statistics for him. "I never do any brainwork that anyone else can do for me."—An axiom which shows organizing but not thinking capacity. Replete with dodges for winning Oldham against the Labor and Liberal candidates. But I daresay he has a better side—which the ordinary cheap cynicism of his position and career covers up to a casual dinner acquaintance. Bound to be unpopular—too unpleasant a flavor with his restless, self-regarding personality, and lack of moral or intellectual refinement . . . But his pluck, courage, resourcefulness and great tradition may carry him far unless he knocks himself to pieces like his father.[50]

A few days later, Churchill founded the Free Food League, which sixty Unionist MP's joined, while only half that number joined the rival Tariff Reform League. On July 16, he attacked Balfour in the *Times*: ". . . While Mr. Balfour silences his followers in the House of Commons Mr. Chamberlain is busy with their constituencies. . . ." He might have included his own constituency of Oldham, where pro-Chamberlain elements disapproved of

Churchill's stand. On August 5 he was reprimanded in a resolution of the East Oldham Conservative Club and went to Oldham to shore up his position, holding eight meetings and winning a vote of confidence from the Central Executive. The working classes, he was pleased to see, seemed drawn to a representative whose name they read frequently in the papers and who conferred distinction on the town.[51]

By this time, Churchill felt that Balfour would break with Chamberlain, and that Joe would leave the government with a certain following and drive on his own wild career as an independent person, which would mean his ruin. He had far more respect for Joe Chamberlain than for the time-servers waiting to see which way the cat would jump. Joe was ready to sacrifice his whole political career for this issue. It made him melancholy to think of it, for Joe had been so kind to him.[52]

In the afternoon debate on August 11, Churchill's ally Hugh Cecil challenged his first cousin Balfour to explain why Chamberlain had been allowed "to publish on a scale of almost legendary magnitude" leaflets on the fiscal issue "and to distribute them broadcast over the whole country." Was this a misuse of Chamberlain's prestige as a minister of the Crown? When Balfour interrupted on a point of order, Cecil lost his temper and interjected, "Oh, muzzle the House of Commons!"[53]

That evening, Jack Seely and Churchill co-hosted a dinner in the House for Balfour and Hugh Cecil and others. The Prime Minister showed no rancor, but chaffed and chatted with them. Later Churchill ran into Chamberlain, who gave him a look of reproach, as if to say, "How could you desert me?" When Churchill wrote to confirm this impression, Chamberlain replied that it was not a reproach but shortsightedness (perhaps his monocle was not on) and that he bore him no malice for his political opposition.[54]

On August 14, the last day of the Parliamentary session, Churchill made his first frontal attack on Balfour. An unworthy doubt had crossed his mind.

"I have sometimes doubted whether the right honorable Gentleman's policy has been so disingenuous, so haphazard, so dictated by circumstances beyond his control, as I would gladly believe, whether in fact it is merely a serious and honest, but a somewhat undignified, attempt to keep the Cabinet together rather than a tactical deployment to commit a great Party to a new policy against which its instinct revolts and distrusts—a policy which in the minds of the wisest and oldest counselors in its ranks would lead to ruin and failure, whether it is an attempt to coax the Party over difficult ground, and to commit it to a position which, had there been full opportunity of debate, the Party would have repudiated. I cannot hold to that view, because to do so would be to say that the right honorable Gentleman has been guilty of bad faith to his followers and friends."[55]

Borrowing from Shakespeare, Churchill used the "but Brutus is an honorable man" approach to charge his Prime Minister with hypocrisy. Balfour did not deign to reply.

In September, Chamberlain exploded another bombshell: he resigned in order to pursue his protectionist campaign without splitting the party. Balfour also obtained the resignations of four of the leading free trade ministers, and may have felt that he had solved his problems by cleaning both sides of his stable. But the damage had been done. As Churchill had predicted, the controversy had reached the constituencies. Nowhere was this truer than in Oldham, where Chamberlain's ideas had won over the local Tory leaders. J. T. Travis-Clegg, the Oldham Tory chairman, warned Churchill in mid-October that the committee was in revolt and that he had the choice of retiring or being thrown out. When Churchill did not respond, Travis-Clegg wrote him again that unless he adopted Chamberlain's policy he would be repudiated by the Oldham Tories.[56]

Faced with the betrayal of his constituents, who preferred Chamberlain's "quack medicine" to his brave stand in defense of the true Tory tradition, Churchill took the final step in his meandering march toward Liberalism. Writing to Hugh Cecil on October 24, he made this astonishing statement: "I am an English Liberal. I hate the Tory Party, their men, their words & their methods." He would not stay inside the party and split hairs. He would not feign friendship where none existed and loyalty to leaders whose downfall he desired . . . it sickened him.[57]

To Hugh Cecil, the guardian of orthodoxy, such words were sacrilege. Like Churchill, Hugh Cecil was a free trader, but he would no more have joined the Liberal Party than he would have converted to Catholicism. Everything about the Liberal Party—its foreign policy, its religious reformism, everything, in fact, except its stand on free trade—repelled him. If the choice was between crossing the floor and losing his seat to a pro-Chamberlain Conservative or a Liberal, he would not hesitate to do the latter. Churchill the political realist knew that "Linky" derived a melancholy satisfaction from being driven out of the House of Commons nursing his wrongs—well, he would have the martyrdom he so devoutly cherished. "Linky" in fact lost his seat and did not gain another until 1909, but his principles were intact.

Balfour had re-formed his Cabinet with pro-Chamberlain men, including Austen Chamberlain, who replaced Ritchie at the Exchequer. Churchill's omission caused comment, for an undistinguished new member named Bonar Law, in the House for only eighteen months, was made Parliamentary Secretary to the Board of Trade. Balfour was rewarding loyalty, not brilliance. Chamberlain thought he was wrong in not silencing Churchill with a minor appointment, and later told Margot Asquith: "Winston is the cleverest of all the young men, and the mistake Arthur made was letting him go."[58]

Churchill was despondent about saving even a remnant of the Conservative Party from the contagion of protectionism. In every constituency, popular feeling seemed to be on the side of Chamberlain. Deciding to carry the fight to Chamberlain's home ground, he agreed to speak in Birmingham in November.[59] Chamberlain's Tory organization threatened a boycott against anyone abetting the meeting, and hawkers walked the streets with bills calling upon people to disrupt it. But Churchill was well received by a largely Liberal audience, one of whom said: "That man may call himself what he likes but he's no more a Tory than I am."

Churchill's attitude toward Chamberlain was one of mingled contempt and admiration, according to Wilfrid Scawen Blunt, the handsome poet and anti-imperialist who had once been jailed for his pro-Irish views. He and Churchill met for the first time on October 31 at the Earl of Lytton's, whose wife was none other than the former Pamela Plowden. Living up to the expectations of her friends, Pamela had married a wealthy lord in 1902. Churchill was friends with them both.

White-maned and white-bearded at sixty-three, Blunt found in Winston a strange replica of his father, with all of Randolph's suddenness and assurance, and more than his ability. As Churchill repeated his conversations with Chamberlain, Blunt seemed once more to be hearing Randolph's monologues on Northcote and Salisbury. There was the same *gaminerie* and contempt of the conventional and the same engaging plainspokenness and readiness to understand.[60]

Churchill was ejecting himself from the Tory Party by stages. There was a by-election in Ludlow, and on December 19 he sent the Liberal candidate, Frederic Horne, a letter of support that said ". . . the time has now come . . . when Free Traders of all parties should form one long line of battle against a common foe."[61] Two days later, he told a free trade meeting at Halifax:

"Thank God we have a Liberal Party!" This was too much for the Oldham Tories, who passed the following resolution on December 23: "That this meeting of the General Purposes Committee of the Oldham Registration Association intimates to Mr. Winston S. Churchill, MP, that he has forfeited their confidence in him as Unionist member for Oldham, and in the event of an election taking place he must no longer rely on the Conservative organization being used on his behalf."[62] This resolution would be submitted to the General Executive on January 8, 1904. Churchill's actions were also too much for Hugh Cecil, who was under the impression that he had agreed to continue the battle inside the party. But now, in one of his thousand foolish passing moods, he was flinging himself into the arms of the Liberals like a seduced woman. Why had he lent support to a candidate of the opposing party at the very moment the Oldham committee was voting on his fitness? His lamentable instability made it impossible to work with him, and unless he cured it, it would be fatal to his career.[63]

Horne lost, but won 3,423 votes in a constituency that had not been contested by the Liberal Party since 1892. It was a straw in the wind. The Liberals were winning seat after seat in by-elections. The message was not lost on Churchill. When the resolution against him carried in January with only one dissenting vote, he wasted no time conferring with Herbert Gladstone, the Liberal Chief Whip, about the possibility of a Liberal seat. What about Central Birmingham, his father's old battleground? He did not want the initiative to seem to come from him. He was getting tender inquiries from Preston and Cardiff, but was keeping himself free. In the meantime, there was no reason for him to resign; he could continue as member for Oldham in the present Parliament.[64]

The Unionist hierarchy was losing patience with Churchill. He no longer received the circulars from the Whips, nor did he get a copy of a letter Balfour sent his party's MP's in January. He wrote Balfour to ask if he was being reprimanded. There had been an article to that effect in the *Daily Telegraph*.

To Balfour, Churchill was a potential troublemaker tending toward schism, like his father, and perhaps, like him, a bit unbalanced. In a fine example of the "Balfourian manner," he wrote Churchill on February 1, stating the case against him without making any accusations:

> I find that the authorities responsible for the issue of the Circular Letters and Whips to members of the party were under the impression,

derived apparently from some of your speeches, that you did not desire any longer to count yourself as among the supporters of the present government . . . This mistake, which happily has been remedied in time, appears not to have been without some plausible justification. A hasty reading, for example, of such a phrase as "Thank God, we have an opposition!" . . . is apt to lead to a misunderstanding. It was rashly interpreted by some as meaning that the policy of the country would be safer in the hands of the opposition than the government, a meaning clearly inconsistent with party loyalty. Obviously it is equally capable of a quite innocent construction. It might for example be a pious recognition of the fact that our heaviest trials are sometimes for our own good. Or again it might mean that a world in which everyone was agreed would be an exceedingly tedious one; or, that an effective opposition made party loyalty burn more brightly. There are, in short, countless interpretations, quite consistent with the position which I understand to be yours, namely of a loyal though independent supporter of our present administration. Exegesis is a harder task to perform in explaining away a letter which you seem to have written to the electors of Ludlow, apparently advising them to vote against the Unionist candidate, but *you* are the best judge of your own meaning: and I have therefore gladly given directions that you are not to be deprived of the daily "whip" which you desire to receive.

Stung, Churchill replied that he had never said he desired to receive it, he had only asked why he was not receiving it. In case any doubt remained in Balfour's mind, Churchill served notice that "my position is that of a wholehearted opponent of Mr. Chamberlain's and his proposals and it is quite possible that in such opposition I may be forced into action . . ."[65]

Balfour was patience itself, but on March 17, in an exchange during the question period, a crack showed in his Olympian detachment. At issue was the committee on spending, about which nothing had been done, for it was one of Balfour's methods to agree in principle to something and then forget about it. Churchill pressed him on the matter, and Balfour said he saw no reason why the government should be specially bound to spare a day to discuss it.

CHURCHILL: "Will my right honorable friend endeavor to secure an opportunity for the consultation with the right honorable Gentleman after Questions this afternoon?"

BALFOUR: "I must say my honorable friend is trespassing on the individual liberties of both sides of the House when he endeavors to prescribe to us the precise hour at which we should come into consultation."[66]

Churchill's peremptory manner in the House had already frayed the tempers of some of his fellow members. On February 4, the Speaker had been interrupted, and the Liberal Unionist member for Bradford Central, James Wanklyn, called for order. Churchill turned around and rebuked him for shouting people down. "Permit me to warn you," Wanklyn wrote him afterward, "that if I have any more impertinence from a young man like yourself, I shall know how to deal with it. Your conduct in using words like 'lie,' 'quack,' 'charlatan,' 'weak,' 'dangerous' of Mr. Balfour and Mr. Chamberlain has disgusted most people, as well as yours truly."[67]

On March 29, 1904, Churchill's isolation from his party was shown in a dramatic scene in the House of Commons. Balfour had spoken and was followed by Lloyd George, who was on the attack, saying that if the Prime Minister "went on clutching at power, in spite of the opinion of the people, he would lose something more important than the confidence of the country, something more difficult to regain, and that was the respect of the country."

As Lloyd George wound up and Churchill rose to speak, Balfour walked out of the Chamber, either angered by Lloyd George's speech or in a deliberate snub to Churchill. "I am very sorry the Prime Minister has left the House," Churchill said, "as I had desired to ask him one or two questions." At this, all the ministers on the Conservative front bench rose and followed Balfour out, as if the whole thing had been orchestrated. Then the Tory backbenchers rose and were herded out by Frederick Banbury, MP for one of the districts in the City of London. Some of them lingered at the door to jeer at Churchill, who stood alone and silent on the government side, which was empty except for about a dozen Tory free traders (including Hugh Cecil), facing the crowded Liberal benches. Rarely had a member been treated with such scathing discourtesy by his own party.[68]

Resuming his speech, Churchill said that he had tried without success to discover what Balfour's policy was on free trade. Having failed, he announced that he had "passed formally from the position of an independent supporter to the position of a declared opponent of the present Government." The time had come for the country to be relieved from Balfour's "shifty policy of equivocal evasion; they had a right to know what public men thought on public questions."[69]

When Churchill sat down, he was cheered on the Liberal benches. Mr. Robson, the Liberal member for South Shields, congratulated him "on the fact that the organized attempt to deprive him of an audience had in no way affected the excellence of his speech." The Tories had reached a pretty pass when they were so apprehensive of hearing one of their own members' views that they fled from the Chamber.

Then Sir John Gorst, Randolph's Fourth Party colleague, and now a Unionist free trader, rose to speak from the vantage point of forty years of membership in the Conservative Party. He wanted to say that those who still adhered to the old orthodox opinions of free trade ought not to be treated with such marked discourtesy. Churchill "was the son of an old colleague of mine, and an old Leader of the House of Commons, who, of all men in the world, deserved well of his party, and, if every other consideration had failed, the member for Oldham's hereditary right to respect and consideration ought to have preserved him from such treatment as he had received at the hands of his party."[70]

The boycott shook Churchill, who had to make a great effort to reach the end of his remarks. Advice came from all sides. His cousin Ivor Guest (the son of Lord Randolph's sister Lady Cornelia Wimborne and a social climber known as the Paying Guest), a free trade Conservative MP, said that such an explosion of envy and malice would have a boomerang effect. His father's old friend Sir Michael Hicks-Beach, who had resigned as Chancellor of the Exchequer in 1902, and who was retiring from politics, told Churchill that a Tory could get on admirably who was more Tory than the Tories, or a Radical who was more Radical than the Radicals, but Radical tendencies in a Tory, or Tory tendencies in a Radical, however agreeable to the conscience, were a severe handicap.[71]

Churchill was not the only young Tory disgruntled with party policy. On March 30, his friend and fellow Hooligan Jack Seely resigned from the Conservative Party over the practice of sending thousands of Chinese to work in South African mines, where they were virtual slaves. There was such an outcry that Churchill objected that "I am quite unable to hear what my honorable friend is saying owing to the vulgar clamor maintained by the Conservative Party," to which the MP from North Islington, Sir George Trout Bartley (founder of the National Penny Bank to promote thrift), pointed his finger at Churchill and shouted angrily: "Allow me to say, Mr. Speaker, that the vulgarest expression came from this honorable gentleman!"

Coming to the same conclusion as Seely, Churchill pondered an offer to run as a Liberal in North-West Manchester. But the strain of being a pariah in his party was telling. On April 22, he spoke for three-quarters of an hour in the debate on the Trade Unions and Trade Disputes Bill. It was a pro-labor speech that the *Daily Mail* called "Radicalism of the reddest type." "It could not," Churchill said, "be said that labor bulked too largely in English politics at the present time. When they considered how vast the labor interest was, how vital, how human, when they considered the gigantic powers which by the consent of both Parties had been given to the working classes, when, on the other hand, they considered the influence in this House of company directors, the learned professions, the service members, the railway, landed, and liquor interests, it would surely be admitted that the influence of labor on the course of legislation was even ludicrously small." At this point in his speech Churchill stopped. *Hansard*, the verbatim report of Parliamentary proceedings, went on to say: "The honorable member here faltered in the conclusion of his speech, and, amid sympathetic cheers, resumed his seat, after thanking the House for having listened to him."[72] Driven to exhuastion by the stress of events, Churchill had fumbled with his notes, sat down, and covered his face with his hands. Some of the younger Tories were tempted to jeer, but others remembered the collapse of his father. He had died less than ten years before, and the memory of his last garbled speeches was still vivid in the minds of many.

Churchill wondered whether he was having some kind of breakdown. Jack Seely consulted a brain specialist, Dr. George Dabbs, on his behalf. Without seeing the patient, Dr. Dabbs diagnosed "a sudden brain anaemia: a sort of syncope of the memory cells. But it always spells overstrain and is not a symptom to neglect or pass by."[73] Seely advised Churchill to take it easy for a few days. Another old friend, Reggie Barnes, now in India as aide-de-camp to Kitchener, wrote him not to be foolish and try himself too high, for there was a limit to everyone's capabilities, only he did not realize what his limit was. It could not be right for him to strain himself to the extent of suddenly losing his memory. Perhaps "the old-fashioned Tory asses" in the House had not been treating him fairly, they were swine of the deepest dye, but all the same the Tory side was the right one on broad principle, and there were plenty of good sound men who would become his friends in due time.[74]

This advice Churchill disregarded, for in late April he agreed to run as a Liberal in North-West Manchester, the citadel of free trade. He had not yet formally joined the Liberal Party and was still a member of the Conservative Carlton Club, but now the final break was only a matter of days. On May 31, when the House reassembled after the Whitsun recess, he entered the

Chamber of the House of Commons, stood for a moment at the Bar, glanced at both government and Opposition benches, and strode swiftly up the aisle. In the twilight of a rainy afternoon, with most of the benches empty from end to end, he bowed to the Speaker and turned to his right, toward the Liberal side. He sat next to Lloyd George, who greeted him amicably, in the seat where his father had sat while in the Opposition, waving his handkerchief in glee at Gladstone's downfall in 1885.[75]

When Churchill crossed the floor, his father's specter crossed with him. This was the settlement of an old debt. He thought of all that Randolph had done for the party, and how he had been treated when they had obtained the power they would never have had except for him. They had flung him aside to spend the rest of his days "wailing along the margins of existence." Randolph had been unable to leave the party that had rejected him, but his son was doing it for him, at no little personal cost. What a wrench it was to break with all that glittering hierarchy. What did he have left? As the free trade issue subsided, his personal ambitions would be left naked and stranded on the beach—they were an ugly and unsatisfactory spectacle, except when borne forward upon the flood of a great cause.[76]

There was more to it than vindicating his father's memory. Churchill was never comfortable with party activities or the party machine, which he called stupid and brutalizing. He never had a party affiliation in the accepted sense, for he was often outside the orthodox party view. As Asquith later said, he was ever hankering after coalitions. Instinctively he saw politics in national rather than party terms. Issues mattered more than party loyalty. If the Tories had been consistent and backed free trade, he would have marched in step.

An early example of his independence of mind takes us back to February 1897, when he was serving as a subaltern in India. Following Britain's traditional foreign policy of maintaining the balance of power in Europe, the Salisbury government had blockaded Crete to prevent Greece from sending reinforcements and supplies to the small Greek expeditionary force protecting the Christians against the Turks. Although a Tory by tradition and upbringing, Churchill did not for an instant accept the Conservative policy. He was shocked that Lord Salisbury, who was serving as his own Foreign Secretary, was supporting Turkey in its brutal suppression of a nationalist revolt in Crete. What an atrocious crime the government had committed! he wrote his mother. That British warships had helped blood-bespattered Turkish troops to escape from Crete was too horrible to contemplate. Such policies would be the ruin of the Conservative Party, and of the two Tory leaders whom he despised and detested above all others (who happened to have been friends of his father)—Balfour, the languid and lackadaisical cynic, and Curzon, the spoiled darling of politics, insolent from undeserved success, the epitome of the superior Oxford prig. It was to that pair that all the criminal muddles could be ascribed. (Two years later, when Curzon was Viceroy of India and Churchill was invited to stay at his palace in Calcutta, his hostility evaporated, and in the revised version, Curzon became "a remarkable man" with "great charm of manner." Three years later, he apologized to Balfour, his party leader, for having lost an election.)

Jennie replied that Britain had been obliged to help Turkey, but Churchill insisted that it was a very wicked thing to fire on the Cretan insurgents and blockade Greece. It would take a lot of whitewash to justify the spectacle of the Seaforth Highlanders fighting by the side of Turkish mercenaries. Surely the people of England did not approve of the use to which their fleets and armies were being put. It was an abominable action, prolonging the servitude of a Christian people to the Turks. Were he in the House of Commons, there would be no lengths to which he would not go in opposing the Tories. Already, he felt that he was a Liberal in all but name. Were it not for Home Rule—to which he would never consent—he would enter Parliament as a Liberal. Lord Salisbury looked at the question from the point of view of profit and loss. But to Winston, it was right and wrong that mattered. As in the Empire Theater dispute and in Protection Against Free Trade, he was on the side of freedom against coercion, the side that *England* should be on. And now, seven years after that youthful yearning for the Liberal Party, he had crossed the floor, swallowing his objections to Home Rule.

In the Smoking Room and the other places where members gathered, Churchill's move was eagerly discussed. Had he made a mistake? It was all right for a politician of Chamberlain's stature to change parties, but Churchill was a raw beginner. The stigma of the turncoat was bound to be attached to him. How would the Liberals welcome him, as a dashing recruit, the hero of free trade, or as an intruder, a latecomer to the vineyard wanting a share in the harvest? To the Tories, he was a renegade who had betrayed class and party to join the enemy, a Blenheim rat who had left the sinking ship, fair game for any Conservative MP or newspaper. Churchill was not the only young Tory to cross the floor, for Ivor Guest and Jack Seely had also defected, but it was on him that the party's anger fell. Among the more moderate comments was that of Alfred Lyttelton, who had replaced Chamberlain as

Colonial Secretary: "One might as well try to rebuke a brass band: he trims his sails to every passing wind." More typical was the remark of Sir Albert Muntz, MP for North Warwickshire, who called Churchill "a wretched rag of a thing." Leo Maxse, the editor of the *National Review*, referred to him routinely as "this ridiculous jackanapes," "a violent and reckless political adventurer," and "the pot-boy of Downing Street." The bitterness was so intense that when Churchill was put up as a polo-playing member of the Hurlingham Club, he was blackballed, an event without precedent in the club's history.[77]

"Churchill crossing the floor" soon entered the repertory of House of Commons humor. Mentioning it was a sure way of injecting laughter into a speech. To give but one example, on February 20, 1907, when Churchill was at the Colonial Office, Sir Charles Dilke spoke on the repatriation of Chinese indentured labor from the New Hebrides. The issue, he said, had "peculiar difficulties . . . It was like repatriating the Under-Secretary for the Colonies to the other side [Laughter]. If they popped him down on one side of the island he was admired, respected, and cheered; but on the other side he was eaten" [Loud Laughter].

Now that he was running in Manchester, Churchill sought to win the backing of its powerful Jewish community. An occasion arose in the fight over the Aliens Bill, which had been introduced in March (coining the term "undesirable alien"), and was aimed at the thousands of Jewish refugees from the terror of Czarist pogroms. Appointed to the Standing Committee on the bill after it had passed its Second Reading, he filibustered against it, saying that he "did not wish to close the door against the unfortunate Hebrew coming from the Continent." The bill was vicious in principle and unworkable in practice, he argued, unless the Russian system of police espionage was established in England. The committee took so long in its deliberations that the bill was withdrawn, which helped Churchill's position in Manchester and established him as the champion of minority rights. He bragged to Captain Rawson, the Tory candidate for Reigate: "Yes, I wrecked the [Aliens] Bill."[78] He saw it as a shabby hoax, a bill that was never meant to pass, because of the opposition within the Tory Party of wealthy Jews like Lord Rothschild.

On June 28, Churchill went to Manchester to speak at the Free Trade Hall. Calling on Barrow Belisha, a prominent Liberal Jew, he strode into the house and came upon a ten-year-old boy, Belisha's nephew. The boy later remembered a pink face topped by reddish hair, an unmistakable lisp, a frock coat with silk facings, and a large winged collar with a black bow tie. Churchill patted the boy on the head and said: "What a nice little boy! Would you like to come for a drive in my carriage?" The drive never materialized, and the boy later reflected that the pat on the head had been a political pat.[79] His name was Leslie Hore-Belisha, and he would serve in the 1939–1940 War Cabinet with Churchill and in the 1945 caretaker government. He was none-theless impressed. So was the audience at the Free Trade Hall when Churchill produced from beneath the platform table a small loaf of bread and, waving it aloft, declared: "This is the loaf you'll get under Fair Trade, and this"—lifting from the same place a larger loaf—"is the loaf you'll get under Free Trade." He then placed the loaves side by side on the table.[80]

In Manchester things were going fine, but in the House Churchill was heckled by the Tories, who had turned him into a sort of public enemy, the butt of their sarcasm and invective. On June 20, he moved an amendment providing that duty should be paid on tea imported from foreign countries, as distinguished from tea imported from the Empire. Balfour had some fun with this, as Churchill seemed to be proposing Imperial preference, and welcomed "this new recruit . . . who desires to speak formally and deliberately against his convictions . . ." Austen Chamberlain, the Chancellor of the Exchequer, chimed in that Churchill did not believe in his own amendment, but had used it only "as a medium for sneering at those whom a little time ago he was glad to claim as his political friends."[81] On July 4, when he spoke in a debate on a Licensing Bill, the Tories succeeded in shouting him down. Churchill protested against this "carefully organized attack upon the liberties of debate in which the right honorable member for West Birmingham was an accomplice and a consenting party—" (Loud cries of "Order," "Withdraw," and cheers.) Rising to a point of order amid more interruption, Joseph Chamberlain asked "whether it is in order for the junior member for Oldham to say that there is a conspiracy against him in which I am an accomplice—a statement which is absolutely untrue." (Cries of "Oh" and "Order" and cheers and countercheers.) The Speaker told Churchill not to make a charge of that kind, and he withdrew it.[82]

Such attacks only whetted Churchill's combativeness. In a few months, he had become a dauntless Liberal skirmisher, leading the troops into battle on many issues. He might have agreed with Mr. Arabin in Trollope's *Barchester Towers* that "I know of no life that must be so delicious as that of a . . . leading member of the Opposition—to thunder forth accusations against men in power; show up the worst side of everything that is produced; to pick holes in every coat; to be indignant, sarcastic, jocose, moral, or supercilious; to damn with faint praise, or crush with open calumny." On August 2, he addressed a committee hearing on capital expenditure four times in three hours, which led an exasperated Tory MP named Renwick to cry out: "Windbag!" Coming to Churchill's defense, Lloyd George objected to this gross breach of order. The chairman remarked that "if a member addresses the Committee very frequently and repeats over and over again the same observations he must not be surprised if he is met with some cries of impatience."[83]

When he was not in the House, Churchill was collecting material for the biography of his father. On August 9, Wilfrid Blunt, the poet and professional romantic, came to Mount Street to talk about him. Churchill had just come in from playing polo and read aloud from Randolph's letters to Blunt while Blunt explained the allusions. There was something touching, Blunt thought, about the way he continued to espouse his father's cause and his father's quarrels. Leadership in the Liberal Party would be an opportunity for full vengeance on those who had caused his father's death.[84]

The opportunity was approaching, for 1905 was the last year of the Balfour government. Wobbling on the tightrope between free trade and protectionism, Balfour now resorted to leaving the Chamber whenever fiscal questions were debated, to avoid committing himself. As the forward on the Liberal team, Churchill developed an increasingly vitriolic and "Randolphian" style, which earned him rebuke in high places. In March, mounted once again on the decrepit nag of army economy, he complained about "those gorgeous and gilded functionaries with brass hats and ornamental duties who multiplied so luxuriously on the plains of Aldershot and Salisbury." His speech was sent to King Edward by the Home Secretary, and the King scribbled in the margin: "What good words for a recent subaltern of Hussars."[85] When Churchill ran into the King at the Newmarket races, Edward told him to tone down his language, and later sent him a newspaper report of a speech Churchill had made in Manchester, which said that "hysterical violence of language is not usually regarded as an evidence of statesmanlike qualities, and that the country expects those who aspire to govern it to show some signs, at least, of their ability to govern themselves."[86]

Some idea of Churchill's reputation may be gained from an exchange in the House with Harry Levy-Lawson, the Jewish manager of the *Daily Telegraph*. During the debate on a new Aliens Bill, Churchill said that Lawson was supporting it in spite of his mixed origins. Lawson, who interpreted the remark as a racial slur, pointed out that Churchill too was of mixed parentage, and added: "It seems a pity that the honorable Gentleman, whose abilities we all recognize, cannot take part in a debate without introducing the bitter venom of acrimonious personality . . . The honorable member always seems anxious to pay off old scores."[87]

In his carefully prepared speeches, which he learned by heart, Churchill kept his best barbs for Balfour, sensing that his tottering government was on its last legs. It was also good tactics to take on the men at the top, as his father had taken on Gladstone. "To keep in office for a few more weeks and months," he said on March 28, "there is no principle which the Government are not prepared to betray, and no quantity of dust and filth they are not prepared to eat." On April 4, he complained about Balfour's absences: "It should be known to what miserable and disreputable shifts the Prime Minister resorted to eke out his remaining weeks and months . . . It was quite unprecedented. The Leader of the House not merely shirked his own duties, but he invented and calculated occasions when he could inflict deliberate and studied insults upon the House of Commons." And again on April 5: "The great majority of voters in the country were sick of the Government. Why did they continue in office? Why did the Prime Minister continue? Office at any price was his motto at the sacrifice of any principle, by the adoption of any maneuver, however miserable or contemptible. For whom? For his Party? No. The genius of his Party was not represented in his Government. But for his friends, his personal backers."

On July 17 it was Balfour's grasp of policy that Churchill scorned, calling attention to "the great ignorance displayed by the Prime Minister on several occasions with reference to matters which came under his own special authority . . . Everybody knew of the case when the Prime Minister informed an astonished and amazed country that we were much more likely to be at war with Switzerland than with the Orange Free State . . . No Prime Minister, certainly not in recorded time, had ever before, in regard to matters of which he should be better informed than anybody, shown such lamentable and extraordinary ignorance . . . gross, unpardonable, and flagrant ignorance."

Balfour ignored these slurs, indeed for many of them he was not in the Chamber. But on July 24, after the government had been defeated several days earlier on an amendment to the Irish Land Act, and Balfour announced that he would neither resign nor dissolve Parliament, Churchill drew blood. "We have been told ad nauseam of the sacrifices which the Prime Minister makes," he said. "I do not deny that there have been sacrifices. The House ought not to underrate or deny those sacrifices. Some of them must be very galling to a proud man. There were first the sacrifices of leisure and then sacrifices of dignity . . . Then there was the sacrifice of reputation . . . It has been written that the right honorable Gentleman stands between pride and duty. Pride says 'go' but duty says 'stay.' The right honorable Gentleman always observes the maxim of a certain writer that whenever an Englishman takes or keeps anything he wants, it is always from a high sense of duty."

Balfour had heard enough. Unfolding his six feet to reply to the accumulated insults of months, his long-fingered hands clasping the satin lapels of his frock coat, he administered a lesson that Churchill would not forget.

"As for the junior member for Oldham, his speech was certainly not remarkable for good taste, and as I have always taken an interest in that honorable Gentleman's career, I should certainly, if I thought it in the least good, offer him some advice on that particular subject. But I take it that good taste is not a thing that can be acquired by industry, and that even advice of a most heartfelt and genuine description would entirely fail in effect if I were to offer it to him. But on another point I think I may give him some advice which may be useful to him in the course of what I hope will be a long and distinguished career. It is not, on the whole, desirable to come down to this House with invective which is both prepared and violent. The House will tolerate, and very rightly tolerate, almost anything within the rule of order which evidently springs from genuine indignation aroused by the collision of debate. But to come down with these prepared phrases is not usually successful, and at all events, I do not think it was very successful on the present occasion. If there is preparation there should be more finish, and if there is so much violence there should certainly be more veracity of feeling."[88]

It was said that Churchill's speech was one of the most insolent ever heard in Parliament. He agreed that there was a good deal of truth in a cartoon that had appeared on April 18 in the *Pall Mall Gazette*, showing Churchill and Lloyd George, with mud in their hands, being addressed by Balfour: "I'm afraid, gentlemen, that in this persistent mud-throwing you only waste your time!" The mud slingers replied: "Not a bit of it, we're qualifying for 'high positions' in the next Liberal Government."

When Hugh Cecil, his ally from the Hooligan days, suggested that he had gone too far in attacking a man who had become a pathetic failure, Churchill replied that he thought of Balfour as a successful man moving gradually but prosperously to the close of ten years of unbroken service. It was only because the ministers were uplifted, guarded, served, and praised that they excited his attacks. He would be truly sorry if he had hurt any man's *private* feelings.[89]

Perhaps what Churchill most admired about the House was its spirit of gentlemanly complicity, "that line of half-chaffing, half-candid intercourse which prevails between people who know each other though on opposite sides, in this country almost alone of modern countries." In their civilized ability to remain on courteous and friendly terms in spite of the free-for-all on the floor, the members seemed to be distilling the best qualities of the English people. No one was more adept at it than Balfour, and Churchill was touched when he heard that at a smart weekend, where everyone was tearing him to pieces, only Balfour spoke in his defense, expressing generous hopes about his future, not with an air of false magnanimity, but simply, genuinely, and naturally, from the heart.[90]

It was Chamberlain, not Churchill, who brought down the Balfour government. In November, he publicly described the Prime Minister's conduct as "humiliating." Having won the support of the National Union of Conservative Associations, he asked Balfour to dissolve Parliament and call for new elections so that the Tory electorate could determine the party position. But instead, Balfour resigned the premiership on December 4 so that the Liberals would have to form a minority government, which he believed would be doomed from the start, for once again, the Liberals were divided, this time over Home Rule, and the Liberal leader, Henry Campbell-Bannerman, was sixty-nine years old, in poor health, and nursing an invalid wife.

The son of a wealthy Glasgow merchant, Campbell-Bannerman was one of those reassuring Radicals who owned a castle in Scotland and a house in Belgrave Square, as well as a social conscience. Like Gladstone, once in office he moved to the left. With Scottish obstinacy he rose to the challenge, and on December 5, 1905, he accepted the King's invitation to form a government. On January 8, 1906, the King dissolved Parliament, which had sat for exactly five years, ending ten years of Tory rule. For the next ten years Britain would have Liberal governments, and for the next seventeen years Liberal Prime Ministers. It was the apogee of the Liberal Party. Churchill could have crossed the floor at no better time.

Campbell-Bannerman drew on a number of remarkable men to form his government, balancing Radicals and Liberal Imperialists. Edward Grey went to the Foreign Office, Asquith to the Exchequer, Haldane to the War Office, John Morley to the India Office, Lloyd George to the Board of Trade, and

John Burns, the first workingman to attain Cabinet rank, went to the Local Government Board. Foremost among the younger men who were picked as under-secretaries were Reginald McKenna and Churchill, who was not passed by, despite his brief service in Liberal ranks, for he had displayed enormous stamina and mental agility in the Opposition.

V

THE COLONIAL OFFICE

For the first of many times, Churchill went through the agony of being "on the doorstep." The process of Cabinet making was a way of humiliating distinguished men, who waited for hours and days for a summons that might never come, fearful of going out lest it arrive in their absence. In the scramble for posts, their careers hung in the balance. They called their friends: Had they heard anything? So-and-so had gotten the India Office, but what good was that, with its one debate a year? What was left? Only a Lordship of the Treasury? They'd be damned before they'd take it. It was theirs if they wanted it? All right, they'd take it.

On December 6, 1905, Campbell-Bannerman offered Churchill the post of Financial Secretary to the Treasury, the most important and best-paid of the junior offices, which would give him the chance to work with Asquith. But he had his eye on the Colonial Office, for the Secretary, Lord Elgin, sat in the House of Lords. As Under-Secretary, Churchill would lead the debates in Commons, unhampered by a superior who could claim the credit. Rather than lurk in Asquith's shadow, he would have a place in the sun. This was a chance to make his reputation, to follow his instinct for going where the action was hottest, like boarding the armored train instead of staying in his tent, for he would be handling the crucial settlement of the South African question. It was a matter he knew from direct experience, while Elgin, who had been Viceroy of India for five years, was unfamiliar with it. There was some difficulty, for Campbell-Bannerman had to reshuffle his lineup, but Churchill got the Colonial Office.

Was he right? he wondered. In any case, no one had ever complained that he was incapable of hard work.[1] Among the letters of congratulations, there was one from John Atkins, who had covered the Boer War with him. How things had marched, he said, since they had pitched their tent at the Estcourt railway station.[2] There was also a word of advice from Hugh Cecil: Churchill needed the sort of reputation Edward Grey had, as a good administrator and industrious official. He also needed to be liked by his colleagues. Harcourt could not be Prime Minister because he swore at his colleagues, while Balfour held his position because of his charm on the front bench.[3]

Elections were scheduled for January. What a catastrophe Joe had brought upon a great party, Churchill thought. But Balfour was even more to blame, never lifting a finger to help forward talent, selfish and cynical—his father had foreseen the Tory's crowning and irretrievable disaster.[4] Campaigning since October, Churchill had run afoul of the suffragettes. It was his bad luck that the movement had started and was most active in Manchester, where Emmeline Pankhurst, the widow of a barrister, founded the Women's Social and Political Union in 1903. Their tactics were to harass the elected officials who refused to give the vote to women. On October 13, Churchill addressed a large meeting with Sir Edward Grey in the Manchester Free Trade Hall. Emmeline's daughter Christabel turned up with a young woman named Annie Kenney, who had started life as a half-timer in a cotton mill at the age of ten. When Grey spoke, small white flags with the words "Votes for Women" bobbed up in the hall. After Churchill had spoken, Annie Kenney rose and asked: "If you are elected, will you do your best to make Women's Suffrage a Government measure?" Churchill, who had recorded his opinion against the measure in the margin of an *Annual Register*, but who had voted in its favor in 1904, did not reply. William Peacock, the chief constable of Manchester, offered to submit the question to Grey if it was put in writing. But Grey, although under the influence of his wife, a fervent feminist, remained awkwardly silent. Women stood on chairs, calling out "The Question, answer the Question," until police hustled them out of the hall, as Christabel Pankhurst cried: "I shall assault you! I shall spit at you!"[5]

"I am not sure that, unwittingly and in innocence, I have not been a contributing cause," Grey explained lamely. "As far as I can understand the trouble arose from a desire to know my opinion on Women's Suffrage. That is a question which I would not deal with here tonight, because it is not, and I do not think it is likely to be, a Party question."[6] When Christabel and Annie Kenney tried to start a meeting in the street, they were arrested. Faced with fines or imprisonment, they chose the latter. Churchill went to Strangeways Gaol and offered to pay the fines, but the women insisted on serving their terms. Thereafter, a chorus of female hecklers attended all of his Manchester meetings, which led him to announce on one occasion, borrowing from Byron's *Don Juan*: "Nothing would induce me to vote for giving women the franchise. I am not going to be henpecked on a question of such grave importance."[7]

Now that he was in the government, Churchill needed a private secretary. On December 14, at a party at Lady Granby's, he was introduced to a dapper little man with a high, reedy voice and bristling eyebrows named Eddie Marsh, who was a First Class Clerk in the West African Department of the Colonial Office. Eddie said, "How do you do, which I must now say with great respect." "Why with great respect?" Churchill asked. "Because you're coming to rule over me at the Colonial Office." Later in the evening, Eddie noticed Churchill gazing pensively in his direction. The next day, Churchill's first at his new job, he asked for Eddie, who was alarmed, for he had heard that the man was truculent and overbearing. He would work poor Eddie to death and turn him into a gray-haired skeleton. Seeking advice, he went to see Lady Lytton, the former Pamela Plowden, who told him: "The first time you meet Winston you see all his faults, and the rest of your life you spend in discovering his virtues." The matter was sealed at a dinner *à deux*, at which Eddie found his new boss charming. He remained Churchill's secretary for twenty years, following him until his retirement to every Cabinet post he occupied, the Board of Trade, the Home Office, the Admiralty, the Duchy of Lancaster, the Ministry of Munitions, the War Office, back to the Colonial Office, and the Treasury. They became close friends, even though on the face of it, they had nothing in common. Two years older than Churchill, Eddie was a direct descendant of the assassinated Prime Minister Spencer Perceval, and had, as a result of that misfortune, inherited a little money through an Act of Parliament, which he disbursed in patronage of the arts, collecting paintings and beautiful young men like Rupert Brooke and Ivor Novello. A boyhood illness had made him impotent, and according to his biographer, he went on to live and die as chaste as the day he was born, but his capacity for friendship often ripened into a devotion that was feminine in its tenderness. Churchill found him a model of tact and efficiency. A patient and gentle soul, Eddie had a gift for allaying his chief's irritability. He put up with his moods as he put up with the London weather, and never much minded having his head bitten off, for he knew that instead of throwing it into the wastebasket, Churchill would very soon be fitting it back on his neck with care and even with ceremony.[8]

Churchill had finished his book on his father, and authorized Frank Harris, the energetic editor who had published the early work of George Bernard Shaw and H. G. Wells, to act as his agent, promising to pay Harris 10 percent of any profit over four thousand pounds. Harris replied with enthusiasm: "Properly worked this book should bring you in 10,000 pounds or I'm a Dutchman!"[9] It went to Macmillan for eight thousand pounds and appeared in the first week of January 1906, at once attaining the stature of a classic. *The Times Literary Supplement* called it "among the two or three most exciting political biographies in the language . . ." Reviewers stressed that it was a far cry from the customary work of filial piety. That much was true; it had been undertaken for more complicated reasons. It was in fact one of the most systematic whitewashings that any biographer, whether related to his subject or not, had ever attempted. The dual motive was to refashion his father according to his own needs and to justify his defection to the Liberal Party. In this, the most deeply felt of Churchill's books, written at a time when he was losing faith in his party, Randolph is portrayed as a Liberal *manqué*. After his resignation, it would have been logical for him to cross the floor, but duty and honor prevented him. Thus, Churchill turned Tory Democracy into a Liberal-leaning splinter movement, whereas it had always been rooted in Tory soil. To portray the Tory Party as one where there was no place for gifted innovators helped to explain his own behavior. Churchill vindicated his father and, through his father, himself. Here was no cynical opportunist, but a Randolph rejected because of his own admirable consistency, just as Churchill had remained consistent in his free trade beliefs, while his party adopted the heresy of protectionism. Here was a Randolph aloof from intrigue, a man of far-ranging strategies, an epic hero undone by a mysterious "pattern of failure." The theme of rejection came up again and again; it seemed to obsess Churchill, himself the object of his father's rejection. In his treatment of Randolph's personal life, there was the same lack of candor. His madness was not mentioned, or his unhappy marriage, or the large sums he borrowed from Lord Rothschild, to whom he owed sixty thousand pounds when he died.

Every editorial trick was used to achieve this laundering of the material. Churchill simply rejected information that did not fit his case. In November 1902, Lawrence C. Tipper, the director of a company that made veterinary medicines, wrote him that Randolph had claimed to be a fair trader (protectionist). Tipper had heard him say in the Committee Room of the Birmingham Town Hall: "Within these walls I am a Fair Trader, outside I don't know anything about Fair Trade. When the Masses shout for Fair Trade then I shall be willing to take up and champion the Cause." Tipper informed Churchill that he had told this story at a public meeting in London. Since it showed Randolph as a cynical follower of a popular cause rather than a man of principle, Tipper's letter received a frosty reply: "The remarkable account which you give of your treatment of the confidences of the late Lord Randolph Churchill does not encourage me to embark upon a personal correspondence with you."[10] Churchill preferred to continue believing the myth that his father had been an authentic free trader, which was the foundation of his own position.

Along with the rejection of pertinent but uncongenial data, Churchill relied on omissions and selective quotations. References to Randolph's great foe, the Leader of the House, Sir Stafford Northcote, as "a cretin" and "a species of earthworm" were deleted. So were letters like those from Blunt, which showed Randolph to be a covert Home Ruler, knocking holes in the castle of consistency. ("He was far more of a Home Ruler than you seem to know," Blunt wrote after reading the book.) There was nothing about Randolph's intrigues, his leaks to the press, or his maneuvers prior to his resignation, which was described as the unpremeditated outburst of a man driven to the wall because of his principles. To make these points required a pattern of textual change. Thus, in a letter to his mother, the words "I should give anything to form a government" become "I should like to form a government," deleting the urgent tone of his ambition. When Randolph wrote "altogether my action is not unjustified by events and the public will soon see it," the latter clause was dropped, so that he was not shown to have planned a calculated appeal to the masses. In these and dozens of other examples, Churchill amended the record of his father's life. A. G. Gardiner, the Parliamentary correspondent for the *Daily News*, praised "that scorn of concealment which belongs to a caste which never doubts itself." In fact, Churchill's occasional revelations served to make his selective presentation more plausible. He succeeded in having his view of his father accepted until very recently, when a new generation of historians like R. F. Foster began taking a fresh look at Randolph and noticing the discrepancies between the book and the material in the archives.

One false note in the medley of praise was the review in the *Daily Telegraph*, the newspaper managed by Harry Levy-Lawson, with whom Churchill had crossed swords in the House. Perhaps Levy-Lawson was continuing their quarrel in the columns of his newspaper, whose anonymous reviewer wrote of Randolph: "His treatment of his friends was often atrocious, sometimes even not honorable; he was very careless of the truth . . ." Sunny Marlborough, the ninth Duke, and Churchill's first cousin, vowed to avenge Randolph's honor. What an insult to the family! Sunny would administer a good and sound trouncing to "that dirty little Hebrew" in the form of a demand for an apology. He did not allow Jews to say members of his family were dishonorable without giving them back more than they expected.[11]

When the *Daily Telegraph* published a withdrawal of the offending passage, Sunny wrote Churchill that he was glad his letter had met with his cousin's approval. Levy had had his head "rubbed in shit."[12] Jews could not be dealt with with that same good feeling that prompts the intercourse between Christians. He had called the publication of the passage "un-English," intending to convey that no one but a foreign Jew would have permitted himself to commit such an error.[13] Sunny's outburst was not untypical of the pent-up anti-Semitism that festered in the British aristocracy, which Churchill, although he condoned his cousin's action in defense of his book, never shared. He deplored anti-Semitism wherever it arose. In September 1898, keeping up with European events from Omdurman, he had in a letter to his mother expressed sympathy for Alfred Dreyfus, the Jewish army officer who had been arrested in France on trumped-up charges of espionage and sent to Devil's Island. Emile Zola's articles had saved Dreyfus, and Winston wrote: "Bravo Zola!" He was delighted to witness the complete debacle of that monstrous conspiracy. Of course, his reaction may have had as much to do with Dreyfus's profession as with his racial origin—like Winston, Dreyfus was a soldier; and like Winston, viewed with disfavor in high quarters because he chased wars, he had been treated unfairly by bigoted superiors.

But in 1905, Churchill spoke out against the Czarist persecution of the Jews, and in 1906, when he was at the Colonial Office, he was one of the first political figures to recognize the principle of a Jewish homeland—"the supreme attraction to a scattered and persecuted people of a safe and settled home under the flag of tolerance and freedom." Indeed, at a time of division between Jewish groups on whether to settle in Palestine or East Africa, Churchill saw that "Jerusalem must be the ultimate goal. When it will be achieved it is vain to prophesy: but that it will some day be achieved is one of the few certainties of the future." That is what he wrote on January 30, 1908, to Alderman Jacob Moser, one of his Manchester constituents, but the phrase was deleted in the final draft of his letter.

What would Sunny have thought of another unfriendly reaction to the book, that of Theodore Roosevelt, who wrote Henry Cabot Lodge on September 12, 1906: "I have been over Winston Churchill's life of his father. I dislike the father and dislike the son, so I may be prejudiced. . . . they both possess or possessed such levity, lack of sobriety, lack of permanent principle, and an inordinate thirst for that cheap form of admiration which is given to notoriety, as to make them poor public servants." Lodge replied that Randolph "was not a man who appealed to me at all and I never thought him a very serious figure . . . The son I know; I have met him several times. He is undoubtedly clever but conceited to a degree which it is hard to express either in words or figures and he was not at all sympathetic to me." Roosevelt also wrote his son Theodore, Jr., that although Churchill's book was interesting, "I can't help feeling about both of them that the older *was* a rather cheap character, and the younger one *is* a rather cheap character."[14]

When Churchill's book came out, he was in Manchester campaigning. He did not have much time left, for Manchester voted early in the three-week election, on January 13. On January 4, he went for a walk with Eddie Marsh and they found themselves in the slums. Looking about at the tenements, Churchill said, "Fancy living in one of these streets, never seeing anything beautiful, never eating anything savory, never saying anything clever!"[15]

With a population of more than six hundred thousand, Manchester was the biggest manufacturing center in Lancashire, divided into six constituencies, with three more in the contiguous borough of Salford. Of these nine seats, eight were held by Tories, and one of them was Balfour's. Churchill's constituency, North-West Manchester, had been represented by a Tory since its formation in 1884. The Tories were so entrenched there that in 1892 and 1900 the Liberals did not contest the seat. Sir William Houldsworth, a powerful figure in Lancashire, seemed to have a lock on it. After a tour of inspection, Campbell-Bannerman told Herbert Gladstone, the Chief Whip, that "things look well at Manchester, but doubts are expressed whether our friend Winston, with all the cleverness and variety of his speeches, is quite the sort of man to capture the quiet non-party voter who went for Houldsworth because of his solidity and stolidity and eminent respectability."[16]

But two circumstances worked in Churchill's favor. First, Houldsworth decided not to run, and in his stead Churchill faced a lackluster London solicitor named William Joynson-Hicks, who had no local following. Second, Manchester was a stronghold of free trade. Its businessmen and cotton brokers had no fondness for tariffs. Churchill won the backing of powerful Tory business groups that crossed party lines to vote for the free trader. At a meeting on January 10 at the Memorial Hall, a leading Tory cotton manufacturer, Tootal Broadhurst, stated the case bluntly: "For Free Trade or against it! There is no halfway house for timid retaliators to shelter in. . . . We do not agree with Mr. Churchill on all points; we do not approve of everything he has said—but I hope no Free Trade Unionist will allow any personal feeling on such points to prevent him from supporting in this election the great cause of Free Trade, of which Mr. Churchill is a most able and courageous champion."[17]

His district consisted of the financial and commercial center of the city, and the prosperous area of Cheetham Hill, where most of the Jewish voters lived. The Jews were on his side, but the women were against him. Of course, the women did not vote, but they agitated. At a meeting on January 9 at St. John's School, Churchill abruptly broke off answering questions to utter the words: "You have got it the wrong way round." Following the direction of his eyes, the audience saw a woman holding up a flag bearing the words "Votes for Women" upside down. Inviting her to come to the platform, he said, "Let us hear what she has to say." When the woman stood up and said, "Men and women—" she was drowned out by cries of "We want to hear Churchill!" "I should like to ask Mr. Churchill as a member of the Liberal government whether he will or will not give a vote to the women of this country," the woman said. There were loud cries of "Never!" Women's voices cried out "You are disgracing us" and "Leave it to the men." "This lady has asked me a question," Churchill said. "She has a perfect right to ask it, but I don't know why she didn't send up a notice of it on paper like everyone else has done." When the woman said she had done that, a voice called out, "And you have had your answer." "We should be fair and chivalrous to ladies," Churchill said. "They come here asking us to treat them like men. That is what I particularly want to avoid. We must observe courtesy and chivalry to the weaker sex dependent upon us." There were shouts of "Hear, hear." "The only time I have voted in the House of Commons on this question," Churchill went on, "I voted in favor of woman's suffrage, but having regard of the perpetual disturbance at public meetings at this election, I utterly decline to pledge myself. . . ."[18]

In most constituencies, the Liberals played up the issue of Chinese slavery, for the Balfour government had committed itself to a program of importing coolie labor for the South African mines. It was a good stick to beat the Tories with, and walls were plastered with billboards of Chinese in chains, while sandwich men dressed as coolies walked the streets and cried out

"Pigtail!" But for Churchill, free trade was the issue, and he made only passing references to the Chinese, although he had been against the program from the start.

When he met his opponent for the first time, he said, "I am so sorry I am coming to Manchester to queer your pitch," and Joynson-Hicks was impressed by the calm assurance that he would succeed in doing so. Joynson-Hicks brought in Oldham Tories to tell the Manchester voters how Churchill, when he had spoken at Conservative clubs, would propose the toast: "A good glass of beer, and confusion to the Radicals." He compiled a pamphlet of statements that Churchill had made while a Conservative, which was used by hecklers. To cries of "Answer it" at one meeting Churchill replied: "I admit I did say so and I admit that it was a very stupid thing to have said. I said a lot of stupid things when I was in the Conservative Party, and I left them because I did not want to go on saying stupid things."[19]

On Saturday, January 13, Churchill waited in the Town Hall in Albert Square for the count. He soon saw that he had won a decisive victory, 5,639 to 4,398, with a majority of 1,241. In all nine seats of the Manchester-Salford area, the Tories lost, seven seats to the Liberals and two to the emerging Labour Party. Balfour himself, the Conservative standard-bearer, went down to a humiliating defeat in the East Manchester seat he had held for twenty years. The results that came in over the next three weeks followed the pace set by Manchester. It was a landslide for the Liberals; not since the Reform Bill of 1831 had the pendulum swung so decisively. It was the defeat of the landed gentry, of the upper-class politicians who considered it their right by birth to govern, and the rise of new men, ready to enact a vast program of reforms that would transform England. It was, said Churchill's cousin Ivor Guest, the Tory Armageddon, and the start of a new social era. Too bad there were so many Labour MP's; they were the salt but a pinch would do.[20]

Society women complained that the new House was "full of strangers." The Liberals had won 377 seats as against 157 for the Tories. The Irish with 83 seats and Labour with 53 seats would vote with the Liberals. But as Ivor Guest had shrewdly warned, the real surprise was the strength of the Labour Party, the first in Europe, emerging as a major political force. French deputies crossed the Channel to study this new phenomenon, *le parti ouvrier* (the workingman's party). A "Lib.-Lab." agreement had in most cases prevented three-cornered races that could only have helped the Tories. Liberal candidates stepped aside to give a chance to the young party that would eventually devour them.

But for the moment, the Liberals, with a strong mandate from the people and an absolute majority in the House, were a formidable party. While the Tories worried that they might remain in opposition for half a century, Campbell-Bannerman supplied them with an epitaph: "For years they've lived on tactics, and now they've died on tactics." An exultant Churchill wrote Bonar Law, whose rise in the Tory ranks had been temporarily halted by his defeat in Glasgow, that "the wheel has swung full circle in the country and we may be at work for some time. I resist all temptations to say 'I told you so!' Perhaps if you had had a clear run you might have gotten across your fence. But the 'double objective' [free trade and the Chinese coolies] was fatal. It would be great fun to be a Tory now. I expect you will not be long out of the House. The wheel may turn again."[21]

This was the only time in his long career that Churchill served in a subordinate post, under a minister who was more of an administrator than a politician. The grandson of the man who had brought the Parthenon marbles to England, Lord Elgin was fifty-six, but with his long beard and severe Victorian manner, he might have been Churchill's grandfather. Eddie Marsh called him "the rugged old Thane." He had been treasurer of the Queen's household in 1886; Victoria complained that he was not talkative. He disliked making speeches and hardly ever spoke up at Cabinet meetings. Other members of the Cabinet reported that all he did was tug at his beard in silence, and that once, to the astonishment of his colleagues, he had put the end of it in his mouth. Describing himself as a foe to display, he did nothing to shine or court favor.[22]

The 9th Earl of Elgin was not overjoyed to have Churchill as his aide. By the standards of Balliol College, which Elgin had attended, Churchill was a badly educated upstart who had shown renegade tendencies to the class into which he had been born. While Elgin was Viceroy of India, Churchill had written a controversial book on the Malakand Field Force, which in viceregal circles was known as "a subaltern's hints to generals." Flamboyant and self-seeking, he would surely try to advance his reputation at Elgin's expense.

Elgin had reached the twilight of his political life, and Churchill the dawn. Elgin had an ailing wife and spent much of his time at home in Scotland. It was soon rumored that Churchill, having completely overshadowed his chief, was running the Colonial Office, a rumor that Elgin did nothing to deflate. In all but title, it seemed, Churchill was the minister, for he spoke from the government front bench, parried questions, led debates, and expounded on policy. He took to writing his minutes in red ink, normally reserved for the exclusive use of the Secretary of State. In a comment that managed to combine self-congratulation and self-mockery, he wrote the leading Liberal journalist J. A. Spender in January: "I hope you admire my Ministerial manner in making colonial pronouncements. Vacuity, obscurity, ambiguity and pomposity are not much less difficult to practice than their opposites."

Churchill had a way of pulling history around him like a blanket. With his usual luck, he arrived at the Colonial Office at a moment that would later be viewed as the watershed between nineteenth-century Empire and twentieth-century Commonwealth. The Liberals were trying to redefine the authoritarian Imperialism of Chamberlain and Milner without making too sharp a break with the past. Everyone agreed that the Empire was a wonderful thing, the agent of progress, a moral force. No one doubted Britain's title to "dominion over palm and pine." But what should the relationship be between the Imperial government and its colonies? How much control should they have over their own affairs? Should the Colonial Office act like the general of an army or like a wise and restraining father? Should it allow a greater latitude to the local governments or intervene more often? What should it do to help nonwhite interests? And what of South Africa? Why couldn't it be more like Canada, where everything was going so well, where self-government had worked, and a long-established minority lived peaceably with the English majority?

In his two and a half years at the Colonial Office, Churchill was caught up in great schemes of Empire. He could not, like his father, annex a new land (indeed, it was his job to deal with the consequences of the game of grab), but he could and did take part in the formulation of policy that paved the way for the unification of South Africa. This was the crowning achievement of his partnership with Elgin. As Churchill wrote the Liberal leader Sir Charles Dilke in January 1906: "Certainly I shall never be among those who having gained power do not wish to use it. And indeed we will now have a fine homogeneous majority. I do not suppose we are at liberty to attain the millennium: but a few Big Acts by way of installment ought certainly to be put on the Statute Book."[23]

It was not surprising that two men of such different temperaments as Churchill and Elgin would try each other's patience. Lord Lugard, the maker of modern Nigeria, told Austen Chamberlain at a party that he was "much struck by Winston's keenness and ability," but that "Elgin could hardly sit in his chair when Winston spoke, snubbed him and interrupted him."[24] A phrase that appeared often in Elgin's correspondence was: "I am sorry that I entirely disagree with Mr. Churchill's minute." When Churchill pressed his case with his customary vivacity, Elgin was not daunted. He had an independent mind, and the sound and cautious attitude of a man experienced in high office. In a way they complemented each other, with Elgin acting as the brake to Churchill's accelerator. But there were many small points of friction, ranging from Elgin's editing outrageous remarks from Churchill's speeches to Elgin's annoyance at Churchill's scribbling on dispatches. "I must formally request you not to place these remarks on papers which have to pass through me back to the office," Elgin wrote. "It does not tend to edification! In this case I suggest you should paste a paper over your remarks of the draft dispatch, and I hope you will not object to do so." Elgin also found him inconsistent, and coined the phrase, "Churchill's latest volte-face." He sometimes seemed to take up a cause out of boredom or inactivity, less concerned with the merits of a quarrel than with the need to be in the thick of a fight.[25]

It was not a question of who ran the Colonial Office, for as Haldane said of Elgin: "He is absolutely master." Churchill was disliked by some of the permanent civil servants, such as the widely respected Sir Francis Hopwood, who said: "He is most tiresome to deal with, and will I fear give trouble—as his Father did—in any position to which he may be called. The restless energy, uncontrollable desire for notoriety, and the lack of moral perception make him an anxiety indeed."[26]

Elgin handled him with tact, was loyal in his dealings, and never forgot that it was Churchill who was on the firing line in Commons, whereas he sat in the relative safety of the House of Lords. Elgin earned the respect of his subordinate, who wrote him in an uncharacteristic pupil-to-master tone after a year in office: "No one could ever have had a more trustful and indulgent chief than I have been most lucky to find on first joining a government: and I have learned a very great deal in the conduct of official business from your instruction and example which I should all my life have remained completely ignorant of, if I had gone elsewhere."[27] Summing up the experience of working with Churchill, Elgin wrote his Cabinet colleague Lord Crewe: "When I accepted Churchill as my Under-Secretary I knew I had no easy task. I resolved to give him access to all business—but to keep control (& my temper). I think I may say I succeeded, certainly we have had no quarrel during the two and a half years, on the contrary, he has again and again thanked me for what he has learned and for our pleasant personal relations, and I have taken a keen interest in his ability and in many ways attractive personality. But all the same I know quite well that it has affected my position *outside the Office*, and the strain has often been severe."[28] It was not Churchill's conduct in office that disturbed Elgin, but his compulsive need to focus attention on himself in his rush to head his own department.

When Parliament opened after the January election, Elgin and Churchill had two hot potatoes in their laps, inherited from the previous government: the Transvaal constitution and the coolie problem. Concerning the first, Churchill urged early self-government. According to the strategy of timely concession in order to retain ultimate control, it was better to give it to them now and to have a say in the drafting of their constitution. In February, he circulated a Cabinet paper pressing for an early decision and linking self-government with the coolie problem, which could be handed on to the Transvaal Parliament once it was elected. On February 8, the Cabinet agreed to grant the Transvaal self-government at an early date.

Chinese slavery had been the burning issue of the election. Headlines in the Liberal press had told of "Terror on the Rand," "Horrible Cruelties," and "Flogging of the Rand Yellow Serf." Campbell-Bannerman had called the importation of coolies "a system indistinguishable in many of its features from slavery," and pledged to put an end to it. But the coolie problem looked rather different from inside the government. As Elgin and Churchill found when they took office, fifty thousand coolies were already in South Africa on three-year contracts, without their families, confined to compounds, drilling rock at the bottom of deep-level mines ten hours a day six days a week for two shillings a day. They were subject to flogging and had no access to courts of law. But how could contracts be canceled that had the authority of the British government behind them? The cure was worse than the illness. When he asked how many new contracts were outstanding, Elgin was shocked to learn that fourteen thousand more had been rushed through in the last few days of a dying administration. These too, it was decided at a Cabinet meeting on January 3, had to be allowed to stand. Campbell-Bannerman admitted that there were cases "where an evil having been done, or an evil practice established, it is impossible, without a possibly greater evil almost, to put an end to it abruptly." Churchill thought up a repatriation scheme allowing the coolies to go home if they could put up seventeen pounds in travel expenses. Unless this modest reform was adopted, he warned Elgin, the indignation of the House at the continued employment of "armed compulsion to maintain an immoral contract" would lead to more drastic measures.[29]

On February 22, he made an impressive presentation of this program to the House, finding a middle ground between the obligations of Empire and humane sympathy for the Chinese, and avoiding the trap of a discussion on slavery. Balfour, back in the House after winning a by-election, had mocked "the subtleties indulged in . . . with regard to the distinction between that which is slavery, that which is semi-slavery, that which can be described as slavery and I know not how many other methods of manipulating that word, which would have puzzled a sixteenth-century casuist." But in doing so, Churchill fell into another trap when he said that the contract with the coolies "cannot in the opinion of His Majesty's Government be classified as slavery in the extreme acceptance of the word without some risk of terminological inexactitude."[30]

Those two words, "terminological inexactitude," were used to ridicule Churchill for months afterward, and entered the language as a euphemism for "lie." As Chamberlain said in response to his speech, "That is English as she is wrote at the Colonial Office. Eleven syllables, many of them of Latin or Greek derivation, when one good English word, a Saxon word of a single syllable, would do!" Chamberlain charged that the Liberals had won the election on the slavery issue, while Churchill was now admitting that the coolies were not slaves: "He had, in effect, to tell his followers that they had all been on the wrong line, that they had all been misinformed, that the charge they had made was only an inexactitude." Churchill himself, Chamberlain added in the heat of oratory, had produced posters and placards, and paraded every street in his constituency with a gang of men dressed as Chinamen and accompanied by some agent got up as a slave driver.[31] In fact, Churchill had purposely refrained from following these widely used tactics and obtained from Chamberlain a written apology.[32]

But this was just a scrimmage compared to what was coming over the censure of Lord Milner. The former High Commissioner and architect of the Boer War had left South Africa in May 1905, but did not make his maiden speech in the House of Lords until February 26, 1906. On the next day, Lord Portsmouth, the Under-Secretary of State for War, asked Milner whether it was true that he had condoned the flogging of coolies. It had come out in some correspondence published in a Parliamentary Blue Book that coolies were subjected to corporal punishment without being convicted of any crime or even appearing in a court. This was contrary to promises made to Parliament and to the Chinese government. The superintendent of foreign labor in the Transvaal, Mr. Evans, had informed Milner of the floggings and received his sanction. In reply to Lord Portsmouth, Milner said: "I fully recognize that I took upon myself the whole responsibility. I think, in the light of subsequent events, that I was wrong, because whatever the drawbacks might have been of not having prompt repression of such offenses, abuses might arise from allowing the punishment in any case."[33]

Milner's predicament incited to righteous anger both sides of the House. To the Tories he was a hero of Empire, a great civil servant who had saved South Africa. To the Liberals, he was "an English Bismarck," ruthless, unbending, fanatical, the symbol of outworn Imperial attitudes. Milner's *mea culpa* gave the Liberal press an opportunity not to be missed. As the *Manchester Guardian* wrote, "He empties the stale dregs of his war vocabulary on to his public and never, apparently, suspects that what used to excite now merely disgusts."

The next day, February 28, in a debate on the rights of natives in South Africa, Churchill said of Milner: "I should not myself be anxious to be forward in attacking him; but I tell the House most frankly that certainly, as far as I am concerned—and I think I speak for others who sit here—I should not put myself to any undue or excessive exertion to defend Lord Milner from any attacks which might be made upon him."[34]

Had Churchill forgotten the time in November 1899 when he was a prisoner of war in Pretoria and pleaded with Milner to do his best to obtain his release? Had he forgotten how he courted Milner's friendship, wrote him long letters, and offered to act as his spokesman? He, more than most of his colleagues, knew the mitigating circumstances of Milner's position. If he was not prepared to defend a man whose favor he had sought, he might at least have remained neutral in the controversy.

But it was Churchill's job to define his department's policy in the House of Commons. When the poet and satirist Hilaire Belloc, one of the new Liberal MP's, asked on March 14 whether Milner had done anything illegal, since there were no written records, Churchill replied: "I think my honorable friend will see that there is no doubt whatever that in authorizing illegal punishment of this character at the same time that his official superiors were denying that such punishment was being permitted Lord Milner committed a grave dereliction of public duty and at the same time an undoubted infringement of the law."[35]

Belloc's question was followed a few days later by a motion of censure proposed by the Liberal member for Salford North, William Byles: "That this House expresses its disapproval of the conduct of Lord Milner as High Commissioner of South Africa and Governor of the Transvaal, in authorizing the flogging of Chinese laborers in breach of the law, in violation of treaty obligations, and without the knowledge or sanction of His Majesty's Secretary of State for the Colonies."[36]

When a number of ministers met on March 17 at 10 Downing Street to discuss government strategy with regard to the motion, Churchill argued that Britain was too great a country and the Liberal victory had been too overwhelming for the government to engage in the task of making martyrs. What would the reaction to censure be in South Africa, where Milner was idolized? Seeking a middle ground that would contain Liberal anger as well as satisfy Tory indignation and South African public opinion, he suggested an amendment deprecating any formal censure of individuals. It would be a difficult job to persuade the House, but he hoped for a chance to try.

On March 21, the day of the debate on the motion of censure, Churchill presented the following amendment: "That this House, while recording its condemnation of the flogging of Chinese coolies in breach of the law, desires, in the interests of peace and conciliation in South Africa, to refrain from passing censure on individuals."[37]

The motion, which had aroused considerable passion on both sides of the House, was debated after dinner. At stake was a certain vision of Empire, which cared more for maintaining the dignity of one of its loyal servants than for the retroactive punishment of alleged illegality. It was Empire as a law unto itself, a closed corporation answerable to no one, that the Liberals were attacking through Milner.

This was Chamberlain's vision of Empire, and it was Chamberlain, as Milner's chief at the Colonial Office, who came to his defense. Did not Churchill realize, he asked, that he must say all that could be said in favor of someone who had served in his department?

"It is not so," Churchill replied.

What a view Churchill had of his duties and of Lord Milner's services, Chamberlain said. It was regrettable that he was representing the government on this occasion, for the head of a department must defend the servants of the department. And besides, was it just to censure a public servant who had given the best years of his life to South Africa because he had confessed to an error of judgment on a single occasion? As Disraeli had once observed, "Great services are not canceled by one act, by one single error, however it may be regretted at the moment."

It was despicable and vindictive to humiliate a man like Milner with a motion of censure, Chamberlain said. As for Churchill's amendment, it was a cowardly insult on the part of someone who had already found Milner guilty of a grave dereliction of duty.[38]

Following Chamberlain, Churchill defended his position: "Can anyone dispute the fact that for a public officer to authorize illegal flogging is to infringe the law? Can anyone deny that an infringement of the law by an officer especially charged to maintain and administer the law is a direct dereliction of public duty?"

In no way did he disagree with the motion of censure, Churchill said. In fact he had admired its truth and moderation. But was it wise or practical to take this step? Milner's offense had been committed under another government, and to censure him in a new House of Commons had the flavor of a retroactive retribution. Was it right, moreover, to censure a man unheard?

In a roundabout way, Churchill was protecting Milner, and offering his amendment as a substitute for a motion of censure which, as he pointed out, was so serious and unusual that it had been used only twice in the last hundred years. But in making a case for Milner, Churchill adopted a patronizing tone that offended the Tories more than any attack: "Lord Milner has gone from South Africa," he said, "probably forever. The public service knows him no more. Having exercised great authority he now exerts no authority. Having disposed of events which have shaped the course of history, he is now unable to deflect in the smallest degree the policy of the day. Having been for many years, or at all events for many months, the arbiter of the fortunes of men who are 'rich beyond the dreams of avarice,' he is today poor, and I will add, honorably poor."

At the words "honorably poor," which seemed to be answering an imaginary accusation that Milner had profited from his service in South Africa, the Conservative benches broke into such prolonged shouts of angry disapproval that for some time Churchill stood silent at the Box; finally he continued: "After twenty years of exhausting service under the Crown, he is today a retired Civil Servant, without pension or gratuity of any kind whatever. [Opposition cries of "Shame."] If it is a shame, there [pointing to the front Opposition bench] is where the responsibility lies for any neglect. But I do seriously say to my honorable friend, is it worthwhile to pursue him any further?" There was also a practical reason, for the censure of Milner "would undoubtedly aggravate social and racial animosity in South Africa."[39]

While Churchill's speech did much to save Milner from censure, it earned him the renewed hatred of the Tories. Balfour, the last speaker before the amendment came to a vote, indignantly referred to "the insulting protection" accorded Milner and called Churchill's amendment "utterly mean and utterly contemptible." It was voted nonetheless by a wide majority, 355 to 135. A week later, a pro-Milner motion in the House of Lords passed in retaliation, 170 to 35. But the Tories remained bitter and so did the King, who wrote

Churchill's Cabinet colleague Lord Crewe: "It is a pity that Lord Elgin does not seem to be able to control the violent and objectionable language of his Parliamentary Under-Secretary. It has made a painful impression on most people."[40] Even Margot Asquith, wife of the Chancellor of the Exchequer, felt that Churchill's speech had been "calculated to hurt and offend everyone."

Probably no single episode had done Churchill as much harm as his attack on Lord Milner, the hero of the British Establishment. On April 5, Hugh Arnold-Foster, who had been Secretary of War under Balfour, and whose army reforms Churchill had criticized, attacked him directly during a debate on civil service estimates. Moving to reduce Churchill's salary, Arnold-Foster called him a young man in a hurry, who made short shrift of the traditional courtesies of politics and presented his views in an unpalatable way. Churchill, he charged, had used "embittered and poisoned language" on the Chinese coolie issue. Above all, he had insulted Milner, "a man whom so many of us esteem, honor and love."[41]

Churchill felt unfairly treated, for he had parried the blow of censure, to the disgust of many Liberals. As the spokesman on colonial matters, he could hardly remove himself from the debate. But he was badly cast as a judge of Milner's conduct, having been his admirer, and having been elected in the "khaki" election of 1900 as a pro-Milner Conservative, with an assist from Joseph Chamberlain, who had come to Oldham to speak on his platform. Already branded a turncoat, he was now seen as having turned against a man whose policy he had once supported and a man who had helped him get elected. If Churchill had set out to prove that there was no gratitude in politics, he succeeded. In politics the page is soon turned is another handy maxim, for Milner and Churchill would later serve in the same coalition government.

At least Churchill was where he liked to be, at the heart of the action, leaping from frying pan to frying pan and from fire to fire. In Natal, the self-governing colony where one hundred thousand white men lived uneasily amid nine hundred thousand native Africans, there was a Zulu uprising on February 8 near Pietermaritzburg. Two white policemen were killed, and two Zulus were sentenced to death and executed on February 15. The local governor, Sir Henry McCallum, asked the Colonial Office for troops and decreed martial law and censorship.

This was a good test case of the colonial policy of the Campbell-Bannerman government. To what extent should the Colonial Office interfere in the affairs of Natal? Churchill felt that as long as Natal had asked for troops, the responsibility of the Crown was involved, and the Colonial Office had a duty to restrain the local government. On February 12 he minuted: "The action of governor and ministers is preposterous. The proclamation of martial law *over the whole country*, causing dislocation and infinite annoyance to everyone, because two white men have been killed, is in itself an act which appears to be pervaded by an exaggerated excitability. The censorship exploit descends to the category of pure folly."[42]

When the Natal authorities informed the Colonial Office on March 28 that it planned to execute twelve more natives for the murders of the same two policemen, Churchill drafted this telegram for Lord Elgin: "Continued executions under martial law certain to excite strong criticism here . . . I must impress upon you the necessity of utmost caution in this matter, and you should suspend executions until I have had an opportunity of considering your further observations."[43]

Finding the telegram's tone peremptory, the Natal government resigned *en bloc*, on the grounds of interference with a decision of a self-governing colony. Lord Elgin backtracked at once, not wanting a crisis on his hands, and wired that he had no intention of interfering, and that the decision rested entirely in their hands. On April 2, the twelve Zulus were executed.[44]

On the same day, Churchill was asked during Question Time whether the government had sanctioned the earlier executions. While preparing his answer to the written question, he had wanted to reply that the decision rested with the government of the colony, but Elgin said that would make it look as if the Colonial Office had deliberately decided not to intervene. The safest answer, he advised, was the plain "No, Sir," which was the answer Churchill gave.

Later that day, in a heated debate, Churchill tried to explain that the Colonial Office had to tread softly because the Natal government was so quick to take offense. "Our policy throughout has been to trust and support the government of Natal," he said, adding: "We more than once felt grave misgivings as to what our duty should be and in what direction we might properly exert ourselves to safeguard the interests of the vast native population." When he pointed to "the enormous liberties and responsibilities which were perhaps too light-heartedly confided to a small white community," there were shouts of disapproval on Opposition benches, while a Labour member cried out: "Make it a Crown Colony."[45]

The Colonial Office had thought the crisis was past and that martial law would soon be lifted, Churchill explained, when on March 28 came the news of the twelve new executions, "which I venture to say would have startled if it did not disgust any man of humanity and moderation." The prisoners had been tried under martial law. "Martial law is no law at all. Martial law is brute force. [Opposition cries of "Oh, oh."] It is ignorance alone that makes those interruptions." The executions, "the echo of which has jarred in all our ears—" [Cries from the Conservative benches of "No."] "In almost all our ears today, all who have ears to hear . . .

"It may be objected," Churchill went on, "that it is a very strong order to kill fourteen persons for the murder of two. I quite agree, but so far as the verdict is concerned the fact that so many persons were implicated is not to my mind an absurdity. Do not let us forget that the bodies of the two white men are before us. The body of Inspector Hunt was pierced by innumerable assegais and every one of the natives concerned had actually blooded his assegai in the body of the murdered inspector."[46]

After the executions, the Colonial Office had been accused of "climbing down," and Churchill had to defend the policy of noninterference with which he disagreed, although he added: "I must say that so vehement an assertion of independence was not altogether compatible and consistent with passionate appeals for the support of British troops and eager acceptance of that support." Chiding the disruptive Tory benches, he said they were "poisoning the hearts of the colonists against us." Of course, whenever he attacked the Opposition, some Tory member would rise to remind him that he had once belonged to the party.

Churchill wanted to make a test case of Natal, to define the rights of the Crown in self-governing colonies. The case he made to Lord Elgin was that those rights were "latent and paramount" and had been called into being by Natal's request for troops. But Elgin did not wish to pursue the matter.

That summer in Natal, open warfare broke out, and the Zulus were put down with a heavy hand. Three thousand Africans were killed, and four thousand prisoners were taken. The Natal government wanted to deport twenty-five ringleaders. Churchill was against deportation, and when the Cabinet did not share his view, he grew petulant, saying he would have nothing to do with drafting answers to Parliamentary questions on the matter, he would only read out the answers Elgin wanted to give. More than ever, Churchill wanted to intervene, "to bring this wretched Colony—the Hooligans of the British Empire—to its senses."[47]

When the ringleaders were deported to St. Helena, Elgin and Churchill urged that they be treated as political prisoners. They should be allowed to weave baskets and grow their own vegetables, Churchill said. This was the first sign of his interest in prison reform. After all, he knew what the inside of a prison looked like. But Galloway, the governor of St. Helena, had no sympathy for "these dusky captives," as Churchill called them. It was the spirit of Hudson Lowe, the mean-minded warden of Napoleon, all over again.[48]

The stubbornness of the Natal authorities confirmed the need for Transvaal self-government, which would lead to the union of South Africa. With its handling of the Zulu uprising and its reprehensible treatment of Africans, the Natal government lost the confidence of the Colonial Office. Natal was the "weak spot" in South Africa. But the Colonial Office could not adopt one policy for Natal and another for the rest. The best solution was a South African federation in which Natal would be submerged.

Throughout the Natal crisis, Churchill remained a loyal though sometimes grumpy second-in-command, curbing his instinct for interference. When his colleague at the Local Government Board, the former riveter John Burns, wrote him that an old black woman had been forced to walk 160 miles to give evidence in a Natal court, Churchill replied: "I am sorry for the poor old lady, but I fear she is not of that 'Imperial importance' which would justify our interfering with a self-governing colony and she must stand, as you suggest, for an instructive instance of native treatment in South Africa."[49]

The Cabinet was drafting the Transvaal constitution, in spite of Tory prophecies that the Boers would win back in the ballot box what they had lost in the war. They could not be trusted, and would evict the British civil servants and form their own autonomous state. Balfour called the constitution "the most dangerous, audacious, and reckless experiment ever tried in the development of a great colonial policy." From his dealings with them, Churchill felt the Boers would be trustworthy partners, who would keep their word once they had given it. For one thing, they trusted Campbell-Bannerman, who had denounced Kitchener's type of warfare as "methods of barbarism." As Louis Botha, the first Premier of Transvaal, would one day say to J. A. Spender: "After all, three words made peace and union in South Africa: 'Methods of Barbarism.' "[50]

In July, when the draft was ready, Campbell-Bannerman told Churchill: "You've done the fighting, you shall have the prize." On July 31, Churchill argued the government's case. The constitution was not framed as a Bill in Parliament, which the Tory House of Lords would have thrown out, but as Letters Patent, which had only to be passed by the House of Commons. His speech, lasting nearly two hours, was regarded even by his foes as statesman-like. C. F. G. Masterman, the brilliant young reformer who would later work with Churchill at the Board of Trade and the Home Office, remembered Churchill's speech as one of the great moments in Parliament, particularly its final appeal to the Tories: "You are the accepted guides of a party which, though in a minority in this House, nevertheless embodies nearly half the nation. I will ask whether you will not consider if you cannot join with us to invest the grant of a free Constitution to the Transvaal with something of a national sanction. With all our majority we can only make it the gift of a party. You can make it the gift of England." The constitution was approved by 316 to 83, with some cross-voting, and the new Transvaal government took office under Botha on March 21, 1907. Churchill could say that he had fought in a war to prevent Boer self-government and that he had also fought for the legislation that returned it to them.

In his appeal to the Tories, he was displaying a new statesmanlike manner, but his reputation still suffered. Herbert Asquith's young daughter, Violet, finding herself next to him at dinner that summer, thought that here was a man famous for putting the cat among the pigeons. Seemingly sunk in abstraction, Churchill suddenly asked her how old she was. Nineteen, she said. "And I," he said with despair in his voice, "am thirty-two already. Younger than anyone else who *counts*, though. Curse ruthless time! Curse our mortality. How cruelly short is the allotted span for all we must cram into it!" He burst into a diatribe on the shortness of human life and the immensity of accomplishment, ending up with "We are all worms. But I do believe that I am a glowworm." Violet was used to the company of brilliant men. Her father was one of the finest Liberal orators and her four brothers had gone to Oxford, which in some quarters was held as sufficient proof of brilliance. But nothing like this had she ever seen. What was it that marked him out? He was unself-conscious and not afraid to be eloquent. His approach to life was full of ardor and surprise. But there was some other elusive quality. She thought of Dr. Johnson's remark: "We all know what light is. But it is difficult to *tell* what it is." Coming home from dinner, she burst into her father's room and told him that for the first time in her life she had come face to face with genius. Chuckling, Asquith replied, "Well, Winston would certainly agree with you there—but I am not sure whether you will find many others of the same mind. Still, I know exactly what you mean."[51]

Parliament recessed on August 5, and Churchill was off to Deauville, where he spent his days in idleness and dissipation, gambling every night until five in the morning.[52] He won 260 pounds, some of which he spent on 267 French books, including the complete works of Balzac and Voltaire, while the rest was spent in certain unspecified other directions. But he took his work with him, and on August 15 wrote King Edward to explain the Transvaal constitution. Through his secretary, Sir Frederick Ponsonby, the King replied in an avuncular tone: ". . . His Majesty is glad to see that you are becoming a *reliable* Minister and above all a *serious* politician. *Which can only be attained by putting country before Party.*"[53]

Invited to the annual German Army maneuvers in Silesia as a guest of Emperor Wilhelm II, Churchill set out for Breslau in early September, having borrowed his cousin Sunny's Yeomanry horse plume and leopard skin for the parade. As he watched the great waves of German infantry and the squadrons of motorcars, then a novelty, Churchill thought of the tiny British Army, in which the parade of a single division was a notable event, and noticed the gloomy face of the French military attaché. Wilhelm II, resplendent in the white uniform of the Silesian Cuirassiers, mingled with his foreign visitors like the solicitous host of an English house party. "Have you seen everything you want?" he asked Churchill. "Tell me, is there anything you have not seen that you would like to see? Have you seen my new gun?" Churchill said he had seen it at a distance. "Oh, but you must see it close to," the Emperor said, and turning to an officer: "Take him and show him our new gun. There is a battery over there. Show him how it works." Churchill left the Emperor's side aware of a perceptible bristling, almost a murmur, among the staff officers in his entourage. He saw the gun, made it clear that he did not want to pry too closely, and, after the usual heel-clicking and saluting, departed, very thankful that there was a sea between the German Army and England.[54]

Back in London in October, he found himself embroiled once more in the coolie question. It was one of the ugliest facts of his service that he had to administer the Chinese Labor Ordinance, that symbol of inequity and greed, which Campbell-Bannerman had called "the biggest scheme of human dumping since the Middle Passage was adopted," pending Transvaal self-government. The more he had to deal with it from day to day the more he disliked "this hideous Chinese monstrosity."[55]

Churchill's policy of voluntary repatriation had been approved on May 1. Proclamations in Chinese were posted in the mines, promising repatriation to any coolie who could give half of one month's wages toward the trip home. It seemed like a viable scheme, but for some reason it did not work. Only twelve coolies had applied by the beginning of June. Churchill became convinced the mine owners were sabotaging the program. Secret pressures were at work. Even the language of the proclamation had been tampered with. The coolies were invited to "tremblingly obey" it, according to a term used in China for prohibitive proclamations and not for those making concessions. For the mining authorities to handle repatriation was like asking poachers to be gamekeepers.[56]

Privately, he felt that repatriation was a fiasco. Elaborate conditions and the verbiage of the proclamation had made it ridiculous. But on June 8 he defended the policy in the House: "I am not prepared to admit that the policy is a failure because only twelve coolies have applied to be returned to China." About three thousand, he pointed out, had been repatriated because of ill health.[57]

Hardly a day went by in the House without a question about the coolies. Inquiries had shifted from the injustice of their contracts to their unruly behavior. The coolies seemed to have brought with them every social evil. They gambled and started riots. They deserted the camps in roving bands and committed robbery and murder. The problem grew so serious that shotguns and rifles were issued to citizens who lived along the Rand railroad line. Explaining the rising crime rate to the House, Churchill said: "The Chinese have a very peculiar code of ethics, which makes them regard it as a more dishonorable thing not to pay a gambling debt than to commit a murder."[58]

Equally shocking to the turn-of-the-century English mind was the crime of homosexuality. In August, Churchill had been asked to comment on reports that the Chinese, deprived of their families, were practicing unnatural vices on a large scale. A Cape Colony solicitor named Leopold Luyt had written several MP's that homosexuality in the compounds was open and scandalous. There was an organized system of homosexual prostitution at a charge of two shillings per coolie (a day's wages), and venereal diseases were rampant. This horrible moral cancer had demoralized the white population and contaminated the native population. It was tolerated, Mr. Luyt asserted, by the police with the knowledge of the government.

Churchill pledged that an inquiry would be made at once. Lord Selborne, the High Commissioner, appointed a committee headed by a lawyer named Bucknill to investigate the conditions of immorality. Twenty-six witnesses and fifteen medical officers were questioned. The report forwarded to the Colonial Office in November was so shocking that on November 15 Churchill told the House that it would have to remain confidential. To this news there was an outcry of protest, for the MP who had originally raised the question in August, F. C. Mackarness, had been allowed by Lord Elgin to study the report, take notes on it, and show extracts to his friends in the House.

Here was the Empire, that brotherhood of nations linked by a common code of honor, fostering the most reprehensible kind of vice. A great moral disaster was being hushed up. The House had a right to know, said another MP, Mr. Lehmann. Did the government have evidence showing that systematic unnatural vice existed in the Chinese compounds? Were there a considerable number of coolies who hired themselves out for this vice? Was it true that these coolies dressed and braided their hair in a special fashion intended to show they could be used for that purpose? Had the prevalence of this vice long been known to the mine inspectors, who would do nothing about it? What a taint on South Africa![59]

Churchill had to maintain the confidentiality of the report while pacifying the House. The charges made by Mr. Luyt were not proved in the report, he said. "It was not true that there was a prevalence of a specific disease of a peculiar nature among the Chinese coolies . . ."

MR. MASTERMAN: "How many cases?"

MR. CHURCHILL: "There might have been five or six cases . . . It certainly was not true that these practices were openly tolerated by the Government, by the police, or by the mine managers, and it was still less true that the native population of South Africa had been contaminated by novel forms of vice, because it was indisputable that those particular forms of vice had long prevailed among the native tribes in South Africa in particular districts and even to a greater extent than it prevailed among the Chinese coolies."

What was true, Churchill went on, was "that this particular offense of sodomy prevailed in most if not all compounds . . . and that there were in those compounds persons who lent themselves to these practices either from habit or for money who were, in fact, proved to be catamites." As to whether persons affected by this form of vice could be identified, reports conflicted. But, Churchill asked, should not this evil have been foreseen from the conditions of Chinese labor, the great number of men confined in compounds without women?

The important thing, Churchill said, was that "the revelations of Mr. Bucknill's report disclosed a sufficiently unhealthy, unwholesome, and unnatural condition of affairs to seal the fate of Chinese labor . . . the system must absolutely, totally, utterly come to a close."[60]

The speech was a great success. Pleased with himself, Churchill told Eddie Marsh: "I smote the Radicals hip and thigh from Sodom and Gomorrha." He also broke new linguistic ground. The word "catamite" had never been used in the House before. Eddie wrote a friend that it was a great puzzle to the MP's; hardly anyone knew that it was just a fancy name for a bugger. It had been rendered "Amalekite" by the baffled shorthand writer, who thought Churchill was referring to the Biblical people who had occupied Canaan before the Jews.[61]

In consequence, Lord Elgin ruled that any coolie suspected of "professionalism" should be repatriated at once. The only lasting remedy, he and Churchill agreed, was to convert public opinion in the Transvaal to repatriation. When Botha came to power after the elections of February 1907, he promised to abolish the system as soon as possible. The coolies went home when their contracts expired. In his first year at the Colonial Office, Churchill had led the government in disposing of its two most serious problems: Transvaal independence and Chinese coolies.

When a Cabinet reshuffle was announced for January 1907, rumors flew that he would be rewarded with the Board of Education. Lord Elgin wrote to say: ". . . I have been dreading every post to find the rumors true and that I was to lose your help. You might think it unkind if I said I 'hoped' not to hear—but however it may turn out I shall always look back on our cooperation during this year of toil & strife with peculiar satisfaction—and with real gratitude to you not only for the courage & ability with which you have fought our cause—but for the invariable consideration you have shown for me & my opinions."[62]

Campbell-Bannerman, however, decided against the promotion. Churchill was better off where he was, for so much was happening at the Colonial Office, and he would be quite unsuitable for the delicate negotiations of the Education Office. In addition, he had not been in the party long enough. The Prime Minister wrote Asquith on January 5: "Very recent convert, hardly justifying Cabinet rise."

At the Colonial Office, Elgin and Churchill had more than sixty territories to look after, and hardly a week passed without some natural or man-made disturbance. In January 1907, an earthquake in Jamaica killed eight hundred persons and destroyed part of Kingston. The commander of a U.S. warship in the harbor, Rear Admiral Charles Davis, landed sailors to help clear the streets and then wrote the governor, Sir Alexander Swettenham, offering to assist "out of common humanity."

Swettenham, who was suspicious of American expansion in the Caribbean, had recently obstructed U.S. efforts to hire Jamaicans to work on the Panama Canal. In a reply dripping with sarcasm, he told Admiral Davis: "I may remind your Excellency that not long ago it was discovered that thieves lodged in and pillaged the house of a New York millionaire during his absence in the summer. But this would not have justified a British admiral landing an armed party to assist the New York police. . . ."[63]

Swettenham's letter found its way into the newspapers on January 21. It was plainly indefensible and wantonly insulting, Churchill said, urging his recall unless he withdrew the letter and apologized for having written it. Lord Elgin wanted to save the man, for although he was rough, he was a good officer who should not be sacked for bad manners. What a nuisance it was! Churchill argued that he could not be allowed to stay when he had expressed such a hostile attitude toward his American neighbors. The man was "an ass," wrong on every point. Noting that Swettenham had made an unkind remark about Admiral Davis' misspelling of the word "thieves," Churchill minuted: "It is characteristic of all his writings—an irrelevant, petty and spiteful kink in his composition—literary and personal."[64]

A telegram was sent to Swettenham instructing him to apologize, for "both in tone and expression, [the letter] is highly improper and especially unbecoming to His Majesty's representative in addressing an officer of a friendly power engaged upon an errand of mercy." Swettenham withdrew the letter but was so dilatory in furnishing a full account of the incident that an exasperated Lord Elgin had him recalled, and he left Jamaica in May.[65]

Usually there was teamwork between Elgin and Churchill, but sometimes there was not. The case of a railway clerk in Ceylon named Serasinghe can serve as an example. Acquitted by the High Court of a charge of theft, Serasinghe brought a countercharge of perjury and conspiracy against the stationmaster who had uncovered the fraud at the station where he worked. The railway's Departmental Committee dismissed him for what it held to be a false charge against the stationmaster. The governor of Ceylon, Sir Henry Blake, confirmed the dismissal. There the matter would have rested had not Churchill's indignation been aroused by the dismissal of a man acquitted of all charges against him, which amounted to saying, on mere departmental authority, that he was guilty after all. Churchill argued for a new trial.

Elgin, who had served five years in India, knew the danger of reversing the disciplinary decision of a governor in an Eastern colony. Ceylon was not the sort of place where every minor clerk should be allowed to defy government rulings. He decided to confirm Serasinghe's dismissal. Disturbed, Churchill wrote him on January 19 that this was a shocking violation of the elementary principles of law and justice. . . . When the case was brought before the House, the brickbats would be about *his* head.

Unswayed, Elgin held his ground, not realizing the extent of his subordinate's persistence. Churchill wrote again on January 23 that he could not agree to a man being treated with wanton illegality and flat injustice. Were not Serasinghe's charges against his accusers strong grounds tending to prove his innocence? A guilty man who had escaped by the skin of his teeth would not reopen his case. But even if he were guilty, the treatment of Serasinghe was a flagrant impropriety.[66]

This letter did no more good than the previous one, so on January 26 Churchill tried again. He had been overruled without reason. Elgin's decision caused him "the most profound disquietude." Distressed by his nagging, Elgin replied that Churchill was not being as fair with him as usual. Elgin had not overruled him; he had simply declined to interfere in the handling of the case by the men on the spot. The Ceylon government could be relied on to give Serasinghe just and lawful treatment.

Churchill then took to coming to Elgin's office to plead his case. He was always "roaming about," Elgin complained; perhaps it was because he had nothing else to do, there being a lull in other matters. They finally had it out in a two-hour discussion on January 29. Churchill was impassioned and excited, but Elgin did not budge. Churchill knew he had lost, but he was a good loser. Calming down, he told his chief: "Well, Lord Elgin—no one can have a conversation with you without advantage!"[67] Churchill's hunger to head his own department showed in his unwillingness to defer to his superior, and in the way he chafed at a decision he did not agree with. If only he had been in charge!

With the South African issue settled, he found the Colonial Office less challenging. He needed great issues as a sail needs a strong wind, but no winds were rising. When Elgin was invited to receive an honorary degree in Cambridge, along with Lord Milner, the event seemed to signal that Imperial problems had entered a more tranquil phase.

At the end of March, Churchill went to Biarritz for a holiday and chanced to meet the King, who said he was watching his career with great interest. In April, he was busy with the Colonial Conference, which brought to London the Dominion Premiers. Among them was a man for whom he reserved a special welcome, Louis Botha, his military foe of the armored train ambush, now Prime Minister of the Transvaal. Botha came with his pretty nineteen-year-old daughter Helen. Churchill took them around London, and tongues began to wag. Rumors of his engagement to Miss Botha were published in the papers. Muriel Wilson, the young woman to whom he had once proposed, wrote him from the south of France that she hoped Winston and Miss Botha and all their little Bothas would come and see her garden, and they would talk of old times and wisteria.[68] But the rumors were unfounded, and Churchill escaped matrimony once more.

At the Colonial Conference, Churchill fought off the Dominion Prime Ministers when they pressed for the adoption of a preferential system. At a political meeting in Edinburgh on May 18, he repeated his stand. The door was closed against taxation on food. The Liberal majority had banged it, barred it, and bolted it. It was a good stout door of British oak. There would not be a farthing of preference on a single peppercorn. He expressed scorn for Tory protectionists like Austen Chamberlain, who "donned an orchid regardless of expense and screwed on an eyeglass regardless of discomfort." Coming to Chamberlain's rescue the Birmingham *Evening Dispatch* of May 22 showed a cartoon of Churchill as a bartender pulling on draft handles labeled "Personalities," "Vulgar Abuse," and "Claptrap."

But Churchill was not pulling quite so often on those handles, and in recognition of his growing stature and maturity, the King named him to the Privy Council, an honor not usually bestowed upon an under-secretary of thirty-two. He could now place the initials PC next to his name, and had the right to be addressed in the House as "the right honorable Gentleman." When Churchill was sworn in on May 7, Almeric FitzRoy, the Clerk of the Council, noticed that he was dressed in a cutaway coat, perhaps to mark his aloofness from ordinary restraints. The King kept them waiting, and Churchill paced up and down the far end of the room with rapid strides, his head bent upon his breast and his hands in his coattail pockets, an odd and fitful figure. To calm him down, FitzRoy explained the nature of the ceremony. As he spoke, Churchill's hands strayed up to FitzRoy's neck, and he found that his tie was being straightened, which he took as another instance of a sedulous restlessness.[69]

Stories about Churchill's restlessness abounded. Eddie Marsh reported that Churchill was lying in bed one morning in gestation for a speech when the telephone rang. He picked up the receiver and said, "Hullo, hullo, *hullo*," getting more and more impatient. At last a voice said, "Yes?" "Christ damn your soul," Churchill shouted, "why do you keep me waiting?" A soft voice, which he recognized as belonging to the wife of the journalist J. A. Spender, asked: "Is that Mr. Churchill?" "No!" roared Churchill, slamming down the receiver.[70]

And yet his restlessness found many useful channels to explore. Botha wanted to present King Edward with the world's biggest diamond, to symbolize his allegiance to the Crown. Named after Thomas Cullinan, the owner of the mine where it had been found in January 1905, it weighed 3,025 carats uncut. Campbell-Bannerman felt it would be inappropriate for the King to accept it, and there was also some criticism in Tory ranks. Such objections annoyed Churchill. Why did they want to drag these wretched Boers inside the Empire if they would not even accept their loyalty so generously tendered? Taking his persuasive pen in hand, he urged the King to accept the diamond, repeating his entreaties until Edward agreed. Presented on his birthday, November 9, the Cullinan diamond was cut later into a number of smaller stones. In thanks for his efforts, the Boers sent Churchill a model of the diamond as a keepsake. He liked to show it to his friends, and one day when Sunny Marlborough's sister Lady Lilian Grenfell came to lunch, he had it sent for. There was some delay, and another topic was being discussed when the butler arrived at Lady Lilian's elbow with what looked like a shapeless lump of white jelly on a tray. Eyeing it with distaste, she said: "No thank you."[71]

With the Parliamentary session "dragging its belly," Churchill looked for new fields to conquer, and resolved to travel to East Africa during the autumn recess. The treatment of natives was a problem all over the Empire, and here was a chance to see things at first hand. Elgin welcomed the plan, which would put several thousand miles between Churchill and the Colonial Office. A cartoon in *Punch* on July 31 showed Elgin helping him pack and saying: "Well, my boy, you see I'm helping you get off, though I shall miss you terribly. You must be sure to have a good rest, and whatever you do, don't hurry back."

When Churchill asked Eddie Marsh if he wanted to come along, Eddie replied with one of his chief's favorite phrases: "Will a bloody duck swim?" Eddie went to ask Sir Robert Chalmers, an official at the Treasury, for a travel allowance, saying that Churchill was taking one. "I dare say he is," Chalmers replied, "but you're not a Blenheim spaniel."[72]

Before his tour of Africa, Churchill went to France in September to attend the army maneuvers, so that he could compare them with the German *Kriegs-spiel* of the previous year. Still fascinated by soldiers, he never missed a chance to attend these live re-enactments of his boyhood deployments and had retained his active service in the Yeomanry. He found that where the German maneuvers had been theatrical, the French were lifelike.

Accompanying him was a new friend, Frederick Edwin Smith. Two years older than Churchill, Smith was a handsome six-footer who had been elected to the House as a Tory in 1906. The son of a provincial lawyer of modest means who had gone to Oxford on a scholarship and acquired the attributes of a Tory aristocrat, Smith got along marvelously with the Duke's grandson accused of betraying his class, for it is not political differences but clashes in temperament that prevent friendship. Churchill and "F.E." would insult each other heartily on the floor of the House, then meet in the bar for a drink. "The Socialists had better not cheer the name of Mr. Churchill," Smith said on one occasion, "for he will most likely in the end steal their clothes when they go bathing—if they do bathe, which I doubt." On another occasion, Churchill described Smith as "invariably vulgar."

Others wondered why they were so close, for Smith was generally regarded as a flippant lightweight, a man "who extracts the honey and escapes the sting." His one principle seemed to be self-advancement. He was brilliant, but as someone said, his brains went to his head. And yet Churchill called his friendship one of his most precious possessions. Drawn to those who possessed the qualities he lacked, Churchill admired Smith's caustic wit and his brilliant forensic mind, the product of an Oxford education of which he had been deprived. He always had a good time with Smith, a hard drinker who was said to empty a bottle of champagne before playing tennis, explaining that it improved his vision. The only apparent similarity between them was that they were both considered "on the make." A cartoon in *Punch* showed them absorbed in *The Life of Disraeli*. "Master of epigrams," Smith said, "like me!" "Wrote a novel in his youth," Churchill responded, "like me!" Together: "Traveled in the East—like us. How does it end?"

Perhaps Smith reminded him of his father. He had the same arrogance, the same impertinent delivery in the House, the same opportunism disguised as principle. Perhaps in Smith, Churchill's dream of making a friend of his father was in some once-removed manner realized. Churchill had acquaintances and colleagues in multitudes, but did not make friends easily. Some people he antagonized, to many more he was indifferent. While he was in France, the former Pamela Plowden, now Lady Lytton, wrote him that although he might not have many friends, those he had loved him with strength and loyalty, and she was perhaps their leader.[73] It was quite true, Churchill replied, he had very few friends, but why should he have more? With his busy selfish life, he failed in the little offices that kept friendship sweet and warm. He could make more, but not like Pamela; she was a demure kitten purring and prinking over the sweet and abundant milk of life.[74]

In October 1907, Churchill left on the first leg of his African journey, to Malta and Cyprus. He had told Lord Elgin that it was a private trip, but it soon took on all the trappings of an official visit. He made speeches, received deputations, passed inspections, and sent a continuous flow of memos and minutes to the Colonial Office. Moreover, he had agreed to write five articles for the *Strand* magazine at 150 pounds each, which he planned to turn into a book. This was the first time a servant of the Crown had combined official business and journalism. Elgin felt that Churchill had not kept his word. As usual, he was chasing after glory. What had been intended as a purely sporting and private expedition had drifted into an official progress over a course strewn with memoranda. Irritated by the glut of communications, Sir Francis Hopwood complained to Elgin: "He can never understand that there is a better way of enforcing an argument than by intrigue & by pugnaciously overstating a case."[75] Hopwood was a curiously two-faced figure who maligned Churchill behind his back while pretending friendliness. Churchill remained unaware of his mischief-making.

From Cyprus, he and Eddie "threaded the long red furrow of the Suez Canal" and "sweltered through the trough of the Red Sea" to Aden. On October 13, the telephone rang in the guard office in Aden harbor, where a noncommissioned officer named Calvert was on duty. "This is Mr. Churchill speaking from the Union Club on the quay," a voice said. "I shall be here for a day or two and would be glad if the camel battery could lend me a camel to ride." "Certainly," Calvert said, and called the battalion sergeant major, who said: "Go down to the gun park and tell them to saddle Number 51 and send it with a Somali boy to the club." Calvert was surprised the sergeant major had chosen Number 51, a bad-tempered kicker. That evening, the Somali boy reported back to Calvert, grinning and holding out a five-rupee note. "Him very good man, sahib," the boy said. "Give me a backsheesh." Calvert asked how the camel had behaved and the boy said: "Sahib camel kick Churchill. Churchill sahib kick camel. Him very good camel now, sahib."[76]

From Aden, Churchill went to Mombasa, Nairobi, and Entebbe, which had that hallmark of British rule, a golf course. In Kampala, he stayed with the Governor of Uganda, Hesketh Bell, keeping him awake by dictating an article while taking his bath. When Bell told him that if he visited one bishop he would have to visit the two others as well, Churchill said: "I'm not going here, there, and everywhere! And I'm damned if you're going to turn me into a blasted starfish!" When Churchill asked the Governor his age, Bell told him he was forty-three. By the time he was forty-three, Churchill announced, he would be Prime Minister.[77]

The hunting was good in Uganda, and Churchill bagged a rare white rhinoceros. Another big-game hunter, President Theodore Roosevelt, was impressed. "The officials who were with Churchill were able to take him to a place where there were plenty of elephants and plenty of white rhinoceros," he wrote the American ambassador in London, Whitelaw Reid. "Now I should consider my entire African trip a success if I could get to that country and find the game as Churchill describes it. . . . The white rhinoceros is the animal I care most to get—even more than the elephant."[78] Roosevelt went to East Africa in 1909 after his second term expired and shot two white rhinoceroses, but was disappointed that they were not as white as they were said to be.

From Kampala, Churchill went to Lake Victoria, where he started on a twenty-day safari northward to Gondokoro, on the way to Khartoum. They had 350 porters, and Churchill was apt to end each day with the phrase "sofari sogoody." Eddie Marsh thought of Lady Cromer's maid, who, on the fourth day in the African bush, had asked: "How long, my Lady, must we tarry in this shrubbery?"[79]

They took a train and a steamer down the Nile, arriving in Khartoum on December 23. Churchill had brought along his valet, George Scrivings, who had been a steward on his mother's hospital ship. He fell ill in Khartoum and died of ptomaine poisoning on December 24, leaving a wife and four children. Churchill's reaction was typical: they had all eaten the same food, but Scrivings had died while he had survived. Scrivings had sprained his ankle at the start of the safari and had been carried in a chair for three weeks. Churchill was sure that his organs were fat and flabby and in a condition to receive bacteriological poisoning. Churchill, by contrast, was wonderfully fit. The only injury he had sustained was a broken front tooth, shorn by a plum pit on Lake Chioga.

Scrivings' death was a shock to Churchill, a keen and palpable loss, casting gloom over an otherwise pleasant journey. He had become dependent on Scrivings for all the little intimate comforts of his daily life. As Jack pointed out, he would never have so faithful a slave again. Alas, alas, few things had grieved him more. He felt responsible, for he had brought Scrivings to Africa, and he thought of the family in London, struck down by ill tidings on Christmas Day. He wanted Jack to tell Mrs. Scrivings not to worry about her future, he would look after her and her children as far as his limited means would allow.[80]

How easily it might have been he, Churchill thought as he walked behind the coffin through the streets of Khartoum on the day of the funeral. He would not have minded that much. If his life had ended there, Jack could have married without delay.

For Jack was engaged to Gwendeline (known as "Goonie"), daughter of a Catholic lord, the irascible old Lord Abingdon. It had to be kept secret until Jack, a junior partner with a firm of stockbrokers, had enough money to propose officially. Jennie had sometimes thought Winston had designs in that quarter, though not serious ones. When he had met her, Winston had been "bowled over" by the vivacious Goonie. Certainly there was a strong sympathy between them, and she wrote him witty and affectionate letters. On December 16 Goonie wrote that it was positively cruel not to see Jack: "I know that you love a woman, Winston, very much, and you know what it means—you can imagine what I am going through not being able to be with Jack—"[81] Winston at the time was in love with the American actress Ethel Barrymore, who often visited England, but who decided that becoming the wife of an English politician was not for her.

The political news was that Churchill had missed the German Emperor's visit, the railway strike (settled by Lloyd George), and the baiting of Balfour in Birmingham. John Burns had silenced a suffragette by roaring at her: "When you are married, my dear, you will understand a great deal more than you do at present." The King and the Emperor had kept Campbell-Bannerman standing for two and a half hours (he joked that Royalties had a special static muscle for state functions), and the next day he suffered a heart attack in Bristol. The succession was considered secure for Asquith. His only possible rival, Edward Grey, refused to budge from the Foreign Office. Churchill was alarmed. A heart attack was serious in a man of seventy-one, who had recently lost his wife. His removal from the scene would lead to many changes. Political circles at home must be buzzing and he was glad to be out of the way.[82] Hopwood wrote him that changes were coming and that he was looking forward to seeing Churchill in the Cabinet.[83] Behind his back, Hopwood wrote Elgin that Churchill had liked one of his telegrams so much that he was "rather alarmed that I may not have detected a latent vice."[84]

Churchill also saw himself in the Cabinet. His mind began to drift from colonial questions to the social reforms that he believed would be the great challenge of the Liberal government that followed Campbell-Bannerman's retirement. In a letter written on the White Nile to his journalist friend J. A. Spender, he revealed the course of his thoughts:

> . . . The people are not satisfied, but neither are they offended with the government . . . All minds are turning more and more to the social and economic issues. This revolution is irresistible. They will not tolerate the existing system by which wealth is acquired, shared, and employed. They may not be able to devise a new system . . . but they will set their faces like flint against a money power . . . and its obvious injustices . . . however willing the working classes may be to remain in passive opposition to the existing social system, they will not continue to bear the awful uncertainties of their lives. Minimum standards of wage and comfort, insurance against sickness, old age, these are the only questions by which parties are going to live in the future. Woe to Liberalism if they slip through its fingers. This is the fruit of my Central African Reflections . . . We have shot lion, rhinoceros, elephant, buffalo, hippopotamus, heartebeast, wilderbeast, roan antelope, gazelle of many kinds, crocodile, zebra etc. 23 species in 10 days' shooting.[85]

In the midst of piling up big-game trophies, Churchill was already plotting the course of the next government. He did not hesitate to challenge the interests of his class, the wealthy landed aristocracy, in proposing a "revolution" to benefit the workingman. Already, he saw the outline of a national policy that the Liberal Party must follow for its salvation and the good of England.

Back in London on January 17, 1908, Churchill was welcomed home after his four-month absence at a dinner in his honor at the National Liberal Club. "I come back into the fighting line," he announced, "in the best of possible health, and with a wish to force the fighting up to the closest possible point." The political situation was murky. Although gravely ill, Campbell-Bannerman clung to office. He attended his last Cabinet meeting on February 12, and thereafter Asquith deputized for him. On March 3, King Edward visited him at 10 Downing Street, a rare tribute from sovereign to subject. It was so clear that the Prime Minister would not last long that the King summoned Asquith to Buckingham Palace the same day and said he had made up his mind to send for him at once should anything happen to Campbell-Bannerman. The King had heard gossip that Winston wanted his under-secretary's job upgraded to the Cabinet level. His mother, the late Queen, had vetoed a similar proposal in favor of Edward Grey when he was Under-Secretary for Foreign Affairs.[86]

Asquith said that Winston had every claim to Cabinet rank. He had been passed over when Reginald McKenna, who had taken the job Churchill had rejected, Financial Secretary to the Treasury, had been promoted in 1907 to President of the Board of Education. Of course, McKenna was eleven years older than Churchill and had been a Liberal MP since 1895. He had been passed over again when Lewis Harcourt, like Churchill a Liberal MP since 1904, had been given a seat in the Cabinet as First Commissioner of Works. The King agreed, but said that Winston would have to wait until a suitable Cabinet office fell vacant.[87]

Churchill knew that the plan to upgrade his post would not work. It was impossible for both him and Elgin to sit in the Cabinet for the Colonial Office, for Elgin was too unassertive. His only hope was that Campbell-Bannerman would resign or die, and that he would be asked to join the new Asquith Cabinet. After his meeting with the King, Asquith began to send out feelers, and had a long talk with Churchill on March 12 about Cabinet possibilities, mentioning the Colonial Office, the Local Government Board, and the Admiralty, an office that "would suit you very well." Two days later, Churchill's reply came in a letter that was halfway between a discourse on the merits of those offices and a response to a "Help Wanted" ad. The Admiralty was the most pleasant and glittering post in the Ministry, but it was held by his uncle and dear friend, Lord Tweedmouth (who had married one of his father's sisters), and he did not want to press for it. It would be unseemly to replace one of his relatives. As for the Local Government Board, he wanted nothing to do with it, for "there is no place in the Government more laborious, more anxious, more thankless, more choked with petty & even with squalid detail, more full of hopeless and insoluble difficulties . . . I would rather continue to serve under Lord Elgin at the Colonial Office without a seat in the Cabinet than go there." What he really wanted, however, was to replace Lord Elgin at the Colonial Office.[88] It was a grave matter for a Prime Minister to dismiss a man serving in the Cabinet, but Asquith had told Churchill that he was dumping Elgin, who had made a poor impression on him with his taciturn ways and his uselessness in debates. Quoting Gladstone, Asquith had said: "The first essential for a Prime Minister is to be a good butcher," adding: "There are several who must be pole-axed now."

Knowing that Elgin was out of the way, Churchill had no compunction in making an unashamed grab, which required belittling the accomplishments of a chief who had shown him constant consideration and support, and exaggerating his own. "During the last two years," he wrote, "practically all the constructive action & all the Parliamentary exposition has been mine." Churchill now saw himself as an indispensable man: "I have been fortunate," he wrote, "to establish excellent relations in many quarters, which will not soon be re-created by another."[89]

In the Liberal Party, pressure was mounting for a new Prime Minister, for there was a sense of drift, and the government had lost several by-elections. On March 27, Campbell-Bannerman sent for Asquith and told him he was dying, even quoting the text he had chosen out of the Psalms to put on his grave. But he did not speak of resigning and said in farewell: "This is not the last of me." But when he took a turn for the worse at the beginning of April, he resigned. The King, not wishing to interrupt his holiday, summoned Asquith to Biarritz to kiss hands and form a government. There was some unfavorable comment about this unusual procedure, which the *Times* described as "an inconvenient and dangerous departure from precedent," but when someone asked F. E. Smith: "Would you kiss hands on foreign soil?" he replied: "I would kiss hands in hell." Churchill would have agreed.

Campbell-Bannerman died on April 22. Although not a great Prime Minister, he had in his seventeen months in office achieved one great thing, the unification of South Africa. Lord Elgin drafted the policy, and Churchill defended it in the House, but Campbell-Bannerman inspired it. Having reached the first place, he rose to the occasion.

The new Prime Minister, who in May 1908 would move into the quiet cul-de-sac off Whitehall known as Downing Street and remain there until December 1916, was destined to preside over nothing less than the transformation of English society. At the age of fifty-five, Asquith had quietly climbed the Liberal ladder to the top. Born in the Yorkshire town of Morley, the son of a modest wool merchant, he was a brilliant classical scholar at Oxford and an equally brilliant lawyer. Winning a Liberal seat in 1886, he had from the start what was known as "the front-bench style." His gifts of measured lucidity, sound judgment, and an easy flow of oratory were exactly those required for Parliamentary leadership. Churchill admired his intellect and said that his mind opened and shut smoothly and exactly, like the breech of a gun. Asquith had none of Churchill's flamboyance, but he understood that patience, calm deliberation, the esteem of one's colleagues, and an almost phlegmatic stolidity were the fountainheads of Parliamentary power. He was ambitious while scorning the limelight, and his ruthlessness had a veneer of bonhomie. In 1894, his first wife having died, he married the hawk-faced and wasp-tongued Margot Tennant, who was his engine and his spur. Where others saw a short, stocky, bulbous-nosed and sandy-haired figure out of Dickens, she saw a leader of Cromwellian stature. His critics said that Asquith was irresolute and slipshod, and Leo Amery described him as having a "speciously transparent lucidity of expression, of saying nothing whatever in the course of half an hour, and yet leaving an impression of business-like conciseness." Austen Chamberlain said that he was at times needlessly brutal.

Brutal indeed was the way he dropped Elgin, a friend since Oxford, who had recently told his wife: "I cannot conceive Asquith wishing to injure me." Elgin read about his dismissal in the newspapers, and soon after received from Asquith a curt note that gave no explanation. Elgin was shocked. Through much of 1907 he had been depressed, saying that he wanted to throw up the sponge because he was all too conscious of his limitations. Perhaps he felt threatened by Churchill, so purposeful and bustling. But no sooner had he decided to hang on than he was dismissed, and (this was the crowning insult) replaced by another lord, Lord Crewe. Elgin was offered the title of marquis, which he refused, and retired to his Scottish estate, where he died in 1917, an embittered man.[90]

Asquith's government, another "Ministry of all talents," was perhaps the most brilliant gathering of men in twentieth-century British politics. Grey, Haldane, and Morley remained at their respective posts, the Foreign, War, and India offices. Lord Crewe, "the man who never gave wrong advice," went to the Colonial Office, with Jack Seely, Churchill's friend from Harrow days, taking over his job as Under-Secretary. McKenna, the son of a civil servant, took the Admiralty, preserve of lords. Walter Runciman, the shipowner's son who had opposed Churchill in Oldham, was President of the Board of Education, and Herbert Samuel, the son of a Jewish banking family, was Under-Secretary for Home Affairs. Looking at the new Cabinet, Lord Esher observed: "Here we are, overwhelmed by the middle classes." The big surprise was that Asquith had made Lloyd George Chancellor of the Exchequer, in order to carry the Radical wing of the party. This left open the Board of Trade, which Lloyd George vacated, a sort of grab-bag department responsible for commerce and industry and a dozen other areas. Rejected in his bid for the Colonial Office, Churchill accepted the Board of Trade. He was thirty-three, three years younger than his father had been upon reaching Cabinet rank.

At the Colonial Office, Churchill left behind him a reputation for frantic activity. Frustrated at not being in charge, he seized on issues where he could make his mark, lavishing his brilliance and style on matters great and small. When he noticed that the education and religion budget of the Seychelles islands was about the same as the income from stamps, he wrote: "And thus Christianity is sustained by variations in the watermark! Such are the unseen foundations of society."[91]

In his conduct of business, he tended to take the side of the individual against the bureaucracy, as he had defended the Sandhurst cadets against collective punishment. Elgin, wanting to maintain the cohesiveness of a great service, was usually against interfering with the decisions of the men on the spot. Churchill judged each case on its merits and did not assume that local authorities knew best. He was a righter of wrongs rather than a company man. Always, he took the large, generous, humane view against the blinkered bureaucratic view. While Elgin tended to worry about the prestige of colonial officials, Churchill's concern was with the subject people. When seven thousand silver medals were struck for the troops that had massacred the Zulus, Churchill described them as a "silver badge of shame." Elgin replied: "Emphatically no. This will be worn by men who did their duty in obedience to orders, and did it well." When a rule was proposed that native cadets entering the Ceylon civil service must be unmarried, Churchill was against it, saying: "The cadets must continue to solve the riddle of life for themselves."[92]

Particularly irritating to Elgin was Churchill's defense of an African named Sekgoma, who had been removed as a local chief in South Africa's Bechuanaland Territory. He was troublesome, and Lord Selborne proposed deportation, but Churchill objected in a minute that combined sarcasm and a hectoring tone:

> We cannot imprison him or deport him without flat violation of every solid principle of British justice. As at present advised I could not undertake even to attempt a defense of the lawless deportation of an innocent man upon an informal *lettre de cachet*. If we are going to embark upon this sort of law-breaking and autocratic action, where are we going to stop? What kind of injustice is there that would not be covered by precedents of this kind? If we are going to take men who have committed no crime, and had no trial, and condemn them to life-long imprisonment and exile in the name of "State policy," why stop there? Why not poison Sekgoma by some painless drug? No argument, that

216

will justify his deportation to the Seychelles, will not also sustain his removal to a more sultry clime. If we are to employ medieval processes, at least let us show medieval courage and thoroughness. Think of the expense that would be saved. A dose of laudanum, costing at the outside five shillings, is all that is required. There would be no cost of maintenance, no charge for transportation, no legal difficulties, no need to apply to the Portuguese, no fear of habeas corpus. Without the smallest money or expense the peace of the Protectorate would be secured, and a "dangerous character" obnoxious to the Government removed.[93]

Annoyed, Elgin replied that the man was a savage and a troublemaker, and that he, at least, was ready to take his share of the responsibility for preserving the peace. But in a tacit compromise between the two men, Sekgoma was detained but not deported. This was one of many examples, for Churchill, although often accused of inconsistency, remained consistent in his belief that local conditions had no bearing upon the rule of law. The Empire existed to govern justly, not to favor the British Raj. Just as he had not been a loyal party man when he felt the Tories to be in error, he did not condone the actions of colonial governors when they violated principle. At the Colonial Office, his independence of mind made him a sometimes lonely and sometimes maligned figure, although everyone agreed that he had talent to burn.

VI

BOARD OF TRADE

In March 1908, Lady Jeune (now Lady St. Helier) gave a dinner party at her home, 52 Portland Place. Churchill was invited, but Eddie Marsh found him soaking in his bath when he should already have left. "What on earth are you doing, Winston?" he asked. "You should be at dinner by now." "I am not going," Churchill announced. "It will be a great bore." "But you can't do that," Eddie said, "especially not to Lady Jeune. Remember how kind she was to you when she got Sir Evelyn Wood to get you to the Omdurman campaign."[1]

As Eddie hustled Churchill out of his bath and got him dressed and on his way, another guest was having similar misgivings. Twenty-three-year-old Clementine Hozier had come home after an exhausting day of giving French lessons at half a crown an hour. "Your Aunt Mary has just sent a message," her mother told her. "She has been let down and is thirteen for dinner, and she would very much like you to go to dinner tonight."

"I really can't," Clementine said. "I don't want to go. I've got nothing to wear and have no clean gloves."

"That is very ungrateful of you," Blanche Hozier scolded. "Your aunt has been extremely kind to you. Let's have no more nonsense, go upstairs straight away and get dressed."[2]

The dinner was in honor of Lady Lugard, wife of Sir Frederick Lugard, maker of Nigeria. As Flora Shaw, she had been colonial editor of *The Times*. Her opinion of Churchill was not high. She had once written her husband that he was "an ignorant boy, so obviously ignorant in regard to colonial affairs and at the same time so full of personal activity that the damage he may do appears to be colossal." Among the other guests were F. E. Smith, Lord Tweedmouth, and Sir Henry Lucy, the Parliamentary sketch writer for *Punch*, who was sitting on one side of Clementine. The other side was vacant until Churchill arrived, in time for the chicken.

Churchill had met Clementine in 1904 at a dance given by Lord and Lady Crewe. His attention was drawn to a beautiful girl, barely nineteen, with lustrous reddish-blond hair and brown-flecked green eyes. Jennie introduced them, but Churchill was gauche and tongue-tied. He did not ask her to dance or to have supper; he just stared. Having heard that he was stuck-up and objectionable, Clementine beckoned to one of her admirers, Charles Hoare, who rescued her.

Perhaps Churchill *was* objectionable in those days. Women, he felt, were lesser beings who did not do justice to the complexity of life. They were so frightfully cock-sure; they saw things in black and white, whereas nature never drew a line without smudging it. Critical also of their appearance, he would huddle with Eddie Marsh at a ball, scrutinizing the new arrivals, and grading them according to Marlowe's line "Was this the face that launched a thousand ships?" "Two hundred ships?" one would suggest. "By no means," the other would reply, "a covered sampan, or small gunboat at most." One of the rare women who, in the eyes of both assessors, scored the full thousand was Clementine Hozier, with whom Churchill kept up a steady stream of conversation all through Lady St. Helier's dinner. Of course, most of the conversation had to do with him. Had she read his life of Lord Randolph? Deciding to be honest, Clementine admitted that she had not. "If I send you the book tomorrow, will you read it?" Churchill asked. She said she would, but he never sent it, which made a bad impression on her. Here was a man who did not keep his promises.[3]

Churchill's interest was so noticeable that the other ladies teased Clementine in the cloakroom. For once, he had not lingered with the men after dinner over a cigar, but had followed her into the drawing room. Determined to see her again, he asked Jennie to invite her for a weekend at Salisbury Hall, Jennie's house near St. Albans. By that time, on April 11, he had been named to the Board of Trade. Winston and Clemmie had long talks, and her impression of him began to change. In her thank-you note to Jennie, she referred to Churchill's "dominating charm and brilliancy."

After years of struggle, Churchill now had a seat in the Cabinet and a sufficient income and could take enough of a breathing space to contemplate marriage. His father had married at twenty-five, and he was thirty-three. His brother was getting married. It was time. Clemmie was not the first girl he had looked at with an eye to the future. He had proposed to Muriel Wilson and been unofficially engaged to Pamela Plowden. He had wooed the actress Ethel Barrymore, but she did not think herself able to cope with the great world of politics. Now he pursued Clemmie with the same single-mindedness that he did everything. She was off on a six-week tour of the Continent, and Lady St. Helier told her mother that she was mad to let her go just when Winston was showing an interest. Churchill wrote her that it had been a comfort and a pleasure to meet a girl with so much intellectual quality and such reserves of noble sentiment. He hoped that they could lay the foundation of a frank and clear-eyed friendship.[4]

Although they did not know it, Churchill and Clemmie had in common an unhappy childhood and a parent who favored their siblings. Clemmie's mother, Lady Blanche Ogilvy, the eldest daughter of the 10th Earl of Airlie, belonged to an ancient Scottish family. Her parents were relieved when in 1878 the twenty-six-year-old Blanche married a dashing former Dragoon Guards colonel, the forty-year-old Henry Hozier, who was working for Lloyd's. They overlooked Hozier's checkered past—he was divorced and had been named as corespondent in another divorce—for they wanted to see their wayward and passionate daughter settle down.

But the marriage was a disaster from the start. Blanche and Hozier did nothing but quarrel and taunt, taunt and quarrel. It was a sorry mismatch of two strong and conflicting personalities. Hozier told Blanche that he did not want children and would not give her any. She waited five years and then decided to find someone who would. She went looking for a man to sire her child, the way a farmer might have shopped for a prize bull, and settled on Captain George "Bay" Middleton of the 12th Lancers, a superb horseman and an escort to the Empress Elizabeth of Austria when she had come to England in 1876. Kitty was born in 1883, followed by Clemmie two years later.[5] As Wilfrid Blunt, who had a brief affair with Blanche, wrote in his diary upon hearing of Churchill's engagement: "Clementine and Kitty, who died, are both Blanche told me long ago her daughters by Bay Middleton, who I believe was a charming man but I never saw him. It is much wiser for a woman who has an inferior husband to choose a suitable sire for her children, and both these girls were delightful, refined and superior in every way." Famed in hunting circles as one of the finest riders to hounds in England, Middleton was killed while riding in a point-to-point.[6]

In 1888 Blanche had twins, a boy and a girl, Bill and Nellie. The father was rumored, probably falsely, to be Blunt. Blanche's behavior was decidedly un-Victorian; she seemed like a throwback to the carefree sensuality of the Regency. Her friend Lady Gregory, one of the founders of Dublin's Abbey Theater, said that she rotated ten lovers. In 1890 her husband found her in bed with a Conservative MP named Ellis Ashmead-Bartlett and asked for a separation.[7] Five-year-old Clemmie was a pawn in the custody battle that left her in the care of her capricious mother. She grew up without a father, and with the constant spectacle of a mother who was ready to sacrifice everything to her own pleasure and often left her children in the care of governesses. Blanche showed a marked preference for the bubbling, outgoing Kitty, as Randolph had preferred Jack to Winston. Realizing that she would always hold a secondary place in her mother's feelings, Clementine developed defenses, such as mother-substitutes and a hardening of the heart against vulnerability. In 1899, afraid that Hozier might try to kidnap her daughters, Blanche moved the family to the French seaside resort of Dieppe, where she gambled away at the casino the allowance her relatives sent her. Clementine acquired a horror of gambling and of all excessive behavior. The foundation of her reserved and judgmental nature was built upon the critical observation of her mother.

Kitty died of typhoid when she was sixteen, and Clemmie grew into a radiantly lovely young woman, who was routinely known as "the beautiful Miss Hozier." Studious, she wanted to go to a university, but her mother would not hear of it. Blanche wanted no intellectuals in the family, and went as far as devising stratagems to prevent her from doing her homework. It was Randolph all over again, telling Winston he did not have the capacity for Oxford. When Blanche returned to London, Clemmie began to go out in society. This woman of abandoned behavior was strict with her daughter, insisting that she get home at midnight from balls that started at eleven, and boxing her ears if she was late, as if she did not want Clemmie to be a replica of herself. Clemmie was so sought-after that her sister Nellie suggested she keep a file entitled "Proposals to Clementine," with the headings "Discussed," "Answered," and "Pending Decision." "Change of Heart" might have been another heading, for Clemmie had been engaged to two men by the time Winston took an interest in her: first to Sidney Peel, a banker-barrister fifteen years her senior, who sent her a bunch of white violets every day of the year, except in August, when no violets could be found in all of England—and then, in 1906, to Lionel Earle, a pompous civil servant nearly twice her age. In both cases she drew back from the brink, which in those days took courage, for lack of love was judged a poor reason to break off an engagement. The emotional stress of breaking two engagements left the high-strung and easily distraught Clemmie feeling humiliated, and made her physically ill. Then, in 1907, Henry Hozier died, a man she had hardly known, who was not her true father. Now, in 1908, she met the man with whom she would spend the rest of her life, sharing the spirals of his career.

While waiting for Clementine to return from her European tour, Churchill had urgent business to attend to. In those days, newly appointed Cabinet ministers had to vacate their Parliamentary seats and submit to re-election. Instead of settling down to the business of governing, they had to hurry off to get elected as soon as they had been named. A promising career could be ruined if a minister was defeated. Sometimes, as a matter of courtesy, the seat was not contested. But the Tories were not about to give Churchill a free ride, and in April he went to North-West Manchester to win back his seat.

He knew that in 1906 he had been swept in on the Liberal tide, and that North-West Manchester was a marginal constituency liable to swing back to the Tories. Although he still had the backing of Tory business groups, free trade was not now so alarming an issue, and his opponent, William Joynson-Hicks, conducted an aggressive campaign. Also, this time it was a three-cornered race, for a Marxist named Dan Irving was running on the Labour ticket.

Joynson-Hicks presented the by-election as a symbol of Conservative resurgence. "Well do I remember that fatal Saturday night," he said, "when we went about with our leader practically slain, with our forces scattered in all directions, and the citadel of Conservatism in South-East Lancashire in the hands of a guerrilla chieftain who was once a Lieutenant of our party."[8]

The guerrilla chieftain had some powerful friends. Lloyd George came and spoke for him, and H. G. Wells wrote in the *Daily News* that Joynson-Hicks represented "absolutely the worst element in British political life at the present time . . . is an entirely undistinguished man . . . and an obscure and ineffectual nobody."[9]

Churchill thought his chances were good. The Tories still seemed divided, and he had the backing of the businessmen and the Jewish community. He told the chairman of the Liberal Election Committee, James Thewlis: ". . . we Churchills die young, and I want to put something more on the slate."[10]

Once again, the suffragettes disrupted his meetings. Just as he was making his best points, a high-pitched voice in the back would ask: "What about the women?" The movement had grown stronger, and he tried to be conciliatory, saying, "Trust me, ladies, I am your friend and will be your friend in the Cabinet." But since he did not promise a franchise bill, the heckling continued.

On election day, April 23, the whole country watched Churchill lose by 429 votes, 4,988 to 5,417. Ninety percent of the electorate had turned out. The 276 votes that went to the Labour candidate could not have saved him. He blamed the Irish Catholic vote, which had changed sides at the last minute under priestly pressure.

Now the full blast of Tory hatred stored against the turncoat was released. Churchill defeat jokes made the rounds, such as: "What's the use of a W.C. without a seat?" Levy-Lawson's normally staid *Daily Telegraph* was delirious: "Churchill out—language fails us just when it is most needed. We have all been yearning for this to happen, with a yearning beyond utterance. Figures—oh, yes, there are figures, but who cares for figures today. Winston Churchill is out, Out, OUT."

Churchill thought there had been an unfair press campaign against him. The *Manchester Courier* had charged him with breaking his parole while a prisoner of the Boers. He sued the *Courier* for libel, and blamed its owner, the press lord Alfred Harmsworth. But Harmsworth chided him for violating their agreement that each should use his stage thunder in the furtherance of his interests. Churchill was free to criticize Harmsworth hotly in Parliament, and Harmsworth was free to say what he liked about Churchill.[11] There was nothing personal in it. Nonetheless, the *Courier* published an apology.

Once his initial disappointment was spent, Churchill saw the Manchester defeat as a blessing in disguise. If he had won the by-election, he would probably have lost the General Election. Now, he was free to run in another constituency. Several safe seats (eight or nine, he bragged to Clemmie) had been placed at his disposal. He could pick one that would be secure for many years. Still, defeat was vexing. The Tory howls of triumph rang in his ears, as did the cries of grief of his friends and helpers. But to explain away defeat was odious. There was only one saving grace, he had done all he could.[12]

Deciding on Dundee, a strong Liberal seat, Churchill left for Scotland the night of his defeat and campaigned against the dual threats of Tory reaction and Labour socialism. It was a splendid occasion to define his own position. First, as a foe of the special interests on the right, as exemplified in the House of Lords, "filled with doddering peers, cute financial magnates, clever wire-pullers, big brewers with bulbous noses. All the enemies of progress are there

. . ." Second, as a friend of the working class and the dispossessed, pursuing the goals of Tory Democracy, but repudiating socialism. With a Labour candidate in the race, there was a danger of being outflanked on social questions, so Churchill described his aims at the Board of Trade, such as an old-age pension scheme for those over seventy, which would cost the Exchequer six million pounds a year. This was greeted with derision by hecklers who shouted that no one in the working classes ever reached the age of seventy, and who asked why he had voted against Ramsay MacDonald's "Right to Work" bill. Churchill drew the line: "Socialism wants to pull down wealth, Liberalism seeks to raise up poverty. . . . Socialism assails the maximum pre-eminence of the individual—Liberalism seeks to build up the minimum standard of the masses. Socialism attacks capital, Liberalism attacks monopoly."[13] On May 9, he won by several thousand votes against the Conservative, Labour, and Prohibition candidates. The Labour and Tory parties, which in years to come would divide the Liberal carcass, polled roughly the same.

Churchill sat for "Bonnie Dundee" for fifteen years. Finally, he was a Cabinet minister, at the heart of the matter. He had arrived at his "true degree." Perhaps he thought of Gladstone's words: "The desire for office is the desire of ardent minds for a larger space and scope within which to serve the country, and for command of that powerful machinery for information and practice which the Public Departments supply. He would be a very bad Minister indeed who does not do ten times the good to the country that he would do out of office, because he has hopes and opportunities which multiply twentyfold, as by a system of wheels and pulleys, his power for doing it." "Bravo!" wrote Lord Curzon, his father's friend, the former Viceroy of India. "At 33 a great record. *Sic itur ad astra* [So shalt thou scale the stars]."[14]

"The stir and fuss incident to a change of government is now near its end," John Morley noted on April 30, "and we are all settling down to the work of the ship, and continuance of our cruise. The weather is a little *thick*, as in politics it is always apt to be; but the new pilot is a sober-minded and most attentive man; the crew are aware that if they play tricks, the ship will founder with themselves in it, and the country is in no hurry about anything in the political line—least of all in a hurry to bring Balfour back again."[15]

As for the crew playing tricks, there was from the start a decided wariness of Churchill in the Cabinet. He already had a reputation as an impulsive meddler, who would just as soon busy himself with the affairs of other departments as with his own. His energy and ability were not in dispute; the fear was rather that he was so able that his own duties would not be enough to absorb him. Charles Hobhouse, the Financial Secretary to the Treasury, said that the whole Cabinet atmosphere had been upset by Churchill, before whose advent there had been no electricity.[16] Edward Grey, the Foreign Secretary, was sure that one thing he did not need was Churchill's advice, for "Winston knows nothing about the Foreign Office work, and thinks that because a Parliamentary Under-Secretary can travel and pick and choose and gallop about the field and toss his head and sniff what breeze he pleases, therefore a Foreign Secretary can do the same."[17] Haldane, the patient and tolerant Secretary of State for War, said that Churchill in Cabinet was "as long-winded as he was persistent."[18] The minister that Churchill most antagonized was the new Colonial Secretary, Lord Crewe. With a continuing interest in colonial affairs born of his recent expertise, Churchill bombarded Crewe with suggestions and scraps of advice. Of one of his memos to Crewe, Asquith said: "A typical missive, born of froth out of foam." Crewe learned, as other ministers would, that he had to guard his prerogatives against Churchill's uncontrollable tendency to overstep his bounds.

Crewe was particularly touchy, having been warned by his predecessor, Lord Elgin, of Churchill's expansionist reflexes. Churchill had been only a few days in office when Asquith asked him to wind up a debate on Natal on May 13, but did not take the trouble to inform Crewe, who, upon finding out, let Churchill know that he did not want him to speak. Churchill protested that he had no intention of interfering in the affairs of his department. Crewe replied that he did not want to be bound by Churchill's views without prior consultation, since he did not have the faintest idea what he planned to say. "No department can be conducted on such lines," he said, "and certainly none ever will by me." The argument flew back and forth on a current of notes. Churchill said that Crewe should be glad to have the help of a colleague. Crewe could not help thinking that when Churchill had been at the Colonial Office, he would have resented someone outside the department conducting a debate. Churchill said the course of the debate was so obvious that there was hardly room for a mistake, except on the assumption which Crewe made so freely that his personal clumsiness would upset a delicate situation. He had devoted two hours of a busy afternoon to preparing the debate and had canceled private engagements in order to be present. He then had received a verbal message through a secretary that he should not speak. There was no need to adopt a method openly discourteous to a colleague and cruelly embarrassing to the young man who had brought the message. Outgunned, Crewe retreated into saying it was all a misunderstanding, but such incidents did not enhance good fellowship in the Cabinet.[19]

In his two years at the Board of Trade, Churchill turned an archaic, sprawling department into an instrument of social reform. His sense of occasion was truly phenomenal. He was like the winner in a game of musical chairs. He always knew exactly where to sit down. Already as a young officer he had shown his knack for finding the action. In his Cabinet career, he had gone to the Colonial Office at the precise moment when great matters of Empire had to be settled. He moved to the Board of Trade when colonial questions were receding and the Liberal government embarked on the reform of an obsolete social order through sweeping intervention. The Liberals had not done much in this direction under Campbell-Bannerman, but now, with Lloyd George at the Exchequer, they initiated a period of active legislation. It was part of the ongoing struggle at the core of British political life between those who oppose all change on principle and those who consider it necessary. The lower orders wanted their seat at the table. It had not been thought until then that the government should do anything to help the poor, who were poor, just as the king was king, by divine right. That was left to churches and private charities. Prodded by Lloyd George, the Asquith government undertook to make matters such as unemployment its concern. It was, after all, in society's interest that something be done for the needy, since the unemployed had a tendency to riot. Churchill saw in social reform "the untrodden field of politics," and embarked on a brief career as a radical, for welfare legislation did not command the wholehearted support of the Asquith Cabinet. The Board of Trade, although it had no mandate for social reform, was a good place to "interfere from."

The world of the dispossessed was one that Churchill did not know first hand; he had to take lessons from the Fabian Socialist couple Sidney and Beatrice Webb, who helped focus his undisciplined reformist energies, and from his young radical friend Charles Masterman, to whom he poured out his hopes and plans and ambitions. Full of the poor, whom he had recently discovered, he felt that he was called by providence to do something for them. "Why have I always been kept safe within a hair's breadth of death," he asked Masterman, "except to do something like this?" "I'm not going to live long" was another refrain. "You can't deny that you enjoy it immensely," Masterman said, "the speeches, the crowds, the sense of increasing power." "Of course I do," Churchill said, "thou shalt not muzzle the ox when he treadeth out the corn—that shall be my plea at the day of judgment." He was just an extraordinarily gifted boy, Masterman thought, with genius and astonishing energy.[20]

It was not only his sense of occasion but his ability to rise to the occasion that singled Churchill out. His reputation was: Give him any job and he will do it remarkably well. Without missing a beat, he had moved from the intricacies of the Transvaal constitution and the importation of Chinese coolies to labor negotiations and trade disputes. His ability to digest great masses of unfamiliar data seemed unlimited. The way he imposed his personal style and pace on an encrusted bureaucracy was equally impressive. After making himself an expert on England's overseas territories, on native uprisings, on the rights of subject peoples, he had to switch tracks and defend his department in the House on topics such as these: hop substitutes in beer, the Port of London, lighthouse-keepers' salaries, the testing of railroad weighing machines, the importation of boneless meat, the advantages of daylight saving time, fat and tallow prices, the cause of death of an Asiatic fireman on a merchant ship, grants to piers and harbors, the lighting of staircases in railway stations, the persons best able to stand stokehole heat in the tropics, the regulation of artillery fire in the Thames estuary, and the import duty on mackerel from the United States.

All the above matters, and many more, were under the jurisdiction of the Board of Trade. And yet Churchill felt deprived. "I've got this pie too late," he complained. "Lloyd George has pulled out all the plums."[21] David Lloyd George—the Welsh wizard, the son of a schoolmaster who died when David was an infant, so that he was brought up by the village cobbler—here was a man to admire, to model himself on. They were both outsiders who did not fit into the ordained slots of English politics, they both had a sense of destiny, and it had been said of both of them that they would be Prime Minister. Both were fiery Hotspurs on the platform, and both had minds unburdened by what Hazlitt called "the regular gradations of a classical education." The renegade grandson of a duke and the Welshman whose whole youth had been a rebellion against the aristocracy shared the true reformist zeal.

This man, short like himself, eleven years older, with a leonine head too large for his body, and bright-blue eyes that saw through the surface of things, was someone to learn from. One day, when Churchill stopped to chat with Violet Asquith in her little sitting room on the garden of 10 Downing Street, she noticed a new inflection in his voice and said, "You've been talking to Lloyd George." "And why shouldn't I?" he asked. "Of course there's no reason why you shouldn't, but he's 'come off' on you. You are talking like him instead of yourself."[22]

Churchill thought Lloyd George was the greatest political genius he had ever met and became his lieutenant and henchman. They were dubbed Cleon (the shoemaker demagogue of Athens) and Alcibiades (the renegade aristocrat who joined the rabble). Churchill considered Lloyd George the greatest master at getting things done and putting things through that he had ever known. He saw a man of great imagination and foresight, with an unlimited capacity for work, whose powers of persuasion were based on the insight that "a man convinced against his will is of the same opinion still." He saw a man who had the power of seeing, in moments when everyone was asking about the next step, the step after that. Everyone called Churchill "Winston"; very few called Lloyd George "David"—Churchill was among them.

He did not for the moment see the unscrupulousness that was bound up with Lloyd George's ambition. When Asquith formed his government, Lloyd George leaked the Cabinet changes to the *Daily Chronicle*. Furious, Asquith asked Churchill to raise the matter with him. Wrapping himself in the cloak of humble birth, Lloyd George wrote Asquith: "Men whose promotion is not sustained by birth or other favoring conditions are always liable to be assailed with unkind suspicions of this sort . . ."[23]

Lloyd George welcomed Churchill as a disciple, while knowing that his ambition equaled his own. Cleon and Alcibiades were at the same time allies and secret rivals for Asquith's succession and the party leadership. When Lloyd George's fellow MP Sir Herbert Lewis asked him if he trusted Churchill, he replied, "I'm afraid I don't." "I would not trust him a yard," Lewis said. "If he saw a chance to pass you he would not hesitate a moment." "I know he would not," Lloyd George said. "It is his nature to go ahead, but I have not the least doubt that he would be willing enough to pick me up afterwards."[24] A Max Beerbohm cartoon showed them on the terrace of the House of Commons. Fingering a coin, Churchill said: "Come, we must toss for it, Davie." Stroking his chin, Lloyd George replied: "Ah, but Winnie, would either of us as loser abide by the result?"

For the moment, however, Churchill sat in his office, the former drawing room of a converted mansion in Whitehall Gardens, with a little bronze bust of Napoleon on his writing table, content to finish up what Lloyd George had started. The first order of business was the Port of London Bill, replacing the many private dock companies with one single Port of London Authority and giving the dockers a charter protecting them from exploitation. Churchill saw the bill through the House, warning that if it was not passed, "the docks which have already been called obsolescent will have to be allowed to obsolesce into obsoleteness." The next order of business was a bill to improve safety conditions in coal mines by reducing to eight the daily number of hours that a miner worked underground. The mines were under the Home Office, but somehow Churchill appropriated the bill and brought it to a successful conclusion. On July 6, winding up the debate on the Second Reading, he introduced the novel idea that workers should have leisure time: "The general march of industrial democracy is not towards inadequate hours of work, but towards sufficient hours of leisure. That is the movement among the working people all over the country. . . . They demand time to look about them, time to see their homes by daylight, to see their children, time to think and read and cultivate their gardens—time, in short, to live. . . ."[25]

One of the Tories who spoke against the bill, a new member making his maiden speech, said that he was an employer "who had never had a strike or a lock-out." As a partner in an established firm of ironmasters, he was against legislation on matters that could be worked out in an amicable way. This champion of paternalism was Stanley Baldwin, who, despite his late start, would be Prime Minister before Churchill. The Coal Mines Bill passed by 390 to 120. Churchill was less lucky with the Licensing Bill, the darling of temperance reformers, which was designed to reduce the number of pubs by thirty thousand over fourteen years by canceling licenses. The lobby of brewers and distillers was too strong and the drinking public too numerous. He was annoyed when Bonar Law, in a speech on July 27, misquoted him as saying "the publicans are all Tories; we will have no mercy on them." After passing in the House of Commons, the bill was thrown out by the Lords in November.

In the meantime, Lloyd George piloted through his Old Age Pensions Bill, which promised five shillings a week for those over the age of seventy whose income was not more than eight shillings a week. This was seen as a reckless measure by the Liberal leader Lord Rosebery, who called it "a scheme so prodigal of expenditure [that it] might be dealing a blow at the Empire which could be almost mortal." With much shaking of heads, the House of Lords let it pass. Although the scheme had been initiated when Asquith was at the Treasury, Lloyd George was remembered as the man who gave the old folk five shillings a week.

Churchill was remembered as the man who gave the unemployed Labour Exchanges. Inspired by the example of Germany, which already had unemployment insurance and clearinghouses for the out-of-work, he wanted to "thrust a big slice of Bismarckianism over the whole underside of our industrial system, and await the consequences whatever they may be with a good conscience." Labour Exchanges were state-run employment agencies that told workers where to find jobs. In a small country like England with good trains it was easy to go where the jobs were.

Beatrice Webb, who with her husband promoted the idea, told Churchill: "If you are going to deal with unemployment, you must have the boy Beveridge." She arranged a dinner on March 10, 1908, where Churchill met twenty-nine-year-old William Beveridge, an Oxford don who wrote editorials for the *Morning Post* and had done social work in London's East End. The dinner conversation that night was eclectic. . . . St. Paul had been the first Fabian . . . Churchill was still unused to being called a Liberal . . . Salvation Army officers were a new religious caste . . . People were divided by temperament into A's (aristocrats, artists, and anarchists) and B's (benevolents, bourgeois, and bureaucrats) . . . When Beveridge got around to explaining about Labour Exchanges, he wasn't sure that Churchill grasped what he meant. Beatrice Webb had warned him, you never quite knew what he would hand back to you as his version of your idea. Beveridge was not that impressed by his cleverness either; he seemed rather tired and inconsecutive— but he was amusing to listen to.[26]

Churchill was impressed enough by Beveridge to hire him in July to set up the machinery for Labour Exchanges. In doing so, he created within the Board of Trade a Ministry of Labour, and became one of the architects of the modern welfare state. Beveridge recalled that ministers considered the Board of Trade a stepping-stone to something better, and that in his first six years there he served under four bosses—Churchill, Sydney Buxton, John Burns, and Walter Runciman. The permanents regarded themselves as the soul of the Board, while the ministers were pleasant though sometimes embarrassing phantoms. Churchill was the exception, for in his short time there, he showed how a strong personality could in a few months change the course of social legislation. It was fun being a civil servant, Beveridge thought, because they had a government that was really doing something. And Churchill was fun to work with. Beveridge remembered going to see him at home one morning with the first list of Divisional Women Officers for the Labour Exchanges. Resting in bed, Churchill took the list, signed it, and said: "Let there be women."[27]

For his colleagues in the Cabinet, however, Churchill was not always so much fun. In June 1908, prompted by Lloyd George, he attacked Haldane's army estimates. It was one of the contradictions in Churchill's makeup that while fascinated with all things military, and rushing off to Europe every summer to attend maneuvers, he continued to advocate economy for the Army. At first he had copied his father. Now, he had another reason: the money saved on the Army could be used for social programs. He also had not forgotten the way he had been treated by Kitchener and other staff officers, and would have agreed with Clemenceau that "war is too important to be left to generals."

Appointed to a Cabinet subcommittee on the estimates with two other retrenchers, Lloyd George and Lewis Harcourt, he produced a long memo on June 18 arguing that the British Army was too large and expensive, and that there must be a reduction of staffs and of the medical, transport, ordnance, and engineer services. Viscount Esher, a confidant of the King and an expert on army matters, of whom it was said that he made a mark on the events of his time through the application of great social gifts, was shocked by Churchill's frontal attack on Haldane. What a strange move for a young minister! Haldane was the most popular Minister of War with senior officers that Esher had ever seen. He would remain in position, but Churchill would be repulsed with heavy losses.[28]

Haldane was not so sure. Churchill was a dangerous rival, who obviously wanted to replace him at the War Office, with the backing of Lloyd George. Haldane was another of those senior officials who had congratulated Churchill on his swift rise and were now biting their tongues. Always serene under attack, he prepared the case for his estimates. Richard Burdon Haldane was one of the strangest Secretaries of War who ever served England, and one of the best. A member of an old Scottish landed family, he had as a young man obtained a doctorate in philosophy from Göttingen University and fallen under the spell of German culture. He knew Kant by heart, translated Schopenhauer, and wrote a book of Hegelian inspiration called *The Reign of Relativity*. In some ways he was the Liberal counterpart of Balfour, a patrician born to wealth with a philosophical bent, and like Balfour a lifelong bachelor. But Balfour was lean and distinguished, while Haldane was so heavy and ponderous, with his smooth, round face, eunuchlike voice and epicene waddle, that he looked and sounded like a stage butler. King Edward, whom self-regard made tolerant of corpulence, said to him as they sat down to dinner at Windsor: "Mr. Haldane, you are too fat." Also unlike Balfour, who had discreet love affairs with wellborn ladies, Haldane had no female attachments other than his mother, to whom he wrote every day until she died at the age of one hundred. He had been engaged to a young woman who broke it off without giving a reason. An admirer of Oscar Wilde, he visited the writer in Holloway prison after his conviction on charges of sodomy to try to boost his morale. When he went to the War Office in December 1905, Campbell-Bannerman, who had doubts about the appointment, said: "We shall now see how Schopenhauer gets on in the Kailyard." A kailyard was a cabbage garden; Campbell-Bannerman saw Haldane dropping from the lofty and theoretical to the earthy and practical. To everyone's surprise, the philosopher got on wonderfully well with the generals. He led by seeming to defer. But the language he used when asked what reforms he had in mind raised some eyebrows. He said that he was a young and blushing virgin just united to a bronzed warrior and that no result of the union would appear for at least nine months.[29]

Skeptical of his own abilities, Haldane once confided to Lord Milner: "I have no gift of expression and no real capacity for managing men—much less leading them."[30] But many said he had the finest mind in the Cabinet. He also had Asquith's backing. They had been young solicitors and young MP's together, and Haldane had been the best man at Asquith's wedding to Margot Tennant.

Refuting Churchill a week after his assault, Haldane pointed out that some of the problems he had raised simply did not exist. Compared to the European nations, the British Army was smaller than it had been in Wellington's time or even in Marlborough's. The army staffs were proportionately smaller than the staffs of the seven leading European powers. The German expeditionary force was far greater than the infant British force Churchill was complaining about. After all, Haldane said in a phrase that would find its full resonance in 1914, Britain had "certain Treaty obligations which might compel us to intervene on the Continent."[31] Haldane was not so easy to catch out. If he had not fought Churchill and Lloyd George in 1908, there would have been no British Expeditionary Force in 1914.

Still the anti-Haldane campaign continued, and on June 25 Esher found him agitated and nervous over a story in the *Times* that said: ". . . In the category of rumors which are not necessarily idle may be put the rumor that there is a possibility of Lord Loreburn's resigning the Lord Chancellorship. Nothing definite can be said upon the subject except that in the event of such a change it is expected that Mr. Haldane will succeed to the Woolsack. In connection with the post of Secretary of State for War, if thus vacated, Mr. Churchill's name is mentioned." Haldane went straight to Asquith and told him that nothing would induce him to leave the War Office. His back was against the wall, and he was resolved not to agree to the reduction of a single infantry battalion, cavalry regiment, or artillery battery. King Edward backed him, saying: "I agree that Haldane must not resign, it would be rank cowardice."[32]

The next day, Asquith took the tactful Esher aside and asked him to speak to Churchill and compose the quarrel. At the Board of Trade, he and Churchill talked for two hours. Churchill was clever and ingenious, Esher thought, but wild and impractical. He thought he was Napoleon. There was Bonaparte's bust on his desk. Thank God Britain was not governed by a Directoire. At last Churchill conceded the difficulty of forcing Haldane's hand and the undesirability of breaking up the government.[33] To placate Churchill, Haldane invited him to the War Office to study departmental papers that were "marked" for him. This unusual procedure led to a Question in the House: "Whether the President of the Board of Trade had a room placed at his disposal at the War Office for the purpose of giving him access to departmental papers?" Haldane saved his army budget, and when Churchill and Lloyd George challenged the Admiralty later that year, they took care to prepare a better case.

Beaten back by Haldane, the "Heavenly Twins," as Churchill and Lloyd George had been dubbed, shifted their attention to foreign policy. Sir Edward Grey, Foreign Secretary since December 1905, was another child of privilege, who had "stepped into generalship without ever doing any soldiering," gliding effortlessly from Winchester to Oxford to Parliament to ministerial rank. When he went to his family estate of Fallodon in Scotland on weekends, he was able to stop trains by request at the tiny station a few hundred yards from his door, an ancient right his family had acquired when the railroad had been given right-of-way through their land. But private means did not obscure a social conscience, and Balfour described him as "a curious combination of the old-fashioned Whig and the Socialist." A thin-lipped, beak-nosed, mournful-eyed man known for his reserve and his passion for fishing, he had sunk into depression since the death of his wife, Dorothy, in a carriage accident in 1906. And yet he was an able if not a great Foreign Secretary, who steadfastly followed the traditional British policy of balance of power in Europe: Britain must be the ally of the second-strongest power on the Continent, at the moment France, defeated and amputated of Alsace-Lorraine (now Elsass-Lothringen) in 1871 by Germany, which was building up its Army and Navy to alarming proportions.

Lloyd George, however, was suspicious of the French and partial to the Germans. He admired German social reforms and German patriotism. He was friendly with the German ambassador in London, Count Metternich, and when he visited Berlin, he was invited to dinner by the German Chancellor, Dr. von Bethmann-Hollweg, with whom he lifted steins of foamy beer, although he proclaimed himself a teetotaler. He was sympathetic to German fears of encirclement by France and Russia, and shared German misgivings about England's ruling caste.

Lloyd George transmitted his fondness for Germany to Churchill, who had no foreign policy experience but was quite prepared to adopt a public position on a matter about which he knew nothing. At a miners' rally in Swansea on August 15, 1908, Churchill made what may have been the most wrongheaded and irresponsible speech of his entire career. Curiously enough, the man who became the symbol of resistance to Germany in two world wars started out as an appeaser of Germany, bent on cutting Britain's military and naval strength because he was blind to the danger of Germany's military buildup. At Swansea he made his case:

"I have been astonished and grieved to read much of the wild language which has been used lately by people who ought to know better . . . about our relations with Germany. I think it is greatly to be deprecated that persons should try to spread the belief in this country that war between Great Britain and Germany is inevitable. It is all nonsense . . . there is no collision of primary interests—big, important interests—between Great Britain and Germany in any quarter of the globe. . . . Look at it from any point of view you like, and I say you will come to this conclusion in regard to the relations between England and Germany, that there is no real cause of difference between them, and although there may be snapping and snarling in the newspapers and in the London clubs, these two great people have nothing to fight about, have no prize to fight for, and have no place to fight in. What does all this snapping and snarling amount to, after all? How many people do you suppose there are in Germany who really want to make a murdering attack on this country? I do not suppose in the whole of that great population of fifty or sixty millions of inhabitants there are ten thousand persons who would seriously contemplate such a hellish and wicked crime; and how many do you think there are in this country? I do not believe there are even that number to be found in our country if you exclude the inmates of Bedlam and writers in the *National Review*. . . . far and wide throughout the masses of the British dominions there is no feeling of ill-will towards Germany. I say we honor that strong, patient industrious German people, who have been for so many centuries a prey to

234

European intrigue and a drudge amongst the nations of the Continent. Now in the fullness of time, after many tribulations, they have by their virtues and valor won themselves a foremost place in the front of civilization. . . . We rejoice in everything that brings them good; we wish them well from the bottom of our heart . . ."[34]

This ode to Anglo-German partnership was received with cheers by Lloyd George and with consternation by the Foreign Office and the Crown. Then touring Germany, Lloyd George telegraphed from Hamburg: "Your Swansea speech was tiptop, and pleased the Germans immensely."[35] Less pleased was King Edward, afraid that such speeches would lull Englishmen into a false sense of security. He wanted Grey to reprove the Heavenly Twins for trespassing on his bailiwick. The King's secretary, Sir Francis Knollys, wrote Sir Charles Hardinge, the Permanent Under-Secretary to the Foreign Office, on August 24: "It is most unfair on Grey that he should be hampered and his Department invaded by a couple of ignorant and irresponsible men like Lloyd George and Mr. Churchill, who are not loyal to their colleagues, who spend most of their time in unprincipled intrigue and who act as they do for their own party purposes."[36] Hardinge replied that Grey had wired Lloyd George in Germany not to discuss naval armaments or any other sensitive subject with his hosts. Grey had also pointed out to Churchill the fallacy of some of the statements in his Swansea speech, and the undesirability of his embarking on questions of foreign policy in his political speeches.[37]

Once burned, Grey was more watchful of Churchill's activities. When Churchill asked the Foreign Office to help him make arrangements to meet French Prime Minister Clemenceau and other political figures while on a trip to Paris in January 1909, Grey warned him not to set himself up as an exponent of government views on foreign policy questions. Churchill angrily responded that he found the warning undeserved and uncivil—Grey had formed a totally false impression. Grey replied that ". . . you, especially you, cannot discuss politics with prominent political people abroad as a private individual. Importance will be attached to all you say, in such circumstances; it will certainly give rise to much talk and probably to some reports in the French Press, which may be misleading. . . ."[38]

On the same day that Churchill made his pro-German speech at Swansea, his engagement to Clementine Hozier was announced on the court page of the *Times*. After her tour of Europe, Clemmie had gone to Cowes on the Isle of Wight, where Churchill sent her letters expressing continuing interest.

Marriage was in the air. His brother Jack had married on August 8, leaving the church on the arm of his beautiful bride, Gwendeline, under an arch of crossed Yeomanry swords. Churchill had thrown an old slipper after the departing car. He was going to Blenheim for a house party with the F. E. Smiths and wanted Clemmie to join him there so that he could learn the secret of her strange mysterious eyes. She need have no apprehension about coming, for he never took steps of which he was not sure. He hoped she would like his cousin Sunny, who was so different from him. Sunny was so absolutely dependent on feminine influence for the peace and harmony of his soul that he went to great lengths to understand the fair sex. Churchill, however, saw himself as a clumsy novice with women. This was, he rationalized, because he was so self-reliant and self-contained that he did not need them.[39]

Although embarrassed to be going to Blenheim without a personal maid, Clemmie accepted. As she rode on the train to Oxford on August 10, counting the telephone posts flashing by the window, she felt shy and tired. She sensed what was coming. It was like a dream. Churchill was solicitous and promised to take her for a walk in the rose garden the next morning after breakfast. But he overslept, and Clemmie was so annoyed she thought of leaving for London. In the afternoon they went for a walk to the lake. A thunderstorm surprised them, and they found shelter in a little Greek temple, where Churchill proposed, as he had planned to, in the grandiose and historical setting of the palace. Emerging from the temple after the rain, Churchill spotted F. E. Smith, and, dancing across the lawn, flung his arms around his neck and blurted out the news that Clemmie had accepted. That night, Clemmie sent him a note with a heart drawn around the word "Winston."[40]

The next day, they took the train to London to ask Clemmie's mother's consent. Churchill waited while Clemmie went to Abingdon Villas alone to break the news to Min (her nickname for Blanche) and to show her the lovely engagement ring, a fat ruby and two diamonds, one of the rings Randolph had given Jennie. Blanche knew it would be a good marriage. Winston was so like his father, hated by those who had not come under his charm, but gentle and tender and affectionate.[41] Returning to Blenheim, they sent love notes to each other's rooms, Churchill sending heaps of love and four kisses,[42] and Clemmie writing *"Je t'aime passionnément"* (I love you passionately)—in French she was less shy.

The wedding date was set for September 12, and Lord Hugh Cecil, Churchill's ally from the Hooligan days, agreed to be best man. In his preachy way, he told Churchill that marriage would be excellent for him mentally, morally, and politically, for a bachelor was regarded as morally unprincipled.[43] During the brief engagement, Clemmie had doubts. Was she doing the right thing in marrying a public figure, an ambitious man who would always put his career first? Was she equal to the task? Consumed by his work as he was, would he have time for her? She thought of breaking off, but a stern letter from her brother, Bill, reminded her that she had already terminated at least two engagements, one publicly, and that it was unthinkable of her to humiliate and make an exhibition of a public figure like Churchill.[44] But more than her brother's letter, it was Churchill's affectionate attentiveness that won her over, and she wondered "how I have lived twenty-three years without you."

At 2 P.M. on September 12, 1908, eight hundred guests filed into St. Margaret's, in Westminster, the parish church of the House of Commons. Arriving late, the poet Wilfrid Blunt could not find a seat and was beckoned to the family pew by Blanche Hozier. She was surrounded by former lovers, Blunt observed: there on one side was Hugo Wemyss, with Baron Redesdale in the next pew.[45] In the vestry, Lloyd George signed the register as Churchill drew him into a political discussion. Good God, thought Lloyd George, even on his wedding day he could not get off the subject.[46] One of the bridesmaids, Clare Frewen (the daughter of Jennie's sister Clara), was chattering about the amours into which Lady Blanche ceaselessly plunged when a burst of music brought the bride into the church on the arm of her brother, who was in his naval sub-lieutenant's uniform.[47] Clemmie's reddish-gold hair was set off by a gown of shimmering white satin, and her flowing veil of soft white tulle was held in place by a coronet of fresh orange blossoms. What a glittering prize, Blunt thought; here was surely one of the nicest and most beautiful women in society. Then came Winston, for once looking pale, and dressed in a manner that *Tailor and Cutter* described as " 'neither fish, flesh, nor fowl,' and . . . one of the greatest failures as a wedding garment we have ever seen, giving the wearer a sort of glorified coachman appearance."

Nearly thirty-four, Churchill had lost hair and gained weight, and his face sometimes settled into that fixed expression of pugnacity the world would come to know. It was a powerful though ugly face, Blunt thought. At least he said the vows clearly, whereas Clemmie was almost unintelligible. And there was Jennie in a beaver-colored satin gown, still beautiful although a bit broad in the hip at fifty-four, but seeming to some as youthful as the bride. Bishop Welldon gave the address and spoke of the beneficial influence exercised by the wives of statesmen. Then the scene shifted to the reception at Lady St. Helier's house. Mr. and Mrs. Winston Churchill stood in an open window, watching the Pearlies dance in the street. As President of the Board of Trade, he had restored some of their ancient rights as street vendors. Then it was off to Blenheim, the place of his birth, for their first night together, leaving behind a roomful of presents: a gold-headed malacca cane from King Edward, a scallop-edged silver tray inscribed with the autographs of his Cabinet colleagues, a silver bowl from Haldane, a silver fruit basket from Lloyd George, a beaver rug from Reginald McKenna, a silver cigarette box from Balfour, the complete works of Jane Austen from Asquith, the complete works of Sainte-Beuve from Eddie Marsh, a pair of old wine stands from the Hooligan Ian Malcolm, a carpet from Nathan Laski, one of the leaders of the Jewish community in Manchester, a card case from his onetime enemy Henry Labouchère, and a cash gift of five hundred pounds from that friendly financier, Sir Ernest Cassel.

Everything had gone well, Churchill wrote his mother after the wedding night. There was no need for any anxiety. From Blenheim they traveled to Italy and spent happy days in Venice, loitering and loving, a good and serious occupation for honeymooners, thought the bridegroom, for which the histories furnished respectable precedents. Churchill wrote his mother-in-law: "I find love-making a serious and delightful occupation,"[48] in the tone of a neophyte reporting to an expert, which seems incredible in a man approaching thirty-four. If he applied himself to love-making as he did to the Transvaal constitution and the Labour Exchanges, he was bound to make up for lost time.

Churchill and Clemmie remained married for fifty-seven years, at a time when divorce and remarriage became accepted in society. It was by all accounts, including his own, a solid and happy marriage. He liked to say that his ability to persuade his wife to marry him had been his most brilliant achievement. In his old age he confessed: "My marriage was much the most fortunate and joyous event which happened to me in the whole of my life. For what can be more glorious than to be united with a being incapable of an ignoble thought?" But Clemmie was no vacant-eyed ornament for a rising politician. Strong-willed and opinionated, she sought and obtained full partnership in her husband's life. They settled, as so many couples do, into complementary roles—Churchill was impulsive and outgoing, Clemmie deliberate and reserved; Churchill was extravagant, while Clemmie, who had always managed on little money, clutched her copy of *House Books on Twelve*

Shillings a Week. Churchill had a fun-loving nature, he liked to drink and gamble, but Clemmie had too often seen her mother squander the family budget at the roulette table. There was a rigid and censorious side in her that would affirm itself with age. She was the wielder of the moral pruning shears, snipping off from the bark of her husband's nature twigs that grew in the wrong direction.

Toward those she disliked, like her mother-in-law, she was cool and distant. She thought Jennie was vain and frivolous and a figure of ridicule for having married a man half her age. Also in her bad books was F. E. Smith, whom she suspected of encouraging Churchill to gamble and drink when they went off to training camp in the Oxfordshire Yeomanry. Nor could she abide his cousins Ivor and Freddie Guest (the sons of Lord Wimborne, who had married one of Randolph's sisters, Cornelia). Once, when Ivor was her bridge partner at Canford Manor, the Wimborne home, he lost his temper and threw his cards in her face. She insisted on leaving the next morning, taking her reluctant husband with her.

With Churchill, Clemmie's reserve melted, and they lapsed into a private language of intimacy. She was the Cat or sweetest Kat, the Catling or Clemmicat. He was the Pug or Amber Pug. Their letters were strewn with these pet symbols. It was a return to the illustrations in children's books, to the warm smells and security of the nursery. The ghost of Mrs. Everest accompanied them into the bedroom. It was as if marriage allowed Churchill to regress innocently to the care and cuddling of infancy. Since his Victorian upbringing had taught him not to talk about sexuality in an adult way, he veiled it with baby talk. Clemmie became an adorable but slightly unreal pussycat. He wanted to stroke her baby cheeks and make her purr softly in his arms.

Upon returning to London, Churchill and his bride moved into his bachelor flat at 12 Bolton Street while they looked for a house and began to go out in society. At a small dinner party at 10 Downing Street, Clemmie complained to Violet Asquith that Churchill was force-feeding her books to complete her education. He had shut her up with Maeterlinck's *The Life of a Bee,* a subject that did not prick her interest. She confided to Violet that she was discovering her husband's odd habits, one of which was his expensive underclothes of finely woven pink silk. When Violet taxed him with self-indulgence, Churchill said: "I have a very delicate and sensitive cuticle which demands the finest covering." Rolling up his sleeve to uncover his forearm, he said: "Look at the texture of my cuticle—*feel* it. I have a cuticle without a blemish —except on one small portion of my anatomy where I sacrificed a piece of my skin to accommodate a wounded brother officer on my way back from the Sudan campaign."[49]

When Beatrice Webb had lunch with the Churchills on a Sunday in October, she thought Clemmie was charming, well bred, pretty, and earnest. It was not a good match, for Clemmie was not rich, which was all to Winston's credit. When Mrs. Webb had first met him, in 1903, Churchill had seemed bumptious, shallow-minded, reactionary, and cynical. Now that he had adopted the Webbs' Labour Exchange scheme, she thought him brilliantly able, not just a phrase-monger, with more intellect than Lloyd George, and a more attractive personality—less of a preacher and more of a statesman.[50] In his urge to accomplish great things at the Board of Trade, Churchill was increasingly drawn to the Webbs' Fabian policies. His concentration on Labour Exchanges and unemployment insurance, and his hypnotic attraction to Lloyd George, made him adopt a strangely parochial position in military matters. After being rebuffed by Haldane, Churchill and Lloyd George turned their paring knives on McKenna and his naval estimates, sparking a three-month government crisis that became known as the "Great Naval Scare." In the heat of battle, the Asquith government tottered but did not fall, and the Heavenly Twins were once again beaten back.

Attacking the Navy was out of character for Churchill, who had always been a believer in the "Blue Water School"—Britain's military supremacy depended on a small army and a powerful navy. The accepted naval policy was that of the two-power standard. That is, Britain must have 10 percent more than the combined number of capital ships of the next two strongest powers. With the advent of the torpedo, the Admiralty, inspired by the First Sea Lord, Admiral Sir John Arbuthnot Fisher, began building floating fortresses called dreadnoughts, with eleven-inch-thick armor and ten 12-inch guns. To critics of these monster battleships, Fisher pointed out that the Germans, who were not fools, were building them too, even though it was a great nuisance since they would have to enlarge the Kiel Canal to accommodate them.

The first two dreadnoughts were laid down in 1905, and the policy was to build four more a year. But construction fell behind, and in 1908, when Admiral von Tirpitz built four all-big-gun ships to Britain's two, the Germans appeared to be entering in a race for naval supremacy. In his push for more dreadnoughts, Fisher was backed by the cunning courtier Viscount Esher, who wrote, in a letter published by the *Times* on February 6, that "there is not a man in Germany from the Emperor downwards who would not welcome the fall of Sir John Fisher." One subscriber to the *Times*, the Kaiser, was so outraged by this remark that he wrote a long personal letter to Lord Tweedmouth, the First Lord of the Admiralty, as one navy man to another and one gentleman to another: "It is absolutely nonsensical and untrue that the German Naval Bill is to provide a Navy meant as a 'challenge to British Naval supremacy.' The German fleet is built *against* nobody, at all. It is solely built *for* Germany's needs." Referring to Esher's onetime post as Secretary of the Office of Works, the Kaiser concluded: "Now I am at a loss to tell whether the supervision of the foundations and drains of the Royal Palace is apt to qualify someone for the judgment of naval affairs in general." There was some truth in the Kaiser's protest, for he and Von Tirpitz had secretly agreed to let a 10 to 6 ratio stand in favor of the British fleet.

In his single-minded pursuit of military economy, Churchill was quite ready to agree with the Kaiser that there was no threat in the growth of the German Navy. He still felt that suspicion of German intentions was shortsighted, and that Germany did not intend to disturb the peace of Europe. Lloyd George, who had been to Germany and sounded out its leaders, bolstered Churchill's convictions. The naval construction that was going on, he told Churchill, was only intended to relieve unemployment in German shipyards.

"Jacky" Fisher thought otherwise. As early as 1906, long before Churchill started making pro-German speeches, Fisher predicted that "Germany is our only possible foe for years to come." In 1908, with uncanny accuracy, he announced that war with Germany would start in the late summer of 1914, when the enlargement of the Kiel Canal was completed and Von Tirpitz had enough ships to risk war. In a conversation with King Edward in March 1908, he seriously proposed doing a "Copenhagen," the same sort of preemptive strike on the German Navy that Nelson had done in 1801 by sinking the Danish fleet in the harbor of Copenhagen. It was better to fight a tiger than its cubs. Since a war with Germany was certain, why let the enemy pick the moment? The King told him he was mad.[51]

Fisher's madness was the subject of lively discussion in naval and political circles. Since his career and Churchill's were intertwined, it is necessary to take a closer look at one of the great outsiders of the British Navy, so at variance with the model of calm and obedient uprightness on the recruiting posters. Fisher was born in 1841 in Ceylon, where his father, an army officer, had settled as a coffee planter. The slightly Oriental cast of his features, the full-lipped mouth and the round gray eyes with the curiously small pupils, led his detractors to spread the rumor that he was the son of a Singhalese princess, which accounted for his cunning and duplicity. In fact, his mother, *née* Sophia Lambe, was from London. Fisher left Ceylon when he was six and went into the Navy as a midshipman when he was thirteen. "I entered the Navy penniless, friendless, and forlorn," he said. "I have had to fight like hell, and fighting like hell has made me what I am." His fighting, however, was not done against a foreign enemy but against all the "anointed cads, no-cheesed clerks, quill-drivers and ink-spillers" who had the effrontery to disagree with him. About the only action he ever saw was the bombing of Alexandria in 1882, when he commanded the battleship *Inflexible*. After that he was put in command of the Mediterranean Fleet and tested his theory that what England needed was "a sea-going Army that we can launch forth anywhere AT AN HOUR'S NOTICE." After an exercise in which eight thousand men were embarked in nineteen minutes, a short, fat, red-haired major, livid with rage, complained to Fisher on the beach that a bluejacket had shoved him into the boat and said, "Hurry up, you bloody lobster, or I'll be 'ung." "The man *would* have been hanged," Fisher told the major.[52]

In 1892, he came to the Admiralty as Third Sea Lord and was promoted to Second Sea Lord in 1902 and to First Sea Lord in 1904. It was during these years that he made his reputation as the first great reformer of the Navy in a century. The Navy was in a rut. It had never fought under modern conditions. Everything was archaic. A sailor was punished because the "S" in the word "Sovereign" on his cap ribbon was not directly over his nose. Spit and polish were more important than war readiness. Burdened with the duties of Empire, the Navy had become a "show the flag" navy.

Fisher's presence was felt like a hundred brooms in a cobweb-filled room. Applying his principle that history was a record of exploded maxims, he adopted everything new, director firing, the water-tube boiler, the long-range-firing dreadnought. Everywhere his hand was felt, from the appointment of an Inspector of Target Practice to a rule that every ship must have its bakery to a regulation limiting the number of ships that could be absent for repairs at any one time from each fleet.

Naturally, this whirlwind of activity caused resentment. Admirals with long years of service grew purple at the mention of his name. Naval clubs rang with the outraged sentiments of officers on half-pay. Critics fired broadsides from the decks of the *Times*. Fisher never explained and never apologized. Two of his favorite maxims were: "It is only damn fools who argue" and "*Qui s'excuse s'accuse*" (every excuse is incriminating). His method was to kick back when he was kicked. Or better yet, to practice the preemptive kick. "If any subordinate opposes me," he said, "I will make his wife a widow, his children fatherless, and his home a dunghill."[53] Favoritism was a deliberate policy. Those who agreed with him belonged to the "Fishpond." Those who did not were grouped in a "Syndicate of Discontents." The price of Fisher's reforms was a splitting of the Navy into two bitter factions that sniped and fought and played dirty tricks on each other. Every squadron, every ship, was divided into pro- and anti-Fisher camps. There was something truly loony in Fisher's compulsive rooting out of enemies. Destroying the opposition sometimes seemed a more urgent priority than the need for change. Here is how Churchill saw him: "Harsh, capricious, vindictive, gnawed by hatreds arising often from spite, working secretly or violently as occasion might suggest by methods which the typical English gentleman and public-school boy are taught to dislike and avoid, Fisher was always regarded as the 'dark angel' of the Naval Service."[54]

His habit of provocative exaggeration was another eccentricity that might have been considered amusing had he not been engaged in constant vendettas and intrigues. For all his blunt, no-nonsense manner, Fisher was a political admiral who courted support in both parties and wrote hundreds of letters to his friends in Parliament and the press, peppered with his favorite expressions: "yours till the angels smile on us," "yours till hell freezes," "yours till a cinder," "yours till we play harps," "yours till charcoal sprouts," and "yours till the next glacial period." He was a great one for exclamation points and capital letters, and for admonitions evoking deep and devious machinations: "Burn this when read!" "Destroy at once!" "Do not talk about this even in your sleep!" Fisher was so excitable that King Edward once asked him during a conversation: "Would you kindly leave off shaking your fist in my face?"[55]

Leading the Syndicate of Discontents was Admiral Charles Beresford, a charming and wealthy Irishman known as "Charlie B." His hatred of Fisher bordered on the pathological. His whole life and being were devoted to undermining the man he called "The Mulatto" and his reforms. There had never been such a rift in the British Navy, such a state of unrest. Each side had its spies. In 1906, Reginald Bacon, a captain serving under Beresford in the Mediterranean Fleet, warned Fisher that Charlie B. was criticizing his reforms to the King. In 1907, when he was put in command of the Channel Fleet, Beresford had asked for war plans to taunt Fisher, who did not believe in a Naval War Staff and had no such plans. Beresford criticized the Home

Fleet and gathered about him a group of admirals plotting Fisher's downfall. When Reginald McKenna replaced the deranged Lord Tweedmouth at the Admiralty in June 1908, he backed Fisher and demanded full cooperation from Beresford. When Charlie B. continued his agitation, he was forced into early retirement and hauled down his flag in March 1909. But he continued to attack Fisher from the floor of the House of Commons, making use of secret documents that were leaked to him by friendly officers. McKenna came to the Admiralty at a difficult time, having to cope with a climate of morose rebellion in the officer corps, and having to fight for a sharp increase in naval estimates owing to what Fisher perceived as a German menace.

On December 8, McKenna asked for an increase of 2,923,000 pounds and recommended a program of six dreadnoughts for the 1909–1910 estimates. Under the new naval law of 1908, German construction was upped to four battleships a year. The Germans were catching up. They would have thirteen battleships by 1912. Britain, if the six dreadnoughts were built, would have eighteen big ships in 1912. Even that was not enough, for the ratio of eighteen to thirteen was an abandonment of the two-power standard. There was evidence that the Germans were increasing the pace of their building. They were buying large amounts of nickel, which was used for guns, armor, and gun mountings.

Lloyd George and Churchill argued for four dreadnoughts at the most. They did not believe the Germans were speeding up their building program. The admirals were cooking up false information to frighten the Cabinet. Fisher had probably written the naval attaché in Berlin to send something that would panic the government and strengthen McKenna's hand. In any case, Lloyd George did not like McKenna, a persistent and hardworking minister who gave complete support to his First Sea Lord. His only expertise in naval affairs was that he had rowed for Cambridge. He was nothing but "a good clerk—or perhaps an accountant."[56]

The battle lines were drawn, with the Cabinet split between four- and six-dreadnought men. Fisher was shocked to find Churchill in the enemy camp, having looked upon him as an ally ever since their first meeting in 1907 in Biarritz, after which he had remarked: "I think he's quite the nicest fellow I ever met and such a quick brain that it's a delight to talk to him." His good impression was confirmed when they had lunched at the Ritz on January 18, 1908, and Churchill had told Fisher that he liked him because he "painted with a big brush." Churchill had even given him a copy of Machiavelli's *The Prince*, of which he made good use. In return, Fisher had invited Churchill aboard the Admiralty yacht in July. It would do him good. He was delighted when Churchill attacked the army estimates and told J. A. Spender: "The sacred fire burns brightly in Winston and you'll no more stop the Great Reformation in the Army than you can stop a glacier." But now Churchill's sacred fire was aimed at him. What had gotten into the man? The command of the sea, the very future of the British Navy, were in jeopardy. Who could Fisher count on? Churchill had betrayed him. Lloyd George was his sworn enemy. Asquith was "as weak as water." Haldane he had always hated, calling him "the soapy Jesuit" and "Saponaceous Napoleon B. Haldane." Every pound that Haldane took for the Army was bread out of his mouth.[57]

By December 19, the navy estimates had been discussed at two Cabinet meetings, and Lloyd George thought he and Churchill had defeated Mc-Kenna. "We have checked him for the moment at any rate," he wrote. "It looked three days ago as if he would ruin my financial plans by his extravagant demands. The danger is, I believe, over." He thanked Churchill for helping smash McKenna's fatuous estimates and for the splendid way he had raked McKenna's squadron.[58]

But the danger was not over. Fisher prepared a revised estimate asking for two more dreadnoughts in 1909–1910, bringing the total to eight. The Tory press took up the cry of "We Want Eight and We Won't Wait." On February 2, Lloyd George sent Asquith a "secret" warning that giving in to the Admiralty would split open the Liberal Party, which was committed to reduce the gigantic spending on armaments brought on by Tory recklessness. On February 8, he wrote again to complain that all their secret discussions were being leaked to the press. The main source of leakage was Fisher, who provided a continuous stream of top-secret data to his good friend J. L. Garvin, the editor of *The Observer*. This way Parliament would be informed, in case cuts were decided in the Cabinet without being brought to the attention of the House. In the meantime, Churchill fought a duel of memos with McKenna, insisting that Britain had a two-to-one superiority. McKenna replied that he had his figures wrong.[59]

The riposte to Fisher's leaks was the threat of resignation. On February 9, Lloyd George reported: "Have had complete success with the Navy. Late last night got a letter from the Prime Minister practically accepting my alternative proposals . . . but Winston, Morley, and myself had to threaten to resign. All's well that ends well."[60] Nothing had ended, and nothing was well. On February 10, Charles Masterman's wife, Lucy, noted in her diary: "There has been, and still is, a Cabinet crisis going on. . . . Lloyd George, Winston,

Morley, and Burns resisted to the verge of resignation. It is the first time the seam in the Cabinet has shown up."[61]

Also on February 10, King Edward's secretary, Sir Francis Knollys, wrote Viscount Esher: "What are Winston's reasons for acting as he does in this matter? Of course it cannot be from conviction or principle. The very idea of his having either is enough to make anyone laugh."[62] Two days later, after lunch, Esher ran into Churchill, who asked him to tell Jacky that although fond of him as ever, he would quit office rather than agree to six dread- noughts—this was not a bluff, the government would break up. Esher did not deliver the message, for he thought it was a bluff. The next day, when he saw Churchill and Lloyd George at the Board of Trade, he told them that he could not find Fisher. The majority of the country was against them, Esher warned. Six dreadnoughts stood for supremacy on the seas. To resign on that issue would ruin them. No one had ever resigned with personal triumph on a negative policy. It would be a betrayal of trust. Lloyd George, Esher thought, realized that Britain was in danger of having a *one*-power standard by 1912. Churchill did not see it, although he seemed to be looking for a way to back off from his position. But could a bridge be found, and would he walk over it? Esher's concluding words were: "If the Admiral was to go back on the six he would be irretrievably damned."[63]

The struggle continued. On February 14 Fisher tried to force the issue by leaking to Garvin the false news that the Cabinet had definitely agreed to six dreadnoughts. Fisher wondered about Churchill's stream of memos, which backed the case for four dreadnoughts with columns of technical data. Where was Churchill getting his information? He finally admitted to McKenna that he was being briefed by Admiral Sir Reginald Custance and the onetime Admiralty designer Sir William White, two of the foremost pro-Beresford men and both outspoken critics of the dreadnought policy. Seeing the dreadnought dispute as a way of forcing Fisher's resignation, they were only too glad to supply Churchill with the ammunition he needed. Fisher was aghast. Not only had Churchill abandoned the cause of the Navy, he had sided with his enemies in the Syndicate of Discontents. "Winston Churchill has been a double-dyed traitor in this business and yet he sends me messages by Esher that he loves me more than ever!" Fisher wrote Garvin on February 16.[64]

Asquith, whose responsibility went beyond the dreadnought issue, for he had to keep the government from breaking up, was beginning to lose patience with the Heavenly Twins, and wrote his wife on February 20: "Winston and

Lloyd George by their combined machinations have got the bulk of the Liberal press in the same camp . . . [they] go about darkly hinting at resignation (which is bluff) . . . but there are moments when I am disposed summarily to cashier them both. E. Grey's a great stand-by, always, sound, temperate, and strong."[65] To those outside the Cabinet, Asquith seemed hopelessly adrift. He had let the crisis drag on for nearly three months. Austen Chamberlain commented that he "jumps about like a parched pea in a frying pan, and doesn't know which way to face."[66]

On February 23, Charles Masterman underlined the gravity of the crisis in a letter to his wife. "All the life and spirit" had gone out of the government. "The uncertainty about the Naval Estimates hangs over all. Our rank and file won't listen to anything more than four Dreadnoughts and if the Government propose six they will have to depend on Tory votes and that will mean the beginning of the end."[67]

No Cabinet minutes were kept in those days, so we cannot eavesdrop on the actual deliberations on the dreadnoughts. But among the Asquith papers there is a report of one meeting on the naval estimates on February 23 in the Prime Minister's room in the House of Commons. The discussion recorded was not about the dreadnoughts but about the burdens of Empire—the great cost of the Navy being due in large part to the Admiralty's need to maintain fleets in China, South Africa, and the East Indies, for the Foreign Office, the Colonial Office, and the India Office. Commerce had to be protected, the sea-lanes had to be kept open, British presence had to be shown—the dreadnoughts were far from the only expense. Churchill was not present, but the meeting gives us a rare glimpse into the tone and substance of an Asquith Cabinet meeting.

LLOYD GEORGE: "What on earth do we want with a fleet in South Africa? What does it mean in terms of money? What is the cost of their upkeep, and of the men and so on?"

McKENNA: "So many hundreds of thousands a year."

GREY: "There are a number of places where we are constantly having to send a ship."

McKENNA: "They are always being used."

FISHER: "We are sending one ship twenty-six hundred miles up the Amazon: she will nearly get to Peru on the other side."

McKENNA: "If you were at the Board of Trade, you would have petitions objecting to any notion of giving them up. Every Chamber of Commerce in the country would petition against it."

GREY: "If a revolution breaks out in South America, we are always expected to be there."

ASQUITH: "If an earthquake happens at Kingston in Jamaica they expect you to have a cruiser on the spot, and there was the greatest indignation because there was none."

FISHER: "We have had to send vessels up the Zambezi."

ASQUITH: "The other day there was a very good case at Monrovia in Liberia. Our consul telegraphed from Monrovia, which is the capital of Liberia, and where there are about one hundred British subjects, 'Our lives are in danger, send a cruiser at once.' Where was your vessel?"

FISHER: "We had to send a vessel which was fifteen hundred miles off."

McKENNA: "Our traders say, you let lines of communication be closed between the Argentine and Great Britain, you will starve the people. They will tell you that and ask you what would happen if one foreign cruiser should get free."

LLOYD GEORGE: "We can do something in the way of cutting down there."

McKENNA: "That is a question for the Cabinet."

ASQUITH: "It is not an Admiralty question at all."

McKENNA: "We do not mind at all."

GREY: "You cannot very well go into it at this moment."

LLOYD GEORGE: "There is no time."[68]

The Cabinet was desperately looking for cuts to defray the cost of the dreadnoughts, but with the Navy committed all over the world, there was not much to be done. The resolution of the crisis was approaching, and the key figure was Grey, whom Fisher had been lobbying, and who had swung over to the six-dreadnought group. In a note that he passed to Morley during one of the critical Cabinet meetings, he said: "I fear if we say 'we lay down six this year' the party will be split. But if we do *not* promise to lay down six, I think with the figures of German shipbuilding disclosed the feeling of apprehension in the country will be such that the country will become ungovernable. There will not be only scare but *panic*. I am convinced that six must be laid for this year, but that by saying it as part of a *definite* program you will diminish the fear of *indefinite* naval expansion. . . ."

At the Cabinet meeting of February 24, it seemed that the Admiralty had lost. Asquith appeared to be siding with the retrenchers. His proposals rejected, McKenna remained behind, wondering what to do next. Grey came in and said, "You look dejected." McKenna said he was sending in his resignation. "Do you really mean that?" Grey asked. "Are you so certain you are right?" "Absolutely certain," McKenna said. "I have no alternative but to go." "If you go, I shall go too," Grey said. "I shall see Asquith."[69] Everything hinged on Grey, who, because of the soundness of his judgment and the calm and undramatic way he expressed his views, had considerable authority. To Grey, it was wrong not to build on the simple faith that the Germans might not speed up their program. At the Cabinet meeting of February 25, Asquith, prompted by Grey, offered a compromise solution. Four ships would be laid down at once and four more when the need was proven. McKenna got his three million pounds and his building program, for the additional four dreadnoughts were adopted in July. As Churchill put it, "In the end a curious and characteristic solution was reached. The Admiralty had demanded six ships; the economists offered four; and we finally compromised on eight."[70] The Great Naval Scare of 1909 was over.

In fact, there was no German acceleration. In 1912, the Germans had only nine battleships. They did not close the gap. Churchill and Lloyd George had been right in the narrow sense. But as Churchill was the first to admit, "We were absolutely wrong in relation to the deep tides of destiny. The greatest credit is due to the First Lord of the Admiralty, Mr. McKenna, for the resolute and courageous manner in which he fought his case and withstood his party on this occasion." It was thanks to McKenna that in 1914, in the first critical months of World War I, when Churchill was First Lord, the British Navy had a margin of security.

Fisher was delirious. Eight dreadnoughts a year—think of it, that was one every six weeks! Glowing with victory, he wrote the King: "I think I am most disappointed in Mr. Haldane, who has been a terrible Judas. Lloyd George and Winston Churchill, bad as they were, fought out in the open. They said they would resign if more than 4 ships—McKenna asked for 6 and we have got 8! Lloyd George is a good attorney, but he is not a Machiavelli! . . . Your Majesty has one splendid servant in the Cabinet—the Foreign Secretary. He is as much above all the rest of them as Mr. Balfour is above all his colleagues."[71]

Two nights after the decisive Cabinet meeting of February 25, Fisher was in the Athenaeum reading a newspaper when Churchill came in. Fisher nodded and went on reading. Wanting to patch things up, Churchill followed him out and was extremely cordial. Fisher told him "as a great secret" that he wanted twenty dreadnoughts before April 1912. Churchill made another attempt at friendship in a letter to which Fisher replied on February 28: "I confess I never expected you to turn against the Navy after all you had said in public and in private. (*'Et tu Brute!'*)"[72]

As Asquith pointed out to Grey, it was a serious setback for the Heavenly Twins: "The fact is that Lloyd George and Winston and John Morley feel that the course of things this week has been a complete debacle for them and their ideas, and the two former cannot help reflecting how they would have looked at this moment if they had resigned with (as Winston predicted) '90 per cent of the Liberal party behind them.' "[73]

As he sometimes did when he was wrong, Churchill fell back on the example of his father, which he invoked in a speech at Manchester on May 23: "The Naval Estimates have risen by three millions this year. I regret it; but I am prepared to justify it. There will be a further increase next year. I regret it; but within proper limits necessary to secure national safety I shall be prepared to justify it; but I hope you will not expect me to advocate a braggart and sensational policy of expenditure upon armaments. I have always been against that, as my father was before. In my judgment, a Liberal is a man who ought to stand as a restraining force against an extravagant policy. He is a man who ought to keep cool in the presence of Jingo clamor."

Churchill's ill-judged resistance to naval spending did not enhance his reputation among his Cabinet colleagues. On March 9, Charles and Lucy Masterman were dining with Edward Grey and Augustine Birrell, the Chief Secretary for Ireland, who agreed that the tendency in Churchill was to see first the rhetorical potentialities of any policy. In other words, as Asquith was to say, "He thinks with his mouth." "I think we are a very forbearing Cabinet to his chatter," Birrell said. Grey observed that Churchill had recently been lecturing him on foreign policy and had come out with: "The longer I live, the more certain I am I know all there is to be known." "Very soon," Grey said, "Winston will become incapable from sheer activity of mind, of being anything in a Cabinet but Prime Minister."[74]

For the moment, however, Churchill was too busy with his social legislation at the Board of Trade to think about higher office. He felt that he had gotten hold of a tremendous thing in the Labour Exchanges. The honor of introducing them in England was in itself a rich reward. When he presented the bill on May 18, he explained to the House: "Modern industry is national. The facilities of transport and communications knit the country together as no country has ever been knitted before. Labor alone has not profited by this improved organization. The method by which labor obtains its market today is the old method, the demoralizing method of personal application, hawking labor about from place to place, and treating a job as if it were a favor, as a thing which places a man under an obligation when he has got it."[75] The Labour Exchanges would change all that. The bill was passed with little opposition (only the trade unions were against it), and William Beveridge was appointed director of the program. When the first exchanges opened in February 1910, Churchill visited the seventeen in London. In their first year, 24,290 jobs were found outside the areas where workers registered, and often they were given travel loans. Churchill succeeded in finding a practical though partial solution for the greatest problem in the nineteenth-century industrial state—unemployment.

He also tackled the disgrace known as "sweated labor," the unskilled, the immigrants, the children, all those who were beyond the reach of trade unions or any other control, from seamstresses to dockhands. In the sweated trades, where the good employer was undercut by the worst, there were no wage negotiations. It was a morbid patch of the economy where the workers, feeble and ignorant, were easy prey to the tyranny of masters and middlemen. Regulating wages by law was only proper, Churchill thought, for these diseased and parasitic trades, where no legal minimum prevailed, and working conditions were prejudicial to physical and social welfare. Fabians like the Webbs had long wanted it. Churchill worked many hours, receiving deputations, drawing up verbatim transcripts of their complaints, and asking his staff how it could all be translated into law. "Draw a line," he told them, "below which we will not allow persons to live and yet above which they may compete with all the strength of their manhood." The Trade Boards Bill passed through the House on April 28 without a division. It covered 200,000 workers, 140,000 of them women and girls, and called for trade boards, made up of an equal number of employers and workers, who would set minimum rates for piecework in designated trades. It was the first attempt in British labor legislation to enforce a minimum wage, and turned out to be the thin edge of the welfare state wedge. In the bill, hundreds of pages of which were drafted in Churchill's own hand, people employed in shops were given the right to light and air and decent pay and their cup of tea. It was Churchill who brought the tea break into labor law. Thus, as he put it, he created "minimum standards of life and wages, of security against going to the Devil through accident, sickness, or weakness of character."

With those matters out of the way, Churchill was free to second Lloyd George in the great battle of 1909 over the "People's Budget." Lloyd George was asking for an increase of fourteen million pounds to cover social programs offering material improvement for the masses, as well as the building of dreadnoughts. How would the money be raised? By soaking the rich.

Income tax would go up from one shilling on the pound to one shilling twopence. Death duties were increased by a third on estates of more than five thousand pounds. There would be a Super Tax of sixpence on the pound for incomes of more than five thousand pounds a year. None of these items was terribly upsetting. The great outcry was over the four new land taxes, which were seen as a shocking assault on the sacred right of property. There was a mineral rights tax, a tax on increased value at the end of a lease, a development tax, and, most horrible of all, a 20 percent tax on added value when land was sold. Lloyd George wanted to skim off some of the profit from properties that had vastly increased in value because of industrial development in cities like Liverpool. He was the first Chancellor of the Exchequer to use the budget as a tool for a more equal distribution of the national income. Some of the money from the landed rich would go to the aged, the sick, the poor, and the unemployed. By one of history's ironies, Britain's purse strings were in the hands of a true radical, born poor, who had grown up believing that "all down history, nine-tenths of mankind have been grinding the corn for the remaining tenth, and been paid with the husks and bidden to thank God they had the husk."[76]

The budget was also a way of joining battle with the House of Lords, with its veto power over legislation. The issue here was constitutional. Would the Lords break the 250-year-old rule that they could not veto money bills? The budget would "kill or cure," Churchill thought. Either they would get the funds for great reforms or the Lords would veto, forcing a dissolution of Parliament and new elections.[77]

It was the Lords' veto power that had led Balfour to boast after the Tory defeat of 1906: "Whether in power, or whether in opposition, the Tory Party will control the destinies of the country." When the Tory leader Henry Chaplin called the House of Lords "the watchdog of the Constitution," Lloyd George retorted: "You mean it is Mr. Balfour's poodle! It fetches and carries for him. It barks for him. It bites anybody that he sets it on to!"[78]

It was time to tackle the Lords with their capricious use of the veto. They had passed some bills like old-age pensions and Churchill's Labour Exchanges and Trade Boards, but they had thrown out the Education Bill abolishing state support of denominational schools, the Plural Voting Bill to end the usage (mainly in Scotland) of giving more than one vote to those who owned land in more than one constituency, and the Licensing Bill, designed to curb alcoholism in the working classes by closing a number of pubs.

As Lloyd George had told Masterman, "First we said, 'We'll have the parson out of the schools.' The House of Lords said, 'No you shan't.' We said, 'What, you say we shan't? Then we'll have a go at the Scotch landlords,' and the House of Lords said, 'Hands off the Scotch landlords.' 'Then we'll go for the brewers!' Then the House of Lords will say, 'Hands off the brewers,' and we shall say, 'You won't let us touch the brewers!'" It was disgraceful, and would lead to dissolution.[79]

Churchill was particularly incensed by the rejection of the Licensing Bill. At dinner at the House of Commons with the Mastermans on November 26, 1908, he was so angry he could hardly speak, stabbed at his bread, and muttered about "the heart of every Band of Hope sinking with them." Then he promised, "We shall send them up a budget in June as shall terrify them, they have started the class war, they had better be careful."[80]

The House of Commons had changed with the times, but the House of Lords was an oak-paneled mausoleum where 544 peers surrounded by stained-glass windows and framed portraits of royalty clung to their privileges. From the start, Churchill saw the budget as a constitutional issue; it had to do with the right of the Lords to reject it. The House of Lords was not being consistent with its historical role. The problem had existed for some time, and Churchill, never shy about discussing national issues that had nothing to do with his department, had spoken of it while still at the Colonial Office, at the Manchester Free Trade Hall on February 4, 1907. He pointed to the "plain absurdities in the composition of our hereditary chamber where a man acquires legislative functions simply through his virtue in being born, where the great majority of the members never come near the place from year's end to year's end, where if they go mad or are convicted of a crime or become mentally incompetent to manage their estates or acquire an unwholesome acquaintance with intoxicating beverages, nevertheless they are still considered perfectly fit to exercise the highest legislative functions." The Lords' veto was "the spoke in the wheel and the dog in the manger." What was to be done? "There are more ways of killing a cat than drowning it in cream," he said, "and I am certainly not in favor of a Liberal Government going on sending up bills to the House of Lords for them to throw out until the country gets exasperated." Again, in a debate in June 1907, Churchill saw the true nature of the crisis: "If we persevere we shall wrest from the hands of privilege and wealth the evil, ugly and sinister weapon of the Peers' veto, which they have used so ill, for so long."

It took Lloyd George four hours to read the budget on April 29, 1909, from a closely typed manuscript of enormous length. After two hours his voice became hoarse and Balfour proposed adjournment to give him a chance to recover. There were audible gasps as one proposal after the other was flung at the Tory benches. When he announced the new Super Tax, a well-known and popular millionaire rose sadly from his seat and walked out of the House, the very picture of dejection. One MP told Haldane that Lloyd George had read mechanically, like a man who did not understand his text. "Of course he doesn't," Haldane said, "why for weeks we've been trying to make him understand clause X, and he can't."[81] But Lloyd George did understand that he was changing England. These were proposals that shattered friendships, decided two elections, maintained the Liberal Party in office, and broke the power of the House of Lords.

For seven months the budget was debated. Five hundred and fifty-four times the MP's left their seats and gathered in the lobbies for a division. "Month after month, we tramped through the lobbies," Churchill said, "night after night, and all day and all night, all through the summer, all through the autumn and into the winter we marched and perambulated in this House . . ." It was a "shameless degradation" of Parliament.[82]

To the disgust of his cousin Sunny, Churchill became president of the Budget League, an itinerant evangelist spreading the gospel according to Lloyd George. "Sometimes when I see Winston making these speeches," Lloyd George confided to Masterman, "I get a flash of jealousy and I have to say to myself, 'Don't be a fool. What's the use of getting jealous of Winston?' "[83]

The Duke of Beaufort said he would "like to see Winston Churchill and Lloyd George in the middle of twenty couples of hound dogs." In Tory ranks, Churchill was the greater villain. Lloyd George's behavior could be explained by his upbringing. But why was Churchill so eager to destroy the class from which he had sprung? Was this the final vindication of his father, who had been discarded by Lord Salisbury and the rest of the Tory hierarchy? Or was he only looking for a big issue upon which to fasten? In fact, gazing through the prism of history, Churchill saw the new social policies and the removal of the Lords' veto as part of a long and necessary process. His rhetoric and pushiness veiled the deeper side of his nature, which understood political battles as chapters in a historical sequence. Reducing the power of the Lords was the correct policy, whether he was a duke's grandson or a foundling. If Churchill was to be blamed, it was not for his lack of sectarian loyalty, but for identifying the good of the country with his own advancement. Once again, just as when he had crossed the floor, he was seen as a traitor to his class, fuming about the Lords during the week and spending the weekend at Blenheim. "What have you got to say for him now—your treacherous little gutter genius?" a friend asked Violet Asquith.[84] Max Beerbohm portrayed him with his hand reassuringly on the shoulder of a dejected Duke of Marlborough, saying: "Come, come. As I said in one of my speeches, 'There is nothing in the Budget to make it harder for a poor hardworking man to keep a small home in decent comfort.' "

The struggle over the budget was momentarily forgotten in July, when Clemmie gave birth to a daughter. Earlier in the year, she and Winston had moved into a house at 33 Eccleston Square, with an eighteen-year lease at 195 pounds per annum. Together they placed the books on the shelves of the library, and arranged their bedrooms. After less than a year of marriage, they had separate bedrooms. Clemmie's reason was that they kept different hours. Churchill, who had a loving and spontaneous nature, was made to observe the protocol of the bedchamber—by invitation only. This was one area where Clemmie would keep the initiative, her last line of defense against her husband's "dominating brilliance." Churchill was placed in the position of pleader, always hoping "to kiss her dear lips" and "curl up snugly in her arms."[85]

A solicitous husband, Churchill worried over her pregnancy. She needed a lot of rest; he did not want her to wear herself out. Out of pain joy would spring, and from passing weakness new strength arise. He hid his trials, the world was good, bad, and indifferent, only his sweet Pussy Cat remained a constant darling.

The PK, or Puppy Kitten, a cross between the Amber Pug and Clemmicat, was born on July 11, 1909, and was named Diana. She was red-haired like her father. Run-down, Clemmie went to stay with her mother in Sussex. The PK and her nurse stayed in London, and Churchill officiated at her bath. Her strength was surprising; her little hands shut like a vise on his fingers. What would she grow into? Would she be lucky or unlucky? She should have some rare qualities of mind and body, but these did not always mean peace and happiness—still, he thought a bright star shone for her.[86] "Is she a pretty child?" Lloyd George asked on the bench in the House of Commons. "The prettiest child ever seen," Churchill said, beaming. "Like her mother, I suppose?" "No," said Churchill gravely, "she is exactly like me."[87]

Six days after Diana's birth, he spoke at Edinburgh and, without consulting Asquith, announced that if the Lords rejected the budget the government would dissolve Parliament. Asquith's strategy was to treat the veto as unthinkable. He did not want an inconvenient election in the dead of winter in which the Liberal majority might be trimmed. At the Cabinet meeting of July 21, Asquith took the unusual step of formally rebuking Churchill for "purporting to speak on behalf of the Government" in a way that was "quite indefensible and altogether inconsistent with Cabinet responsibility and Ministerial cohesion."[88]

Even so, it began to seem likely that the Lords would veto, goaded and taunted as they were by the Heavenly Twins, who seemed to be holding a contest in invective. In his July 30 Limehouse speech to four thousand Cockneys on the London docks, Lloyd George ridiculed the nobleman who "has one man to fix his collar and adjust his tie in the morning, a couple of men to carry a boiled egg to him at breakfast, a fourth man to open the door for him in and out of his carriage, and a sixth and seventh to drive him." There was more of the same, and in the Tory press, which called it the "Slimehouse" speech, he appeared as a highwayman, poacher, pirate, and anarchist.

Not to be outdone, Churchill on September 4 at Leicester spoke of "the small fry of the Tory Party splashing actively about in their proper puddles." It was too easy to bait the dukes, he said, "almost like teasing goldfish. . . . These ornamental creatures blunder on every hook they seek, and there is no sport whatever in trying to catch them. It would be barbarous to leave them gasping on the bank of public ridicule upon which they have landed themselves. Let us put them back gently, tenderly into their fountains—and if a few bright gold scales have been rubbed off in what the Prime Minister calls the variegated handling they have received, they will soon get over it."

Lord Knollys wrote the *Times* to complain about this speech. Churchill thought that he and the King must have gone mad to intervene so directly in political matters. It showed the bitterness that was felt in royal circles, but he would take no notice of it, for it would defeat itself.[89]

Churchill was off to Germany to attend military maneuvers and visit Labour Exchanges. He still saw it as a friendly nation, the beacon and model of social progress, even though fear of Germany was an oft-sounded theme in English life. The hit play in London that year was *An Englishman's Home,* which dramatized an invasion of England by "The Emperor of the North." Invasion jitters spread to the writer Henry James, living on England's south coast, who worried that "when the German Emperor carries the next war into this country, my chimney pots, visible to a certain distance out to sea, may be his very first objective."

Born in one of Blenheim Palace's three hundred rooms, Winston Churchill had an American mother, *née* Jennie Jerome, and a father who was the second son of an English duke, Lord Randolph Churchill.

The beautiful Jennie flanked by her two sons, nine-year-old Jack, who became a stockbroker, and fourteen-year-old Winston, then at Harrow.

In September 1893, when l was eighteen, Churchill we to the Royal Military Colleg at Sandhurst, where he is shown with two fellow offic cadets.

In the last demented stage of tertiary syphilis, Randolph insisted on taking Jennie on a tour around the world, along with one of his doctors, George Keith.

Herbert Henry Asquith, Liberal Prime Minister from 1908 to 1916, was Churchill's political mentor and a father figure.

Jennie with Jack and Winston, who holds an unidentified dachshund, at the start of Winston's political career.

The Third Marquess of Salisbury, who was Conservative Prime Minister when Randolph Churchill was Chancellor of the Exchequer in 1886 and again when Winston Churchill entered Parliament in 1900.

When he was a lieutenant in the South African Light Horse, during the Boer War, Churchill tried to grow a mustache, but the result was so unimpressive that he shaved it off. (He wanted one because all the members of his squadron football team had them.)

Churchill, second row center (*without mustache*) as a member of his squadron football team.

Captured by the Boers in 1899 when the armored train he was on was ambushed,
Churchill escaped. He reached Durban on December 23, described his adventures to
a cheering crowd (*opposite page, bottom*), and was photographed on one of General
Sir Redvers Buller's remounts at the scene of his capture, which had just come under
British control.

£25

(Twenty-five Pounds stg.) REWARD is offered by the
Sub-Commission of the fifth division, on behalf of the Special Constable
of the said division, to anyone who brings the escaped prisoner of war

CHURCHILL,

dead or alive to this office.

For the Sub-Commission of the fifth division,
(Signed) LODK. de HAAS, Sec.

ON DECEMBER 30 the following newspaper story appeared:

Dec. 30, 189.   PEARSON'S ILLUSTRATED WAR NEWS.   3

HOW I ESCAPED
FROM PRETORIA.

By Winston Churchill.

THE *Morning Post* has received the following telegram from Mr. Winston Spencer Churchill, its war correspondent, who was taken prisoner by the Boers and escaped from Pretoria.

LOURENCO MARQUES, December 21st, 10 p.m.

I was concealed in a railway truck under great sacks.
I had a small store of good water with me.
I remained hidden, chancing discovery.
The Boers searched the train at Komati Poort, but did not search deep enough, so after sixty hours of misery I came safely here.
I am very weak, but I am free.
I have lost many pounds weight, but I am lighter in heart.
I shall also avail myself of every opportunity from this moment to urge with earnestness an unflinching and uncompromising prosecution of the war.

On the afternoon of the 11th the Transvaal Government's Secretary for War informed me that there was little chance of my release.
I therefore resolved to escape the same night, and left the State Schools Prison at Pretoria by climbing the wall when the sentries' backs were turned momentarily.
I walked through the streets of the town without any disguise meeting many burghers, but I was not challenged in the crowd.
I got through the pickets of the Town Guard, and struck the Delagoa Bay Railroad.

I walked along it, avoiding the watchers at the bridges and culverts.
I waited for a train beyond the first station.
The eest 11.10 goods train from Pretoria arrived, and before it had reached full speed I boarded it with great difficulty, and hid myself under coal sacks.
I jumped from the train before dawn, and sheltered during the day in a small wood, in company with a huge vulture, who displayed a lively interest in me.
I walked on at dusk.
There were no more trains that night.
The danger of meeting the guards of the railway line continued; but I was obliged to follow it, as I had no compass or map.
I had to make wide *détours* to avoid the bridges, stations, and huts.
My progress was very slow, and chocolate is not a satisfying food.
The outlook was gloomy, but I persevered, with God's help, for five days.
The food I had to husband very precariously.
I was lying up at daylight, and walking on at night time, and, meanwhile, my escape had been discovered and my description telegraphed everywhere.
All the trains were searched.
Everyone was on the watch for me.
Four wrong people were arrested.
But on the sixth day I managed to board a train beyond Mulibilorg, whence there is a direct service to Delagoa.

Three kings of England: Edward VII (*center*) died in 1910. He was succeeded by George V, "the sailor king." George's oldest son, the Prince of Wales, who later became Edward VIII, would abdicate in 1936.

Loves of the Churchills: In 1900, Jennie married George Cornwallis-West, who was half her age. Winston, a few years later, proposed to Ethel Barrymore, with whom he is shown in front of Blenheim Palace in a previously unpublished photograph. Miss Barrymore turned him down.

As Member of Parliament, Churchill (*above*) broke with the Conservative Party over the protectionist policy of Joseph Chamberlain (*below,
right*), and joined the Liberal ranks. His reward was an appointment as
under-secretary for the Colonial Office in the 1905 government of Sir
Henry Campbell-Bannerman (*below, left*).

Silk-hatted in Malta, Churchill was on the way to East Africa in October 1907 with his secretary Eddie Marsh, an "unconditional Churchillian" who served with him in every government office he held from 1905 to 1929.

The Dominion Premiers came to London for the Colonial Conference of 1907 and posed for a group photograph. Among the group are the bearded Colonial Secretary, Lord Elgin (*seated center*); Lloyd George, President of the Board of Trade (*seated extreme right*); and Herbert Henry Asquith, Chancellor of the Exchequer (*seated extreme left*). Standing behind Asquith is the 32-year-old Colonial under-secretary, Winston Churchill, already balding; next to him is the Colonial Office permanent under-secretary, Sir Francis Hopwood, a curiously Machiavellian figure who praised Churchill to his face and sniped at him behind his back.

Led by Emmeline and Christabel Pankhurst, the suffragettes were most active in Churchill's constituency of Manchester. They were arrested when they disrupted his meetings because he would not come out in favor of votes for women.

Campaigning in North-West Manchester in April 1908, Churchill was defeated and had to run again in Dundee, where he found a safe Liberal seat.

In 1909, Churchill attended war games in Germany as a guest of the Kaiser, with whom he is shown here shaking hands.

Sometimes friend, sometimes foe, Arthur James Balfour, the nephew of the Marquess of Salisbury, became Prime Minister when Churchill was a young Tory, and in 1915 succeeded Churchill as First Lord of the Admiralty.

Much sought after, Clementine Hozier had already broken two engagements when she decided to marry Churchill in 1908.

Criticized in the press when he was Home Secretary for ordering the Army out against a besieged gang of burglars—which resulted in fatalities—Churchill gave evidence at the inquest on January 18, 1911.

ABOVE: As First Lord of the Admiralty, Churchill had run-ins with the Secretary of War, Lord Kitchener (*left*), seen here on a tour of the Dardanelles, as well as with his First Sea Lord, the irrepressible Jacky Fisher (TOP, RIGHT), the first authentic genius the British Navy could boast of since Nelson.

LEFT: The Dardanelles expedition was commanded at sea by Admiral John de Robeck and on land by General Ian Hamilton, whose withered left hand was the result of a wound at the battle of Majuba in South Africa in 1881.

During World War I, Hamilton wanted the poet Rupert Brooke (ABOVE) as a member of his staff, but Brooke insisted on regular duty; he died of a mysterious illness before the troops landed.

Churchill as First Lord of the Admiralty, with Lloyd George, who became Prime Minister in 1916 during World War I.

When he was First Lord, Churchill took up flying, to the dismay of Clementine, who nonetheless accompanied him when he inspected an early glider model.

In 1915, the First Lord of the Admiralty—who would soon be forced to resign—inspected a unit of fourteen-year-old naval cadets, many of whom would be killed when the ships on which they served were torpedoed by German U-boats.

This previously unpublished photograph shows the actual landing at Cape Helles on April 25, 1915, the first time in the twentieth century that a landing in open boats was attempted against a defended beachhead.

Before leaving, Churchill had lunched with Count Metternich, the German ambassador, and explained the rise in the naval estimates. The disquieting fact that the Germans were working on eleven dreadnoughts, two in excess of their own Naval Law, had caused some public anxiety. It was no good shutting one's eyes to facts; however hard governments worked to build trust between two countries, they would make very little headway while there was a booming naval policy in Germany.

Metternich ventured that the navy scare had been part of a deep policy to rally the British Empire, obtain contributions for the Navy from the colonies, and influence public opinion for the building program.

That was quite wrong, Churchill said. His colleagues' anxieties were real, even if he did not share them all. The Liberal government did not play games. Armaments races were not popular with the rank and file.

Arms limitations were only possible when there was a spirit of trust, Metternich said; it was no good having them between powers who regarded each other as likely antagonists.

Why should they be antagonists? Churchill asked. They had nothing to quarrel about, and no alliances to involve them.

Metternich was skeptical. The German government knew perfectly well that the closest plans had been concerted between the French and the British War Office for joint action.

Churchill, who knew nothing of such plans, said he did not believe that was true.

Up until a few years ago, Metternich said, the German Intelligence Department drew up contingency plans for war with every major European power except England, but now that they had discovered the close military ties between England and France, they were making plans for England too.

Churchill was unimpressed. It was the job of every decent Intelligence Department to make plans for contingencies, no matter how remote and improbable.[90]

On September 12 in Strasbourg (wrested from France in the 1870 war), the ringing bells of the old city reminded him of the chimes that had saluted his wedding exactly one year ago. He hoped that his "lovely white pussy-cat" had no cause, however vague and secret, for regrets. His marriage was everything he had wished for. He felt so safe with his precious Clemmie that he did not keep the slightest disguise.[91]

Three days later, mounted on a very good horse from the Emperor's stables, he watched the maneuvers at Würzburg and was impressed by the size and the armament of the German Army. It could march thirty-five miles in a day. Much as war attracted and fascinated his mind with its tremendous situations, he felt more deeply each year what vile and wicked folly and barbarism it all was.[92]

On October 1, the Churchills were invited to Newbuildings, Wilfrid Blunt's country house in Sussex, for a shooting party. Blunt, who was nearly twice Churchill's age, had become a close friend. They were both nonconformists and had a high regard for each other, although Churchill did not follow Blunt in his anti-Imperialist views. Long and far-ranging talks were the order of the day when they got together, as they had a month before, with Churchill doing most of the talking. On that occasion, he had told Blunt that the budget was very popular and the Lords would not fight it. They were the debased products of public schools, which he hated: "I never learned anything at school, and to be high up at Eton is enough to ruin any boy, and give him a narrow view of life." Another object of his sustained hatred was Kitchener: "I always hated Kitchener, though I did not know him personally. Kitchener . . . had behaved like a blackguard in that business [of the Mahdi's head]. He pretended to have sent the head back . . . in a kerosene tin, but the tin may have contained anything, perhaps ham sandwiches. He kept the head, and has it still." This was pure fabulation, for the head had been buried by Lord Cromer. When Blunt talked about his imprisonment in Ireland, Churchill said, "I am dead against the present system, and if I am ever at the Home Office I will make a clean sweep of it." Then the talk turned to the suffragettes, who had vowed to chain themselves to railings outside the House of Commons until they got the vote, and Churchill told the story of the man who said, "I might as well chain myself to St. Thomas's Hospital and say I would not move till I had had a baby." Blunt liked him very much, and liked the way he took all possible care of his wife. Clemmie was afraid of wasps, and when one settled on her sleeve, Churchill took it by the wings and thrust it into the fire.[93]

Churchill shot very well at the October party, though of course it was easy shooting. His old friend Harry Cust, the editor of the *Pall Mall Gazette*, was there, and that night at dinner they tied one on. Churchill drank seven glasses of Blunt's best Madeira, as well as quantities of champagne, and was moved to make an extended comparison between Balfour and Asquith.

Asquith was simpleminded, but a workhorse, with a clear head for business. He could sit up playing bridge and drinking until the small hours, and in the morning his head would be clear to work on the most complicated business. He would attend committees and draft amendments in his clear handwriting without altering a word in clause after clause. But his power came from being far and away the best speaker in the House. Arthur, by contrast, was hard by nature, and could be cruel, although he was the most courageous man alive. If you held a pistol to his head it would not frighten him. He was not affected by adverse circumstances, or by the number of his enemies, among whom Churchill counted himself. The difference between Balfour and Asquith was that Balfour was wicked and moral, while Asquith was good and immoral.[94]

Heavy drinking did not blunt the edge of Churchill's discourse, for he had a phenomenal ability to absorb alcohol, but Cust was so drunk that he talked incoherently about the moon and wandered about the house trying to find his room. The next night Clemmie stole the show in a tight dress of crimped silk. When Blunt remarked that she looked as if she had nothing on underneath, she whispered that it was almost true.[95]

On October 3, Winston and Clemmie went to the Webbs' for dinner to meet a party of young Fabians. Beatrice Webb thought Churchill was taking on the appearance of a mature statesman, even though he was not yet thirty-five, and was still in love with his own phrases. Critical of the Webbs' political agitation, Churchill said: "You should leave the work of converting the country to us, Mrs. Webb, you ought to convert the Cabinet."

"That would be all right," she said, "if we wanted merely a change in the law; but we want to really change the mind of the people with regard to the facts of destitution, to make them feel the infamy of it and the possibility of avoiding it. That won't be done by converting the Cabinet, even if we could convert the Cabinet—which I doubt. We will leave that task to a converted country."[96]

Churchill was a trifle uneasy in his role of Danton to Lloyd George's Robespierre. He wanted reforms, but not upheaval. One night at dinner, Lloyd George and Masterman were chaffing him about the revolutionary measures they would propose—the guillotine in Trafalgar Square, and who would be in the first tumbril. When Churchill became indignant, the others told him he could be the Napoleon of the British revolution, an idea that was not entirely distasteful. Walking home with Masterman after this merry dinner, Churchill said with great solemnity, "If this is what it leads to, you must be prepared for me to leave you." Then he added, tongue in cheek, "You are at the bottom of all this revolutionary talk, Masterman."[97]

Campaigning in Dundee on October 17, Churchill received a deputation of suffragettes. "I am bound to say I think your cause has marched backwards," he said. The movement had opted for violence, attacking Asquith on the golf course and Lloyd George in his car. A month later, Churchill was attacked at the Bristol railway station by Miss Theresa Garnett, who had recently been charged with biting a wardress. Cracking a dog whip, she cried, "Take that in the name of the insulted women of England!" Churchill seized the whip and calmly put it in his pocket. Miss Garnett was arrested and sentenced to a month in prison.

The dog-whip incident led a Scotsman from Leith, Mr. W. Newlands, to write Churchill suggesting "a punishment which I think would cure the trouble. Shave their heads as bare as a bald-headed crane, and let them go. I think the hair would take at least six months to grow. It would not harm their health, simply cool that part where brains should be."[98]

Churchill hoped that Clemmie, a suffragette sympathizer, would not be angry with him for having been stern. The one woman he would never oppose was his beautiful pussy cat that "purred and prinked" before him so that he felt as proud and conceited as three peacocks to possess it. He wanted to take her in his arms, all cold and gleaming from her bath. Left too much alone by her campaigning husband, the beautiful pussy cat was having pangs of jealousy, wondering if there was another woman. Why did she nurse such absolutely wild suspicions, Churchill asked, which were so dishonoring to all the love and loyalty he bore her, and unworthy of them both. They filled his mind with feelings of embarrassment to which he had been a stranger since he was a schoolboy. He knew that her jealous feelings originated with her love, but at the same time they depressed and vexed him—he did not live in a world of small intrigues but of serious and important affairs. He could not conceive of forming any other attachment than her. Why did she indulge in small emotions and wounding doubts—she must trust him, for he could never love any other woman in the world.[99]

Perhaps Clemmie was jealous of her sister-in-law, Goonie, who was witty and amusing, and who shared an easy intimacy with Winston. Churchill would learn to live with his wife's unreasoning jealous rages. In the opinion of her grandmother Lady Airlie, Clemmie's behavior was sometimes hysterical. The calm of her being would be broken by sudden, irrational storms. She could lose her temper at the slightest thing—if the soup was cold, or a servant had made a small mistake—and the tantrum passed as soon as it had arisen. It required great patience and understanding for Churchill to help her through these episodes, and in later life she experimented with medication and diet to alleviate her recurring fits.

On November 25, 1909, the budget passed its Third Reading in the House of Commons by 379 to 149 and went to the Lords. The *Times* warned that it would be highly unconstitutional for the peers to meddle with a money bill. There had already been a civil war in England to decide who controlled the public purse. But Tory dialecticians argued that this was not a true money bill; it was a blueprint for socialism. Sure that the Lords would reject, Churchill said in Bristol on November 14: "All the House of Lords can do—if they go mad—is to put a stone on the track and throw the train of state off the line and that is what we are told they are going to do."

On November 30, after six days of angry debate, by a vote of 350 to 75, the Lords threw the train off the line. Lloyd George was delighted, telling the National Liberal Club, "Their greed has overborne their craft, and we have got them." New elections would return a Liberal majority that would hand the Lords not only the People's Budget but legislation to end their veto powers. They could not refuse once the people had spoken. By rejecting the budget, the Lords were sawing off the branch they were sitting on.

November 30 was also Churchill's thirty-fifth birthday, and they were six for dinner at Eccleston Square, gathered around a cake with the appropriate number of candles. Churchill sat all evening with a paper hat on his head. If only the thousands who went to his meetings could see the queer sight, Viscount Esher thought. The Churchills had a cook, two maids, and a man, but Clemmie ran down to the kitchen before dinner to see that everything was all right. Winston and Clemmie sat on a sofa holding hands. He had never seen two people more in love.[100]

On December 2, Asquith moved in the House of Commons that the Lords' rejection of a money bill was a breach of the Constitution. Parliament was dissolved on the fifteenth and an election was scheduled to begin on January 14, 1910. Assuming that the Liberals would win and that Asquith would be returned to office, there was likely to be a Cabinet reshuffle. Churchill felt that he was in line for a promotion. He had fought the good fight over the budget, speaking incessantly in its defense, which had moved Asquith to write Lord Knollys: "I hope you have noticed the moderation of tone, and the absence of personalities and bad taste—as well as the conscious ability— which have characterized Winston Churchill's campaign . . ."[101] There was no doubt where Churchill wanted to go—the Admiralty. He deeply regretted having let it go by in 1908, when it was run by his uncle. Now he saw himself as a First Lord devoted to curbing expenditure, fighting hard inside and outside in an ugly and thankless job. Still, he could do it, juggling Westminster, Downing Street, Whitehall, and the North Sea. It would be better for everyone if McKenna went to the Home Office and left the Admiralty to him. He would have to convince Asquith.

One reason Churchill felt that he could lead the Admiralty in a program of economy was that Jacky Fisher had been forced into retirement. When Admiral Charles Beresford had hauled down his flag in March 1909, he agitated in the House of Commons for an investigation of the Admiralty. Asquith appointed a subcommittee of the Committee of Imperial Defense, which held meetings between April 27 and July 13. It was a way to silence Beresford, who had a small political following, but many in the Navy felt that it was shocking that a Board of Admiralty should be put on trial and have to defend itself against the charges of an undisciplined subordinate. The subcommittee's report in August neither sustained Beresford's charges nor vindicated Fisher, who was chided for his opposition to a Naval War Staff. Considering the jealous and proprietary way he ran things, how could there be any cooperation with the Army? Fisher was shunted to the House of Lords, as Baron Fisher of Kilverstone, and retired on his sixty-ninth birthday, on January 25, 1910.

By that time, the election was in full swing, and Churchill spent January campaigning in Dundee with his faithful secretary Eddie Marsh. It was a dog's life, Eddie thought; Churchill said the same things over and over again —he was as familiar with the speeches as Mr. Clutterbuck had been after eighteen years of married life with the appearance and manner of Mrs. Clutterbuck—there were times when he longed for a little needlework. It did amuse him though when Winston said that he had read one of Austen Chamberlain's speeches, "which the Conservative papers for once had . . . the humor to report in full."[102] Eddie attended to all the little chores, and Clemmie spread the vile rumor that he had mixed up his telegrams, wiring Churchill's wine merchant "May God defend the right" and the editor of the *Daily News* for "more champagne."[103]

"Peers against the People" was the election's theme. As Churchill put it on December 8 in Liverpool: "There are four hundred or five hundred backwoods peers meditating upon their estates on the great questions of government or studying *Ruff's Guide* [to the Turf] and other Blue books or evolving problems of Empire at Epsom. Every one of them, a heaven-born or God-granted legislator, knows what the people want by instinct and every one of them with a stake in the heart of the country."

But when the votes were counted, the great Liberal majority of 1906 had vanished. The two great parties were almost equal, the Conservatives having polled 273 seats to the Liberals' 275. It was a lesson on the resilience and grass-roots strength of the Conservative Party, and a terrible blow to the Liberals, who were now condemned to rely on the 41 Labour and 71 Irish Nationalist seats for their majority. Holding the balance of power, the Irish swallowed their distaste for the budget, for with the removal of the Lords' veto, they could make a deal with Asquith to force the passage of Home Rule. Margot Asquith, behind whose extravagance and gossipmongering there lurked a keen political mind, was deeply grieved to see the splendid majority smashed. A little less violence in the budget, a little less baiting of the Lords, and this horrible crisis would *never* have come. She was a "very *very* sad woman watching Henry with his loyal kind splendid nature drowning slowly."[104]

In Dundee's two-member constituency, Churchill was returned with the Labour candidate, a ship's carpenter named Alexander Wilkie. Each of them polled more than ten thousand votes, more than twice the Tory vote. But Churchill too was disheartened by the outcome. He wondered whether the system of staggered polling to which they were wedded gave less satisfaction to the Liberals or their opponents. For the Liberals, it was a process not unlike the pulling out of teeth day by day with every circumstance of pain, while the Tories were like a man swimming bravely and successfully and yet knowing that he has no chance of reaching the shore.[105] It might be a Liberal victory, he told Haldane, but it was Wagram, not Austerlitz.[106]

Taking the sun and reconstructing his Cabinet in Cannes on February 1, Asquith offered Churchill the Irish Office. It was one of the most delicate and difficult posts and had been held in the past by men of the weightiest caliber, Morley and Balfour. Of course, if he did not want it, he could always stay at the Board of Trade, where he was doing such useful work.[107]

Churchill felt that he was in a strong enough position to write his own ticket. He did not want the Irish Office, which did not offer great prospects, for the time was not ripe for a Home Rule Bill, and he did not wish to be a mere administrator. Augustine Birrell might as well stay there; he had already been through the unpleasant process of being disillusioned and had all the threads in his hand. Still obsessed with repeating his father's career as the great parer of the army and navy cheeses, he wanted the Admiralty—if it was vacant—or barring that, the Home Office. Lecturing Asquith, he pointed out that ministers should occupy positions that corresponded with their influence in the country. With grave struggles impending, there should be a generous application of the real forces that had contributed to the strength of the party and the government.[108]

But Asquith, who had saved the dreadnoughts with his four-plus-four compromise, did not want Churchill dismantling the naval program, and offered him the Home Office. Margot Asquith, who seems to have held Churchill partly responsible for the loss of the Liberal majority, hoped that he would turn over a new leaf now that he held a major Cabinet post. After all, he had an affectionate heart, and a wife who was not vain of her marvelous beauty, which was rare. Instead of being known for cheap shots, hen-roost phrases, and squibs and crackers, he should cultivate loyalty, reserve, and character. He should thrive on being liked rather than loving abusive notice and rotten notoriety. Only then would the King and the West and East ends of London change their view of him.[109]

VII

HOME OFFICE

CHURCHILL WAS in the ascendant. In two years, he had risen from Colonial Under-Secretary to a position of leadership in the government. Outdistancing senior statesmen like Haldane, Grey, and McKenna, he now formed a troika with Asquith and Lloyd George. Not only had he done a remarkable job at the Board of Trade, he had actively promoted the long-range aims of his party, the People's Budget and the dismantling of the Lords' veto. His delivery in the House had become more rounded and statesmanlike, less cutting, owing perhaps to his appointment to a higher office. The Tory leader Walter Long congratulated him on the vast change in his manners.[1] Charles Masterman, the brooding and untidy radical with the loose lock falling across his brow, who had moved to the Home Office as Churchill's Parliamentary Under-Secretary, thought that his great weakness was love of the limelight. He always wanted to be in the public eye. He also showed signs of losing the great assiduity of learning he had as a younger man, and was content to delegate, complaining that he did not want to be bound up in details. Masterman's wife, Lucy, noticed a tinge of amused indulgence in Churchill's colleagues toward this "extraordinarily gifted boy." He did not seem to realize the danger of prolonged boyishness, the clamor for the attention of his elders.[2]

It must be said in Churchill's defense that the year 1910 opened with a situation of enormous Parliamentary complexity. The Liberal Party was weakened; its supporters were disheartened. They could govern only by paying off the Irish, who, spying the shores of Home Rule in sight, insisted that the government fight the battle of the veto before the battle of the budget. But to win against the Lords, Asquith needed a secret weapon: a threat that if they refused to curtail their own powers, the King would create enough additional Liberal peers, perhaps as many as five hundred, to swamp the Upper House and make it more compliant. When Edward declined to employ this stratagem, Asquith informed the House on February 21 that he had no guarantee on the creation of peers. The Liberal advance was paralyzed. They could not move on the veto, and the Irish dragged their feet on the budget. Asquith's prestige fell. Morale was low. Resignation was in the air.

Churchill tried to reason a way out of the maze. On February 22, in the debate on the King's Address, he argued that the budget must be the first completed business of the new Parliament. To coerce the Lords by refusing to send them a budget until they had agreed to give up their veto, as the Irish were suggesting, was as absurd as saying "if you do not do what we wish we will punish you by not doing what you do not wish . . . I should almost have ventured to say that this suggestion for coercing the Lords had somewhat of a Hibernian flavor about it."

"None the worse for that," said the Irish leader John Redmond.

"You were very glad of the help of the Hibernians at Dundee, my boy," added William Redmond.

"Have your taxes a Hibernian flavor?" asked Tim Healy. "Will you refuse them on that account?"[3]

Churchill was crestfallen. There seemed to be no straw to make bricks with, no way out of the constitutional deadlock. On February 25, he ran into Austen Chamberlain, who observed that in the Liberal camp, there were plenty of people taking and seeking offense.

"Oh, yes," Churchill said, "just look at the Irish. You know how ready they are for chaff generally, but you saw how touchy they were on Tuesday. Oh! you won't have to wait long! A few weeks."

"Oh, you'll last longer than that," Chamberlain said.

"How can we? Why, the Irish send us a fresh ultimatum every day. We're at the fourteenth now! I don't see how we can last beyond April. I thought you might have beaten us on hops today. It would have suited me very well to hop it on hops."

"Yes, I daresay, but it didn't suit us," Chamberlain said.[4] Having lost the last two elections, the Tories did not particularly want to form a minority government, in the event of Asquith's resignation, with the prospect of losing a third.

In the Cabinet, however, Asquith rallied his ministers to a course of action. There was no point in resigning until an effort had been made to move the budget and the veto through. The Irish were told that the budget would come first. But there would also be put before the House three resolutions to curb the Lords: (1) They could neither amend nor reject a money bill, and the Speaker of the House of Commons would determine what was and was not a money bill. (2) The veto on other bills would be overruled after they had been passed in three successive sessions of the House of Commons. This gave the Lords a two-year delay on nonmoney bills. (3) The maximum duration of Parliament would be reduced from seven to five years. Irish cooperation was won on the promise that if the Lords rejected the three resolutions the government would launch a strong constitutional attack on their position. Asquith wrote the King that if the Lords balked, then he would either have to accept the government's resignation and let Balfour form a minority government or agree to a dissolution and new elections with a guarantee that if the Liberals were returned he would create new peers.

As Churchill put it on March 17 in a speech at Manchester, it was now a matter of "the Crown and the Commons acting together against the encroachment of the Lords." Through his assistant secretary, Sir Frederick Ponsonby, Edward let it be known that he did not appreciate being brought into the controversy. But Churchill was already drawing up lists of peers, and offered Wilfrid Blunt a peerage if only he would vote against the veto. He shocked Grey by saying that he would not object to a single-chamber government. Grey was all for reform, but this talk of doing away with the House of Lords altogether was too much. The Cabinet was at sixes and sevens. Grey did not see how they could possibly get over the next three weeks without breaking up.[5]

As for the King, recovering from chronic fits of coughing in Biarritz, he was resolved to oppose any creation of peers and wrote Lord Knollys on April 9: "I do not suppose the Prime Minister will suggest my making a quantity of Peers, but should he do so I should certainly decline as I would far sooner be unpopular than ridiculous." When Asquith did suggest it, Knollys said he was about "to commit the greatest outrage which has ever been committed since England became a Constitutional Monarchy." That loyal courtier Viscount Esher agreed. This was no more and no less than a coup d'état the King was being asked to take part in, a combination of blackmail and bribery. A pretty pass! The King said he would never agree to the plan unless required to do so by the nation after a referendum. The creation of hundreds of new peers was preposterous, ridiculous. He felt alienated from his ministers, who were ruining the country and maltreating him personally, and he would neither forgive nor forget.[6]

The resolutions were presented on March 29, and from the Tory benches, F. E. Smith asked: "Why three times? If you may be wrong once or twice, I cannot imagine why you cannot be wrong three times." Churchill responded that the power of delay was a real power, for "I cannot think of any greater restraint that could possibly be imposed on reckless or sectional legislation than that it should be hung round the neck of its authors, not merely as something attempted and failed in, but as an actual real living issue when they next present themselves to the electorate."[7]

Passed on April 14, the resolutions were incorporated into a Parliament Bill that would be sent to the Lords. Reintroduced, the People's Budget passed on April 27 by 324 to 231, and the Lords bowed their heads, submitting to the beast that would devour their lands without a vote, in keeping with the verdict of the 1910 election. What a victory for Asquith and the Heavenly Twins! It had taken them two Parliamentary sessions and one election to get the budget through, but now there was no going back on the new taxes.

Next on the agenda was the House of Lords, which Churchill described as "a weapon, an engine, which is used by one party to vex, harass, humiliate and finally destroy the other; and it has been employed so cruelly, so violently, and so brutally in recent times that there is not a single man on this bench who will consent to hold office on these conditions . . . except with the reasonable hope of effecting a change in these conditions."

Returning to England on April 27, King Edward wanted nothing to do with a government that was trying to use him to break the back of the House of Lords. He wrote Knollys that he would be greatly relieved if Asquith, Lloyd George, and Churchill did *not* meet him at Victoria Station. They were so puffed up with self-conceit they thought they were infallible.[8]

Laid low by bronchitis, the sixty-eight-year-old monarch was mortally ill. One of his last acts was signing that disgraceful mess they called a budget. Refusing to take to his bed, he gave an audience on the morning of his death, May 6, 1910. Edward VII had kept the nineteenth century alive in England. His natural sympathies were with his class, the lords who were being plundered and stampeded, the old order, the calm and stable age of aristocratic rule. Caught in a crisis where it was impossible not to be partisan, he ended his life as the final stumbling block in the reform of the Upper House, which did the bidding of the Conservative Party. He was a man of pleasant little wickednesses, Wilfrid Blunt thought when he heard of Edward's death, but he performed his duties well. He never tired of putting on uniforms and taking them off, and receiving princes and ambassadors, and opening museums and hospitals, and attending cattle shows and parades. He had the popularity of an actor who plays his part in a variety of costumes.[9]

Nine kings, all related to Edward, rode in the funeral procession on May 20. Following his coffin, they were the unknowing pallbearers of the era of great European dynasties. Austen Chamberlain felt a great admiration for the Kaiser, who turned neither to the right nor to the left as he rode through the streets, his eyes fixed on the coffin. He stood for the whole service as steady as one of his own grenadiers till he knelt for the benediction. He was conspicuous because he was so utterly oblivious of all but the king who was gone.

On May 7, the day after the King's death, Margot Asquith was dining with the Crewes, the Harcourts, Jennie and George Cornwallis-West, and Churchill. At the end of the dinner, Churchill said: "Let us drink to the health of the new king." "Rather to the memory of the old," responded Lord Crewe.[10]

Also on May 7, while on a cruise with the McKennas aboard the Admiralty yacht *Enchantress*, Asquith learned that the King was dead. They were leaving Gibraltar for Plymouth, and it was almost dawn when he went up on deck. The first thing he saw was Halley's Comet blazing in the sky, the symbol of a new reign and perhaps a new age. The news had stunned and bewildered him. The only thing that lightened the shock was that now there would be no clash over the creation of peers. Now he would deal with George V, who was without political experience. The country was on the verge of a crisis without example in constitutional history. As the *Enchantress*, with two fast escorting cruisers, steamed across the Bay of Biscay, Asquith wondered: What was the right thing to do?[11]

At forty-four, George V was an unassuming man of plain tastes who liked to brew his own early-morning tea. Indistinguishable from the great majority of his countrymen, he seemed to sum up the attitudes of the average Englishman; he was what you might call "a decent chap." His experience was in the Navy, which he had entered as a naval cadet at the age of twelve. He knew the seaport towns where ships stopped to coal better than the cities of Great Britain, and the quarterdeck better than the Throne Room. He did not inherit his father's worldliness, but as those who observed him at length discovered, he was like good sailcloth, made for wear.

When Churchill went to the Home Office in February 1910, he was the youngest man ever to serve there with the exception of Robert Peel, who had been Home Secretary at thirty-three, and the only one who had ever been in prison. He succeeded Herbert Gladstone, youngest son of the Grand Old Man, who was made a peer, and who wrote him a long memorandum, a sort of Introduction to the Home Office, on February 19, in which he said that the most difficult work was the supervision of sentences. It was worth taking the time, offered Gladstone, "to lift up not a few miserable creatures out of trouble and disgrace."[12] Like the Board of Trade, the Home Office was a great lumpy bag of duties that incorporated most of the criminal justice system (police, prisons, courts, and reform schools), the fire brigades, the immigration services, public morals, mines and fisheries, roads, bridges, and canals, dangerous drugs, explosives, and firearms. It also fell upon the Home Secretary to write letters to the King summing up each meeting of the House of Commons. With all this and the crisis with the Lords to boot, Churchill had his hands full. One day found him reviewing a clemency appeal for a murderer sentenced to death, while on the next he had to deal with thousands of striking Welsh miners.

Some inkling of the variety of his duties can be gained from a tiny sample of the Questions he answered in the House:

February 28: Was he aware that a suffragette named Selina Martin had been put in irons during her detention in Liverpool Gaol while awaiting trial, and that she had been frog-marched and forcibly fed? Churchill said she had been treated "in strict accordance with the rules for untried prisoners. No force was used towards her beyond what was rendered necessary by her very violent and destructive behavior, and her resolve to starve herself."

April 19: When a child was whipped in a reform school, were the strokes inflicted upon the naked body? Churchill: "I believe that when a boy is birched it is usual to divest of clothing that part of his body on which the birching is administered."

June 21: Could something be done to relieve Mr. Francis Lascelles, who had been run over by a vehicle while riding a bicycle? His right ear was nearly torn off, his collarbone was broken, his legs were badly bruised, and after suffering all these injuries he was arrested for using the word "damn" and fined one pound and costs at the Ivybridge Sessions.

Churchill: "I made an inquiry in the case some time ago and found that the newspaper reports give a somewhat euphemistic account of the language used by the defendant. In view of the facts given in evidence I see no reason for advising any reduction of the penalty imposed."

May 22, 1911: In view of the value to farmers of the peewit or lapwing in reducing the number of snails, wireworms, beetles, aphids, and the larvae of various insects, destructive of roots, cereal crops, and pasture, and of the large and increasing exportation from this country to the United States of the eggs of these birds, could an order be issued for the protection of this rapidly decreasing bird and its eggs? Ahead of his time in protecting endangered species, Churchill replied: "It rests with the respective county councils to apply to me for an Order protecting the birds and their eggs if they consider that such an Order is called for in their area."

With his need to leave a mark on everything he touched, Churchill at once set out on an ambitious reform program. But he also had to tie up the loose ends left by his predecessor, three or four bills that had to be seen through the House, and a capital case in which the King took an interest. The case was that of a former navy man who had murdered a child. Neither the judge nor the jury nor Gladstone had recommended mercy. No doubt, Churchill thought, the harsh conditions of his life and the hopelessness of his outlook had roused him, and prompted him to commit a terrible act as an expression of the spite and hatred with which suffering had filled his heart, and as a ferocious demonstration similar in its character to anarchistic crimes against society in general. Nonetheless, he agreed that the man must die.[13]

Churchill's ethical code was based on the elementary concept of fairness. People should get what they deserved. He believed in capital punishment. As a young officer in India, writing in the margins of old *Annual Registers*, he had made the point that murderers should lead the way in being against the death penalty. But he took great care in reviewing capital cases and exercised clemency whenever there was a doubt or a mitigating circumstance. In his twenty months at the Home Office, he ruled on forty-three cases of capital punishment and recommended commutation in twenty-one.

In other areas, he felt the same concern for the individual whiplashed by an impersonal bureaucracy as he had at the Colonial Office, where he had taken up with such tenacity the quixotic cause of a minor civil servant in Ceylon. Inspired by Blunt, who had sent him a long memo on the subject within two weeks of his appointment, he wanted to create a special category of political prisoners. As Blunt pointed out, it would save him persecution at the hands of the suffragettes. In contrast to every other class of prisoner, these gallant ladies wanted to be sent to jail to draw attention to their cause, and went on hunger strikes to achieve complete martyrdom. Force-feeding, a method unpleasantly reminiscent of the Inquisition, involving rubber hoses and rough matrons, was in use. The Home Secretary was a brute who tortured women. Gladstone was relieved to be rid of the office, the most unpleasant in the Cabinet.

When Churchill presented his plan for political offenders, Sir Edward Troup, the Permanent Under-Secretary, pointed out that motive was a dangerous heading, for political murderers would be among the beneficiaries. It would be preferable to list a category of offenses that did not involve dishonesty, cruelty, indecency, or serious violence.[14] On March 10 Churchill announced in the House this new category of prisoners, including suffragettes, who would not have to wear prison uniforms or take the regulation bath, and who could order food from the outside and have library books. Force-feeding, however, was maintained. Churchill did not want any dead suffragettes on his hands.

Gladstone, who had been working along the same lines before leaving office, was stunned by Churchill's announcement, which gave the impression that the whole thing was his idea. Now the newspapers were saying that Churchill had acted in a wise and humane manner while Gladstone had not. Churchill should have acknowledged his debt to his predecessor. Churchill replied that Gladstone had been misled by incomplete newspaper accounts, but added: "I think it might interest you to read the series of Minutes which led up to the decision. They will show you that my action was independent, and will perhaps enable you to see how it was I failed to ascribe proper importance to your point of view."[15] ". . . if you had been through 3 years of a vexatious and nasty movement I faced with a minimum of public support from my colleagues," Gladstone explained, "you would understand that I felt nettled at the invidious comparisons drawn at my expense in consequence of the form of your answer as reported in *The Times*."[16]

It was not hard to find room for improvement in the prison system, which remained largely unchanged since the days of Dickens. The problem was where to begin. John Galsworthy, who had written a prison drama called *Justice*, which the civil servants at the Home Office thought was a gross misinterpretation, wrote Churchill in February to ask for an end to solitary confinement: "I need not say to you that, in prison as in life, men can only be reformed by kindness, by calling out the best that's in them; nor need I say that torture is not confined to the body. The whole tendency nowadays is to paint the outside of the house, and leave the inside to rot. Closed cell confinement is an illustration of that lamentable fact. I beg you to strike a crushing blow at a custom which continues to darken our humanity and good sense."[17] Accordingly, solitary confinement was reduced to one month, except for "old lags" (recidivists).

Churchill seemed to have an idea a minute. He wanted concerts for the convicts, and books. "They must have food for thought," he told Violet Asquith. "Plenty of books—that's what I missed most—except of course the chance of breaking bounds and getting out of the damned place—and I suppose I mustn't give them *that*."[18] He would announce his whole program to Commons in July. Because of the crisis with the Lords and his own short time in office (he went to the Admiralty in October 1911), he was never able to get a single bill on the Statute Book, but he did get the engine of reform turning. Sir Edward Troup, who had to convert his brainstorms into legislative language, said: "He drives me crazy sometimes, but he's the first great Home Secretary we've had since Asquith."[19]

It was Troup who handled the first Home Office crisis of the year that May, when Churchill was in Switzerland on a week's holiday, having left things in the nominal charge of his War Office colleague, Haldane. In the busy South Wales harbor of Newport, up the Bristol Channel, where twenty-nine shipping lines operated, the stevedores working for the Empire Transport Company had gone on strike when their employers, Messrs. Houlder, abruptly changed from piece rates to time rates. They refused to load the steamer *Indian Transport*. The Houlders brought in blacklegs, whom the strikers assaulted. When the strike spread, local authorities asked the Home Office for police reinforcements. Churchill's reaction was not in favor of the employer. The Empire Transport Company should be made to realize, he cabled on May 19, that hiring large droves of men from London to break the strike is a very strong order, which the Home Office should not give the impression of approving. On May 20, the chief constable of Newport asked for 250 men. It was an emergency. The docks were at a standstill and there were reports of looting. More blacklegs were arriving up the channel on the *Lady Jocelyn*. The major was anticipating serious riots. Troup promised, with Churchill's assent, that if needed, he would send 250 foot and 50 mounted police. In the meantime, on May 21, F. H. Houlder came to see Troup in a state of great excitement. His men were trying to save the steamer from attack by getting her off to a buoy in the river. Forty of his men were being murdered and Troup must send police at once. In the Argentine, Houlder said, they managed these things better, they sent machine guns and artillery and gave their subjects proper protection. Troup found his manner offensive and bullying. He seemed to think that at any moment an unlimited supply of horse, foot, and artillery should be placed at his disposal. A Board of Trade negotiator was dispatched to Newport and reached agreement on the twenty-second with representatives of owners and strikers. Orders for sending police were countermanded. Work resumed on the Newport docks on the twenty-third, except on the Houlders' ship, for they refused to abide by the settlement and once again said they would bring in blacklegs. The Home Office tried to persuade them to reconsider, explaining that their behavior was contrary to the public interest. When he reported the incident to the House a month later, Churchill displayed a vestigial knowledge of the Latin he had so hated at Harrow, referring to "the ancient and respectable maxim of law, *sic utere tuo ut alienum non laeadas*, which I will translate as meaning that you should use your own rights so as not to injure the rights of others."[20]

In the end, the dispute was put up to arbitration, and it was decided that the owners had the right to pay time instead of piece rates so long as wages were raised. The strikers went back to work, and the crisis ended without the movement of police.

Around this time, there was another minor fracas. Home Office inspectors wanted to clear the London streets of hawkers. Christopher Addison, the Liberal MP for Shoreditch, some of whose constituents were street sellers, appealed to Churchill, who invited them to come to the Home Office to state their case. "Let 'em all come," he said, "provided they are genuine hawkers." On the appointed day, a long and ragged line of the lame, the halt, the blind, and the infirm stretched up Whitehall, two abreast. They crowded into the biggest room in the Home Office and told their tale so movingly that Churchill decided to help them. The officials who wanted them off the streets said, "No, Home Secretary, you ought to sanction the bye-law as it is." "I'll see you to Hell first," Churchill exploded. He ruled that licenses would be given to hawkers with three years' experience.[21]

When Asquith had introduced the Parliament Bill in April, with its three resolutions to diminish the Upper House, Churchill had told Wilfrid Blunt that the King had no reason to complain, for the Liberals in office were always more polite to him than the Tories. The Tories were in the habit of considering that they were doing quite enough for the King by being in office and protecting him from the Radicals and the Socialists without showing special politeness, while the Liberal ministers showed him the greatest consideration, thus balancing things between the parties.[22]

At this point Lloyd George and Churchill were thinking in vague terms about coalition governments and a reform of the House of Lords that would be acceptable to both parties. Their friendship was still close, although Lloyd George was now less of a father-figure and more of an equal. They made an entertaining pair, with their humor and extravagance and their different sorts of childishness. At a weekend in Folkestone in February, Churchill, overtired and suffering from a chill, worried about having every mortal disease under heaven. After absorbing some whisky, champagne, and port, he took a more cheerful view of life. "I am all for the social order," he pronounced. "No! I'm against it," Lloyd George replied. "Listen. There were six hundred men turned off by the G.W. works last week. Those men had to go out into the street and starve. There is not a man in that works who does not live in terror of the day when his turn will come to go. Well, I'm against a social order that admits of that kind of thing." Churchill cocked his nose in the way that he did when he knew he was going to be impertinent. "That's just what I say," he replied, "you are not against the social order, but against those parts of it that get in your way." Lloyd George crumpled up with laughter.[23]

After Edward's death, Churchill seemed to waver from day to day on how to handle the Lords. On May 11, Austen Chamberlain reported that he was "pressing for the fight at once." Lloyd George proposed a political cease-fire and a bipartisan conference. Asquith approved. He did not want the new and inexperienced King, at the outset of his reign, to be faced with the unpalatable decision of creating hundreds of new peers. The warring parties entered into a "Truce of God." The so-called Constitutional Conference met on June 17 and continued to meet, twenty-two times in all, until the fall. Lloyd George circulated among his colleagues a proposal for a coalition government. After the deluge, a rainbow would form, in which the various tints of party would be combined. Lists of a coalition Cabinet were drawn up. Churchill at first was all for it and discussed the coalition with Masterman, meeting his objections with: "Oh, you are in one of your soup-kitchen moods." He got quite worked up about it, Masterman thought, praising government by aristocracy and revealing the aboriginal and unchangeable Tory in him. But when he learned that he was not on the list, he flew into a rage, telling Lloyd George: "You can go to hell in your own way. I won't interfere. I'll have nothing to do with your damned policy."[24] Lloyd George calmed him down by suggesting that he might take the War Office. But Balfour gave in to the Tory Old Guard, who balked at this unholy alliance with the two pirates who had made them walk the plank of the People's Budget. The "Truce of God" was shattered. It was back to the fight over the veto.

The grace and favor period, sheltering the King from unpleasant realities, was coming to an end. George V would have to swallow the medicine his father had choked on. Churchill could imagine the King's plight. Most of his friends, the social circles in which he moved, resented the "monstrous" creation of new peers. Hereditary nobles would be manufactured on a scale that would be fatal to the whole institution of the peerage. But the lamentable expedient had to be faced. No doubt the King would suffer the deepest distress.[25]

On November 10, the Cabinet decided on the immediate dissolution of Parliament and new elections, which would give the government, if it was returned, a specific mandate to go ahead with the Parliament Bill. The next day Asquith went to spend the night at York Cottage in Sandringham, one of the King's country residences, and told the King that all the dates had been arranged and he had to make the announcement at once so that the election would be over by Christmas. Why was this necessary, the King asked, since Parliament was still very young and the government had a good majority? Asquith said there was no use sending the veto resolution to the Lords, for they would only reject it. It would be a waste of time. The King, in open conflict with his Prime Minister, refused to grant the dissolution until the veto had been submitted to the Lords. They had dinner, and Asquith came back on the attack, but the King, feeling he was being bullied, remained obstinate. The next morning, however, having slept on it, he changed his mind but pointed out: "Remember I only give you the dissolution. I give you no guarantee as to the creation of peers." "No," said Asquith. "I quite understand that. I would not dream of asking you for that."[26]

The King thought he was off the hook. He was wrong. Asquith knew that without the royal guarantee the resolutions were stillborn. On November 16, he went with Lord Crewe, a personal friend of the King's, to deliver the bad news. The King complained that a pistol was being put to his head and asked what Asquith would do if he refused. "I should immediately resign and at the next election should make the cry 'The King and the peers against the people.' " The King was shocked. On the throne for only six months, he was being blackmailed by his own Prime Minister. Had he known that his father had refused even to consider a guarantee, he would have had a precedent to follow. But his father had never mentioned the subject. He appealed to Crewe, who said that the entire Cabinet was behind Asquith. They were not asking the King to do anything unconstitutional, Crewe said. The King asked to be allowed to consult with Balfour and Lord Landsdowne, the Leader of the House of Lords, but Asquith said that was out of the question. Finally, after a discussion that lasted an hour and a half, with Asquith and Crewe very bullying, thought the King, he agreed to give the guarantee if the Liberals won a majority in the election. But he added: "I have been forced into this and I should like the country to know it." Asquith and Crewe told him that the pledge must be kept secret. It might never have to be used. If they were beaten, the question would not arise, and if they had a working majority after a third election, the Lords would give way, and the King would not have to be involved. Crushed, the King told Asquith that if he had to create 450 peers, he would never hold up his head again. That evening he wrote in his diary: "After a long talk, I agreed most reluctantly to give the Cabinet a secret understanding that in the event of the Government being returned with a majority at the General Election, I should use my Prerogative to make Peers if asked for. I disliked having to do this very much, but agreed that this was the only alternative to the Cabinet resigning, which at this moment would be disastrous." The intensity of his resentment was not committed to his diary, but he confided to Lord Derby that Asquith and Crewe had "behaved disgracefully to me."[27] Hidden in the folds of his strategy, Asquith now had a loaded gun to point at the Lords' heads.

Three days after Asquith's showdown with the King, Lloyd George and Churchill were playing golf on the Walton Heath links, about fifteen miles south of London, when they ran into Joseph Lawrence, the Conservative MP for Monmouth Boroughs. The following conversation took place:

LLOYD GEORGE: "Hello, Lawrence, why aren't you electioneering?"
LAWRENCE: "I am waiting for you."
LLOYD GEORGE: "What's the betting?"
LAWRENCE: "Two to one on us."
LLOYD GEORGE: "I'll take you."
LAWRENCE: "In Sovereigns?"
LLOYD GEORGE: "All right!"
LAWRENCE: "Agreed."
CHURCHILL: "Will you lay me the same odds?"
LAWRENCE: "Yes—in Sovereigns."
CHURCHILL: "Right!"[28]

Parliament was dissolved on November 28. Churchill saw extinguished the pallid flickering life of a House of Commons that had lasted less than a year. It had never really lived, and now it had died. No one cared about it anymore.[29] The members were hurrying to their constituencies, for the voting would take place between December 2 and 19. The voters were bored with being asked to go to the polls on exactly the same issues for the second time in a year. If there was any theme to the election, it was "let's get it settled."

"Really," sighed Eddie Marsh, "two elections with Winston in one year are more than enough for an ordinary young man." He could not understand why the Tories were so optimistic. They were betting all takers that the government majority, including Labour and the Irish, would be less than sixty, and were paying one pound for every seat above that. It was too good to turn down.[30]

Campaigning in Sheffield on November 30, his thirty-sixth birthday, Churchill saw the Tories on the run: "Frantic appeals for quarter and mercy rend the air, the white flag hangs over the Tory club, over many a noble residence and public house. All the colors, tents, baggage, and ammunition are scattered along the line of flight. . . . Balfour is now like Charley's aunt, still running."[31]

He took the time to lend a hand to the Liberal candidate in his former seat, North-West Manchester, where Bonar Law, rising to eminence in his party, had replaced the commonplace Joynson-Hicks. Born in New Brunswick, the son of a Presbyterian minister, Bonar Law had done well running an iron-works in Glasgow, and represented the new merchant order in the Conservative Party. Asquith called him "the gilded tradesman," for he retained the manner and outlook of an industrious provincial businessman. His austere nature clashed with Churchill's, and they conducted a running feud, while observing all the marks of mutual courtesy. During a debate on Welsh Disestablishment, Bonar Law had said that the Liberal Party had no more right to take away the property of the church "than I have to take away the coat of Mr. Winston Churchill—even if he has turned it"[32] (loud cheers).

It was impertinent of Churchill to come poaching on his territory, Bonar Law thought, and challenged him to fight for North-West Manchester in person, with the provision that the loser would remain out of the House for the duration of the next Parliament. It was a good thing Churchill did not take him up on it, for Bonar Law was beaten, and the 1910 Parliament lasted until 1918, becoming known as "the Long Parliament." As it was, Bonar Law found a safe seat. When they ran into each other in the lobby of a Manchester hotel as Churchill was on his way to address a meeting, Bonar Law said, "I suppose I had better speak to you tonight because I imagine after I've read your speech tomorrow we shan't be on speaking terms."[33]

In Dundee, Churchill won by a comfortable margin, ahead of the Labour candidate Wilkie by a few hundred votes, and of the two Tories and the eternal Prohibitionist by thousands. Those waiting for the pendulum to swing were disappointed, for it stood still. Tories and Liberals now had 272 seats each. But with their Irish and Labour allies, the Liberals had a working majority of 126. Eddie Marsh collected sixty-six pounds just in time for Christmas. The people's verdict was clear. The House of Commons must get on with the Parliament Bill. The King could not side with the Lords in their continued obstruction. Churchill wrote his wife on December 17: "Well, we are through. I am resolved that nothing shall turn me from the veto *sans phases, sans trêve, sans merci* [without interruptions, peace, or mercy]. The slightest wavering would be absolutely fatal."[34]

While the great constitutional crisis with the Lords held stage center, in the wings the day-to-day matters of the various departments and the House of Commons were being fought out. Women's suffrage seemed to make headway in 1910 when a Parliamentary committee brushed with every party hue was formed to further the cause. Lord Lytton, brother of the suffragette leader Lady Constance Lytton, husband of Churchill's early love Pamela Plowden, and an old friend of Churchill's, was the chairman. It was known as the Conciliation Committee, and its members, in the spring and summer of 1910, busily concocted a bill that might find favor with the new House. To make it palatable to the Conservatives, they restricted the vote to women who owned property. There was no vote for the working woman or for the housewife who did not own her home.

The Second Reading of the bill, on July 11 and 12, found F. E. Smith, the Tory picador, arguing for once on the same side as Churchill. Smith made the point that if women had the vote they might be able to impose duties on men, like conscription, which their own sex prevented them from carrying out. This was typically clever Smith reasoning, but it was Churchill who went to the heart of the matter. He was voting against the bill because it was undemocratic. In their efforts to rope in Conservative support, the committee had produced a bill that was worse than no bill at all. Money was the yardstick. Only one woman in thirteen would get the vote. It would lead to faggot-voting: that is, a wealthy man could give property to his wife and daughters and enfranchise them. A prostitute could enjoy the vote on her premises and then lose it when she made a respectable marriage. He was also voting against it because he did not think women were ready. "I do not believe that the great mass of women want a vote," he said. "I think they have made singularly little use of the immense opportunities of local and municipal government which have been thrown open to them. Although there are numerous brilliant exceptions, these exceptions do not alter the actual facts."[35] The bill was pigeonholed in committee. At least the issue had finally been awarded a full-dress debate. But Lord Lytton, laboring under the impression that Churchill favored the bill, felt betrayed, and there was a distinct chill in their friendship. Aside from the merits of the bill, Churchill felt that the suffragettes had less claim on him than on any other public man, having for five years tried to break up every meeting he ever addressed, having opposed him in four elections, having treated him with the vilest discourtesy and unfairness, having attacked him in insulting terms, and having assaulted him physically.

On July 20, Churchill presented to the House a program of prison reforms that would make him remembered as the first great Home Secretary of the twentieth century. What he asked for seemed obvious—time to pay debts instead of being sent to prison, and suspended sentences for trivial offenses—but in five years in power, the Liberals, who were supposed to have reform in their blood, had done nothing. Now Churchill, the turncoat Tory, the duke's grandson, came along and in less than a year pushed through reforms that are still the basis for English prison law.

The outstanding problem was that too many were sent to prison for minor offenses such as drunkenness or debt. Out of 205,000 committals in 1909, 61 percent, or nearly 125,000, had been for a fortnight or less, and nearly half of those were first offenders. It was a terrible waste of public money and human character. "The first real principle which should guide anyone trying to establish a good system of prisons," Churchill said, "should be to prevent as many people as possible getting there at all." It was better to fine a drunk than jail him, for release was often an occasion for celebration, while a fine effectively enforced meant a period of temperance. And what was the point of jailing a man for the nonpayment of a fine? Was it not preferable to give him time to pay it? The Tory argument was that without imprisonment for debt, workmen would not be able to obtain the necessary credit to tide them over strikes in bad times. By their going to jail as human collateral their debts were canceled. But it was not the business of the state, Churchill said, to facilitate strikes on credit by insolvent workmen. Trade union leaders agreed that workmen should find credit without pledging their bodies. Only working people were sent to prison for debt. Ernest Hooley, a well-known London stockbroker whose bankruptcy had made headlines, was thriving in opulent insolvency. In the meantime, touts and tallymen (who sold goods on the installment plan) went around pressing cheap jewelry, musical instruments, and other unnecessary articles on the workingman's wife in his absence, and then the man was sent to prison for nonpayment of debts run up by his wife. When the measures Churchill proposed were enacted in subsequent years, the resulting reduction of imprisonment for nonpayment of fines was dramatic, from 95,686 in 1908–1909 to 5,624 in 1918–1919. Convictions for drunkenness were also reduced.

Another shocking abuse was the treatment of youthful offenders between the ages of sixteen and twenty-one, who were sent to prison to mingle with the adult convict population. Each year, five thousand of these youths were shoveled into the prison system, convicted of such offenses as stone-throwing or playing football in the streets. This was pure waste, Churchill said. It was an evil "which falls only on the sons of the working classes. The sons of other classes may commit many of the same kind of offenses and in boisterous and exuberant moments, whether at Oxford or anywhere else, may do things for which the working classes are committed to prison" (as Randolph in his Oxford days had caused a disturbance in a hotel). "In my opinion no boy should go to prison unless he is incorrigible or has committed some serious offense."[36] Here again the results were telling: in 1910, there were 12,367 boys in prison; in 1919, 3,474.

As Churchill continued to explain what he had in mind on that July 20, 1910, grumbling was heard from the Tory benches that he was making prison life too comfortable. Why, the Somerset Light Infantry had given a concert at Dartmoor! And now he wanted to set aside money for four lectures a year in each prison, and for books, arguing that because of the Education Act many of the convicts were now literate and needed "brain food," and remembering perhaps how glad he had been in Pretoria to have access to books and newspapers.

But Churchill had the House with him when he ended with a passage that noted lawmakers since, in Great Britian and the United States, have committed to memory: "The mood and temper of the public in regard to the treatment of crime and criminals is one of the most unfailing tests of civilization of any country. A calm and dispassionate recognition of the rights of the accused against the state, and even of convicted criminals against the state, a constant heart-searching by all charged with the duty of punishment, a desire and eagerness to rehabilitate in the world of industry all those who have paid their dues in the hard coinage of punishment, tireless efforts towards the discovery of regenerating processes, and an unfaltering faith that there is a treasure, if you can only find it, in the heart of every man—these are the things which in the treatment of crime and criminals mark and measure the stored-up strength of a nation, and are the sign and proof of the living virtue in it."

Churchill's brief tenure at the Home Office left its stamp on the prison system for years to come. But on one occasion his intervention in favor of the downtrodden came too close to home. That August, he very improperly used the power and influence of his office in favor of his brother-in-law, twenty-two-year-old naval lieutenant William Ogilvy Hozier. Young William, in the Navy since 1903, had been serving for twenty-eight days aboard the H.M.S. *Mars* when his captain, F. E. C. Ryan, gave him the rating "inexperienced and highly inefficient," which would cripple his career. Convinced that Captain Ryan was prejudiced against him, Hozier wanted a transfer to another ship. Churchill took the matter up with the First Lord of the Admiralty, Reginald McKenna, writing him on August 8: "I am sure any good-hearted man who had young people's interest and fortunes in his care would feel a strong sense of fatherly responsibility to all of them. Most of all would this be so in a great Service like the Navy. But I found no trace of such a sentiment in Captain Ryan's certificate, and I am very pleased to read all you say about it on other grounds."[37]

A captain was well within his rights in reporting the performance of his subordinates; indeed, it was his duty to do so. Churchill was not addressing the substance of the matter—whether Hozier had deserved the rating—but shifted instead to an attack on the Captain for daring to criticize his brother-in-law. Even in those days, when it was common for Cabinet ministers to ask favors of one another on patronage matters, and allowing for the possibility that Ryan was one of those captains who liked to single out young officers of privileged background for harsh treatment, Churchill's interference was a clear example of abuse of office, quite out of character with his exertions for fair treatment in other areas.

When Lieutenant Hozier was transferred to the *Hibernia*, he wrote Churchill: "I did not mean you to know anything about the affair except to let you know that I wished to get out of the *Mars*. I feel that I have had every advantage given me thanks to you as most fellows could not get away from a bad Captain except by going on half-pay."[38]

In October, Hozier heard from McKenna that if he thought the certificate was unfair he should apply for a reconsideration. Captain Ryan at first refused, but then, thinking perhaps that with all this meddling in high quarters it might be in his own best interest to comply, he agreed to omit "inexperienced and highly inefficient." The new certificate said that Hozier's performance had been "unsatisfactory." Knowing he had Churchill behind him, Hozier sent an appeal to the Admiralty. Again Churchill wrote McKenna in his support: "I hope you will see your way to press this matter to a conclusion. You have told me that Captain Ryan's original report was irregular in form and open to objection on every ground. If this report is furthermore found to have no justification or no sufficient justification in fact behind it, I trust you will then consider whether an officer who shows himself ready to blacken and injure the reputation of young men under his care and charge callously, recklessly, and I daresay spitefully, ought not to be himself the subject of a severe reprimand . . . It is not on personal grounds any longer, but as a matter of principle that I venture to address you."[39] Churchill had turned the tables. The accused was no longer Hozier, but the evil Captain, who was now charged with behavior that deserved a reprimand, whereas all he had done was write a routine report on one of his junior officers. In his zeal to come to the aid of a relative, Churchill improperly interfered in an Admiralty matter.

Of course it might be argued that he was genuinely concerned with rooting out all cases of injustice, but the Admiralty was not his department, and it would have been appropriate to abstain from pressuring a Cabinet colleague in favor of an in-law. Churchill's instinct was generally on the side of the individual against the institution. With an ego of imperial dimensions, how could he not have defended individual dignity? There was another case at the time where he took the part of the accused against the accusing, but this time he was well within his bounds. Two warders at Warwick Prison were about to be fired for stopping off at pubs while escorting prisoners to the Police Court. The recommendation had been made by the prison commissioners and their respected chairman, Sir Evelyn Ruggles-Brise. Churchill had the warders reinstated, even though misbehavior on escort was considered a grave offense. He reasoned that although their conduct had been grossly improper, it was unlike cruelty to prisoners, giving false evidence, or insubordination, and that they should be given another chance.[40]

In August, Winston and Clemmie left on a cruise of the eastern Mediterranean. But before going, Churchill was presented with the case of a man who had killed the woman he lived with in a fit of drunken rage and was sentenced to death. It had become a nightmare for him to exercise his power of life and death over condemned criminals. This time, he saw that although the man had committed a terrible act, the rest of his life was unblemished. He was a good-natured fellow, popular in the neighborhood, and in the habit of giving sweets to children. Churchill commuted his sentence to life imprisonment. A few weeks later the man hanged himself in his cell. Churchill pondered the case. He was not sure that his grounds for a reprieve had been adequate. Now he realized that to most men, including the best, a life sentence was worse than a death sentence. The gulf was not that wide, there was almost as much torment in life imprisonment. He retained for the rest of his life the belief that capital punishment was necessary, and might be preferable to a life sentence.[41]

During his six-week holiday in the world of ruined civilizations and harshly jumbled races, Churchill left the Home Office in the care of Sir Edward Grey, who reported on August 21 that things were quiet. Two men had been hanged. This was the beastly part of the job. On the eve of the execution Grey kept wondering what sort of night they were having, until he felt that he could not let them hang unless he went to be hanged too. Aside from that, an incorrigible tramp had been given twelve lashes for having bashed a warder in the face with a pair of loose handcuffs, bitten a second, and pulled a third to the ground by the testicles.[42]

When he returned in September, the Home Secretary faced the worst social unrest in years. Between twenty-five thousand and thirty thousand miners went on strike in November in the Rhondda and Aberdare valleys of South Wales over wage differentials in the working of hard and soft seams. There was a tradition of violence in the mines. The owners were alarmist and provocative, and treated the local police like flunkies. The miners were prone to riot. One November dawn, they formed a cordon around the pitheads, preventing the enginemen from going to work. They turned off the ventilating machines, endangering the lives of hundreds of pit ponies in their underground stalls. On November 7 and 8, attacks on the Glamorgan Colliery were repulsed by the county police. The rioters foiled in the colliery attack wrecked some houses and shops and stormed a pithead in the town of Tonypandy. This was reported in the pro-management *Times* as "an orgy of naked anarchy."

On November 10, the chief constable of Glamorgan asked for troops from the local Army Command, without consulting the Home Secretary. A small force was sent, and the constable then notified Churchill, who got in touch with Haldane at the War Office and prevailed upon him to stop the movement of troops. On August 15, he had said in the House: "There can be no question of the military forces of the Crown intervening in a labor dispute." Instead, Churchill proposed to send three hundred police, one hundred of them mounted. They were unarmed and picked for handling crowds. They had an instinct for prevention rather than cure. If troops were sent, rifles would go off, sabers would cut, and families would mourn their dead. With a General Election due in a month, the last thing the government wanted was to be accused of murdering workingmen.[43] General Sir Nevil Macready was seconded to the Home Office and sent to South Wales to take command of both military and police forces. Macready did not for a moment believe that the British workingman would sink to the level of Irishmen or foreigners by the use of lethal weapons against unarmed police.[44]

In an appeal to the miners, Churchill promised an immediate Board of Trade inquiry, warning that "rioting must cease at once so that the inquiry shall not be prejudiced and to prevent the credit of the Rhondda Valley being injured. Confiding in the good sense of the Cambrian workmen we are holding back the soldiers for the present and sending police instead." The police contained the rioters, and the troops were held in reserve, not to be used as strikebreakers but to rescue the unarmed constables. There was a hard fight on November 21, when the police drove the mob back along the main road, under heavy stoning, and six policemen were badly injured. General Macready used a little gentle persuasion with the bayonet in rounding up strikers and herding them into the arms of the police.[45]

One might have expected Churchill to be commended for his restraint. Instead, he was attacked on the left for using too much force and on the right for not using enough. The *Times* of November 9 wrote: "The Home Secretary took upon himself a grave responsibility in interfering with the arrangements demanded by the Chief Constable and acceded to by the military authorities . . . if loss of life occurs, which we fear is more than possible, the responsibility will lie with the Home Secretary." The *Daily Express* found that his message to the miners was "the last word in a policy of shameful neglect and poltroonery which may cost the country very dear." On the left, the leader of the Labour Party in the House of Commons, Keir Hardie, himself a coal miner, attacked Churchill for "letting loose troops upon the people to shoot down if need be whilst they are fighting for their legitimate rights." Hardie's call for an inquiry, on March 6, 1911, was defeated by 238 to 23. When Clem Edwards, the Labour MP for Glamorgan, spoke in Churchill's defense, Hardie became so incensed that he called Edwards "a reptile of the viper kind," an expression that was ruled out of order.

For the next forty years, the albatross of Tonypandy hung around Churchill's neck. At every election he would be accused of having sent troops to attack the miners. Tonypandy was the start of the break between Churchill and the trade-union movement. Although it was unfair to focus on and distort that single incident, Tonypandy was a convenient way to embarrass Churchill, who was seen as unsympathetic to the aims and methods of trade unionism.

General Macready, the man on the spot, wrote in his memoirs that "it was entirely due to Mr. Churchill's forethought in sending a strong force of Metropolitan Police directly he was made aware of the state of affairs in the valleys that bloodshed was avoided, for had the police not been in strength sufficient to cope with the rioters there would have been no alternative but to bring the military into action."[46] Churchill defended himself convincingly when the matter came before the House of Commons in February 1911: "For soldiers to fire on the people would be a catastrophe in our national life. Alone among the nations, or almost alone, we have avoided for a great many years that melancholy and unnatural experience. And it is well worth while, I venture to think, for the Minister who is responsible to run some risk of broken heads or broken windows . . . to accept direct responsibility in order that the shedding of British blood by British soldiers may be averted as, thank God, it has been successfully averted in South Wales."

A week after Tonypandy, on Friday, November 18, when Asquith announced new elections, the suffragettes realized that the Conciliation Bill was dead, and that they would have to start from scratch in the next Parliament. Some three hundred women stormed Parliament Square and fought with the police for six hours. There seems to have been a breakdown in the chain of command between the Home Office and the London police chief, Sir Edward Henry. Churchill said he had wanted to arrest large numbers of women right away and then release them. The opposite was done. Police roughed up the women but did not arrest them. The incident became known in the suffragette movement as "Black Friday," because the police had acted with such deliberate brutality. Women were punched, kicked, pinched, knocked down, and grabbed by the breasts. One constable, seizing a woman in an affectionate hug from behind, said, "My old dear, I can grip you where I like today." When a suffragette leader was arrested, an inspector was heard telling a constable: "Take the cow away." In the course of the fracas, two hundred arrests were made. Churchill was held responsible and occupied a special place of villainy among the militant female population.[47]

Four days later, the suffragettes attacked Asquith and Augustine Birrell as they came out of 10 Downing Street. Arriving on the scene, Churchill saw a suffragette leader pinned against a railing by police and called out: "Take that woman away, she is obviously one of the ringleaders." "That woman" was Mrs. Cobden-Sanderson, daughter of the great Cobden, champion of free trade, who had often been Churchill's hostess and was a close friend of his wife's family.

Overhearing Churchill, a twenty-one-year-old sympathizer named Hugh Franklin swore to avenge the insult to Mrs. Cobden-Sanderson. A few days later, Churchill was campaigning in Bradford. Returning to London on the train, he was on his way to the dining car when Franklin loomed, raising a dog whip and shouting, "Winston Churchill, take that, you cur." The blow was intercepted by a detective, and Franklin was sentenced to six weeks in jail.[48]

Campaigning in Dundee on December 1, he had it out with three suffragettes who came to call: Agnes Husband, a prominent member of the Dundee Labour Party; Lila Clunas, secretary of the Dundee branch of the Women's Freedom League; and a Miss Grant.

Miss Clunas said that Asquith had given a "sort of a pledge" that there would be a woman's franchise bill in the next Parliament.

"Why do you call it a sort of a pledge?" Churchill asked.

"I do not think it is a pledge," Miss Clunas said. "What we want is a pledge for the first session of 1911."

"You will not get that," Churchill said. He was in favor in principle of women being enfranchised. But he utterly declined to pledge himself to any particular bill. He would not support any bill that would alter the balance of parties by favoring the property vote. He would not vote for any bill unless he was convinced that it had behind it the genuine majority of the electors. He did not want to extend any encouragement which might afterward afford grounds for their reproaches. Whatever he said on the subject only served as an excuse for renewed abuse and insult.

"You referred to hostility," Miss Husband said.

"I call it hostility when meeting after meeting is disturbed, when people who come miles and miles to hear a speaker find the proceedings interrupted by senseless and deliberately planned interruption. I call it hostility when threats of violence are used and personal violence is offered."

"The Liberals are hostile to us," Miss Clunas said.

"But you are working your utmost to defeat me."

"Yes."

"What right have you to come here at all? If a body has definitely taken a part against a man, it is not usual for that body to come and examine the candidate. A neutral body free, free to take action in any way, and ready to be conciliated by the answer it receives—such a body may come, but I know you will do your best, as you have done on every occasion, to prevent my return. I make an exception for you, but if you were men I would not have received you on these conditions. I don't think that any body which has continued an active campaign has a right to be received."

"Anyone working actively against you would not be allowed to your meetings to ask questions," said Miss Clunas.

"If you find difficulty in getting into meetings it is because you have gone to wreck them," Churchill concluded.[49] He had met with the enemy and found it exasperatingly obstinate.

Churchill shuttled between his campaign in Dundee and the Home Office, where the staff was working on measures that had been shelved because of the political crisis. There was a Mines Accidents Act to deal with pit disasters, which had cost the lives of nearly five hundred miners that year, and a Coal Mines Act compelling owners to take safety measures against gas and coal dust. Both these acts were incorporated into a Coal Mines Bill that was passed in 1911. There was the Shops Bill, to protect shops assistants, for whom there were no health regulations or limitations on the hours of work. Their tuberculosis rate was one of the highest in the nation, and their woeful condition had been dramatized by H. G. Wells in *Kipps* and *Mr. Polly*. Eddie Marsh found the Shops Bill intensely interesting. Churchill was receiving deputations and getting the most thrilling revelations about how the poor live. What a difference it would make to all the "counterjumpers"; it really was one of the things that were worth doing.[50]

There was a day during the debate on the Shops Bill when Horatio Bottomley, editor of the scandal sheet *John Bull*—which ran items such as "Who are the two Front Bench men who are in the habit of coming down to the House in a state of alcoholic stimulation?"—got the better of Churchill. Bottomley rose in righteous wrath to inveigh against the harshness of a clause that would prevent a poor old woman from buying a twist of tobacco at the very hour when her need was greatest. Churchill whispered to Charlie Masterman, who briefly left the floor and returned to whisper to Churchill, who asked Bottomley if he was aware that the provision he objected to had been a part of the law since eighteen hundred and something. "No, sir," Bottomley said, "I was not aware of it. Nor was the right honorable Gentleman himself till a moment ago; for I saw him send the Under-Secretary to inquire of the officials."[51] Poorly drafted, the Shops Bill fell prey to various lobbies. The Jews did not like it because it specified that Jewish shops open on Sunday should serve only Jewish customers. The Archbishop of Canterbury did not like it because it proposed Sunday opening in large towns. It was so deci-mated in committee that Churchill complained about the long succession of pages that were now wastepaper.

In such a fertile mind as Churchill's some of the rubies were bound to be garnets. One of his most bizarre plans, apparently derived from the study of eugenics, would have been better suited to the Germany of the Third Reich than to the England of George V. He wanted to lock up or sterilize the feeble-minded, whom he saw as a grave threat to the health of the British race, for he was convinced that they bred like rabbits.

This is the proposal he made to Asquith in December 1910:

> I am convinced that the multiplication of the feeble-minded . . . un-checked by any of the old restraints of nature, and actually fostered by civilized conditions, is a very terrible danger to the race. The number of children in feeble-minded families is calculated at 7.4 whereas in normal families it is but 4.2. The feeble-minded girls and young women are the easy prey of vice and hand on their own insanity with unerring and un-failing fertility . . . The males contribute an ever-broadening streak to the insane or half-insane crime which darkens the life of our towns and fills the convict prisons. It will be expensive to keep the feeble-minded but it will be much cheaper than multiplying them. The unnatural and increasingly rapid growth of the feeble-minded and insane classes, coupled as it is with a steady restriction among all the thrifty, energetic and superior stocks constitutes a national and a race danger which it is impossible to exaggerate . . . I feel that the source from which the stream of madness is fed should be cut off and sealed up before another year has passed.[52]

Nothing more was heard of the plan, although Churchill told Wilfrid Blunt that he was a strong eugenist concerned about the decay of the race, and that he had drafted a bill to shut up the mentally retarded. He wanted to sterilize both men and women with roentgen rays, although the women might require an operation, to which they would happily submit as a condition of having their liberty restored. This must stand as Churchill's wildest scheme and points to curious notions of race and irrational fears, connected perhaps to his father's madness. The inherent danger of Churchill's brilliance and ascendancy over many of his colleagues was that he could defend a sound or an unsound idea with equal persuasiveness.

The year 1911, a year that saw a war scare with Germany and the worst labor unrest that England had known in the twentieth century, opened with the sound of gunfire for Churchill. His thoughts were on the Parliament Bill, the King's secret pledge to create peers, the chance at last to reduce the Lords. On the morning of January 3, at home in his study at Eccleston Square, he was mapping out strategy in a letter to Asquith. Cabinet ministers saw one another every day but communicated by letter, and Churchill wrote his colleagues a dozen letters a day, for which biographers are grateful. "We ought as early as possible to make it clear that we are not a bit afraid of creating 500 Peers—if necessary . . ." he wrote. "Such a creation would be in fact for the interest of the Liberal Party, and a disaster to the Conservative[s] . . . The wealth and importance of British Society could easily maintain 1000 notables . . . If the Bill does not make proper progress we should clink the coronets in their scabbards. . . ."[53] (As mixed a metaphor as was ever penned.)

At 10:45, the telephone rang. It was the Home Office with an urgent message. The Houndsditch gang was surrounded in a house at 100 Sidney Street, in Stepley, and was firing at police. Two weeks before, on December 16, a gang of burglars had been surprised by police as they tried to break into a jewelry shop in the East End district of Houndsditch. They opened fire on the unarmed constables, killing three and wounding two others. There was an outcry in the press. The compact that allowed the "bobbies" to carry out their duties unarmed had been broken. It was not only criminal, it was un-English. Churchill authorized the issue of automatic revolvers, and soon after, a member of the gang was killed in a gun battle. The gang, it developed, was part of a tiny colony of Latvian anarchists from Baltic Russia, led by a shadowy figure known as "Peter the Painter," a sign painter from Riga.

At the Home Office, Churchill gave the authority to use twenty Scots Guards armed with rifles. The Horse Artillery was also brought in with its cannon. Unable to resist seeing for himself, he left with Eddie Marsh for 100 Sidney Street, a mean house in a bleak district, arriving at noon in his silk hat and fur-lined overcoat. He did not interfere with the arrangements of the police, but told the gathering crowd to stay back and reconnoitered the rear of the house for escape routes. At 1 P.M., the house caught fire. The fire brigade was ready, but the gang was still firing. A junior officer asked

Churchill if they were right in not putting out the fire. "Quite right," he said, "I accept the full responsibility." It was too dangerous to let the firemen operate their hoses at close quarters.[54] How extraordinary, thought Eddie, to see a fusillade going on in a dim London street, and the fire brigade standing by encouraging the house to burn.

Hundreds watched the flames billow skyward. A twenty-eight-year-old social worker assigned to a boys' club in the East End was taking the headmaster of his former school for a walk when they ran into one of the boys, who said, "I can't get to work; they're shooting like anything down the street." "Let's go and see," said the social worker, whose name was Clement Attlee, and they joined the crowd viewing the scene.[55]

Two bodies were picked out of the smoking ruins, one shot and one asphyxiated, but neither was Peter the Painter, who was not heard from again, and may not have existed.

Churchill went home to finish his letter to Asquith: "I was interrupted in copying out this letter by the Stepney affair from which I have just returned. It was a striking scene in a London street—firing from every window, bullets chipping the brickwork, police and Scots Guards armed with loaded weapons, artillery jingling up &c. I thought it better to let the house burn down rather than spend good British lives in rescuing these ferocious rascals."[56]

His presence at the scene was the subject of indignant commentary in the Tory press. Would the First Lord of the Admiralty command a ship when the fleet was sent out? Would the rotund Secretary of State for War march at the head of the Army? What was the Home Secretary doing there, and why did he call out the troops? Churchill complained that the *Times*, which had blamed him for stopping the troops from going to Tonypandy, was now blaming him for sending soldiers to Sidney Street. Their doctrine was apparently that soldiers should always be sent to put down miners in trade disputes, but never to apprehend alien murderers engaged in crime. And why should he not have gone to the scene? Was it not the Home Secretary's responsibility to be physically present at a siege involving troops and loss of life taking place in England's capital?

At the Palace Theatre, Eddie Marsh saw himself and Winston animated with the fluttering gestures that early newsreels lent to human motion. Their appearance on the screen was greeted with unanimous boos and shouts of "Shoot him" from the gallery. Why, Eddie wondered, were London music-hall audiences so uniformly and so bigotedly Tory?[57]

In the House of Commons, where Churchill's zest for action was the subject of debate, Balfour commented: "We are concerned to observe photographs in the illustrated newspapers of the Home Secretary in the danger-zone. I understand what the photographer was doing, but why the Home Secretary?" Churchill replied that Balfour had been the victim of similar publicity when he had risked his valuable life in a flying machine. He acknowledged that he would have been better advised to follow the action from his office but insisted that he had not directed the operations.[58]

When it was all over, Charles Masterman, back from a trip, burst into Churchill's office and asked, "What the hell have you been doing now, Winston?" "Now, Charlie, don't be cross, it was such fun," Churchill said.[59]

Having fought against tighter measures for aliens when he was running in Manchester, Churchill now agreed with the views conveyed by Sir Arthur Bigge, the King's private secretary, in a letter on January 5, expressing the King's hope "that these outrages by foreigners will lead you to consider whether the Aliens Act could not be amended so as to prevent London from being infested with men and women whose presence would not be tolerated in any other country." He drafted a bill that would expel aliens convicted of a criminal offense, and would restrict their right to own guns, but it came to nothing, and aliens' regulations were not revised until after the start of World War I.

The true significance of the Sidney Street affair was not in Churchill's presence at the scene or in his decision to let two criminals die in order to save British lives. The origins of his visceral anti-Communism can be traced to the Houndsditch gang. They represented everything that threatened the ordered society, the rule of law, the Parliamentary government, the very marrow of English life. The English had evolved a civilized way of managing their affairs, which these hoodlums upset. They were the same sort of men who were soon to overthrow the established order in Russia. In one great sweep, Anarchy and Bolshevism combined in his mind. They were the enemy.

The right way to do things was through debate, the use of language rather than the use of arms. On February 23, there was a motion of censure against Churchill for not dismissing the superintendent of a reform school near Liverpool who was accused of cruel and unusual punishment. Captain Beuttler, who ran the Heswall Reform School, sounded like one of the sadistic child-floggers in Victorian novels. He used nonregulation canes for birching and stifled the boys' cries by covering their mouths with blankets. Of eighty-eight boys caned in the period of a year, scars disfigured twenty-seven. At the Home Office, Churchill, Masterman, and Marsh spent an amusing afternoon birching one another with the "sealed pattern" birches used at Heswall to see if they hurt. They didn't, Eddie thought, but wouldn't it be awful if there was a birching scandal at the Home Office? He could see the headlines: "Brutal cruelty of a Minister to his Private Secretary."[60]

In the House of Commons, there were members who did not find the Heswall matter quite so amusing. On one occasion, Captain Beuttler had made the boys stand by their hammocks from ten at night until five in the morning, alternating every fifteen minutes between attention and at ease. This one action should have warranted his immediate dismissal. One boy had been taken out on a cold night in November and had fifteen pails of icy water thrown on him. This was inhuman treatment. Three boys had died of illness, improperly attended, and another boy had died after being drenched with water. Clearly, the superintendent was a brute and must go.

Although quick to defend those unjustly punished (his brother-in-law was only one example) and knowledgeable in matters of birching (he had been birched at his first school), Churchill had no intention of dismissing Captain Beuttler, who had done wonders for the Heswall reformatory. It was run along nautical lines, and shipping companies were now willing to hire the boys it released. But by laying all the facts before the House, and by giving the impression that he might dismiss the Captain, he escaped censure, by a vote of 244 to 67.[61]

On that occasion his rhetorical gifts saved him, but just as often they mired him in senseless disputes. On February 10, in his nightly letter to the King on the work of the House, he proposed Labour Colonies for tramps and wastrels, adding: "It must not however be forgotten that there are idlers and wastrels at both ends of the social scale."[62] George V saw this remark as a gratuitous dig at the Lords and perhaps even an implication that he was a *roi fainéant*. He had his secretary, Lord Knollys, inform Asquith's secretary that it was quite superfluous to talk of idlers and wastrels at both ends of the social ladder.

Mortified, and feeling that the King was ungrateful for the great trouble he took over the letters, which were a burdensome addition to his regular duties, Churchill's reply on February 13 showed him at his most petulant: as he had been in the habit of writing freely and frankly, he now would have great trouble continuing for fear that in a moment of inadvertence or fatigue some phrase or expression might escape him that would produce an unfavorable effect. He hoped that the duty could be transferred to some other minister. As for the offending remark, he felt that all persons whether rich or poor should render some service to the state. Most of the wealthy class did their duty; he only wanted to point to those persons whose idle and frivolous conduct and lack of public spirit brought a reproach to the meritorious class to which they belonged. He did not withdraw the remark and adhered to the sincerity of his opinion.[63]

Lord Knollys replied on the fourteenth that the King was sorry Churchill's feelings were hurt, though he still wished Churchill had suppressed the remark about idlers and wastrels on both ends of the social scale, for obviously the cost of support in one case fell on the state but not in the other. It was not a good idea for a Cabinet minister in a communication to the King to express his own views on important questions, which might not be in agreement with the views of his colleagues. The King would be sorry if he were to receive no further letters from him. At the same time he did not want him to continue if he was disinclined. Churchill had said that he had never been offered any guidance in the form of his letters. Lord Knollys said he would be pleased to show him the bound volumes of letters from previous Home Secretaries such as Palmerston, Disraeli, and Gladstone.[64]

There was too much arrogance in Churchill, Lord Knollys thought, and too little deference to the King. Why did he always insist on being right? By this time, Churchill had received from Asquith a formal notification of the King's displeasure. The rebuke led him to write again, on February 16, that the serious and exceptional step of a letter to the Home Secretary from the Prime Minister was utterly undeserved and out of proportion to any error unconsciously committed. This was why, feeling pained, he had asked to be relieved of a duty that might expose him to further possibilities of forfeiting the King's favor. However, in view of Lord Knollys' letter, he agreed to continue.[65]

Knollys supposed that this was the closest that Churchill could come to an apology. He was rather like a bull in a china shop, and quite wrong in complaining about the King going through the Prime Minister. Surely that was the proper way of conveying a reproof from the King to a member of the Cabinet. Queen Victoria always used to send remonstrances to her Foreign Secretary, Lord Palmerston, through her Prime Minister, Lord John Russell.[66]

In the midst of these skirmishes with the House of Commons and the King, the central issue was still the Parliament Bill. The new Parliament had opened on February 6, 1911, and the bill with its three resolutions had gone through Commons two weeks later for the second time, by 351 to 227. All spring it was discussed, and more than nine hundred amendments were defeated. It was a laborious process. An entire week was devoted to four lines of one paragraph. When was the real conflict in the House of Lords going to begin? Churchill wondered; every week it seemed to recede a stage. When the Second Reading was carried on March 2, Balfour called the bill a fraud. His use of the word created a storm, but Churchill approved. The House of Commons must not be mealymouthed. Such accusations were not beyond the limits of debate.[67]

In addition to his Home Office work, Churchill had a great deal to do with piloting the Parliament Bill through the House. He was often deputized by Asquith, on whom the burden of leadership was beginning to tell. The stress and restraints he was under as Prime Minster led him to seek release in drink and the company of young women. He had begun his flirtation with the twenty-three-year-old Venetia Stanley, the camellia-skinned and luminous-eyed daughter of a Liberal lord (and Clementine Churchill's cousin), which would flower into a grand passion. He was already known to his detractors as "Squiff," for his bibulous evening habits. In Asquith at fifty-eight, the dignity of the statesman alternated with the comic figure of the drunk. One night he was so drunk he had to be carried off the floor of the House. During the debate on April 22, he was all right until dinner, but thereafter he was so deep in his cups he could hardly speak. Churchill squirmed with embarrassment, for a hundred Members of Parliament at least had seen the Prime Minister incapable of leaving the House unassisted. What an awful pity it was; only the freemasonry of the House of Commons prevented a scandal. It was nonetheless a terrible risk to run, for if the negotiations had fallen to him the consequences would have been disastrous.[68]

On May 15, when the bill passed its Third Reading, Churchill said: "We regard this measure as territory conquered by the masses from the classes—a province won by the people in two elections which have been fought upon it. . . . We shall no longer face each other as master and servant. We shall meet each other on a true and proper basis of responsible partners in the trust and inheritance of our country and Empire." On the day after Churchill spoke these words, John Burns, the President of the Local Government Board, had an audience with the King, who expressed his fear that Churchill had not been entirely successful in conciliating the House. "Well, Your Majesty," Burns said, "Winston Churchill does not exactly walk about the House with an oil-can in his hand."[69]

The bill went to the House of Lords, where it was smothered in amendments, as if no election had been held, and was sent back to Commons completely mutilated. Churchill would be glad when the crisis came. What could you do with men whose obstinacy and pride had blinded them to their interests and every counsel of reason? It would not be surprising if they actually had to create five hundred peers.

In a Cabinet meeting on July 14, it was decided that the only recourse was to bring in the King, who was notified that the dreaded moment had arrived. Like a man under sentence of death pleading for a reprieve, George V asked that the Lords be advised and given a chance to reconsider. Accordingly, on July 20, letters went out to the Conservative leaders of both houses, Balfour and Lansdowne, warning that this was not a bluff. The Lords split between Ditchers, who thought Asquith was bluffing and who vowed to die in the last ditch before surrendering, and Hedgers, who advised strategic retreat. At last, here was the showdown that Churchill longed for.

The degree of anger could be measured by the temperature of the House of Commons and July 24, when Asquith rose to move that the Lords' amendments be considered. He was immediately assailed by cries of "Traitor." When the Speaker tried to restore order, a knot of Tories led by Lord Hugh Cecil, the former Hooligan and Churchill's best man, prevented Asquith from going on.

LORD HUGH CECIL: "Mr. Speaker, the right honorable Gentleman [Interruption] . . . King's name [Interruption] . . . House of Commons . . . [Interruption] has prostituted ordinary Parliamentary usage . . . [Interruption]. Therefore, there is no discourtesy to him."

MR. SPEAKER: "The House has not yet heard what the Prime Minister has to say. It would only be according to the ordinary rules of courtesy to hear him."

LORD HUGH CECIL: "This is not an ordinary occasion."

ASQUITH: "Mr. Speaker, in offering . . ." [Disorder.]

SIR E. CARSON: "I beg to Move the Adjournment."

MR. SPEAKER: "I cannot take any notice of the Motion of Adjournment of the right honorable and learned Gentleman as we have not yet begun on the Debate."

ASQUITH: "This proposal . . ." [Disorder.]

AN HON. MEMBER: "Write another letter."

ASQUITH: "Once more . . ." [Interruptions.]

MR. SPEAKER: "My appeal is that the decencies of debate shall be observed on both sides of the House."

ASQUITH: "The principles on which this Bill is drawn were all affirmed and approved by the House of Commons as long ago as the year 1907."

AN HON. MEMBER: "It ought to have known better."

MR. CROOKS: "Many a man has been certified as insane for less than half of what the Noble Lord [Lord Hugh Cecil] has done this afternoon."

From the Ladies' Gallery, Margot Asquith scribbled a note to Edward Grey, sitting next to her husband: "For God's sake, defend him from the cats and the cads."

But what could Grey do? The situation was impossible. Every time Asquith opened his mouth, he was shouted down by furious Tories.

ASQUITH: "We were to have the application of the Referendum. . . ."

HON. MEMBERS: "Let the people decide."

ASQUITH: "Another General Election followed in December 1910. . . ."

HON. MEMBERS: "On the old Register."

ASQUITH: "The electors of this country had before them—"

HON. MEMBERS: "Black bread."

ASQUITH: "—the Bill itself with all its details . . ."

HON. MEMBERS: "And the Preamble."

ASQUITH: "On the other hand they had before them the counterproposals—"

HON. MEMBERS: "Limehouse."

ASQUITH: "—of the Opposition, which . . . were vigorously defended and as vigorously attacked in every constituency in the country. What was the result?"

MR. HAROLD SMITH: "Sods and souls."

On it went, until Asquith, abandoning his speech, said: "I will not degrade myself by attempting to address arguments to Gentlemen who are obviously resolved not to listen . . ." He only wanted to say that unless the Lords accepted the bill as it stood, the government would invoke the prerogative of the Crown, that is, the creation of peers. The bill must take its place on the Statute Book without further delay.[70]

Reporting the brouhaha to the King, Churchill wrote: "The ugliest feature was the absence of any real passion or spontaneous feeling. It was a squalid frigid organized attempt to insult the Prime Minister . . ."[71] Perhaps he remembered that Balfour had once accused him of rehearsing his insults and delivering them without spontaneity. The bill went back to the Lords in an either/or situation. Either they passed it or the King would create enough new peers to ensure its passage. Already, the Liberal Whips were compiling lists of more or less willing volunteers for the peerage. Churchill thought he saw indications that the bill would be carried by a coalition of Liberal peers, bishops, and friends of the King. Balfour and Lansdowne beat the drum for the Hedgers. The Ditchers, led by that excellent symbol of the old order, eighty-seven-year-old Lord Halsbury, recruited among the backwoods peers, who were said to have three talents—they knew how to kill a fox, evict a bad tenant, and get rid of an unwanted mistress.

On August 7, Churchill made what he called a "wretched-man-I-do-not-wish-by-any-words-of-mine-to-add-to-the-anguish-which-you-no-doubt-feel" speech, stressing the bill's moderation. The Lords would have plenty of power left.[72]

On August 10, the Lords voted. It was one of the hottest days of an extremely hot summer, 97° in the shade. Usually half empty, the House of Lords was packed. Some of the backwoods peers, it was said, had found Westminster only after asking directions. The speeches droned on, the shadows lengthened, the candles were brought in. Finally, at 10:30 P.M., the Ditchers and the Hedgers filed out into the lobbies on either side of the Chamber, and tellers with white wands tapped them on the shoulder as they emerged from the division lobbies. The count was 131 to 114 for the Parliament Bill. The power of the peers had come to an end with a whimper, by a majority of 17. It was not only that the Lords had lost their right to obstruct legislation, and that the way was now open for a Home Rule Bill, which would be introduced in the next session. There was an intangible sense of loss. It was goodbye to the men who did not believe in Lord Acton's dictum that the only possible attitude of statesmanship was "to watch with hopefulness the prospect of incalculable change." The two-year crisis was over. "I am spared any further humiliation," the King said.

Having lost three elections in a row and been beaten on the Parliament Bill, the Tories turned against their leader. "B.M.G." was the slogan— "Balfour Must Go"—and in November he went, quite willingly. Bonar Law, the square-jawed Presbyterian, replaced him, illustrating the transfer of power from the landed gentry to the merchant class; from Balfour, who loved Handel and house parties, to Bonar Law, a teetotaling widower who had once shocked his hosts in the country by not recognizing a pheasant. On November 17, Churchill sent his congratulations. "If ever a national emergency makes party interests fade," he said, "we shall find in the leader of the

Opposition one who in no fictitious sense places the Country and the Empire first."[73] They both belonged to a dining club called the Other Club, and Churchill expressed the hope that one of its members would someday become Prime Minister. The Other Club had been thought up by Churchill and F. E. Smith, who decided to bring together in relaxed and informal surroundings political and intellectual leaders of the time, irrespective of their views and party affiliations—it was a deliberately cross-party club. Each year while Parliament sat, however bitter the debates, men of all political hues—but the brilliant ones—gathered on alternate Thursdays for dinner at the Savoy Hotel. The total membership was about fifty, a dozen from each major party and a couple of dozen from outside the House of Commons, and twenty or so usually turned up in full evening dress or uniform. Women were not asked, and, according to the bylaws, members of the Executive were "wrapped in impenetrable mystery." At the Other Club, Churchill could expand his range of interests and contacts. He could meet men with whom he fought in the House on convivial terms, and men of a different generation, like Lord Londonderry. He could exchange views with men as different as the Duke of Westminster, J. L. Garvin (editor of *The Observer*), Lord Kitchener, James Barrie (author of *Peter Pan*), and the rising young Liberal Josiah Wedgwood (a direct descendant of the celebrated potter). Wedgwood thought of the Other Club as a pleasant brotherhood, where men who did not want anything from one another and who did not hope to change anyone's mind about anything met in the unspoken conviction that if they did not rule the world it was the world's misfortune.

Aside from the Parliament Bill and the new Tory leader, the House of Commons changed in 1911 in another significant way. An annual salary of four hundred pounds was voted into the Budget, marking the end of the MP as an unpaid gentleman's profession. There were working-class men in the House of Commons now, like the coal miner Keir Hardie, who could, thanks to their salary, afford to remain in politics. It would come in handy for Churchill, who had the expense of a growing family without the relief of a large private income.

Diana was almost two, and on May 28, 1911, Randolph was born. His parents, who dubbed him Chum Bolly, had been expecting a boy. Clemmie hoped he would not inherit the Pug's unpunctual habits. Sir Edward Grey and F. E. Smith were the godfathers. Grey and Churchill had become good friends. They went swimming in the Automobile Club pool, and Grey filled in at the Home Office when Churchill went on trips. "He likes and wistfully admires our little circle,"[74] Churchill wrote of him to Clemmie, for Grey was a sad and solitary man, still mourning his wife.

In June, Churchill drilled with the Oxfordshire Hussars. His poor face hurt from sunburn and he missed his family. He hoped his precious pussy cat was not sitting up or fussing; she must get well and strong and enjoy the richness of the new event. The Chum Bolly must do his duty and help Clemmie with the milk, at his age greediness and even swinishness at table were virtues.[75] Clemmie reported that he grew more darling and handsome every hour and put on weight with every meal, so that soon he would be a little round ball of fat. Catching sight of her nose when she was kissing him, he suddenly fastened and began to suck on it, no doubt thinking it was another part of her person.[76] Everything was going fine, except that the nurserymaid was a hussy. Don't hesitate to sack, Churchill advised. He sent two thousand kisses to his sweet birdling and wished he could see her in her most transparent Venetian bathing dress—how glorious she would look. When he got back, he wanted to have dinner with her in her room and give her lots of kisses on her dear cheeks and dearest lips.[77]

On June 22, an overcast day, George V was crowned. As a mark of favor to Churchill, Clemmie, the nursing mother, was invited to attend the ceremony in the King's box. It was the last prewar coronation. George V would rule for twenty-five years. His son and successor, the Prince of Wales, would rule less than a year before abdicating. Churchill formed a good impression of the seventeen-year-old Prince when he read out the Letters Patent at his investiture on July 13 at Carnarvon Castle in Wales.[78] While playing golf with Lloyd George at Walton Heath, Churchill had recited the proclamation he had to make, and there was considerable discussion as to what emphasis should be placed on the words "know ye." Churchill experimented with three or four different renderings.[79] Now, amid the sunlit battlements, with Lloyd George as Constable of the Castle standing at the side of the three thrones, Churchill proclaimed young Edward's style and titles, and his reading was much praised. The little Prince, he thought, looked and spoke as well as it was possible. He made a little speech in the Welsh tongue, rehearsed by Lloyd George, and they sang "God Save the King" and "The Land of My Fathers." Churchill loved the ceremonial side of the monarchy. It was in his blood. This was a happy event that would live in the memory of all who took part in it. For the dangerous Radical Lloyd George, cordial relations with the royal family were a new departure. "I 'ear Lloyd George has 'ousemaid's knee from cringing to Royalty," John Burns said.[80]

From Carnarvon, Churchill went to stay at Penrhos, on the Holyhead Peninsula in northwest Wales, with Lord and Lady Stanley of Alderly. Three of their daughters were there, Blanche, Sylvia, and Venetia, as well as Asquith, his daughter Violet, and his daughter-in-law Cynthia. Asquith and Violet teased Venetia, accusing her of flirting on the golf course with Reginald McKenna, who had said, "Come along my little mascot," to which she had replied, "I wish I were—and then I could hang on your watch chain." Venetia was furious and denied having said any such thing.[81] In the afternoon they motored to a large sandy bay, and Churchill mobilized the party into building fortifications in the sand according to Vauban's first system. The cliffs were lined with people observing this strange spectacle through field glasses. Watching Churchill, Cynthia noticed the intensity of his eyes, and his alternating periods of brooding and surging talk. He looked older, as if the weight of the world and his own destiny were already on his shoulders.[82]

The lightheartedness of such occasions and the snug harbor of his family were Churchill's escapes from the cares of office, for as J. A. Spender said, "Never in the memory of men living had a Ministry been beset with so many and great dangers as Asquith's government." Two days before the Coronation, seamen at Southampton had struck, and were followed in Liverpool and Cardiff and Hull. Warehouses went up in flames and the London dockers "downed bales." It looked to Churchill like the beginning of a general strike, with a multiplication of Tonypandy incidents. The police and the military were being asked for at town after town. There was the danger of a railway strike, for transport workers everywhere were getting to know their strength, and had new leaders. Sympathy strikes were called. Shipping, coal, railways, and dockers were uniting and striking together.

In August the crisis came. This time Churchill decided that troops were needed, for there were fifty places in the country where violence might erupt, but he ordered them to fire over the rioters' heads. On August 13, the National Transport Workers Federation held a mass meeting in front of St. George's Hall in Liverpool. The head constable was ready with a large number of police and one hundred men of the Royal Warwickshire Regiment. Demonstrators felt that the spirit of the meeting was being violated by a cart that was being loaded with scenery at the back of a theater to be taken to the railroad station. The cart was overturned, and the rioting began. The disturbance spread to Lord Nelson Street, where three policemen were attacked. The Riot Act was read, and the area was cleared. On the next day the riots continued, and soldiers fired at individuals who were throwing missiles from windows and roofs of houses. There were no casualties. But when a detachment of two officers and thirty-two men of the 18th Hussars escorting a Liverpool prison van was attacked, the soldiers fired and one civilian was killed. At Llanelly, in Wales, there were bloody riots, and two men were killed when troops repelled an attack on a train.

This was more like a revolution than a strike, thought George V. He deprecated the halfhearted employment of troops. If called upon they should be given a free hand and the mob should be made to fear them.[83]

On August 18, two-thirds of the nation's railway workers went on strike. Nothing like this had ever occurred before. The railway system was England's lifeline. Without it, food could not be distributed, and industry would come to a standstill. Churchill saw the railroad strike as a national disaster, "an abyss of horror which no man dared to contemplate." No blockade by a foreign enemy could produce such terrible pressure on England's population. In the history of the world, he could not think of a worse catastrophe. It was like the breaking of the great Nimrod Dam in the valley of the Euphrates in the fifteenth century, which had wiped out a huge population from the book of human life.[84]

In such an emergency, strong measures had to be taken. The railways had to be kept running at all costs. Already, there had been at least six attacks on stations, many damaged signal boxes all along the line, nine attempts to wreck trains, and innumerable cases of train stonings, cut telegraph and signal wires, and looting. Accordingly, on August 19, Churchill gave the military authorities instructions that amounted to martial law: "General Officers commanding the various military areas are instructed to use their own discretion as to whether troops are, or are not, to be sent to any particular point. The Army regulation which requires a requisition for troops from a Civil Authority is suspended."

The same man who had gone to such lengths to prevent the use of troops at Tonypandy was now deploying fifty thousand men in a vast strikebreaking force. In his determination to keep the trains running, Churchill ignored the unions' struggle for recognition by the companies. To him, there was only one issue: the strike was a threat to the life of the nation.

To his aide Charles Masterman, Churchill had rather a "whiff-of-grapeshot" attitude. He enjoyed mapping the country and directing troop movements. He issued disastrous bulletins that exasperated the unions. Sometimes Masterman thought he was longing for blood.[85] Lloyd George, fearful that

Churchill's bringing in the military to settle an industrial dispute "should bring open warfare in the streets," used his remarkable talents as a negotiator to settle the railroad strike in two days. It was all over by August 20. "I'm very sorry to hear it," Churchill told him. "It would have been better to have gone on and given these men a good thrashing."[86]

In the House of Commons on August 22, there was an outcry against Churchill led by the Labour Party leaders Ramsay MacDonald and Keir Hardie. "The Department which has played the most diabolical part in all this unrest was the Home Office," MacDonald said. ". . . This is not a medieval state, and it is not Russia. It is not even Germany . . . If the Home Secretary had just a little bit more knowledge of how to handle masses of men in these critical times, if he had a somewhat better instinct of what civil liberty does mean . . . we should have had much less difficulty during the last four or five days in facing and finally settling the . . . problem." Keir Hardie charged Churchill with unlawfully instituting martial law and using armed force to intimidate the workers and support the railway companies. As usual, Churchill gave a spirited defense. "No Government could possibly sit still with folded hands and say, 'A trade dispute is going on. We must remain absolutely impartial . . .' It was not a question of taking sides with capital against labor, or with the companies against the employees. We took sides only with the public."[87]

Churchill recalled that he had been criticized earlier for not using troops in South Wales. But that had been a local disturbance. In this case, the whole country was concerned. To protect the railroad stations, the signal boxes, the goods yards, and other points, it had been necessary to give each general responsible for a strike area the full liberty to send troops out, without being summoned by local authorities. In all the disturbances, no more than twenty shots had been fired with serious intent, and four or five persons had been killed by the military. But what was not seen was the number of lives saved, and the number of tragedies averted. In their drunken frenzy, the Llanelly rioters had wrought more havoc and shed more blood and produced more serious injury than all the fifty thousand soldiers all over the country.[88]

Churchill made his case, but his reputation with the trade-union movement, which had already suffered after Tonypandy, sank very low. He had made no effort to communicate with the strikers, although he was in correspondence with one of the railroad bosses, W. Guy Granet, the general manager of the Midland Railways, who informed him that a German agent was behind the strikes. According to Granet, the agent was a man named

Bebel, a waiter in a railroad station hotel, who had distributed about five thousand pounds to assorted unions and their leaders.[89] Churchill swallowed Granet's report without verifying it and went around London saying that he had proof that all the labor unrest was being fomented by German gold. In his eyes, there was a hint of treason in the strike action, at a time of mounting international tension with Germany.[90]

Churchill's faith in a peaceful Germany had gone up in the smoke of the Agadir incident. Following the conquest of Algeria, Morocco had become a target of French expansion. Britain gave the French a free hand in North Africa in exchange for the same treatment in Egypt. Germany, which had stayed out of the scramble for North Africa, now began to show some interest in the area. When a French expedition was sent to occupy Fez in 1911, the Kaiser responded on July 1 by sending a warship, the *Panther*, to Agadir, ostensibly to protect German merchants there. This example of gunboat diplomacy set the alarm bells ringing through the chancelleries of Europe, focusing attention on Germany's growing sea power and ambitions. The Germans did not respond to Sir Edward Grey's repeated requests for an explanation. The great question, said Eddie Marsh, was would there or would there not be a war? He was like Mr. Micawber, hoping that something would turn up to avoid it.[91]

If there was a war between Germany and France, what would Britain's position be? No word came from the Foreign Office. On July 21, however, Lloyd George was speaking at the annual dinner given by the Lord Mayor of London at Mansion House to the bankers of the City, and this occasion was used to alert the Germans as to British intentions. Lloyd George showed his speech to Asquith, Grey, and Churchill, all three of whom approved. It was fitting that the warning to the Kaiser should come from England's leading Germanophile. In Lloyd George, Churchill saw a man convinced that they were drifting toward war. Germany was acting as if England did not count, ignoring its representations.

This was the key passage: ". . . if a situation were to be forced upon us in which peace could only be preserved by the surrender of the great and beneficent position Britain has won by centuries of heroism and achievement, by allowing Britain to be treated, where her interests were vitally affected, as if she were of no account in the Cabinet of Nations . . . then I say emphatically that peace at that price would be a humiliation intolerable for a great country like ours to endure."

The warning was clear: if Germany went to war, she would find Britain against her. The Kaiser saw the Mansion House speech as a contingent declaration of war and soon recalled his ambassador, the courtly Count Metternich, who had been assuring him that thanks to Lloyd George's strong pro-German sentiments, England would not interfere between Germany and France.

Four days after the speech, at five-thirty in the afternoon, while walking by the fountains of Buckingham Palace, Lloyd George and Churchill were intercepted by a messenger. Sir Edward Grey wanted to see the Chancellor of the Exchequer at once. "That's my speech," Lloyd George said. "The Germans may demand my resignation as they did Delcassé's." (The French Foreign Minister had resigned in 1905 under German pressure.) "That will make you the most popular man in England," Churchill said.

They found Grey in his rooms in the House of Commons in a state of uncommon excitement. "I have just received a communication from the German ambassador so stiff that the fleet might be attacked at any moment," he said. "I have sent for McKenna to warn him!" Grey had seen Metternich, who had voiced a long complaint that Lloyd George's speech had been a warning bordering on menace.[92]

Churchill saw the danger behind these diplomatic exchanges, these "exactly-measured phrases in large peaceful rooms." In some of his finest prose, he described the anxiety running through many minds:

> So now the Admiralty wireless whispers through the ether to the tall masts of ships, and captains pace their decks absorbed in thought. It is nothing. It is less than nothing. It is too foolish, too fantastic to be thought of in the twentieth century. Or is it fire and murder leaping out of the darkness at our throats, torpedoes ripping the bellies of half-awakened ships, a sunrise on a vanished naval supremacy, and an island well-guarded hitherto, at last defenseless? No, it is nothing. No one would do such things. Civilization has climbed above such perils. The interdependence of nations in trade and traffic, the sense of public law, the Hague Convention, Liberal principles, the Labour Party, high finance, Christian charity, common sense have rendered such nightmares impossible. Are you quite sure? It would be a pity to be wrong. Such a mistake could only be made once—once for all.[93]

Churchill, who had followed Lloyd George in his pro-German phase, now adopted the new line. The Germans had sent their *Panther* to Agadir, and the British had sent their little panther to Mansion House. Germany's action had put her in the wrong and forced England to review her position. If Germany were to make war on France, Britain should join France. He told Clemmie that in the Cabinet they had decided to use pretty plain language to Germany and tell her that if she thought Morocco could be divided up without John Bull she was jolly well mistaken.[94]

Agadir awakened the dormant strategist in Churchill. He was inclined to think that the chances of war were multiplying and that they had better get ready. Here was the young lieutenant again, waiting for the sound of the bugle, and wondering What would Russia do? What would Belgium do? Bringing himself up to date on Britain's foreign policy position, he learned that there was a vague Anglo-French entente, less than a formal alliance, more than an understanding. But Britain was bound by treaty to defend Belgium. As for himself, Churchill did not want to take part in the terrible business of war for the sake of Morocco or Belgium. Only one cause could justify his adherence, to prevent France from being trampled down and looted by the Prussian Junkers, a disaster ruinous to the world and swiftly fatal to England. It was astonishing, the train of thought that could result from the presence of one German warship in Moroccan waters.

In August, General Sir John French, whom Churchill had met during the Boer War and saw regularly at the Other Club dinners, gave him a report on his meeting with the Kaiser during German war maneuvers. The Kaiser had said that Lloyd George's speech was dangerous to the peace of Europe. He deplored the differences between Germany and England, but they were not of his making. If the British interfered with the actions of Germany, they must take the consequences. In any case, the great wars of the future would be racial, and Europe should be as strong as possible against such dangers as the Yellow Peril. One had to support one's policies with the sword, and the sword must be kept sharp. He could overrun France when he liked. France would not attack unless egged on by the British. The Kaiser gave French a photograph of himself, saying: "Here is your arch enemy, here is the disturber of the peace of Europe."[95]

In Churchill, the possibility of war was sometimes indistinguishable from the hope for war, which he saw as a promising arena for high deeds. After the great domestic reforms and the crisis with the Lords, he sensed the direction events were taking and became absorbed in military matters. Never one to confine himself to the duties of his department, he prepared a long memorandum for the Cabinet on the forthcoming war in the form of a game plan: there was an alliance between Britain, Russia, and France, which was attacked by Germany and Austria. With more troops than the French, the Germans would break through the line of the Meuse on the twentieth day. The French would fall back on Paris. By the fortieth day the German Army would be so extended that it could be beaten with British help. Britain should send 107,000 men as soon as the war broke out and 100,000 more by the crucial fortieth day. Churchill was not far off. When war broke out in 1914, the Germans did break through the Meuse line, on the twenty-first day, and the French did fall back on Paris, to be saved on the thirty-third day at the Battle of the Marne, the turning point of the war.[96] Recalling the Churchill memorandum in the early days of the war, Balfour called it "a triumph of prophecy."

But General Sir Henry Wilson, the Director of Military Operations at the War Office, and as unrepentant an intriguer as Jacky Fisher, dismissed Churchill's carefully reasoned paper with the contempt of the professional strategist for the amateur, and wrote in his diary in mid-August: "Winston has put in a ridiculous and fantastic paper on a war on the French and German frontier, which I was able to demolish. I believe he is in close touch with Kitchener and French, neither of whom knows anything at all about the subject."[97]

By this time, the crisis was abating. It did not look as though France and Germany would go to war over Morocco. But Agadir had strengthened the ties between France and England, while Germany suspected that England had encouraged the quarrel, hoping to join it. Churchill and Lloyd George felt let down. At Balmoral Castle, Lloyd George electrified the King and Queen by observing that it would be a great pity if war did not come now. According to Sir Arthur Nicolson, who had replaced Sir Charles Hardinge as Permanent Under-Secretary to the Foreign Office, Churchill and Lloyd George were "a little disappointed that war with Germany did not occur . . . I was struck with the determination of both of them not to permit Germany to assume the role of bully and at their belief that the present moment was an exceedingly favorable one to open hostilities."[98] Sir Edward Grey was just as alarmed by their present saber rattling as he had been by their past fondness for Germany, although he specified, "let me not be supposed to imply that Churchill was working for war, or desired it . . . It was only that his high-mettled spirit was exhilarated by the air of crisis and high events."[99]

It is hard to see why Churchill and Lloyd George thought that England was in a good position to go to war. The opposite was true. The woeful inadequacy of British military planning was dramatically illustrated when

Asquith convened a secret meeting of the Committee of Imperial Defense on August 23 to discuss what action to take should France be attacked.

The meeting, which lasted from 11:30 A.M. to 6 P.M., was a shocker. Henry Wilson opened it with a briefing on army plans. His tall, gangling frame standing by an enormous map, the spaniel-faced, mustached Wilson unfolded the British plan for helping France. Following Clausewitz' theory of supporting the largest allied force engaged against a common enemy, an expeditionary force would be prepared. Six infantry divisions and a cavalry division would be sent across the Channel as soon as war was declared, about 160,000 men in all. It had all been worked out with the French General Staff. Haldane said that the timetable had been made out in such detail that the French had even allowed for *dix minutes d'arrêt pour café*.

The Army was ready. Now, what about the Navy, which would have to carry these troops to France? It was the turn of Sir Arthur Wilson, the First Sea Lord, a much-admired admiral, considered by some to be the greatest figure the British Navy had produced since Nelson. Sixty-nine years old, he had won the Victoria Cross fighting on land against the Dervishes. But he was a sturdy old sea dog, known as "Tug" Wilson. What this eminent sailor had to say caused consternation in the Cabinet: the Navy could not spare a single man, a single officer, a single ship to assist the Army.[100] The whole force at the disposal of the Admiralty would be absorbed in keeping the enemy within the North Sea.

Stunned, General Sir William Nicholson, Chief of the Imperial General Staff (CIGS), said he had presumed that the Army could count on the ungrudging assistance of the Transport Department of the Admiralty.

He had presumed wrong, Sir Arthur Wilson replied, unyielding. The Navy could not furnish any ships.

McKenna backed up his First Sea Lord. No assistance could be given during the first week of war. The whole effort of the Admiralty would be absorbed in mobilizing the Navy, and the Transport Department especially would be fully occupied in taking up fleet auxiliaries. The Admiralty could not be expected to undertake two operations simultaneously.

Arthur Wilson and McKenna acted as if the expeditionary force was an annoying sideshow that would hamper the important, that is to say, naval, operations of the war. Arthur Wilson said that he had not been told of any plan for an expeditionary force. He knew that a scheme for dispatching such a force had been mooted, but thought that it had been abandoned.

McKenna said the Admiralty had actually recorded in a Committee of

Imperial Defense paper its inability to guarantee the transport of troops on the outbreak of war.

General Sir Henry Wilson emphasized that the dates fixed for embarkation were from the second day of mobilization to the twelfth day. It was expected that the Germans would deploy eighty-four divisions against sixty-six French divisions.

Asquith said the simultaneous mobilization of the French and British armies and their immediate concentration in the theater of war were essential features of the scheme.

Churchill said the Germans would attack through Belgium.

Admiral Sir Arthur Wilson thought the expeditionary force was a poor idea. Apart from the smallness of its numbers, the Army would labor under disadvantages due to the difference of language and training, and the diversity of ammunition, arms, and equipment. It would be handicapped by its dependence for supplies on the French railways. In the early days of the war, the French would also be mobilizing, and there would be congestion on the railways.

What would happen to the British forces in the event of a French retreat? Churchill asked.

General Sir Henry Wilson said that British command of the sea would enable them to change their base as they required. The British Army would retain absolutely its freedom of action.

Churchill said he did not like the idea of the British Army retiring into France, away from its own country.

McKenna thought the British force should be placed under French command.

Churchill dissented emphatically. The whole moral significance of British intervention would be lost if its Army was merely merged with that of France. If they had to retreat, they could retreat to the sea. And what of the chance of making terms with Turkey and bringing Russian troops through the Dardanelles?

Asquith said the passage of the Dardanelles was an insuperable difficulty.

Grey agreed. The Turks were in close relations with the Germans, and they certainly could not force the Dardanelles under those circumstances.

Once more, Asquith asked for the views of the Admiralty.

Admiral Sir Arthur Wilson said he was against the expeditionary force. If the entire regular Army was dispatched abroad at the start of war there could be an outbreak of panic. The Navy needed troops for its own operations. The policy of the Navy at the start of the war would be to blockade the whole of the German North Sea coast. He foresaw troop landings in Germany with naval support, as well as an attack on Heligoland, for which the Admiralty would need one division.

To land detachments at points on the German coast was hopeless, Haldane pointed out, because any troops that were landed would be immediately surrounded by ten times the number of enemy soldiers, brought up by train.

Keeping his temper with difficulty at Admiral Wilson's view of the war, in which the Army's role was to supply troops for amphibious operations, General Sir William Nicholson asked if the Admiralty would continue to press for landings on the German coast if the General Staff expressed its opinion that such military operations were madness. Did the Admiralty have a map of the German railways? Nicholson asked. Sir Arthur Wilson disdainfully replied that it was not their business to have such maps. "I beg your pardon," said Nicholson, "if you meddle with military problems you are bound not only to have them, but to have studied them."

The discussion was growing acerbic. McKenna agreed with his First Sea Lord that the absence of the British Army from the country would have a great moral effect, that the Navy needed the Army at home, and that it could not provide transport at the outbreak of war without hampering its initial operations. He objected most strongly to denuding the country of all regular troops in the early days.[101]

Haldane said that if they had nothing to fear but small raids, the risk of denuding the country of regular troops could be taken. But the meeting ended in a deadlock between the two services. Haldane was terrified by what he had heard. The situation was highly dangerous. The grave divergences between generals and admirals could lead to disaster. The Navy did not grasp that this would be a land war, and that its first duty was to transport troops. The Admiralty did not want to know the Army's plans and was reluctant to divulge its own, if it had any. Cooperation was an alien concept. Naval strategy was 150 years behind the times. This talk of landings in the Baltic went back to the Seven Years' War. Admiral Wilson had shown a startling ignorance of elementary military principles. Unless the cobwebs were swept out of the Admiralty, Britain did not stand a chance. There must be a Naval War Staff, along the lines of the staff he had created at the War Office. And the First Lord, McKenna, must go, for he was too closely associated with Admiral Wilson's views.

Right after the meeting, Haldane took Asquith aside and voiced his misgivings. He felt so strongly about the matter that he said he must resign unless there was a sweeping reform at the Admiralty. The admirals must cooperate with his General Staff and form a staff of their own. There must be a new First Lord.[102]

Haldane thought he was the man. In five years at the War Office, he had reformed the Army and given it a brain. He knew how to handle senior officers. He was the logical choice, a senior Cabinet member with experience in running a service department.[103]

There were times when a Prime Minister felt like saying "anything for a quiet life." Now Asquith had to sacrifice McKenna or lose Haldane, his oldest and closest friend in the Cabinet. He agreed that there must be changes, and wrote Lord Crewe: "The present position, in which everything is locked up in the brain of a single taciturn Admiral, is both ridiculous and dangerous."[104]

But who was the right man to replace McKenna? There were two objections to Haldane. First, having recently been made a viscount, he sat in the House of Lords. The First Lord of the Admiralty should be in Commons, where he could lead the debate on the estimates and other naval matters. Commons was full of Little Navy men, retired admirals, and antiquated naval specialists whom the First Lord would have to silence. Second, with interservice rivalry running high, he could not send the Secretary of State for War to reform the Navy. You could not sweep the Navy with the same broom that had been used for the Army. It was too much like a vote of censure and was too likely to cause friction with the admirals.

For more than a month, Asquith wrestled with the problem. In the meantime, smelling a Cabinet shake-up, Churchill saw his chance and began running down Admiralty operations to his colleagues. On September 13 he asked Asquith whether he was sure that the Admiralty realized the serious situation in Europe. They were all nearly on leave at the present time. After Wilson's revelations the other day, how could one place confidence in a man who had answered so foolishly? The Admiralty had ample strength, but one lapse, as stupid as that revealed at the meeting, and it would be the defense of England rather than France.[105] On September 14 he told Lloyd George that Sir William Nicholson had expressed his surprise to Admiral Wilson that he had left the office so denuded. Wilson had explained that everything was ready; all that was necessary was to press a button, which a clerk could do. Churchill certainly hoped that was the case.[106] On September 15, Lloyd George replied: ". . . I had a long talk with Balfour. He is very much worried—as you are—about the Navy. He is by no means happy about the Admiralty. He has no confidence in Wilson's capacity for direction and leadership. He thinks the Admirals too cocksure."[107]

In September, with Parliament recessed, Asquith escaped to Archerfield, a lovely Adam house on the East Lothian coast of Scotland. It was paradise because of its private golf course, stretching down to the sea. There he continued to ponder the Admiralty change. Lloyd George came to see him, insisting that McKenna must be replaced, and plumping for Churchill.

In late September, Churchill and his wife went to Scotland. He was invited to Balmoral, the royal castle in Aberdeenshire, and had long talks with the King, who was worried that Lloyd George seemed to want war. On September 24, Churchill stood in the Ministers' Room at Balmoral, surrounded by all the portraits of departed Premiers, perhaps wondering whose faces would be added to the illustrious gallery. Attending to an urgent Home Office matter, he approved an injunction against the Empress Hall in Earl's Court to stop a fight between the British boxer Bombardier Wells and the American Negro world heavyweight champion Jack Johnson.[108] It was feared that if Johnson won, there would be racial strife in various parts of the Empire. Johnson's victory over a white antagonist in Reno the previous year had set off race riots.

Wives were not asked to Balmoral, and Clemmie went to stay with her formidable eighty-one-year-old grandmother, the Countess of Airlie, who pointed out all her defects "for your own good." Like Winston, she found Clemmie's handwriting detestable and said "a gentlewoman of consequence should not write like a housemaid." She gave Clemmie samples of good handwriting to copy, like those of two former Prime Ministers, Lord Melbourne and Lord Palmerston.

On September 27, Churchill motored from Balmoral to Archerfield in the new red Napier that had set him back 610 pounds. In the golden autumn sunshine, with sea gulls circling overhead, he played golf with Asquith and his daughter. As Violet sliced the ball with her driver, Churchill counseled "complete abandonment, absolute self-surrender." When they reached the sea at the ninth hole, a silvery shrub with orange berries caught Churchill's eye. Violet told him it was buckthorn, sometimes known as "the olive of the north." "The olive of the north," Churchill mused, "that's good. The buckthorn of the south—that's not so good." During the rest of the game, he embroidered on this theme, his attention deflected. A delighted Asquith reported at lunch: "Winston was four up at the turn but once he heard about the 'olive of the north' he never hit another ball and lost the game."[109]

Another guest was expected. Haldane was arriving from Cloan, his small estate in Perthshire, a fisherman's paradise with its brooks and pools. He was coming to press his case for the Admiralty, not knowing that Churchill had gotten there first. It was to be a clash between two temperaments and two generations. At fifty-five, Haldane was at the end of his career, and had suffered, the year before, an attack of iritis so grave that the doctors feared he would lose an eye. At the time, Churchill had reproached him for working too hard. Not quite thirty-seven, Churchill was brimming over with energy and eager to expand his scope. Haldane was philosophical, reflective, lacking Churchill's drive. He believed he was the best man for the job, but could not match Churchill's appetite for office. It was a struggle between two species of animal, one ruminant, the other carnivorous.

As Haldane drove up the avenue of lime trees that led to the house, he saw his rival's slightly hunched silhouette framed in the doorway and guessed that Churchill, hearing of possible Cabinet changes, had come to Archerfield to propose himself for the job he wanted.[110]

Confirming his fears, Asquith told him that Winston was immensely keen to go to the Admiralty. As forcefully as he knew how, Haldane presented his case. As far as he was concerned, the prospect of the Admiralty yacht and of moving his house was distasteful, but it was not a question of his or Churchill's keenness. It was a grave issue, more urgent than social reform. The Admiralty must be put on a better intellectual footing than Fisher's cry of "seek out and destroy the enemy's fleet." The admirals could not be ordered to do it; they must be guided, more *Socratico*, by gentle leading. They could only be led if the person entrusted with the task had knowledge and experience of this special problem. He was the only person available who was equipped to cope with the problem of the Naval War Staff. Would Winston do it better than the man who had succeeded at the War Office?[111]

Asquith said that Churchill had argued that the First Lord must be in Commons. Obviously, Haldane thought, Churchill had been pressing hard. Haldane said the situation was too critical to permit any such difficulty standing in the way. Asquith suggested that Haldane might take the post of Lord Chancellor, which he had once sought. Haldane brushed the offer aside. The interest of the state was the only thing that mattered.[112]

Asquith wanted to think things over and asked Haldane to return on the following day. When he did, Asquith's Solomon-like solution was to shut up Haldane and Churchill in a room together. Haldane took the initiative, saying that he knew Churchill's imaginative power and vitality were greater than his own and that physically he was better suited to be War Minister. But at this critical moment it was not a question of such qualities. The Navy had to be convinced to change, by someone who had already done the job with the Army. He offered Churchill a deal. He was satisfied that he could accomplish the needed reforms within a year. If Churchill would look after the Army for a year, he would return to it, and then Churchill could take over the Admiralty. To be frank, he did not think that Churchill's type of mind was best for planning a war staff.[113]

Churchill countered with an offer of his own. If Haldane withdrew his insistence on going to the Admiralty to fashion a war staff, he was prepared to ask him to come over to the Admiralty and sit with him and the admirals and fashion the new staff with them. As Churchill at his most persuasive described their forthcoming collaboration, Haldane could not help thinking that it had only been a year since he had done his best to cut down Mc-Kenna's estimates, and that the Admiralty would receive the news of his appointment with dismay. They would think, wrongly or rightly, that as soon as the pinch came, he would want to cut down. Churchill was too apt to act first and think afterward, though one could not speak too highly of his energy and courage.[114]

They parted on friendly terms, still not sure whom Asquith would pick. On the afternoon of the day after Haldane's second visit, Churchill and Asquith played golf. Violet was finishing tea when Winston came in, looking radiant. Did he want tea? "I don't want tea—I don't want anything—anything in the world. Your father has just offered me the Admiralty."[115]

Churchill wanted to walk, and as they crossed the darkening woods down to the sea, he told Violet: "Look at the people I have had to deal with so far—Judges and convicts! This is a big thing—the biggest thing that has ever come my way—the chance I should have chosen before all others. I shall pour into it everything I've got."[116]

When they reached the sea, the Fidra's lighthouse was flashing out its signals. In the fading light of evening, they could see the silhouettes of two battleships steaming slowly out of the Firth of Forth. To Churchill, they were invested with a new significance.[117]

VIII

THE ADMIRALTY
IN PEACE

IT WAS AN ODD TURN of the wheel that brought to the Admiralty the impenitent scoffer of war scares and merciless critic of bloated army and navy estimates, who only two years earlier had almost brought down the government in his resistance to eight dreadnoughts. Central to Churchill's nature was his ability to "box the compass," and he now embraced the cause of naval might as eagerly as he had retrenchment. His reputation for economy may have been reassuring to the Germans, but he had other ideas: he intended to prepare for an attack as if it might come the next day. The two dolphins that flanked the entrance of the Admiralty building in Whitehall were the symbols of his newly acquired nautical purpose. On the wall behind his desk, he mounted an open case with folding doors that spread a large chart of the North Sea. Every day a staff officer marked with flags the position of the German fleet. The first thing Churchill did when he came in was study the chart. Not to keep himself informed, for there were many other channels of information, but to inculcate in himself and his staff a sense of ever-present danger. Alarmed at having seen the Admiralty almost deserted, save for the proverbial clerk ready to push the proverbial button, he decreed round-the-clock seven-day-a-week duty officers. From the day he took office, the Admiralty was in a state of war readiness, although war would not start for three years.

Churchill, who in 1902 had scorned Austen Chamberlain's wish to be First Lord as "a poor ambition," called his three and a half years at the Admiralty the most memorable of his life. His rise in the Cabinet had been dazzling. He had hopped from post to post like a mountain goat from rock to rock, staying still just long enough to gain a secure foothold. Other senior ministers were identified with their departments through long service. Grey was at the Foreign Office from 1905 to 1916, and Haldane was at the War Office from 1905 to 1912. But Churchill stayed at the Board of Trade barely two years and at the Home Office only twenty months, pausing just long enough in his ascent to put a few "Big Acts" on the statute books. Not yet thirty-seven, he was by far the youngest of the senior ministers, for in 1911, Lloyd George was forty-eight, Grey was forty-nine, Haldane was fifty-five, and Asquith was fifty-nine. To repeat what Churchill had written about his father, he had been found equal to all the varied tasks which are laid upon an English minister. If he was thus armed and equipped at thirty-seven, what would he be at fifty? "The sun shone fair. The clouds were parted to the right and to the left, and there he stepped into the center of the world's affairs—amid the acclamation of the multitude and in the hush of European attention—the Grand Young Man."[1]

Until now, Churchill had not been completely his own man. He was weighed down with the inherited political luggage of his father. On too many occasions, he had taken a position out of loyalty to Randolph. He had been the good son, carrying the blunted lance of his father's outdated crusades. Besides that ghostly presence, there was the ardently admired figure of Lloyd George, his mentor on social and foreign policy issues. Churchill was reluctant to make any decision without consulting "Davie," who said: "Very often I hear him come stalking down the hall at Downing Street, and then I see him put his head inside the door and look round the room. I know from his face that something has happened, and I always say, 'What's wrong now?' "[2]

It was at the Admiralty that Churchill shook off the two helmsmen who had guided his career. Jettisoning their borrowed cargo, he pulled out on the tide of his destiny, at last under his own steam, at last spared of the residual boyishness that Lucy Masterman had mocked. Fame was a balm for resentment. As Earl Winterton, his longtime foe in the House of Commons observed, it was difficult when you held high office at an early age and were married to an exceptionally beautiful and charming woman to believe that your mission in life was to fight the world at large because your father had been badly treated.

Still the label of turncoat and the charges of opportunism and unscrupulousness clung to him and were trotted out on suitable occasions. After his appointment, the right-wing and peppery *Spectator* wrote: "We cannot detect in his career any principles or even any consistent outlook upon public affairs. His ear is always to the ground; he is the true demagogue, sworn to give the people what they want, or rather, and that is infinitely worse, what he fancies they want."[3]

Before his immersion in naval affairs, Churchill fought against a Reform Bill proposed by Asquith for the 1912 Parliamentary session, which would have extended the franchise and given the vote to women. Stridently against it, he wrote long letters predicting calamitous consequences to Asquith, Grey, and Lloyd George. What a ridiculous tragedy it would be if this strong government were to perish like Sisera (the Canaanite captain who was slain by an Israelite woman while he slept) at a woman's hand. How terrible it would be for the government to go down on petticoat politics. It was damnable. He could not understand why Lloyd George wanted to add eight million women to the electorate. He was just like Joe Chamberlain in 1903 splitting the party on free trade.[4]

The Reform Bill did not get through. The real reason Winston hated the suffragettes, Lloyd George said, was they spoiled his beautifully prepared speeches. They might just as well have cut his daughter Diana's throat. "The truth is," Churchill told his golfing partner George Riddell, owner of *News of the World*, "we already have enough ignorant voters and we don't want any more."[5]

George Riddell was a good example of how close to the center of power a newspaper proprietor could burrow in Asquith's England. By doing favors for politicians, such as obtaining a house for Lloyd George at the edge of the Walton Heath golf course, and by being always available to make up a foursome and pass on the latest political gossip, Riddell was admitted into the inner circle, and made a practice of dropping in on Churchill and Lloyd George at their offices. Insatiably curious, he cross-examined everyone he met, and committed the results of his inquiries to a diary.

Bitter at being ousted from the Admiralty, Reginald McKenna resented Churchill's pushiness and the sudden and unexpected manner in which he himself was being shunted to the Home Office. At first he resisted the transfer, and took a sardonic pleasure in reflecting that while he delayed the drafting of the new Admiralty Warrant, he would draw two salaries while Churchill would draw none. But the day came at the end of October when McKenna went to the Home Office to be introduced to the staff in the morning, and Churchill went to the Admiralty in the afternoon.

Churchill was in charge of the greatest naval establishment in the world, with its fleet patrolling the seven seas, and its training schools and dockyards and warehouses and harbors forming a service that embodied British might. But the Navy had been too long at peace, showing the flag, rescuing ships in distress, and helping the victims of natural disasters. Its fighting spirit had not been tested. It carried out its obsolete strategy at maneuvers in quadrille-like exercises, where "follow the Admiral's motion" was a fetish. It was split into factions, for Jacky Fisher had weakened the band-of-brothers feeling. Churchill found that there was no moment in the career and training of a naval officer when he was obliged to read a single book about naval war or pass the most rudimentary examination in naval history. The "Silent Service" was not mute because it was absorbed in thought and study, but because it was weighed down by daily routine.

All this he would have to remedy. He was pledged to create a Naval War Staff, even though he knew that it would take a generation to form the proper habits of mind, for there was a violent prejudice against "ink-slingers." New appointments had to be made. Some admirals had to be "poached" and others would be "scrambled." But how to go about it? For all his powers of assimilation, Churchill was a newcomer to naval problems. His education and experience had been in the Army. He needed help. There was one man who had all the secrets of the Navy locked in his brain, and that was Jacky Fisher, since 1909 Baron Fisher of Kilverstone, who was enjoying the quiet pleasures of retirement in Lucerne. On October 25, while still at the Home Office, Churchill cabled: "I want to see you very much. When am I to have that pleasure? You have but to indicate your convenience & I will await you at the Admiralty."[6]

Fisher was loyal to McKenna, who had stood by him in the dreadnought crisis, and who had been tricked in a dirty low way. He would stand aloof. At the same time, he was glad that the Little England Churchill of the 1909 Naval Scare was no more. From the time he had first met Churchill he had known that he was right for the Admiralty, because he was a brave man. The whole secret of success was plunging, it stupefied foreign Admiralties; once you had a lead, a stern chase to pick up was hell. He thought he could be a help. He didn't claim to be a genius, but he knew a damned fool when he saw one. And yet, he did not want to horn in or play second fiddle. The greatest Napoleonic maxim was *j'ordonne ou je me tais* (I command or I remain silent). He must be first violin. He wasn't going to be understudy to anyone—it was Caesar or nothing.[7]

Amid these contradictory and megalomaniacal musings, there was one overriding factor. Fisher had a demon who told him things, and one of the things the demon kept repeating was that there would be war with Germany. He knew the year, the month, and the day—October 21, 1914. By that time the Kiel Canal would be dug, and the year's harvest would be gathered (as it turned out, he was about three months off). Fisher remembered his first day as First Sea Lord, when he was brought a two-feet-high pile of papers. "Take 'em away," he had said, "I'm going to attend to the fleet and not what a lot of damned old women have written in these papers." He had known what to do, and now he must help Churchill navigate amid the shoals and shallows of all the mediocrities and intriguers who clung to their Admiralty offices.[8]

In a stream of letters, and in a three-day meeting at the end of October in Reigate, a small town south of London, when he and Churchill stayed up talking until two in the morning, Fisher outlined his program, peppering his new pupil with his favorite aphorisms: "Armor is vision," "Never rely on an expert," "The secret of successful administration is the intelligent anticipation of agitation," and "Somebody must be hung for every little thing that goes wrong." He was a veritable volcano of knowledge, a volcano in vehement eruption. On the train back to London, Churchill was on the brink of saying, "Come and help me," and offering him the job of First Sea Lord. But Fisher was seventy, and Churchill did not feel sure of the poise of his mind. Bringing him back would mean reviving old feuds. He decided against it, wondering whether he was right or wrong.[9]

First and foremost, Fisher said, Winston must have the right kind of board. The Navy was run by a board of four Sea Lords under a ministerial First Lord. The First Sea Lord was responsible for war preparations and the distribution of the fleet. The Second Sea Lord manned the fleet and trained the men. The Third Sea Lord directed naval construction, and the Fourth Sea Lord was responsible for stores and ammunition. The whole Admiralty Board must be changed—*Totus Porcus!* Admiral Wilson was able, but no good ashore. Winston could get rid of him by telling him on the first of January that he must go because of the estimates, as he would be going in March in any case because of age. Louis of Battenberg, a naturalized German prince who had married one of Queen Victoria's granddaughters, would be ideal as First Sea Lord; he had the German faculty for organizing a staff. Bred to the sea, Prince Louis had spent a large proportion of his forty years' service afloat.[10]

Fisher drew up long lists of appointments, peppered with comments on admirals who had incurred his disfavor. Berkeley Milne was a sneak of the dirtiest kind. George Warrender was off his head and had a sister locked up. Sir George Egerton, the Second Sea Lord, was an ass who had done irreparable mischief, and Fisher hoped he would have appendicitis. Charles Briggs, the Third Sea Lord, was a servile copyist, one of those who added on half an inch to the latest design. His favorite was John Jellicoe, who was as great as Nelson, but not senior enough. In three years it would be Armageddon. Jellicoe must be Admiralissimo. No more seagoing appointments of men senior to Jellicoe should be made, so that in 1914 he could be put in command of the Home Fleet. If Jellicoe was in the right place, Churchill could sleep quiet in his bed. Fisher insisted that Winston must take all his advice. If he left out a single appointment, the arch would cave in, for each one was a keystone, and he would be a damn fool and make the mistake of his lifetime.[11]

Apart from appointments, they must have bigger dreadnoughts—they were the armadillos that put out their tongues and licked up the ants, and the bigger the ant, the more placid the digestive smile. They must have the 15-inch gun. What had enabled Jack Johnson to knock out his opponents? The big punch. They must switch from coal to oil. Oil meant a savings of 50 percent in the stoker personnel, no going into harbor for coal, and no smoke to alert the enemy. Why was England behind on internal combustion? It was a scandal. They could have a dreadnought driven like a motorcar by the captain on deck and only half a dozen damned chauffeurs down below instead of four hundred stokers and engineers and why didn't they? It was all that damned stupid Briggs. You must always push the experts over the precipice. They were always straining at the gnat of perfection and swallowing the camel of unreadiness.[12]

On the issue of a Naval War Staff, Fisher did a turnabout. He had always been against it, believing that war plans should be drawn up in great secrecy, known only by the First Sea Lord, and divulged to the Army on the eve of war. "No such rubbish has ever been talked as about the Naval War Staff," he had written. "A Naval War Staff at the Admiralty is a very excellent organization for cutting out and arranging foreign newspaper clippings." Now, seeing that there was no resisting the idea, he said that with a War Staff the country would not be ruined if you had a damned fool as First Sea Lord. Privately, Fisher still had doubts. Could Winston evolve a War Staff out of his own head? *Nous verrons*[13] (We shall see).

Working with Haldane, Churchill drafted a long memorandum on the

Naval War Staff. It was odd, Haldane recalled, to think that only two years ago he had had to fight Churchill for every penny of his army estimates. Now it was delightful to work with him. Even Lloyd George, who used to call him "the Minister for Slaughter," was friendly.[14]

Admiral Wilson had not changed since the disastrous CID meeting of August 23. He wanted nothing to do with a Naval War Staff; it would lead to an elite of brooding officers poring over maps and memos and withdrawn from the day-to-day work of the Navy—a bunch of intellectual landlubbers. His reply on October 30 made that clear: "The Navy has learned, by long experience, thoroughly to distrust all paper schemes and theories that have not been submitted to the supreme test of trial under practical conditions . . . The Service would have the most supreme contempt for any body of officers who professed to be specially trained to think. . . . The whole spirit and training of the Navy is to make officers, whatever their position, do their thinking for themselves . . ."[15]

Churchill knew he had to get rid of Wilson, for he did not want the issue of the War Staff to unravel into a personal controversy. Discussing the various moves with Fisher, he worked in secrecy forming the new board, so that no whisper should reach the present men. Sir Francis Bridgeman was asked to be First Sea Lord. Commander of the Home Fleet for less than a year, he did his best to decline, but Churchill insisted. Against the grain, Bridgeman had to consent. Fisher loved Bridgeman. Although he had no genius for administration, he was a splendid sailor and a gentleman, and he would command immense confidence. Battenberg was brought in as Second Sea Lord. *Entre nous*, Viscount Esher wrote Fisher, he was NOT a first-class intellect, but he might be the best of an indifferent lot. But Lord Selborne, who knew Prince Louis well, having been First Lord from 1900 to 1905, told Churchill he was the ablest officer in the Navy. If his name had been Smith, he would have filled a high office long ago, but his career had been maimed because of his German origins. And yet a better Englishman did not exist.[16]

Against Fisher's harangues, Churchill decided to keep the Third Sea Lord and Controller, Admiral Charles Briggs, although he would fire him the following May—he had been in office a year and seemed to have the facts at his fingertips. As his Naval Secretary, he rescued from half-pay the youngest rear admiral in the Navy, forty-year-old David Beatty, against the advice of his Sea Lords, for Beatty had turned down an appointment as second-in-command of the Atlantic Fleet. It would be contrary to precedent to make him a further offer. Besides, he had got on too fast and had too many interests ashore. Married to the Chicago department-store heiress Ethel Marshall Field, who had a dowry of eight million pounds, the handsome Beatty spent much of his time fox hunting and was said to have "an eye for country." Like Churchill, he had a knack for being at the right place at the right time, and had been promoted in the Egyptian and China wars. Perhaps Churchill remembered a bottle of champagne tossed from a gunboat on the Nile on the eve of Omdurman. Summoning Beatty, he said: "You seem very young to be an admiral." Beatty, who was three years older than Churchill, replied: "And you seem very young to be the First Lord of the Admiralty." He moved into the office next to Churchill's, the First Lord being struck by "the shrewd and profound sagacity of his comments expressed in language singularly free from technical jargon."[17]

When the new board was installed on November 28, Churchill was delighted, and so was Fisher. It had been like a brilliantly effective *coup d'état* that had dumbfounded and dazed everyone and been swallowed like an oyster. Winston was splendid. As the great Napoleon said, *les hommes sont rares* (men are rare). The only shadow was Briggs, the Slug who wanted to perpetuate obsolete battleships of the Tortoise type, all armor and no speed. Fisher was sorry Churchill had kept him, for he was timid as a rabbit and silly as an ostrich.[18]

But the disappointment over Briggs was tempered when Churchill brought on board his colleague from the Colonial Office, Sir Francis Hopwood, as Civil Lord. Fisher was delighted. It was a way of cutting the detested Briggs in two, for Hopwood would take on some of his duties. Hopwood should be warned that every head of department jammed on a big sum at estimate time to be on the safe side, for there was a hell of a row if he underestimated. Hopwood was the Iago-like intriguer who, while pretending friendship, had maligned Churchill behind his back to Lord Elgin. He had not changed, and soon became the King's spy at the Admiralty.

Jellicoe was made second-in-command of the Home Fleet under Vice Admiral Sir George Callaghan, passing over the heads of four or five of the most important senior admirals on the active list. Churchill could not put him in command; he was not sufficiently practiced in the handling of a fleet to justify what would be seen as a startling promotion. Fisher was pleased. No other First Lord in history could have done it. Jellicoe had all the Nelsonic attributes, self-reliance, fearlessness of responsibility, fertility of resource, and power of initiative. In two years, he would be Nelson's age at the Battle of Trafalgar, and he would win the Battle of Armageddon on October 21,

1914—Churchill should make a note of the date.[19] (In fact, Nelson was forty-seven when he was killed at Trafalgar, whereas in two years Jellicoe would be fifty-four.)

Lloyd George was concerned about Battenberg, and Asquith warned Churchill that "Lloyd George is an excellent foolometer and the public will take the same view."[20] The expected outcry came in Horatio Bottomley's jingoistic *John Bull*: "Should a German 'boss' our Navy? Bulldog breed or Dachshund?" It would be "a crime against our Empire to trust our secrets of National Defense to any alien-born official. It is a heavy strain to put any German as a ruler of our Navy and give him the key to our defenses."[21] This had always been the problem, and as early as 1906, Prince Louis had written Fisher: "I heard by chance what the reasons were which [Admirals] Beresford and Lambton and all the tribe gave out . . . against [me] . . . that I was a damned German, who had no business in the British Navy and that the Service for that reason did not trust me."[22]

The new board was agreed on the policy of preparing for war against Germany. The Navy's obsolete tail must be cut off to develop teeth and claws of terrible strength. The feeling that war was coming was in the air. The French ambassador, Paul Cambon, kept repeating *"Nous allons vers la guerre* [We are heading toward war]." The press lord Sir Alfred Harmsworth, now Lord Northcliffe, saw the determination of the Prussian Junker class to force some foreign complication in order to prevent the destruction of privileges by internal reform. Toward the end of November, Churchill received from Captain Kell of the War Office Secret Service a thick sheaf of reports proving that an extensive network of German spies was operating in England.[23] This information was largely the result of a decision Churchill had made at the Home Office to authorize a general warrant for the Secret Service to open the mail of suspects. The move had paid off, and now Churchill knew that Britain was the subject of a minute and scientific study by the German military and naval authorities.

Churchill followed Napoleon's axiom: If you want peace, prepare for war. Prodded by Fisher, he took risks that no other First Lord would have taken. He changed the fuel from coal to oil. The old women at the Admiralty would have a nice time of it, Fisher warned, when the new American battleships were at sea burning oil and the first German motor battleship "cocked a snook" at the British Tortoises. Churchill agreed. The advantages of oil were clear. It gave greater speed, and saved space and manpower. On the average coal-driven battleship, one hundred men were constantly occupied shoveling coal from one bunker to the other. With oil, a few pipes sucked in fuel with hardly a man having to lift a finger. But it was a formidable decision, requiring much planning and expense, for Britain had plenty of coal but no oil. A reliable source of supply must be found.

Plunging ahead, Churchill ordered a Fast Division of five oil-powered battleships that could cruise at twenty-five knots—the *Queen Elizabeth, Warspite, Barham, Valiant,* and *Malaya.* The 15-inch gun, firing shells that weighed 1,920 pounds, was another unheard-of innovation. No 15-inch naval gun had ever been made. The usual procedure was to build a prototype and to see if it worked, but that took a year. To save time, Churchill ordered 15-inch guns built and mounted on the Fast Division ships. He would not know for a year and a half whether the gamble was a triumph or a disaster. Fancy if the guns failed entirely. He could imagine the accusations: "rash, inexperienced"—"before he had been there a month"—"altering all the plans of his predecessors"—"this ghastly fiasco." And yet it was worth the risk; courage in design might win a battle later on.[24]

Churchill resolved to visit every dockyard and important ship. He could be seen having a "yarn" with a submarine crew or taking Arthur Balfour down into one of the turrets of the *Orion* to show him how the guns of a super-dreadnought worked—he wanted to know what everything looked like and where everything was. He would ferret into every department, purge the war plans of foolishness, track down wasted money, probe, prune, and prepare. It was too bad he had to trust so much to others, when he knew he could do it better himself. In his first eighteen months as First Lord, he spent 182 days aboard the Admiralty yacht *Enchantress,* a miniature ocean liner of four thousand tons with a good cellar and a board room, spacious cabins for guest ministers and their wives, and a crew of 196. There were questions in Parliament about his constant use of the yacht. Sir Clement Kinloch-Cooke asked "whether the First Lord's unofficial visits could be more easily undertaken by rail, at a considerable saving of time to himself and expense to the State." Churchill replied somewhat testily that the annual charge was about 2,900 pounds for officers, 6,900 pounds for the crew, and 4,000 pounds for fuel and stores, and that it could not be reduced.[25]

His surprise visits and poking about were not always appreciated. On one occasion he visited a cruiser and asked the first lieutenant on duty to show him the punishment cells. When the lieutenant returned to the wardroom, his messmates shouted: "Why didn't you lock him up?"[26] Another time, while inspecting a ship's company, he asked the commander: "So you know your men by name?" "I think I do, sir; we have had many changes recently, but I think I know them all." "What is the name of this man?" "Jones, sir." "Are you quite sure that the man's name is Jones?" Churchill turned to the seaman and asked, "Is your name really Jones or do you say so only to back your officer?" "My name is Jones, sir," the seaman said. When the First Lord left, the commander and his officers were in a state of choking wrath. Once again, Churchill was displaying his "bull in a china shop" side, barging into the encrusted caste system that was the Navy. Although he bruised some egos, he was genuinely concerned with conditions in the lower ranks. Fisher had warned him that he would have a mutiny on his hands if he did not attend to their grievances concerning low pay, poor food, brutal punishment, and primitive living conditions.

Clemmie pitched in and launched the battleship *Centurion* on November 18. Her main concern was to delay the move to Admiralty House, an eighteenth-century mansion she knew they could not afford, for it would take a staff of at least twelve.

In just a few months, Churchill had brought in a new board, embarked on a program of building fast oil-driven battleships with 15-inch guns, and created a Naval War Staff (which, it must be said, existed more on paper than in reality). Viscount Esher thought it was the most pregnant reform of the Admiralty since the days of Lord St. Vincent, the great nineteenth-century First Lord. In January 1912, Churchill informed Fisher that he was going ahead with a naval aviation unit. Fisher had seen the possibilities of planes for observation missions. They would supersede small cruisers and intelligence vessels. At first relying on "various shifts and devices," and then by wheedling funds out of the Treasury, Churchill created the Royal Naval Air Service under Captain Murray F. Sueter.[27]

He was so absorbed in his Admiralty work, said Lloyd George, that all he thought about was boilers. This was not quite true, for as a leading member of the government, he played a part in all the important issues of the day, and in domestic politics, none was then so crucial as Home Rule for Ireland. Having beaten the Lords with Irish support, Asquith was pledged to move a Home Rule Bill, which the Upper House could no longer veto. It was on this issue that Churchill broke with his father's memory. Resisting Home Rule was the Ulster Protestant, that stubborn fellow the Orangeman, who despised his Catholic neighbors as a lower order of human species. Only the nine Ulster counties stood between Ireland and Home Rule. Randolph Churchill, in his efforts at the time of the first Home Rule Bill to split the Liberal Party and break Gladstone's majority, had in 1886 played the "Orange card" and uttered these famous words: "Ulster will fight, and Ulster will be right." The Tories acquired the alias of Unionists, which meant those who did not want Home Rule. The Whigs and some of the Radicals broke away from the Liberals and gathered under the umbrella of Liberal Unionists. Gladstone's bill was rejected and he dissolved Parliament. Randolph's tactic had worked, for the Liberals lost in the General Election.

Churchill, whose earliest memories were of evil Fenians in Dublin, had started his political career as a Conservative and a Unionist. "The millstone of Home Rule" had at first prevented him from joining the Liberal Party. Even after crossing the floor, he clung to his father's beliefs. But after the election of January 1910, when the Liberals were returned with only two seats more than the Tories and needed the support of the eighty-two Irish and forty-one Labour seats, he bowed to political reality and embraced Home Rule. He once told the Irish leader John Redmond that it was the ambition of his life to bring in a Home Rule Bill as Chief Secretary for Ireland.[28] Redmond said on another occasion: "All of us count on *you* to put Home Rule through."[29]

When the local Liberal Association invited Churchill to speak in the Ulster capital of Belfast on February 8, 1912, on the virtues of Home Rule, he accepted. It was a provocation, for he would be speaking in the very hall where his father had lent his support to the Orangemen. The Belfast Unionist press accused him of "dancing on his father's grave." On January 17, the Ulster Unionist Council said that it had observed "with astonishment the deliberate challenge thrown down by Mr. Winston Churchill." It was resolved to prevent his meeting from being held in Ulster Hall. The Orangemen booked the hall for the previous night and swore to hold it by force if necessary.[30]

To avoid rioting, Churchill's hosts shifted the meeting to the Celtic Football Ground in the Catholic working-class district. In spite of warnings that his life was in danger, Churchill insisted on going, and wrote Clemmie on January 23: ". . . *coûte que coûte* [at all costs] I shall begin punctually at 8 o'clock on the 8th of February to speak on Home Rule in Belfast."[31] At last, after nearly a dozen years in the House of Commons, he was taking a stand in direct defiance of his father. His debts were paid. He no longer had to give obeisance. He was free of the past. As if insisting on his refusal to be intimidated, he announced that Clemmie would go with him. Friends begged him not to take her. It was too risky. Police reports were alarming—revolvers were being taken out of pawn, and great quantities of bolts and rivets had been stolen from railway yards. Ten thousand troops had been massed in the inflammable Ulster capital for the First Lord's protection.[32]

On February 7, Winston and Clemmie left London by train for the Scottish port of Stranraer, where they would cross the North Channel to Belfast. Reading the paper in the station, Churchill saw that in Germany the Kaiser had opened the Reichstag. One sentence in his speech stood out as though in bold print: "It is my constant duty and care to maintain and to strengthen on land and water, the power of defense of the German people, *which has no lack of young men fit to bear arms.*" This last clause was like an invitation to war. Churchill thought of France with her declining birth rate peering out from her fortresses at populous and bellicose Germany. There was no doubt that deep and violent passions of humiliation and resentment coursed beneath the glittering uniforms that thronged the palaces through which the Kaiser moved. Germany was the enemy.[33] Only a few days earlier, Churchill had told Wilfrid Blunt over lunch: "I never could learn their beastly language, nor will I till the Emperor William comes over here with his army."[34]

On the boat from Stranraer to Belfast, suffragettes ran around the decks all night shouting "Votes for women" into their cabin windows. Berthing at Larne at 7:30 A.M. on February 8, Winston and Clemmie found the walls around the quay splattered with anti-Home Rule slogans. A hooting crowd greeted them and sang "Rule Britannia" as they disembarked. There was a similar unfriendly reception at the station in Belfast. The lobby of their hotel was crowded with fist-shaking businessmen. That afternoon, on the way to the football grounds, angry crowds lunged at their car, lifted it off the ground, and almost overturned it. The police rapped the hands on the bumpers and running boards with canes. Clemmie worried that the car windows might break and that flying glass would disfigure her lovely face for life. When they reached the Falls, the Catholic district, the scowls turned to smiles and they found themselves surrounded by ardent supporters. In a variation on Randolph's famous words, Churchill showed that he was no longer bound to honor his father's views: "It is in a different sense that I adopt and repeat Lord Randolph's words, 'Ulster will fight and Ulster will be right.' Let Ulster fight for the dignity and honor of Ireland; let her fight for the reconciliation of races and for the forgiveness of ancient wrongs . . . Then indeed Ulster will fight and Ulster will be right." After the meeting, which took place without incident, in a downpour, Churchill was driven in haste to the station, where a special train sped him to Larne before his enemies realized that he had fled.

One Ulster Protestant businessman, Samuel McFadzean, although paying lip service to the Ulster political faith, was so struck by the boldness of Churchill's visit that he named his son Winston.[35]

Churchill had made his point that a minister of the Crown could not be prevented from speaking on Home Rule wherever he chose to go. Now, in a speech in Glasgow on February 9, he addressed himself to the equally urgent issue of Germany. "This island," he said in response to the Kaiser's challenge, "has never been and never will be lacking in trained and hardy mariners bred from their boyhood up in the service of the sea . . . the purposes of British power are essentially defensive. We have no thoughts . . . of aggression and we attribute no such thoughts to other great Powers. There is however this difference between the British naval power and the naval power of the great and friendly Empire . . . of Germany. The British Navy is to us a necessity and from some points of view the German Navy is to them more in the nature of a luxury. Our naval power involves British existence. It is existence for us; it is expansion to them."

The Germans received the news that their fleet was a luxury with an indignation that had not been seen since Lloyd George's Mansion House speech. The Kaiser demanded an apology. The *"Luxus Flotte"* became an expression passed angrily from lip to lip. The timing was awkward, for Haldane, who was in Berlin on a goodwill mission, had to explain that the English word "luxury" did not have the offensive connotation it had in German, where it meant something approaching debauchery. According to the veteran Cabinet-watcher Almeric FitzRoy, several of Churchill's colleagues were upset by his remarks. What mischief had been caused by such a strange lapse from ordinary prudence![36] But Asquith, although dubious about Churchill's use of words, felt that he had made "a plain statement of an obvious truth."[37]

Whether it was the strain of the Belfast trip, or the fox hunting to which she had become increasingly addicted while Winston roamed the oceans aboard the *Enchantress,* Clemmie suffered a miscarriage at the end of February. It was so strange to have all the same sensations as a real baby, with no result. She hoped she would never have such an accident again. Badly treated by her doctor, who let her get up too soon, she was in poor health and in need of further treatment for most of the year. Going from doctor to doctor, she was depressed at not being able to share her husband's life, and Winston was grieved to see her subjected to such a cruel trial, always hoping to get better and then relapsing. As the months drew out and she did not improve, Clemmie began to fear that she would become a permanent invalid. "I am a poor wrecked ship," she told Winston. "You must take me in hand as if I were one of your battleships. Think my case over carefully, and decide what is to be done." Churchill sought advice from his friend Ernest Cassel, whose niece had suffered the same problems following a curettage.[38] Another doctor was brought in, and after changing Clemmie's treatment, he cured her. Churchill was relieved. To friends who saw them, they still seemed like young lovers, full of affectionate banter. Lunching with them, George Riddell mentioned that he had met Lady Kitty Somerset, who was descended from Charles II, a king notorious for the number of his illegitimate children. Clemmie laughed and said everyone was; she was too, through the bastard son of the Duchess of Cleveland. Churchill laughed and said, "Yes, old Charles II was a splendid fellow in that way." Clemmie made some remark— Riddell could not recall what it was—whereupon Churchill said: "That's how you caught me." "That does not matter," Clemmie said, "I've got you. The real question is how to keep you now that I've made my capture." "Well, my dear," Churchill replied, "you don't have much difficulty in doing that."[39] Underlying the banter was the very real anxiety Clemmie felt that she might not be able to hold her husband.

Aside from his wife's illness, Churchill was living on top of happy hours, stretching his talent taut, absorbed in high deeds. In a talk with Riddell and another journalist, T. P. O'Connor, the latter said: "Apart from grinding poverty, happiness does not depend on environment and it is fairly equally distributed amongst all classes." "I don't agree with you," Churchill said. "When I was at school I was miserable. I was dragooned for seven years. I was made to do work I did not like. Since then I have always done work which is a pleasure to me and I have been happy. Happiness does depend a great measure upon environment."[40]

On March 18, Churchill presented his estimates for 1912–1913. As a gesture of goodwill, the Kaiser had sent him the text of the new German Navy Law, but Churchill was alarmed. Although the law did not introduce that much new building, it amounted to putting four-fifths of the German fleet permanently on a war footing. It was like a mobilization order. And yet Churchill held to the figure proposed by his predecessor, forty-four million pounds. His speech, promising a policy of two keels to one on all increases in German ships, was much applauded. Fisher admired the phrase: "We must always be ready to meet at our average moment anything that any possible enemy might hurl against us at his selected moment." How straight and daringly truthful, that backstairs policy-shaper Viscount Esher noted. Captain Maurice Hankey, the rising young strategist who had become secretary of the Committee of Imperial Defense, wrote Fisher that Churchill's estimate speech had made a profound impression on the country. He was a really great man, although Hankey suspected he got his inspiration from Fisher. He was far more brilliant than McKenna, a bit impetuous, but extraordinarily hardworking.[41]

Less pleased with the speech were the Germans, who saw Churchill as a wild man bent on an arms race. The Chancellor, Bethmann-Hollweg, said that he seemed "a firebrand past praying for." And yet when Churchill proposed a Naval Holiday ("supposing we both introduced a blank page in the book of misunderstanding"), the Kaiser refused, saying that such arrangements were only possible between allies.

Churchill still believed that war between two civilized European nations was out of the question. If it did come, they would be heartily sick of it before they came to the end of it. But surely, the best deterrent was a strong Navy. In Portland harbor, on March 24, he viewed the assembled fleet, conquering his seasickness with a patent medicine called Mothersill.

It was a stirring sight to watch the streaks of white foam at the bow of each vessel as the ships filled the bay, and the cables roaring through the hawser holes, and the anchors falling, and the miles of ships all in a line so straight it might have been drawn with a ruler. The flags of a dozen admirals and the pennants of 150 ships flew together. On these ships, Churchill reflected, floated the majesty and power of Empire.[42]

Even the *Titanic* disaster on April 14, when the White Star liner, the largest ship afloat, struck an iceberg on her maiden voyage to New York, with a loss of more than fifteen hundred lives, inspired positive thoughts in Churchill. The way the women and children had been saved showed that in spite of all the inequalities and artificialities of modern life, British civilization was humane and Christian. How differently Imperial Rome would have settled the problem—the swells and potentates would have gone off with their concubines and pet slaves and soldier guards, and then the sailors would have had their chance, headed by the captain; as for the rest, whoever could bribe the crew the most would have had preference and the rest would have gone to hell.[43]

The mutual admiration society with Jacky Fisher was still going strong. Fisher thought Churchill was Napoleonic in audacity, Cromwellian in thoroughness. Churchill was nourished by his letters of advice. As the man wrote his tailor about the white leather hunting breeches he had ordered, Churchill said, "Keep continually sending."[44] He was pleased with the results so far. They would have sixteen ships with 13.5-inch guns before the Germans had anything bigger than 12 inch. On paper it looked more like murder than war.

Immersing himself in technical details, Churchill advised Fisher that he did not want broader battleships that would throw all the docks out of use. They were at the limit, especially if good bilge keels to give stable gun platforms were provided. He traipsed from port to port looking for first-class men to promote, but what a dearth there was in the vice admirals and rear admirals list. On the whole he was content, and only wished there were forty-eight hours in every day.

In April, however, their warm collaboration cooled. When Fisher learned that Churchill had promoted three admirals he had no use for, Berkeley Milne, Reginald Custance, and Hedworth Meux, he took it as a personal affront. Milne was utterly useless, Meux was a courtier, and surely Churchill knew that Custance was one of the leading Beresford men. That was it. The mischief had been done—it was irreparable and irremediable. Churchill had arranged a naval Colenso (the terrible Boer War defeat). "I fear this must be my last communication with you in any matter at all," he wrote on April 22. "I am sorry for it but I consider you have betrayed the Navy in these three appointments, and what the pressure could have been to induce you to betray your trust is beyond my comprehension. . . ."[45]

In a letter to Esher, he was more explicit: Winston, alas, fearing for his wife the social ostracism of the court, had succumbed to the appointment of two court favorites. He had sold his country for a mess of pottage.[46] Fisher was done with him, and would move to the United States. The appointments had in fact been made after a conversation on March 28 between the King and Churchill. But it would not have been in character for Churchill to rubber-stamp the King's wishes, for he did not think much of his opinions in naval matters. After welcoming George V aboard the *Enchantress* in May, he reported to Clemmie that the King had talked more stupidly about the Navy than anything he had ever heard before. It was disheartening to hear the cheap and silly drivel with which he let himself be filled up. Battenberg agreed that the sailor King understood nothing of naval strategy.[47]

The harsh and accusing tone of Fisher's letter was inexcusable. But Churchill did not want a break with the old curmudgeon and replied on April 27 that surely it argued some want of proportion to write such a letter about appointments, none of which touched on vital matters, and all of which rewarded eminent services. Although he regarded Fisher as a man of genius, Churchill would participate in no vendettas. The high patronage of the Admiralty must be evenly, representatively, and not unkindly administered.[48]

A reconciliation was not long in coming. On May 22, Churchill left for a Mediterranean cruise aboard the *Enchantress* with Clemmie (still unwell), Asquith, his daughter Violet, Prince Louis of Battenberg, and the First Lord's three secretaries, David Beatty, Eddie Marsh, and James Masterton-Smith. One of the trip's aims was to woo Fisher, who was in Naples. The floating house party first sailed from Genoa to Elba, where Churchill visited the house of his hero, Napoleon, and saw his death mask.

David Beatty, the man of action, was bored to tears. Prince Louis was *not* terribly exciting. Winston talked about nothing but the sea and the Navy, and bragged about all the great things he was going to do. As for Mrs. Winston, Beatty had never met a better specimen of the Amiable Fool. Old Asquith read extracts aloud from his Baedeker to an admiring audience. He was so ordinary that Beatty was embarrassed to introduce him as the Prime Minister of Great Britain when they went ashore. Beatty could bear it no longer. He liked Winston the best; he was sincere and appreciative of the Navy, and did not enthuse.[49]

On May 24, they steamed into the Bay of Naples; the town looked to Violet like a Scottish shipping town. The sky was overcast, hiding Vesuvius. Beatty saw that old rascal Fisher arrive on board. He never stopped talking and after lunch remained closeted with Winston. Prince Louis hated having him there and stayed out of the way. There Fisher was, noted Violet, in the flesh but not yet in the bag. His eyes, like smoldering charcoals, lit up at his own jokes, a stock of puns of the sort that came out of birthday firecrackers.[50]

Fisher was secretly delighted by the attention. His old cabin as First Sea Lord had been all arranged for him. They must want him very badly. They had done everything but kidnap him. Churchill was most friendly and told him that he had defended him when the King said that Fisher was wedded to certain ideas of which he could not approve. Churchill had replied that the German 12-inch gun was only a peashooter compared with the British gun. That had silenced the King. Churchill promised Fisher that the highest positions in the Admiralty and in the fleet would not be governed by seniority. The future of the Navy rested in the hands of men in whom they both had confidence. They parted once again on friendly terms.[51]

On May 26, the First Lord's party visited the ruins of Paestum and saw the great temple of Zeus with its double rows of Doric columns. Unmoved by the sight, Churchill concentrated on trying to catch the little green-backed lizards darting in and out of the crevices. When they eluded him he pressed Beatty into service, advising him that "we must be more scientific about our strategy. There is a science in catching lizards and we must master it."[52]

Back on board the *Enchantress*, Churchill expounded on the Greeks and Romans, whose languages he had detested since Harrow. "They are so over-rated," he said. "They only said everything *first*. I've said just as good things myself. But they got in before me." It was a lovely sunny day, and as he and Violet leaned against the taffrail and gazed out at the coastline of the Adriatic, she remarked: "How perfect." "Yes," Churchill replied, "range perfect—visibility perfect."[53]

After dinner they played bridge. Churchill's game was untrammeled by conventions, codes, or rules. To be his partner was an agonizing experience, as he recklessly doubled and redoubled. His secretaries, when they played with him, watched with respectful dismay: "But, First Lord, you discarded the knave . . ." "The cards I throw away are not worthy of observation or I should not discard them. It is the cards I *play* on which you should concentrate your attention."[54]

Reaching Malta on May 30, they sailed into the "harbor of harbors," bristling with strongholds and fortifications. A stream of grandees came aboard, including Churchill's old friend Ian Hamilton, who was governor of Malta, a lot of admirals, who complained that Churchill was stripping the Mediterranean to reinforce the North Sea, and Lord Kitchener himself, not quite so martial in a civilian suit and homburg. He and Churchill seemed to get on quite well, considering they disliked each other.

On June 1, Asquith, Churchill, and Kitchener boarded the *Cornwallis* to watch battle practice. They were given little glass stoppers with anchors on them to plug their ears as the big guns fired at a target towed by another ship. Great bursts flashed from the ship's side, and fountains higher than Nelson's column rose from the water where the shells landed. Then they went below-decks to wash their faces, pitch-black from the "smokeless" powder. Churchill was itching with impatience to know how many hits had been scored. Admiral Sir Edmund Poe told him there had been none. "Not *one*? *All* misses? How can you explain it?" "Well—you see, First Lord," the Admiral said, "the shells seem to have either fallen *just* short of the target or else gone just a *little* beyond it."[55]

Bizerta, in the French protectorate of Tunisia, was their next-to-last port of call. It was disappointingly un-African, without sand or palm trees or camels or tigers. Churchill rounded up ten Marines whom he dressed up in scarlet uniforms and placed at the head of the companion ladder to bugle and salute and present arms when the French brass came aboard. There was a phenomenal amount of hypercourteous bowing, and Churchill carried on a confusing conversation with a French admiral:

> ADMIRAL: *"Vous avez fait une bonne traversée?* [Did you have a good crossing?]"
> CHURCHILL: "Yes, yes, very fine fortifications."
> ADMIRAL: *"A la bonne heure—enchanté de vous voir.* [Wonderful— delighted to see you.]"
> CHURCHILL: "How many torpedoes have you got?" Then, with a great effort: *"Où sont vos sous-marins?* [Where are your submarines?]"[56]

Upon his return, Churchill set up a Royal Commission on Oil Fuel and Oil Engines for the Navy and asked "the Oil Maniac," as Fisher was known, to chair it. He needed a big man to crack the nut, if it was crackable. Fisher had to find the oil and show how it could be stored cheaply and bought regularly and protected from aerial attack. His gifts belonged to the Navy. He needed a plow to draw. His propellers were racing in the air.[57]

Fisher agreed to come back to England and start plowing. What a comfort it was to Churchill that he was driving ahead and butting into this gigantic question. But Fisher knew that there were still bloody fools who wanted to stem the tide of internal combustion. The resistance of the admirals to anything new was appalling, but it had always been so. There was an Admiralty minute of bygone days prohibiting the introduction of steam! There was another minute saying that as wood floated, iron did not, and there could be no iron ships. Lord Charles Beresford had called submarines playthings. Sir Arthur Wilson hated oil and loved coal.[58]

It was the same with buying oil. The procrastination was quite damnable. Deals fell through with California and the Dutch company. They were like the Foolish Virgins of the Bible; the door was closing and they would find no oil. Why couldn't they conclude with Deterding, the Napoleon of oil, who had a fleet of sixty-four tankers? Couldn't they realize once and for all that like the colored worsted thread that ran through all the government rope made in the dockyards, the oil engine ran through all the phases of sea fighting from blockades to battles? It was like the motorcar—no fuel consumption when at rest, and instantly ready to go full speed with the engines cold, whereas coal engines needed eight hours to warm up—*what a fighting advantage!*

Finally the Admiralty entered into a twenty-year contract with the Anglo-Persian Company to buy six million tons at thirty shillings a ton. This turned out to be one of the best deals ever made by a government agency, for by investing two million pounds to develop the Persian oil fields, the government acquired a controlling interest in the company. It was a continuing source of wealth and the start of British influence in the Middle East. Indeed, it was the only measure of defense ever entered into by the British government that, instead of costing the taxpayers a great deal of money, brought in an enormous profit.

And yet when Churchill carried through the House of Commons the bill authorizing the Anglo-Persian Oil Convention, he was fought by an opposition of confusing variety: economists deprecating naval expenditure; members for mining constituencies who wanted ships to burn coal; oil magnates objecting to government interference in their monopolies; Conservatives who disapproved of state trading; and partisan opponents who stooped so low as to accuse the Admiralty of corruption. It was never easy to win acceptance for a new idea.[59]

When he had introduced the estimates in March 1912, Churchill had gone along with his predecessor's low figures. But now, with the implications of the German Navy Law, the increase in dockyard wages, and the reforms he wanted to put through, he needed more money. In July, he asked for five million pounds in supplementary estimates, preparing the ground in CID meetings and letters to Lloyd George. Losing his temper at a CID meeting on July 4, he said he would leave the government and stump the country if he did not get his way. The ultimatum fell quite flat, but one or two of his colleagues said they wished to goodness he *would* go.[60]

Lloyd George told Churchill: "You have become a water creature. You think we all live in the sea, and all your thoughts are devoted to sea life, fishes, and other aquatic creatures. You forget that most of us live on land." Churchill was too concentrated on his particular office. He did not understand the fine art of the Welsh footballer's passing game. When he was opposed, he talked of resigning. Lloyd George knew that he had been very near going back to the Tories some little time ago, but that would have been a mistake. He would have been like a woman who had run away from her husband and then gone back after a long interval.[61]

At a CID meeting on July 11, Grey came to Churchill's defense, explaining that foreign policy depended on a strong Navy: "Foreign policy and naval policy are now most intimately connected. The smaller our naval power, the more difficult our foreign policy. If our naval power dropped to such a point that we were in an inferior position in home waters, our foreign policy would be impossible . . . We should have to give way on every diplomatic question, and no self-respecting Empire could hold together . . . the weaker our Navy is, the more difficult foreign policy becomes; the stronger our Navy is, the easier foreign policy becomes. That is really the intimate connection between the two."[62]

And what of the naval point of view? Asquith asked. "The main factor in the naval situation," Churchill said, "is, of course, the growth and the development of the Germany Navy, and it is necessary that I should say a word or two on that. For fifteen years Admiral von Tirpitz has been the Minister of Marine, and during the whole of that period one ruling idea has been perseveringly and unswervingly pursued step by step to a conclusion which clearly has not yet been reached. . . ." Churchill quoted from the German Navy Law of 1900: " 'Germany must possess a battle fleet of such a strength that even for the most powerful naval adversary a war would involve such risks as to make that Power's own supremacy doubtful.' " The Germans said their fleet was to protect their trade and colonies but in fact "it is designed for aggressive and offensive action of the largest possible character in the North Sea or the North Atlantic." Churchill added that he was conscious of "the very heavy burden which the Naval Estimates throw upon the people of this country. . . . Our Annual Estimates, which a few years ago were in the 30's . . . are 45 million pounds today [and] will go up considerably next year; I cannot say how much because the Chancellor of the Exchequer is here, and I should not like to give him a shock for which I have not properly prepared him . . ."[63]

It was enough of a shock that Churchill had asked for supplementaries, and at a Cabinet meeting five days later Lloyd George passed him a note that said: "Bankruptcy stares me in the face." Churchill replied: "Your only chance is to get 5,000,000 pounds next year—and put the blame on me. Then you will be in clover again for the rest of the Parliament."[64] When McKenna questioned some of his facts, Churchill was most abusive and insulting, according to Charles Hobhouse, the Chancellor of the Duchy of Lancaster, who thought he was just a spoiled child endowed by some chance with the brain of a genius. McKenna was on Churchill's enemies' list, having several weeks earlier submitted a memo to George V criticizing Admiralty dispositions in the Mediterranean and the North Sea.

After a year in the Cabinet, here is the way Hobhouse, a somewhat acerbic observer, summed up his colleagues:

Asquith had an admirable intellect but was a drifter, nearly always in favor of the last speaker.

Grey was narrow and obstinate but carried weight.

Lloyd George was quick and humorous, and had a wonderful talent for managing men, but knew not the meaning of the words "truth" and "gratitude."

McKenna was quick-minded, and put out a kind of false bonhomie.

Churchill was ill-mannered, boastful, unprincipled, without any redeeming qualities except his amazing ability and industry. He would, without hesitation, desert a sinking ship.[65]

When Churchill introduced the supplementaries in the House of Commons on July 22, they passed easily. The press praised his refusal to evade the problem and the way he spoke to Germany with the firm courtesy of one strong nation talking to another. The next day, he was off to Portsmouth to watch the fleet at its tactical exercises. During the submarine attack there was a near-tragedy when a submarine overturned a small yacht. The Asquiths came along, and Margot talked nonstop; anything and everthing that came into her head slipped off her indiscreet tongue. If you wanted to flatter her, you had only to say that her husband was growing quite like Gladstone. Asquith loved the war games; he would have made a much better admiral than most of those Churchill had to work with.

Getting along with the admirals was a branch of naval science he could not master. Impatient with the traditions and ceremonious discipline of the Navy, he stepped on too many toes. In his eagerness for information, he broke the chain of command, asking junior officers to inform on their captains. When he did this while visiting the problem-ridden battleship *Lion*, which had failed its speed trials that February, it came to the ears of the *Lion*'s commanding officer, Vice Admiral Lewis Bayly. He took Churchill to the bridge and told him that even though he was First Lord, on the ship the captain was supreme, and he would have him removed if there was any repetition of such inquisitorial methods.[66] Churchill was always rushing where he had no business. After the naval maneuvers that summer, he lectured the flag officers on how they should have conducted themselves before the umpire had completed his report.

Inside Churchill's hand-picked Admiralty Board, there was a state of near-mutiny. The Sea Lords were outraged by his peremptory manner and the bossy language of his official minutes: "I will want to see you on so-and-so" or "I want you to make a series of proposals." He was treating them like flunkies. Hopwood, who had his ear to the ground, tried to warn Churchill in October as tactfully as possible. It was mainly a question of language. To secure the application of a speedy remedy, Churchill dictated a forcible indictment, condemning the subject matter, but the Sea Lords assumed he was reflecting on them as individuals.[67]

Sir Francis Bridgeman and Prince Louis of Battenberg met and agreed the situation could not continue. Bridgeman confronted Churchill and told him that if he did not mend his manners the board would take action. He pointed out that the First Lord was no more than *primus inter pares* and could not give a single order outside the Admiralty building without the board's consent. He must stop using these improper methods. When Churchill argued that he was well within his rights, Bridgeman said he would take the matter to Asquith and the King. Bridgeman was stunned to see Churchill suddenly become so melancholy and weepy that he thought he must be ill.[68]

Behind Churchill's mercurial changes of mood, from anger to sympathy-induced mawkishness, there was the conviction that the Sea Lords were hidebound creatures of routine, looking through the wrong end of the telescope. Only he, Churchill, saw the big picture, but he was constantly interfered with by these gnats in uniform. On October 18, he opened his heart to General Sir Henry Wilson. He was hamstrung for want of a staff of superior leaders. If only he could borrow a couple of Wilson's boys, he would have the finest Navy in the world.[69]

After the run-in with Bridgeman, Churchill resolved to get rid of his contentious First Sea Lord. By November 14, he had told Prince Louis that he would be moved up a notch into Bridgeman's place and that Jellicoe would be brought in as Second Sea Lord. Stunned, Prince Louis wanted to be alone with his thoughts. This would be the last great turning point in a long career.[70]

It so happened that Bridgeman was depressed about his health. Appendicitis, followed by two attacks of bronchitis within a few months, had weakened his constitution. On November 25, while convalescing in the country, he wrote Prince Louis that sometimes he felt inclined to resign. He wished he could go somewhere warm to spend the winter, but that was impossible as long as he remained at the Admiralty. On November 26, he wrote David Beatty that he had actually taken up his pen to write out his resignation, but, feeling better the next morning, he had changed his mind.

Following up on these signals, Churchill wrote Bridgeman on November 28 that he was aware that only his high sense of duty kept him from retiring and that he would not stand in Bridgeman's way if he chose to do so. If there was a war, the burden would be too great.[71] Churchill meant this as a demand for Bridgeman's resignation, but it was expressed with such considerateness that Bridgeman misapprehended its character, thinking it left him an option, and wrote back that he was much better. His doctor said there was nothing organically wrong; he was just run-down. He did not think there was any need to resign. But by this time, Churchill had consulted Asquith and submitted Bridgeman's resignation to the King, without yet having obtained it. On December 2, abandoning all pretense about not standing in his way, Churchill informed him that his resignation was final.[72] Bridgeman may not have thought he was too ill to serve, but Churchill told him that he was. Stunned that the matter had already been settled with the Prime Minister and the King, Bridgeman complied, feeling that he had been treated in a most unfair and insensitive manner. Curiously on the defensive, Churchill accepted the resignation on December 6, protesting that he had acted with loyalty and sincerity. When he had been wrong he had admitted it. He felt no prick of conscience.[73]

Any hope that the Bridgeman resignation could be kept behind Admiralty doors was shattered on December 11 when a Question in the House of Commons came from that self-appointed naval watchdog Lord Charles Beresford. Ever since Churchill had come to the Admiralty, Beresford, who saw in him the willing tool of his archenemy Jacky Fisher, had been making wild speeches. Churchill thought he did a great deal of mischief, not only in spreading discontent and want of confidence through the Navy but in leading the Germans to think the British Navy was thoroughly inefficient. All talk of making Beresford an admiral of the fleet was now forgotten, for he had injured his profession and disgraced himself too much.

For months, Churchill had ignored his mischief-making, but now he had to answer.

CHURCHILL: "Reasons of health led to the resignation from the Board of Admiralty of the late First Sea Lord. The regret which is felt personally by me and by my colleagues on the Board at the withdrawal of so distinguished an officer is only tempered by the fact that no difference in view or policy had led to any disagreement."

BERESFORD: "Might I ask the First Lord if it is a fact that ill-health and no other cause at all was the reason for the First Sea Lord's resignation?"

CHURCHILL: "So far as I am aware, no other cause whatever."

BERESFORD: ". . . Might I ask on which side the proposal for resignation emanated—from the Admiralty or from the First Sea Lord?"

CHURCHILL: "I should like, before answering such a question, to know whether the Noble Lord is speaking on behalf of Sir Francis Bridgeman."

BERESFORD: "That is a very fair question. No, sir, I have not had any communication from Sir Francis Bridgeman of any sort or kind since his resignation. I merely ask this question in the interest of the Service, because so many Sea Lords have left during the last year. It is a question in which the Service is very interested."

MR. LANE-FOX: "Might I ask whether the statement that the resignation of Sir Francis Bridgeman is owing to causes of ill-health is made with his authority?"

CHURCHILL: "No, sir, I take full responsibility for the statement that the cause of ill-health led to the retirement of Sir Francis Bridgeman. For that I take full responsibility, and I require no other responsibility to cover it."

BERESFORD: "Might I ask for an answer to my question—on which side the proposal for the resignation emanated?"

CHURCHILL: "Very well, since the Noble Lord presses it; the proposal emanated from me."

SIR C. KINLOCH-COOKE: "Will the right honorable Gentleman tell the House whether it is not a fact that the Sea Lords have threatened more than once during the last month to resign?"

CHURCHILL: "There is absolutely no truth in that statement."[74]

Now that the resignation was out of the bag, Beresford would use it as a stick to beat the Navy with. It could only be a matter of days before the press seized on it. On December 14, the *Morning Post* wrote, "on the very best authority," that Bridgeman had resigned over conflicts with Churchill, notably on the subject of pay and living conditions for sailors.

Churchill, who could now expect a full-scale debate in the House, saw that in Bridgeman there was a real potential for trouble. Accordingly, on the day the article appeared, he wrote the Admiral a threatening letter. Unless Bridgeman stated that in no way had differences with the First Lord led to his resignation, Churchill might be forced to bring into the open the painful facts of his poor health. If challenged, he would have to prove to the House, inch by inch, that Bridgeman's strength and energy were no longer equal to the duties of his office. Surely Bridgeman remembered that he had accepted the proposals on improved pay, subject to getting more if the money was to be found? He had been willing to resign if necessary to strengthen Churchill's hand, but no resignation had been tendered by him or any other member of the board.[75]

The proposals for a pay increase had in fact come from Churchill via Jacky Fisher. It was a sore point that the pay for able seamen and petty officers had not changed in sixty years. In a budget approaching 50,000,000 pounds, all Churchill wanted was 470,000 pounds for pay raises, but Lloyd George balked, complaining that Churchill was "looking out for opportunities to squander money." Churchill found it hard to understand Lloyd George, who usually took big views. Perhaps it was because there were so few Welshmen in the Navy. In any case, he had known all along that the Treasury would try to smother his plans by saying, "What about the Army?" At a Cabinet meeting on November 27, Charles Hobhouse noted in his diary: "We had the usual display of bad manners and bad temper from Churchill. He proposed a fortnight ago an increase of 500,000 pounds for navy pay. The Estimates Committee cut this down to 300,000 pounds. At this he stormed, sulked, interrupted. Like an ill-bred cub. The P.M. treated him admirably and finally reduced him to silence."[76] The Sea Lords' resignation would have been Churchill's trump card, but the funds were obtained, and the small increases in pay went into effect in December.

Bridgeman replied on December 15 that he could give Churchill no blanket endorsement, as "you will recollect that on more than one occasion such differences have arisen on matters of serious importance. For example, I need only refer to a recent question of an appointment which involved so grave a conflict of opinion that I felt obliged to suggest my resignation."[77] This was the choice of Arthur Farquhar to command the Coast Guard, which Churchill had finally agreed to. But appointments were a point of friction with the Sea Lords. According to Dudley De Chair, who had just been named Naval Secretary to succeed David Beatty, gone to sea to command a battle-cruiser squadron, Churchill thought he knew more about naval personnel than men who had spent their entire adult lives in the service. Once, when De Chair had tried to dissuade him from making a disastrous appointment, Churchill announced that as he had instituted the Labour Exchanges, he could tell in a five-minute conversation whether or not a man was suitable.[78] It was this sort of shooting from the hip that made the Sea Lords seethe with frustration.

Furious, Churchill wrote Bridgeman on December 18 that it was unworthy of him not to dissociate himself from statements that were unfounded, and known to be unfounded by his colleagues. He had never tendered his resignation. No resignation was threatened or impending at the time he retired.[79]

By this time, the Bridgeman resignation had been blown up into a full-scale scandal, and when the word went out that it would be discussed on December 20 in the House, the promise of a duel with the buttons off the foils between Churchill and Beresford brought a crowd of spectators. There was an uneasy feeling in people's minds that Bridgeman had been unfairly treated. It was bad for the service that a man with a long and honorable career, who had attained the topmost rung of the ladder, was cast aside without consideration. And he was but the last of five Sea Lords who had been retired since Churchill had taken office a year ago—the others were Admiral Sir Arthur Wilson as First Sea Lord, Vice Admiral Sir George Egerton as Second Sea Lord, Rear Admiral Sir Charles Briggs as Third Sea Lord, and Rear Admiral Sir Charles Madden as Fourth Sea Lord. Churchill had retired an entire Admiralty Board and was now starting on the new one. Was this any way to run the Navy, by firing Sea Lords? The press was saying that Churchill and Bridgeman had differed on three questions, the manning of the fleet, the pay of the sailors, and the Canadian proposal to build dreadnoughts. The House had been told that Churchill was a tyrant, that no one could work with him unless prepared to be subservient. This would be a true war of words. If Churchill could be shown to have acted improperly, he might have to resign.

The sixty-six-year-old Beresford, who had first entered the House of Commons in 1874, the year of Churchill's birth, gave the first thrust by charging that Churchill had led the House to believe that Bridgeman had resigned voluntarily, whereas Churchill had forced him to resign in a letter that said in effect: " 'You are ill; you shall be ill; I order you to be ill. . . . Then if you keep silent . . . I will make you a G.C.B. and an Admiral of the Fleet.' . . . The First Lord of the Admiralty's policy, as I have explained, is a policy of bribes and threats. . . . What was the real reason why Sir Francis Bridgeman had to go? Because he did not agree with the autocratic methods of the First Lord, and because he thought on technical questions expert opinion should be taken."

What technical questions? Churchill asked.

CHURCHILL: "What I ask the Noble Lord to do is to state specifically what he has in his mind, if he has anything in his mind."

BERESFORD: "The First Lord suggests that my mind is a hollow blank. What I have in mind . . . is that the . . . right honorable Gentleman is doing at the Admiralty exactly what he did wherever he has been placed. . . . the reason so many officers in the Service do not trust his administration is that he will always assume the executive as well as the administrative. This was well exhibited . . . in the Sidney Street riot. . . . He does the same thing at the Admiralty. On many occasions he took charge . . . and he took charge during the maneuvers."

CHURCHILL: "That is absolutely untrue. No order, instruction or directions, directly or indirectly, were sent by me."

HON. MEMBERS: "Withdraw."

BERESFORD: "I do not see why I should withdraw, because 'taking charge' is a naval expression, which a landsman would not understand. If a ship's rudder carries away, you say the ship 'takes charge.' If a man goes and interferes on the forecastle with work that is not his own . . . we say he 'takes charge.' "

The dismissal of five Sea Lords since he had taken office was fatal to Churchill's authority, Beresford went on. What a fatal disaster the present system would be if they went to war.

The time had come for Churchill to bring up his 15-inch guns, to show Charlie B. that in the battle of rhetoric he was hopelessly outgunned.

CHURCHILL: "It is his habit in matters of this kind to make a number of insinuations—"

BERESFORD: "That is not true."

CHURCHILL: "Insinuations of a very gross character, some of which transgress the limits of Parliamentary decorum; to cover the Order Paper with leading and fishing questions, designed to give substance and form to any gossip or tittle-tattle he may have been able to scrape together, and then to come down to the House, not to attempt to make good in fact or in detail . . . but to skulk in the background, waiting for an opportunity . . . I have not ever since I became First Lord of the Admiralty made any reply to the Noble Lord's scurrilous and continuous personal attacks, none. I sought no quarrel with him. . . . but within a fortnight he made a speech in which he said I had betrayed the Navy . . . and ever since he has been going about the country pouring out charges of espionage, favoritism, blackmail, fraud, and inefficiency."

BERESFORD: "I deny that entirely. I never used the word 'blackmail.' Give the date and the place."

CHURCHILL: "Certainly; in the constituency of the honorable member for Eversham [Mr. Eyres-Monsell]—my memory is very good on these points—he used the great bulk of those offensive expressions, needless to say, unsupported by any facts or arguments. . . . I have never taken these things too seriously. I am not one of those who take the Noble Lord too seriously. I know him too well. He does not mean to be as offensive as he often is when he is speaking on public platforms. He is one of those orators of whom it was well said, 'Before they get up, they do not know what they are going to say; when they are speaking, they do not know what they are saying; and when they have sat down, they do not know what they have said.' . . . Under a genial manner . . . the Noble Lord nourishes many bitter animosities on naval matters. He is the last man who ought to make the Navy either a party or a political question, and, as far as I can make out, he is about the only man in the House or either side who does it."

Churchill went on to explain the steps leading up to Bridgeman's resignation. "I am sorry," he said, "that the Noble Lord should have gone out of his way to insult Sir Arthur Wilson and Sir Francis Bridgeman by saying the one was bribed by an Order of Merit and the other by a Grand Cross of the Bath. Such expressions applied to officers who receive marks of distinction from the Crown are odious."[80]

Since Beresford was getting the worst of it, the new leader of the Tory Party, Bonar Law, came to his rescue. He could hardly congratulate Churchill on his treatment of Beresford in the early part of his speech:

BONAR LAW: "He made upon him one of those attacks which I think are most futile. He pretended to treat him with contempt, while at the same time he showed an amount of venom which made the House understand there was no contempt in his feeling . . . Rightly or wrongly, my Noble Friend has raised the question that the right honorable Gentleman is a dictator in his department, and that he cannot stand any interference with his views, and that, for that reason, he was glad to get rid of Sir Francis Bridgeman . . . I am at a loss to make what the right honorable Gentleman has said coincide with the information which has reached me . . . I was told yesterday that Sir Francis had said quite recently, on some question within his department, that if the First Lord insisted on carrying out his views, he would resign."

CHURCHILL: "Sir Francis never made any such statement to me. If the right honorable Gentleman will state the specific matter, I am quite willing to trace it to its course and reduce it to its proper proportion."

BONAR LAW: ". . . The important thing to me is that Sir Francis thought any subject of sufficient gravity to make him say he would resign . . . If the idea were spread that it was dangerous for the First Sea Lord to be independent, nothing would be worse for the Service."[81]

[Churchill then quoted the two letters he had sent Bridgeman.]

BONAR LAW: "I do not want to use strong language, but I am bound to say that, if anyone had sent me that second letter following the first, I should have considered I was brutally ill-used . . ."

CHURCHILL: "My conclusion was, 'if by misadventure, we should be involved in war, the burden might be more than you could bear.'"

BONAR LAW: ". . . I think that is brutal treatment for anyone in the position of Sir Francis Bridgeman."[82]

And there the debate ended, in what was considered the most exciting Parliamentary session of the year, full of lively invective, thrust and counter-thrust. Both sides had been bloodied. Beresford had shown himself to be an embittered old man, obsessed with his vendetta against Fisher's Navy. But he and Bonar Law had brought out that the working relationship between Churchill and the Sea Lords was not a happy one, due to Churchill's inclination to run a one-man show. There was a lesson to be drawn, which Churchill ignored. As his Naval Secretary, Captain De Chair, who probably saw more of him than did anyone else, including his wife, recalled in his memoirs, published in 1936: "He had a misconceived impression of his own importance, overriding and silencing the wise and matured reasoning of his advisers on the Board."[83] Oddly enough, Bridgeman bore no grudge, and wrote Lord Stamfordham on December 28: "I do hope the whole business is now at an end, but I hear rumors of a deep-laid agitation against Churchill; I am using every bit of influence I possess to arrest it . . . I am afraid Beresford is difficult to hold and I unfortunately can do nothing with him."[84]

As new dreadnoughts burned oil, Churchill burned pugnacity. Anyone who fought him had to be brought to his knees, whether it was Bridgeman or Beresford. He illustrated Jacky Fisher's axiom that the man who wanted something badly enough usually got it. Churchill was ready to cross swords

345

with the King if he had to, over a relatively minor matter like the naming of ships. In October he proposed that the four new dreadnoughts, the most powerful ships ever built, should be named after these great English warriors and sovereigns: *King Richard the First, King Henry the Fifth, Queen Elizabeth,* and *Oliver Cromwell.* Through his secretary, Arthur Bigge, now Lord Stamfordham, the King replied that surely there must be some mistake. He could not agree to Cromwell, who, after all, had sanctioned the execution of Charles I.[85] Churchill insisted: Cromwell was one of the founders of the Navy. There was no chapter of British history from which the King should feel himself divided.[86] But the King's view did not alter, as Lord Stamfordham informed Churchill on November 4. He still felt that it was inappropriate to name a ship after a regicide.

On November 5, Churchill launched an inquiry into the expense of refitting the royal yacht, the *Victoria & Albert.* Was the timing a coincidence? Or was it a way of putting pressure on the King to make him more amenable in the matter of ship's names? The King would be surprised to see the enormous charges that were made for quite small things, Churchill said. Sure that His Majesty would disapprove of anything in the nature of wasteful or extravagant expenditure (and conveniently forgetting that he had also been accused of extravagance in the use he made of the *Enchantress*), he was sending Sir Francis Hopwood and the Director of Dockyards to Portsmouth to audit the new estimate for thirteen thousand pounds presented by the yacht's commodore.[87] Showing no signs that he was vexed by such an unprecedented investigation, the King acknowledged the commodore's extravagance and promised that in the future he would tell him to report how little was required and not how much.[88]

In the meantime, Prince Louis warned Churchill not to persist with *Oliver Cromwell.* The Sovereign's decision as to names for ships had always been accepted as final by First Lords.[89]

But just as he had done when bombarding Lord Elgin with letters over the release of an African chief, Churchill would not let go. On November 16, with quotations from historians to back him up, he argued that it was right to name a battleship after a man who had never failed to make the enemies of the King tremble.

At his wit's end, Lord Stamfordham replied on November 20: "You will, I am sure, realize how very distasteful it is to the King not to approve of recommendations coming from any of his Ministers . . . But nothing which has been said or written since His Majesty discussed the matter personally with you some months ago has induced him to alter his strong opinion as to the undesirability of including among the coming additions to the Royal Navy *His Majesty's Ship Oliver Cromwell*. In these circumstances the King must ask you to consider and submit some other name."[90]

Churchill could go no further. He could not force George V to resign on grounds of health, or debate ship's names in the House of Commons. Bowing to the King's wishes, he submitted the name *Valiant*. But the argument raged again the following year when he proposed for two new battleships the names *Ark Royal* and *Pitt*.[91] The King did not like *Ark Royal* because it sounded like Noah's Ark, which was not suitable for a ship made of metal. As for *Pitt*, the name was neither euphonious nor dignified. The King, who had spent fifteen years in the Navy, knew enough of the lower deck to realize that the bluejackets would find ill-conditioned four-letter nicknames rhyming with *Pitt*. Churchill found the suggestion that sailors might dub one of his beautiful new battleships *Shit* "unworthy of the royal mind."[92]

Again, he insisted. There had been a *Pitt* and an *Ark Royal* before, and both vessels had important historical associations. He was strongly of the opinion that the names should be approved. The King was not of that opinion. He hoped that Churchill would have no difficulty in selecting two other old names in place of the two he disliked.

Churchill was sorry the King did not like the names but remained convinced that they were the best choice. *Pitt*, suggested by the Prime Minister, recalled the two famous statesmen under whom the most martial exploits of the British race had been achieved. The *Ark Royal* had been the flagship at the defeat of the Spanish Armada. Churchill reminded the King that as First Lord of the Admiralty he had a definite responsibility to give advice. He regretted that on several occasions the names he had submitted had not met with the King's favor. Consequently, he had examined the custom of bringing the names of battleships to the Sovereign's notice, and found that it did not exist during the reign of Queen Victoria, and had only been introduced in the reign of Edward VII. It occurred to Churchill that the King might prefer not to be troubled at all in the matter, reverting to the practice followed up to a quite recent date. This was gall, for Churchill was in effect suggesting that rather than accede to his monarch's wishes when they disagreed, the King should resign his privilege of naming ships.[93]

Stung, the King replied through Lord Stamfordham that he yielded to no one in his concern for all that affected the daily life of the sailor, including the name of his ship. The King could not help thinking that the officers and men of the Royal Navy would like to feel that the ships were named with the approval of the Sovereign, all the more so as the King had been for many years in the service. Under the circumstances, the King hoped that Churchill would see his way to carrying out his wishes and submitting two other names.[94] After carrying the fight for the usual three rounds, Churchill had to retire from the ring. Why did he waste so much time and energy resisting a higher authority on a marginal matter? As Viscount Esher, an intermittent admirer, said: "For so clever a man, he is sometimes exceedingly foolish."[95]

During Churchill's first year at the Admiralty, the barometer was set at "stormy." He fought the admirals and won; he fought the King and lost. In a third fight, over the Irish question, he emerged bloodied but victorious. The Home Rule Bill, the third such bill proposed by a Liberal government, had been introduced on April 11. It made no provision for Ulster, four of whose nine counties were solidly Protestant. Like Randolph in earlier days, the Tories played the Orange card. Ulster was the cure for their humiliation, after the setbacks of the budget and the Parliament Bill. Deprived of the Lords' veto, the Tories sought to kill Home Rule by direct action, if need be by force of arms. In this bizarre period of English politics, the Tory leadership, custodians of tradition, moved into open revolt against the Parliamentary system. Bonar Law, the Glasgow businessman who had succeeded Balfour, was an unlikely revolutionary. But he was the son of an Ulster Presbyterian minister, and all the passions and prejudices of that stubborn minority coursed in his veins. With Edward Carson, a noted lawyer who had prosecuted Oscar Wilde, and who was now the chief of the dour Belfast bigots, Bonar Law took the stand that insurrection was preferable to the rule of a Catholic Parliament in Dublin—Home Rule was Rome Rule.

On April 30, when the bill was given its Second Reading, Churchill addressed the House, asking that prejudices and passions be shed. "At one sweep of the wand," he said, the Ulstermen "could sweep the Irish question out of life and into history and free the British realm of the canker which poisoned its heart for generations. If they refuse, if they take to the boats, all we say is they shall not obstruct the work of salvage and we shall go forward at any rate to the end."[96]

Referring to the speeches that Carson and Bonar Law had been making around the country, he accused them of "almost treasonable activity: had British statesmen and leaders of great parties in the past allowed their thoughts so lightly to turn to projects of bloodshed within the bosom of the country, we should have shared the follies of Poland."

If he thought his words would serve to calm the Tory leader he was wrong. Sounding more like an insurrectionist than the leader of a great party, the party of Old England, hereditary titles, the Anglican Church, and country squires, Bonar Law on July 27, at a Tory rally at Blenheim, said: "They may, perhaps they will, carry their Home Rule Bill through the House of Commons but what then? I said the other day in the House of Commons and I repeat here that there are things stronger than Parliamentary majorities . . . I can imagine no length of resistance to which Ulster can go in which I should not be prepared to support them . . ."[97]

When Parliament reconvened after the summer break, the Conservatives were in open rebellion and there were threats of civil war in Ulster. On October 10, Churchill berated the Opposition for using language of derision and violence. Had not his friend F. E. Smith asserted that the great majority of the Irish nation were people unable to manage a bucket shop or a second-hand clothes shop? Had not Sir Edward Carson talked of the need for British bayonets? He viewed such tactics with the strongest feeling of reprehension.

CARSON: "I do not care twopence whether you do or not."

CHURCHILL: "There are so many things the right honorable Gentleman does not care twopence about—"

CARSON: "You will say the opposite tomorrow."

AN HON. MEMBER: "You were jolly glad to get out of Belfast."

CHURCHILL: "I do think . . . that he [Carson] should show towards others some of the courtesy which he expects to be shown towards himself."

CARSON: "You do not know what courtesy means."

CHURCHILL: "I have never said a discourteous word about the right honorable Gentleman. . . . He comes here to grumble about Parliamentary procedure . . . when he has just elsewhere declared his intention to defy an Act of Parliament and to levy war upon his fellow countrymen."[98]

On November 11, with Liberal attendance slack and the front bench dozing, the Tories called for a snap vote on the financial provisions of the Home Rule Bill and defeated the government by twenty-one votes. Two days later, Asquith moved that the Tory amendment be rescinded. When his motion was carried, a great uproar resulted. Sir Rufus Isaacs, the Attorney General, was shouted down as he tried to speak in Asquith's support.

AUSTEN CHAMBERLAIN: "We want fair play on both sides and they will not give it us."

THE SPEAKER: "Those who appeal for fair play ought to show it."

Mr. Wyndham: "Civil War."

Sir Rufus Isaacs: "You have ruled, Mr. Speaker [Interruption]. The honorable and learned member has challenged us [Interruption] —to quote precedents [Interruption]—Mr. Speaker, you have pointed out—[Interruption] . . ."[99]

At this point, Churchill and Jack Seely, who had replaced Haldane as Secretary of State for War, left their seats and were assailed by cries of "Rats." In ironic acknowledgment of these cries, Churchill waved his handkerchief at the Opposition benches. That was too much for Ronald McNeill, the tall, distinguished Ulsterman who had been editor of St. James' Gazette. Shouting "Why do you not sit down?" he picked up from the elbow of the Speaker's chair a small leather-bound copy of the Standing Orders and hurled it at Churchill. The book struck him in the face, drawing blood, and Seely shepherded him off the floor. Adjourning the House, the Speaker said: "In my opinion, grave disorder has arisen."[100]

The following day, November 14, McNeill apologized.

"Political feeling was very high [he said], and taunts were exchanged between members upon both sides of the House. Under the influence of a momentary loss of self-control, I regret to say that I discharged a missile which struck the First Lord of the Admiralty. As soon as the heat of the moment had passed, I fully realized my action was entirely reprehensible, and returned to the House at a later hour, and, with the assistance of the President of the Local Government Board, I endeavored to find the First Lord, in order that I might express to him my regret, and ask his pardon. I was unsuccessful in finding him, and I am anxious to take this, the first opportunity, of saying how extremely I regret having lost my temper, and of tendering to the right honorable Gentleman and to the House a full and unreserved apology."[101]

Churchill assured McNeill that he had no personal feelings in the matter (the two would become Cabinet colleagues in the twenties). One explanation of McNeill's rage appeared in the Daily Chronicle, which said that the Tories "had come back from dinner flowing with insolence and wine." But the Speaker, when asked about the article, repudiated the suggestion that any members had been intoxicated, however regrettable the scene may have been.[102]

As the year 1912 ended, Churchill found himself at the hub of the country's two great issues—the Irish muddle at home and the German menace abroad. In preparing for a possible war, he and the other members of the CID had to act as if war with Germany was a certainty. Their minds became accustomed to grappling with its strategic and logistical problems. Discussed incessantly, the conflict took on a character of inevitability.

Looking in on a few such meetings helps re-create the mood of urgent concern. On one occasion, the topic was trade with the enemy.

LLOYD GEORGE: "We could not hurt Germany except through her in-
dustries and by cutting off her supplies of corn and meat."
HALDANE: "The question of which would be the most advantageous
to us, the neutrality or hostility of the Low Countries, has been
much discussed."
CHURCHILL: "Their neutrality is out of the question. They must be
either friends or foes."
ASQUITH: "In the old French wars the Low Countries were treated
practically as foes."
CHURCHILL: "If the Germans violated Belgian neutrality, Belgium
would be compelled to take one side or the other. If those countries
were friendly to us they would certainly be overrun by the
enemy."[103]

The meetings show the innocence with which England's leaders were ap-
proaching the first great war between industrialized European nations. It was like a game the rules of which had yet to be invented. Discussing the control of enemy aircraft, Churchill said he was working on a semiautomatic 3-inch gun that could fire thirty rounds a minute at an angle of elevation of eighty degrees and had a range of seven thousand yards. Although there was no name for it yet, it was the first antiaircraft gun.

McKenna wanted to know what would become of the fragments once the shell had exploded.

Churchill said that of course the pieces might fall on their own people but that could hardly be helped.

Colonel Seely said the fragments would be very small.[104]

When it came to the infant arm of aviation, they could not decide whether to concentrate on planes or airships. Churchill later wrote in *The World Crisis* that "I rated the Zeppelin much lower as a weapon of war than almost anyone else. . . . I was sure the fighting airplane . . . would harry, rout and burn these gaseous monsters. . . . I therefore did everything in my power in the years before the war to restrict expenditure upon airships and to concentrate our narrow and stinted resources upon airplanes." In fact, the exact opposite was true. In the CID meetings, Churchill was the principal backer of airships. He wanted them because the Germans had them. They had built two models, the Zeppelin and the Parsifal, which they were using to carry passengers. In wartime they could carry troops. What if the Germans sent their fleet of twenty-four airships over London? England must be ready to meet and attack them. They could no longer afford to neglect airships.[105]

Admiral Sir Arthur Wilson, who although no longer a Sea Lord was still a member of the CID, said airships were useless. Unable to keep an accurate dead reckoning, they would lose their position as soon as they were out of sight of land. Churchill argued that they could easily keep in touch with a specially detached ship. He was alarmed at the impression Wilson made on the CID with his stubborn and well-argued disparagements of the airship's capacities. Impatient to catch up, he had the Admiralty order a Parsifal airship from the Germans, to be delivered in March 1913.[106]

No item was overlooked. With the Secretary of State for War, Jack Seely, Churchill called a conference to discuss building horse stalls in the ships that would carry the expeditionary force to France. It was agreed that stalls would be made for twenty thousand horses.[107]

While the horse stalls were put up, while the antiaircraft guns were built, while the first airships were launched after the German model, British leaders listened anxiously for warning signs from Europe. In January 1913 the French ambassador, Paul Cambon, told Churchill that the state of Europe was infinitely graver than it had been at any time since 1875. Churchill thought it would be almost impossible to keep Russia and Austria from going to war but hoped that Germany and France might be kept out of it. If they joined in, how could England stand to one side without being hated and despised throughout Europe?[108] They would never be forgiven. Grey was watching for Austrian mobilization. He did not think the Austrian military party could hold out against the pressure of the other powers for peace.[109]

As the curtains of the new year parted, Britain's leaders had no way of knowing what the next act in the European drama would bring, but they prepared for a violent finale. After a year in office, and despite occasional grumbling from the Sea Lords, Churchill was in full charge of his sprawling department. If genius can be described as an infinite capacity for detail, he was not wanting. His mind was equally at home with sweeping abstractions and small technical particulars. His eye fastened on such minutiae as whether a recreation center for airmen should be called a "canteen" or an "institute," on the erection of colored and numbered metal signs to make landing strips visible to pilots, and on the uniforms of the Naval Air Service—an eagle instead of an anchor on buttons, cap badges, epaulets, and sword-belt clasps.[110]

In turn, he was kept attentive to all naval activities by the Questions in the House of Commons. On January 8, 1913, for instance, there was a Question concerning the court-martial of a sailor named H. C. Day serving aboard H.M.S. *Hearty*. He had been sentenced to eight months' detention for striking a lieutenant after discovering that a letter from his mother had been opened. While in detention, he struck a chief petty officer, adding nine months to his sentence. Could something be done to reduce it? And was it the policy of the government to allow private letters to be opened? Pointing out that the original sentence had been reduced from eight to four months, Churchill defended the disciplinary measures: "I am not prepared to recommend any further exercise of clemency in this matter. Striking a superior officer is one of the gravest offenses anyone can commit . . . There is no excuse whatever for behaving in such an extraordinary manner."[111]

In another Question, Major Archer-Shee chided the First Lord for wasting the taxpayers' money by his ostentatious use of the Admiralty yacht.

ARCHER-SHEE: "It seems to me that the time has come when this very expensive yacht should be done away with . . . When we want every man and every penny we can get for the Navy it seems to me we ought not to be spending on this yacht what amounts to something like the interest on a million of money, for the yacht must cost 30,000 pounds a year at least . . . The usefulness of this yacht appears no longer to exist. I am not making any sort of personal attack on the First Lord . . . We heard the other day that the right honorable Gentleman had been 186 days afloat in the yacht. That is certainly a tribute to his energy, but my point is that it is not necessary for the First Lord of the Admiralty to go to sea at all. If he has to inspect naval stations around the coasts of these islands he can do it more quickly and better by rail. The naval stations are not out at sea, they are dotted round the coast."

CHURCHILL: "I can only refer the honorable Gentleman to the answer which has frequently been given in this House on the subject and say that the whole of the personnel of the yacht, officers and men, would be appropriated by the war fleet in time of war, and disposed of in fighting vessels, and that the vessel itself would be used as an auxiliary hospital ship."

When the cook on the *Enchantress* was granted a raise in pay by the Privy Council, Lord Morley, the president of the council, wrote Churchill that he ventured to hope that "if his own emoluments should ever be assailed, on the ground that his office is of the nature of a sinecure, Mr. Churchill will defend Lord Morley in whatever of the various parliaments of the UK his salary may be grudged."[112]

The *Enchantress* had become Churchill's preferred form of transportation. He used it not only on naval business but also to visit his constituency of Dundee, a bustling port and the center of the jute trade, where he spoke on January 30. He loved the luxuries that went with the office, adding to its grandeur, and looked forward to moving into stately Admiralty House that April. Clemmie was not quite so delighted as she went through the grim catalogues of Admiralty furniture to pick what she needed for the bedrooms, sitting rooms, and nurseries. She wished they had a woman at the head of the Office of Works. She worried about the expense of running such a mansion, and the added servants, and prevailed on her husband to seal off the first floor with its endless suite of reception rooms. Money was always a problem, for Churchill was no economist when it came to his personal exchequer. Once, to balance the house books, she had sold a diamond-and-ruby necklace he had given her as a wedding present. He rushed to the jeweler's to buy it back, but he was too late.

After five years of marriage, communication by baby talk had not abated. The Amber Pug was still offering cream to the Sweet Kat. When they quarreled, the milk and honey of mutual goodwill was quickly poured. Churchill liked to quote the Biblical precept "let not the sun go down upon your wrath." He knew that Clemmie was easily agitated and prone to anxiety. He told her that it was not worth worrying about things that might not even happen and enjoined her to cast care aside. Only with him did she lower her barriers of reserve.

There had been an argument before he left for Dundee, and he was quick to admit that he had been stupid, a prey to nerves and prepossessions. It was a great comfort for him to feel absolute confidence in her. He wanted to kiss her dear face and stroke her baby cheeks and make her purr softly in his arms. Only she could break the loneliness of a bustling and bustled existence.[113] Clemmie too was apologetic; when she got excited and cross she always said more than she meant instead of less—it all came to the top and boiled over. The only time she felt low was when there were too few breaks in Winston's bustling existence. She was a very greedy Kat and liked a great deal of cream.

For Clemmie, leaving Eccleston Square was the end of a chapter in her life. Moving into an official residence seemed an indication that she would see less of her husband, that their privacy and time together were the price of his ambition. Luckily, they leased Eccleston Square to Sir Edward Grey. Clemmie settled into the mansion life. In the morning, as in a scene from a Fragonard, the cook appeared in her white apron bearing the menu book, which Clemmie in her lace cap and bed jacket scrutinized. Winston might pop in, saying, "Let's have Irish stew with lots of onions," wearing his new dressing gown, a gift from his cousin Sunny, who was tired of seeing his pink and corpulent form roaming naked in the halls of Blenheim from bedroom to bathroom. In many ways, Winston and Clemmie were opposites. She liked to be up early and in bed early, while he kept late hours. When she retired, she left notes, specifying whether she wanted him to visit her bedroom.

Winston was an affectionate father, lavishing the same care and attention on his son and daughter that he did on official business. He had his mother's warm and giving nature rather than his father's cold and forbidding one. Raised by nurses, the children were brought out for his approval. He had a preference for the radiant Randolph. Diana was a darling too, but somehow Randolph seemed a more genial and generous nature, while she was mysterious and self-conscious. But the day would come when everyone would admire her and grumble about him.[114]

While Churchill was circling the British Isles in the *Enchantress*, Clemmie was befriended by the Asquiths, who often asked her for weekends at their riverside house, The Wharf, at Sutton Courtenay. With her puritan streak, she did not entirely approve of the Prime Minister. She disliked his habit at dinner parties of ogling down "Pennsylvania Avenue," as a lady's cleavage was then called. She disapproved of his flirtation with the twenty-six-year-old Venetia Stanley, which he camouflaged by pretending that she came to see his daughter, Violet. Asquith, while adopting his most cordial manner, also had reservations about Clemmie, and wrote Venetia that although he was quite fond of her, she was "*au fond* a thundering bore."[115] Not that he was in the least anti-Clemmie, but he thought her sister-in-law, Goonie, was worth one hundred Clemmies. What a prig she was—on one occasion, she had turned down a couturier dress offered by the gracious and beautiful Mrs. Keppel, who had been the last mistress of Edward VII.[116]

On March 31, Churchill presented his estimates for 1913–1914 to the House of Commons. Each year naval expenses leaped alarmingly by millions of pounds. The new estimates amounted to some forty-eight million pounds. He had won Cabinet approval for the sum, in spite of Lloyd George's grumbling about bankruptcy. In the House, concern that Britain was losing her naval supremacy over Germany smothered any residual feelings about economy. Aside from a skirmish with Lord Beresford, everything went smoothly. When Beresford charged that the Navy was twenty thousand men short, Churchill replied: "Ninety percent of the whole fighting strength of the Fleet is manned without the use of a single Reservist."

> BERESFORD: "There again, in one of those charming sentences which take in the House, the right honorable Gentleman is perfectly right in what he says, but what are these crews? The ships' companies consist largely of boys and young stokers. The First Lord knows it."
>
> CHURCHILL: "It is not true."
>
> BERESFORD: "To make up what the right honorable Gentleman calls the fighting fleet, he will have to put in Reservists."
>
> CHURCHILL: "Not in the First and Second Fleets."[117]

Jacky Fisher thought Winston had never made a better speech in his life and sent him an article from the *Daily Telegraph* that said, "The Navy has never in its long history had a more persuasive spokesman in Parliament than the present Minister."

No sooner had the victory of the estimates been won than Churchill was dipped into the muck of a political scandal that had been stirring for about a year. In March 1912, the Postmaster General, Sir Herbert Samuel, concluded a contract with the English Marconi Company to build a chain of wireless stations across the Empire. The company's shares, which were at forty-six shillings in July 1911, had risen to eight pounds by April 1912. Its director, Godfrey Isaacs, was the brother of the Attorney General, Sir Rufus Isaacs, of whom Frances Stevenson, Lloyd George's live-in secretary, said that he had a "cafeteria mind—self-service only." He was in her view devoted only to obtaining advancement.

There was also an American Marconi Company, 10,000 shares of which Godfrey Isaacs offered to his brother at below the market price. The American company did not benefit from the contract, but as if by osmosis, when the British shares rose so did the American ones. Sir Rufus Isaacs sold 1,000 of his shares to Lloyd George and another 1,000 to Alexander Murray, the Master of Elibank, who was Chief Liberal Whip. All three members of the government speculated in the shares, hoping for a quick profit.

When stories alleging improper conduct appeared in the press, instead of admitting what they had done, they denied having traded in Marconi shares, privately making the specious distinction between the British and the American companies. In October, when the contract came up for ratification by the House, charges were made about the disgraceful and scandalous gambling in shares, and a bipartisan Select Committee was appointed to investigate the matter.

It was a shock to the Asquith government, and the Prime Minister's concern was to keep his Cabinet together. What an unpleasant and distasteful business, thought Haldane, the newly appointed Lord Chancellor. He was thankful that he had never had any temptation to try to make money by investments—it was a slippery business.[118] Churchill's involvement consisted in trying to save Lloyd George. In a spontaneous act of friendship, he went to see Lord Northcliffe, the owner of the *Daily Mail*, assuring him that there was nothing to the charges, and obtained his promise that the story would be played down.[119] Having muzzled Northcliffe, Churchhill prevailed upon F. E. Smith to act as Lloyd George's lawyer in a libel suit against the French newspaper *Le Matin*, thereby neutralizing the principal Tory firebrand.[120]

In their friendship, Churchill had until now been the disciple, somewhat in the Welshman's shadow, although he had affirmed his independence upon reaching the Admiralty. His intervention in the Marconi affair made them equals at last. Having helped rescue Lloyd George from political disgrace, Churchill no longer had to play second fiddle.

On April 28, Churchill was summoned by the Select Committee, after Mr. Powell, the editor of *Financial News*, had testified that his name had been mentioned in connection with the shares. Powell was asked: "In what form did the rumors come to you with regard to Mr. Winston Churchill having investments in Marconi's?" "Precisely the same effect as in relation to the other ministers," Powell said. "Namely, that he had been operating very successfully in the Marconi market."

Quivering with rage, and protesting that he had been dragged in with ten minutes' notice, Churchill told the committee chairman, Albert Spicer, that it was a most insulting charge. It amounted to saying that he had sat silent while his colleagues disclosed their position, that he had sulked in the background keeping his guilty knowledge to himself.

"I have never at any time," he said, "in any circumstances, directly or indirectly, had any investments or any interests of any kind—however vaguely it may be described—in Marconi telegraphic shares, or any other shares of that description, in this or any other country in the inhabited globe;

and if anybody at any time has said so, that person is a liar and a slanderer; and if anybody has repeated this statement and said he had no evidence and he believed it to be false but that there it was, the only difference between that person and a liar and slanderer is that he is a coward in addition."

Churchill on the attack was a fearsome spectacle. He had burst into the committee room like a cyclone, one of the reporters said. The committee was sympathetic. Sir Richard Essex said that not one of its members suspected him, for his name stood for chivalry, high feeling, and courage, and he had shown his innocence by laying about him so lustily.[121]

Vindicated, he was not asked to appear again. Viscount Esher congratulated him on knocking the last remaining worm-eaten plank out of that ludicrous committee. If only he could have kicked an editor![122] Wilfrid Blunt wrote: "It is in affairs like these that breeding asserts itself."[123]

The committee exonerated Lloyd George and the others from all charges of corruption, although one of its Tory members, Lord Robert Cecil, accused them of having committed a grave impropriety. But although the charges had been exploded, "the deadly after-damp remained," as Lloyd George put it. Asquith was heard to remark of his Chancellor of the Exchequer: "I think the idol's wings are a bit clipped."[124] Clipped, but not broken, for Lloyd George went on to replace Asquith as Prime Minister, while Rufus Isaacs was promoted to Lord Chief Justice a few months later.

The government having weathered the Marconi crisis, it was time for a holiday. On May 9, Churchill took the *Enchantress* on a Mediterranean cruise with the Asquiths, Violet, Clemmie, Eddie Marsh, and his mother. Jennie was unhappy, for her young husband, George Cornwallis-West, had deserted her for Mrs. Patrick Campbell, and she had filed for divorce. It would do her good to get away from England and bask in the Mediterranean sunshine.[125]

In Venice they went sightseeing in a gondola, in Dubrovnik they drank beer, and in Vallona Bay, on the Albanian coast, Churchill organized a fishing expedition. First he tried stunning the fish with depth charges. The tactics were repetitious and the victims unresisting. Then he recruited fifty sailors to drag the bay with a large net. Wading through the water, they pulled with might and main as he gesticulated and orated, enlarging on first principles. Expecting an abundant catch, he caught four fish. Nonetheless, they ate a splendid lunch, as Churchill quoted Gray's "Ode to Spring": "*At ease reclined in rustic state . . .*"[126]

In Athens, when they visited the Parthenon, Churchill was indignant at seeing so many tumbled columns and suggested that a posse of bluejackets from the *Enchantress* should be detailed to prop them up, but the archeologist in attendance was not responsive. Eddie felt that having seen Athens gave a man what Swift called Invisible Precedence over his fellows. Then it was on to Sicily, Sardinia, and Corsica, where Churchill observed a minute of silence in the house where Napoleon had been born.[127]

He stayed away from the incessant prattling of Margot Asquith, who complained that he kept himself out of range. Discussing homosexuality with Eddie Marsh, she said she could see no sense to it, since "they can't even produce a paper-parcel between them, and I think the only point of that sort of thing is to have rows of jolly little children."[128]

On the last day, Asquith asked Eddie's advice about tips, wondering whether he should do anything for the doctor who had attended their maid, Coats. "I understand he has twice diagnosed her," he said, "once for ptomaine poisoning and once for cardiac debility—in both cases I believe falsely—but the *vis medicatrix naturae*, which is fortunately strong in Coats, triumphed over both his diagnosis and his remedy."[129] Eddie was in awe of the Prime Minister's polished sentences.

What a magical cruise, Violet thought as it ended, combining "the time and the place and the loved ones all together"—never guessing that in little more than a year the curtain would drop on the world they had always known.[130]

The estimates were on Churchill's mind. He knew that further increases would be fought in the Cabinet, and he wondered where economies might be made. Prince Louis had long been pressing for a full mobilization of fleet reserves, and Churchill saw that in 1914 this could be an inexpensive substitute for the usual Grand Maneuvers. In June, he sent Prince Louis one of his "as you know" memos: "As you know, this has been in my mind for a long time. I should hope next year to obtain a mobilization of the whole of the Royal Fleet Reserve . . ."[131] Mobilization would cost 50,000 pounds compared with 230,000 for maneuvers. This decision, based on the need to save money, and unconnected to the European situation, had an unexpected result, for in August 1914, when war broke out, the fleet was mobilized and ready. It was another example of the way Churchill sometimes hit the bull's-eye without even taking aim.

By July, the Home Rule Bill had passed twice in the House of Commons and been rejected twice in the House of Lords. Under the Parliament Act, if it passed a third time it was bound to become law. But Ulster was up in arms.

Half a million Orangemen had signed a "Solemn Covenant" pledging to use "all means" to defeat Home Rule.

The last wild hope of the Conservatives was that the King might refuse the bill his Royal Assent or force a dissolution by dismissing his ministers. George V worried that whatever he did he would offend half the population. He told Lewis Harcourt, the Secretary of State for the Colonies, that if he signed a Home Rule Bill he would be hissed in the streets of Belfast. Harcourt replied that if he did not sign it he would be hissed in the streets of London. Influenced by the Tory case against Home Rule and by the advice of his secretary, Lord Stamfordham, the King's greatest fear was that in case of rioting in Ulster, the Army would be used to suppress disorders, subjecting the loyalty of the troops to a severe strain.

At a Cabinet meeting on August 8, Churchill said he had heard rumors that the King intended some unconstitutional action. Asquith said he had seen no sign of such an intention. Everyone lamented the loss of Sir Francis Knollys and the advent of Lord Stamfordham, whose wings Asquith desired to be clipped.[132]

A few days later, Asquith reminded the King that no recent monarch had ever dreamed of reviving the ancient veto of the Crown. As for the right of the Sovereign to dismiss his ministers, perhaps it still existed, but Queen Victoria during her long reign had never used it, nor had the King's father. The stability and regard for the throne were based almost solely on its abstention from political quarrels.[133]

The King invited leaders of both parties to meet at Balmoral in September to try to reach a compromise. There were signs that the Tories might accept Home Rule if Ulster was left out. Churchill went on September 17 and saw Bonar Law and the King. Asquith warned him that he would find the royal mind obsessed and the royal tongue exceptionally fluid and voluble.[134]

Churchill was conciliatory. He had always admitted that Ulster had a case. If Ireland could claim separate government from England, Ulster could not be refused a similar exemption from Irish rule. But he strongly resented the talk of civil war and the men who were stirring up rebellion. Naturally the Opposition wanted to turn out the government, but it was not playing the game to raise a threat of civil war. Personally he would take a very strong line if the Army or the Navy hesitated to put down uprisings in Ulster. Ireland had been waiting for the fulfillment of her dream for thirty years. Could she now stand by and see the cup, almost at her lips, dashed to the ground?[135]

Churchill was agreeably surprised by his talks with the King, who favored a settlement on the basis of excluding Ulster for a time. He seemed more reasonable and able to see both sides, and nothing in his conversation hinted at an unconstitutional intervention by the Crown. Bonar Law too, he thought, seemed full of a spirit of courage and goodwill. Bonar Law, however, was not at all sure that the exclusion of Ulster would work, for it would abandon the Protestant minorities in the rest of Ireland to the tender mercies of a Roman Catholic majority and hand over the Catholic minority in Ulster to an Orange mob.[136]

Bonar Law warned Churchill that as soon as Home Rule became law, Carson would take control of Ulster. Churchill spoke of stopping sea and rail communications, but Bonar Law said that would interfere with all of Ireland. If the Tories supported Ulster and were turned out of Commons, there would be civil war. Did he suppose the Army would obey orders to exercise force?

The days at Balmoral were pleasant. Churchill played golf with Bonar Law, leaving it to his sense of decency to fix Churchill's handicap. He made friends with the nineteen-year-old Prince of Wales, going through the Admiralty dispatch boxes with him. He was so nice, Churchill thought, but very spartan, eating hardly anything. He needed to fall in love with a pretty young cat.[137]

Arthur Balfour, who at sixty-five was becoming the Grand Old Man of the Tory Party, was at Balmoral too, and saw the disturbance in Ireland as one more example of a general loosening of the ordinary ties of social obligations. The suffragettes and the syndicalists were other symptoms of this malady. The government in its criminal folly was now apparently prepared to add to these a rebellion in Ulster. He did not argue that Ulstermen were wrong to act as they did, but he felt strongly that nothing was more demoralizing to a society than that some of its very best and most loyal members should deliberately organize themselves for the purpose of offering armed resistance to persons holding the King's commission and representing lawful authority. Balfour was pessimistic about the country in general. He hoped that some of his gloom was due to a day of steady rain.[138]

Bonar Law secretly met with Asquith three times in October and November, but their talks decided nothing. Asquith rejected the indefinite exclusion of Ulster, and Bonar Law rejected its temporary exclusion.

On November 26, Austen Chamberlain was invited on board the *Enchantress*, and the next day, in the train from Portsmouth to London, they had one of those frank, free, and unfettered conversations that Churchill liked. He said that he and Lloyd George had proposed to the Cabinet from the start to exclude Ulster. The then Lord Chancellor, the Earl of Loreburn, had been particularly opposed to the idea. "I asked them," Churchill recalled, "but how far are you prepared to go? Are you ready to plant guns in the streets of Belfast and shoot people down?" Loreburn said pompously: "I shall be prepared to do my duty."

Churchill said that though he was prepared to put down disorder ruthlessly, he did not feel they had the right to coerce Ulstermen into submission to Home Rule. Public opinion must have a shock, he said. A little red blood would have to flow, and then public opinion would wake up, and then . . . ! Time was on their side. They would give no provocation. The Ulstermen would have no excuses, and public opinion would not support them if they wantonly attacked.

Chamberlain said that was a dangerous gamble in bloodshed. Why didn't Asquith resume his talks with Bonar Law? Oh, said Churchill, he would. But they could not scrap their bill before they had a substitute. Asquith was supreme in the Cabinet, but very self-contained and reserved. He held the casting vote but did not use it until everyone had spoken.

Chamberlain said his root objection to Home Rule was the idea of Ireland as a nation. There would be no nation, Churchill argued, as long as the Irish accepted a subsidy and could be brought to book by its being withheld. But to deny them the enjoyment of their Parliament was to act like the Roman Catholic Church, which admitted the necessity of the marriage bed while holding that no pleasure should be found in the enjoyment of it.[139]

On the same day, November 27, in a speech at Leeds, Asquith took a firmer stand, saying that he stood by the Home Rule Bill and would not be intimidated by violent threats. Chamberlain, who had been lulled by Churchill into thinking that Asquith wanted a settlement, felt that the Prime Minister had slammed the door in Conservative faces. He had blown conciliation to the winds. If Chamberlain had known, he would have talked navy shop or fashions or feminism with Churchill, anything *except* the Irish question. For the moment, the forces on both sides remained deadlocked.[140]

It is hard to conceive of the passions that these issues stirred, the extent to which party hatreds invaded private life. There was a social apartheid between Tories and Liberals. A certain duchess complained that she had been forced to sit in the Peeresses' Gallery "in plain sight of the wives of two members of the Cabinet." To the Tories, Asquith was the embodiment of all political evil. He had let his wild Chancellor of the Exchequer use the budget to make a social revolution. He had sold himself to the Irish enemy. He was pictured as drinking champagne and playing bridge while England burned.

Friendships were broken and families were torn apart over politics. On October 22, Lloyd George spoke at Swindon on land reform. Clemmie was at Blenheim without Winston. The next morning in the Great Library she read reports of the speech with loud expressions of approval. In retaliation, her host, Sunny Marlborough, teased her at lunch about Asquith's drinking habits. Clemmie asked him not to make jokes in such poor taste in front of the servants. He repeated them in a louder voice.

Just then, a telegram arrived for Clemmie from Lloyd George, and she got up from the table, saying that she must reply at once. They were in the Green Room, where informal meals were taken, and which was furnished with writing desks. "Please, Clemmie," Sunny asked, "would you mind not writing to that horrible little man on Blenheim writing-paper?" Clemmie huffed out of the room, rang for the maid, packed her cases, and ordered a "fly" from Woodstock to take her to the station. As she descended the staircase like wrath itself, Sunny apologized and asked her not to go, but it was no use.[141]

Churchill when he heard of the incident wished that she had been more forgiving; now there was bad blood between him and his cousin. On November 2, Clemmie wrote that she could not bear his disapproval. If he ceased to love her, she would be raw and unhappy inside, and like the prickly porcupine outside, instead of the cat with soft fur. Churchill could not stay annoyed and replied that he only wished he were more worthy of her and more able to meet the inner needs of her soul.[142]

One of *his* soul's needs, a craving for adventure and physical danger, suppressed during the years of his climb to high office, was indulged when he organized the Naval Air Wing. The airplane was ten years old—the Wright brothers' first flight in a power-driven, heavier-than-air plane had occurred in 1903. Six years later, Colonel Louis Blériot had flown across the English Channel. The early planes were unreliable, with rudimentary instruments and landing gears, and fatalities were high. There were no headphones, and once aloft pilot and copilot shouted at each other, hoping the wind would carry the words over the open cockpits. Churchill, as an important member of the Cabinet, approaching the age of thirty-nine, had no business going up in them. But he resolved to learn to fly, as he had charged with the Lancers at Omdurman; the prospect was irresistible. In the air, he was freed from the cares of office; he could forget about party politics, awkward by-elections, unfavorable newspaper editorials, sulky Orangemen, obnoxious Tories, and the "little smugs" in the Cabinet who opposed him on the naval estimates.[143]

In March 1913, he lost what he called his "ethereal virginity." On October 6, as Asquith and Jack Seely waved from the ground, he went up in a naval hydroplane at Cromarty Firth. On October 23, at the Eastchurch Royal Naval Flying School near the Sheerness naval base, he flew with the pioneer aviator Charles Samson in an Astra-Torres airship, so easy to manage that he steered for an hour. When he expressed the wish to qualify as a pilot, no instructor wanted him. They were scared stiff of having a smashed-up First Lord on their hands, and he was bucketed about from one pilot to the next. As Captain Eugene Gerrard, one of his instructors, explained: "Churchill has had as much as twenty-five hours in the air. But no one will risk letting him solo. If anything happened to him the career of the man who had allowed him a solo flight would be finished."[144]

Clemmie was aghast that Winston would do anything so reckless. F. E. Smith warned him repeatedly what a foolish thing it was to fly. Sunny Marlborough said that he must for the sake of his friends and family desist from a pastime fraught with so much danger to life. Churchill paid no heed. In the young Captain Gilbert Wildman-Lushington, he found an instructor who was willing to stick with him. Six months before, Wildman-Lushington had nearly quit the Royal Naval Air Service. One day as he was preparing to take off, his friend Lieutenant Berne checked the engine. Thinking that Berne was clear, Wildman-Lushington turned it over. The propeller struck Berne, killing him. Broken with shock and sorrow, Wildman-Lushington swore he would not fly again. Every time he saw a plane he felt the horrible despair of having killed his dear friend. But Commander Samson persuaded him to stay.[145]

On November 29, Churchill went up with Wildman-Lushington around noon. He got so bitten with it he would not leave the machine. He showed great promise, the Captain thought, although he complained that the rudder was stiff and hard to work. The Captain told him he had fallen into a common error of beginners, of pushing against himself. Such little faults would rectify themselves in time. Churchill hoped Clemmie would not be vexed, for with twenty machines in the air and thousands of flights made without mishap, he could not look upon it as a serious risk.[146]

It was not so bad instructing Churchill, thought Wildman-Lushington, for that night he was invited to dinner on the *Enchantress* and sat on the great man's right. The next day was Churchill's thirty-ninth birthday, and a plane was sent to Whitstable for oysters. The evening was convivial, and the Captain showed Churchill a snapshot of his fiancée, Airlie Hynes. When was it coming off? Churchill asked. When he had saved some money, the Captain replied.[147]

Two days later, flying the same plane that he had taken Churchill in, Wildman-Lushington sideslipped as he was landing, crashed, and was killed.[148] It was the same story all over again. Those around Churchill fell, like the Lancer at his side at Omdurman, or his valet on the Nile, while he was spared. The accidents that happened to those who flew with him, he reflected, were out of proportion. Besides the Captain, a lieutenant who had taken him up had been killed. It made one think.

To be killed instantly without pain or fear in the service of one's country was not the worst of fortunes, Churchill wrote Miss Hynes. But to some who were left behind, the loss was terrible.[149]

Fifty years later, in 1963, Airlie Hynes, now Mrs. Airlie Madden, a woman in her seventies, still cherished his words. In 1918, she had married Major J. G. Madden. They had lost two sons in World War II. She often thought of her pilot fiancé. His vivid personality did not fade. She was sure that some of those he had instructed had contributed to the victory of World War I. Pride was a great help in old age. What a mercy for England that Churchill's flight had not been the fatal one.[150]

Pride was a great help in old age.

Here was a woman who had lost the man she loved and two sons in the service of their country, and who said without rancor or regret that her loss was not in vain because they had contributed to the common effort. Perhaps nothing more stirring was ever written to describe England than those eight words. For alone among the nations of Western Europe, England after World War II could hold up her head without shame. She had not been occupied. Her government had signed no dishonorable armistice. Her King had not gone into exile. Her leaders had not collaborated with the enemy. The swastika had not flown from London's public buildings. Her young men had not joined units to help Hitler on the eastern front. She had not rounded up Jews for delivery to the death camps. She had fought. She had remained unconquered. And Churchill was the heart and sinew of that fight. For nations as well as individuals, pride was a great help.

Churchill continued to fly with unconcealed delight. In April 1914, his pilot had to make an emergency landing on the water close to Clacton jetty. That day, on holiday in Spain, Clemmie had a premonition and was seized with a dreadful anxiety. She sometimes felt what her husband was doing before she knew about it. She was very "ears down" about his flying, particularly when she heard that the distinguished British aviator of French extraction Gustav Hamel had disappeared over the Channel in late May. It was Churchill who had invited Hamel to fly from Paris to Portsmouth, where he would give a demonstration to the Navy pilots at their air station. As he waited for Hamel's plane to appear, the sky grew darker, and it became evident that something had gone wrong, and that Hamel would have to be added to the lengthening casualty list of aviation's infancy.[151]

Pregnant with her third child, Clemmie went to stay with her mother in Dieppe. Nervous and unhappy, every time a telegram arrived she was sure it would announce that her husband had been killed flying. On June 5, she dreamed that her baby had been born, but that the doctor and the nurse had hidden it. She ran all over the house searching for it and found it in a darkened room. It looked all right, and she feverishly undressed it and counted its fingers and toes. She ran out of the room with the baby in her arms, and in the daylight she saw that it was a gaping idiot. She wanted the doctor to kill it, but he was shocked and took it away.[152]

When Churchill heard about the nightmare, he promised that he would fly no more, at least until she had recovered from her "kitten." It was a wrench to give it up, for he was on the verge of taking his pilot's certificate; he needed only a couple of calm mornings to qualify. But the many flying fatalities of the year justified her complaint. He gave it up as a gift to his wife that cost him more than anything he could have bought with money, which he laid at her feet knowing it would rejoice and relieve her heart. Even if he did not fly again, he now knew a good deal about this fascinating new art and could manage a machine with ease, even with high winds. He knew the difficulties and dangers, having been up nearly 140 times in all kinds of machines.[153]

Grounded, Churchill could no longer escape from the cares of office. In two years at the Admiralty, he had not improved his methods of dealing with the naval brass, which continued to cause resentment. He tended to treat admirals a generation older than himself as a stern schoolmaster would treat dull pupils. In one instance, Rear Admiral Arthur Limpus, the naval adviser to the Turkish Navy, who was doing the best he could to combat German influence in Constantinople, had managed to obtain an important dock-building contract for a British firm and wrote to tell Churchill of his success. While congratulating him on his part in the negotiations, Churchill replied that he was alarmed by the chaotic character of his letter. It did not have the proper seriousness and formality. It should have been neatly written or typed on good paper. The sentences should be complete. Mere jottings hurriedly put together without sequence gave a poor impression.[154] Such reprimands to highly respected officers with long years of service did not help his popularity.

Declared enemies like Lord Beresford were fed information about Churchill's supposed misdeeds. Humbled in the House, Beresford pursued him with a manic obstinacy, making speeches and sending letters: Churchill had destroyed the morale and discipline of the service; his firing experiments in deep waters were a wasteful expenditure; his cruises at the taxpayers' expense, his tinkering with ships under construction running into the thousands, all this and more would cause a panic by and by.[155]

Beresford was not an isolated critic. There was a growing anti-Churchill clan in the Navy. Rear Admiral Rosslyn Wemyss, who would command the cruiser squadron that would escort the British Expeditionary Force to France, believed that Churchill's methods were doing incalculable harm and that his removal would be worth two dreadnoughts to the country. His chief objection was Churchill's habit of extracting in one form or another from officers and even from men their opinion of their superiors—how they handled their ships, men, and machinery.

It was precisely this practice of breaking the chain of command to obtain firsthand information that led in November 1913 to the most serious confrontation Churchill had yet had with his Sea Lords, when all four threatened to resign. While inspecting the huge naval base of Sheerness, on the Isle of Sheppey (which sailors called "Sheer Necessity" because it was such a dull place compared with Chatham and Portsmouth and other naval bases), Churchill interviewed a lieutenant serving on the H.M.S. *Hermes*, the parent ship of the Naval Air Service, who criticized his captain, G. W. Vivian, for some decision having to do with the use of a strip of land on the banks of the Medway River. Churchill sent for the Captain and told him that the young Lieutenant's views should be forwarded to him. When the Lieutenant drafted his report, the Captain refused to forward it, and the young officer said: "Then I shall send it direct to Mr. Churchill, who invited me to do so . . ." Such a breach of discipline was intolerable to Captain Vivian, who complained to the commander in chief of the Sheerness base, Admiral Sir Richard Poore. The Admiral passed the matter on to the Second Sea Lord, Sir John Jellicoe, with a covering letter criticizing the First Lord's methods.[156]

Somehow, perhaps through a message from the young officer that he was in trouble, Churchill got wind of what was going on and sent his Naval Secretary, Captain De Chair, to tell Jellicoe that he wanted to see immediately any communication that came from Admiral Poore on the subject.

But when Jellicoe saw Admiral Poore's letter, he found it too strongly worded to show Churchill and returned it for amendment, with a letter of his own. Learning that the dispatch had been sent back, Churchill felt that he had been disobeyed and sent a telegram to the General Post Office asking that the letter be found at once and returned to him. That was done, and although he claimed not to have read Jellicoe's letter, Churchill was so angry with Admiral Poore that he said he would make him haul down his flag.[157]

It was in this frame of mind that Captain De Chair found him one morning in the second week of November. "Good morning, First Lord," he said, "you seem disturbed this morning."

"Disturbed!" Churchill fumed. "I have been insulted by the commander in chief at the Nore [Sheerness], and I am dictating a telegram to him to haul down his flag at sunset and give up his command."

De Chair suggested that it was a matter for the board.

"Do you think I am going to humiliate myself before the Sea Lords?" Churchill asked. "I will not be insulted. Either his flag comes down or I go. I refuse to discuss the matter further."[158]

On November 12, however, an ultimatum came from Prince Louis, the one Sea Lord who had always sided with Churchill in previous controversies: "You have informed us that it is your intention, whether we agree or whether we do not, to issue an order to the C in C, Nore, to strike his flag forthwith.

"According to the very clear terms of the Patent under which we act, the First Lord has not, in our opinion, the power to issue such an order.

"We, therefore, cannot share the responsibility for such an act and we have no alternative but to resign our seats on the Board."[159]

Faced with the signed resignations of his entire Admiralty Board, Churchill backed down. If the Sea Lords resigned, the outcry in Parliament and in the press would drag him down too. The timing could not have been worse, for he was about to do battle in the Cabinet for the next year's estimates and needed a strong and united board. The next step was to persuade Admiral Poore not to resign. If he had resigned and asked for a court-martial, Churchill would have had to defend himself against the accusations of one of his senior commanders. The Sea Lords prevailed upon the Admiral to remain at his post, arguing that Churchill was so much off his head over the whole business that Poore should take no notice of it.[160]

One marginal aspect of the crisis was that Sir Francis Hopwood, whom Churchill trusted and had brought to the Admiralty as Civil Lord, kept the King's secretary, Lord Stamfordham, informed in great detail. Just as he had done at the Colonial Office six years before, Hopwood disparaged Churchill behind his back while pretending to be his loyal aide. As Hopwood explained it to Stamfordham, "Churchill very foolishly travels round the coast holding reviews and inspections and so forth without reference to Naval opinion and regulation. He is also much addicted to sending for junior officers and discussing with them the proceedings of their superiors; this naturally enrages the latter and is very mischievous to the former. It is on the score of breaches of discipline that the present trouble has been founded." When the crisis passed, it was "no thanks to the First Lord," Hopwood wrote. ". . . it is over for the time but we shall have it again in some form. Jellicoe will not put up with it for long."[161]

Churchill's 1913–1914 estimates had passed almost without a murmur. This time, when he proposed an expenditure of 50,694,800 pounds, an increase of nearly three million pounds, a section of the Cabinet rebelled. It was not only that each year there was a huge increase in naval spending, which went against the Liberal grain, for the party of Gladstone was a party of social reform, not weapons races. The violent reaction to Churchill's proposals was also due to his overbearing personality. He grated on his colleagues. Charles Hobhouse's diary is full of comments about his monopolizing Cabinet meetings: Churchill had given "the usual lecture on the country"; "we were favored by addresses from Churchill on Education, Finance, Navy, Aviation and Electioneering and finally there was a general revolt summed up by the P.M. remarking that his views were pure 'cynicism defended by sophistry.'" Of course Hobhouse, who never went higher in the Cabinet than Postmaster General, was full of the small man's envy of the larger one, like the frog in the La Fontaine fable that wanted to be an ox.

Churchill had no better friend in the Cabinet than Asquith, but even the Prime Minister sometimes lost his patience, complaining that in one three-hour Cabinet meeting, Churchill had held the floor for all but a quarter hour. Finally, there was uneasiness among some members of the Cabinet concerning Churchill's views on Ireland. He was beginning to sound like a Tory. At Dundee in October he had said that the claim of Ulster for special consideration could not be ignored. It was feared, Hobhouse thought, that he might give up on Home Rule to win over Ulster.[162]

The first rumbling of discontent came on December 11 when the Attorney General, John Simon, told Jack Seely that the estimates were scandalous. Seely asked what practical criticism he had to make. "What we want is a clear statement showing what Germany was spending four years ago and what she is spending this year," Simon said, "and the same figure for ourselves; you will then see that our advance in expenditure is out of all proportion to theirs."[163] Herbert Samuel, the Postmaster General, proposed that only two capital ships be built instead of four.

At meetings on December 8, 15, and 16, Churchill flooded the Cabinet with memos, position papers, and statistics. His voluminous calculations, Hobhouse said, were difficult to refute and even more difficult to verify. But under cross-examination he admitted that he had doctored his figures, making the German advance seem greater by not including two old and slow British ships while including ten German ships that were even slower and older. On December 15, Churchill offered reductions of 700,000 pounds, and Lloyd George agreed to a naval budget of 49,700,000 pounds.

At the December 16 meeting, Churchill was stunned when he was asked for further cuts, and Lloyd George sided with the malcontents. In two years, Lloyd George had moved quite a way from his Mansion House speech. He no longer believed in the war menace and had become a leader of the peace movement. He thought the needs of the Royal Navy were less urgent than those of pensions, health insurance, and education.

Churchill, who thought he had an understanding with his old friend, felt betrayed and passed a note to Lloyd George that said: "I consider that you are going back on your word: in trying to drive me out after we had settled, and you promised to support the estimates."[164]

Lloyd George had this reply: "I agreed to the figure for this year and I have stood by it and *carried it* much to the disappointment of my economical friends. But I told you distinctly I would press for a reduction of a new program with a view to 1915 and I think quite respectfully you are unnecessarily stubborn. It is only a question of a six months' postponement of laying down [keels]. That cannot endanger our safety."[165]

Another note shot back from an angered Churchill: "No. You said you would *support the estimates*."[166]

When the Cabinet asked Churchill to cut two battleships from his building program, he said he would resign unless the figure remained at four. He left in a huff, banging his dispatch box and the door as loud as he could when he went out.[167]

The Heavenly Twins had come to a parting of the ways, no longer struggling together over a common cause, but bickering over the estimates. And yet, despite the tug of issues, the strands of friendship were not rent. "I shall be no party to driving Winston out of the Cabinet," Lloyd George told George Riddell. "I do not agree with some of my colleagues."

"He was very loyal to you over the Marconi business," Riddell said.

"Yes, I know," Lloyd George said, "and I shall never forget it. Of course I have been too easy during the past two years regarding the naval estimates. When he went to the Admiralty I made a bargain with him about expenditure. He has not kept it. He has been extravagant. Now the feeling against him is very strong. I think, however, he will amend his figures to meet the views of the party."

Sir Francis Hopwood lost no time reporting the crisis to Lord Stamfordham. The Cabinet was putting pressure on Churchill to reduce his program, but this he could not do "for the simple reason that he was fool enough to tell the world what his program was going to be for about half a dozen years ahead. To this he is bound hand and foot." Of course, Hopwood pointed out, the Cabinet was in bad faith in asking for reductions, for not one member had dissented when Churchill had stated his intention to build four battleships each year. "They are odd people indeed!" he commented. "Is it possible they are riding for a fall or do they merely want to shed Winston?"[168]

Churchill said more or less the same thing to Asquith on December 18. How could he go back on his public declarations and his promise to keep a 60 percent standard over Germany? It really was too stupid of Lloyd George to throw the car off the track. A weakening now would upset everything, as there was a chance of a naval understanding with Germany.[169] Asquith was uncertain. The feeling among the rank and file was definitely against more naval spending. On December 17, he had faced a deputation of one hundred Liberals protesting over the estimates. At the same time, if Lloyd George introduced a new policy of disarmament, he might split the Liberal Party. Looking for support, Churchill turned to his friend the Foreign Secretary. Grey should remember what a strong Navy meant to England's position in Europe. To desert a program already set up while Germany continued on her path unmoved and unwavering would be to mar seriously England's prestige abroad.[170]

Just before Christmas, Lloyd George circulated a paper to the Cabinet insisting on the need to cut down and abandon the 60 percent margin. It was, thought Churchill, a terrible challenge to Admiralty policy. He would have to resign if the building program was reduced,[171] and he would not remain discreetly silent; he would bring down the government and precipitate a General Election.

Churchill could not know that Lloyd George was being pressured on all sides. Margot Asquith had written him on November 17: "Don't let Winston have too much money—it will hurt our party in every way—Labour and even Liberals. If one can't be a little economical when all foreign countries are peaceful I don't know *when* we can."[172] C. P. Scott, the editor of the *Manchester Guardian,* told him that "of course Churchill can play the mischief with this or any other plan, but it won't be so easy and you can bring him to book. I feel it in my bones that the time has got to be now or never."[173]

On New Year's Day 1914, while Churchill was on holiday, shooting wild boar with his friend Bendor, the Duke of Westminster, Lloyd George aired the Cabinet quarrel in the pages of the *Daily Chronicle.* He saw hardly a cloud in the European sky. Anglo-German relations were more cordial than ever. There was no friction with France. The common people throughout Europe were against the idea of war. It was true that the Continental Powers were wasting their money on the "organized insanity" of armaments, but they were concentrating on land forces. The time was right to reconsider England's "overwhelming extravagance of our expenditure on armaments," and Liberals should seize it.

Then came the direct attack on Churchill's program: ". . . it seems to me that we can afford just quietly to maintain the superiority we possess at present, without making feverish efforts to increase it any further. The Navy is now, according to all impartial testimony, at the height of its efficiency. If we maintain that standard no one can complain, but if we went on spending and swelling its strength, we should wantonly provoke other nations."[174]

The Chancellor recalled that a distinguished predecessor in his office, Lord Randolph Churchill, had resigned in 1887 rather than assent to "bloated and extravagant" service estimates. What an irony! Lloyd George taking the crazed Randolph as an example, and using the memory of the father against his son. Churchill's political survival depended on a struggle with his old friend and mentor to impose a policy that would have made his father whirl in his grave. The days of carrying on Randolph's policies were indeed over.

A shocked Churchill felt that the interview was a fine illustration of Lloyd George's underhanded methods and would deeply vex the Prime Minister.[175] Asquith did not seem overly vexed, although Grey, Seely, and Samuel all muttered severe words about the interview's needless folly. Asquith was glad to see that Churchill was back from hunting the boar, with his tusks well whetted and his bristles in good order. There would be "wigs on the green" (a lawyer's term for a serious disagreement) before his tussle with Lloyd George was over.[176]

According to Hopwood, reporting on January 5 to Lord Stamfordham, the Cabinet, sick of Churchill's perpetually undermining its policy, was picking a quarrel with him. As a colleague he was a great trial. The only remaining point was the conduct of the Sea Lords in the event of Winston's resignation. He would press them fiercely to go with him. But Hopwood felt they should not waste themselves on Winston but on his successor. If they did not agree with his successor's program, then was the time to resign. The government could not stand the double shock. The whole affair might blow over but it looked very ugly. Winston realized that his back was against the wall.[177]

Calling on Churchill at the Admiralty on January 18, George Riddell found him dictating replies to messages of condolence regarding the loss of a submarine and marveled at the careful way he constructed his words. "I don't know how long I shall be here," Churchill said. "The position is acute. I cannot make further economies. I cannot go back on my public declarations . . . I can make no further concessions. I cannot agree to any concealment of the actual figures. I think I know the English people. The old Cromwellian spirit still survives. I believe I am watched over. Think of the perils I have escaped . . . If I resign, I shall take a small house at Carnoustie, near Dundee, and deliver a series of speeches setting out my political views . . ." Riddell asked whether he would go back to the Tory Party. "Certainly not!" Churchill exclaimed. "I am a Free Trader, and quite out of sympathy with their attitude to the working classes."[178]

Hopwood was treacherous but astute. He saw that the fight over the estimates had escalated into a "dump Churchill" movement organized by half a dozen Cabinet members—Attorney General John Simon, Postmaster General Herbert Samuel, Home Secretary Reginald McKenna, 1st Commissioner of Works the Earl Beauchamp, Chancellor of the Duchy of Lancaster Charles Hobhouse, and President of the Agriculture Board Walter Runciman. Personal animosities aside, Churchill's demands threatened their slices of the budget pie. Churchill called them "the crew"—he knew them—they had no stomach for a fight. But into their camp had moved a more formidable opponent, Lloyd George. In Churchill's opinion, the Chancellor was accustomed to dealing with people who could be bluffed or frightened, and he did not count himself among that number.[179]

Finding no ground for compromise, Lloyd George thought a crisis was unavoidable. He had asked Churchill for reductions in 1915–1916 to offset the increase in the current estimates. Churchill had replied that he could not undertake such a task, for no First Lord had ever been asked for forecast estimates. He would not buy a year of office by a bargain under duress on future estimates. Indeed, he now wanted supplementary estimates that would raise the total to 52,850,000 pounds.

When Churchill spoke of resigning, Lloyd George asked: "What will you resign upon? Everything has been conceded to you. You have your four ships; your estimates are up to over 53 millions. You are not satisfied. You want more. And you go out of office on the top of that and expect the country to support you."[180] Lloyd George wanted 1915–1916 estimates of forty-six millions but would settle for forty-seven millions. He would require a pledge, not from Churchill but from the Prime Minister. "Why?" asked Churchill. "Because I do not trust you," Lloyd George said. "I had your promise for this year and you have broken it; my whole budget was based on your estimates and now it has proved wholly delusive."

On January 21, Lloyd George, Simon, Samuel, and Beauchamp approached Asquith and suggested that the only way to guarantee against extravagant naval spending was to get Churchill to retire from the Admiralty and preferably from the Cabinet altogether. "Oh," said Asquith, "this is a personal question." "No," said Simon, "a question of temperament."[181]

The situation changed from day to day. On January 26, Lloyd George told his colleagues that Churchill had promised to keep expenses down in 1915–1916. The others found that hard to believe, pointing out that large increases in maintenance costs this year were not a good prelude to reductions next year. Hobhouse wrote the Chancellor: "I served under you so long that I think I ought just to let you know that I find myself still unconvinced by Churchill's figures. If I get a chance at Cabinet tomorrow I wish to express my dissent from and my distrust of them. My fear is that between them—him, the Labour Party and the Tories—we may come to hopeless grief."[182]

Churchill then told Lloyd George that while he would try to keep spending down in the next two years he could not be bound by any irregular obligations. Lloyd George felt driven to despair. Before Christmas Churchill had wanted fifty millions; now it was up to fifty-three. Churchill's idea of a bargain was to bind the Treasury while imposing no obligation on the Admiralty. Lloyd George had been repeatedly told he was being made a fool of, and now he saw the justice of the taunt. This was the greatest tragedy that had ever befallen Liberalism.

Acting more like a referee in a cricket match than a Prime Minister, Asquith called for a spirit of mutual accommodation. A sort of preresignation letter signed by five members of the anti-Churchill camp—Simon, Hobhouse,

McKenna, Beauchamp, and Runciman—insisted that they could not accept the estimates. Another letter from John Simon warned that a split in the Cabinet could lead to dissolution and the possibility of losing a General Election. The loss of Churchill, while regrettable, would strengthen rather than split the party, because it would show that the Cabinet had fought for economy while pursuing Home Rule. The lines were drawn: it was dump Churchill or lose half the Cabinet.[183]

On January 29, there was a fierce two-hour wrangle, but no agreement was reached. Asquith warned the Cabinet of the disastrous consequences of a split and asked both sides to re-examine their positions. Privately, he pleaded with Churchill: could he not throw a baby or two out of the sledge?[184] The sledge was bare of babies, Churchill replied, and though the pack crunched the driver's bones, the winter would not end.[185] It was at this point that Lloyd George approached him and said, "Come to breakfast tomorrow at Number 11 and we shall settle the matter." When Churchill arrived, expecting to resign, Lloyd George greeted him warmly and said, "Oddly enough my wife spoke to me last night about this dreadnought business. She said, 'You know, my dear, I never interfere in politics; but they say you are having an argument with that nice Mr. Churchill about building dreadnoughts. Of course I don't understand these things but I should have thought it would be better to have too many rather than too few.' So I have decided to let you build them. Let's go in to breakfast."[186] Churchill never learned whether the Chancellor, who was not always so receptive to wifely advice, had simply found a graceful way to retreat from his position without losing face. Churchill obtained most of what he wanted. On February 11 the estimates were fixed at 51,580,000 pounds. In all the months of bickering, he had lost only three small cruisers and twelve torpedo boats for harbor defense. A promise was made for substantial cuts the following year, but when the time came, he was not pressed to keep it.

The result was largely due, he thought, to the unwavering patience of the Prime Minister and to his solid, silent support. Rather than force the issue, Asquith had let it unravel in Churchill's favor.

It was normal practice for Churchill and Lloyd George to pass notes during Cabinet meetings when someone was speaking. The following exchange commented on Churchill's victory:

LLOYD GEORGE: Philip Snowden [a Labour MP who would later serve as Chancellor of the Exchequer] in his weekly letter today says that had there been any other Chancellor of the Exchequer your Naval Bill would have been cut by millions.

CHURCHILL: There would also have been another First Lord of the Admiralty! And who can say—if such gaps were opened—that there would not have been another Government—which does not necessarily mean lower estimates.[187]

Aware that increased naval spending was unpopular in Liberal ranks, Churchill mingled actively in the Irish controversy, in order to strengthen his position in the party. As it became clear that the Home Rule Bill would become law in its third passage through the House of Commons, Ulster prepared for armed resistance, applauded by the Tory leadership. On February 5, 1914, the King warned Asquith that Ulster would never agree to a Dublin Parliament. Army officers would resign rather than enforce Home Rule. Would not a General Election clear the air? Asquith was driven to propose an amendment that would excuse Ulster counties from Home Rule for six years. But when the bill got its Second Reading on March 9, Sir Edward Carson said: "We do not want a sentence of death with a stay of execution for six years." Nonetheless, the amendment was embodied in the text of the bill. Churchill's position was that although he would never coerce Ulster to come under a Dublin Parliament, he would not let Ulster keep the rest of Ireland from having the Parliament it desired.

In Ulster they seemed to be saying, "Give us a clean cut or come and fight us." On March 12 the Cabinet met to discuss the alarming military situation. Police reports indicated that Ulster Volunteers might attack arms depots or seize military barracks. The depots were hardly held at all. Carrickfergus Castle had eighty-five tons of small-arms ammunition guarded by a dozen men. At Omagh and Armagh, about eighty men guarded thirty tons of ammunition, and at Dundalk a few men watched over eighteen guns of the Royal Artillery. A small committee including Churchill was appointed to deal with this emergency.

Churchill was due to speak in Bradford on March 14. Here was the chance for a strongly worded warning to Ulster. Lloyd George told him, "You can make a speech that will ring down the corridors of history. I could not do it. You are the only member of the Cabinet who could make such a speech. You are known to have been in favor of conciliation for Ulster. Now you can say that having secured a compromise Ulstermen will have to accept it or take the consequences."[188]

Spurred on by Lloyd George and Asquith, Churchill accused Sir Edward Carson of "a treasonable conspiracy" and condemned Bonar Law as "a public danger seeking to terrorize the government and to force his way into the Councils of the Sovereign." "We are not going to have the realm of Great Britain sink to the condition of the Republic of Mexico," he went on. ". . . If all the loose, wanton and reckless chatter we have been forced to listen to these months is in the end to disclose a sinister revolutionary purpose, then I can only say to you, 'Let us go forward and put these grave matters to the proof.' " The Tories saw the Bradford speech as a declaration of war on Ulster.[189]

On March 18, the Cabinet committee on Ulster reported that four arms depots were in danger of being rushed. They offered too great a temptation to be left unprotected. Reinforcements would have to be sent from southern Ireland, for there were only nine thousand troops in Ulster. Churchill, who moved ships with the same facility that he had once moved toy soldiers, offered to send the 3rd Battle Squadron, consisting of eight battleships, from Spanish waters to Lamlash, on the Isle of Arran, off the Scottish coast, seventy miles from Belfast. The ships could be used for troop movements in case the Orangemen blocked the trains.

General Sir Arthur Paget, the commander in chief for Ireland, was summoned to London the same day. He feared that troop movements might be seen as a provocation. He was not sure he could count on his officers. There was a strong Ulster element in the Army. Many officers owned property or had family ties there. Garrisoned in Ulster, they had become sympathetic to its aims. How could it have been otherwise, when rabid pro-Ulster sentiments were voiced by such eminent spokesmen as the Tory leadership and Field Marshal Lord Roberts, who had commanded the British Army in the Boer War? He had signed the Covenant, an oath promising to prevent the armed forces from being used to deprive the people of Ulster of their rights, and encouraged his fellow officers to sign it, an amazing act of sedition on the part of a British field marshal.

Aware that the Army was divided, the Secretary of War, Jack Seely, felt that Asquith was partly to blame for having stated that he had no difference in principle with the leader of the Ulster minority, Sir Edward Carson. If there was no difference, the soldiers could pick and choose the orders they liked. One man would say he would shoot an Ulsterman but not a Trade Unionist; another would shoot a Trade Unionist but not an Ulsterman. It would be fatal to discipline.[190]

Seely was of the happy-warrior sort, more at home on the battlefield than in Cabinet rooms, although he confessed that when he spoke in the House he had the same metallic taste in his mouth as when he went into combat. His political career had run a little behind Churchill's, whom he thought of as someone he would go tiger hunting with. There was no higher accolade. When Seely was omitted from the Campbell-Bannerman government, Balfour had said, "I wonder to what political group you will now belong; perhaps the Outside Left."[191] "Oh, no, sir," replied Seely, "a more formidable party, the left outside." Like Churchill, he had crossed from the Tory to the Liberal camp, and like Churchill, he now ran one of the service departments. Unlike Churchill, who committed all his decisions to paper, knowing he might have to justify them, and who never made a move without informing the proper authorities, Seely had an impulsive and disorderly mind. He gave General Paget verbal instructions that the military depots would have to be secured. Officers who refused to obey orders would be dismissed from the Army. Exceptions would be made for officers who were domiciled in Ulster or had a special connection there.

On March 19, in a tense House, Bonar Law said that Ireland was being turned into "a new Poland," a reference to Czarist tyranny against the Jews. Carson stormed off the floor, saying his place was not in Westminster but at the head of his troops in Ulster.

On March 20, General Paget held a conference with seven senior officers at the Royal Hospital in Dublin, briefing them in alarmist terms. He had obtained a concession for officers living in Ulster, he said, but he wanted to know the intentions of the others. They must be prepared to do their duty or face dismissal. The seven should go back to their regiments and give their officers two hours to decide whether to take part in Ulster operations or resign. General Paget's briefing provoked what became known as the "Curragh mutiny." He had turned a precautionary operation to guard arms depots into a loyalty test. He felt that he had to know whom he could count on, although there was no need at this stage to raise the issue. He could have quietly asked the senior officers to recommend loyal units. Instead, he chose to stage a dramatic showdown.

Returning to the Curragh training camp, thirty miles southwest of Dublin, Brigadier General Hubert Gough, a distinguished cavalry officer and the most fervent of Ulstermen, presented the ultimatum to the seventy officers of the various units garrisoned at the camp in a cruder form than he had heard it. Fifty-seven of the seventy chose to resign. Losing his head, General Paget went to the Curragh on March 21 to turn the officers around. His orders, he lied, had come direct from the King and not "those dirty swine of politicians."

In his emotional appeal, Paget promised that he would never give the order to fire at Ulstermen until his own units had been attacked and suffered losses. He would walk out at the head of his troops and be shot down by the Orangemen before ordering any firing in reply. It did no good. The resignations stuck.[192]

Hearing the news in London on March 22, Asquith at first was sanguine. It was all a misunderstanding. The officers seemed to think from what Paget had said that they were about to shed the blood of the Covenanters, but they would not object to doing duty like protecting depots and keeping order. It would all be cleared up in a few hours. But as more news came in, Asquith's spirits fell. There was no doubt in his mind that if the government ordered a march on Ulster half the officers in the Army would strike. What with Paget's tactless blundering and Seely's clumsy phrases, and the general army position, he would have a tough job to handle.[193]

On March 22, General Gough and three colonels from pro-Ulster regiments, the 5th and 16th Lancers, and Churchill's old regiment, the 4th Hussars, were summoned to London. In a meeting with Seely, Field Marshal Sir John French, and Adjutant General Sir J. Spencer Ewart, Gough refused to budge. When he was asked to go back and carry on as though nothing had happened, he demanded a written assurance that the Army would never be used to enforce Home Rule in Ulster. Incredibly, Seely agreed, and brought a draft of the assurance to the Cabinet meeting on Monday morning, March 23. Asquith amended it so that it said nothing more than that officers should obey orders. Seely, who had been summoned by the King, returned to the Cabinet meeting as it was breaking up. Asquith gave him the amended document and left the room to go to lunch. Seely went over it with Lord Morley, the Lord President of the Council, and they added a paragraph that gave Gough what he had asked for: "His Majesty's Government . . . have no intention whatever of taking advantage of the right to crush political opposition to the policy or principles of the Home Rule Bill." Why had Morley, that model of rectitude, coauthored an unwarranted redrafting? He was deaf, he had not heard what had gone on, and he was due to speak that day on Ireland in the House of Lords and wanted to be sure that he would say the right thing. When he sat down with Seely to go over the government position, they drafted what was later called "the peccant paragraph," which turned up, word for word, in his speech.[194]

Seely showed the document to Churchill, who approved it, saying that "nothing in the statement would prevent the Army Council from ordering troops to aid the lawful civil powers against any unlawful authority engaged in breaking the law or committing acts of violence."[195] But it was not good enough for Gough, who asked for a more specific assurance that the paragraph meant that troops would not be called upon to enforce the Home Rule Bill. General French wrote in the margin: "That is how I read it. J.F." As General Sir Henry Wilson, the pro-Ulster intriguer who was supplying Bonar Law with military information, wrote in his diary: "So long as we hold the paper we got on Monday, we can afford to sit tight."[196]

Asquith was appalled. Army officers had extracted a policy concession from the government as the price of doing their duty. Seely would have to go; so would French and Ewart. For the moment the crisis was over. The troops had been moved to the depots without incident. But what were the long-range consequences for the Army? Now that Gough had defied the War Office, any officer could refuse to obey orders.[197]

In the meantime, the ships that Churchill had ordered to the Scottish coast had been turned back. An order to embark field guns aboard the flagship of the 3rd Battle Squadron was canceled. The reason for the change in plans, as Churchill explained in the House of Commons on March 25, was "because the precautionary movements of the military in Ireland had been effected without opposition from the army of 100,000 which has been raised to resist the authority of Crown and Parliament."[198]

In the Tory view, however, the combined military and naval operations had been nothing less than an attempted invasion of Ulster. Seely had worked General Paget up into a state of bellicose agitation on the plea that a short and bloody war would be better than a long one later. Here, under the pretext of restoring law and order, was a chance to smash the Ulster Volunteers and enforce Home Rule.

It was with the conviction that the government had plotted to suppress resistance in Ulster that Leo Amery (the boy pushed into the pool at Harrow and a fellow correspondent at Estcourt) rose to address Churchill.

AMERY: "Will the right honorable Gentleman state whether he expected and hoped that purely precautionary measures to look after stores would lead to fighting and bloodshed?"
CHURCHILL: ". . . I may repudiate that hellish insinuation."
HON. MEMBERS: "Withdraw!"
SPEAKER: "The First Lord of the Admiralty must see that that was

hardly a proper epithet to apply. I hope he will see his way to withdraw it . . ."

CHURCHILL: ". . . I have been in this House for fourteen years, and in that time I have never been asked from the Chair to withdraw any expression which I have used, although I have been in many stormy Parliamentary scenes. Of course, if you say the epithet 'hellish' . . . cannot be permitted, then I must bow to your ruling. But I earnestly trust you will permit it to be used."

SPEAKER: "It would be impossible to permit an expression of that sort to pass."

CHURCHILL: ". . . I withdraw the expression 'hellish.' "[199]

Counterattacking, Churchill said that "every effort has been made with the greatest dialectical skill by the right honorable Gentleman the Senior Member for the City of London [Mr. Balfour] and by the Leader of the Opposition [Mr. Bonar Law], who emulated his dialectical force without his dialectical subtlety, to show that it is always right for soldiers to shoot down a Radical or a Labour man—[Hon. Members: "Liar!" "Withdraw!" "Rub it in!"] . . . But in any matter where Liberals are concerned, then of course no gentleman would ever demean himself by doing his duty to the Crown and Parliament."[200]

That weekend, at The Wharf, Asquith told Churchill that Seely must resign and that he would take on the War Office himself, in addition to being Prime Minister. "I need not tell you," Asquith wrote Venetia Stanley, "that Winston's eyes blazed and his polysyllables rolled, and his gestures were those of a man possessed."[201]

Seely felt he was a scapegoat. The government had determined to take military action but had lost its nerve. Churchill was just as responsible as he was, having sent ships. Churchill said he was grieved and would do what he could to save him, but they had all turned their backs on him. He was tempted to tell the whole story . . .[202] Churchill was sorry to see Seely going about like a disembodied spirit. He was terribly hard hit and losing poise. The world was pitiless to grief and failure.[203]

In the debate on Monday, March 30, the Tories repeated the charge that Churchill had moved troops in expectation of a collision. F. E. Smith affirmed that a serious invasion of Ulster had been contemplated: "The scheme was Napoleonic, but there was no Napoleon."

It fell to Churchill to defend the government. They had done no more than reinforce arms depots. Augustine Birrell, the Chief Secretary for Ireland, had not thought troop movements would be provocative. There had been a mis-understanding between General Paget and the officers.

> BONAR LAW: "Rubbish."
> CHURCHILL: "Do I understand the right honorable Gentleman to say rubbish?"
> BONAR LAW: "Yes."

The issue threatened to divide the Army, Churchill explained. One young officer had written his father a letter that had been published in the *Pall Mall Gazette*:

"I have decided to stay on . . . Although as you know my sympathies are absolutely with Ulster, I think that at a time like this the Army must stick together. If we once start to disintegrate the service, then goodbye to the Empire and anything else that happens. Moreover, in case of strike duty, the men whose sympathies are fairly obviously with the strikers have to carry on and do their duty so that now it is up to us to do the same."[204]

Curragh left a legacy of bitterness and unrest in the Army, and the Tories designated Churchill as the villain of what they called the "Ulster Pogrom." He was the mastermind who had summoned eight battleships and field guns, with Asquith and Seely as weak accomplices. It was Churchill who had told Sir John French on March 20 that if Belfast showed fight his fleet "would have the town in ruins in 24 hours."[205]

Not since he had crossed the floor had he been subjected to so much abuse. At a Tory rally in Hyde Park on April 4 Lord Charles Beresford called him a "Lilliput Napoleon—a man with an unbalanced mind, an egomaniac—whose one absorbing thought was personal vindictiveness towards.Ulster." Sir Edward Carson, at the same rally, called him "Lord Randolph's renegade son who wanted to be handed down to posterity as the Belfast butcher who threatened to shoot down those who took his father's advice." Bonar Law was convinced that Churchill had plotted an invasion of Ulster. Lord Robert Cecil, third son of Lord Salisbury, spoke of his "dark and tortuous mind."[206]

The Tory case was summed up in a letter Beresford wrote Rear Admiral Rosslyn Wemyss on April 7: "We have evidence that the Churchill plot was an accomplished fact. That he was the moving spirit in the whole question, that he took charge of the Army, the Cabinet, and the Government for the time being, that arrangements were made to seize all the strategical points around Belfast by means of the Army associated with the Navy, and that arrangements had been made to arrest Sir Edward Carson, Walter Long . . . and the leading people associated with the Ulster organization. If Sir Edward Carson had not left for Dublin on the Monday night, he was to have been arrested the following morning. The resignation of the officers brought the matter to a climax. The fleet was stopped by wireless, and the infamous plot fell through. . . . Churchill ought to be hanged. I am not going to let him go, and shall never cease exposing him in my speeches. As you know, there were plenty of ships at home that they might have sent to Lamlash and Belfast, but the Admirals in command gave it distinctly to be understood that they would not fire on Ulster, so Churchill fell back on Bayly, who is supposed to be a great Radical, and the Government knew he would obey orders . . ."[207]

None of the supposed "evidence" that anything more than troop reinforcements had been planned ever came to light, although sending eight battleships with field guns into Ulster waters had unfortunate implications. Churchill bore the attacks with equanimity, explaining that Vice Admiral Bayly, commanding the 3rd Battle Squadron, had asked for the field guns to exercise his men on shore in case of bad weather (the Tories said "bad weather" was a code for "disturbances in Ulster"). The Ulster Pogrom was in full swing, he wrote Clemmie on April 23. Bonar Law had exceeded himself in rudeness, and feelings on all sides were bitter to a degree hitherto unknown.

On April 24, two steamers unloaded an estimated thirty-five thousand rifles and three million rounds of ammunition at the Ulster port of Larne. This daring action, conceived and carried out by Carson's Ulster Volunteers, showed that the government's precautions had been warranted. For a month, the government had been on the defensive, but the gun-running escapade gave Churchill a Parliamentary advantage that he exploited on April 28 and 29 when he responded to a vote of censure proposed by Austen Chamberlain.

"What we are now witnessing in the House," he said, "is uncommonly like a vote of censure by the criminal classes on the police."

An Hon. Member: "You have not arrested them."
Churchill: "Is that the complaint—that we have been too lenient?"

It was no longer a question of coercing Ulster, Churchill went on, "it was a question of our preventing Ulster from coercing us . . . All this talk of civil war has not come from us; it has come from you. For the last two years we have been forced to listen to a drone of threats of civil war with the most blood-curdling accompaniments and consequences. Did they really think that if a civil war came it was to be a war in which only one side was to take action? . . . I wish to make it perfectly clear that if rebellion comes we shall put it down . . ." But then Churchill's tone changed, and he held out an olive branch to Sir Edward Carson, acknowledging Ulster's needs for safeguards and urging Carson to agree to the six-year amendment.[208]

Pleased with himself, Churchill felt that his offer was an inspiration, a daring and perilous stroke that had transformed the political situation. Never had he taken a greater risk. The Irish were saying he had betrayed their cause. The Radical wing of the Liberal Party was comparing his action with Seely's surrender to Gough. Having been the Tory villain, Churchill was now condemned in his own party. What in fact did he want? A military defeat in Ulster or an agreement with Sir Edward Carson? The apparent contradiction was a deliberate policy. Churchill was willing to go further than Asquith in taking action against illegal violence in Ulster. He was also more forward than the left wing of his party in seeking conciliation, so long as Ulster remained within the law. His policy was one of appeasement from a position of strength.

But with the Army divided, and the two great political parties at each other's throats, was it surprising that German agents reported that England was drifting into civil war and was so preoccupied by the Irish problem that it was no longer a factor in the European situation?

Europe, for the moment, seemed calm, and Churchill busied himself with the many cubicles of his department. He wanted to revive singing in the fleet. There should be songbooks, an officer in charge on each ship, singing once a month, and a silver wreath for the best singing ship; singing should be carried out as routinely as gunnery practice. Then there was the sailor's wife. More attention should be paid to her needs in order to develop a naval caste whose children would return to the service their fathers had taught them to respect. Then there was the expense of railway travel for men on leave, and incentives to encourage them to stay in the Navy after serving twelve years.[209] Then there was the submarine. Should they build more? Jacky Fisher had heard that in Germany, Von Tirpitz was digging out submarines wherever he could find them. Fisher wanted Churchill to drop one dreadnought secretly and build twenty submarines instead. But Churchill was not sure. The 1914 submarine was in many ways a primitive vessel. The image on the periscope was inverted, so that the commanding officer had to attack a target that he saw upside down. Live white mice were kept on board as a way of detecting toxic air. Imbued with Victorian notions of honorable warfare, Churchill was genuinely shocked at Fisher's forecast that submarines would be used to sink unarmed merchant vessels. No civilized power would ever do such a thing. If ever a nation were vile enough to adopt such methods, it would be necessary to employ the extreme resources of science, to spread pestilence, poison the water supply of great cities, and proceed to the assassination of individuals.[210] But these were unthinkable propositions, and Fisher was being morbidly unrealistic. Knowing better, Fisher wrote Asquith on May 8: "I have said all this to Winston till I am sick (and made him sick too I fear!) . . . There are a lot of idiots who lecture at the Naval War College and write in the papers that Tirpitz won't use his submarines to sink merchant ships—the civilized world they say would execrate him . . . [but] the essence of war is violence."[211]

Fisher took Churchill to visit the submarine base at Portsmouth. The officer in charge was Captain Roger Keyes, a diminutive, ferret-faced man with large elfin ears, noted for his outspokenness. He disliked Churchill for encouraging young officers to talk and getting themselves in trouble, and because as an Ulsterman he felt that the First Lord had divided the Navy by calling out a battle squadron. Churchill was in an aggressive mood, showed no interest in the latest submarines, but glared at Keyes and asked why more were not being built. Keyes said it was Fisher's fault for giving an absolute monopoly on construction to Vickers, which took two and a half years to build one. With scathing emphasis, Fisher said, "Very interesting!" and turned his back on them.[212]

At the end of June, in keeping with the relaxed European situation, Admiral Sir George Warrender took the 2nd Battle Squadron to Kiel, the chief German port, for the festive opening of the canal, which had been widened and deepened so that the new German dreadnoughts could go from the mouth of the Elbe in the North Sea to Kiel in the Baltic, sparing them the dangerously exposed detour around Denmark. The sixty-mile inland route across the neck of Schleswig-Holstein, which Jacky Fisher had been dreading for years, gave Germany unchallenged control of the Baltic. Some of the finest ships in the British and German navies were berthed side by side. By mutual agreement, undue curiosity in technical matters was banned. Under sunny blue skies, the Kaiser presided over races, banquets, and speeches. Officers and men of the two navies strolled arm in arm through the hospitable town, dined in goodwill in messes and wardrooms, drank together in beer halls, and stood bareheaded and silent at the funeral of a German officer killed while flying an English seaplane.[213]

On June 28, in the midst of these festivities, came the news that Archduke

Francis Ferdinand, the heir to the Austro-Hungarian throne, had been assassinated in Sarajevo, capital of the annexed territory of Bosnia-Herzegovina. Out sailing, the Kaiser returned in a state of agitation and left Kiel that night.

There was no cause for alarm. What did the crack of bullets in a Balkan town have to do with England? Not one Englishman in a thousand knew where Sarajevo was. All they knew was that it was very far away. Europe was still a continent of principled societies, each the mirror-image of the other, with the same conventions and values. The Kaiser was related to the Czar of Russia, who was related to the English King. They belonged to a European family of rulers who would keep peace and order. There was an accepted diplomatic system for smoothing out disturbances. In the chancelleries of Europe, men trained in the nuances of official communications made the necessary adjustments in the machinery. Words counted, even whispers. It was a working system of equipoise. In case of imbalance, a communiqué could be placed on the scales.

Such was the old world in its sunset, with its naval visits and exchanges of military data, its court life, and its royal funerals, upon which converged the extended family of monarchs. Behind this venerable patinaed façade, the nations of Europe were arming: France with its three-year service, Russia with its strategic railways, England with its dreadnoughts, and Germany with its mighty standing Army. Austro-Hungary, beset by nationalistic agitation, was in a state of decay. Germany, in Churchill's words, looked at Europe and its gaze became a glare.

On July 15, the test mobilization that Churchill had ordered as an economy measure in place of Grand Maneuvers began. More than twenty thousand reservists answered the Admiralty's call. Churchill and Prince Louis inspected the great naval base at Chatham and saw the reservists draw their kits and proceed to their ships in eager confusion. The old battleships and cruisers of the Third Fleet coaled and raised steam and sailed for Spithead, the channel between Portsmouth and the Isle of Wight, where they joined the gleaming new ships of the First and Second Fleets. Aboard the *Enchantress*, Prince Louis and Churchill followed. On July 17 and 18 the ships lay at anchor, and with the King, they inspected the greatest assemblage of naval power the world had ever seen, fifty-three battleships and a total of four hundred pennants of all classes. On July 19, the mighty fleet put to sea for exercises, bands playing, each ship crowded with bluejackets and decked with flags, while overhead planes circled. It took more than six hours for the armada, steaming at fifteen knots, to pass before the royal yacht, as the Sailor King waved them on, identifying each unit, and watched them melt out of sight.[214]

On July 23 the exercises were over, and on July 26 the ships of the Third Fleet were due to return to their home ports, where the reservists would disband. On July 23 Lloyd George gave a speech urging naval economy because relations with Germany were better than they had been for years.

On Friday afternoon, July 24, the Cabinet was huddled over the Irish problem. A bipartisan conference called by the King had broken down. The disagreements seemed as fierce and hopeless as ever, and yet the margin of dispute had been narrowed down to the boundaries of two religiously mixed Ulster counties. It depressed Churchill to think that the political future of Great Britain turned on the dreary steeples of Fermanagh and Tyrone. He had hoped that the events at the Curragh would have sufficiently shocked public opinion to bring about a settlement; apparently not. The conflict would have to be carried one stage further. Not since the days of the Blues and the Greens in the Byzantine Empire had partisanship been carried to such absurd extremes.

The Cabinet was about to separate when a messenger handed Edward Grey a "most immediate" dispatch, which he read aloud. It was the text of an ultimatum to Serbia from the Austrian government. Grey had been reading for several minutes before Churchill could disengage his mind from the bewildering debate that had just ended. They were all tired, but gradually it began to dawn on him that this was an ultimatum such as had never been penned in modern times. No state in the world could accept it, and no acceptance, however abject, would satisfy the aggressor. The Ulster parishes faded back into the mists and squalls of Ireland, and in their place Churchill saw, bathed in a strange light, the map of Europe.[215]

For Asquith the ultimatum was the gravest event in European politics for many years past. But happily there seemed to be no reason why Great Britain should be anything more than a spectator. The Austrians were quite the stupidest people in Europe—as the Italians were the most perfidious—and there was a brutality about their procedure that made it seem as if a big power was wantonly bullying a little one.[216]

Churchill went at once to the Admiralty and took stock of the situation with Eddie Marsh and James Masterton-Smith. The reservists of the Third Fleet had been paid off and were on their way home. But the whole of the battle-ready First and Second Fleets was at Portland and would remain there until Monday morning at seven, when the First Fleet would disperse by squadrons for exercises and the Second Fleet would proceed to home ports to discharge its balance crews (the men taken on in addition to the skeleton crews for the exercises). A word by wireless before Monday could give the order to "stand the fleets fast."

Churchill had the Navy well in hand, as even the German naval attaché in London, Captain Erich von Müller, acknowledged. In a June 4 dispatch to Admiral von Tirpitz, he wrote: "On the whole the Navy is satisfied with Mr. Churchill, because it recognizes that he has done and accomplished more for them than the majority of his predecessors in office. There is no doubt that there has been friction between Mr. Churchill and the officers at the Admiralty, as well as those at sea. That is not surprising with such a stubborn and tyrannical character as Mr. Churchill." But naval power had increased under his guidance and the Navy was "very much aware of it."

That night, July 24, after the Austrian ultimatum had been read in Cabinet, Churchill dined with Albert Ballin, the head of the Hamburg-America Line, in Sir Ernest Cassel's great house on Park Lane. Ballin was on a fishing expedition to find out under what conditions Britain would stay out of the war. "I remember," he said, "old Bismarck telling me the year before he died that one day the great European war would come out of some damned foolish thing in the Balkans." Then he added: "If Russia marches against Austria, we must march; and if we march, France must march, and what would England do?" What could Churchill say? England was not bound by treaty to France. England's foreign policy was the great question mark. No one knew which way the British lion would jump. There was a strong popular impulse to stay out of European affairs. There was also the ancient policy of maintaining the balance of power on the Continent. Churchill said it was a mistake to assume that England would do nothing. His last words to Ballin, almost with tears in his eyes, were: "My dear friend, don't let us go to war."[217]

Churchill was due to spend the weekend with his pregnant wife and their two children at Pear Tree Cottage in Cromer, on the Norfolk coast, 138 miles away from London and three and a half hours by train. He took the train on Saturday at 1 P.M. Asquith, Grey, Haldane, and Lloyd George were also away, not overly alarmed at the rumblings of war. On duty at the Admiralty, Prince Louis reflected on the peculiar insouciance of British statesmen and told his young son Dickie that "Ministers with their weekend holidays are incorrigible."[218]

On Saturday afternoon, July 25, the news came that Serbia had accepted the ultimatum, and Churchill went to sleep in his bedroom at Pear Tree

Cottage feeling that things might blow over. Could Austria demand more? And if war broke out, could it not be confined to Eastern Europe? There was still time for conciliation. If the call came, the British Navy had never been in greater strength.

The next morning he went down to the beach to play with the kittens, so dear and caressing. Diana was such a sweet child. One day at the Admiralty, when George Riddell had turned up, his finger bound up in plaster, she had said, "It does hurt me to see your poor finger." It was a beautiful day, with the North Sea sparkling to a far horizon. The tide was going out, and as they dammed the little rivulets that trickled down to the sea, Churchill thought of the German High Seas Fleet, cruising off the Norwegian coast, and of all the great ships of the British Navy, *his* Navy, waiting behind the torpedo-proof moles of Portland harbor.

When he called Prince Louis at nine and again at noon, the situation was confused. Messages were pouring in from foreign capitals. There were rumors that Austria was not satisfied with the Serbian acceptance. He decided to return to London, authorizing Prince Louis to do whatever was necessary in the meantime. While waiting for Churchill, Prince Louis took it upon himself to order the First Fleet to remain mobilized. At five minutes past four, he sent this telegram to Admiral Sir George Callaghan: "Admiralty to C in C Home Fleets. Decypher. No ships of First Fleet or Flotillas are to leave Portland until further orders. Acknowledge." When Churchill got in, at about nine in the evening, he gave the order his instant approval and went to see Sir Edward Grey, who had rented Churchill's house at 33 Eccleston Square. Grey viewed the situation gravely. Churchill asked whether it would be helpful to disclose that the fleet was being kept together. Grey said it might have a sobering effect on the Central Powers, and Churchill went back to the Admiralty and drew up the communiqué, hoping the Kaiser would get the message when he saw it in the papers.[219]

On Monday, July 27, there began the series of daily Cabinet meetings specifically devoted to the European crisis. Three-quarters of the Cabinet was determined not to be drawn into a European war unless Great Britain was attacked. There was no scarcity of wishful thinking: Austria and Serbia would not come to blows; Russia would not intervene; Germany would stay out of it; France and Russia would neutralize each other; half a dozen possibilities to wrangle over, about none of which any proof could be offered except the proof of events. While the ministers talked, war crept up like the players in the children's game of Grandmother's Footsteps, who must be caught moving. You look away, and they are distant and motionless. You look back, and they are still motionless but a bit closer. The game continues until one of the players is spotted in motion or until the final pounce.

It was not in Churchill's nature to wait for the final pounce. On July 27 he started putting the Navy on a war footing, and wired Admiral Sir Berkeley Milne, in command of the Mediterranean Fleet, to be prepared to shadow possible hostile men-of-war. On Tuesday, July 28, the First Fleet was ordered to sail secretly for its northern station, while the Second Fleet remained at Portland. Patrol flotillas were ordered to their war stations. The two Irish blockades were abandoned. Naval aircraft were stationed around the Thames estuary. Minesweepers were collected. Oil tanks and arms depots were guarded against aerial attack and sabotage. Two dreadnoughts ordered by the Turks at a total cost of 3,680,650 pounds were seized in their British shipyards. A Turkish crew of five hundred lay waiting in a steamer on the Tyne to board one of them, the *Sultan Osman*. Not wanting a diplomatic incident in which the Turks would brush aside the Armstrong workers and hoist the Turkish flag, Churchill ordered military guards to be placed aboard the vessel. When Ahmed Tewfik Pasha, the Turkish ambassador to London, called on the Foreign Office to ask why the ships had been embargoed, he was told that in view of the serious situation abroad, it was not possible to allow battleships to pass into the hands of a foreign power. The ambassador seemed puzzled, and said that three million pounds had been paid. He was assured that he would not lose the money. He asked how long the ships would be detained and was told that they stood before the unknown. It was later charged that holding these ships had helped bring Turkey into the war on the side of Germany, but the Turks were already negotiating a secret alliance, which was signed on August 2.[220]

Still hoping that war could be averted, Churchill wondered why those stupid kings and emperors could not assemble together and save the nations from hell. On Wednesday, July 29, the strategic concentration of the First Fleet was begun with its transfer to Scottish ports. Eighteen miles of warships steamed slowly out of Portland harbor, squadron by squadron, steel castles moving unlit in absolute blackness through the Strait of Dover into the North Sea, like giants bowed in anxious thought. By July 31 the fleet had reached its battle stations: the battleships at Scapa Flow, in the Orkney Islands, and the Cromarty Firth, in northern Scotland; the battle cruisers at Rosyth, in the Firth of Forth.

The Cabinet authorized Churchill to put into force the "precautionary period" regulations. Harbors were cleared of pleasure craft, bridges were guarded, steamers were boarded, and watchers lined the coast. Churchill knew through the intercept of letters that a network of agents kept the German naval attaché informed on British naval measures. For the moment, he did not arrest them; it was useful that Germany should know how seriously Britain viewed the situation. The time would come soon when all the petty traitors willing to sell their country for a few pounds would be laid by their heels.

War plans were under way, but Churchill still believed in an orderly Europe under the leadership of kings who would not permit a conflict to break out. At the Wednesday Cabinet meeting, he urged Asquith to call for a conference of kings to avoid the appalling calamity that civilized nations were being forced to contemplate, but the idea came to nothing.

Churchill had lunch that day with Kitchener, who was on a rare visit to England from his post as British Agent and Consul General in Egypt to receive an earldom. Kitchener told him that the Germans were preparing to use great quantities of high-explosive shells, which not only would kill French gunners but would blow to pieces the guns and carriages. It was the first time Churchill had heard of this disagreeable possibility. Kitchener was eager to sail for Egypt, but Churchill told him: "If war comes, you will not go back to Egypt." The old hostilities of the Sudan campaign had vanished. Churchill felt sure that Asquith would not continue to hold the two offices of Prime Minister and Secretary of State for War, and that Kitchener's presence in a War Cabinet would be a great asset.[221]

On Thursday, July 30, the Second Reading of the Amending Bill for Home Rule was to have been moved. In the Ladies' Gallery, Violet Asquith saw women who she knew were attending Red Cross classes, learning to roll bandages and make splints in preparation for the impending civil war. Asquith announced that the Amending Bill would be put off because of the danger of general war. For the moment, the Irish problem was put away and wrapped in mothballs. Home Rule was placed on the Statute Book, but its operation was suspended for the duration of the war. Tyrone and Fermanagh would have to wait while more distant place names captured the imagination.

That morning, at his daily staff meeting with the Sea Lords, Churchill learned that the First Fleet was heading toward its war stations in the North Sea. The nightmare of the fleet caught napping in its home ports, as the Russian fleet had been surprised by a torpedo attack off Port Arthur by the Japanese, had been preying on his mind. Now, he was filled with a sense of relief and passed on the good news to Jacky Fisher, who had dropped by the Admiralty. The old boy's delight was wonderful to see.[222]

On Friday, July 31, summonses were sent to the naval reservists for a complete mobilization. There was no deficiency of officers, and the sailors were thrilled and confident. Everyone was awake and ready to the tips of their fingers. If war came the Germans would get a good drubbing.

Churchill was in a state of high excitement. He never felt more alive than in a crisis. He had to admit that the war preparations held a hideous fascination for him. Just at the time when everything was tending toward catastrophe and collapse, he was geared up and happy. It was horrible to be like that. And yet he would do his best for peace; nothing would induce him to strike the first blow. The British on their island were not responsible for the wave of madness that had swept Christendom. They were drifting on in a kind of dull cataleptic trance, as if watching someone else's operation.[223]

As the last week of European peace began to unfold on Friday, July 31, Churchill felt that there was still hope, although the clouds were blacker and blacker. Germany seemed tardily to restrain her idiot ally, and the British were working to soothe Russia. The City had broken into chaos. The world's credit system was suspended. You could not sell stocks and shares or borrow money. Soon it would not even be possible to cash a check.[224] Prices were rising to panic levels. At lunch at Admiralty House, Kitchener told Churchill and Asquith that the real danger was not a Balkan war but a German attack on France. If England did not back up France when she was in real danger, she would never exercise power again.

On Saturday, August 1, ministerial weekends were suspended as the Cabinet sat for two and a half hours. Asquith ruefully noted that Winston occupied half the time. He was very bellicose, demanding immediate mobilization. Of course, Charles Hobhouse thought, he was in favor of any enterprise that gave him a chance to display the Navy as his instrument of destruction. The Cabinet was dividing into three main groups: Churchill, Asquith, Haldane, Grey, and Hobhouse were in favor of war if Belgian neutrality was violated; Harcourt, Simon, Beauchamp, Morley, and Burns said that under no circumstances should Britain get involved; McKenna and Lloyd George, the only Cabinet minister who could have swung a majority of the Cabinet, and even a majority of the Liberal Party in the House of Commons, behind neutrality, were undecided.

The sticking point was Belgium, as can be seen from the following exchange of notes between the First Lord and the Chancellor of the Exchequer:

LLOYD GEORGE: Would you *commit* yourself in public *now* to war if Belgium is invaded whether Belgium asks for our protection or not?

CHURCHILL: No.

LLOYD GEORGE: If patience prevails & you do not press us too hard to-night we might come together.

CHURCHILL: Please God—It is our whole future—comrades—or opponents. The march of events will be dominating.

LLOYD GEORGE: What is your policy?

CHURCHILL: At the present moment I would act in such a way as to impress Germany with our intention to preserve the neutrality of Belgium. So much is still unknown as to the definite purpose of Germany that I would not go beyond this. Moreover public opinion might veer round at any moment if Belgium is invaded & we must be ready to meet this opinion.

LLOYD GEORGE: I am most profoundly anxious that our long cooperation may not be severed. . . .

CHURCHILL: . . . I am deeply attached to you & have followed your instinct & guidance for nearly 10 years.[225]

News of the Cabinet divergences was leaking out. Geoffrey Robinson, editor of the *Times*, thought that Saturday was a black day for England, with half the Cabinet rotten and every prospect of a disastrous and dishonoring refusal to help France. Churchill had done more than anyone to save the situation.

That evening Churchill dined alone at the Admiralty, reading the foreign telegrams as they arrived in a continuous flow of red dispatch boxes. There was still hope. No frontiers had been breached. No shots had been fired.[226] At nine-thirty F. E. Smith and the Canadian businessman and Conservative MP Max Aitken came to see him, and he told them there was still a chance. They sat down at a card table to play three-handed bridge. The cards had just been dealt when another dispatch box arrived. He opened it and read: "War declared by Germany on Russia." It was all up. Germany had quenched the last hopes of peace. The next step would be a declaration of war against France. The world had gone mad.

He walked across the Horse Guards Parade to 10 Downing Street, where, finding Asquith with Grey and several other ministers, he announced his intention of mobilizing the fleet instantly. Asquith did not say a single word, but it was obvious from his expression that he approved. As Churchill left Downing Street with Sir Edward Grey, the Foreign Secretary said: "You should know I have just done a very important thing. I have told Cambon that we shall not allow the German fleet to come into the Channel."[227]

All Sunday morning, August 2, the Cabinet sat, and it looked to Churchill as if the majority would resign. At one point, John Burns, the workingman minister, leaned over the table, shaking his clenched fists, and said the choice was between neutrality and war with both hands, naval and military. "But *which* is your policy?" Lloyd George asked. Turning very white, Burns replied: "Neutrality, under the circumstances." John Morley, the lifelong pacifist, said: "You all know my views . . . I cannot renounce [them,] and if you persevere in intervention, I cannot return to this room." No one took him seriously, for he threatened to resign once a month.[228]

During a lull, the two Oxford classicists, Asquith and Simon, discussed the parallel between Britain's pledge to Belgium and that of the little town of Plataea in the second year of the Peloponnesian War, when its integrity was guaranteed by the great powers of Greece. When Sparta threatened to occupy it, Plataea appealed to Athens. Asquith, who in Simon's opinion satisfied Macaulay's definition of a scholar as "a man who could read Thucydides with his feet in the fender," said the analogy was striking. "But I trust the outcome will be different," he added, for the Plataeans had been butchered and their city razed to the ground.[229] Simon wanted to resign. England had behind it a century of wonderful progress with no involvement in Europe since the Napoleonic Wars, except for the Crimean War. They had stayed neutral in the war of 1870. Why not stay neutral now?

At another Cabinet meeting on Sunday evening, the ministers learned that German troops had invaded Luxembourg. Belgium would be next, and Britain would be drawn in because of its written pledge. Asquith authorized the mobilization of the Army. Churchill instructed his commanders in chief to make direct contact with their French opposite numbers in case of combined action.

When the Cabinet met again on the morning of Monday, August 3, Churchill could see no hope for peace. France was behaving well, holding back her covering troops a good distance behind her frontier, and delaying mobilization. But Germany had asked her to break her treaty with Russia. Even if she had agreed, she would be going from shame to shame, for, as it was later learned, the Germans would have demanded as a guarantee of French neutrality the surrender of the fortresses of Toul and Verdun.

While the Cabinet was in session, news came that Belgium had refused the German ultimatum. King Albert had made a personal appeal to King George.

Poor little Belgium became gallant little Belgium. England was bound by treaty to defend Belgian neutrality, but there were loopholes, which the pacifist wing of the Cabinet seized on. Was the violation "substantial" and an "interference with Belgian independence," as the wording of the treaty required? The threat to Belgium nudged some of the waverers on the side of intervention. Men who had objected to being drawn into a Central European war, and who were even willing to accept an unresisted "traverse" of the Lowlands, drew the line at letting Belgium fight alone.[230]

The remaining pacifists—Morley, Simon, Burns, and Beauchamp—resigned. Churchill told Morley that if he would only wait a few days, all would speedily be made plain, for Germany would overrun Belgium. He offered to show him on the map. "You may be right," Morley said, "perhaps you are—but I should be no use in a War Cabinet. I should only hamper you. If we have to fight, we must fight with single-hearted conviction. There is no place for me in such affairs."[231]

That was four gone, Asquith thought, wondering if there would be any more. Offsetting the defections was Lloyd George's shift toward intervention; his sympathy for Belgium's plight and his feeling that Britain should honor her treaty obligations weighed more heavily than his pacifism and his fear that war would bankrupt England. Lloyd George appealed to the four to delay their resignations, and that afternoon in the House of Commons they sat on the front bench in a show of government unity that did not in fact exist.

Churchill was pleased that the Welsh miners, who had at first denounced the war, were now behind it, promising to cut all the coal that would be needed. He urged Lloyd George to send them a strong Welsh message about the need to help small nations.[232]

The Cabinet agreed that Sir Edward Grey should make a policy statement in the House that afternoon. But no decision was taken to declare war on Germany or to send an army to France. Some ministers still hoped that Germany would recall her armies. You might as well recall an avalanche, thought Churchill. Still, it was a frightening decision to make, committing England to the unknown evils of a European war, and they preferred to back into it, responding to events over which they had no control. Lord Crewe, whose judgment Asquith held in such high esteem, felt an overpowering sense of unreality, as if they were all characters in a novel by H. G. Wells.[233]

All over the country, in pubs and classrooms, in the City and on farms, in barracks and factories, across back yards and the card tables of London clubs, the same question was being asked: Would England go to war? At his camp, wearing a light-gray uniform with blue facings, a seventeen-year-old member of the Eton College Officers Training Corps named Anthony Eden was filled with a sense of foreboding. But his platoon commander said: "There won't be any war. The City would never allow it. Even if fighting did break out, it couldn't last more than a few days, the money would run out."[234]

At three that Monday afternoon, as the brilliant sun of a bank holiday filtered through the tall windows of the Chamber and buses rumbled over Westminster Bridge, Sir Edward Grey rose to speak. Only once before in his thirty years as a Member of Parliament had he seen the House so crowded that chairs had to be placed in the aisle, and that was when Gladstone had introduced his first Home Rule Bill. Now, on a wave of emotion, he felt the sorrowful passage of time, and his personal misfortune—the death of his dear wife, Dorothy—fused with the misfortune of Europe, and the hopes of peace blasted. But he gave no hint of his distress when he began to speak in a calm and uninflected voice, soberly appraising the situation in a tone completely lacking in rhetorical flourishes. A hush fell over the audience as he described Britain's historic and vital interest in the independence of the Low Countries. He read the Belgian King's plea to King George V: "I make a supreme appeal for the diplomatic intervention of Your Majesty's Government to safeguard the integrity of Belgium." If Belgium fell, Holland and Denmark would follow. What would Britain's fate be if France was beaten to her knees? Britain had no formal commitment to France, only close ties. "Let every man look into his own heart," Grey said, "his own feelings, and construe the extent of that obligation to himself. . . . If in a crisis like this we run away from those obligations of honor and interest . . . I doubt whether, whatever material force we might have at the end, it would be of very much value in face of the respect we should have lost."[235]

The effect of Grey's words in the House was electric. Everyone sensed that a bridge had been crossed and there was no going back. Britain had not declared war, but after Grey's speech she was *at war*. Immediate pledges of support came from the Tory Party and the Irish members. Asquith was pleased with his Foreign Secretary. There had been the usual ragged ends, but on the whole he had been tactful and cogent.[236] Watching from the gallery, the French ambassador, Paul Cambon, told a friend: "Now we can breathe."

As they left the House, Churchill asked Grey: "What happens now?" "We shall send them an ultimatum to stop the invasion of Belgium within twenty-four hours," Grey said.[237] Lord Hugh Cecil, the ally of his early days in Parliament, the best man at his wedding, and now a fervent pacifist, came up and grabbed Churchill violently, beside himself, outraged, and accused him of being responsible for all that had happened. Nothing Churchill said could calm him.

Upon reaching the Admiralty, Churchill, with the approval of Asquith and Grey, made a decision that effectively ended Britain's long period of isolation from Europe: he put into force the dispositions for full Anglo-French naval cooperation. It was done without the approval of the Cabinet or the House of Commons, and without a written treaty, but it meant that Britain and France were now military allies. Although no warlike action was contemplated, secret signal books were to be distributed to the French, mutual regulations for the entry of allied ships into each other's ports were to be issued, and British naval bases were placed at the disposal of the French.[238] This was a typically Churchillian *ad hoc* method of forging practical links where no formal alliance existed.

Grey was in his office at dusk when the Liberal journalist J. A. Spender came to see him. Standing at the window, they watched the sun set on St. James's Park and the lamps being lit in the streets below. "The lamps are going out all over Europe," Grey said. "We shall not see them lit again in our life-time."[239] It was the only memorable phrase that Grey ever uttered. The Foreign Secretary was a strange mixture of caution and resolution, attached to Victorian codes of honor and gentlemanly behavior. Churchill and Lloyd George wondered on one occasion whether he was as interested in foreign affairs as he was in the tame squirrels on his family property of Fallodon. "He is a firm sort of chap," Churchill said. "Supposing the Germans turned up at his house suddenly and put a revolver at his head telling him to sign a peace, he would not do so." "That's not what the Germans would say," Lloyd George replied; "they would say, if you don't do it we will skin your bloody squirrels—and Grey would probably capitulate."

From her seaside cottage, Clemmie knew that Churchill was tingling with life "to the tips of his fingers" through the anxious days. She had tried three times to call him that day at the office but each time the line had been busy.

On the morning of Tuesday, August 4, Churchill went to see Asquith at 10 Downing Street and pointed out that if war came, he could not hold the seals of office of the Secretary of State for War, as he had done since the Curragh mutiny, as well as those of Prime Minister. There would be a constant flow of interdepartmental work between the War Office and the Admiralty, which would have to be transacted between ministers, and with which Asquith could not possibly be burdened.[240] Churchill asked whether Asquith would consider the appointment of Lord Kitchener, and saw that his mind was moving along the same lines. But Kitchener had left that day for Dover, where he would board a fast destroyer returning him to Cairo. Asquith had him intercepted and brought back to London.

On that steamy, sultry August day, the last grains of sand ran out of the European hourglass. The Germans had invaded Belgium. The forts of Liège were under the fire of German howitzers. In the Reichstag, the Imperial Chancellor announced that "necessity knows no law, we must hack our way through."

Gottlieb von Jagow, the German Foreign Secretary, sent Grey a transparently bogus telegram explaining that Germany had been forced as a matter of life and death to disregard Belgian neutrality because of unimpeachable information that the French were planning to attack across Belgium.

Reading the telegram to the House, Asquith observed: "We cannot regard this as in any sense a satisfactory communication. We have, in reply to it, repeated the request we made last week to the German government that they should give us the same assurance in regard to Belgian neutrality as was given to us and to Belgium by France last week. We have asked that a reply to that request, and a satisfactory answer to the telegram of this morning—which I have read to the House—should be given before midnight." It was Asquith's turn to deliver an ultimatum. If the Germans did not reply by midnight, Britain would go to war. There was a great wave of cheering as Asquith's stocky figure walked slowly to the Bar and he faced the Speaker to read the King's proclamation calling out the army reserves. When Violet Asquith heard the words "units and individuals," she realized that war was no longer an abstraction, war was hundreds of thousands of young men who would be sent to France to fight and die, men like her friends and her four brothers.[241]

To the old anti-Imperialist poet Wilfrid Blunt, following events from his great Sussex estate, war was folly. What were they fighting for? For Serbia, a nest of murderous swine who had never listened to a word of English remonstrance? For Russia, the tyrant of Poland? For France, Britain's fellow brigand in North Africa? For Belgium, with its Congo record? And all this was being done in the name of England's honor.[242]

For Churchill, war was both horrible and fascinating. Ever since his arrival at the Admiralty in 1911, he had been preparing for this moment. He had staked his political survival on huge sums for the Navy. He had not hesitated to remove admirals who were not up to the task. He had gambled with 15-inch guns and started an air wing from scratch. He had honed the Navy's cutting edge to razor sharpness, and now the great cutlass was poised to strike. Walking from Downing Street to the Admiralty with Spender that afternoon, Churchill was in high spirits: "At midnight we shall be at war," he said, "at war. Think of it—if you can—the fleet absolutely ready, with instructions for every ship, and the word going out from that tower at midnight. Within a week enemy airships may be sailing over this spot on which we stand and dropping bombs on the seats of the mighty."[243]

As Admiral Percy Scott (who had once told Churchill that he had the two required qualities to become Prime Minister, genius and plod) would later point out, it was not so much that the fleet was ready, but that it believed itself to be ready. In terms of equipment, the fleet did not have an efficient mine, or up-to-date minelayers, or properly fitted minesweepers. There were no arrangements for guarding ships against mines and no efficient method for using guns at night. There were no anti-Zeppelin guns or antisubmarine defenses. Only a few ships had director firing, and torpedoes were so badly fitted that they passed under German ships instead of hitting them. All these inadequacies would become apparent with time, but for the moment the ships were in their war stations and ready to fight.

Returning to the Admiralty at ten to six, and fearing a German surprise attack, Churchill sent this telegram to every ship in the Royal Navy: "The war telegram will be issued at midnight authorizing you commence hostilities against Germany. But in view of terms our ultimatum they may decide open fire at any moment. You must be ready for this."

He dined at Admiralty House with his mother, his brother, Jack, and Geoffrey Robinson, the editor of the *Times* who had singled him out that morning as the one minister "whose grasp of the situation and whose efforts to meet it have been above all praise."

Sitting after dinner in the Admiralty War Room, hung with maps showing ship positions, Churchill listened to the clock tick. Now it was a matter of hours. Every ship was at its station, every man at his post. The minutes passed slowly. It was like waiting for election results. The votes were being counted and in a few moments the announcement would be made. One could only wait.

Prince Louis brought in two French admirals who wanted to use Malta as a base for the French fleet. That same Malta, Churchill thought, for which the British had fought Napoleon. "Use Malta as if it were Toulon," he said,[244] advancing cooperation between the two navies.

Marching through Belgium in order to defeat the French Army before turning eastward against Russia, the Germans ignored the British ultimatum, which expired at midnight German time, or 11 P.M. Greenwich Mean Time. As the moment approached, the windows of the War Room were flung open to the warm night air. Along the Mall, from the direction of the Palace, came the murmur of many voices singing a chorus of "God Save the King." Suddenly, above the chorus, the deep chimes of Big Ben boomed out the first stroke of the hour. The clock struck eleven and England was at war. Churchill went over to 10 Downing Street, where some of the ministers waited.[245] Two of the straying pacifist sheep, Simon and Beauchamp, had returned to the fold.

Gloom hung heavily over the Cabinet Room. Asquith sat with darkened face and dropped jowl. His head between his hands, Grey showed in his careworn face the strain of the last few days. The silence was oppressive. The hour having struck, they tried to realize what it meant for the days and months and perhaps years to come. Through the double doors Churchill burst upon the grave assembly, radiant, his face bright, his manner keen, pouring out a stream of words on how he was going to send telegrams to the Mediterranean and the North Sea. There, Lloyd George reflected, was a really happy man.[246]

From the Admiralty, at 11 P.M. precisely, the following message had been sent to all ships and naval establishments:

"COMMENCE HOSTILITIES AGAINST GERMANY."[247]

IX

THE ADMIRALTY IN WAR

Eᴺɢʟᴀɴᴅ ᴡᴀs ᴀᴛ ᴡᴀʀ in Western Europe for the first time since the Napoleonic conflicts of a century before. Thanks to Haldane, the Army had six divisions of professional soldiers ready to embark for France and an ample reserve of Territorials. Thanks to Churchill, the Navy was "the nation's sure shield," best summed up in the names of its ships: *Invincible, Inflexible, Implacable, Indefatigable.*

In Berlin, the news of England's entry came as a shock. Only a month before, British and German ships had lain peacefully at anchor in Kiel harbor. What did England have to gain? She had no territorial incentive, no *revanchard* urges. Crowds surging through the Unter den Linden threw stones at the British Embassy and attacked diplomats on their way home from work. The next day, one of the Kaiser's aides conveyed this message to the British ambassador, William Goschen:

"His Majesty the Emperor commands me to express his regret for the demonstration last night against the British Embassy, but bids me to add that it is an indication of the general feeling through Germany at England's faithless conduct. His Majesty begs you to inform King George that although he has in the past been proud to wear the uniform of the British Navy and Army [he was an honorary admiral of the fleet and field marshal], that is all now at an end."[1]

Churchill had not waited for England to be at war to replace Sir George Callaghan with John Jellicoe as commander in chief of the First Fleet. The decision had been made on July 30. Callaghan, almost sixty-two, was too old to lead the fleet in time of war. Jellicoe was Jacky Fisher's choice, and Fisher was delighted. He adored the English principle of having a civilian First Lord, having read how Lord Spencer, against navy tradition, and over the heads of senior admirals, had sent Nelson to the Mediterranean, giving England the finest victory at sea since the world began, the Battle of the Nile. And now they had Jellicoe as Admiralissimo![2]

On July 31, Jellicoe was in possession of a letter naming him commander in chief of the Grand, or First, Fleet and ordering him to repair on board his flagship, the *Iron Duke,* and arrange for the succession of command. The letter was to be opened only on receipt of telegraphic instructions, which arrived August 1, saying, "Open secret personal envelope taken with you from London."

Jellicoe was aghast. To remove the commander in chief on the eve of war would have terrible repercussions throughout the Navy. Between August 1 and August 4 he peppered the Admiralty with telegrams urging Churchill to reconsider. Instead of being pleased at his promotion, and the chance to lead a great fleet into battle, he did his utmost to avoid the job.

August 1: "Am firmly convinced after consideration that the step you mentioned to me is fraught with gravest danger at this juncture and might easily be disastrous owing to the extreme difficulty of getting into touch with everything at short notice."[3]

August 2: ". . . am more than ever convinced of vital importance of making no change." Wondering why the man he had chosen over many senior admirals was so curiously reticent, Churchill told him he had forty-eight hours to be ready.[4]

August 3: "Can only reply am certain step contemplated is most dangerous. Beg that it may not be carried out . . . Hard to believe it is realized what grave difficulties change Commander-in-Chief involves at this moment. Do not forget long experience of Commander-in-Chief."[5]

August 4: "Feel it my duty to warn you emphatically you court disaster if you carry out intention of changing before I have thorough grip of fleet and situation."[6]

August 4: "Fleet is imbued with feelings of extreme admiration and loyalty for C-in-C. This is a very strong factor."[7]

Losing patience, Churchill replied that Jellicoe must make the change quickly. Personal feelings could not count, only what was best for all.

Hearing the news on August 4, Admiral Beatty, in command of a battle-cruiser squadron, was indignant at the rude way his old chief and brother

Irishman had been sacked. What a curse it was to change horses in mid-stream! Jellicoe might be the better man, but he did not have the fleet at his fingertips. Beatty wired the Admiralty that the move would cause "unprecedented disaster—the moral effect upon the Fleet at such a moment would be worse than a defeat at sea."[8] Churchill brushed aside the warning.

From Pear Tree Cottage, Clemmie added her note of concern, hoping that Churchill would not be vexed. She had been cogitating over the "Callico Jellatine" crisis. There would be a deep wound in an old man's heart, and if Churchill put the wrong sort of poultice on it, it would fester. To a proud and sensitive man, a decoration would be an insult. Churchill must offer him a seat on the board. It might be true, as Churchill had said, that Callaghan "cannot say Boo to a Goose"—but surely he did not want a small clique of retired people to feel bitter and cackle. The whole service must see that Callaghan was not being humiliated. This would prevent the people at the top of the tree from feeling "In a few years *I* shall be cast off like an old shoe." Also, Clemmie added, he should not underrate the power of women to do mischief. Lady Callaghan and Lady Bridgeman might form a league of "Retired Officers' Cats" to abuse him. But if Callaghan was still employed, his wife would keep silent.[9]

Heeding Clemmie's advice, Churchill offered Callaghan an advisory post at the Admiralty and named him commander in chief at the Nore on January 1, 1915.

Jellicoe was in command of the fleet in the North Sea, where the clash with the German High Seas Fleet was expected, but the first naval action of the war took place in the Mediterranean. At the end of July, the battle cruiser *Goeben*, flagship of the German Mediterranean Squadron commanded by Admiral Wilhelm Souchon, was undergoing repairs in Pola, the Austro-Hungarian naval base at the northern end of the Adriatic. On August 1, the *Goeben* headed down the Adriatic and tried to coal at Brindisi and Taranto, in the heel of the Italian boot. But the Italians, who were neutral, turned her away.

Joined by the light cruiser *Breslau*, the *Goeben* then headed west toward the coast of North Africa, where French transports were embarking colonial troops from Algerian ports to Marseilles. With her ten 11-inch guns and her top speed of twenty-seven knots, the *Goeben* could outrun and outgun all the ships in the French Mediterranean Fleet. Churchill, ready for war to be declared at any moment, ordered Admiral Berkeley Milne, commander of the Malta-based British Fleet, to shadow the *Goeben* with two battle cruisers.[10]

This was the same Berkeley Milne, known as "Arky-Barky," whose promotion had so upset Jacky Fisher, who thought of him as a sneak of the dirtiest kind, distrusted by everyone.

On the morning of August 4, Milne wired that the *Indomitable* and the *Indefatigable* were shadowing the *Goeben* and the *Breslau* at 37.44 north by 7.56 east, which was west of Sicily. Churchill replied: "Good. Hold her. War imminent."[11]

Germany had by this time declared war on France, and the two German ships boldly sailed to the Algerian coast and bombarded the ports of Bône and Philippeville. What a coup it would be if Churchill's battle cruisers, shadowing at a safe distance, their guns loaded and trained, could move in and sink them. He pressed Asquith and Grey to let him retaliate, and, anticipating a favorable response, he wired Milne at midday on August 4: "If *Goeben* attacks French transports you should at once engage her. You should give her fair warning of this beforehand."[12]

The Cabinet met immediately after this telegram was sent. Winston had on all his war paint, Asquith thought; he was aching for a sea fight that would give him the first victory of the war.[13] But the Cabinet would not allow him to commence hostilities before the British ultimatum had run out. The moral integrity of the Empire could not be compromised for the sake of sinking a single ship. There could be no act of war until after midnight, and Italian neutrality must be respected.

If only they could take immediate action, Prince Louis urged, they could sink the *Goeben* before dark. Eager as he was, Churchill could not ignore a Cabinet decision, though he feared that the spirit of honorable restraint would be costly. New orders went out to Milne: he must not attack the *Goeben*, even if French transports were fired on. Also, "The Italian Government have declared neutrality. You are to respect this neutrality rigidly and should not allow any of HM ships to come within six miles of the Italian coast."[14]

As night and the end of the ultimatum approached, the hunter and the hunted cleaved the waters of the Mediterranean. Churchill suffered the tortures of Tantalus, knowing that at any moment his two battle cruisers could have opened up with sixteen 12-inch guns at a range of ten thousand yards. In the gathering dark, the *Goeben* increased her speed past the twenty-four knots that the battle cruisers could steam and shook them off.

On the morning of August 5, the *Goeben* and the *Breslau* reached the Sicilian port of Messina, where German colliers were waiting to begin coaling operations. Admiral Souchon was ordered by the German Admiralty to proceed to Constantinople, an alliance having been concluded between Germany and Turkey. At 3:35 P.M., the light cruiser *Gloucester*, watching off the southern exit of the Strait of Messina, reported on the basis of intercepted wireless signals that the *Goeben* must be at Messina.

Having received this information, Milne, who had assembled three battle cruisers and two light cruisers between Sicily and the African coast, did not close in on the *Goeben*. He followed orders: respect Italian neutrality and aid the French in the transport of their African army. He reported his dispositions to the Admiralty, which approved them, and did not order him to follow the *Goeben* into the Strait of Messina.

At 5 P.M. on August 6, having completed coaling, made his will, and deposited his valuables (including a signed portrait of the Kaiser) with the German consul, Admiral Souchon sailed out of Messina harbor, cleared for action, bands playing. He expected to find the route blocked by British ships, but Milne was on the other side of Sicily. Still, the British had a squadron of four armored cruisers and eight destroyers in the Adriatic under Rear Admiral Ernest Troubridge—smaller ships admittedly, but twelve mosquitoes against one hornet.

Not knowing of the Turkish alliance, Troubridge expected the *Goeben* to steam up the Adriatic back to Pola, and was positioned for interception. Instead, the *Goeben* took a southeasterly course toward Greece. Troubridge had received no orders to leave his station, and was hoping to be sent a battle cruiser. In the early hours of August 7, he decided on his own initiative to pursue. At 2:45 A.M., one of his officers asked: "Are you going to fight, sir? Because if so, the squadron ought to know."

"Yes," replied Troubridge. "I know it is wrong, but I cannot have the name of the whole Mediterranean Squadron stink."

But an hour later, having received no reply from Milne, he called off the chase.

He had become convinced that if he engaged the German ships in broad daylight, his smaller vessels would be picked off one by one while the *Goeben* remained outside the range of the 9.2-inch British guns. By 6 A.M., the fastest capital ship in the Mediterranean was steaming an unobstructed course for the Dardanelles.[15]

Three days later, the *Goeben* and the *Breslau* were anchored off Constantinople. Their arrival was hailed by the Turks as proof of German naval superiority. The Kaiser at once offered the ships to the Turkish Navy, to make up for the two dreadnoughts that Churchill had embargoed. It was a stunning military and diplomatic coup, although Asquith tended to think that it did not much matter, since the inexperienced Turkish crew could only navigate the *Goeben* on rocks or minefields.[16] Still, Churchill's mouth had watered for the *Goeben*, in vain.

Jacky Fisher was appalled. The wording of the telegram to Milne should have read "Haul down your flag and come on shore!" He and Troubridge should both be shot *pour encourager les autres* (to encourage the others). After the next naval battle in the Mediterranean, no doubt the telegram they would get at the Admiralty would read:

> *"The French Admiral shot himself*
> *The English Admiral 'shit' himself."*[17]

The *Goeben*'s escape seemed to Churchill the omen of a sinister fatality. The terrible "if's" accumulated: if they had opened fire on the afternoon of August 4, if they had been less solicitous of Italian neutrality, if the Admiralty had sent Milne more forceful instructions on the fifth, if Troubridge had not been afraid to fight . . . things might have been different.[18] For the most combative of ministers, to whom prudence was "that ugly old maid, courted by incapacity," his admirals' timorousness was an insult. He placed the blame on Milne for not having telegraphed: "I believe *Goeben* is at Messina. Submit since she has entered Italian territorial waters I may follow her, observing that otherwise I shall be much hampered in my operations."

But Milne had only followed orders. In fact, the blame was the Admiralty's, for not voiding its Italian neutrality telegram and for not giving precise orders to track down the *Goeben* as soon as she was reported at Messina. Churchill's forcefulness and spirit of initiative as First Lord made the admirals particularly careful of observing the chain of command and not acting on their own, but in this case the Admiralty drifted and then Churchill blamed Milne for not soliciting the orders he should have been sent.

Although absolved of misconduct, Milne was ordered to strike his flag and got no further command. Troubridge went before a court-martial and was acquitted, although his conduct was described by a court of inquiry as "deplorable and unworthy of the traditions of the Service." His career at sea was ended, and his next assignment was to accompany a shipment of naval guns to Serbia.[19]

The lesson of the *Goeben* was that war was not like maneuvers. The dreadnoughts might be built, the fleets might be at their war stations, the naval might of Britain might be at its most impressive state of readiness, but inexperience, human error, and the unexpected factors of this new war would jam the finely tuned machinery. All this came home to Churchill in the midst of the *Goeben* chase as the details of the first naval disaster of the war arrived at the Admiralty.

Patrolling the approaches of the Channel, the light cruiser *Amphion* had sighted the German minelayer *Königen Luise* at 11 A.M. on August 5 and sunk her, taking survivors on board. Returning triumphantly to her base, the *Amphion* hit one of the mines laid by the ship she had just sunk and went down with a loss of one officer and 150 men.[20] Churchill was shocked by the indiscriminate scattering of contact mines about the seas, which might just as easily destroy peaceful merchantmen flying neutral flags and carrying supplies to neutral countries as enemy warships. Such methods were indeed disconcerting.

In the meantime, all over Europe, millions of men were converging and forming into lines of battle: across Rhine bridges and along French roads, from the sunny Midi northward, from the Russian steppe westward, from the cold German plain southward, from the British Isles eastward. Wonder of wonders: when the troops and reservists marched through Belfast to embark on August 5, Churchill's name was cheered wildly. Differences were sunk in defense of the country. In joining a world war, England was saved from the threat of civil war.

On August 5, the newly formed War Council met at 10 Downing Street at 4 P.M. to answer this simple question: How should the war be fought? Sir John French, the field marshal commanding the British Expeditionary Force, said the troops would be ready to leave in a few days. Known for his boldness and bad temper, French had been a cavalry general in the Boer War, galloping through enemy lines to relieve Kimberley. The plan was, French said, that the five divisions of the BEF should concentrate behind the French at Maubeuge by the fifteenth day of mobilization. But Maubeuge was right on the border, and French preferred Amiens, about sixty miles from the border. As an alternative he was inclined to consider a landing at Antwerp with a view to cooperating with the Belgians and the Dutch. This was a startling suggestion for the commander of the BEF to make. It would mean improvising a new campaign and jettisoning years of staff work. Churchill pointed out that Antwerp was a different proposition entirely. The Navy could carry troops to French Channel ports in its protected sea lanes. But it could not protect the passage of transports across the North Sea and up the Scheldt River to Antwerp.

General Sir Charles Douglas, Chief of the Imperial General Staff, said that all plans were ready for landings at French Channel ports. A change of destination at the last moment would be grave.[21]

Kitchener had by this time taken over at the War Office. Sitting at his desk on August 6, he held a broken pen before his secretary and said: "Dear me, what a place. Not a scrap of Army. Not even a pen that will write."[22] Soon, the Alfred Leete poster appeared on the hoardings: the flinty eyes, the mustache that hid the mouth, the outstretched arm and the pointing index finger: "Your Country Needs YOU."

On August 6, Kitchener called on Churchill to discuss the carrying of the troops. What would happen if the Germans made a dash into the Channel, attacking the transports with their fast ships? Their movements would be known in time to hold back the transports until they had been dealt with, Churchill assured him. What of the danger of submarines? Kitchener asked. The danger would be less at night than during the day, Churchill said. Without further discussion, Kitchener turned to General Douglas and ordered him to suspend day crossings.

Churchill was impressed. Here was a man ready to take unlimited responsibility, ready to give an important order by word of mouth as if on the field of battle, but who also had a limited knowledge of his job, never having before exercised command in Europe. Looking into the matter, Churchill found that because of the railway timetables, night crossings would take twice as long. The risk of submarines would have to be faced, he told Kitchener.[23]

This was the honeymoon period between the heads of the two service departments. The Secretary of War held out the hand of friendship, asking Churchill to address him as just plain Kitchener, dropping the Lord. Churchill was still estranged from his cousin Sunny. Since the incident over Lloyd George, he and Clemmie had not been spending Christmas holidays at Blenheim. He asked Kitchener to find Sunny some sort of army job, and Kitchener did—Special Messenger at the War Office. Churchill knew the two departments would pull well together. Kitchener said they were only one department really.[24]

On August 7, sitting in on his first War Council meeting, Kitchener had some sobering thoughts. It was his belief that the war would not be short. It would only be ended by great land battles on the Continent. Millions of men would have to be put into the field. He would form six new divisions, all volunteers. Conscription was a dirty word. England had fielded a volunteer army ever since the Duke of Wellington had ordained that recruits for foreign service "must be volunteers." Kitchener wanted nothing to do with the Territorials, and would create a new army. The Territorials were "a town clerk's army." As an observer in the war of 1870 he had seen French Territorials routed. In any case, at the moment they had more men than weapons to arm them with. Eager recruits were being handed staves to march with.[25]

In the most notable British naval feat of the war, not a shot was fired. Between August 12 and 22, in an unbroken bridge of ships that spanned the Channel, the Navy ferried across 80,000 men, 30,000 horses, 315 field guns, and 125 machine guns. Not a single man or a single horse was lost. For Churchill, it was a period of acute tension. Every day he expected to hear that ships had been blown up by mines or sunk by submarines. Incredibly, and in spite of German agents and reconnaissance planes, the secret of the ten-day passage was kept.

On August 13, General Sir Henry Wilson, leaving for France, called on Churchill to say farewell. They had never been afraid to cross swords, he said, but Churchill had behaved like a hero on August 5 when he urged the immediate dispatch of the BEF. Wilson's departure brought home the great troop movement that was under way, and Churchill broke down and wept.[26] By August 14, Sir John French had reached Amiens, and the five British divisions were assembling. By August 21, the German high command still doubted that any significant move of British troops had taken place.

Lurking behind Germany's commitment to its Austro-Hungarian ally were hopes of territorial expansion, while the French wanted revenge for 1870, and the return of Alsace-Lorraine. The British were fighting not to change the boundaries of Europe but to preserve the balance of power. In coming to the aid of a tiny ally, Britain appeared to be acting in a gallant and selfless manner and conforming to a chivalric ideal that appealed to the idealistic young men who shrugged off their university robes and their factory smocks and lined up by the thousands at recruiting offices in the East End, the West End, and all over England. The spectacle of a million men volunteering in the first eighteen months of the war almost made one forget that there was a ruling class; the son of a lord might serve in the same battalion as a coal miner, and be killed by his side. To die for a noble cause abolished class differences.

Kitchener had more volunteers than he could arm and train. The fever to serve that swept the country, the eagerness and lightness of heart with which so many volunteered seem baffling unless one remembers the century of popular chivalry that saturated British life. Young men went to war, as had medieval knights, in the belief that it was a proving ground for nobility. Rupert Brooke wrote:

Now God be thanked who has matched us with His hour
And caught our youth, and waken'd us from sleeping . . .

God be thanked . . . the prevailing sentiment was gratitude. They were grateful for the chance to go to France and be killed in trenches, although they had no inkling of the horror to come. Francis Grenfell, a thirty-four-year-old lieutenant, embarked with his twin brother, Riversdale, or "Rivy," on August 15. His regiment was the 9th Lancers, which had fought at Omdurman in 1898. An older brother, Robert Grenfell, had fallen in that fray. Francis Grenfell wrote Churchill, who was a friend of the family, that they were leaving with great enthusiasm. He could hardly believe his good fortune at being a soldier. They must once again teach these foreigners what a great nation they were and what "England" meant.[27] There it was: they were not fighting for gain but for an abstract conception of their country. Francis Grenfell won the Victoria Cross at Messines and was killed at Ypres on May 13, 1915. Rivy Grenfell was killed less than a month after leaving England, on September 11, 1914.

Another pair of Grenfell brothers, Julian and Billy, cousins of the twins, two more eager young warriors, also left for France. It was the best fun one could dream of, Julian wrote home, like a picnic without the objectlessness of a picnic. He had never been so well or happy. He adored war. There was a sincerity, a truth to war that he had not found elsewhere, and always something to joke about. Passing some soldiers, the driver of one of the London buses that Churchill had sent over, with all the playbills and ads still on them, called out, "Oxford Street, Bank." Julian laughed when he heard a corporal say: "What tires me in this bloody country is Jesus Christ and all his relatives in glass cases at every bloody corner." His brother Billy saw, as he tramped through the Lowlands, Hobbema landscapes.[28] What an echo of upbringing there was in that—Eton, Oxford, a country house full of heirlooms, a life devoted to the appreciation of fine things.

Julian Grenfell, elder son of the 1st Baron Desborough, and author of the famous poem "Into Battle," was killed on May 26, 1915, at the age of twenty-seven. His brother, Billy, was killed on July 30, 1915. The Grenfells were one English family, not atypical, among thousands. Death at an early age seemed inconsequential. Parents would live into old age as if they had inherited their sons' normal life-spans. "None of us who give our sons in this war," said Sir Edward Grey, "are so much to be pitied as those who have no sons to give."[29]

Those who would mourn and grieve, and would later lead England into appeasement because they had never come to terms with the death of their sons, were eager to send them into battle. Churchill identified closely with this attitude—how he wished he could be at the front fighting—which was translated by the generals, those accountants of death, in terms of "intake" and "outgo."

While Churchill conducted the naval war, Clemmie and the children stayed at the cottage in Cromer. She knew that Winston was under a strain, and told him to get to bed before midnight, not to wake up each time a Belgian killed a German, and not to smoke too much. Invasion jitters were causing tourists to flee the seaside resort, to the distress of landladies and shopkeepers. Local authorities flashed this message on the local cinema screen: "Visitors! Why are you leaving Cromer? Mrs. Winston Churchill and her children are in residence in the neighborhood. If it's safe enough for her, surely it's safe enough for you!"[30]

Robert Houston, a wealthy shipowner and Tory MP, and an admirer of Churchill and his beautiful wife, sent Clemmie as a patriotic compliment an emerald-and-diamond ring that she priggishly returned, thinking what an illogical world it was: because she had a Pig who was a genius and a "Poodle-Ching," she was given a costly jewel, where if she had an inferior husband and needed consolation she would get nothing. Winston was proud of her high and inflexible principles.[31]

Clemmie's mother, Blanche, came to stay at Cromer because Dieppe was not safe. Nellie, Clemmie's sister, went to France to get Blanche and then left for Belgium to join a nursing unit. Clemmie was furious; she had been counting on Nellie's help. This running off to Belgium was all cheap emotion, she was not trained, she would be just another mouth to feed, she should have stayed, instead of dumping Blanche on her when she was one month away from giving birth. What a tax on the nerves it was! She longed to put her arms around Winston's neck; he would calm her hurt and angry feelings. Nellie had not been at the front two weeks when she was taken prisoner in Mons.[32]

Still sore about the *Goeben*, Churchill wanted to sink her in Constantinople's harbor. Could not a torpedo flotilla be sent into the Dardanelles? he asked at a Cabinet meeting on August 17. Kitchener and the others were against it. They should wait for the Turks to make the first move. Grey still hoped for Turkish neutrality.

Asquith was rather bored with all the details about the war at the August 21 Cabinet meeting. The divisiveness of the Cabinet was annoying. Everyone had an axe to grind. Kitchener felt that Rumania was the pivot of the situation, while Masterman (now Chancellor of the Duchy of Lancaster) thought Bulgaria was the key. Lloyd George was keen for a Balkan federation. Grey was judicious, Haldane was misty, Simon was uninspiring, Hobhouse was assertive and irrelevant, and Runciman was instructive and juiceless.[33] Winston was violently anti-Turk, jumping from topic to topic, Hobhouse thought, backing and filling without rhyme or reason. Asquith, although against aggressive action in Turkey, was moved to comment: "A very queer set of people, these Turks."[34]

On August 23, for the first time since the eighteenth century, British and German soldiers fought, between Mons and the French border. At 7 A.M. the next morning, Churchill was sitting up in bed at Admiralty House going through his boxes when his bedroom door opened and Kitchener appeared, holding a slip of paper in his hand. Churchill watched his gigantic frame poised in the doorway and knew that something was wrong. There was a distortion in his face, as if it had been punched. "Bad news," he said, laying the telegram on Churchill's bed. Namur, pivot of the allied line, had fallen. Sir John French and his five divisions, in battle for only a day, were in full retreat.[35]

Churchill found it hard to believe that Namur had been taken in a single day. If strong fortresses melted like wisps of vapor in the morning sun, where would it stop? What of the naked Channel ports, Dunkirk, Calais, Boulogne? Poor Kitchener! It was like seeing old John Bull on the rack![36]

Shaken by the army reverse, Churchill felt an intense need to see his old comrade-in-arms Lloyd George, to be buoyed up by his sense of purpose, so he walked across the Horse Guards Parade to the tunnel entrance of the Treasury Board Room. Lloyd George was in conference but came out when Churchill beckoned. They went into an adjoining room, and Churchill was heartened by his friend's resolute confidence. Here was the Lloyd George of the Mansion House speech, sure that Britain would triumph.[37]

As the British retreat continued through August 24 and 25, Churchill wondered what he could do, and thought of his Naval Division. This unit, known as "Churchill's Pets," had been hastily formed in the first weeks of August from the thousands of leftover naval reserves for whom there was no room at sea. It was intended as a sort of commando force that could seize and hold temporary bases the fleet might need, but it was soon labeled Churchill's private army. A free-floating unit of two Naval Brigades and one Marine Brigade, the division recruited on the principle of *la carrière ouverte aux talents* (unrestricted placement). Every friend of Churchill's with a son or a nephew to place found an opening. Even his ex-stepfather, George Cornwallis-West, joined, as did some of Eddie Marsh's friends, notably Rupert Brooke. The Royal Naval Division was formed to fight on land but had nautical customs and a hybrid khaki uniform with a seamanlike shape. Bells recorded the passage of time, and to leave their camp the recruits asked for leave to go ashore. When they returned, they came aboard, and when they did not, they were reported as adrift. The Army was clean-shaven, but Churchill's Pets could ask for "leave to grow." When ill they attended sick bay.[38]

Not everyone at the Admiralty thought the Royal Naval Division was a good idea. Captain Herbert Richmond, the Assistant Director of Operations, called its members a bunch of undisciplined amateurs. Soon there would be a shortage of seamen and here was Churchill training troops. "I really believe Churchill is not sane," Richmond wrote in his diary on August 20. ". . . What this force is to do, Heaven only knows . . . The whole thing is so wicked that Churchill ought to be hanged before he should be allowed to do such a thing."[39]

On August 26, Churchill sent the Marine Brigade of three thousand men to Ostend, supported by four battleships, to create the illusion that British reinforcements were about to land en masse in Belgium. After an aimless week of patrols and digging trenches, they went home.

At the August 26 Cabinet meeting, Churchill raised the delicate matter of conscription. He felt it was essential if defeat was to be avoided. Why should the married Territorials be sent to the front while unmarried young men who had not volunteered did nothing for their country but loaf and cheer? The rest of the Cabinet listened to his harangue, much bored. Asquith said conscription would divide the party and the country from one end to the other. Lloyd George said the people would not listen. Kitchener said he had 120,000 men although he had asked for only 100,000, but that conscription might come later.[40] In addition, he was sending the last division of the professional Army, the 6th, to reinforce French. Churchill had assured him that the Navy alone could secure England against invasion.

In the first three weeks of war, the Grand Fleet under Jellicoe was almost continually at sea, making sweeps through the North Sea and daring the Germans to come out and fight. But the German High Seas Fleet did not venture forth. The Grand Fleet was an awe-inspiring sight: twenty battleships in five columns, zigzagging at eighteen knots from starboard to port with military precision, each column screened against submarine attacks by destroyers and preceded by light cruisers covering a 120-mile front. But the strain of seeking the Germans and not finding them was heavy. Aboard the battle cruiser *Lion*, Admiral Beatty was bored and disappointed. For thirty years he had been waiting for the day, and now, after three weeks, not a single German had come out to be whacked.[41]

Commodore Roger Keyes, the head of the submarine unit, had been penetrating German waters and going up into the mouths of German rivers, gathering information about enemy movements and systems of defense. On August 23 he proposed a combined attack of submarines and destroyers in the Heligoland Bight, an indentation of Germany's north coast, where the bulk of the German fleet was anchored. They would take advantage of the German practice of sending out their light cruisers to meet the returning destroyer guard at daybreak, ambush them, and hopefully stir the Germans into action.[42]

On August 28, with the North Sea overcast and gloomy, Keyes's submarines and Commodore Reginald Tyrwhitt's flotilla of sixteen destroyers moved into the Bight. Tyrwhitt's flagship, the *Arethusa*, had left the building yard only three days before. Beatty's 1st Battle Cruiser Squadron was in support, forty miles away. Almost everything that could go wrong did. At 6 A.M., alarmed by submarine movements, the Germans sent out their 5th Destroyer Flotilla. At thirty-four hundred yards, the *Arethusa* opened fire on the *Frauenlob*, and all but one of her 6-inch guns jammed. She was hit in the engine room but kept firing until the *Frauenlob*, also hit, retired. Because of faulty communications and bad visibility, there were hair-raising errors of identity. One of Keyes's submarines attacked a British light cruiser, but no damage was done. In the midst of the confusion, the German counterattack came at 11 A.M. The situation was not promising. The small British force was outnumbered and outgunned. Four German cruisers were converging on the crippled *Arethusa*.[43]

Out of the mists in the northwest appeared the providential shapes of Beatty's battle cruisers. Beatty had worried about bringing his fine ships into such a hornet's nest. The loss of a capital ship meant an automatic court-martial, but he had to risk it. To Oswald Frewen, Churchill's first cousin (his mother was Jennie's sister), serving aboard a destroyer, the battle cruisers were like elephants marching through a pack of hounds, great and grim and uncouth. Their big guns blazing, they quickly dispatched three cruisers and a number of destroyers, with a loss of more than a thousand officers and men, including two flag officers. Then Beatty gave the order to retire, to tow his lame ducks out of the Bight. British casualties were thirty-five killed, and Beatty returned to his base without the loss of a ship.[44]

After the retreat from Mons, this was heady stuff. With amazing boldness, a raiding party had knocked on the German front door and found it ajar. The fighting took place twenty miles from the main German naval base. The whole High Seas Fleet could hear the boom of the guns. Admiral von Tirpitz' son was among the prisoners. The Kaiser did not want losses of this sort and restricted the fleet's movements. There was a parting of the ways with Tirpitz, who complained that his Navy was being muzzled.

Victory though it was, the Battle of Heligoland Bight showed up a dismal failure in staff work. Churchill's much-vaunted Naval War Staff existed on paper only. Ships had failed to report the enemy's and their own positions. There was no coordination of strategy among naval units. A brand-new ship like the *Arethusa* should never have been sent into battle.

All that was forgotten in the glee of the moment. When Tyrwhitt brought the damaged *Arethusa* into Sheerness, an overjoyed Churchill "slobbered all over" him and offered him any ship he wanted.[45]

On the very day that the battle raged off the German coast, a verbal battle was fought in the paneled hall of the Carlton Club, a Tory sanctuary, between the embittered retired Admiral Lord Charles Beresford and an Army colonel and Conservative MP, Arthur Lee. The conversation had turned to German spies, and Beresford said that all Germans, including highly placed ones, ought to leave the country, as they were in close touch with Germans abroad.

"Prince Louis is the First Sea Lord," Lee said. "Do you suggest that he should be removed?"

"No," Beresford said, "his good taste should tell him to resign." He was an exceedingly able officer, Beresford went on, but nothing could alter the fact that he was German, and as such should not be occupying his present position. Why, he kept German servants and owned property in Germany.

Lee protested that Prince Louis was as loyal and patriotic as Beresford himself.

"I admit all that," Beresford said, "but nonetheless he is a German and he entered the Navy for his own advantage, not for ours. Feeling is very strong in the Service about his being First Sea Lord. It is strongly resented."

When Lee expressed surprise at such a statement, Beresford said: "If things went badly at sea, as they well may, there would be a howl in the country and the mob would attack Prince Louis' house and break his windows."

Lee expressed total disagreement with Beresford's views, which he reported to Churchill, who wrote Beresford a warning letter on August 29: Spreading reports to cause mistrust or despondency in time of war was a military offense. Unless he received an absolute retraction and a written promise not to repeat the offense that same day he would take serious action.[46]

Beresford lamely explained that all he had done was express regret about Prince Louis' German birth, and Churchill let the matter drop. But the Prince's days were numbered. Already, in that scurrilous publication *John Bull*, he was routinely referred to as "the GermHun."

Churchill soon found himself arbitrating another personality conflict, this time between Sir John French and Lord Kitchener. In seven days, French had been pushed back 150 miles, nearly to the suburbs of Paris. On August 30, under the headline "BROKEN BRITISH REGIMENTS," a *Times* correspondent wrote: "Our losses are very great. I have seen the broken bits of many regiments." On August 31, French telegraphed that his troops were "shattered." He intended to fall back behind Paris, and refused to cooperate further with the French.

Asquith called a midnight conference of ministers, fearing a complete breakdown of the Anglo-French alliance. The only thing to do was send Kitchener right away to unravel the situation and put the fear of God into them all. Kitchener was a real sportsman, thought Asquith, he went straight home to change his clothes and collect his kit and started by special train from Charing Cross at 1:30 A.M. Churchill had a fast cruiser waiting for him at Dover.[47]

The change of clothes turned out to be the sticking point, for Kitchener showed up in Paris wearing his field marshal's uniform. To French, also a field marshal, this was an affront meant to show that he was no longer trusted.

Trying to mediate between the two field marshals, Churchill wrote French on September 2 that the Cabinet had been bewildered by his intention to retire from the line, coming as it did on top of a casualty list of six thousand and French's previous reports that the spirit of the troops was good. They wondered whether he had quarreled with Joffre, and felt that a personal consultation was indispensable.

Not at all, French replied, he was on the best of terms with Joffre, but Kitchener's visit had been most unfortunate. He had been dragged away from the front on a critical day. He begged Churchill to do his utmost to stop this interference with field operations. Kitchener knew nothing about European warfare.[48]

At this low point for the Army, with the names of the dead published daily in the London newspapers, the situation improved. On September 3, even as the commander in chief was complaining about Kitchener's meddling, French and British forces drove across the Marne. The Germans were overextended, having diverted troops to meet a Russian penetration into East Prussia. In five days of hard fighting, the French and the BEF drove them back from Paris. The chance to fell France with a single blow was lost.

Field Marshal Alfred von Schlieffen's plan, designed for war on two fronts, which called for a gigantic flanking movement to defeat France in six weeks, so that German troops could mass against Russia, could not be carried out. Moltke stopped his troops for two days on the Marne, and the course of the war was changed.

It was five days of simple hell for the Germans, French informed Churchill. What a change to be pursuing instead of pursued! Joffre's strategy had been just right.[49]

In 1911, Churchill had forecast that on the fortieth day after the German push, they would be beaten back. In fact, the decisive battle took place on the thirty-third day. Jacky Fisher, another writer of prophecies, thought that Churchill's accuracy was astonishing. Balfour thought it was a triumph. But when he dined with Asquith and Churchill on September 8, the Tory leader found the First Lord full of hyperbole, talking airily of a British Army of a million men, and of making siege mortars bigger than the German ones in order to crush the Rhine fortresses.[50] The need for a large army, which Churchill had seen from the first, but which would require conscription, was still repugnant to most British statesmen.

While the war was being fought on land, Churchill's fertile mind turned on operations that would involve the Navy. One possibility was an attack on the Gallipoli Peninsula, at the entrance of the Dardanelles. Major General Charles Callwell, Director of Military Operations and Intelligence at the War Office, informed Churchill that such an attack would be extremely difficult. It had been examined in 1906 and declared unfeasible. The garrison on the peninsula was estimated at twenty-seven thousand men with 136 guns, and the Turks could easily bring up reinforcements from the mainland. It could not be done with less than sixty thousand men.[51] Also, Turkey was now clearly in German hands, and the Gallipoli troops might be strengthened by Germans.

Gallipoli was momentarily forgotten as Churchill turned his attention to the Channel ports. What if the Germans in their retreat made a dash for Calais or Dunkirk? At the end of August, he had sent Commander Charles Samson to Dunkirk to set up an air base for shooting down German Zeppelins on their way to England. The daring young men who had been his instructors at Eastchurch made occasional sorties, dropping one or two bombs, which often did not explode. Aerial warfare was becoming accepted as useful, and the same people who had once scorned the airplane now expected it to work wonders. As Lieutenant Richard Davies said: "They have pissed on Churchill's plant for three years—now they expect blooms in a month."[52]

On September 10, Churchill made a secret visit to France to inspect his flying base. A few days later, he sent the Marine Brigade, just back from its week at Ostend, to Dunkirk on another "show the flag" mission. Kitchener contributed a regiment of Yeomanry, the Oxfordshire Hussars, in which Churchill's brother, Jack, and his cousin Sunny were serving. Helping out this family enterprise, Churchill gave the Hussars a fleet of trucks and armored cars from naval stores, which did not endear him to the War Office. Adding to the unit's *panache* were fifty double-decker London buses, following up the success of the Marne taxis. Asquith had little faith in the fighting powers of the Oxfordshire Yeomanry. He hoped they would meet no Germans, and would follow the example of the good old Duke of York, who led his men to the top of a hill and led them down again.[53] The interservice mix of Marines, air squadrons, and Yeomanry soon became known as "Churchill's Dunkirk Circus."

Five days later, he went to France again, at Kitchener's request, to convince French to move his army from its position north of Paris to its "natural station" on the Channel coast, in contact with the Royal Navy. Sitting on a haystack near Soissons with Major General Sir Henry Rawlinson, commander of the 4th Division, Churchill watched the fire of the French artillery, the planes threading their way among the smoke puffs, and the big black German shells bursting near the ridge where the British batteries were dug in. It was his first taste of the war, and he was thrilled. French agreed to the new strategy, perhaps because Churchill rather than the hated Kitchener suggested it.[54] Through his force of intellect and character, Churchill dominated the rather humdrum French, and Kitchener soon began to see in the First Lord a meddler challenging his own authority.

Returning to naval matters on September 17, Churchill visited the Grand Fleet at its fueling station on the western coast of Scotland, Loch Ewe. As he reviewed the fleet, he heard Commodore Keyes, one of the heroes of the Heligoland Bight, comment on the "live-bait squadron." What was that? he asked. Only some old cruisers of the Bacchantes class, Keyes said, that were patrolling near the Dogger Bank, a sandbank in the North Sea between England and Denmark, and in the "Broad Fourteens" off the Dutch coast. Keyes had long thought they were sitting ducks for the Germans. They hadn't fired their guns in years and were manned in the most extraordinary way. Twice he had gone to the Admiralty and protested, but back they always came, parading up and down the Broad Fourteens, surrounded by Dutch fishing craft—often within sight of Holland. You could set your watch by their movements! He had begged the War Staff to believe they were a gift to a German submarine. What good could they do? Keep the Scheldt open, came the answer. Who wants to block the Scheldt? Keyes responded—not the Germans; their one object was to preserve Dutch neutrality. So they gave him some wild story that had to do with ships filled with sand at Hamburg.

Appalled at the risk, Churchill wrote Prince Louis on the eighteenth: "The *Bacchantes* ought not to continue on this beat. The risk to such ships is not justified by any services they can render. The narrow seas, being the nearest point to the enemy, should be kept by a small number of good modern ships. The *Bacchantes* should go to the western entrance of the Channel . . ."[55]

On September 19, bad weather forced the destroyers that normally protected the *Bacchantes* squadron into harbor, while the three cruisers, the *Aboukir*, *Cressy*, and *Hogue*, were ordered away from the Dogger Bank to patrol the Broad Fourteens without their flotilla screen. On September 22, the sea subsided. A German submarine, prowling down the Dutch shoreline, spotted the cruisers steaming along placidly, one behind the other, at under ten knots. At 6:30 A.M., a torpedo struck the *Aboukir*. Some of her lifeboats were destroyed by the explosion, and hundreds of men jumped into the water or clung to the wreckage. With heedless chivalry, the *Cressy* and the *Hogue* came to a standstill a few hundred yards away and lowered their boats. The same submarine sank first the *Hogue* and then the *Cressy*. The old cruisers were of no value, but like all Third Fleet ships, they were manned by reservists, mostly married men, and young cadets from Osborne, posted to low-risk ships that would not be engaged in great battles. Of some twenty-two hundred men on board the three cruisers, more than fourteen hundred died.[56] Captain R. W. Johnson, in command of the *Cressy*, had known what he was in for, Keyes reflected. They had all known it was only a matter of days— they were bound to get it in the end on such a ridiculous parade.

The U-boat commander, Lieutenant Otto Weddigen, was proclaimed a national hero. He and his twenty-five men were awarded the Iron Cross. What sort of fame was it, Churchill wondered, to have with his own fingers destroyed fourteen hundred lives? A Court of Inquiry was convened, and the two rear admirals responsible for the patrol, Arthur Christian and Henry Campbell, were placed on half-pay. In the meantime, Thomas Gibson Bowles, the editor of a scandal sheet called *Candid Quarterly Review*, published a brochure charging that "despite the warnings of admirals, commodores and captains, Mr. Churchill refused, until it was too late, to recall [the cruisers] from a patrol so carried on as to make them certain to fall victims to the torpedoes of an active enemy." This was patently false, but it was widely believed, and because the information on an operation of war was classified, there was nothing Churchill could say in his defense. In the Cabinet, his only comment on the three lost cruisers was: "very provoking." If only his observations on other matters were equally brief, thought Hobhouse, they would get through the day's business much more easily.[57] To Asquith, it was the worst news since the start of the war. To have lost three good and powerful cruisers of an old but not obsolete type was a blow because the Navy in general was not doing well. Too many British merchantmen were being sunk. The Admiralty had not been clever in its outlying strategy.[58] Churchill was always off to France on some furtive mission; he was never around when he was needed, as when, on September 22, the Cabinet learned that New Zealand would not send its expeditionary force to Europe unless the British provided a destroyer escort. How irritating it was!

The plight of the cadets, some of whom went to sea at fourteen, was particularly striking to Lord Crewe, who was now at the India Office, and who asked Churchill if something could be done to keep them off warships. In the old days, the midshipmen could take their chances of being hit by a round shot or piked in a boarding attack. But in these days of mines and submarines, when ships went down with all hands, it was painful to have the poor lads aboard. What could they do on board a big cruiser or battleship beyond improving their knowledge of navigation and gunnery? It seemed a terrible waste.[59]

Churchill disagreed. The boys wanted the experience of being at sea, where they rendered useful service. This was an ancient custom of the Navy, supported by naval opinion. He had actually received deputations of parents asking that their fourteen-year-old midshipmen sons be given the same conditions of service as the other sailors. He could not in any case see much difference between the tragedy of a young life cut off at fourteen and one cut off at seventeen, the normal recruiting age. The lads would be kept at sea to take their chances, and he hoped that not all days would be as fatal as September 22. In the future, ships would be ordered to steam away in opposite directions rather than go to the rescue of their comrades, and sailors would be issued rubber bladders (an early version of the life preserver) to keep them afloat in the water.[60]

After the action in the Heligoland Bight, the German fleet stayed in its harbors. The big battle that Churchill hungered for did not come. Despondent at the inactivity, officers feared a drop in morale. On the eve of the *Bacchantes* disaster, Churchill gave vent to his frustration at a recruiting rally in Liverpool, saying that "although we hope the Navy will have a chance of settling the question of the German Fleet, yet if they do not come out and fight in time of war they will be dug out like rats in a hole." It was time for plain speaking, he thought, and he was cheered wildly.[61] But in more exalted circles, the remark seemed ill-judged, particularly when on the following day the rats did come out of their hole and sank three ships. King George V thought the phrase had been unfortunate and undignified.[62]

Churchill's relations with his sovereign were strained. There was in him a touch of Randolph's congenital rebelliousness to the Crown, expressed in small things, such as insisting on naming a ship after Cromwell. His worst offense, however, was his loose tongue. The King had once confided to Churchill that although he respected Asquith, the Prime Minister was "not quite a gentleman." Churchill promptly repeated the remark to Asquith, which George V thought was a monstrous thing to do. Thereafter, nothing could shake him from the conviction that Churchill was irresponsible and unreliable, and something always seemed to come up, such as the "rats in a hole" speech, to confirm his opinion. Another point of friction was naval decorations. The King wanted sailors to wait until the war was over. Churchill argued that a man might be dead by then, and that bravery should be rewarded after each action, as was done in the Army, rather than posthumously. The King reluctantly agreed.[63]

On September 26, Churchill was off to France again. His trips across the Channel and his marginal "circus" operations were seen by some members of the Cabinet as signs of chronic restlessness and irresponsibility. Why didn't he stay in his Admiralty office where he belonged? Why, he went to France more often than Kitchener, who was supposed to be running the Army. But because of his forays, Churchill, alone in the Cabinet, had a personal experience of the war and knew that it was not like previous wars. The war of movement was settling into a war of position, where cavalry units were useless and artillery fire was paramount. To challenge German artillery, he offered Kitchener naval guns that would outrange the German heavy howitzers. Surely it was wrong to have to oppose flesh and blood to German cannon when they could match them with naval artillery. But the offer was never taken up.[64]

Once again offering political advice, Clemmie urged Churchill to be sure to tell Asquith about his trips, or he would be displeased and hurt. He must also consult Kitchener, or else each trip would be like a weekend jaunt rather than a mission. What would Churchill think if Kitchener slipped off to visit Jellicoe on his own? She wished he did not crave these trips. It made her grieve to see him so gloomy and dissatisfied with the high position he had reached, when he was the only young and vital member of the Cabinet, on whom the Prime Minister leaned more and more. It was wicked of him not to be swollen with pride at being First Lord during the greatest war since the beginning of the world. The Army was only a small fraction of the allied forces, whereas he ruled the great Navy that would decide the outcome.[65]

Taking Clemmie's advice, Churchill sent Kitchener a note asking whether he had any objection to his having a talk with General French on the general situation and on the Dunkirk business. No objection, Kitchener replied, although he was beginning to resent Churchill's outings. Churchill spent Sunday, September 27, touring the fifteen-mile-long British front on the north bank of the Aisne River. It seemed an impregnable position, protected by one thousand guns. Only three hundred yards separated the German and British trenches, and every night there was a skirmish, in which, Churchill was told, three Germans were killed for every one of theirs. After the Marne victory, General French had developed a blind faith in the inherent superiority of the British soldier. The German was more of a machine, kept in working order by a rigid system of discipline. They were not as good individual shots as the English, nor did they lay the same stress on the value of good individual shooting. Colonel Charles Bulkeley-Johnson of the Scots Greys told Churchill that he had not lived in vain, for he had seen officers and men of the Prussian Guard, an elite German corps, kneeling on the ground and begging for mercy.[66]

The Marine Brigade was moved from Dunkirk to Lille, with orders from Churchill to overwhelm some detached enemy force and "hit hard." They wandered about the countryside for a week but did not engage the enemy.

When Churchill returned to London on September 29, Asquith told him it was time to mine the neutral waters of the North Sea, without stinting, on a Napoleonic scale.[67] Churchill was reluctant, although his notions of chivalric warfare were fast vanishing. He was coming to realize that it was a dirty, ruthless war. The Germans were using the white flag of surrender as a trick, shooting the trustful British troops who came forth to take prisoners. Sir John French had to issue orders to fire on any German white flag, and Churchill gave the same order for white flags hoisted on German ships. Things had come to a pretty pass when the acknowledged emblem of surrender was habitually abused.[68]

There was something else Churchill found hard to swallow, and that was the attitude of the Dutch. By a geographical irony, German access to the sea on its greatest river, the Rhine, and Belgian access to the sea from its principal port, Antwerp, passed through Dutch waters. Antwerp could be reached only through the Dutch River Scheldt, and the Rhine meandered past Rotterdam and through half of Holland before entering Germany. From the start of the war, Churchill had wondered what the Dutch would do. What if they closed the Scheldt, blockading Antwerp, while allowing supplies for Germany up the Rhine? he asked Grey on August 5.[69]

On August 19, the British ambassador to Belgium, Sir Francis Villiers, reported that the Dutch were allowing food for Germany up the Rhine while turning back merchant ships trying to reach Antwerp.[70] Churchill's fears were confirmed. If Holland was trying to strangle its small neighbor, she would lose all claims to British sympathy. The Admiralty would be happy to keep the Scheldt open to merchant vessels.[71] But Grey feared that if Churchill started patrolling the Scheldt, Holland would become Germany's ally.

Churchill argued that a state of war with Holland was preferable to neutrality. Holland's contribution to German naval forces was negligible, but once war was declared, the British Navy could open the Scheldt and blockade the Rhine. As things stood, the supply of Antwerp required a line along the coast from an unimpeded Channel port, which could only be maintained on sufferance from the enemy. Why keep this line open when the Germans could cut it off at will with a powerful punch? The Dutch were responding to German pressure. If they had been free agents they would have been relieved of the odious task of strangling Belgium. They should be "seized by the throat" and told that Britain would keep the Scheldt open by force. It was folly to keep peace with Holland and give up the advantage of blockading the Rhine. Antwerp could not be allowed to be choked and murdered and to fall into German hands.[72]

Holding Antwerp was an article of faith for Churchill. Imbued with a sense of historical precedent, he must have remembered that during the Napoleonic Wars, the British had landed on Walcheren Island, only thirty miles from Antwerp. Their presence had been described as "a British pistol pointed at the heart of Europe." Here was a chance to aim the pistol again. There was another reason. With Brussels overrun, Antwerp had become the seat of the Belgian government. Britain had gone to war to defend Belgian neutrality, and Churchill felt strongly that Britain had a moral commitment to save Antwerp, the fall of which would leave all of Belgium at the mercy of the Germans.

Attention focused on Antwerp in the last week of September. At the August 5 War Council, Sir John French had suggested sending the BEF there. Now, after their great wheeling movement across Belgium, and having reached the suburbs of Paris, beaten back to a line fifty miles from the French capital, the Germans threw nine infantry divisions and 175 heavy guns against Antwerp, which was defended by the Belgian Field Army of eighty thousand and a garrison of seventy thousand. By September 28, the Germans were firing on the city's outer forts with seventeen-inch howitzers. What could Britain do to save the city? Having been stunned by the fall of the fortresses of Liège and Namur, Churchill had no illusions about Antwerp.

On September 30, Churchill dispatched Admiral Henry Oliver, the Director of Naval Intelligence, to destroy merchant ships at anchor in the Scheldt, for the ships would have been recovered by the Germans once they took the city.[73] In five days, placing explosive charges in the propelling machinery, Oliver destroyed thirty-eight. Churchill had also been sending guns and other matériel to Antwerp, circumventing Holland's neutrality by disguising the supplies as goods from private firms, and by using a Great Eastern Railway boat that made a regular refugee run between London and Antwerp.

Asquith was anxious. The fall of Antwerp would be a great blow. The Germans were pounding away with their big guns, and the Belgians had lost their morale and nerve and were making the most piteous appeals for help. Each German soldier was equipped with a small disk of compressed benzine, no bigger than a lead pencil, which could be thrown into houses and would flare up into a big explosive flame. There was always Winston's little army, but it would be idle butchery to send them into the inferno.[74] It was decided at a Cabinet meeting on October 1 that if the French sent a division, the British would send their 7th Division to raise the siege.

Entrenched in a triple line of forts, the Belgians defended the city. But on the night of October 2, a shocker from Ambassador Villiers reached London: the Belgian King and government had decided to leave on the following day for Ostend.[75] Once they were gone, resistance was sure to collapse. Kitchener and Grey received the news in London with consternation. Asquith was away at Cardiff giving a speech. Churchill had just left on another trip to France to review his Dunkirk Circus.

Something had to be done. Twenty miles out of London, Churchill's train was recalled. From Victoria Station, he was taken to Kitchener's house at Carlton Gardens. Kitchener feared that with Antwerp lost the Germans would sweep down the coast, take the Channel ports, and invade England. With Paris unobtainable, the Channel ports shone like bright available jewels, and the second phase of the war would begin—the race to the sea. Also, if Belgium fell unaided, other neutrals might wonder about promises of British support.

For several hours they discussed what measures to take. Churchill suggested that his Marine Brigade be sent at once to Antwerp. Since he was on his way to Dunkirk, why didn't he go to Antwerp instead, where he could report on the situation at first hand? Kitchener agreed, Grey briefed him, and once more he was off on the train to Dover.[76]

Back in London on October 3, Asquith approved of Churchill's mission. He would beard the King and his ministers and infuse into their backbone the necessary quantity of starch. How fluent was Winston in French? he wondered. If he could do justice to himself in a foreign tongue, the "Belges" would listen to a discourse the likes of which they had never heard before. Ah, well, this was but one of the many unconventional incidents of the war.[77]

Unconventional it certainly turned out to be, since Churchill remained in Antwerp four days to mastermind the military operations that might save the city, a mission that was not part of his patent as First Lord. But Churchill's impassioned defense of Antwerp, with the approval of Kitchener, Grey, and Asquith, was based on two strategic misconceptions. First, that Belgium had an independent policy and an independent Army. Instead of defending Antwerp, a pocket cut off from the rest of the allied front, the Belgians should have seen themselves as part of an overall Continental strategy and pulled back their Army to fight jointly with the French. If the Belgian Army had retreated at once to Dunkirk, it could have been saved. But the patriotic urge to defend their homeland was too great. Second, what was the point of holding a port that could not be used without violating Dutch neutrality, which Sir Edward Grey was not prepared to do? Antwerp was a poor prize, since the Scheldt remained closed. As Churchill himself had pointed out, it was too far east and impossible to hold unless it could be supplied by sea. It would have been far better to make a stand at Dunkirk or Calais, and stop the German coastal advance from a base where reinforcements and supplies could arrive across the Channel. For the Germans, the attack on Antwerp was a feint conducted with poorly trained reserve troops, to mask the main advance south of Brussels toward the coast.

In a hasty and emotional decision, Kitchener and Churchill chose to defend Antwerp. Kitchener did not consult with any member of his staff, although the decision went against orthodox army strategy, which was to defend France and avoid sideshows like Antwerp. Fearful that the loss of Antwerp could lead to the invasion of England, Kitchener momentarily departed from the Army's long-standing strategic views. Holding Antwerp was more in keeping with the Navy's strategy, which was to administer the Germans a "left hook" via Belgium or the island of Borkum. In going to Antwerp, Churchill could, for a brief time at least, combine the roles of military leader and naval strategist.

In the light of his stated wish to declare war on Holland, it must be assumed that if Antwerp could be held, Churchill hoped to force the issue of Dutch neutrality by sending supplies up the Scheldt. During the days of the crisis, however, when the arrival of British troops into the besieged city was urgently awaited, neutral waters were respected.

Learning that Churchill was on his way, the Belgian government agreed at a predawn meeting on October 3 to delay their departure. When he arrived at midday, he immediately saw the Belgian Prime Minister, Charles de Broqueville, who told him that the outer forts were falling one by one to shellfire and that the Army was dispirited. Churchill could see that the Belgian ministers were worn and weary men who would collapse unless relief from England arrived promptly. He promised to commit his entire Naval Division, while efforts were made to coordinate the arrival of British and French divisions.[78]

In a whirl of activity, Churchill propped up the Belgians, visiting the front lines and sending requests for guns and cars and two million rounds of ammunition. He was in his element, at the center of the action. Jack Seely, commanding a Canadian cavalry brigade, visited Antwerp and found him ensconced in the Hôtel Saint-Antoine, happily giving orders and eating an excellent dinner. At the Admiralty, the hypercritical Captain Richmond noted in his diary on October 4: "The 1st Lord is sending *his* army there; I don't mind his tuppenny untrained rabble going, but I do strongly object to 2000 invaluable marines being sent to be locked up in the fortress and become prisoners of war if the place is taken. . . . It is a tragedy that the Navy should be in such lunatic hands at this time."[79]

On the morning of October 4, the two Naval Brigades were roused and marched from Deal to Dover with full equipment. They had just had their antityphoid shots and were feeling wobbly. They had no bandages or medical stores. Officers had no ammunition for their revolvers. The men had no ammunition pouches, and carried cartridges loose in their trouser pockets, where they rubbed sores into legs on long marches. The ammunition not being in clips, the rifles could be used only as single-loaders. Many of the men, recruited only days before, had never fired a rifle or dug a trench. None of them had more than two days of musketry training. Included in this strange amalgam of naval reservists, Welsh miners, and the well-born off-spring of Churchill's friends were Arthur "Oc" Asquith, the Prime Minister's son; Denis Browne, a well-known London organist and composer of Latin church music; the writers A. P. Herbert and Charles Morgan; and the poet Rupert Brooke, who had the first draft of his sonnet "If I should die think only this of me" in his kit bag. Asquith worried about his son, but was pleased that Churchill had bucked up the "Belges."[80]

As the Naval Brigades left, the Marine Brigade was already in position in trenches. The line had to be held at the Nethe River to keep the Germans from shelling the city. Famed for the medieval splendor of its spires and galleries, Antwerp still had the prosperous air of a great merchant capital. A few miles away, German shells were reducing the forts to rubble, but inside the city, the shops were open and it was business as usual.

Dressed in a dark coat and box hat, and chauffeured in a Rolls-Royce, Churchill visited the defense perimeter. Large areas had been flooded to keep the Germans at bay, and the ground was too waterlogged to permit the digging of trenches. The Belgian troops were disheartened. The line was too thinly held. For the first time, in the suburb of Lierre, Churchill saw German soldiers, creeping from house to house. Discussing the situation with Belgian officers, he waved his stick and thumped the ground and asked: "Where are the bloody men?" Then it was back to his hotel for a good dinner. Things looked bright. Kitchener was sending the 7th Division, eighteen thousand good men, and Major General Sir Henry Rawlinson, whom Churchill had known since Omdurman, and with whom he had shared a haystack at Soissons, would command the Antwerp force.

In Churchill's absence, the Admiralty was in the hands of Prince Louis. He should have been getting back. He had already been criticized often enough for his jaunts to France. But he was kept in Antwerp by the promise of battle and the prospect of commanding a great army. He thought of his famous forebear, the 1st Duke of Marlborough, who had fought in Lille, not far from Antwerp, in August 1708, as besieger rather than besieged, reducing the great fortress that held the key to the French frontier.[81]

Deciding to stay and see it through, Churchill telegraphed Asquith on October 5 and offered his resignation as First Lord, provided he be given the necessary military rank. Deeply involved, he felt that his presence was necessary for a victorious result. As his replacement, he proposed Walter Runciman, President of the Board of Trade.

Asquith at once replied that he was needed at home. What a bit of tragi-comedy, he thought, that Winston, a mere lieutenant in the Hussars (actually, at the outset of war, he was a major), should ask to be in command of a distinguished major general. At the Cabinet meeting that day, when everyone, including Kitchener, asked when Churchill was coming home, Asquith read his telegram (except for the sentence about Runciman), which was greeted with Homeric laughter. Only Kitchener appeared to take the suggestion seriously and offered to promote Churchill to lieutenant general.[82]

Clemmie wondered what had gotten into her husband. His departure had been unwise in the first place, but his wild telegram was almost frivolous. His sense of proportion seemed to have deserted him. How could Antwerp be balanced in the scale of events with his responsibilities at the Admiralty? This escapade would harm him in the eyes of his colleagues and the public.[83]

The useless game of Churchill's trips was known as "'ewe-lamb' hunting," the ever-disloyal Hopwood reported to Lord Stamfordham. There was a rumor that twenty thousand marks and an Iron Cross had been put on his head. How annoyed he would be when he learned that the sum was equal only to one year's salary. Stamfordham thought Churchill was quite off his head.[84]

On the evening of October 5, the Germans attacked. The Marines stood firm, but some Belgian regiments fell back under shellfire and the Germans succeeded in crossing the Nethe. That night at the Council of Ministers, Churchill exerted himself to prevent an exodus. The Belgians were very downcast.

By the morning of October 6, the Naval Brigades had arrived, after an exhausting trip in crowded transports and trains, from which they disembarked "to port and starboard." How much quicker and easier it would have been had they sailed up the Scheldt into Antwerp. The population cheered them with cries of *"Vive les anglais"* and handed out chocolate and sardines. Rupert Brooke's unit bivouacked in the deserted garden of a château and dug latrines in the rose garden, surrounded by stone statues of Cupids and Venuses.[85]

The 7th Division was disembarking at Dunkirk and Ostend, but the promised French troops had not materialized. On the sixth, as the Naval Brigades took up their positions, the Belgian front caved in. Now within range, the Germans began to shell the city. That evening Churchill made a last tour of the trenches. Shivering in their oilskins in the severe frost, British troops cursed the First Lord as he drove by in an open touring car with a broken windshield and a driver with a bandage around his head.[86] He had to get back to London and the conduct of the Admiralty. Asquith did not trust Prince Louis and his board. Winston had done a good job of starching and ironing the "Belges" but must come home.[87]

When he arrived in London on the morning of October 7, Churchill learned that he had become the father of a redheaded daughter named Sarah. But his head was still full of Antwerp. Going at once to Downing Street, he implored Asquith not to take a conventional view of his future. Having tasted blood, he wanted to be relieved at the Admiralty and given a military command. Asquith said he was needed as First Lord, but Churchill insisted that the naval part was over. His mouth watered at the thought of Kitchener's new armies. Were those "glittering commands" to be entrusted to "dug-out trash" bred on the obsolete tactics of twenty-five years ago—mediocrities who had led a sheltered life moldering in military routine? Asquith wished he had a shorthand writer to take down the priceless stream of Winston's invective. He certainly had "a zigzag streak of lightning in the brain" that some called genius, but he also had a curious streak of schoolboy simplicity.[88]

In Antwerp, it was all over. The French, consolidating their front and protecting their Channel ports, could not divert troops to an isolated battle. The Belgian Army was in complete disarray. Left in command of the British contingent, General Archibald Paris asked for permission to evacuate the trenches on October 8. Furious, Churchill got on the phone to put the fear of God into him but later had to agree that it was the only thing to do. Antwerp was in flames. The King and his ministers had fled to Ostend.[89]

On the night of the eighth, the Royal Naval Division retreated from Antwerp in some confusion, crossing the Scheldt on pontoon bridges and marching to a suburb west of the city where they hoped to find a train.

Through a mix-up, the 1st Brigade was not given the order to retreat in time and found the route cut off. Its leader, Commodore Henderson, marched his fifteen hundred men into neutral Holland, where they were interned for the rest of the war. Among the prisoners was Charles Morgan, who in his novel *The Fountain* set a scene in a Dutch internment camp. Upon reaching the border, a lieutenant named Mawby turned to Commodore Henderson and said: "This means we shall be interned; no use for the rest of the war!" "You will obey orders," he was told. "I will be damned if I do," Mawby said. "Come on any man who will follow me." And off he went, with several dozen men—much to Churchill's delight when he heard the story.

Another group of 936 stragglers was captured on a train by the Germans. The others got away after a forced march through the night. The scene would have appealed to the Flemish painter of the fantastic, Hieronymus Bosch: the enveloping darkness lit by Antwerp in flames, and the road congested with the city's fleeing population, the old leaning on the young, priests and nuns, farmers pulling mules, children gripping their mothers' hands, copper pots jangling on the sides of carts piled high with mattresses, a great and forlorn crowd of refugees through which pushed the exhausted British troops, loaded down with boxes of ammunition and trench stores. All night they marched, for there was no train at the first place they reached, and they had to trudge on, losing all semblance of military formation, discarding their equipment, ignoring the orders of their officers. George Cornwallis-West shouted at his men that he was ashamed of their cowardice, but they were quite out of control and intent only on escaping home to England. It was, thought Rupert Brooke, like several kinds of hell. An endless white-faced procession of refugees crawled out of the city, turning for one last look at the ruined houses and dead horses, lit by an infernal glare.[90]

Upon hearing from his son a firsthand account of the rout, Asquith's amusement at the unconventional episode turned to wrath. Nothing could excuse Winston for sending in this "callow crowd of the rawest tiros." Oc said that his commander, George Cornwallis-West, was incompetent and overbearing and was hated by officers and men. It was like sending sheep to the shambles. The "Belges" had to be forced to fight at the point of a bayonet, while the Germans thundered away with their colossal howitzers. They had marched for seven or eight hours—the one thing sailors couldn't do—over cobbled roads bursting with refugees. What cruel and terrible risks! And what of the fifteen hundred who, "dead beat," had in despair crossed the border into Holland?[91]

The Prime Minister's reaction was mild compared to the press outcry. Why was Churchill directing military operations? Why had he sent untrained Naval Brigade men? It was deliberate murder. Old Tory hatreds were revived. No Cabinet minister in wartime was ever vilified as Churchill was over Antwerp. It was the first break in the political truce that had lasted since the start of the war. His closest friends in the Cabinet, Asquith and Lloyd George, joined the chorus of detractors. Lloyd George thought he had behaved in a swaggering way, posing for photographers in the midst of bursting shells, and promoting his cronies.[92] There was much muttering in the Navy. Beatty thought this flying about and putting his finger into pies that did not concern him was bound to lead to disaster. If only they had a Kitchener at the Admiralty the present state of chaos in naval affairs would not exist.[93]

A typical Tory reaction came from the distinguished mathematician and Conservative MP Joseph Larmor, who wrote Bonar Law on October 13: "I am not an admirer of Winston Churchill's brilliant though somewhat erratic and dashing genius . . . as a leader of cavalry he would have my entire confidence. But as a strategist he gives me ground for much trepidation . . . For a year past I have been accustomed to hear chaff from naval officers who are not entirely out of touch, as to when we will promote Churchill to another Cabinet office. The unfortunate phrase about 'digging them out like rats' made one smart when one read it. He might have become the German Emperor . . ." The leader of the Conservative Party replied: "I agree with the estimate you have formed of Churchill. I think he has very unusual intellectual ability, but at the same time he seems to have an entirely unbalanced mind, which is a real danger at a time like this . . ."[94]

Discouraged, Churchill unburdened himself to Haldane. Perhaps he should leave the Admiralty. The systematic undermining had hurt him. It had given a handle to his enemies and reduced his power to be useful. Haldane urged him not to go, for he was unique and invaluable, and should not pay attention to the fools who write and talk in the press.[95]

As the member of the government in charge of the Antwerp expedition, Churchill drew most of the fire. But he had gone with the full authority of the Cabinet. Kitchener was not criticized, although Kitchener had sent a division to save Antwerp, and had authorized the dispatch of the Naval Brigades. Churchill had specified that the brigades be sent "minus recruits," but this condition was ignored in the bustle of departure. His eagerness to take the initiative made him the obvious target when things went wrong.

In conclusion, the defense of Antwerp was an improvised sideshow, without a unified command. As General Rawlinson noted in his diary: "I have had a trying time under the various orders of Winston, Kitchener, and French."

The British lost 57 dead, 158 wounded, and 2,500 taken prisoner and interned. The Belgians had 20,000 men captured. Once taken by the Germans, Antwerp was no longer a factor in the war. Maurice Hankey, the secretary of the Committee of Imperial Defense, who had promoted himself to the position of military strategist, thought the defense of Antwerp had been worth it because it had delayed the enemy advance. It had not been intended as a delaying action, but now, in a classic example of excusing a mistake *post facto* by clutching at an unforeseen fringe benefit, it was justified as one. The five-day delay had given Rawlinson a chance to get his troops into position on the Yser River, barring the way to Channel ports. It had covered the retreat of the Belgian Army. Antwerp could be seen as an episode in the race to the sea. By mid-October the Germans had taken Ostend, occupying golf courses, casinos, and vacation villas. There was hard fighting on a north-south line from Ypres to Armentières. Sir John French wrote Churchill on October 25: "The Germans will never get further west."[96] He was right. The German thrust stopped at Ypres. The lines froze, and the allies kept Dunkirk and Calais. The armies settled into trenches from which they would not move for four years. On aerial photographs could be seen, snaking across France from the English Channel to the Jura Mountains, an almost unbroken line of trenches that showed up so clearly that even the latrines were visible. New combat techniques would have to be developed to end the stalemate, which Asquith called "this prolonged and bloody pull devil, pull baker business," for in trench warfare the attacker lost three times as many men as the defender. Whatever part Antwerp had played in sealing the front, the result had nothing in common with the intention.

Kitchener had invasion jitters. At a Committee of Imperial Defense meeting on October 7, the day Churchill returned from Antwerp, he pointed out the danger of a possible German invasion. If there was a general fleet action in progress away from the Channel, the German transports could then cross.

Churchill said there was no operation he would so gladly see undertaken by the Germans.

Grey said that in the event of a deadlock on the Continent, Germany could devote her energies to invasion; her transports were fitted, and she could risk one hundred thousand men.

Asquith said that if Germany could spare 100,000 men from the main theater of war, the British could withdraw an equal number to oppose them.

Churchill did not think one hundred thousand men could land. If the danger of invasion became extreme, he would lay mines along the coast.[97]

Again, at the Cabinet meeting on October 21, Kitchener expressed his fears of invasion and demanded that Churchill prepare for the contingency. Churchill defended the orthodox naval policy that the function of a great fleet was not to prevent the landing of an invading force but to strike and destroy the enemy's fleet.[98]

But that was the rub. The German fleet would not come out to be destroyed. Churchill's greatest fault was the need to be always on the attack. He did not grasp that the Grand Fleet's hold over the North Sea was an offensive act in itself. There had been no decisive battles, but the German flag had been swept from the seas. German freighters had taken refuge in neutral ports, while daily traffic between French and British ports continued uninterrupted, with transports and cargo moving across the Channel as secure as buses between Marble Arch and Hyde Park Corner. In spite of all this, at the end of October, after three months of war, the Admiralty's record was a string of misfortunes, which sapped Churchill's authority and made it appear that he had no understanding of the new naval war.

The *Goeben* had escaped, the three *Bacchantes* cruisers had been sunk, and the defense of Antwerp had failed with the loss of one-third of the Royal Naval Division. On September 20 the light cruiser *Pegasus* had been sunk off Zanzibar by the light cruiser *Königsberg*. On October 15, the cruiser *Hawke* had been torpedoed in the North Sea with a loss of five hundred lives. In October, a single German light cruiser, the *Emden*, wreaked havoc in the Indian Ocean. Coaling from captured steamers, and disguising itself with a dummy fourth smokestack when pursued, the *Emden* boldly raided Madras harbor, shelling its oil depots, and sank a merchant ship carrying two million pounds' worth of tea. That was the unkindest cut, to deprive the British of their tea. What bad luck for Winston, Asquith thought. That infernally elusive *Emden* had moved from Madras around the tip of India to the west coast, south of Bombay, mopping up six or seven merchant ships, even though hunted by two British ships and an unpronounceable Japanese cruiser (the *Chikuma*). The *Emden* was eventually sunk by an Australian cruiser in November 1915, but its adventures contributed to the growing alarm at the Navy's incompetence. Asquith also wondered about the three British submarines that had managed to slip into the Baltic, only to attack a *Danish* vessel.[99] It was one of the paradoxes of the war that the Germans were better on water and the British were better on land. At the October 15 Cabinet, when Churchill said it was impossible to control the German U-boats, Asquith outraged him by saying: "You mean we have lost command of the sea."[100]

But Asquith continued to support his First Lord. He ignored the "idiotic" critics who clamored for an expert instead of a civilian at the Admiralty, just as an expert was running the War Office. Experts were good servants but bad masters. Who else had Winston's spirit and resourcefulness? He had all kinds of schemes against submarines, such as a wire hen coop where ships at sea could take refuge from torpedo attack.[101]

Accustomed to praise for the dynamic way he handled his department, indeed needing acclaim as a man with a goiter needs iodine, Churchill was in low spirits. He knew the question was being asked: What is the Navy doing? The Army was fighting for its life while the Navy lay passive and inert except for an occasional mishap. Every hour brought the chance of some new disaster. It was a hopeless situation. He could not strike at the German fleet, and his ships were vulnerable to submarine attacks. He envied his brother, Jack, in the front line at Ypres. He wished he could be there. He would be very frightened, but he would dissemble. As things stood, he felt like a spectator, cheering the efforts of the rowers from the bank.

On October 27, another disaster came. One of the new dreadnoughts with 13.5-inch guns, the *Audacious*, hit a mine off the northern coast of Ireland, near Lough Swilly. Taken in tow by a passenger liner, the *Olympic*, she stayed afloat for eight hours and her crew of one thousand got off safely. But it was a cruel blow to lose such a vital unit. To offset the expected drop in morale, Churchill wrote Jellicoe that it was not surprising to have lost a capital ship after three months of war—the Army too was holding its own in spite of fourteen thousand killed and wounded.[102]

Jellicoe asked that the loss of the *Audacious* be kept secret, and the Cabinet met on October 28 to discuss the matter. Asquith thought it was bad policy not to take the public into one's confidence in reverses as well as successes. Lloyd George too was against concealment. How could the loss be kept secret, Hobhouse asked, when the *Olympic*, with one thousand passengers on board, had tried to tow the *Audacious* to land? Let the Germans collect their own information, Churchill said. Japan had concealed the loss of the battleship *Yashima* off Port Arthur in 1904. Backed by Kitchener, he prevailed. The news was kept quiet until November 14, when the *Philadelphia Public Ledger* published a photograph of the *Audacious* sinking, taken by one of the passengers aboard the liner.

Another passenger was Charles Schwab, chairman of the Bethlehem Steel

Corporation. The sight of the mighty dreadnought sinking so impressed him that he pledged the support of his factories to the allied cause, and built submarines in five and a half months instead of the usual fourteen, assembling them in Montreal to avoid violations of neutrality.[103] Out of catastrophe some good could come.

The October 28 Cabinet meeting was also notable because of a quarrel between Lloyd George and Kitchener. The little Welshman had taken a dislike to the great soldier, who delivered with hauteur his obscure reports in a loud staccato voice, as if he were at drill, a remote look in his eyes. His main idea, it seemed, was to say as little as possible and get back to the War Office as soon as possible. He did not take his Cabinet colleagues seriously, referring to them as "twenty-three gentlemen with whom I am barely acquainted." Matters came to a head over Lloyd George's request for an all-Welsh regiment. Apart from the linguistic difficulties, Kitchener intimated that the Welsh were not to be trusted en masse. Lloyd George was enraged at this ethnic slur. High words were exchanged and Kitchener threatened to resign. You might have thought the Welsh were enemy aliens, Lloyd George complained to Churchill, who ought to be interned until they had mastered the intricacies of the English language sufficiently to converse on equal terms with an East End recruit. Did Kitchener want men? If he did not, let him say so, then they would all be spared much worry and trouble.[104] Kitchener wanted men. What he did not want was to discuss strategy with politicians who could not be trusted to keep secrets.

What a royal row, thought Asquith. The whole thing could have been settled in ten minutes with a modicum of common sense. Kitchener was much the most to blame, for he was clumsy and noisy. He had spent so much of his life in the Orient that he did not understand English conditions.[105] But with some prodding from Churchill, Kitchener relented, and Lloyd George got his all-Welsh unit.

In his quest to improve the Navy's performance, Churchill had been toying with the idea of bringing back Jacky Fisher as First Sea Lord. He had a great fondness for the old boy, and admired his lack of pomp, his sense of fun, and his absolute devotion to the Navy. He was probably the greatest sailor since Nelson. He had been a valuable adviser when Churchill had first come to the Admiralty, on everything from the 15-inch gun to the conversion to oil. His mind brimmed with ideas, and Churchill needed someone with ideas. Contact with Fisher was like breathing ozone. But could he rely on a man of seventy-four? Would he crack under the strain?

Churchill decided to risk it. Prince Louis was worn down by attacks and innuendos in the press, by anonymous letters and talk in the clubs about his German origins. It did not help that his wife's brother-in-law was the German Emperor's brother, Prince Henry, High Admiral of the German Navy. Although a fine sailor, Prince Louis was not a man of ideas, and had been lukewarm about Antwerp. As the naval setbacks mounted, Churchill made up his mind: he would bring back Fisher and Sir Arthur Wilson. The poor blue-eyed German, as Asquith called him, somewhat disparagingly, would be replaced by two well-plucked chickens of seventy-four and seventy-two.[106] The present board had no initiative, Asquith felt; if they had any insight they would be devising "hen coops" and torpedo-proof harbors.

But Churchill had not counted on George V, who had an unconquerable aversion to Fisher, and had always been a Beresfordite in the old quarrels. When he went to Windsor to propose Fisher on October 27, the same day the *Audacious* was sunk, the King was adamant. Fisher was too old and did not have the confidence of the Navy; although he had done much as First Sea Lord, he had created a state of unrest and bad feeling among the officers of the service. Churchill said there was no one else. The King proposed Sir Hedworth Meux, one of Fisher's enemies. Churchill said he could never work with him. Two other admirals whom the King suggested, Henry Jackson and Frederick Sturdee, Churchill also vetoed. Here was yet another clash between the willful First Lord and his wary sovereign. The King said he would not approve of Fisher until he had seen the Prime Minister.[107]

On October 28, Lord Stamfordham, the King's emissary, went to Downing Street and told Asquith: "His Majesty knows the Navy and considers . . . the proposed appointment would give a shock to the Navy which no one could wish to cause in the middle of this Great War." Defending Churchill, Asquith said the present board was "weak and incapable of initiative." Only Fisher could fill the gap. Meux would not inspire the confidence of the Navy, Henry Jackson had no personality, and Sturdee was more suited to command a fleet than to be in office. Lord Stamfordham said Sturdee was not liked because he stood up to Churchill. Fisher's appointment would place the King in an awkward position, for the Navy would know that he had not sanctioned it. Asquith replied that he would be in an equally awkward position if Fisher was not appointed, for Churchill would resign. Lord Stamford-ham pointed out that Churchill had told the King that the Admiralty was no longer congenial to him and that he would be pleased to leave it. Not at all, Asquith said, the truth was that Churchill could not be dispensed with or replaced.[108]

The impasse was total. On October 29, Asquith went to Buckingham Palace determined to humor the King and bring him around. He had to listen to an exhaustive recital of Fisher's crimes and defects. In addition, the King said, Fisher would never get on with Winston. Asquith himself had misgivings on that point, but since Winston would have no one else, he stuck to his guns until the King gave his reluctant consent, expressing the hope that his fears would prove groundless.[109]

Prince Louis walked the plank without a murmur and was made a Privy Councillor. The whole business was painful for Churchill, all the more so because Prince Louis' nephew, Prince Maurice of Battenberg, a lieutenant in the King's Royal Rifles, had been killed in France on October 27. Churchill always felt that he owed a debt to Prince Louis, which he paid by helping the career of his son, Dickie Mountbatten.

What fun it was being back, Fisher thought. He was getting even with the damned fools who thought he was dead and buried.[110] Arthur Wilson had signed on as an unpaid consultant, also known as "Fisher's slave," and Rear Admiral Henry Oliver, a hard worker whom Churchill held in high esteem, was named Chief of Staff. Let everyone be optimistic, Fisher wired Jellicoe, and shoot the pessimists!

But optimism was on short rations in the first days of Fisher's return. On October 30, the seaplane carrier *Hermes* was sunk eight miles northwest of Calais. Churchill was furious. She had been ordered to come back under cover of dark but had waited until daybreak. Worse was to come. At 7 A.M. on November 4, Churchill saw what was to him the most terrible telegram of the war thus far: off the coast of southern Chile, near the Bay of Coronel, a German squadron had sunk two British armored cruisers with all hands, for a total loss of 1,560 lives. How could such a thing have happened?

At the outset of the war, Admiral Maximilian von Spee, the commander of the German Far Eastern Squadron, had started across the Pacific from the German naval base of Tsing-tau, on the China coast, with his flagship, the *Scharnhorst*, another battle cruiser, the *Gneisenau*, and the light cruiser *Nürnberg*. These three fast, well-armed ships left their calling cards, bombing Papeete, the capital of Tahiti, in September. At Easter Island they were joined by two other light cruisers, the *Leipzig* and the *Dresden*. It soon became apparent to the Admiralty War Staff tracking down ship movements that von Spee's squadron was making for South America.

Off the coast of Chile was stationed Rear Admiral Sir Christopher Cradock, an officer known for his daring, with a squadron consisting of two armored cruisers, the *Monmouth* and the *Good Hope*, a light cruiser, the *Glasgow*, a merchant cruiser, the *Otranto*, and the only British battleship in South American waters with 12-inch guns, the *Canopus*. Heavily armored, the *Canopus*, with its four big guns, was a citadel that von Spee could not storm.

On October 5, Cradock was ordered to prepare to meet the Germans, keeping his ships together. He could not hope to catch von Spee with the *Canopus* along, for she was an 1899-vintage battleship, ready for the scrap heap, and could not do more than fifteen knots. But he needed her firepower. All he could hope to do was sight the Germans and alert other British forces in the area. Rear Admiral Archibald Stoddart, commanding a squadron on the east coast of South America, had an armored cruiser, the *Defence*, that could be brought in. There was a good game to play, since von Spee would need to coal after a five-thousand-mile trip across the Pacific.

On October 11, Cradock confirmed that he had understood the need to keep his ill-assorted ships together: "Have ordered *Canopus* to Falkland Islands, where I intend to concentrate and avoid division of forces."

But by October 26, with von Spee approaching, and the smell of battle in his nostrils, Cradock had decided to discard the *Canopus* and have her replaced with the *Defence*. His telegram threw Churchill into perplexity:

"At sea. Admiralty telegram received 7th October. With reference to orders to search for enemy and our great desire for early success, I consider that owing to slow speed of *Canopus* it is impossible to find and destroy enemy's squadron. Have therefore ordered *Defence* to join me after calling for orders at Montevideo. Shall employ *Canopus* on necessary work of convoying colliers."[111]

In the midst of changing First Sea Lords, Churchill may not have given the change in Cradock's plan the attention it required. He simply minuted to Admiral Oliver: "This telegram is very obscure, and I do not understand what Admiral Cradock intends and wishes." A half fear had formed in his mind that perhaps Cradock would fight without the *Canopus*. But that was so improbable he did not even commit it to paper.[112]

On October 29, however, Cradock reaffirmed his intention of keeping his ships in supporting distance of one another. In the meantime, Admiral Stoddart protested giving up the *Defence*, saying he would need two fast cruisers in exchange. Even though British naval strategy was based on the concentration of a superior force to destroy an enemy, Churchill denied Cradock the *Defence*. Stoddart would need her if von Spee escaped around the Horn. Making ship dispositions was not Churchill's job, but the First Sea Lord's. Churchill was a civilian without experience at sea, aside from his cruises aboard the *Enchantress*. In the interregnum between First Sea Lords, however, he enlarged his responsibilities by doing the professional's job. Had Fisher by then been First Sea Lord, the decision would have been different, for it was one of his axioms to overwhelm the enemy with as many ships as possible. But Fisher did not arrive until October 30. Churchill at once took him into the War Room and gave him a two-hour briefing on the position and mission of every ship in the Navy. As they went over the great map, it was clear that South America was the critical point.

"You don't suppose he would try to fight them without the *Canopus*?" Churchill asked. Fisher did not reply.[113]

Without waiting to hear whether he was getting the *Defence*, Cradock was steaming up the Chilean coast without the *Canopus*, although he had taken the armed merchant cruiser *Otranto*, which was almost as slow. On October 27, he coaled at Vallenar, with the *Glasgow* patrolling off Coronel to intercept German shipping.

On November 1, the captain of a Chilean merchant ship was stopped by the *Nürnberg* about sixty miles north of Coronel Bay. This was the first solid information locating von Spee's squadron. He had not slipped past Cradock round the Horn as had been feared. When Churchill received the news via the British consul in Valparaiso, he ordered the *Defence* to join Cradock at once. The order went out on November 3.[114]

In the late afternoon of November 3, minus the *Canopus*, which was three hundred miles away, Cradock spotted the Germans, and decided at once to attack, although he had time to avoid contact and make for the protection of his battleship. Was he, as Churchill thought, carried away by a reckless nature? Or did he feel that the Admiralty would blame him for not fighting, as Troubridge had been blamed for not going after the *Goeben*? He had written a friend, also a naval officer: "I will take care I do not suffer the fate of poor Troubridge."

At 6:18 P.M. he signaled the *Canopus*: "I am now going to attack the enemy." The sun was dropping out of sight, and von Spee had the inland station, shrouded in the darkening twilight, while Cradock's ships were silhouetted against the sunset's afterglow, easy targets for the long-range German guns. The *Scharnhorst* and the *Gneisenau* were manned by long-service seamen, the pick of the German Navy, renowned for their gunnery. The *Good Hope* and the *Monmouth* had not fired their guns since being commissioned, and were manned by reservists. As Fisher was fond of saying: "Gunnery, gunnery, gunnery! All else is twaddle. Hit the target!"

Von Spee opened fire at 6:43 P.M., at eleven thousand yards. The swell was so heavy it obscured his gunners' aim, but their fire soon grew accurate. The *Monmouth*'s front turret was shot away and caught fire. When darkness fell, the burning *Monmouth* lit up the sea for the German gunners. An explosion ripped the stacks of Cradock's flagship, the *Good Hope*. Both ships went down, the *Good Hope* with 867 men and the *Monmouth* with 693. Rescue operations at night and in a heavy swell were not possible. The two other British ships slipped away in the dark.[115]

Von Spee was fervently acclaimed by the German colony in Valparaiso. Presented with flowers, he said: "They will do for my funeral."

At the Cabinet meeting on November 5, heads shook in disbelief. If Cradock had only followed instructions, Churchill explained, he would have kept his superiority. His adventurous nature had led him to attack a vastly superior force.

He had gone to the bottom, Asquith thought; otherwise he richly deserved to be court-martialed. Still, all of this was not creditable to the Navy. It was time Churchill bagged something and broke some crockery.[116]

Kitchener was bewildered. What can the Admiral have been thinking of? he wondered.[117]

It was typical of Churchill to blame Cradock, who had gone down with his ship and could not clear himself, Lloyd George thought. In his eagerness for a flashy success, Churchill was too busy to attend to the real business of the Admiralty.[118]

Poor old Kit Cradock was gone, poor old chap, Admiral Beatty lamented from his North Sea station. His death and the loss of the ships and the gallant lives in them could be laid at the door of Admiralty incompetence. They had as much idea of strategy as a School Board boy, and had broken over and over again on first principles.[119]

Churchill had been aching for a battle, complaining that the Germans did not come out, and when they did, he had hesitated to commit sufficient forces. Cradock had followed a suicidal impulse and disregarded clear and repeated orders to keep his ships together. But because of poor staff work (once again) and because Churchill was absorbed in other matters, the Admiralty did not effectively deal with Cradock's problem: how to carry out his orders to engage the Germans while held up by a slow battleship, when the Admiralty would not give him the faster ship he had asked for.

Fisher knew it was not numbers that told but gunnery. The *Scharnhorst*'s salvos had done the trick on Cradock. Now the same trick had to be worked on von Spee. On November 5, Fisher ordered two battle cruisers, the *Invincible* and the *Inflexible,* to hunt down the Germans. Churchill wanted to send only one, and Jellicoe was afraid of thinning out the Grand Fleet, but Fisher insisted. They went to the Devonport dockyards for repairs, under the command of Admiral Sir Frederick Sturdee, who had been replaced as Chief of Staff by Admiral Oliver. Fisher blamed the pompous Sturdee, who never listened to advice, for Coronel. There had never been such rot as he had perpetrated in his worldwide dispersal of weak units. They were strong nowhere, weak everywhere. One battle cruiser in each ocean would have cleared the world of German pirates. On November 9, Sturdee informed Churchill and Fisher that the earliest date he could sail was Friday the thirteenth. Imagine being such damned fools as to sail on a Friday and on a thirteenth, the superstitious Fisher raged. They would sail on Wednesday the eleventh. But the yard needed the extra time to finish the brick bridges of the *Invincible*'s boilers, Sturdee wired. Fisher told him to put the bricks and the bricklayers on board and finish the job at sea. His motto was "get on or get out." "Hustle" was a good word. Nelson said the whole secret was being there one-quarter of an hour before the other chaps.[120]

As the *Invincible* and the *Inflexible* steamed across the Atlantic on November 11 for their rendezvous with von Spee, Churchill received some disappointing news from his friend Sir John French. Jealous of his authority over European operations, French decided that from now on the Army's Royal Flying Corps and not the Royal Naval Air Service would attack Zeppelin sheds in Germany; French would order the attacks himself.[121] Churchill was furious at being deprived of authority over air bases he had set up. What poor recognition of the dangerous work they had done! But one last raid was already in the works, and he was not about to cancel it. The objective was Friedrichshafen, on the German side of Lake Constance, not far from the Swiss border, where there were some Zeppelin sheds and a hydrogen factory. The British planes, in crates, were sent by train to the French city of Belfort, close to the Swiss and German borders, where they were reassembled. Three planes took off on November 21 and dropped nine bombs, destroying the hydrogen factory and probably one Zeppelin.[122] One of the planes was shot down and its pilot was captured. Churchill was pleased with the raid, but the Swiss complained that the planes had violated their air space and that a Swiss national had been killed. If a Swiss had been killed in the Zeppelin factory, Churchill told Sir Edward Grey, it served him right.[123] In Parliament, it was not the remarkable feat of aerial initiative that provoked comment but the Swiss complaint. Why had neutral territory been flown over? Churchill was asked on November 26. "When machines are flying at a great height," he replied, "it is almost impossible for any but a skilled observer to determine with any accuracy the course the aircraft are taking unless he is directly beneath them."[124]

When Grey told him the Foreign Office would have to apologize to the Swiss, Churchill said they were lucky to have Englishmen fighting the battle of the small states. The least Switzerland could do was not be querulous, when everyone else was struggling and suffering. This was no time for hedging neutrals to give themselves airs. When the British minister in Berne suggested that a few words in the House of Commons would have a calming effect, Churchill replied in a note to Grey: "Tell them to go and milk their cows."[125]

At Lympne, Philip Sassoon's house in Kent, Clemmie was giving mother's milk to the newly born Sarah, and worrying about the military situation. The Germans were horribly powerful and cunning. They had devoted for years the best intellects to preparing for war while the British always thought of soldiers and sailors as brave and bluff and simple, not to say stupid. Kept in London by the press of events, Churchill was delighted to hear from his "Sweet Kat." It gave him so much joy to feel that with all his shortcomings, absorption, and sunlessness, she could still find in him the pith and nourishment that her soul sought.[126]

As if responding to Clemmie's plea that the best British intellects should concentrate on military planning, Asquith convened a War Council, a gathering of senior ministers and military men, which met on November 25. The members were Asquith, Lloyd George, Grey, Kitchener, Churchill, Balfour (as elder statesman and the only Conservative), Fisher, and the new CIGS, Lieutenant General Sir James Wolfe Murray, whom Churchill thought of as Kitchener's flunky, dubbing him "Sheep" Murray. Thanks to the secretary, Maurice Hankey, formal notes of ministerial discussions were taken for the first time in British history, although Cabinet meetings continued unrecorded. As keeper of the secrets, Hankey had an influence beyond his title of secretary. A short man with a large bald head, Hankey was liked for his tact, intelligence, and phenomenal calm. He was never angry or put out. Whenever a problem arose in the War Council, Lloyd George would say: "I'm sure Hankey can find the answer in that little bag of his."

What a difference it made to have Fisher with his dash and initiative instead of poor Prince Louis, Asquith thought as he studied the faces around the table. Fisher's, with its twisted mouth and round eyes, was strangely un-

English, suggesting the legend that he was half-Singhalese. Kitchener's was brick-red, short-nosed, blue-eyed, and Grey, with his well-cut, hawklike face, looked rather pinched. Most people would have called Winston ugly, but his eyes had the glow of genius.[127]

Reviewing the situation at the Admiralty, Churchill said that 260 vessels assured the defense of the coast, and that this force was distinct from Jellicoe's Grand Fleet, which was maintained at greatly superior strength to the German High Seas Fleet.

For the first time, Churchill proposed an attack on the Gallipoli Peninsula, which, if successful, would give the allies control of the Dardanelles, allowing them to dictate terms to the Turks. None of the other members commented on the Gallipoli plan, except for Fisher, who asked whether Greece could undertake it on behalf of the allies.[128]

On November 27, Parliament adjourned for two months, and during the motion for the adjournment, Lord Charles Beresford rose to discuss the war at sea, with the Admiralty under the cloud of a new disaster. The day before, the battleship *Bulwark*, lying in harbor at its Sheerness base, had blown up for reasons unknown. Only 12 men out of a crew of 700 were saved. These deaths could be added to the total of 4,327 that the Navy had suffered since the start of the war, the dismal litany of which Churchill had recited two days before in response to a question: 149 killed on the *Amphion*, mined on August 6; 259 killed on the *Pathfinder*, torpedoed on September 5; in numbing repetition the list went on, ships lost off the west coast of Africa, off the Dutch coast, off Chile, reconnoitering missions in picket boats, transport work in Belgium, seaplanes lost, ships sunk in action; and now this, a mysterious explosion.[129]

The *Bulwark* had been one of Beresford's flagships, and its loss gave him a springboard to attack the Admiralty. "There is a doubt in the public mind," he announced, "and a want of confidence in the Navy to carry out its duties. Things have occurred which have caused that doubt . . . This is not the time to criticize, if mistakes were made. We must back up authority as well as we can . . ." Ignoring his own advice, he then went on to pick apart what the Navy had done, from the escape of the *Goeben* to Cradock's defeat.[130]

Churchill replied that the Admiralty could not be drawn into any "acrimonious discussions," because too much information was still classified, but that he had confidence in the power of the Navy to continue the war indefinitely. One reason for his confidence he could not divulge. In September in the Baltic, the Russians had found the secret cipher and signal book of the

443

German Navy on the body of a drowned German signalman and had turned "the sea-stained priceless documents" over to the Admiralty. Churchill set up a special intelligence branch called "Room 40," which was soon able to decipher some of the messages, providing the Navy with advance warning of German ship movements in the North Sea and elsewhere. The reports from Room 40 were marked "Exclusively Secret" and were seen only by Churchill, Fisher, Wilson, and Oliver. After a while the Germans grew suspicious and changed their code.[131]

On November 30, Margot Asquith congratulated Churchill on his fortieth birthday. He had done a great deal for a man his age. As the traditional dreary peer in the House of Lords started his speeches, she put herself this question: What set Winston apart? It was not his mind. He had a noisy mind. It was not his judgment. He was constantly wrong. It was his courage, his enterprise, his amazing ability always to throw himself in the pool. He never shirked, hedged, or protected himself. He took huge risks. While others were shriveled with grief, he was happy and buoyant, dreaming of war.[132]

Dreams of war meant dreams of victory, but in France the front was frozen. A French general told Jack Seely: "This war degenerates . . . into a war of siege, and the battery commander with his telephone in the front trench holds the grand secret."[133] Some alternative had to be found to these attacks that gained five trenches of which four were lost the next day at a cost of 150 casualties. Something must be done to stop the wasteful bloodshed.

The search for alternative strategies began. At the December 1 War Council, Balfour proposed seizing the island of Borkum, off the German coast, with twenty thousand men from a Home Defense unit.

Kitchener said Home Defense soldiers would not do; men would have to be withdrawn from the Continent, where the British role was to contain as large a German army as possible in order to prevent them from transferring sufficient troops to beat the Russians.[134]

Here were the two main strategic concepts summed up: whether to throw all of British strength into the French front or mount operations in other parts of Europe.

Churchill and Fisher favored Balfour's plan, for a captured island could be used as a naval and flying base. It was important for the Navy to adopt the offensive. The present defensive attitude was bad for morale. But for the moment, the island strategy was postponed.

Churchill was juggling different plans, the island, the Dardanelles, and a combined military and naval attack on the Belgian coast, which he went to

France to discuss with Sir John French on December 5. Kitchener and Asquith did not object, although Kitchener spent an hour on December 4 complaining to the Prime Minister about Churchill's visits to the front. The Army thought he interfered in military matters, while the Navy complained that he was away at critical moments. Asquith was disposed to agree.[135]

So was Jacky Fisher, who did not hold with Winston's outings. Of course Churchill enjoyed them, and of course Fisher was not afraid of the responsibility. But his trips were too venturesome and gave his enemies cause to blaspheme at a time when the Admiralty badly needed a victory.[136]

The victory came on the day of Churchill's return from France, December 8. That morning, Sturdee's battle cruisers were coaling in Port Stanley, the principal harbor of the Falkland Islands, a British Crown Colony off the southern tip of Argentina, desolate and treeless, whose inhabitants called themselves "kelpers," after the seaweed, up to fifty feet long, that grew on its shores. Sturdee was preparing to hunt down von Spee, who was about to make a dash for home waters.

With its unfortified coaling base and wireless station, Port Stanley was an inviting target. Rounding the Horn on his way across the South Atlantic, von Spee reached the Falklands on the morning of December 8 and could not resist the temptation. His five ships closed in to shell the harbor. As he moved within sight of the bay, in a calm sea, under a clear sky, he could make out the sand hills of Port Stanley, and docks and houses. There were ships in the harbor, warships. Two of them had the tripod masts characteristic of dreadnoughts.

Edward Smyth-Osbourne, a lieutenant commander aboard the *Invincible*, could hardly believe his eyes. They were expecting a search that would take weeks, and here was von Spee saving them the trouble and delivering himself into their hands.[137] But as soon as he had identified the battle cruisers, he turned tail. Sturdee started his engines and pursued without haste, at a speed of twenty knots. It was morning, and he had all day. Faced with the prospect of having his ships picked off one by one, von Spee turned to face the battle cruisers and was pounded with 12-inch guns.

Working in his Admiralty office, Churchill was brought the message that von Spee was in action with Sturdee's fleet, which was coaling at Port Stanley. There had been so many unpleasant surprises in the past that shivers went up his spine. Had Sturdee been taken by surprise and attacked while at anchor?[138]

Sturdee began firing at 12:55 at sixteen thousand yards, and the battle lasted five hours. The *Scharnhorst* listed to port until she lay on her beam ends and disappeared, going down with her admiral. The *Gneisenau* keeled over and lay on her side, her men clambering over her hull, then slowly sank out of sight. Other ships in Sturdee's flotilla sank the *Leipzig* and the *Nürnberg*, but von Spee's courageous decision to stand and fight allowed the *Dresden* to escape (she was hunted down and destroyed three months later in the same area).

Churchill's door opened, and Admiral Oliver came in, the normally somber cast of his face relieved by the hint of a grin. "It's all right, sir," he said. "They are all at the bottom." With one exception, he was right.[139]

Helping in rescue operations, Lieutenant Commander Smyth-Osbourne was surprised to see that the German sailors expected to be hanged or shot. Although they had fought marvelously, they seemed to cordially hate their officers. There was some good-natured chaffing between battle cruisers. A boat from the *Inflexible* came alongside and the men shouted that it was lucky for the *Invincible* that they had been there. Smyth-Osbourne was happy that he had taken part both in the action off Heligoland and in the Falkland victory, and hoped to be in time for "the day" in the North Sea. He was, aboard the *Invincible* at the Battle of Jutland in 1916, where she was sunk with 1,026 dead, including himself.[140]

Churchill was pleased that the last German naval squadron outside the North Sea had been destroyed. Coming five weeks after Coronel, the victory would have a great impact in England. Always generous in his praise when things went well, he congratulated Fisher—it had been his show and his luck. His flair had been quite true.[141] Falkland was the last naval action of the war between surface ships by gunfire alone, without mines, torpedoes, submarines, or aircraft. It was the nearest thing in the whole war to the great victories of Nelson's day; perhaps, some naval historians would say, the greatest sea victory since Trafalgar.

But Fisher was furious with the way Sturdee had handled the battle. He had sighted the enemy at 8:20 A.M., with lovely weather, so evanescent and rare off Cape Horn, but instead of pressing for action at once had made the signal "Ship's Company have time for the next meal," and did not go into action until 11:32. The *Dresden* had escaped and informed the German Admiralty that Sturdee had only twenty rounds of 12-inch ammunition left for his two battle cruisers, for he had expended a phenomenal number of shells—1,174 rounds. Sturdee replied to Fisher's telegrams that he had bagged four out of five. Fisher was apoplectic. Sturdee had lost the *Dresden* because he had started too late and the weather had turned after 4 P.M., reducing visibility. When Nelson had been told that fifteen out of twenty enemy ships had struck their colors at Trafalgar, he had said: "That won't do —we want the twenty." *And he got them!*[142]

To punish him, Fisher wanted to leave Sturdee in South America, aboard the cruiser *Carnarvon* (since the battle cruisers had to be recalled), until he had hunted down the *Dresden*. Churchill vetoed this plan, for it was insulting and woefully out of harmony with his achievement. Fisher always wanted heads to roll, while Churchill felt that a single failure was insufficient for getting rid of an officer. Men often learned by their mistakes, and it was bad policy to have admirals always worrying that their jobs were in jeopardy. More good news came on December 13. Operating in the Dardanelles, Lieutenant Norman Holbrook had navigated his submarine under five lines of mines and torpedoed the Turkish battleship *Messudiyeh*, winning a Victoria Cross.[143]

On December 16, Churchill was in his bath when news was brought that German cruisers were bombarding three coastal towns in northern England, Hartlepool, Whitby, and Scarborough. Throwing his clothes on over a damp body, he ran to the War Room, his sympathy for the bombed civilians mingling with the anodyne of contemplated retaliation. Surely, this was a reply to the Falkland Islands. The prestige of the German Navy had to be re-established.[144] But of retaliation there was none, for the German ships vanished into the North Sea fogs, after another communications blunder. Commodore William Goodenough's light-cruiser squadron saw the Germans in the mist and opened fire. Had he gone on, the noise would have drawn the rest of the fleet and there would have been a general engagement. But a signal from Admiral Beatty was misinterpreted, and Goodenough thought he had been ordered to draw away. It was like a game of blindman's bluff. Beatty felt terrible. He had lost a chance to finish the war from a naval point of view.[145]

One hundred and thirty-three civilians were killed and sixty-four were wounded, among them women and children, in the forty-minute bombardment. Such was German *Kultur*, George V noted in his diary. All Churchill could do was write the mayor of Scarborough, Christopher C. Graham, that "whatever feats of arms the German Navy may hereafter perform, the stigma of the baby-killers of Scarborough will brand its officers and men while sailors sail the seas."[146] What a lot of cheap rhetoric, thought Asquith when he saw the letter, with Churchill's usual snarling undertone.[147] There was a great public outcry. Why had the Navy failed to prevent the raid? But Churchill avoided the trap of splitting up the Grand Fleet to take up defensive positions along the English coast.

Whenever he could, Churchill escaped to France. He liked the change of scene, always received a warm welcome from Sir John French, and felt the need to keep up with military operations. He was quite unable to confine himself to the activities of his own department, although he always found a naval pretext for the trip, in this case the clearing of the Belgian coast. As a matter of routine, he asked permission of Asquith and Kitchener before leaving, and until now they had given it. But both of them were fed up with his cross-Channel shuttle, and this time, on December 17, when he proposed to go again, Asquith told him that while he could go to Dunkirk to look into naval matters, he should not attempt to see French. Kitchener had been to see Asquith to complain that Churchill's visits were producing friction between French and himself.[148]

Furious that Kitchener had gone behind his back, Churchill poured out, in Asquith's words, "a kettle-full of opprobrious epithets."[149] How could Kitchener say that he was the cause of friction, when he had always promoted goodwill and confidence? But Kitchener was not to be swayed. In a letter to Churchill, which Asquith convinced him not to send, Kitchener wrote:

> I ought to tell you frankly that your private arrangement with French as regards land forces is rapidly rendering my position and responsibility as S of S impossible. I consider that if my relations with French are strained it will do away with any advantage there may be to the country in my holding my present position and I foresee that if the present system continues it must result in creating grave difficulties between French & myself. I do not interfere with Jellicoe nor do I have a private correspondence with him. [This last sentence was crossed out before Asquith saw the letter.] I am suggesting to the PM that you should take the WO [War Office] and let Fisher be First Lord then all would work smoothly I hope.[150]

In the face of Kitchener's strenuous objection and threat of resignation, Churchill canceled his trip. But the friendly confidence he had shared with Kitchener in the first months of war was lost. Perhaps Kitchener remembered the upstart subaltern who had attached himself to the Nile expedition. He was a born meddler, going behind his back, undermining his authority, and setting

himself up as a parallel Secretary of State for War. As for Churchill, he felt
that Kitchener was being very unfair to a colleague who had worked with him
with the utmost loyalty.[151]

Instead of concentrating on the conduct of the war, Asquith had to mediate between his stormy petrels.[152] Such small tempests illustrated the crucial
role of personality in wartime. Victory did not depend only on manpower and
firepower. It depended on whether Churchill got along with Kitchener,
whether Kitchener got along with French, and, all along the line, whether
leaders worked together loyally, or undercut one another, stalling the machinery of warfare. It was sad to think that the outcome of a battle could
depend on hurt vanity, ruffled tempers, and strong words exchanged across a
Cabinet table. Churchill could not grasp that even if there was nothing underhanded in his meetings with French, the fact that Kitchener resented them
should have been enough to keep him out of the Army's bailiwick. Clemmie
had asked him to put himself in Kitchener's shoes. How would he have liked
it if the Secretary of State for War went around visiting admirals? But seeing
a problem from someone else's point of view was not Churchill's long suit.

French saw Churchill when he came to England for talks on December 20.
The question was, they decided, were the Russians so smashed that the whole
German Army would come down on their necks? Churchill said he would no
longer go to France, for it weakened his influence on events to have to ask
Kitchener for so small a thing, and it was better to deal with him on equal
terms.[153] While professing great friendship for Churchill, French agreed
with Asquith that his visits were an interference and estimated his judgment
as "highly erratic."[154] Churchill, on the other hand, always spoke well of
French and defended him in the Cabinet.

Another point that grated on Kitchener was the naval units that Churchill
still operated in France, independently of army control. The Dunkirk Circus
consisted of an aerial squadron, three squadrons of armored motorcars, three
armored trains, four 15-inch howitzers, about sixty buses used for carrying
troops, and a total of 350 men and 15 officers. The morale of the Army was
affected by these irregular units, Kitchener informed Churchill on December
23; they caused discontent and trouble to the staff out of proportion to their
utility. Churchill had packed the units with friends and friends of friends. "If
these irregular formations are only a means to enable certain officers, and
gentlemen without military experience and training, to get to the front and
take part in the war," Kitchener wrote, ". . . [then] they should form part
of the Army, and not claim to be separate entities under the control of the

Admiralty . . ."[155] Once again, Churchill ran out of counterarguments and had to acquiesce.

In addition to his quarrels with Kitchener, the strain was beginning to tell at the Admiralty between Churchill and Fisher. As Beatty had predicted, two such forceful personalities could not both run the show. When he did not get his way, Fisher fumed and fretted and threatened to resign. He brought a lifetime of naval experience and tremendous flair to the job, but at seventy-four his mind had lost its resilience, and he magnified small adversities into obsessions. Why couldn't the vital wireless stations be built? Why did they have a regular menagerie of charity admirals on ships when the Admiralty was crowded with young officers who ought to have been at sea? Why couldn't slow ships be scrapped? All over the world they had distributed tortoises to catch hares. They must be brought home and put in the zoological garden as specimens. Fisher began to blame Churchill when anything went wrong. Perhaps it relieved him to find a focus for his anxieties. Churchill had so monopolized all initiative, he complained, and fired off such a multitude of memos, that the Sea Lords were atrophied.

One of Fisher's threats to resign came as the result of two minor air raids at Christmastime. On December 24, a Zeppelin dropped a bomb on Dover, and on December 25 a plane flew up the Thames. Fisher was horrified. Why wasn't the Admiralty, which was responsible for aerial defense, doing anything? Churchill had received information that twenty Zeppelins, with a ton of explosive each, were about to bomb London. They would, Fisher believed, cause a terrible massacre and wreck the Admiralty building. There was only one thing to do: announce beforehand that German prisoners would be shot in reprisal if bombs were dropped. Since this had not been done, Fisher was resigning.[156] Churchill replied that he could not support reprisals, but sympathized with Fisher's feelings of exasperation at their powerlessness to resist certain forms of attack.[157] Fisher withdrew his resignation, but Churchill began to wonder about their ability to work as a team.

Fisher was also concerned that too many operations were bungled and too many ships were sunk. On Christmas Day, nine seaplanes took off to bomb the Zeppelin sheds in the German port of Cuxhaven, at the mouth of the Elbe, but could not find them in the dense fog. Only two planes returned to their carriers, the rest landing at sea, and four planes were lost. What a *coup manqué* (lost opportunity), Asquith grumbled. On January 1, 1915, the battleship *Formidable* was torpedoed off the south Devon coast, losing six hundred of her crew of eight hundred. Her captain, Arthur Loxley, who drowned with his men, had signaled to another ship not to stand by, to avoid a repetition of the *Bacchantes* disaster. It was a bad night, and Admiral Sir Lewis Bayly, commander in chief of the Channel Fleet, ought to have taken his squadron of eight battleships into Portland, but instead he moved them west in a close column toward Torbay, in the full glare of the Start lighthouse, one of the most powerful in England, steaming at only ten knots, and a German submarine picked off the well-lit target of the last ship in line. An autocrat of rigid mind, "Luigi" Bayly did not believe in submarines. Appointed only sixteen days before, he was ordered to haul down his flag for want of prudence and poor seamanship.

Churchill had thought of him as an admiral after his own heart, who belonged to the "yes" school.[158] But the loss of a dreadnought was unforgivable. Nonetheless, he appointed Bayly president of the Royal Naval College at Greenwich, not for his own sake, as Churchill wrote Jellicoe, "but because to terrorize Admirals for losing ships is to make sure of losing wars." A letter that Bayly circulated to the Sea Lords protesting his dismissal infuriated Fisher. When you gave your housemaid warning—however excellent she might be—you didn't have to explain. You didn't like her so she went![159]

As the year ended after five months of war, perhaps the brightest spot was the Admiralty's record as a carrier of men and matériel. In a paper circulated on December 29, Churchill gave the statistics: 809,000 men, 203,000 horses, 250,000 tons of stores, 20,000 vehicles, 65,000 wounded, 5,000 refugees, and 4,884 German prisoners of war carried without the loss of a single man.

One evening at twilight, as Asquith sat in the Cabinet Room at 10 Downing Street, wondering what triumphs and disasters 1915 would bring, he looked out the window across the parade ground and saw the Admiralty flag flying and the lights begin to twinkle in the rooms where Churchill and his aides were beating out their plans.[160]

X

THE DARDANELLES

I n December 1914, Churchill became convinced that a condition of stalemate had been reached in France. They were playing the German game by
incurring losses in driving them from one entrenched position to another.
Was there no alternative to sending British armies to chew barbed wire in
Flanders? Was there nothing the Navy could do but sit in its Scottish war
stations waiting for the day when the German fleet would steam out of the
Heligoland Bight for the great seagoing joust?

In fact, trench warfare was not the German game—it came as a shock to
both sides that entrenchments could not be attacked without heavy losses.
Like the allies, the Germans were tied down, unable to release their divisions
in the West to fight the Russians, as planned. Churchill, who had observed
the fighting in France and drawn on his experience as a soldier, believed that
it would take several hundred thousand casualties to convince the military
mind that there would be no decisive change on the western front. A letter
arrived from his friend Valentine Fleming (the father of Ian Fleming), a
major serving in the trenches, confirming his views. From the Channel to the
Swiss border at Basel, Fleming said, there was a ten-mile-wide strip of land
where nothing grew, where no animals grazed, where no houses stood, a
killing ground littered with corpses and rude graves. On either side of this
inhuman and cratered hell ran lines of trenches, where men in brown or gray
or blue crouched, mud-coated, unshaven, hollow-eyed, deafened and crazed
by the rain of shells fired four miles away by an unseen cannon, and positively welcoming an infantry attack as a chance to fight a human assailant.[1]

And yet even in this no-man's land oddly picturesque scenes were to be observed. Riding up the reverse slope of a wooded hill on a clear starlit night, Major Fleming had come upon a camp that showed what a Babel the war was—French cuirassiers with their glistening breastplates and lances, London Scottish in their kilts, an English howitzer battery, a battalion of Sikhs, a squadron of African Spahis in long robes and turbans, all sitting around the campfire chattering and smoking like actors who had just been to the costume wardrobe. Then he saw the remnant of an English line battalion marching back through the trenches, a limping column of bearded, muddy, torn figures, bent with fatigue, wool caps instead of helmets covering their heads, but able to stand the cold and the strain and the awful losses, which other nations *could not do*. It was going to be a long war.[2]

The price for this test of British gallantry was the slow extinction of a nation's youth. Searching for another theater where naval action might shorten the war, Churchill seized on the capture of Borkum, a German island off the Dutch coast. From Borkum, the northernmost German province of Schleswig-Holstein could be invaded, threatening the Kiel Canal, bringing Denmark into the war, and throwing open the Baltic. How an island so close to the German mainland could be held long enough to prepare the next step was not for the moment explained, although Captain Herbert Richmond confided to his diary that the scheme was *"quite mad*. The reasons for capturing it are NIL, the possibilities about the same. I have never read such an idiotic, amateur piece of work as this outline in my life. Ironically enough it falls to me to prepare the plans for this stupendous folly. . . . It remains with the army, who I hope will refuse to throw away 12,000 troops in this manner for the self-glorification of an ignorant and impulsive man."[3]

This was the operation that Churchill proposed on December 29 to Asquith, who was by this time receiving alternative plans from all sides. Lloyd George had reached the same conclusion. The war in the West was bogged down in mud. Not a yard of German territory was in the hands of the allies, while all of Belgium, as well as parts of France, was in German hands. The Russian steamroller was at a standstill. "Little Willie" was not, as expected, goose-stepping back to Berlin.[4]

Studying maps of Europe, Lloyd George's eyes wandered from France eastward toward the Balkans. What if the neutral Balkan states could be induced to attack Austria? Or, failing that, what of an attack against Turkey to break the stalemate in the West? Another proposal for an attack on Turkey came from Maurice Hankey, who was respected as a sound and unflamboyant strategist. Three army corps could be sent to capture Constantinople, which might bring in the fence-sitting Balkan states.[5]

As the War Council went over these various schemes, all agreed that some new operation must be mounted to hit Germany, but which one? Churchill told Hankey that their conclusions were not incompatible, even though one wanted to capture a German island and the other Constantinople. In both cases, the aim was a speedy victory without enormous bloodshed. To Jacky Fisher, the War Council meetings were like a game of ninepins. Everyone had a plan, and it was a matter of seeing which ninepin would fall, knocking over its neighbors.[6]

As it happened, it was Russia that caused the ninepin to fall, for on December 30, Grand Duke Nicholas, commander in chief of the Russian Army, informed the chief of the British military mission, Sir John Hanbury-Williams, that Turkish troops were threatening the Russians in the Caucasus —what could the British do to help? Hanbury-Williams told the British ambassador, Sir George Buchanan, who wired Sir Edward Grey that the Grand Duke wanted ". . . Lord Kitchener to arrange for a demonstration of some kind against the Turk elsewhere, either naval or military, and to spread reports which would cause Turks, who he says are very liable to go off at a tangent, to withdraw some of the forces now acting against Russia in the Caucasus, and thus ease the position of Russia."[7]

Kitchener was concerned. The Grand Duke's appeal could not be ignored. Russia had to be kept in the war. If Russia dropped out, the German armies on the eastern front would be moved to France. On the same day he received the Russian appeal, January 2, Kitchener wired French that it might be better to divert troops from the western front since no breakthrough of the German lines had been made. "The German lines in France may be looked upon as a fortress that cannot be carried by assault and also cannot be completely invested," Kitchener told the commander in chief. ". . . The question of where anything effective can be accomplished opens a large field and requires a good deal of study . . ." French replied at once that "not a man should be diverted from the Western theater without the full and ungrudging concurrence of the French command in chief." He was against the use of the British Army anywhere but in France. There was no other theater in which decisive results could be obtained. "To attack Turkey," French said, "would be to play the German game, and to bring about the end which Germany had in mind when she induced Turkey to join in the war, namely, to draw off troops from the decisive spot which is Germany herself."[8]

Faced with French's refusal to give up a single soldier for an expedition against Turkey, Kitchener passed the Russian appeal on to Churchill. Did Churchill think a naval action would be possible to prevent the Turks from sending more men into the Caucasus? He had no troops to land anywhere. The only place where a demonstration might have some effect in stopping Turkish reinforcements from going to the Caucasus would be the Dardanelles, the forty-mile-long strait connecting the Aegean Sea with the Sea of Marmara, and the gateway to Constantinople. The Army would not be ready for anything big for some months, Kitchener said.[9]

Churchill wasn't sure what he felt about the Dardanelles. It was one of those issues where he could take both sides with equal persuasion, and had. In a memo four years earlier, arguing against the need for a strong naval force in the Mediterranean, he had written: "It is no longer possible to force the Dardanelles . . . nobody would expose a modern fleet to such perils." This was the accepted naval thinking, based on reports provided by Admiral Sir Arthur Limpus, who had trained and organized the Turkish Navy, and who had, incidentally, advised the Turks to strengthen their Dardanelles defenses. But much had happened since the 1911 memo. Turkey had fallen under German influence, Limpus had gone home, and the *Goeben* and the *Breslau* were in Constantinople. Churchill had posted a squadron off the strait under Vice Admiral Sackville Carden with orders to sink the two elusive German ships if they ventured into the Mediterranean, but on September 29 the Germans sealed off the strait with minefields, blocking Russia's warm-water ports in the Black Sea. On October 29, the *Goeben* and the *Breslau*, flying the Turkish flag but commanded by Admiral Souchon, bombarded Odessa and three other Russian ports. Five days later, Carden's squadron bombarded the outer Dardanelles forts for ten minutes, badly damaging one, which impressed the Sea Lords, for it showed that naval guns could demolish forts on land. On November 5, Turkey and Great Britain were at war, and Churchill began studying with his Sea Lords the best way to force the strait, using old battleships that could fire their guns at a static land target. At the first War Council meeting on November 25, he had proposed an attack on the Gallipoli Peninsula commanding the strait, which would have given England control of the Dardanelles, but it was agreed that such an operation would require a large force.[10]

Now, on January 3, 1915, responding to Kitchener's request for a naval action, Churchill sent Carden a routine query: "Do you consider the forcing of the Dardanelles by ships alone a practicable operation? It is assumed older battleships fitted with minebumpers would be used preceded by colliers or other merchant craft as bumpers and sweepers. Importance of results would justify severe loss. Let me know your views."[11]

Churchill's attention still focused on the Borkum expedition, and he was annoyed with Fisher, who had drafted a grandiose plan of his own for invading Turkey with military and naval forces. On January 4, he told Fisher: "I think we had better hear what others have to say about the Turkish plans before taking a decided line. I would not grudge 100,000 men because of the great political effects in the Balkan peninsula: but Germany is the foe, and it is bad war to seek cheaper victories and easier antagonists."[12]

Carden's reply came the next day: ". . . I do not consider Dardanelles can be rushed. They might be forced by extended operations with large number of ships."[13]

This was the crucial telegram of the entire Dardanelles affair. If Carden had replied "I do not think it can be done," that would have been the end of it, for it was not believed at the Admiralty that ships without military support could get through the forts, cannon, and mines that defended the strait. If Carden had agreed with this negative assessment, no further thought would have been given to the plan. But the man on the spot said that he might be able to do it, and Churchill accepted his appraisal.

Sackville Carden, the man who opened the Pandora's box of the Dardanelles, was a lackluster fifty-eight-year-old rear admiral who had been transferred from his job as superintendent of the Malta dockyards to command of the eastern Mediterranean. Grey had vetoed Admiral Limpus, who as adviser to the Turkish Navy had actually helped design the Dardanelles fortifications, on the ground that it would be ungentlemanly to take advantage of his knowledge of the enemy. Roger Keyes, who had left the submarine command to serve as Carden's chief of staff, and who shared Churchill's enthusiasm for offensive action, had a poor opinion of Carden. Keyes had laughed when Churchill told him, before he left, that "Carden will, I know, be too busy to write. You must send me a long telegram every night—two hundred words at least." If only Churchill knew that all Carden did was read novels and take naps! He was *maddening* to work with—a gentleman, but very coldhearted, without a trace of ambition, and he never gave credit to anyone. It was his assistants, Captains Godfray and Rankin, who got him to send the telegram that the Dardanelles could be forced, and then he retired to his novel.

The irony was that by then, the reason for the naval action no longer existed. Caught in the terrible Caucasus winter, the Turkish armies were being decimated, and the Russians would win a decisive victory at Sarikamish on January 16. They no longer needed a diversionary British thrust to draw off Turkish troops.

But at the War Council on the afternoon of January 5, the day Carden's telegram was received, momentum was building for some form of alternative strategy. Everyone seemed to have a plan, thought Asquith as he mulled over the array: F. E. Smith, to whom he had spoken that morning, wanted to withdraw the Indian troops from France, where the severe winter made them useless, and attack Smyrna; Sir John French favored a diversion to help the Montenegrins; Churchill still wanted to capture Borkum; Lloyd George was bent on attacking Salonika; and Kitchener backed a naval attack on the Dardanelles, which would not cost him a single soldier. In support of Kitchener, Churchill read out the telegram that he had received from Carden an hour before. Returning to the Admiralty, he found that Carden's "extended operations" were supported by two members of the War Group, Admirals Henry Jackson and Henry Oliver. With the backing of these two eminent sailors, and knowing that Kitchener and the War Council wanted to follow up the opportunity, Churchill gave Carden the go-ahead on January 6: "Your view is agreed with by high authorities here. Please telegraph in detail what you think could be done by extended operations, what force would be needed and how you consider it should be used."[14]

To Churchill at that point, the Dardanelles was no more than a vague contingency plan that he stored in the back of his mind. The greatest hope was in the north, by bringing Holland and Denmark in through attacks on Borkum and the Belgian coast. An aggressive naval policy could beat the Germans out of the North Sea. Not until all the northern possibilities had been exhausted did he want to look at the south of Europe. The "Southerners" were Lloyd George and Kitchener. At the War Council on January 8, Lloyd George insisted that no victory was possible in France in trench warfare. As far back as 1879 the Turks had held up the Russians at Plevna. Trench warfare was the power of the defensive. Some alternative theater must be found. He proposed a landing in southern Austria. Austria was out, Kitchener said, making, as usual, a final and peremptory remark on the strength of his authority as a great soldier. The only alternative to the western front was the Dardanelles. An attack there with 150,000 men and the fleet would help Russia, bring in the Balkan states, and release wheat and shipping locked up in the Black Sea.[15]

Something had to be tried in view of the deadlock on the western front, but the War Council could not decide where. Churchill went over the possibilities with Asquith when they met on Sunday, January 10, at Walmer Castle, the official home of the Warden of the Cinque Ports (the governor of Hastings, Romney, Hythe, Dover, and Sandwich), Lord Beauchamp. Built on a rock overlooking the Channel, within earshot of the guns in France, the castle was one of the Prime Minister's favorite weekend retreats. He could confer with the other war leaders there and watch the ships go about their business in the Channel.

That evening at dinner, the discussion turned on who should succeed Lord Hardinge as Viceroy of India, a post that Churchill had once told Margot Asquith he wanted above all others. But now he told her: "I've given up all desire for that . . . do you think this is a sign of more modesty or more ambition?"

"More ambition, certainly," Margot replied. "No one sinks into greater insignificance than a retired viceroy, aged in arteries, pickled by the climate, poor and bewildered by another kind of political public life—he retires to small and drab quarters in Eaton Place."

"My God!" Churchill exclaimed. "This, this is living history. Everything we are doing and saying is thrilling—it will be read by a thousand generations, think of that! Why I would not be out of this glorious delicious war for anything the world could give me." His eyes glowed, Margot noticed, while detecting in his expression a slight anxiety that "delicious" might be misunderstood. "I say, don't repeat that I said the word 'delicious,' " Churchill added. "You know what I mean."[16]

Had their conversation been overheard and leaked to the press, it would have created a major scandal. What, the man whose strategic errors and blundering admirals had sent thousands of sailors to the bottom of the ocean, calling the war *delicious!* The men aboard the *Audacious*, the *Formidable*, and all the other ships sunk as a result of naval operations might have another word for it.

But only Churchill among the ministers was entitled to say such a thing. War could be delicious—pleasing to the taste and smell—only to a man who had tasted and smelled it. He had seen war from both sides, as a soldier in India and Africa, led into battle by officers whose orders he did not question, and as head of the Navy. He knew what it was to be under fire, and to be wounded, and to be alive among the fallen. He had derived from pity and envy mixed a child's relief that he himself had incredibly survived, converting survival into proof that he was destined for greatness. As First Lord, although he had never fought at sea, he gave no orders that he would not willingly have carried out. His greatest complaint was that the Germans were cheating him of battle, and that all the fighting was on land. In Churchill's capacious mind, where room could be made for two contrary ideas, the barbarism and slaughter of war were as sincerely condemned as the opportunity for high deeds was eagerly desired.

On January 12, there arrived at the Admiralty what Churchill later considered to be *the* most important telegram of the entire protracted, disastrous Dardanelles affair. Vice Admiral Carden said that it might be possible to force the Dardanelles in about a month. Here was a man who had been sitting off the strait for weeks, turning over the possibilities in his mind, and studying every angle, and who had produced a detailed and novel plan in four stages:

• Reduce the defenses at the entrance.
• Clear the defenses within the strait.
• Reduce the defenses at the Narrows.
• Reduce the forts and clear the minefields at the Narrows, and advance into the Marmara Sea toward Constantinople.[17]

Here was a plan that seemed to present a myriad of benefits. It would use old battleships that had been detached to protect shipping and could be spared by Jellicoe. Obsessed by the weakness of his fleet and the insufficiencies of his margins, Jellicoe was averse to the capture of Borkum, and preferred to remain in what Churchill called an attitude of "inactive expectancy." Here was a chance to fight in the Mediterranean, that "old womb of empire" where English power had traditionally made itself felt, independently of Jellicoe's prudent leadership. Here was a viable plan of attack in response to Kitchener's request for a naval action. It gave the Navy the spotlight and satisfied Churchill's longing to be on the offensive. Carden's fleet could force the strait, attack Constantinople, obtain the surrender of Turkey, bring in the neutral Balkan states, outflank the Central Powers, and win the war without the help of a single soldier. At first glance, the Dardanelles shone with the promise of victory.

Was not England after all an amphibious power, taught by history that wars could be won at sea? The Dardanelles campaign was in the best Imperial tradition of far-off wars with light casualties, such as the Nile campaign, with ten thousand Dervish losses against forty-seven British, under the command of the nation's greatest living soldier. That was the thing, a foe who came on bravely but injudiciously. After the smoke of battle had settled, Kipling could write a poem about their gallantry. The era of cheap victories with little loss of precious British lives had ended with the Boer War, but there was a great nostalgia for it. Perhaps the Turk would fit the bill.

It certainly seemed that he was not a fierce enemy. The Turks had been defeated in the war of 1911–1912 by the Italians, who had seized Libya. If the Italians could beat them, it would be a romp for the British, which early encounters bore out. On November 7, British Indian troops had captured the town of Basra, at the head of the Persian Gulf (in present-day Iraq), and in extending their hold over the area had taken one thousand Turkish prisoners and killed three hundred Turkish soldiers against five British and sixty Indian killed.[18] On December 18, Captain Frank Larken landed the light cruiser *Doris* at Alexandretta, at the northeastern tip of the Mediterranean, cutting railway lines and destroying bridges. Under the threat of bombardment from the *Doris*'s 6-inch guns, Turkish authorities agreed to blow up two railway engines and some military stores, borrowing explosives from Larken because they had none. This farcical cooperation between the attacker and his victim, a full account of which was circulated to the Cabinet on February 8, helped convince Churchill that Turkey was not an efficient military power, and that resistance at the Dardanelles might collapse as it had at Alexandretta.[19]

With his instinct for the deep tides of feeling that swayed the English people, Churchill changed the nature of the war by backing a limited operation that would spare British lives. It was better to gamble with a small risk and large prospects than to continue the slaughter in the trenches. It was a clever and humane solution, a way to avoid conscription, and rescue the concept of limited warfare on the Continent. Of course, as Sir John French talked himself hoarse repeating, operations in secondary theaters had no bearing on major operations except to weaken the force there engaged. The point of the war was to kill Germans, not Turks. But the Dardanelles might be different, because of all the political strings: Russia, Greece, Bulgaria, Rumania. And anyway, the Dardanelles would be a British show with French help, rather than the other way around. If it did not work out, it could be easily abandoned.

When the Admiralty War Group discussed Carden's plan on January 12, no one opposed it. In fact, Fisher suggested that the newest and most powerful dreadnought, the *Queen Elizabeth*, be sent out to the Dardanelles to test her 15-inch guns. She could fire her 1,920-pound shells at the forts instead of spending them uselessly into the sea.[20]

At the War Council on January 13, which lasted from noon until after sunset, Churchill forcefully presented Carden's plan: the Admiral would concentrate his fire on the entrance forts and then deal with the inner forts. His thinking was based on the fact that the forts were armed mainly with old .35-caliber guns, and that the ships could fire their more powerful guns without coming into range. Three modern ships with the heaviest guns and twelve old battleships would do the job. Once the forts were reduced, the minefields would be cleared, and the fleet would proceed to Constantinople and destroy the *Goeben.*

A contagious sense of euphoria that a feasible alternative had been found swept the War Council. It was as if the Carden plan answered each man's heartfelt need. All critical faculties were suspended. No one asked about the weather in the strait, or the tides and currents. No one wanted to know whether German help to the Turks, new guns or floating mines, would increase the difficulty. No one asked what was the strength of the Turkish garrison at Gallipoli. No one wanted to pick holes in the plan, because they were desperate. The bad news on the western front was being kept from the British public. The Dardanelles, they all hoped, would be the providential new theater, a merciful change from the slugging match in France.

Lloyd George liked the plan.

Kitchener thought it was worth trying.

Grey said it might force Italy's hand.

Even that stalwart foe of secondary operations, Sir John French, in England for the day, and disheartened by the lack of success in France, said it was desirable to seek new spheres of activity.[21]

Asquith said nothing, although he believed that there were two things fatal in war: one was to push blindly against a stone wall; the other was to scatter and divide forces in separate and disconnected operations—they were in danger of committing both blunders.[22]

The conclusion, drafted that day by Asquith despite his misgivings, was that the Admiralty should prepare for a naval expedition in February to bombard and take the Gallipoli Peninsula, with Constantinople as its objective.[23] The absurdity of the Navy's taking a defended peninsula with ships and of expecting Constantinople to surrender after a few shells had been fired was overlooked amid the general optimism.

On January 15, Churchill approved the plan of attack, committing to it fifteen battleships, three light cruisers, sixteen destroyers, six submarines, one seaplane ship, and a large number of minesweepers. He sent Carden intelligence reports on Turkish strength and morale, and a Russian blueprint of the Dardanelles forts. Spirits at the Admiralty were high.

Even the captious Captain Richmond liked the plan, writing in his diary: "With our modern long-range heavy guns we can outrange the Turkish forts and a useful bombardment can be carried out. If we can force the passage we have Constantinople open, and the result will I hope be a revolution in Turkey." Richmond's only reservation was the constancy of Churchill's commitment: "Meanwhile Winston is busy thinking out pinpricks in the shape of air raids which he seems to think will produce wonderful results, and fails to appreciate that their proper value is reconnaissances, and no more. He also has still his silly Borkum scheme in mind and wants [it] worked out. I have made one or two remarks upon it which I hope will go some way towards damning it."[24]

On January 17 Churchill went to dine with the Asquiths at Walmer Castle. One of the weekend guests was Henry James, then seventy-one, who would become a British subject that year, with Asquith as a sponsor. The novelist, who boasted that an outsider could not tell whether he was an American writing about England or an Englishman writing about America, and the half-English and half-American First Lord had met the previous month at dinner. On that occasion, Churchill had told him that the British were not building airships, "because the airship is essentially a bad ship, and we English can't make a bad ship well enough." This time, Churchill was annoyed at being displaced by James from the center of attention. He ignored and interrupted the master, whose works he had not read, and showed him "no conversational consideration." Asquith asked James the next morning what he had thought of Winston. In his slow oracular way the master replied: "I never had the lively interest of seeing so much of this remarkable young man before. . . . I confess I am often struck at the limitations with which men of power pay the price for their domination over mankind."[25]

If there was one exception to Churchill's domination it was Jacky Fisher, who was as stubborn and intractable, as intolerant of criticism and easily offended as he was. Fisher was having dark thoughts about the Dardanelles. A lifetime of naval experience told him that it was a terrible blunder. What miasma was it that clouded men's minds into thinking that cutting off the enemy's big toe in the East was better than stabbing him in the heart in the West? He thought of the Nelsonian dictum: "Any sailor who attacks a fort is a fool." Rushing through minefields would be a naval Balaclava charge. The fifteen battleships and dozens of other vessels that were being sent to the

Dardanelles were all urgently required at the decisive theater at home, but it was hopeless to argue with Winston. When he observed that Jellicoe had only twenty-nine battleships available, Winston replied: "Why do you send so many away at once for repairs and refit?" Because Jellicoe had no alternative, Fisher said, to which Winston complained that Jellicoe ran the ships to death and they never got rest.[26]

Actually, Fisher was muddying the waters, for only two of the fifteen battleships were dreadnoughts—the others were old and expendable. But Fisher could not accept risking ships in the Dardanelles. Like a compass needle reverting always to north, his mind was obsessed with the great battle that was bound to take place in the North Sea. Because of England's dependence on naval might, Jellicoe was the one man who could lose the war in a single afternoon.

Fisher was against the project tooth and nail from the start, knowing it was an abomination, but there was nothing he could do; it was high policy, requested by the Russians. He wanted a combined operation, two hundred thousand men in conjunction with the fleet, but Kitchener said that no troops were available. There was only one way out, and that was to resign, but he could not resign because Jellicoe needed him, which meant that he had to stay on against the grain and become a consenting party to a project with which he absolutely disagreed.[27]

Fisher's frustration came from not being able to get the naval point of view across to Churchill, who invariably outtalked him. Fisher lived by instincts and hunches, which he was unable to sustain in argument. He knew he was right, for his gift of prescience had been tested—had he not predicted almost to the month the outbreak of the war? But he felt helpless before Churchill's fluency. Churchill told him that it was not right to condemn operations of war simply because they involved risk. Of course the Dardanelles was risky, but so had been sending the fleet to its war stations by the eastern route on July 29, and throwing the whole British Army across the Channel in the early days of the war, and withdrawing two battle cruisers from the Grand Fleet to destroy von Spee at the Falklands. It was idle to condemn operations because they involved hazard. All war was hazard.[28]

Fisher vented his frustration to Hankey, complaining that he was overruled on technical grounds and that his objections were dismissed. Hankey informed Asquith, who thought that although the old man was difficult, there was some truth in what he said.[29] Captain Richmond, however, observing Fisher's behavior on a daily basis, thought he was worn-out and nervous, a failing old man afraid of mishaps that might be put down to his dispositions.[30]

On January 23, the quarrel between the two uppermost figures at the Admiralty was set aside. Churchill was in his office at noon when Admirals Wilson and Oliver came in with charts and compasses. "First Lord, these fellows are coming out again." "When?" Churchill asked. "Tonight. We have just got time to get Beatty there." Room 40 had intercepted German signals. They thought it was another raid on the British coast. Beatty and Tyrwhitt would join forces at Dogger Bank, off the Danish coast, where German battle cruisers were expected. It would be the first battle between super-dreadnoughts.[31]

At dawn on January 24, with a calm sea and good visibility, the British forces were at Dogger Bank, Beatty with five battle cruisers, Tyrwhitt with three light cruisers and thirty-five destroyers, and Commodore William Goodenough and his 2d Light Cruiser Squadron. On the exact course forecast by Room 40, they spotted four German battle cruisers with four light cruisers and twenty-two destroyers out on patrol. When Admiral von Hipper saw the British ships, he turned his fleet homeward, and Beatty gave chase, fourteen miles behind. As a "touch of spur," he signaled a speed of twenty-nine knots, one knot more than the designed speed of his fastest ship. It was a race between the fastest vessels of the two navies (the battle cruiser was less heavily armored and thus faster than a battleship). Beatty gained, avoiding the wake for fear of dropped mines, and at 9:48 the Admiralty received this telegram from his flagship, the *Lion*: "Am engaging enemy battle cruisers. Range 16,000 yards."

While ships fought on the ocean, in Whitehall the clock ticked and quiet men entered rooms with quick steps, laying slips of penciled paper before other men. Beatty had caught up with the lagging German battle cruiser *Blücher*, but gunnery was poor because of the spray and funnel smoke. Other German ships, including von Hipper's flagship, the *Seydlitz*, fired on the *Lion*, which took fifteen hits.

A message came into the Admiralty and someone said, "The *Lion* is knocked out." Churchill thought of the memorial services he had so often attended in Westminster Abbey—the crowd and the uniforms, and the coffin draped with the Union Jack.[32] In his mind, Beatty's face appeared, his visored admiral's cap at a jaunty angle.

But Beatty was alive, standing on the open bridge of his ship, which listed to port, its wireless shot away, its searchlights smashed, with only two signal halyards left, crippled and dumb. He wanted to tell his fleet to pursue the

Germans, but enough of his signal flags had been shot away so that the message was garbled. The ships stopped following the German force.

Beatty tried to hoist another signal, ENGAGE THE ENEMY MORE CLOSELY, but found to his dismay that it had been removed from the signal book since Nelson had last used it at Trafalgar. The only alternative was KEEP NEARER THE ENEMY. To try to save the situation, he jumped aboard the destroyer *Attack*, hoisted his flag, and attempted to catch up with the battle he thought was still raging, but it was like trying to win the Derby after a bad fall at Tattenham Corner. The other four battle cruisers had gone after the already wrecked *Blücher*, which rolled over and sank with a crew of twelve hundred, while the rest of the German fleet made for Heligoland, eighty miles away. At 12:45 the battle was over. The *Lion* was taken in tow by the *Indomitable*, protected by Tyrwhitt's destroyers, and reached Rosyth at dawn on the twenty-sixth.[33]

The Battle of Dogger Bank was accepted as proof of British supremacy in the North Sea, but Churchill knew that it was a missed opportunity. Why did everything always go wrong, from the mix-up in signals to Jellicoe's piles? The Admiral had to be operated on for an abscess and was out of commission for three weeks. Taking the somatic view of history (Napoleon's liver, Luther's flatulence), Churchill wondered whether Jellicoe's gloomy views were in part the result of his piles.[34] To Fisher, for whom the dour and precautious Admiral could do no wrong, the piles were a proof of his indomitable nature. He had kept working until he had dropped with pain and fatigue. He had suffered like Nelson at Toulon, doing battle with an amputated right arm, after being shot by the Spaniards at Tenerife.[35]

Fisher had decided not to resign, but to make a formal protest over the Dardanelles. On January 25, he produced a long memorandum with a covering note that said: "I have no desire to continue a useless resistance in the War Council to plans I cannot concur in, and I would ask that the enclosed may be printed and circulated to its members before the next meeting."[36]

Fisher argued along the same lines as Sir John French: subsidiary operations played into German hands. But he added the classic naval argument that the first function of the British Army was to help the fleet obtain command of the sea. At present, the Army was bogged down in France, where it no more helped the Navy than if it were at Timbuctoo. He asked for military cooperation in the Dardanelles.

Churchill replied on January 26: The ships going to the Dardanelles in no way weakened British naval dominance in the North Sea. Surplus ships must be used for other operations. Not to use them because of some fear that there would be an outcry if a ship were lost, or if officers and men were lost, would be wrong. They ought not to shrink from it if important objects of the war could be achieved, saving a much greater loss of life among their comrades and allies on shore. A personal appeal was coupled with this reply: "There is no difference in principle between us. But when all your special claims are met, you must let the surplus be used for the general cause."[37]

Fisher wanted his memo and Churchill's reply circulated to the War Council. But Churchill proposed that they be shown to Asquith first. By this time, the Prime Minister had become a strong supporter of the Dardanelles operation. He was sometimes accused of being bored by the war, but this excited him. It would smash up the Turks, let through Russian wheat, and lower the price of bread in England. Not wanting to publicize the dissent between his two top naval men, Asquith refused to allow either of their papers to be circulated. Thus the War Council was kept in the dark about Fisher's objections, and Fisher felt cheated; once again his views had been ignored.[38]

In the meantime, at British naval stations all over the world, ships were being made ready. The *Canopus* had left South America, the *Albion* had left St. Helena, the *Triumph* was in Colombo taking on supplies, the *Ocean* and the *Swiftsure* were in Egypt. Fisher's mind was divided, for although he objected to the operations in principle, in practice he could not help but get involved, and in fact suggested adding two more battleships, *Lord Nelson* and *Agamemnon*, to the Dardanelles fleet. The French Navy was brought in, and all the arrangements, naval and diplomatic, were complete. Churchill expected that Carden could open fire by February 15. There remained only the formal approval of the War Council, which was meeting on January 28.

That morning Fisher wrote Asquith to say that he would not be attending, for he could not condone purely naval actions such as the Dardanelles and the proposed attack on the Belgian port of Zeebrugge. Only military cooperation could justify the risk in ships and men. He was reluctant to leave, but unity of views was essential in war, and he did not want to be a stumbling block.

He also wrote Churchill that he wanted to go back to the roses at his country house in Richmond. He made no objections to operations accompanied by the military so that the Dardanelles could be permanently occupied, but did not agree to draining the Grand Fleet for a naval action.

Churchill did not want to lose Fisher. Though he disagreed with him on the Dardanelles, he respected his judgment. He dreaded working with Admiral Sturdee, whom he feared would be forced upon him if Fisher resigned. Both

Asquith and Churchill felt that Fisher was being petulant, and that his presence at the War Council was indispensable. It was arranged that they meet in Asquith's office beforehand and thrash out their differences.

At ten minutes past eleven, twenty minutes before the start of the War Council, they met in Asquith's study. Worried about the friction between the two, Asquith acted as arbitrator, hearing their grievances and engineering a trade-off: Zeebrugge would be dropped but the Dardanelles would go forward.[39] Fisher agreed, but understood that the Dardanelles would not be discussed at the War Council. Then they went downstairs to join the others in the Cabinet Room.

After some discussion of various topics, during which Lloyd George asked with sarcasm "whether the French intended to attack the German Army," Churchill described the French and Russian reactions to the Dardanelles project and asked "if the War Council attached importance to the operation, which undoubtedly involved some risks."

Fisher said he had understood the question would not be raised, and that the Prime Minister was well aware of his own views in regard to it.

Asquith insisted that "the question could not well be left in abeyance."

Fisher had had enough. He had been betrayed once again. These politicians said one thing and did another. He felt that he was at the War Council in an advisory capacity, to answer technical questions and not to argue with the First Lord over policy in front of the others. But it was impossible to listen to men who knew nothing about the Navy pass opinion on a venture to which he was opposed. He rose, left the council table, and made for the door. Kitchener went after him and, drawing him by the window, asked him what he intended to do. Fisher said he would resign. Kitchener pointed out that he was the only dissentient, and that the Dardanelles operation had been decided upon by the Prime Minister. Surely his duty to his country was to do his job as First Sea Lord. Fisher reluctantly gave in and returned to the table. Aside from Asquith, Churchill, and Kitchener, none of the others realized what had happened, for Fisher's opposition had not been made public. Asquith was amused to see Kitchener take up the role of conciliator, for which he was not naturally cut out.[40]

As soon as Fisher had sat down, Asquith asked the members of the War Council to comment on the Dardanelles. Again, there was a general feeling of euphoria.

Kitchener said the naval attack was vitally important. If it failed, it could be broken off.

Balfour said it was difficult to imagine a more helpful operation, and listed five advantages: it would cut the Turkish Army in two; it would put Constantinople under British control; it would give England Russian wheat; it would restore Russian exports and exchanges; and it would open a passage to the Danube.

Grey said it would settle the attitude of Bulgaria and the rest of the Balkans.

Balfour asked if Austrian submarines could get down the Adriatic to the Dardanelles, and Churchill said he had been told by the French that they could not.

Haldane asked if the Turks had any submarines, and Churchill said that as far as he knew they did not. He explained the plan of attack on a map. The ships were on the way. The man on the spot said he would need three weeks to a month. Some losses must be expected in sweeping for mines and attacking the Narrows.

In a rare burst of elation, Grey said that the Turks would be paralyzed with fear when they heard that the forts were being destroyed one by one.[41]

Fisher listened in stony silence to Balfour sketching out the great prizes to be won, and to Churchill piping seductive notes of success. What a flabby lot they were. All he could think of was the cold gray water of the strait, which he had seen during the Russo-Turkish war, with the current flowing at three knots against the ships, and the minefields laid in neat and lethal rows, and the forts that could fire point-blank at the ships coming through. His views represented the convictions of a lifetime. They played into Germany's hands if they risked fighting ships in any subsidiary operations such as coastal bombardments or attacks on fortified places without military cooperation, for they increased the possibility that the Germans would engage Jellicoe's North Sea fleet with equality of strength. If troops *were* needed, at least they would not have to worry about transports, for the Germans would be only too happy to supply all the transports necessary to carry British troops away from the main theater of war.[42] Fisher had been fond of Churchill, signing some of his letters "Yours till hell freezes." Every day it was becoming more likely that the improbable event would occur.

Early that afternoon, concerned about Fisher's sulkiness, Churchill had an hour's meeting with him, and after a heated discussion, Fisher agreed to support the Dardanelles. He gave his consent without reserve, he said, the whole hog, *totus porcus*.[43]

When the War Council met again that evening at six-thirty, Asquith presided over a united body, determined to carry out the Dardanelles operation.

Admiral Oliver said the first shot would be fired in a fortnight. The fleet would use Port Mudros, on the Greek island of Lemnos, as a base.

Churchill announced to his delighted colleagues that with the approval of Lord Fisher and the rest of the board, the Admiralty had decided "to undertake the task with which the War Council has charged us so urgently." Now there was no going back. The naval attack on the Dardanelles was under way. The original Russian request was by now forgotten, but it had not been Churchill's idea. Kitchener had proposed it as an action that would not involve troops. Admiral Carden said that it could be done. The Sea Lords had agreed, Fisher against his will. But now that the plan was operational, Churchill pressed it forward with his customary zeal. He believed that the Navy could do it alone, and that he would not need troops. In his view, a landing under fire now that the Turks were fully awakened was riskier than a naval attack with old ships. The chance of the naval attack producing revolutionary effects in Constantinople and through the Balkans made it worthwhile to try, even though, if it failed, a subsequent military operation would be more difficult. He was so eager for the Navy to start that he dismissed the idea of a combined operation.[44]

But to win over Fisher, Churchill had promised to urge Kitchener to commit troops. Thus, Fisher, who now supported the scheme *totus porcus*, wrote Churchill on January 29: "I hope you were successful with Kitchener in getting a Division sent to Lemnos *tomorrow*. Not a grain of wheat will come from the Black Sea unless there is military occupation of the Dardanelles! And it will be the wonder of the ages that no troops were sent to cooperate with the Fleet with half a million of soldiers in England!"[45] Churchill planned to ask Kitchener, but for the moment he saw a greater need for troops to rescue Serbia and to occupy Salonika and bring in the Greeks and the Rumanians.

In the first week of February, as British ships steamed across the Mediterranean, the Admiralty drafted its instructions to Carden: destroy the forts at the entrance; clear a channel of mines; proceed to the Narrows, destroying the forts along the way; use two battalions of Marines for small landing operations; use caution; speed was not important; the slow, relentless creeping forward of the attacking force mile after mile would shake the morale of the fort garrisons.[46]

While these plans were being worked out, Churchill turned his attention to the Balkans, where Serbia seemed in danger of being crushed. On February 7, he sent one of his "prophet of doom" letters to Asquith: the Balkan situation was at stake. Asquith might not feel the impact of the projectile, but it had already left the gun and was traveling toward him. Three weeks from now Asquith and Kitchener and Grey would face a disastrous situation, and, as at Antwerp, it would be beyond their power to retrieve it. Churchill often used strong language with Asquith, but in this letter there was a sentence so close to insult that he deleted it: "Surely in your position you cannot be content to sit as a judge pronouncing on events after they have taken place."[47]

The next day Grey gave a lunch for the French Foreign Minister, Théophile Delcassé, whom Lloyd George described as "that fussy little haberdasher." Again they discussed Serbia, and in his fractured French Churchill asked Delcassé "S'ils savent que nous sommes gens qu'ils peuvent compter sur [Do they know they can count on us?]" They agreed to send two divisions, one English and one French, to Salonika.[48]

On February 8, in response to Fisher's prodding, Churchill discussed troops with Kitchener, and, as was his custom, put his thoughts in writing later that day:

> If our operations at the Dardanelles prosper, immense advantages may be offered, which cannot be gathered without military aid. The opportunity may come in three weeks' time, and I think at least 50,000 men should be within reach at three days' notice, either to seize the Gallipoli peninsula when it has been evacuated, or to occupy Constantinople if a revolution takes place. We should never forgive ourselves if the naval operations succeeded and the fruits were lost through the army being absent. In these circumstances I hope earnestly that you will send the 29th Division complete either to Alexandria or Lemnos as convenient. Before it arrives, we shall know how the naval operations are going to turn out . . . The troops can always live on the transports for 10 days or a fortnight, and all the matériel can be left on board, only the horses and men being exercised on shore to keep them fit. It seems to me from what you said this morning that the 50,000 men could be provided as follows—29th Division, 18,000; Australian and other troops from Egypt, 22,000; 9 battalions of Royal Naval Division, 10,000—total 50,000. You would then have a force within two days' steam of Salonika or Constantinople, which having regard to the political circumstances of Turkey and the Balkans might produce very great results.[49]

At the War Council the next day, Kitchener gave the assurance that "if the Navy requires the assistance of the land forces at a later stage, that assistance will be forthcoming."[50] Thus, the Dardanelles operation changed dramatically from a purely naval action to one where the Army would come in and follow up on the gains made by the Navy. Churchill, who had wanted the Navy to do it alone, now saw the advantage of troops. The same thought occurred almost simultaneously in three other quarters.

On February 13, Maurice Hankey went to see Asquith to urge that the naval operations be supported by a strong military force. Asquith agreed. Without denuding French, they could scrape together from Egypt, Malta, and elsewhere a sufficiently large contingent. If only those heartbreaking Balkan states could be bribed or goaded into action, the trick would be done with the greatest of ease. It was essential for this reason that they carry through a *decisive* operation.[51]

On February 14, Captain Richmond circulated a memorandum insisting that the bombardment of the Dardanelles would be only a local success without an army to carry it through, which bolstered Hankey, who wrote him: "Your Memo. is absolutely A.1 and is most opportune. I am sending it to Jacky. You are preaching to the converted but it may ginger him up." "YOUR PAPER IS EXCELLENT," Fisher responded. Richmond recorded in his diary: "Thirty thousand men at the Dardanelles next week would make more impression on the continental campaign than five times that number on the banks of the Yser."[52]

On February 15, Sir Henry Jackson circulated *his* memorandum, which concluded that "the naval bombardment is not recommended as a sound military operation unless a strong military force is ready to assist in the operation, or, at least, follow it up immediately the forts are silenced." Both army and navy strategists were swinging to the view originally propounded by Fisher.[53]

Still unsure of the need to divert troops to a distant eastern operation, overruling the needs of the commander in chief in France, Kitchener summoned one of his intelligence officers, Captain Wyndham Deedes, who had served four years with the Turkish Gendarmerie. What were the prospects of a naval attack at the Dardanelles? he asked. The operation was fundamentally unsound, Deedes told him. Furious at not getting the response he wanted, Kitchener interrupted Deedes to tell him that he did not know what he was talking about and terminated the interview.[54] But when the War Council met on February 16 in an emergency session with six of its ten members, Deedes's words lingered in Kitchener's mind. He agreed that the 29th Division should go to Lemnos "at the earliest possible date," sailing from England "within nine or ten days." It was further decided that the Australian and New Zealand troops stationed in Egypt and the battalion of Royal Marines already on its way should be available to support the naval attack. The Admiralty would build transports suitable for the landing of a force of fifty thousand men. Kitchener's parting words to Churchill were: "You get through. I will find the men."[55]

Asquith saw the Dardanelles as the only hope in an otherwise dreary military situation. In the last *ten days* French had lost one hundred officers and twenty-six hundred men on the western front with very little to show for such losses. The Russians were doing badly (although they had wonderful powers of recuperation), and the wretched little Balkan states were bickering and cowering and holding their hands like Italians.[56]

What had started as a naval diversion to help the Russians had now become a full-fledged joint enterprise committing more than fifty ships and fifty thousand men, although it was not planned as the combined attack that Fisher wanted. The sequence was that the Navy would force the strait and then the Army would land. So much depended on the goodwill between Kitchener and Churchill, which had already been strained by the First Lord's visits to France.

Kitchener was a national hero, the man the people trusted, but to many of his colleagues, he was a cipher. He was the first active professional soldier in a modern Cabinet, the first great general to hold high civil office since the Duke of Wellington, but was he anything more than a recruiting poster? Lloyd George said he had a mind "like a revolving light-house. Sometimes the beam lights up all Europe and the opposing armies in a vast and illimitable perspective. Then the shutter comes round, and for several weeks you get blank darkness."[57]

Kitchener did not seem to take his fellow ministers seriously, and often could not remember their names. It made the generals in the War Office break out in a cold sweat when they heard him say, "A fellow . . . I don't know his name, but he's got curly hair, said . . ." Asquith complained that he did not have the useful corrective of humor. The only time Kitchener got a laugh in the Cabinet was during a discussion on the employment of women in wartime. Lloyd George pointed out that many trades were barred to them, such as miners and dockers. "But they do such work in Zanzibar," Kitchener interjected.[58]

At the War Office, Kitchener simply bludgeoned everyone into agreement, his chief of staff, Wolfe "Sheep" Murray, mumbling assent. Underlings slunk about the corridors whispering, "He's in a good mood today." In the Cabinet he behaved like an honest man trapped in a den of thieves. He was reluctant to part with information, jealous of his authority, disinclined to take advice, and suspicious of his colleagues. After the Battle of Dogger Bank, Churchill showed the Cabinet a photograph of the *Blücher* as she gave her last sideways roll, her crew scrambling up the deck to the taffrail. As Churchill told his story, Kitchener looked bored and uninterested, as if he had a far better story to tell, if only he could disclose it in such suspect company.[59]

As the head of the other fighting department, Churchill was a rival who could not be trusted. He had, Kitchener was sure, plotted with French behind his back, envenoming an already difficult relationship. Kitchener was as touchy as if he had a toothache when it came to Churchill, and it was one of the tragedies of the Dardanelles that at the very moment when their cooperation was crucial they became enmeshed in another jurisdictional squabble.

On February 17, Kitchener learned that Churchill had offered French a brigade of the Naval Division and two squadrons of armored cars.[60] French did not know what to do with these unwelcome gifts, for the naval battalions were still raw and ragged and the only use he could find for the famous armored cars was to remove their Maxim guns for the men in the trenches. But aside from that, Churchill was at it again, going over Kitchener's head and dealing directly with French.

As was his habit, Kitchener complained to Asquith, who was rather vexed with his First Lord. Winston was intolerable. It was all *vanity*—he was devoured by vanity.[61] It was most trying, for he and Kitchener had reached a *modus vivendi*. And it came at a time when they were confronted with difficulties on all sides, Serbia, Russia, the Dardanelles. Truly trouble did not come as single spies but in battalions.[62]

The whole thing was a mare's nest, Churchill told Asquith. He had no power to offer troops to French. All he could do with Admiralty units was hand them over to the War Office. In any case, the offer to French was null and void since the Naval Brigades were now earmarked for the Dardanelles, which Kitchener knew perfectly well. This was not the first time Kitchener had made trouble over nothing.[63]

Nonetheless, on February 18, he wrote the War Secretary a soothing letter. He could not conceive why they should quarrel. Surely Kitchener knew what care he had taken in the last few months to avoid anything that could cause difficulties with the War Office. Even little things, such as whether Admiral Bacon should go to France to find out where French wanted the howitzers put, or whether his cousin Freddie Guest should go to the Dardanelles, had been referred to the War Office for permission.[64]

Kitchener would not be soothed, so Churchill wrote again the following day. It would be a pity to have an argument on the letter of a phrase. If French's letter had begun "I have heard that there are some armored cars available," instead of talking about "the offer of the First Lord of the Admiralty," the whole wearisome incident would have been avoided.[65]

To Kitchener, it was one more example that Churchill was not to be trusted. He had known this since the Sudan, when a brash and bumptious subaltern had used his London connections to worm his way into the Nile expedition, and had written defamatory reports about him. Churchill had not changed; he was as unreliable as ever.

It was in this hostile frame of mind that Kitchener attended the War Council on the afternoon of the nineteenth, which was meeting to confirm the decision to send the 29th Division to the Dardanelles. Churchill could not believe what he heard: Kitchener reneged on his commitment to send the division. He preferred to substitute the thirty thousand Australians and New Zealanders stationed in Egypt, he said. In view of the Russian setback in East Prussia, he was averse to sending away the 29th Division at present.[66]

It was true that Kitchener took a gloomy view of the Russian situation. The Germans had given them a bad knock and taken a large number of prisoners. Happily the German pursuit was hampered by swampy terrain. The Russians said they had nine hundred thousand men ready to fight, clothed and equipped, but they had no rifles.[67] Kitchener's decision made sense on strategic grounds. If the Germans inflicted a decisive defeat on the Russians, they would be able to bring back masses of troops to France. If the 29th was sent to Lemnos, it might sit there for months, when it might be desperately needed on the western front. Kitchener's pique and mistrust of Churchill served to reinforce his decision to keep his division close to hand.

Churchill appealed to the War Council to confirm the decision of February 16. It would be a great disappointment to the Admiralty if the 29th was not sent out. The attack on the Dardanelles was a very heavy naval undertaking, and it would be a thrifty disposition to have fifty thousand men in the region. He was sending out the ten trained battalions of the Naval Division. But neither these nor the Australians and New Zealanders could be called first-rate troops at present, and they needed a stiffening of regulars. They would never forgive themselves if this promising operation failed owing to insufficient military support at the critical moment.[68]

To send or not to send, that was the question of the hour. The persuasive powers of Churchill, Lloyd George, and Asquith combined to try to sway Kitchener, but all their arguments drifted like puffs of air over the stiff and uncompromising figure with a field marshal's rank. All that Kitchener would say was that he was willing to let the division go if holding it back compromised the success of the Dardanelles attack. However, the troops already in Egypt would be sufficient at first. The War Council deferred its decision, which was tantamount to giving Kitchener what he wanted, and agreed that transports should be sent to Alexandria to convey the Anzac (Australian and New Zealand Army Corps) troops to Lemnos.

The thrust of the February 19 War Council was twofold: it established the Dardanelles as a major operation committing important military and naval forces, but it withheld for the moment the division of regular troops that might have made success more certain. For three weeks, Kitchener persisted in his refusal to send the 29th. Even if he had sent it at once, the fiasco of the Dardanelles could not have been avoided, for it had been agreed that the troops would land only *after* the Navy had attempted to force the strait, whereas the best chance of success was in a combined operation. In the Dardanelles attack, the Army and the Navy were caught in the dilemma of the little boy eating bread and cheese. The little boy asks his mother, "Can I have some bread to finish my cheese?" and a little later, "Can I have some cheese to finish my bread?" At the Dardanelles, first the Navy acted without the help of the Army, and then the Army landed without a corresponding naval attack. There was never enough bread for the cheese, and never enough cheese for the bread.

On February 19, as the War Council deliberated, Carden began his bombardment of the four outer forts with their nineteen primary guns. Ships anchored at twelve thousand yards fired their big guns, making no direct hits on the forts, but blowing up two ammunition dumps. After this initial but modest success, a gale prevented further operations, which were not resumed until February 25.

It was a terrible six-day interruption, giving the Turks a chance to prepare, and losing the psychological and material advantage of continuous bombardment. New factors, unforeseen, kept disturbing the expectations of the Admiralty. Perhaps Churchill, who knew Napoleon's campaigns by heart, recalled the exchange after Bonaparte's defeat in Russia. "Which of your generals do you blame?" he was asked, and he replied: *Le Général Hiver* (General Winter).

In the meantime, Churchill prodded Kitchener about the troops, and also about appointing a general to take their command. When the War Council met on February 24, and Haldane asked whether the Turks could be driven out of Gallipoli by naval attack, Kitchener replied that "if the fleet succeeded in silencing the forts, the garrison of Gallipoli would probably be withdrawn," for otherwise "they would run the risk of being cut off and starved out." This made no sense at all unless troops were landed to cut them off.

Once again, Churchill asked for the 29th Division. The results of the Dardanelles operation might be so far-reaching that many troops would be needed to follow it up.

The attack on the Dardanelles had been planned as a naval one, Kitchener said. Did Churchill now contemplate a land attack as well?

Churchill said he did not. But if the naval attack was held up by mines, some military operation might be required.

What would all the troops do when they reached the Dardanelles? Kitchener wanted to know.

Churchill said they could occupy Constantinople, or move toward the Bulgarian border, or toward Salonika, or be sent up the Danube. There were several possibilities.

Lloyd George agreed that a force should be sent to occupy Gallipoli or Constantinople. But what if the naval attack failed, since it was something of an experiment? Should the Army be used to undertake an operation in which the Navy had failed? He did not think the Army should pull the chestnuts out of the fire for the Navy.

Churchill said there might be a case where the Navy had almost succeeded and a military force could tilt the scales.

Kitchener repeated that he did not understand why so many troops were needed. When the British fleet had forced its way through the Dardanelles, the Turkish garrison would evacuate and the Sultan and the Turkish government would flee Constantinople. Victory would be achieved by naval guns alone.

Grey agreed. There might even be a coup d'état in Constantinople.

Churchill pointed out the diplomatic victory to be won. If the Turks were on the run, a million Balkan soldiers might be brought into the allied armies. Surely it was worthwhile to send a hundred thousand British troops to attain this objective.

Asquith asked whether the Australians and New Zealanders were good enough for such an operation.

Kitchener replied that "they were quite good enough if a cruise in the Sea of Marmara was all that was contemplated."

Asquith felt that more troops should be sent, for this was a unique opportunity, but to overrule Kitchener's judgment on a military matter was a great responsibility.[69]

Even when the entire War Council was against Kitchener, no one dared challenge his authority. He was a soldier whose opinions carried the weight of long experience. He had first been to Turkey in 1874, and had served as British vice-consul in Anatolia. In India and Egypt, he had been concerned with Moslem problems, and he spoke Arabic. By contrast, Churchill was a civilian without any record of naval experience prior to his appointment as First Lord, or expertise on Turkey, whose authority was diluted by attacks in the press, persisting Tory enmity, and hostile feeling among some of his Cabinet colleagues. It was an unequal combat. Kitchener's imperturbable presence dominated the War Council. Only Churchill and Lloyd George dared to disagree with him, and Asquith could not overrule him, for he could not afford to lose the face on the recruiting poster.

On February 25, when Carden was at last able to resume the naval bombardment, the four outer forts were destroyed. As the ships' guns blazed with accurate fire, Churchill was on the downs of Blandford Camp, in Dorset, reviewing the Royal Naval Division with the King and the Asquiths on the eve of the division's departure. It was a splendid sight, thought Margot Asquith, the ten thousand men drawn up in formation, and her stepson Arthur, or "Oc," standing in front of his men and looking quite wonderful. They stood waiting for what seemed like hours, and finally Colonel John Quilter, the commander of the 7th Battalion (who would be killed that May in Gallipoli), let the men off to smoke. The King arrived at eleven-thirty with his equerry, Sir Charles Cust, who made disobliging remarks about the division, but sailors who gave up the sea for the court, thought Margot, were not critics to be frightened of.[70]

Over uneven ground, the thousands of young men marched past the King, their backs straight, their bayonets glinting in the winter sunlight, their heads snapping to the order "Eyessss RIGHT!" How lucky they were, thought Asquith, to escape Flanders and the trenches and to be sent to the gorgeous East.[71]

Later, after the distribution of sun helmets, Violet was reunited with her brother and her friend Rupert Brooke, who saw the Dardanelles in Homeric terms: would the sea be wine-dark, and would the battle be a turning point in history? Brooke was leaving with travel books on Turkey and an amulet from a London grande dame. Despite the amulet, he told all and sundry that he would not return alive. Violet went off with Oc to shop for maps and compasses and tinderlights and Fox's special puttees and Keating's powder and the Constantinople Baedeker.[72] It was all going to be such a romp. The Turks were not good fighters. According to the divisional notes, they did not like night attacks because they were afraid of the dark.[73]

At the War Council of February 26, the tug-of-war between Churchill and Kitchener resumed. Churchill made "the strongest possible appeal" that the 29th Division not be withheld. In three weeks, Constantinople might be at their mercy, and they would not have the troops to force a surrender.

Speaking with an authority that no one could challenge, Kitchener predicted, "from his knowledge of Constantinople and the East," that the whole situation would change "the moment the fleet had secured a passage through the Dardanelles." The Turkish government would probably evacuate Constantinople, and the Turkish Army would probably surrender.

The War Council was split: Lloyd George and Hankey backed Churchill, while Balfour and Grey sided with Kitchener. Asquith saw merits in both views. Neither side would budge. It was a mirror-image of the situation in France, with the British leaders stalemated in their own version of trench warfare.

Unable to get his way, Churchill retreated into petulance. If there was a disaster in Turkey because of insufficient troops, he disclaimed all responsibility. He wanted it placed on record that he dissented from keeping the 29th Division in England. It would not make the difference between failure and success in France, but it might well make the difference in the East.[74]

What could one do, Churchill wondered, with a man who had absorbed the whole War Office into his spacious personality, and who was surrounded by petrified yes-men? They saluted like subordinates on a drill ground. There was no strategic thinking in the War Office. The only army policy was "kill Germans." But you could not argue with Kitchener, who had always held independent commands far from England where his authority was absolute. He was aloof under questioning and oracular in his pronouncements, and the confidence in his professional judgment and the belief that he had deeper plans than he was disclosing silenced misgivings and disputes.[75]

Asquith had now swung to Kitchener's side. Kitchener was right to insist on keeping his division at home, free to go either to the Dardanelles or to France, wherever the need was greatest. The War Council had been right to accept his view, much to Winston's immense and unconcealed dudgeon. Winston had been at his worst—noisy, rhetorical, tactless, and bad-tempered.[76] The Prime Minister confided to his wife that Churchill was by far the most disliked man in the Cabinet. "Oh! he is intolerable," Asquith exclaimed. "Noisy, long-winded and full of perorations. We don't want suggestion—we want wisdom."[77] Churchill never knew of Asquith's dislike, for to his face the Prime Minister was always cordial and full of praise.

Churchill was placed in the position of having predicted disaster if the operation went on without troops, while going ahead with the naval attack that had already begun. While urging Carden to pursue the bombardment, he argued in the War Council that it would fail. He contributed to the climate of self-deception by first believing that a naval action would suffice, and by not calling it off when he no longer believed it. Fisher sat through the debates in stony silence, although with each day he liked the Dardanelles less. No one directing public affairs had the courage of a louse or the backbone of a slug, thought Fisher, except Winston, whose courage was that of the Evil One.[78]

At the beginning of March, however, good news lifted Churchill's spirits. On March 1, Violet Asquith was visiting Clemmie at the Admiralty when he came in wild with joy. Pledging them to secrecy, he displayed a telegram from Greek Premier Venizelos, promising three divisions for Gallipoli. "Is the King sound?" Violet asked, for the Greek King was married to the Kaiser's sister, Sophie. "Yes," Churchill replied, "our minister said Venizelos had already approached the King and he was in favor of war."

Churchill totted up the combined forces: the Anzac troops on the spot, the Royal Naval Division on the way, the French division, the promise of three Greek divisions and a Russian army corps, the 29th still in the balance. It was a mighty force that had flowed from their naval enterprise. Violet left the Admiralty treading on air. She saw Turkey encircled by a host of enemies, the German flank turned, the Balkans united on the allied side, the war shortened perhaps by years, and Churchill's vision vindicated.[79] It was, thought her father, the Prime Minister, really *far* the most interesting moment up to now in the war.[80]

There was more good news from Carden, who had landed a small party of Marines at the entrance of the strait. The Marines destroyed nineteen heavy guns, eleven light guns, four Nordenfelt machine guns, and two searchlights, and returned safely to their ships.[81] All the forts at the entrance were now practically demolished, and Carden was in the process of destroying the forts in the strait and clearing the mines. He estimated that he would need fourteen days of good weather to force the strait. There were smiling faces at the Admiralty. In Constantinople, the German Military Mission, under General Liman von Sanders, expecting the British fleet to break through, had made arrangements for the Sultan and his court to take refuge in the interior of Asia Minor. Across the Atlantic, wheat prices fell on the Chicago stock exchange.[82]

With the reduction of the forts proceeding and the Greeks pledged to bring in troops, the Dardanelles looked promising, and the members of the War Council met on March 3 anticipating a speedy conclusion to the naval action. Already seeing Constantinople captured and Turkey occupied, they proceeded to sell the bear's skin before the bear had been shot. The discussion turned on the future of Constantinople. Should it be given to Greece or Russia? Should it be a neutral or an international zone? And who should control the strait? Balfour proposed making a deal with the Turks: if they offered no resistance their mosques would not be damaged. He also wanted the bridges from the native quarter cut to prevent a massacre in the European quarter. Churchill wanted to hire Turkish soldiers as mercenaries, but Lloyd George said they did not fight well outside their own country. The Admiralty had already drafted leaflets to drop over Constantinople, saying, "When Germany is beaten, as she is going to be, who will have a word of pity for her miserable allies . . . ? The forts of the Dardanelles lie in ruins: the great guns are silent never to speak again. . . ."[83]

Amid the glow of elation, only Asquith sounded a cautionary note: the Turks and their German masters would not give in easily. Jacky Fisher, who had elected to keep silent, liked the Dardanelles less and less. Even if they got through the strait, how would they get back out? And it was a wonder that a hostile submarine had not appeared.[84]

Kitchener and the War Council were still getting mixed messages from Churchill. On one hand he clamored for more troops at once; on the other he said the strait could be forced without troops in two weeks. On March 4, still trying to dislodge the 29th Division, he wrote Kitchener that since the transports would be ready by March 15, his decision should be made by March 10. The need of one good division of regular infantry in an army of so many different elements and containing only British and Australian troops raised since the war still appeared to him to be grave and urgent.

Kitchener had sent his favorite general, Sir William Birdwood, who had served as his secretary in South Africa and India, and whom he trusted as much as he could trust anyone, to the Dardanelles to serve as his eyes and ears. Birdwood's first impression was that when the fleet arrived before Constantinople, resistance would collapse. But if troops were required on the hilly, rocky, trackless Gallipoli Peninsula, major operations would be necessary, for the country was big and difficult and even an entire division could lose itself. Kitchener ordered Birdwood on March 4 to concentrate all the sixty-five thousand troops waiting in Egypt (the Anzacs, the French, and the Royal Naval Division) on transports off the island of Lemnos. There they should remain, ready to strike, but "unless the Navy are convinced that they cannot silence the guns in the Straits without military cooperation on a large scale, in which case further orders will be issued, there is no intention of using the troops enumerated above to take the Gallipoli peninsula." In Kitchener's view, it was still Churchill's show.[85]

The Dardanelles predicament was not only military, but diplomatic, in that other nations were involved. British plans depended on Russia and Greece, who had conflicting aims in the area. Control of the Dardanelles, and thus access to the Mediterranean, was a centuries-old Russian dream. Unwilling to take the chance that a Greek army might reach Constantinople first, Russia vetoed Greek participation. Churchill's hope of Greek divisions shattered on the wall of Russian intransigence. He urged Sir Edward Grey to take a strong stand, but diplomatic maneuvering became irrelevant when the Venizelos government resigned on March 6 because of the King's reluctance to go to war.[86] The Greek card would not be played. Not one Greek soldier would set foot on the Gallipoli Peninsula, and not one Greek ship would take part in the bombardment.

As the telegrams flew back and forth between the chancelleries in Athens, Petrograd, and London, Carden was doing his best to cope with unforeseen problems. He had been sent to the Dardanelles with outdated maps, without any information about weather conditions or any up-to-date intelligence on the reinforcements of the strait's defenses by the Germans, to muddle through as best he could. The operation had been encouraged in the hope that the Turk would not put up much of a fight, which turned out not to be the case. On March 4, a demolition party with a covering force of Marines met unexpected resistance in two villages. Under heavy rifle fire that they could not locate, the British were forced to retire with nineteen killed, three missing, and twenty-three wounded.[87]

Working in the strait, which was only a few miles wide, with forts on both sides, was not like shelling the outer forts from the open sea. It was not at all what had been imagined. Naval guns were designed to pierce the armor of other ships with direct fire, and were incapable of the plunging fire that would have permanently knocked out the forts, which had been solidly built, under the direction of the British adviser to the Turkish Navy, Admiral Arthur Limpus, who had been shunted to Malta as superintendent of the dockyards.

Howitzers would have done the trick, but there were no howitzers aboard battleships. The Turks had concealed howitzers that were moved as soon as they were located. Their plunging fire was very destructive, and the battleships *Agamemnon* and *Lord Nelson* were seriously hit. When the *Queen Elizabeth* moved in too close, the howitzers found her range at once, and she was hit, though not badly. She had to shift her berth and move out of range, as far as twenty-one thousand yards, resorting to indirect firing from outside the strait, with a spotter ship in the strait protected by three other ships. The spotter ship, at anchor, was too good a target. Everything seemed to be conspiring against Admiral Carden. The weather was bad, with gale-force winds whipping up the sea; the reconnaissance planes were crippled with accidents and engine trouble; the guns on shore could not be permanently destroyed unless demolition teams were landed; and the minesweepers could work only at night because of fire from the field guns. The minesweepers consisted of twenty-one unarmed wooden trawlers, too slow to make much headway against a strong current, and manned by untrained fishermen hurriedly recruited from the fishing fleets of Grimsby and Hull. The sweeping system was cumbersome—a wire sweep intended to cut the moorings of the mines was towed between two trawlers five hundred yards apart. But until serrated wire was introduced in 1916, the trawlers often had to circle around a mine and drag it out to sea and then sink it with gunfire—it was complicated enough in daylight, but to do it at night, under heavy gunfire at ranges of three thousand yards and the glare of searchlights, would have tested the nerve of the most experienced sailors, not to mention civilian fishermen asked to do the Navy's job. An added menace was mines that came loose from their moorings in the three-knot current and floated about the strait haphazardly. Still, Carden reported that in spite of heavy bombardment and damage to several ships, he was silencing the forts one by one.[88]

It did not take General Birdwood long to realize that Carden's two-week estimate was wildly optimistic. He now wired Kitchener that he was doubtful that the Navy could force the strait alone. The Army would have to land and help them do the job. This was what Hankey and Fisher had said all along. The operation could not succeed without a large force to take the forts on the Gallipoli side in reverse.[89]

But at the March 10 War Council, dwelling on the progress made and skimming over the difficulties, Churchill announced that "the Admiralty still believed that they could effect the passage of the straits by naval means alone, but they were glad to know that military support was available, if required."[90]

Kitchener stunned his colleagues by announcing that "he felt that the situation was now sufficiently secure to justify the dispatch of the 29th Division."[91] Impressed by Birdwood's pessimistic reports, he was adhering to the transport schedule that Churchill had recommended on March 4. If the 29th was to leave on the fifteenth, the decision must be made on the tenth. Even so, it would take a month before they would be ready to fight at Gallipoli. Churchill felt relieved that after three weeks of quarreling, the 29th had been pried loose. They would provide a vital contingent of crack troops in the battle to come.

This was the meeting to which, in a friendly show of bipartisanship, the Tory leaders Lord Lansdowne and Bonar Law were invited. For the Dardanelles was no longer merely an alternative to the stalemate in the West; it had become a land grab in the best Imperial tradition. The War Council felt it might be advisable to have a few Tories sit in on the division of the spoils.

Asquith thought that so long as both Britain and France got a substantial share of the Turkish carcass, Russia's claim to Constantinople should be accepted.

Churchill said that Britain should get Alexandretta, the only good harbor between Smyrna and the Suez Canal. Why should they give Constantinople to Russia and Syria to France and receive nothing in return? Kitchener agreed. Alexandretta also had military value, for troops could be dispatched from there to India and Mesopotamia. Fisher agreed. Alexandretta was important as an outlet for Persian oil.

Lloyd George disagreed. He wanted a British occupation of Palestine, which Kitchener dryly informed him "would be of no value to us whatsoever."

Finally, the War Council decided to accept Russia's demand for Constantinople, provided British demands were met. And so it was that, before any victory had been won, Asia Minor was carved up by British leaders over a council table.[92]

Having decided to send the 29th Division, Kitchener appointed a general to command the growing Dardanelles army; he turned out to be Churchill's old friend Ian Hamilton, the trim and elegant Scotsman with the long, thin face and the handlebar mustaches. Churchill thought highly of the sixty-two-year-old general, but Asquith suspected there was too much feather in his brain.[93] He was a bit of a courtier, taking Churchill's brother on his staff and sending Asquith reassuring letters from the front about his son.

On the morning of March 10, Hamilton was summoned to Kitchener's office, and waited as the great soldier kept writing with studied casualness, not looking up from his desk, until finally he said: "We are sending a military force to support the fleet now at the Dardanelles, and you are to have command."

Hamilton had served under Kitchener in the Boer War and knew his tight-lipped ways. Kitchener probably expected him to bow, leave the room, and head eastward, as he had done years before when Kitchener had said, "You had better go out to the Western Transvaal." But this time Hamilton had questions. What was the enemy strength? About forty thousand, Kitchener said. How many guns? No one knew. Who was in command? Kitchener was not sure. Hamilton's instructions were so vague they amounted to a blank check. They moved to a map on the wall where Hamilton was shown a plan of attack that had been drawn up by the Greek general staff. We soldiers were clearly to understand that we were string number two, Kitchener told him. The sailors said they could force the strait on their own, and the soldiers were not to chip in unless the Admiral chucked up the sponge. He hoped Hamilton would not have to land at all. If he did, then the powerful fleet would be the prime factor in his choice of time and place. "If the fleet gets through," Kitchener said, "Constantinople will fall of itself and you will have won not a battle but the war." Kitchener already saw Hamilton's army floating home-ward up the Danube. "Let the French and the Russians garrison Constantinople and sing their hymns in Santa Sophia," he said. When General Walter Braithwaite, Hamilton's chief of staff, joined the conversation and pleaded for a squadron of planes, Kitchener turned on him and said, "Not one!"[94]

Kitchener had greater hopes for the Navy than did the Navy itself, which was having doubts. At the Admiralty War Group meeting on March 11, attention focused on a minute by Sir Henry Jackson, who had until now supported the naval action. Impressed by Carden's difficulties, Jackson proposed that troops occupy Gallipoli with the support of the Navy. Once the peninsula was captured, the forts on the Asiatic side could be more easily dealt with. But to advance farther over unswept minefields, in waters commanded at short range by heavy guns and howitzers, would involve serious losses in ships and men.[95]

Churchill explained that Carden was not being asked to advance over unswept minefields; his orders were to move his battleships up only when the minefields had been cleared. He expected Fisher to seize on Jackson's memo to discredit the whole plan. But Fisher did not say a word; for once, he was in a pro-Dardanelles mood because the Admiralty had intercepted several German messages revealing that the forts badly needed ammunition, which could not arrive for several weeks. The mercurial Fisher was now so excited by the prospect of victory that he wanted to leave at once and take command of Carden's forces. The time had come, Fisher urged, for Carden to press on and for Kitchener to occupy the deserted Gallipoli forts and mount howitzers there![96]

On the basis of this intelligence, Carden was urged on March 11 by Churchill and Fisher to press the naval attack more vigorously, even if it meant a loss of ships and men. He should not hesitate to use his whole force at one time.[97]

But Churchill still hoped to bring in the Army, and when he saw Ian Hamilton at the Admiralty on March 12, the eve of Hamilton's departure, promising to give him the planes that Kitchener refused to provide, he made a strong case for a combined military attack with whatever troops were available. Hamilton was caught between hammer and anvil. Kitchener had ordered him to go slow, to let the Navy continue to pound the strait, and to wait for the 29th Division. Churchill was telling him to rush the strait with the troops he had on hand. But when Churchill tried on March 13 to get authorization for such an attack, Kitchener's reply was final: ". . . no operations on a large scale should be attempted until the 29th Division has arrived and is ready to take part in what is likely to prove a difficult undertaking in which severe fighting must be anticipated."[98] Kitchener kept putting spokes in the wheel. It was he who had initially promoted the Dardanelles as a naval action. Then he had refused to send the 29th Division in the belief that it would not be needed. Now he refused to let the other troops fight *without* the 29th because the Turks were too strong. What was one to make of him? Disappointed, Churchill saw Hamilton off on the afternoon of March 13 at Charing Cross Station. In the train crossing France, Hamilton wrote him that he had been reading all the papers and "I don't see how these concealed howitzers are to be tackled without storming the plateau."[99]

On March 13, Churchill received a telegram that made him wonder whether Carden was losing his grip. Minesweeping operations on the previous night, reported the Admiral, had not been satisfactory owing to heavy fire, with no casualties. Why would minesweeping be interfered with by fire that caused no casualties? Churchill asked. The sentence made him squirm. He

485

replied that two or three hundred casualties would be a moderate price to pay for opening up the strait. Carden must press forward night and day against an anxious and harassed enemy.[100]

To Churchill, sitting in his office and studying maps, the situation seemed simple. All Carden had to do was sweep a good clear passage through the minefields so the forts could be attacked at close range. But to the man commanding the ships on the cold gray sea, it was an Alice in Wonderland dilemma. There were fixed and movable guns defending the minefields. To destroy those guns brought the ships under fire of the heavy guns in the forts, which had to be dealt with first. But they could not be attacked at close range until the mines had been cleared. And the mines could not be cleared until the guns defending them were destroyed. Around and around one could go.

To escape the dilemma, Carden tried minesweeping by night, but the Turks had strong searchlights that could not be knocked out for more than a few minutes. It was heartbreaking to send the sweepers through a lethal field of fire lit by searchlights, but in response to Churchill's prodding, Carden tried again on the night of the thirteenth, asking for volunteer crews only.[101]

After the battleship *Cornwallis* had bombarded the searchlights and batteries for an hour, the sweepers moved into the minefield with five picket boats and a destroyer escort. The current was so strong they had to pass through the lighted area, under the withering fire of four forts and about twenty-five light guns on either side of the strait. The damage to the sweepers' winches was such that only two were able to get out their sweeps. In two sweepers the entire crew was either killed or wounded. A number of mines were destroyed, but the cost was high: four sweepers and one picket boat out of action, twenty-seven killed and forty-three wounded. Churchill had the casualties he had asked for, while Carden was convinced that efficient sweeping by night was impossible.[102]

As Carden tried in vain to sweep the minefields, the Cabinet, sure of success, was confidently partitioning the Turkish Empire. Sir Herbert Samuel, President of the Local Government Board, suggested that Britain occupy Palestine and turn it into a homeland for the Jews. Asquith could just see the scattered Jews swarming back to that barren place from all quarters of the globe. What an attractive community that would be! was his sarcastic evaluation. Lloyd George, who Asquith knew did not care a damn for the Jews, supported the plan because he did not want the Christian Holy Places to pass into the possession of atheistic France. How odd, thought Asquith, that the same conclusion could be reached by such different roads. The most violent opponent of the plan was Asquith's close friend and confidant Edwin Montagu, Chancellor of the Duchy of Lancaster, and one of the three Jewish members of the Cabinet, the others being Samuel and Lord Reading. Montagu, a foe of Zionism, thought the idea of a Jewish national home was presumptuous and almost blasphemous.[103]

Maurice Hankey was not thinking about Palestine but about the Dardanelles. As brilliantly conceived as the operation was, it was not being carried out in the best possible manner. As soon as the outer forts had collapsed, the troops should have come in as a bolt from the blue to capture the Gallipoli plateau. He had urged this from the start, but his suggestions had fallen on deaf ears. Now the Turks had been given time to assemble a vast force, to pour in field guns and howitzers, to entrench every landing place, and the operation had become most formidable.[104]

On March 16, there was another setback, which Hankey could not have foreseen—Carden went on the sick list with "atonic indigestion" and had to be relieved of command.[105] The bearded fifty-eight-year-old Admiral, who had originally affirmed that ships could force the strait alone, and who had worked out the plan with the Admiralty, left the Dardanelles never to return, and never again held a seagoing command. Carden's "atonic indigestion" was in fact a nervous breakdown. He had cracked under the strain. The mines, the searchlights, the current, the bad weather, the hidden howitzers, all the obstacles to the operation had made him a wreck. He worried so about losing a capital ship that everything he ate gave him a severe pain.[106] It was, he told his chief of staff, Roger Keyes, that beastly suet-and-treacle pudding that had done him in. Keyes advised him to diet and eat more wholesome food. He hadn't been fit that day for a meeting of captains and admirals, and the doctors said he would break down completely if he did not have rest. Keyes thought the ship's doctor was a "mug-wump" afraid of responsibility, and urged Carden to get a second opinion from the Harley Street specialist serving on the hospital ship Sudan, which he did. Birdwood had informed Kitchener that Carden was "very second-rate"—there was no go in him, no ideas or initiative. Clearly, he had not been equal to the command. Kitchener, however, was convinced that Churchill had driven Carden off his head with his impulsive and headstrong ways.[107] The sad fact was that not everyone who reached the rank of admiral had the ability to command an operation as complex as the Dardanelles. Indeed, the reverse was often true.

Churchill immediately appointed Carden's second-in-command, Rear Admiral John de Robeck, to succeed him. Birdwood thought de Robeck was "worth a dozen of Carden."[108] Certainly, he had greater clarity, drive, and substance.

Ian Hamilton arrived at the Dardanelles on March 17 aboard the light cruiser *Phaeton* and got his first glimpse of the Gallipoli Peninsula, a chain of hills running down from the Thracian mainland between the Aegean and the Sea of Marmara, with peaks rising to about eight hundred feet. He could see that the whole slope of the peninsula's neck was scarred with spadework. Clearly, the go-as-you-please Turk was marching to German orders. Every night, under German supervision, the Turks repaired their fortifications. Both coasts bristled with howitzers and field guns, and the channel was sown with constantly renewed minefields. In his first telegram to Kitchener, Hamilton expressed doubts that a naval action would succeed.[109]

Churchill, however, was committed to the large-scale naval attack that Carden had prepared and that de Robeck planned to launch on March 18. If it succeeded it would change the course of the war and vindicate his reputation. If the ships blasted their way through he would be as great a hero as when he had escaped the Boers.

On the morning of March 18, it seemed as if all the ships in the world were gathered at the Dardanelles, from the majestic *Queen Elizabeth* to the smallest tramp steamer that ever carried yeast from Edinburgh to Grimsby. At 10:45, six British and four French battleships steamed up the strait and subjected the forts on both sides to a massive three-hour bombardment.

Keen to see the fun, Ian Hamilton watched from the *Phaeton*, positioned one mile inside the strait. He could see the *Queen Elizabeth* moving up in the front line of battleships, spouting flame and smoke. The echoes of those detonations mingling with explosives of smaller caliber seemed like a strange orchestra that made the hills, which had been fought over since the Trojan War, quiver to their foundations.[110]

By 1:25 P.M., when the battleships reached Kephez Bay, two-thirds of the way to the Narrows, not one fort under attack was still firing. De Robeck had silenced the Turkish defenses covering the Kephez Bay minefields with a loss of less than forty men killed and wounded. It was time for the minesweepers to clear a nine-hundred-yard channel through the five layers of mines in the bay, so that the battleships could advance to the final set of forts around the two villages flanking the Narrows, Kilid Bahr and Chanak. The first line of ships withdrew to make way for the minesweepers.

Passing out of the strait with the rest of the French squadron, the battleship *Bouvet* blew up at 1:54 P.M. in a cloud of smoke and steam. She heeled over and sank in thirty-six fathoms in less than three minutes, and more than six hundred of her sailors were drowned. Unknown to de Robeck, a small Turkish steamer had on the previous night, after the final seaplane reconnaissance, laid a new row of twenty mines, not across the strait, like the other minefields, but parallel to the Asiatic shore, in an area that the allied ships used to emerge from the strait when they had finished firing. This little line of mines changed the whole course of the Dardanelles campaign. Admiral de Robeck assumed that the *Bouvet* had been sunk by a shell exploding in her powder magazine and continued the attack. At 2:36 P.M. six relief battleships again engaged the forts and the minesweepers were ordered in. By 4 P.M., the batteries guarding the minefields had been put to flight and it seemed that at last the mines would be cleared. Orders were given to move to Chanak before dusk. If things continued to go well, the fleet could force the Narrows that very day and be in the Sea of Marmara, heading for Constantinople, on the nineteenth.

But at 4:09 P.M. the *Irresistible* was seen listing to starboard, and at 4:14 the *Inflexible*, de Robeck's flagship, reported having struck a mine on the starboard side. Watching from the *Phaeton*, Ian Hamilton gazed spellbound at the *Inflexible*, not knowing whether she would dive into the depths. All the crew and stokers stood on the main deck at attention, facing death in perfect order. The *Inflexible* was towed out of the strait, but the *Irresistible* had to be abandoned as she sank, after her crew had been transferred to the *Queen Elizabeth*. At 6:05, the battleship *Ocean*, which had been covering the rescue operation aboard the *Irresistible*, also struck a mine and sank to the bottom of the strait. The French Admiral Guépratte reported that one of his battleships, the *Gaulois*, had been so badly damaged by gunfire that she had to be beached.[111]

The presence of unlocated mines led de Robeck to call off the attack. He had lost only fifty British killed, but the loss of the battleships *Irresistible* and *Ocean* was a disaster. Years of mental training and outlook had taught him that losing a capital ship was the worst disgrace possible, leading to an automatic court-martial. He was sure that he would not remain in command for another day.[112] After March 18, Roger Keyes would later remark, de Robeck ceased to exist as a fighting admiral.

When the French and British ships started pulling out of the strait, the Turks and Germans in the forts were stunned. Demoralized and expecting defeat, they watched the mighty fleet vanish out of sight. Surely the ships would be back the next day to finish the job. That night, Associated Press correspondent George A. Schreiner was at the Dardanelles front, where he talked to the chief German technical officer, General Mertens. "We expect that the British will come back early tomorrow morning," he said, "and if they do, we may be able to hold out for a few hours." They were almost out of armor-piercing shells. What were they going to do? Schreiner asked. "I should advise you to get up at six o'clock tomorrow morning," the General said, "and take to the Anatolian hills. That's what we are going to do." The troops had orders to abandon the forts after firing their last shells.[113]

Once the forts were abandoned, the only obstacle was the minefield, through which de Robeck's minesweepers could have cleared a channel in a few hours. The British fleet could have appeared before Constantinople on the morning of the twentieth. But the ships did not return. Paralyzed by his losses, and baffled as to whether his ships had been sunk by submarines or mines, de Robeck lost an opportunity that would not come again.

Churchill was visiting the Belgian coast on March 18. The corpses he saw entangled in barbed wire, covered with seaweed and washed by the tides, confirmed his faith in the Dardanelles operation as a means of shortening the war.[114] On the morning of the nineteenth, at work at the Admiralty, he was shown de Robeck's report. The Admiral said his squadron was ready for immediate action, although means would have to be found to deal with what he thought were floating mines. The losses were unpleasant, but Churchill felt sure that de Robeck would continue the attack, for they had decided that it was worth risking ten or twelve ships to force the strait. Although hostile to the operation, Fisher still had bursts of enthusiasm, and agreed that they should fight it out, and ordered two more battleships to the Dardanelles to make up for losses. "De Robeck really better than Carden," he minuted to Churchill, "so Providence is with us."[115]

But after reading de Robeck's report, Fisher had second thoughts. Why had de Robeck hoisted his flag on the *Inflexible* and taken her into close action? She should have been protected, like the *Queen Elizabeth*. She was there to sink the *Goeben*, not to get sunk by a mine. And why had he endangered his beloved battle cruiser further by using an old destroyer, the *Talbot*, to tow her, when he should have used a larger ship?[116] Fisher's life in the Navy had been devoted to matériel. He had a passion for his ships and could not bear to see them risked. He wavered between supporting the operation when the news was good and denouncing it when the news was bad.

When the War Council met at 11 A.M. on March 19, Churchill announced the bad news, but was authorized to inform de Robeck "that he could continue the operations against the Dardanelles if he thought fit." Not a single voice rose against the plan. Fisher said that a loss of twelve battleships was expected before the strait could be forced. No one suggested that the attack be broken off, or postponed until the Army arrived.

Asquith asked Kitchener whether any general plan had been worked out for landing troops.

Kitchener replied that the question had been examined in the War Office, but that they had not sufficient information to form a detailed scheme of disembarkation. This would have to be done by Sir Ian Hamilton and his staff in concert with the naval commander in chief.[117]

This was a damning admission for Kitchener to make, indicating a total lack of preparation at the War Office. He was treating a major operation with the same breezy shift-for-yourself attitude that he would have maintained in a skirmish against the Dervishes.

Later, when the Dardanelles Commission reviewed the wreckage, it reported: "All the evidence laid before us points to the conclusion that Lord Kitchener was not in the habit of consulting his subordinates, that he frequently gave orders over the heads of the Chiefs of Department, and sometimes without the knowledge of the Chief of the General Staff. The result was to throw on the hands of one man an amount of work with which no individual, however capable, could hope to cope successfully."[118] At the Dardanelles, Ian Hamilton was the man who had to improvise a strategy.

On the afternoon of March 19, Churchill was standing by the fireplace in his office with Fisher when Captain William Hall, the Director of Naval Intelligence, came in with a message, and said, "First Sea Lord, we've just received this." Fisher took it and read it aloud. It was an intercepted message from the Kaiser to Admiral Souchon begging him to hold out at all costs and promising to send ammunition. It seemed clear that the ammunition shortage was critical and that the Germans were in a state of near panic. Waving the message over his head, Fisher shouted, "By God, I'll go through tomorrow."

Churchill seized the telegram and read it through again. "That means," he said, "they've come to the end of their ammunition."

"Tomorrow!" Fisher repeated. "We shall probably lose six ships, but I'm going through."

"Then get the orders out," Churchill said.

Captain Hall was about to return to his office when Churchill asked him whether he had any secret contacts with the Turks. Hall said he had two

British agents, a businessman named Edwin Whittall and a civil engineer named Griffin Eady, both of whom had spent many years in Turkey, who were negotiating with the Turkish Minister of the Interior, Talaat Bey.

"They have with them," he said, "a letter from me guaranteeing a large sum of money in the event of a successful outcome of the negotiations."

Churchill stared in bewilderment.

"Four million pounds," Hall added.

"Who authorized this?" Churchill asked with a frown.

"I did, First Lord."

"But—the Cabinet surely knows nothing about it?"

"No, it does not. But if we were to get peace, or if we were to get a peaceful passage for that amount, I imagine they'll be glad enough to pay."

Churchill turned to Fisher: "D'you hear what this man has done? He's sent out people with four millions to buy a peaceful passage! On his own!"

"What!" shouted Fisher, starting up from his chair. "Four millions? No, no. I tell you I'm going through tomorrow." Turning to Hall, he said: "Cable at once to stop all negotiations. All. No. Offer two million pounds for the *Goeben* and one million for the *Breslau*. But nothing else. We're going through." Hall gave up his scheme to bribe the Turkish government.[119]

The attack did not go through the next day, or any other day. The impetus had been lost, and it was never regained, although at first de Robeck seemed eager to try again. Fisher's telegram of March 20 said that "it appears important not to let the forts be repaired or to encourage enemy by an apparent suspension of the operations."[120] De Robeck replied on the same day that he hoped to renew the attack in three or four days. In both British and French battleships, officers and men were anxious to re-engage the enemy. On March 21 he repeated his intention to clear the Kephez minefield and attack the forts in the Narrows. The only thing holding him up was the organization of his minesweeping force.[121]

But a creeping pessimism was spreading among the principals. Ian Hamilton, writing Kitchener on the day after the naval action, was reluctantly driven to the conclusion that the Navy would not force the strait without the help of troops. The Army's part would be more than a mere landing of parties to destroy forts; it would be a full-strength operation to open a passage for the Navy. Churchill's brother, Jack, serving on Hamilton's staff, sounded the same warning. The fleet could not get through without cooperation on land. Carden's stories of forts being silenced had been greatly exaggerated. It was no good bombarding on Monday and having to do it again on Thursday.[122]

On March 22, de Robeck took the *Queen Elizabeth* to Lemnos to confer with the three generals, Hamilton, Birdwood, and Braithwaite. Before they went aboard, the generals agreed that whatever they might think as landsmen, they must leave the sailors to settle their job, and say nothing for or against land operations or amphibious operations until the sailors themselves abandoned the idea of forcing the passage by naval operations alone.

According to Hamilton, the moment they sat down de Robeck told them he was now quite clear that he could not get through without the help of all of Hamilton's troops. De Robeck felt that unless the guns in the strait were destroyed by troops, once he got through the Narrows he would be trapped in the Sea of Marmara. Only if the Gallipoli Peninsula was in British hands could he get back out. How soon could the troops be ready for a joint operation?

Birdwood wanted to land at once, "even without ship-shape band-o-bast [an Indian Army expression meaning order and discipline], and make good the south point of the peninsula." There was a lot to be said for that view, Hamilton agreed, but his instructions from Kitchener were most specific. He was not to make a piecemeal operation, but to wait for the 29th Division, their pièce de résistance. By the time the 29th arrived, everything would be ready for a smashing simultaneous blow. Hamilton told de Robeck that the troops would not be ready for action until April 14.[123] This would mean a delay of nearly a month, during which the Turks could reinforce their positions.

Hamilton and de Robeck reported the change of plans to their respective bosses. Kitchener felt the postponement was far too long. Reversing his original position, he wanted Hamilton to get on shore as soon as possible, without waiting for the 29th. He should provide landing parties wherever necessary to destroy silenced guns and demolish forts, for it was important to keep up the attempt to pass the Narrows by ship. Once the ships were through the strait, the military position would cease to be important.[124]

On March 23, having abandoned all hope of a speedy landing, Hamilton replied that he would need the whole of his force, for the strength of the enemy on the Gallipoli Peninsula was estimated at forty thousand, with a reserve of thirty thousand. Landing a large force in the face of certain opposition was too risky in March, when the weather was bad. It would be more settled in April.[125] Kitchener deferred to the opinion of the man on the spot, even though Hamilton had thirty thousand men on hand without the 29th.

De Robeck's telegram announcing a joint effort in mid-April reached the Admiralty on the morning of March 23. Churchill read it with consternation.

Why give up the naval attempt? Loss of life had been small. The old battle-ships were destined for the scrap heap. Why wait for the Army to arrive and give the enemy three weeks' additional notice? For most of the morning the Admiralty War Group went over the issues. Fisher's position was that the opinion of the man on the spot must be accepted. His enthusiasm for "going through tomorrow" was gone. Both Sir Arthur Wilson and Sir Henry Jackson backed him up.

Churchill did not agree. Another naval attack could succeed. The Turks were short of ammunition, and their German advisers expected defeat. De Robeck himself had wanted to renew the attack after March 18. It was pathetic to give up with victory in sight. He drafted a telegram telling de Robeck to renew the attack at the first favorable opportunity, but the three old sea dogs were obdurate. For the first time since the start of the war, harsh words were used around the octagonal table.[126] Churchill was reminded that he could not afford another Antwerp.

When Churchill put his case before the Cabinet, which met later that morning, Asquith agreed that the Navy ought to make another big push as soon as the weather cleared. If they waited until the Army was ready, they might fall into a spell of bad weather, or (what was worse) find that enemy submarines had arrived on the scene. It seemed that Admiral de Robeck was rather in a funk.[127]

Returning to the Admiralty with the Prime Minister's support that after-noon, Churchill still could not budge his three senior naval advisers. Again he appealed to Asquith, who was not prepared to overrule the opinion not only of Fisher and the others, but of the admiral in command, who thought the operation was dangerous and undesirable.[128] All his instincts were for re-newing the attack, but as a layman he could not assess the danger of the mines, the technical difficulties of dealing with them, and the resources at de Robeck's disposal.

Churchill thought of resigning, as his father had resigned over military spending, but what good would it do? It would only make matters worse. The admirals had "stuck their toes in." They had only to point to the losses of ships and everyone would side with them. He was therefore prevented from asking de Robeck to renew the attack.[129] Instead, with Fisher's reluctant consent, he sent the Admiral a long telegram marked "Personal and Secret" in which he sought to rekindle de Robeck's enthusiasm for passing the strait. What had happened to make him change his mind? They had never contem-plated a reckless rush over minefields, but a careful and deliberate advance. Why was this no longer possible?[130]

Before receiving Churchill's appeal, de Robeck wired on March 25 that he planned to keep up the naval offensive with limited objectives. He would clear the area where the minesweepers would operate. With the help of aerial reconnaissance, he would destroy the howitzers and other concealed guns, while the *Queen Elizabeth* would bomb the Chanak forts by indirect firing. And he would send planes to attack Turkish supply depots and vessels above Chanak said to be loaded with mines. But there was no mention of forcing the strait.[131]

Faced with a revolt of his senior advisers, Churchill held in his reins. His own feeling, he wrote Fisher on March 25, was that de Robeck should not force the strait until he had succeeded in clearing the Kephez minefield and smashed the forts at the Narrows. The point was to press on methodically while the Army went ahead with its preparations.[132] There were hard facts that Churchill could not ignore. Ships had been sunk by mines. Minesweeping had not been a success, and there were many more minefields ahead. The failed attack of March 18 created a mental barrier against trying again. A do-nothing principle became established, crushing with its deadening weight what Churchill believed was the hope of the world.[133] Despite his repeated intentions of pursuing a "vigorous offensive," de Robeck's combative spirit had flagged. Once the joint operation was decided, the Dardanelles became an army show. Instead of the Navy forcing the strait to be followed by the Army, the Army would try to capture the Gallipoli Peninsula to protect the Navy's passage. Absorbed in his plans for landing the troops, de Robeck dropped his sights from the strait.

The Army was gathering at Alexandria, which Hamilton preferred to Lemnos as a base. He knew now that he would have to lead an amphibious landing against a strongly defended beachhead, an operation that had never before been attempted in the annals of the British Army. It was fine to go by the book, but in this case there was no book. To be sure, the British had made an amphibious landing in the Crimean War, but it had been uncontested. It was one thing to land on a beach where the friendly natives greeted you with bottles of the local wine, and quite another to land when Turkish machine guns were cutting you down.

Despite the loss of time involved, Hamilton had moved to Alexandria because the ships bringing the troops were not combat-loaded. This simple principle, which means essentially having available what the troops will need on the first day of fighting in terms of munitions, food, and medicine, rather than loading all the munitions at the bottom of the ship for seaworthiness, had not been thought of. Everything had to be improvised in this new kind of warfare. (For comparison, it might be noted that some ships were combat-loaded six months in advance for the 1944 D-Day landings, which probably would not have taken place without the instructive precedent of the Dardanelles fiasco.)

The Royal Naval Division landed on March 26, and the long-awaited 29th Division arrived on the twenty-seventh. Jack wrote his brother that the sailors now agreed that they could not get through without troops. Long-range firing at forts was useless unless infantry occupied the forts afterward. Stronger minesweepers were necessary against the current. The airplane spotting was very bad. The whole thing was a very tough proposition.[134]

Also arriving on March 26 on the Gallipoli Peninsula was the German general Liman von Sanders, who, finding the five Turkish divisions weakly distributed along the entire coast, re-formed them into three mobile battle groups. "The British gave me four full weeks before their great landing," he later wrote. "The time was just sufficient to complete the most indispensable arrangements."

On March 27, Churchill received the reply to his "Personal and Secret" telegram. It was vital, de Robeck said, for the Army to occupy Gallipoli, and the landing would require the help of all his naval forces. The flaw in the original plan was the assumption that gunfire would destroy the forts. They might bomb a fort heavily for two days and its guns would still be fit for service. It was therefore necessary to land demolition parties. Even if the fleet did get through the strait, how would it maintain itself in the Sea of Marmara without colliers and other unprotected supply ships that could not get through unless the Army held Gallipoli? The delay was worth it.[135]

Accepting the Admiral's reasons, Churchill no longer urged an independent naval action. In his reply on March 27, he told de Robeck that "the reasons you give make it clear that a combined operation is now indispensable." In another telegram sent later the same day, he wanted to know what the fleet would do in case the Army was checked. Would de Robeck push through separately if the Army was at a standstill, or did he consider that his attack could only be delivered once the Army had succeeded?[136]

De Robeck's reply on March 28 was conclusive: "In my opinion Gallipoli Peninsula will have to be taken and held by land force before Dardanelles can be passed with certainty by capital ships fitted to deal with *Goeben* and by the colliers and other vessels without which the utility of capital ships is very limited."[137]

Churchill was hamstrung. It still seemed to him that since the War Council had decided on a naval attack, and since the Admiralty had made the attempt, and since heavy losses had been foreseen and provided for, they should put the matter to the supreme test. But he could not overrule the professional caution of his advisers and of the military and naval commanders in the field. There had been nothing like the slaughter and stalemate on the western front, there had been no decisive action proving that a naval passage was impossible, but all the negative forces had banded together to defeat the project. Henceforth the tables were turned, and the Navy became spectators and subsidiary assistants to the Army. The power of decision passed from Churchill's hands into Kitchener's. The Army would remain in the Dardanelles nine months and suffer a terrible defeat, but the Navy never again tried to sweep the minefields or break through the Narrows into the Sea of Marmara. Its moment of glory came when it had to evacuate the Army under fire, "steaming away under the cloak of darkness from the scene of irretrievable failure."[138]

While the Navy lost the initiative in the Dardanelles operation, the rustle of intrigue was heard in Whitehall. It came to Asquith's ears that Churchill was maneuvering to have Balfour replace Grey, whom he did not think was forceful enough, and who went on too many fishing holidays.

"Young puppy," Asquith raged to his wife, "let him come and suggest this to me and I'll tell him what I think of him! He really is the greatest donkey! He goes gassing about, abusing Kitchener to Arthur and I've no doubt abusing me, giving him much too much information. He thinks he knows Arthur Balfour, he has not the foggiest idea of what Arthur really is . . . a futile feminine brain [who] takes his hat off, says he is ill and leaves his unfortunate friends to be led by a man of fifth-rate quality like Bonar Law."[139]

Foremost among the peddlers of intrigue was Reginald McKenna, the Home Secretary, who still resented Churchill for having taken the Admiralty away from him. On March 29, McKenna told Asquith that there was a press campaign to replace him with Lloyd George, and that Churchill was part of it.[140] Deciding on a showdown, Asquith summoned Lloyd George, McKenna, and Churchill to his office. Lloyd George accused McKenna of always seeing imaginary plots, as in Churchill's supposed campaign against Grey. McKenna rejoined that the villain was Balfour, with whom Winston was much too intimate. Churchill did not attend, writing Asquith: "I feel that my case is safe in your hands."[141] In one of his frequent turnabouts, Asquith decided that Churchill really was loyal. He had never doubted that he was.

With the Army in charge, Churchill's responsibility in the Dardanelles was getting the troops on shore. He was not involved in the military planning. As the Army prepared, the great fleet waited outside the strait, to Fisher's mounting concern. After all, the main show was still in the North Sea. It had looked for a while as if Germany would invade Holland, and what would they have done with sixteen battleships and as many destroyers at the Dardanelles? What a waste of resources! Already the *Inflexible* was *hors de combat*, being towed to Malta, and the *Queen Elizabeth* with its one engine was a prey for submarines. The other ships were wearing out their guns bombarding the forts. They were all needed in the North Sea. But Churchill wanted to keep sending de Robeck more ships and supplies, further draining the Grand Fleet. Fisher was also furious at the "private" telegram Churchill had sent de Robeck. It was marked private, but it dealt with public matters that the board should have discussed. On March 29, Fisher kept Hankey in his study for an hour complaining about Churchill, and said he wanted to resign.[142]

On April 2, Fisher's seething resentment exploded. They could not send even another rope yarn to de Robeck, he wrote Churchill. They had gone to the very limit! He must be told emphatically that no further reinforcements of the fleet could be looked for! A failure in the North Sea would be ruin! But he didn't want to be pessimistic, and hoped that Gallipoli would not be Plevna[143] (the 1877 siege when Russia captured the city from the Turks after 143 days of fighting). In fact, the British fought longer on the Gallipoli Peninsula than the Russians at Plevna, and never captured it.

When he wasn't complaining to Churchill, Fisher was pouring out his woes to Jellicoe. The Cabinet had taken the bit between its teeth and decided that the Dardanelles was a question for the ministers and not for the experts, and Kitchener had been led on by thinking it would be a purely naval operation, which Fisher had never agreed to, and there they were, with Grey gone trout fishing and Asquith in the country![144]

Churchill's patience with his First Sea Lord was wearing thin. He was depressed at losing the initiative and weakened after a bout of influenza. On April 3, he replied with sarcasm that it was necessary to fight a battle, a thing that had happened before in war, and abide by the results.[145]

To which Fisher responded on April 5: ". . . You are just simply eaten up with the Dardanelles and can't think of anything else! Damn the Dardanelles! They'll be our grave'! . . . We shall be as usual 'Too late'! We could have had the Greeks and everyone else at the right time but we are 'too late' ALWAYS! This war might be described as '*Procrastinations—vacillations —Antwerps*' (That's copyright!)."[146]

Upset by Fisher's constant picking, Churchill was nervous and out of sorts, and on April 5 he quarreled with his old friend Lloyd George over a minor matter, the King's Pledge. George V had gone on the wagon for the duration of the war, an example that was followed painlessly by the teetotaler Lloyd George and with stoicism by the bon vivant Haldane. Discussing the pledge with Lloyd George, Herbert Samuel, and Edwin Montagu, Churchill said the whole thing was absurd, he was not going to give up his liquor just because the King had.

Lloyd George, who felt that drink was doing more damage in the munitions factories and shipyards than all the German submarines put together, started to explain a point when Churchill interrupted. "I don't see . . ." he began. Lloyd George broke in sharply: "You will see the point when you begin to understand that conversation is not a monologue." Churchill blushed scarlet and was silenced.[147] Lloyd George felt rather ashamed for having taken him up so sharply in front of the two minions and sent a letter of apology. He had gotten angry because he was rattled after a disappointing interview with Kitchener.[148] Churchill replied at once that it was *he* who had been churlish and difficult, and the friendship was healed. On the matter of drink Churchill offered a compromise—why didn't they restrict the quantities of alcohol in particular beverages? After all, the French were drinking their wine and the Germans their beer, and the British had never been a drunken and inefficient nation like the Russians.[149]

Two days later, Churchill fought with Kitchener in the Cabinet over munitions shortages. For more than a month Churchill had been asking the War Office when he could expect deliveries of explosives for the Navy, and had received no answer. It really was intolerable when reasonable and necessary inquiries by one department were not taken notice of by the other. How could he arrange for the ammunition of the fleet, the explosive sweeps, and the supply of mines?[150] Why did Kitchener always keep everyone in ignorance on vital matters?

No sooner had the angry words passed his lips than Churchill sent an apology. He knew how touchy Kitchener was and did not want to roil the calm waters of cooperation, for on their mutual trust hung the outcome of the Dardanelles. He was sorry he had allowed himself to become angry. It was a very anxious time and they all had their worries.[151]

The day after their quarrel, Churchill tested Kitchener's goodwill with a request for a 15-inch howitzer that could be landed with the troops and be used to bombard Chanak from a fixed position with all the accuracy of fire attainable only in a shore gun. He urged Kitchener to send Sir John French, who was reluctant to part with such an important piece of equipment, an imperative request.[152] This Kitchener did, to Churchill's gratification.

After studying various plans, the Army had decided to land on the beaches at the tip of the Gallipoli Peninsula. The Navy would carry them ashore and provide a shield of fire. Once Hamilton had taken the high ground, there would be a combined naval and land attack on the Narrows. The Turks would be driven from Chanak and de Robeck could sail his fleet through as easily as through the Dover Strait. Kitchener was certain of success, and had no Jacky Fisher to undermine his plans.

Fisher's resistance took various forms. On April 8 he proposed giving up the Dardanelles and attacking the Syrian coast instead. It would be a great coup that would bring Italy into the war. Churchill replied with a quotation from *Hamlet*:

> *"And thus the native hue of resolution*
> *Is sicklied o'er by the pale cast of thought,*
> *And enterprises of great pith and moment*
> *With this regard their currents turn awry*
> *And lose the name of action."*

He then quoted a remark Napoleon was said to have made after Trafalgar: "We are defeated at sea because our Admirals have learned—where I know not—that war can be made without running risks."[153]

On April 10, Fisher asked Churchill to restrict de Robeck's use of the *Queen Elizabeth* to long-range firing from outside the strait. Churchill replied that it would not be right to make a rigid prohibition of her entering the strait, but that she would not follow into the Sea of Marmara. Fisher persisted, asking on April 11 that a telegram be sent at once. De Robeck should also be warned against using the battleships *Lord Nelson* and *Agamemnon* in preference to older ships, and should be told that the return of the *Queen Elizabeth* and other ships might be imminent.[154] In addition to Fisher's stated policy of "not another rope yarn," he wanted to deprive de Robeck of his best ships.

Fed up by his carping, Churchill replied the same day: "Seriously, my friend, you are not a little unfair in trying to spite this operation by sidewinds and small points when you have accepted it in principle. It is hard on me that you should keep on like this—every day something fresh: and it is not worthy of you or the great business we have in hand together."[155]

Fisher was startled by the rebuke. Never in his whole life had he so sacrificed his convictions as he had done to please Churchill. That was a fact! The outside world was quite certain that he had pushed Churchill and not Churchill he. He thought the undertaking would be a success, but he wanted the oldest ships used first.[156]

This was the closest Churchill could get to a pledge of allegiance, but no sooner had he patched things up with Fisher than he was sniped at from other directions. His old foe Lord Charles Beresford complained to Asquith that the Dardanelles operation was a muddle and that they had only arrived at partial command of the sea because the Germans were incompetent. Church-ill told Asquith on April 16: "In the middle of a great war we cannot waste time with this old clown."[157]

He could not so easily dismiss his other critic, the King. On the theory that submarines did not adhere to the code of honorable warfare, Churchill had ordered that the captured crews of German U-boats should not be treated as ordinary prisoners of war. They were kept in solitary confinement in six-by-twelve cells and were not allowed to talk to one another or to smoke. On April 14, the King expressed concern that these measures had been made public, for they invited reprisals. Already, captured Scots Guards had been placed in solitary in Cologne Fortress. A letter had come from Captain Stewart-Menzies, saying: "I think our government ought to do something for us, considering we fought for our country and have done no criminal act to deserve this fate." Refusing to back down, Churchill replied to the King on April 14: "Our treatment of prisoners must be regulated by what we consider right in all circumstances, and not by the treatment which the Germans may choose to mete out to our own officers and men." Each man had a room to himself, Churchill added, followed the prison routine, and could order German books.[158] He had not forgotten the indignity of his own imprisonment fifteen years before.

In the meantime, the original date of April 14 for the Gallipoli landings had passed, and the fleet's long wait in unfriendly waters was proving hazardous. On April 16, the transport *Manitou*, carrying one thousand men of the 29th Division from Egypt to the Dardanelles, was attacked by a Turkish torpedo boat out of Smyrna. The Turk came up close showing no colors, then hoisted the red crescent and gave the captain ten minutes to abandon ship. In lowering the lifeboats, one of the davits broke and sixty men were drowned. The Turk fired his three torpedoes at close range, but miraculously they all missed and the troops were re-embarked. More than a million men had been transported over the sea since the start of the war, and this was the first time there had been losses. How, Asquith wondered, could the navy people have been so intolerably careless as not to know the Turks had a vessel there, or if they did know, why did they not provide protective escort for the transports? Coming on top of so many mishaps and miscalculations and incomplete successes, it shook one's confidence.[159]

In the Cabinet, there was a good deal of nervousness over the forthcoming operation. It was a formidable undertaking to land seventy-five thousand men on open beaches in the face of an entrenched and expectant army. Tempers were short, and there was a row on April 16 when Kitchener accused Lloyd George of having disclosed to the newly formed Munitions Committee the statistics on the number of soldiers in the field, which he had confidentially communicated to the Cabinet.[160] Lloyd George attacked Kitchener for his inaction on the munitions shortage and accused him of cooking his figures. Kitchener rose from the Cabinet table to his full six feet, the picture of wounded dignity, and said that since he appeared to have lost the confidence of some of his colleagues, he would retire. The President of the Board of Education, Joseph Pease, raced him to the door and barred his way, just as in January Kitchener had stopped Fisher. Kitchener's prestige was so great that his resignation would have brought about the fall of the government.

Surveying the storm with his customary detachment, Asquith thought that clumsy and tactless as he was, Kitchener had come out the best, showing an admirable largeness of mind and temper. One had to understand the man, all his life he had been accustomed to take or to give orders, it was hard for him to get used to the give-and-take and comradeship of Cabinet discussions. The people who ought to have known better had shown themselves at their worst. Winston had been borne along on the flood of his too-copious tongue, and in the end had made amends. The two who came out worst were Lloyd George, who *au fond* was not quite a gentleman, and who had almost gotten down to the level of a petty police court advocate, and McKenna, who played the part of a wrecker pure and simple. It would take Asquith a long time to forgive and forget their attitude.[161]

By April 20, plans for the landing were complete, and Hamilton gave his orders to the troops: "We are about to force a landing upon an open beach in face of positions which have been vaunted by our enemies as impregnable." Hamilton knew what he was up against. Surprise was out of the question. The Turks had had five weeks to dig in and bring up reinforcements. They were commanded by German officers. His troops were an amalgam of 29th Division, Royal Naval Division, Australians and New Zealanders, French and Senegalese, whom Hamilton referred to as "niggy-wigs," and such picturesque units as the Assyrian Jewish Refugee Mule Corps. Churchill had sent a naval air squadron under the dashing Commander Samson and the armored-car unit commanded by Churchill's friend and fellow member of the Other Club, the fierce Josiah Wedgwood. How would Hamilton get them all ashore under fire? But his generals were anxious to "have a go." Now it was only a matter of waiting for the weather to clear. De Robeck's ships would back up the Army.[162]

Churchill wished he were with his brother and the others at Gallipoli instead of sitting in his Admiralty office in a secondary role. It was a huge gamble that Winston had shoved everyone into, Fisher thought, but what a coup to get Constantinople. They had to hope for the best. The German general might make a mess of it, or the Turks might run out of ammunition. *Even Homer nodded!*[163]

On April 22, the murderous second battle of Ypres broke out. Launching their first successful poison gas attack, the Germans routed the British. The battle lasted until May 25, when the front stabilized. Sir John French was hampered by ammunition shortages, for which he blamed Kitchener, writing Churchill that he ought to be shot.[164] British losses were 737 officers and 26,000 men. It was this kind of slaughter, with barely perceptible results, that made the Dardanelles seem worthwhile.

Waiting in the transports, the men of Churchill's Royal Naval Division were eager for battle. "I say," they repeated to one another, "do you think this is going to be a bloody good show? *I* do." Josiah Wedgwood, who saw the war as a "blessed distraction," expected the Dardanelles to be a picnic. An easy landing at Constantinople, and they would roll up to Vienna, "getting at their soft side." During idle days in the great hill-circled bay of the harbor where they were anchored, as bugle calls floated from ship to ship, they bought fruit from Greek farmers and took sailing lessons, while on the Gallipoli Peninsula, Turkish soldiers lined the beaches with barbed wire.

Rupert Brooke, who had turned down a cushy appointment on Hamilton's staff to slog it with the other chaps, seemed the embodiment of every noble and disinterested instinct. "Splendid Rupert," said Henry James, "to be the soldier that could beget his sonnets on the Muse! And lucky Muse, not less, which could have an affair with a soldier and yet feel herself not guilty of the least deviation!"[165] Prone to fevers, Brooke had sunstroke and dysentery in

Egypt and was put on a diet of arrowroot, but he did not improve. Comatose by April 22, he was transferred to a French hospital ship, where he died on April 23, two days before the landing, his death an omen of the bad luck to come. What had he died of, sunstroke or blood poisoning? No one really knew. High fever, a boil on the neck, and he was gone.[166]

Rupert Brooke was a handsome young man with a gift for writing pretty sonnets and a foolishly romantic conception of warfare. He had sought death just as foolishly, and found it without having smelled gunpowder, but he was turned into a hero, in part thanks to Churchill, who made the unusual gesture of writing his obituary for *The Times*. For Churchill, Brooke was the poet of abnegation, the bard of glorious death, who transformed the dirty fact of being killed in battle into a noble deed. "A voice had become audible," he wrote, "a note had been struck, more true, more thrilling, more able to do justice to the nobility of our youth in arms engaged in this present war, than any other—more able to express their thoughts of self-surrender, and with a power to carry comfort to those who watched them so intently from afar. The voice had been swiftly stilled. Only the echoes and the memory remain; but they will linger . . ."[167]

Violet Asquith was heartbroken, and moved by Churchill's tribute. Rupert had been the most radiantly perfect human being she had ever known—so flawless that she sometimes wondered whether he belonged to the ragged scheme of things. He had never had a doubt about his death, mentioning it in two of the letters she had received since his departure.[168]

The night before the landing, General Hunter Weston, commander of the 29th Division, known to his friends as "Hunter Bunter," asked Josiah Wedgwood aboard his flagship and showed him his plans. In orderly fashion, they would land the guns at 8 A.M., line the crest at 9, cover the advance on the village of Krithia, and later cover the attack on the heights of Achi Baba.

"Good Lord," exclaimed Wedgwood, wondering that the general seemed to think the Gallipoli Peninsula would be a walkover, "how far do you expect to get tomorrow?" Hunter Weston drew a line on his map east and west through Achi Baba and said: "I will be on the heights tomorrow night."[169]

In fact, none of the units that landed on April 25 reached their objective; but Hamilton was able to put ashore thirty thousand men, who by nightfall held precarious beachheads. The tip of the Gallipoli Peninsula is shaped like a canine tooth, with one side on the Aegean and the other on the strait. In perfect weather and a calm sea, Hamilton's men landed at five beaches on the tip and one about fifteen miles up the Aegean coast. For the first time in the twentieth century, a modern army landed on defended beachheads in open boats. Watching from his observation post aboard the *Queen Elizabeth*, Hamilton at dawn could see the boatloads pulling for the land. He could see men up to their necks in water, men falling as they ran, men pinned down on the beach. Standing by his side, Roger Keyes snapped his telescope shut—he could watch the scene no longer. They were taking a terrible beating. There was barbed wire in the surf, and men were shot hip-deep in water as they groped for their shears, and too many of the boats, under fire from concealed machine-gun nests, arrived on the beaches carrying nothing but corpses. Landing at Cape Helles, the first seventy men of the Lancashire Fusiliers were bowled over to a man.[170]

The Australians had intended to land near Gaba Tepe point, where the ground rose gently from the shore across the entire peninsula, but the current took them down the coast about half a mile, opposite a series of steep ridges. As they approached the shore, they could see Turks running along the beach fixing their bayonets. They leaped out of their boats under intense fire, threw down their kits, and stormed up the first ridge, at the top of which they found a beautifully dug Turkish trench, into which they gratefully fell.[171] Soon, men could be seen carrying munitions and tins of water up the zigzag paths to the crest.

At Sedd-el-Bahr, a green amphitheater of crumbled and grass-grown slopes, falling away to the sea and ending in low undulating ridges of sand, the Turks were positioned in a crenelated castle and in trenches and dugouts. Updating the Trojan horse trick, the British ran aground an old collier called the *River Clyde*, its decks covered with coal, but loaded belowdecks with two thousand men. When they tried to break ashore, they were pinned down by Turkish fire, and other units landing in open boats were slaughtered. Some were drowned by the weight of their equipment, and those who reached the shore could get no farther than a ridge a few yards inland. On board the *River Clyde*, Josiah Wedgwood returned the fire with his Maxim guns. The shallow water was filled with the dead and dying, and wounded men crying as they tried to keep their heads above water. Men jumped ashore over submerged bodies and could be heard shouting: "Give me your rifle—and your shovel—your left hand—jump wide—keep clear of that man's legs, can't you?"[172]

Why not dozens of *River Clydes*? Wedgwood had written Churchill before the landings. It seemed so much the least risky way of landing troops. Now, as the bursts from the Maxims drowned out the cries of the wounded, Wedgwood remembered from his schoolbooks that the Civil War battle of Antietam in Pennsylvania in 1862, where one-third of the Union and Confederate soldiers had been left on the field, was, for the numbers engaged, the bloodiest battle in history, and thought: Antietam was a joyride compared with Sedd-el-Bahr.

Coming to the rescue, the *Queen Elizabeth* fired off a few 15-inch rounds at about 8:30 A.M. Jack Churchill was standing on the searchlight bridge, and the force of the firing sent his cap and notebook and pipe flying in different directions. He saw about 150 yards of houses rise in the air in a great cloud of smoke.[173]

That night, the British held a thin defensive line between the heights of Achi Baba and the sea. They unloaded stores and ammunition, and buried the dead in the sand, on beaches that stank of decay, littered with heaps of rifles and equipment salvaged from the casualties. Hamilton was surprised by the Germanization of Turkish tactics. They came in German attack formation and seemed to have some of the German energy. The conduct of his troops, he felt, had been half heroic and half lamentable. They were far from out of the wood.[174]

On the morning of the twenty-sixth, observing from the *Queen Elizabeth*, Jack Churchill saw the Anzac force up the coast holding a little triangle near the shore, and clinging to the scrubby ridge, unable to advance because of Turkish fire from higher ground. At 4:30 that afternoon they steamed past Sedd-el-Bahr, and Jack saw tiny figures in the open. From the way they stood, they could only be English. Clearly the ridge was theirs, and from the ridge, Achi Baba could be seen for the first time: The line must be complete, and the beaches could link up. The coast was held and the guns were disembarking.[175]

Sifting the news at the Admiralty, Churchill was distressed by the heavy losses and the failure to reach the heights of Achi Baba. He wanted very badly to tell Kitchener to send another twenty thousand men. A successful attack could go well for a time, but there had to be some *stuffing* behind it, even if Hamilton never needed it. On second thought, he refrained from comment, for Kitchener might think he was interfering.[176]

Asquith was pleased by the news. The Trojan-horse incident satisfied the classicist in him. It was quite one of the romantic by-episodes of the war.[177]

The troops settled in on their fringe of beach and their precarious hold on the cliff top, but it was not romantic. It was true hell, made up of bare rations, dysentery, millions of flies, bandage-littered beaches, unburied corpses, and the perpetual buzzing of shells. Hamilton's small force clung to the tip of the Gallipoli Peninsula, with the prospect, Jack Churchill feared, of fighting the whole Turkish Empire.

They had to capture the heights of Achi Baba from Cape Helles and the heights of Sari Bair from the beachhead, and they could not. After the first four days of hard fighting, they had rested on the twenty-ninth and the thirtieth. On May 1 the Turks attacked in close columns, running in a long line at a heavy jog trot with bayonets gleaming, chanting La Illah Illah Allah (There is no God but God) as they went, and took heavy losses. The British captured three hundred prisoners. On May 6 and 7, there was a combined French and British attack with savage fighting, pitchforking Turks out of trenches with bayonets. Turkish artillery broke the attack. Losses were heavy. Sometimes it took stretcher parties three days to get the wounded back from the front lines. Among the Hood Battalion's casualties was Asquith's son Oc, who was shot in the knee, the bullet luckily passing through without touching the bone or injuring the joint. Also hit, at the top of the left groin, Josiah Wedgwood lay on the field of battle wondering whether he was bleeding to death. When the stretcher finally came, the Liberal member for Newcastle-under-Lyme said, "Thank heaven my seat is safe." From Bighi Hospital in Malta, he wrote Churchill that having got it "comfortably in the balls," he could go back to the study of archeology.[178]

Hoping to gain miles, they had gained only a few yards. All hopes were dashed of capturing Achi Baba. It was like France all over again, trenches and wire covered by machine-gun fire, siege warfare, with the Turks dug in and resisting well. The British lost their fighting spirit. Two men were shot for leaving the firing line, and there was a rash of self-inflicted wounds in fingers and feet.

They were tied up and knotted into the cursed trench warfare, thought Hamilton. The Turks had previously laid lines of fortifications and could replace worn-out and demoralized units with fresh formations, while the British regiments panicked and ran and men had to be shot for cowardice. What a change since Kitchener had sent him off with a bagful of hallucinations—naval guns sweeping the Turks off the peninsula, the Turkish Army running for the mainland as soon as they saw the Union Jack, Russian help in hand, Greek help on the *tapis*. And here they were, bogged down in the same kind of unrewarding war they were fighting in France, with the same shortage of shells—the French had christened the British artillery *un coup par pièce* (one shot per gun). The Gun History Sheets of some of the 5-inch howitzers showed that they had been used at the Battle of Omdurman in 1898.[179] The Australians had three obsolete antiaircraft guns with the range tables printed in Japanese. Still, Hamilton did not give up hope, and was heartened by a letter found on a dead Turk, which he had been writing to his wife, and which said: "These British are the finest fighters in the world. We have chosen the wrong friends."

When it became evident that Gallipoli was not going to be the easy victory the Cabinet had been led to expect, Lloyd George blamed Churchill. "Winston is a difficult fellow," he told Margot Asquith. "He has not merely bad judgment but he has none. . . . The Turk is a formidable fellow and I don't believe we shall get out with less than 200,000 men. . . . Now Fisher goes about all over the place saying he was against this expedition and he *was*, but he should have said so . . ."

"Winston," replied Margot, ". . . is very dangerous because he has no real imagination in the sense of seeing deeply into events and probabilities. I've seen it all through his life—when he was a little Navyite and intrigued against McKenna, how wicked and above all how foolish and shortsighted! When he thought out loud over the Curragh affairs pre-Curragh and talked so loud about what He—Winston—would do in the event of such and such that it almost amounted to a plot. He muddled his Antwerp and he will again muddle this I fear. What a strange being! He really likes war. He would be quite damped if he were told now 'The war is over.' He has no imagination of the heart."[180]

Still suffering from the effects of influenza, Churchill went to Paris on May 5 to take part in the secret negotiations to bring Italy into the war. During his absence, Fisher was in charge at the Admiralty. Clemmie tried to persuade her husband not to leave, arguing that the strain would be too much for the seventy-four-year-old Admiral, but Churchill said, "Just look after the old boy for me." Clemmie asked Fisher to lunch, and he seemed as nervous as a kitten. After lunch, when she thought he had gone, she found him lurking in a hallway. "What is it?" she asked. "You are a foolish woman," Fisher replied. "All the time you think Winston's with Sir John French he is in Paris with his mistress."[181] "Be quiet, you silly old man, and get out," Clemmie replied. She was sure Fisher's mind had become unhinged and that he was on the verge of a breakdown, but when she reported the incident to Churchill upon his return on May 10, he brushed the old Admiral's foolish behavior aside. It was Fisher, Churchill knew, not he, who had the mistress—Nina, the Duchess of Hamilton. He often wished that she would exert a calming influence on the First Sea Lord.

Outside the Dardanelles strait, the fleet was helplessly gathered. There was very little the ships could do when it was a matter of trenches and machine guns. With the troops stuck, de Robeck thought of renewing the naval attack. On May 9, he telegraphed for instructions. Should the Navy try again? If he advanced into the Sea of Marmara he risked being cut off, and in any case he did not think the appearance of the fleet off Constantinople would prove decisive.[182]

In March, when the Admiralty had pressed for a renewed attack, de Robeck had said no. Now the Admiral was making a halfhearted offer, but the Admiralty said no. When one was hot or lukewarm, the other was cold. The situation had changed. The ships were needed to keep the sea-lanes open for supplies of food and ammunition. As part of the bargain with Italy, Churchill had promised that four battleships and four light cruisers would reinforce the Italian fleet in the Adriatic, and these would have to be subtracted from de Robeck's armada. He could not push de Robeck into a risky operation while weakening his force. But he did want the Admiral to clear the area as far as the Narrows of forts and mines. When this was discussed on May 11, Fisher was vehement in his objections, fearing that it was just a first step in trying to break through the strait again. Churchill used every argument and made every appeal, but the deadlock was total.

In a highly agitated state, Fisher later summoned Hankey and told him there had been a terrible row. Hankey relayed to Asquith Fisher's message that he would resign if Churchill got his way. Asquith authorized Hankey to say that there would be no naval action without Fisher's concurrence.[183]

With Asquith's promise as his trump card, Fisher took a hard line. In a memo to Churchill written the same day, he said: ". . . I cannot, under any circumstances, be a party to any order to Admiral de Robeck to make an attempt to pass the Dardanelles until the shores have been effectively occupied. I consider that purely Naval action, unsupported by the Army, would merely lead to heavy loss of ships and invaluable men, without any reasonable prospect of a success in any way proportionate to the losses or to the possible further consequences of those losses. I therefore wish it to be clearly understood that I dissociate myself from any such project."[184]

Churchill replied with a letter to buck up his First Sea Lord's sagging spirits. They were committed to one of the greatest amphibious enterprises of history. A great army was "hanging on by its eyelids" to a rocky beach, confronted with the armed power of the Turkish Empire under German military guidance. The whole *surplus* fleet of Britain was bound to that army and its fortunes. Fisher too must be bound, and support the operation with goodwill. They must present a united front.[185]

But Fisher, believing he had Asquith behind him, was deaf to Churchill's plea. He had decided that he wanted no more to do with the Dardanelles, and if that caused a break with Churchill, so be it. On May 12, he ran into Sir Francis Hopwood near the Duke of York's Column. Taking him like a conspirator into a private room at the back of the Athenaeum, he said: "I have resigned and I am off. I've asked for rooms at Nice . . . and I'm off there in the morning. I'm not going to do another stroke of work with that little fellow." Fisher was on his way to see Hankey at his office in Whitehall Gardens, and showed him Churchill's letter, which he said had much dissatisfied him. It *was* rather a slippery letter, Hankey thought. Should Fisher send his memo to Asquith? Hankey said he would discuss the matter with Hopwood, who once again went behind Churchill's back and recommended that he should. He and Hankey both felt that it was necessary to bring Churchill to his bearings.[186]

Fisher then wrote Churchill again to state his position: "Until the Military Operations have effectively occupied the shores of the Narrows . . . no naval attack on the minefield can take place. . . . With reference to your remark that I am absolutely committed—I have only to say that you must know (as the Prime Minister also) that my unwilling acquiescence did not extend to such a further gamble as any repetition of March 18 until the army had done their part."[187]

Sensing that Fisher was near the breaking point and that his resignation could have the direst consequences, Churchill that afternoon gave in on the point of Fisher's greatest concern—the *Queen Elizabeth*. With German submarines reported in the eastern Mediterranean, Fisher wanted her brought back to home waters. Churchill agreed that she would be replaced by two armored ships with 14-inch guns.[188]

That evening at six, Kitchener arrived at the Admiralty on another of his invasion scare missions. He felt that not enough ships were assigned to defend the east coast of England. But instead of discussing fleet distribution, he found himself confronted with the *Queen Elizabeth*'s recall. As they sat around the octagonal table with other officers of high rank, his usual composure left him and he protested furiously at being deserted by the Navy at a critical moment. The withdrawal of the principal naval unit engaged in the operations would have a serious and depressing effect on the Army. It would also please the enemy, who would conclude that the British did not intend to prosecute the operation to a conclusion.[189]

Fisher's capacity for wrath equaled Kitchener's. The *Queen Elizabeth* would come home, he stormed. She would come home at once; she would come home that night. If she was not ordered to head direct for England at full speed within twelve hours, he would leave the Admiralty.[190]

Kitchener said he had to face the loss of fifteen thousand men in an operation that had been initiated to help the Navy. The *Queen Elizabeth* might run greater risks on her homeward voyage than by remaining with the fleet in the Dardanelles. To even the score, he suggested with heavy sarcasm that troops might have to be pulled back to Egypt in the event of a Moslem uprising.[191]

Returning to the War Office in high dudgeon, Kitchener unburdened himself to General Callwell: "They rammed that ship down my throat," he said. "Churchill told me in the first place that she would knock all the Dardanelles batteries into smithereens, firing from goodness knows where. He afterwards told me that she would make everything all right for the troops as they landed. And now, without 'with your leave' or 'by your leave,' old Fisher says he can't let her stop out there!" Since Churchill had oversold the "Lizzie's" potential, Callwell advised, there was little point in contesting her departure.

Keeping Fisher happy was more important than risking Kitchener's wrath, thought Churchill. That night, he telegraphed de Robeck that the *Queen Elizabeth* must sail for home at once. He hoped the Admiral would not be discouraged at losing his most powerful ship. The two armored ships being sent out were the last word in bombarding vessels.[192]

The *Queen Elizabeth* was not the only ship de Robeck lost on May 12, for that night the battleship *Goliath* was sunk, with a loss of 570 sailors, off Sedd-el-Bahr, by a Turkish destroyer with a German crew that had cleverly slipped down the strait undetected. The incident was proof to Fisher that he was right in recalling the *Queen*. That same night he wrote Asquith to remind him of his attempted resignation at the War Council of January 28. "With extreme reluctance," he said, "and largely due to earnest words spoken to me by Kitchener, I, by not resigning (*as I see now I should have done*), remained a most unwilling beholder (and indeed a participator) of the gradual draining of our naval resources from the decisive theater of war."[193]

Like a man who must repeat something over and over to convince himself of it, Fisher kept saying that he would resign. He could not remain much longer, he wrote Asquith on May 13, as long as Churchill was engaged in the ceaseless prodding of everyone in every department afloat and ashore in the interests of the Dardanelles. He was writing to the one person who ought to know that he felt his time was short. He also went to see Asquith to explain why he now insisted that de Robeck be sent firm instructions not to embark upon any independent naval initiatives. He was waiting in the secretary's room outside Asquith's office at 10 Downing Street when Margot Asquith came by and asked how things were going.

"As badly as they can," Fisher said, "thirty thousand casualties in the Dardanelles, sixteen thousand English, fourteen thousand French, sixty percent of the French engaged. I was always as you know against this mad expedition. . . ."

"You know you have talked too much," Margot admonished, "all London knows you are against the Dardanelles expedition. Why didn't you resign at the time?"

"It's a lie," Fisher retorted, "I've seen no one, been nowhere, I'm far too busy."

". . . Well, we're in for it and *must* see it through."

"Oh, yes, it may turn out all right but I doubt it."

"It's helped to bring Italy in. Has she good ships?"

"Mere organ-grinders! No use whatever, but it's no good looking back-wards!! . . . Come along and have a valse."[194]

Apparently stirred by the mention of organ-grinders, Fisher clasped the Prime Minister's wife in a firm embrace and proceeded to waltz her around the tiny office until he was called in by Asquith. He thought his interview had been the most satisfactory of his life, reporting to Hankey that the Prime Minister had told him: "Rely on me. I will never fail you."[195]

Returning to the Admiralty with Asquith's backing, of which Churchill knew nothing, Fisher was in no mood to compromise. Churchill wanted to send de Robeck a telegram allowing him some initiative, but Fisher called that a *"casus belli."* Churchill then said he would send de Robeck a telegram coming from himself. "Surely I can send a private letter to a friend without showing it to you," he told Fisher. But Fisher would not have it, and finally a telegram went out at 8:40 P.M. that went against Churchill's most deeply held convictions: "We think the moment for an independent naval attempt to force the Narrows has passed and will not arise again under present condi-tions."[196] Signed by Churchill, it had been inspired by Fisher. But Fisher was alarmed when Churchill reasserted his conviction that in six weeks the fleet would have to do it alone, urging Fisher to stay on at least that long. So now, thought Fisher, he was to aid and abet for six weeks! What was one to do with such a determined mad gambler?[197]

On May 14, when the War Council met for the first time in more than a month, Kitchener was in a gloomy mood. That morning, he had been directly attacked in the *Times* as responsible for the munitions shortage in France. The article, by Colonel Repington, the paper's military correspondent, had been inspired by Sir John French, who was convinced that the absence of artillery support was trebling British losses. The offensive against Aubers Ridge on May 9, Repington wrote, had failed because of the lack of high-explosive shells. On the very day that his troops were thrown against the German trenches, French had been ordered to send 250,000 rounds of 18-pounder ammunition and 100 rounds of heavy ammunition to the Dardanelles. Asquith had said in a speech on April 20 that there was no ammunition shortage, which led General Sir Henry Wilson to note in his diary: "This is a real object lesson in the value of minor operations and Squiff's lie about ammunition."[198] The *Times* article was the strongest criticism to date of the Asquith government's conduct of the war.

Kitchener was equally upset by the removal of the *Queen Elizabeth*. He had agreed to the Dardanelles enterprise, he said, only because of statements made about the power of that ship. He could not believe that the Navy would withdraw the principal naval unit upon which they and the Army relied. He wished that he could withdraw from the Dardanelles, but that was not practicable. He did not see how they would ever drive the Turks off the heights.[199]

Asquith asked what Fisher's views were, knowing perfectly well what he thought, but wanting him to express himself in the War Council. Fisher said the *Queen Elizabeth* was vitally important to the fighting predominance of the Grand Fleet, for the Germans now had ships with 15-inch guns. He reminded the War Council that he had not been a party to the Dardanelles operation.[200]

One of the strongest supporters of the Dardanelles now expressed his doubts. Lloyd George wondered whether the Army could force the position. The Turks appeared to be fighting well and to be well led by good German officers. He did not want to abandon the enterprise, but he wanted to know the dimensions of the problem, for it was dangerous to go on from day to day merely drifting.

Kitchener and Crewe said it was impossible to abandon the project because of the effect on the Moslem world and India, where Britain had more than sixty million Moslems under direct rule.

Haldane and Balfour agreed that it was out of the question to withdraw. They must hold the line.

In Churchill's opinion, the outlook was by no means gloomy. The eighty thousand men in the Dardanelles were a small affair compared with the 560,000 men in France. He did not see the slightest reason for believing that either the British or the French lines in France could be pierced. He did not share Kitchener's grounds for pessimism and objected strongly to despondency.

Grey said that without being depressed they had to look the facts in the face. He did not wish to abandon the Dardanelles, but he thought they must avoid an excessive drain on their resources.

In conclusion, Kitchener agreed to send a telegram to Sir Ian Hamilton asking what force he would need to insure success.[201]

It was not the military situation that depressed Hankey, but the bickering among ministers, particularly Churchill and Fisher. He was sick of them,[202] and wished they would all work honestly for their country only. Fortunately, Churchill's stout attitude had done something to hearten his colleagues.

Churchill did not know that Fisher had been seeing Asquith behind his back, but he could sense that his First Sea Lord was in an agitated state. He thought they had settled their differences. He had agreed to the recall of the *Queen Elizabeth* in exchange for Fisher's support, but Fisher had undermined him in the War Council by affirming that he had been against the operation from the start. As soon as he returned to the Admiralty, Churchill wrote the Prime Minister to remind him that Fisher had agreed in writing to every telegram on which the operations had been conducted. If the admiral on the spot decided to run a risk with the fleet, Churchill did not want to be paralyzed by Fisher's veto. Any man who could say that he disclaimed the responsibility for failure could not be the final arbiter of measures that might be vital to success.[203]

That afternoon, after a nap, Fisher poured out his woes to his Naval Secretary, Captain Thomas Crease. He could not remain at the Admiralty much longer because of the continual drain of the Dardanelles. Since he could not stop it, he had better clear out and let Churchill carry on alone.[204]

As Fisher and Crease chatted, Churchill came in to discuss reinforcements for de Robeck. In an amicable conversation that lasted for several hours, he agreed to bring more battleships back from the Dardanelles into home waters as long as he could send de Robeck nineteen more armored ships. Churchill was conciliatory, limiting his request to what Fisher found acceptable. When he left Fisher's room, he said: "Well, good night, Fisher. We have settled everything, and you must go home and have a good night's rest. Things will look brighter in the morning and we'll pull the thing through together." Fisher told Crease that he wanted to sign his papers and go home, and that things were friendly again, adding jocularly that "I suppose he'll soon be at me again."[205]

Churchill remained in his room working on the list of reinforcements. To the ships Fisher had agreed to, he added two submarines, which de Robeck had in recent weeks been urgently requesting. Intending to hold the list for Fisher's approval, Churchill added this covering note: "I send this to you before marking it to others in order that if any point arises we can discuss it. I hope you will agree."[206]

Just before midnight, Masterton-Smith took the list to Crease, telling him to show it to Fisher first thing in the morning. Going down the list and spotting the submarines, Crease said that Fisher would resign at once if he saw it—in his frame of mind, this would be the last straw. Masterton-Smith took the list back to Churchill to explain Crease's anxieties. Churchill asked him to tell Crease that he was sure Fisher would not object, and that in any case the reinforcements must be made. His covering note made it clear that the list was not an order and that they could discuss it further. Churchill went to bed in the small hours of May 15 feeling that the situation was not that bad. In the War Council he had countered Kitchener's gloom. The Italian alliance, a result of the Dardanelles, was now a fact. De Robeck would soon have more armored ships, and Asquith had been notified that Churchill did not intend to let Fisher obstruct further operations.[207]

At nine o'clock on the morning of May 15, Churchill awoke at Admiralty House and went at once to the Foreign Office to go over the Anglo-Italian agreement. Returning to the Admiralty across the Horse Guards Parade, he met a breathless Masterton-Smith, who said: "Fisher has resigned, and I think he means it this time," and he handed Churchill the letter of resignation, written earlier that morning:[208]

"After further anxious reflection I have come to the regretted conclusion I am unable to remain any longer as your colleague. It is undesirable in the public interests to go into details—Jowett [Benjamin Jowett, Master of Balliol College, 1870–1893] said 'never explain'—but I find it increasingly difficult to adjust myself to the increasingly daily requirements of the Dardanelles to meet your views—As you truly said yesterday I am in the position of continually vetoing your proposals. This is not fair to you besides being extremely distasteful to me. I am off to Scotland at once so as to avoid all questionings."[209]

After months of fuming and threatening, Fisher had done it. The submarines had, as Crease had predicted, been the last straw. Every concession that Fisher made was followed by fresh demands. As soon as he left Fisher's office, Churchill proceeded to move the fleet behind his back. Fisher's cumulative annoyance over the First Lord's methods finally exploded.

Churchill was not particularly alarmed. Fisher had been First Sea Lord for six and a half months and this would be his ninth resignation. Churchill had always been able to talk him out of it. But this time, Fisher was nowhere to be found. He was neither in the Admiralty building nor at home. Perhaps, someone suggested, he was at Westminster Abbey, where he went to attend Matins whenever he was agitated and disturbed. But he was not there either. Churchill went to Downing Street and reported to Asquith that the First Sea Lord had vanished. Asquith showed impatience, which he rarely did. It was a grave dereliction of duty for an officer holding the foremost naval place in time of war to desert the post assigned to him by the King and be unavailable for the conduct of urgent and immediate naval business. Asquith sent his secretary, Maurice Bonham Carter, to find him, with a letter that said: "In the King's name, I order you at once to return to your post."[210] By the time Bonham Carter found him, holed up at the Charing Cross Hotel, Asquith had gone off to the wedding of a Liberal Whip at St. Margaret's, in Westminster. While Fisher was waiting at 10 Downing Street, Lloyd George turned up and was struck by his grimness. His lower lip was thrust forward, and his brow was creased by a sinister frown. "I have resigned!" he said, and on being asked why, replied: "I can stand it no longer." Lloyd George urged him to stay on at least until the next War Council, when he could air his complaints, but Fisher said he would not wait another hour. At that point Asquith returned and persuaded Fisher to remain in London. But he could not make him go back on his resignation. Fisher left 10 Downing Street without saying where he was going.[211]

Lloyd George saw at once that Fisher would drag Churchill down with him. The Tory Opposition would not let Asquith keep him at the Admiralty if he lost his First Sea Lord. Churchill had brought in the man who was now his nemesis. In Lloyd George's view, Churchill was being destroyed by his own ambition. When the war came, he saw a chance of glory for himself and accordingly embarked on a risky campaign without caring a straw for the misery and hardship it would bring to thousands, in the hope that he would prove to be the outstanding man of the war. Coming as it did from one of Churchill's closest friends, this was a harsh view, but it was shared by many.[212]

Asquith knew that unless Fisher returned, a political crisis was unavoidable. The shell scandal was already a threat to the government, and now this. Perhaps a letter from Churchill would bring him back. The letter went out. Churchill did not understand why Fisher had resigned. When they had parted last night, he thought they were in agreement. The proposals he had sent over were open to discussion. He had scrupulously adhered to their agreement to do nothing important without consultation. He had a proposition to make, with the assent of the Prime Minister, which might resolve some of the difficulties Fisher felt about the Dardanelles.[213]

Fisher in his hideaway did not get Churchill's letter until ten that night, and the reply arrived at the Admiralty on the morning of the sixteenth. The fresh naval arrangements Churchill had sent him, Fisher said, had convinced him that it was time for a final decision. "YOU ARE BENT ON FORCING THE DARDANELLES AND NOTHING WILL TURN YOU FROM IT—NOTHING," Fisher went on. "I know you so well! . . . *You will remain* and I SHALL GO—It is better so." He did not want to listen to any propositions.[214]

Fisher told Crease to get his pictures and boxes ready. The Second Sea Lord could do his work until Churchill found a replacement. Crease must impress on Masterton-Smith the utter futility of his seeing Winston.[215]

Fisher honestly believed that Churchill loved him, but "kind words buttered no parsnips!" Nothing would change him! At every turn Churchill would be thinking of the military and not the naval side—he had never done otherwise. His heart was ashore, not afloat! The joy of his life was to be fifty yards from a German trench![216]

Seeing at last that Fisher's departure would place his own political life in jeopardy, Churchill tried again, using all the rhetorical power at his command to describe the gravity of the situation. His resignation would be seen everywhere as proof that the military and naval operations at the Dardanelles had failed. It would give sustenance to the enemy, and might prove the deciding factor in the case of Italy, now trembling on the brink. At the very least, Fisher owed him a personal interview, if only to settle the explanation he would have to give to Parliament.[217]

Unmoved, Fisher replied: "Please don't wish to see me. I could say nothing as I am determined not to. *I know I am doing right.*"[218]

Having resigned in a fit of temper, Fisher now began to take stock of the situation. What if the Asquith government fell? If the Tories came back to power, they might make him First Lord. Finally a professional sailor would control naval policy, as a professional soldier controlled military policy. His resignation had not been made public, but he alerted the Tory leader Bonar Law with an anonymous message containing only an old newspaper clipping with this sentence marked: "Lord Fisher was received in audience of the King and remained there about half an hour." Bonar Law drew the proper conclusion that Fisher had resigned.[219]

On May 16, since there was no budging Fisher, Churchill replaced him with Sir Arthur Wilson. He had a board, and felt sure that on Monday, May 17, he could present Parliament not with a crisis but with a solution. Going to see Asquith at The Wharf, his country place at Sutton Courtenay, near Oxford, he announced that Fisher's resignation was final. He would resign too if Asquith wanted a change. "No," Asquith said, "I have thought of that. I do not wish it, but can you get a board?" Churchill said he had one, and began to think the crisis had passed. But the Prime Minister's private secretary, Maurice Bonham Carter, who was also present, warned that the combination of the shell scandal and the Fisher resignation was so grave that Asquith might have to consult the Conservatives. Churchill, however, still believed that in speaking to the House, he could limit the debate to Admiralty policy and prevent a more serious crisis, just as he had weathered Bridgeman's dismissal.[220]

Having received Fisher's hint, Bonar Law on Monday morning called on Lloyd George for confirmation. On being told that the information was correct, Bonar Law said "then the situation is impossible." The Conservatives had supported the government without seeking party advantage, but there was a growing discontent over the munitions shortage and the failure of the Dardanelles expedition. It was getting to the point where he could not restrain his followers. Particularly in the case of Churchill there was bound to be a Parliamentary challenge. If Fisher went, Churchill would have to go.[221]

Lloyd George knew that a concerted Tory attack on military and naval policy would bring down the government. Asking Bonar Law to wait, he went to see Asquith next door and argued that only an immediate coalition could save them. Asquith knew that Churchill had cleaned house, that with Fisher gone Admiralty business would no longer be a matter of two steps forward and one step back, and that Churchill was a formidable presence in the House of Commons, capable of defeating almost any onslaught. But almost automatically, wearily, Asquith agreed to a coalition.[222]

The fight had gone out of the Prime Minister. He was in a state of acute personal distress, for he had learned five days before that Venetia Stanley, the young woman he loved passionately, ridiculously, the balm of his days, the force that sustained him, was about to commit the cruelest act that destiny could devise: she was marrying his close friend and confidant, the one accomplice of his secret love, Edwin Montagu.

Venetia Stanley, the soulful-faced daughter of the Liberal baron Lord Sheffield, was a post-Victorian young woman who displayed alarming symptoms of modernism. She proclaimed that her guiding principle was to get the maximum fun out of life, though sometimes she wondered whether the query was worth the quest. She was a pagan, she said; she had no sense of sin, no penitential moods, no waves of remorse. Asquith, who was more than twice her age, had begun writing her when she was twenty-three. In 1913, he wrote her fifty letters. Smitten by a beguiling mixture of beauty, candor, and seductiveness, he wrote her every day from July 1914, in spite of his great wartime responsibilities. In the first three months of 1915, he sent her 141 letters. In a single day, Tuesday, March 30, he wrote her four times. In the fall of 1914, Venetia came to London to train as a nurse in a hospital in Whitechapel. Asquith saw her whenever he could, driving to the hospital at the height of a political crisis on the off-chance of spending five minutes with her, or arriving at country houses where he knew she was invited.

His love was never consummated, for Venetia was repelled by his drooling, thigh-stroking advances, but for the sixty-three-year-old Asquith, physical fulfillment was less important than the emotional comfort Venetia provided in her letters.[223] To hold her interest, like a man doing card tricks to keep a child amused, Asquith sent her detailed accounts of Cabinet meetings, the disputes and intrigues, the personalities and their shortcomings. He would write these letters, which were longer and livelier than his daily account of Cabinet business to the King, in the middle of a meeting. A messenger would come into the Cabinet room with a letter from Venetia, and he would read it in great concentration, and then settle down to reply at length, ringing for the messenger, who would take the reply for dispatch. Other members of the Cabinet, particularly Lloyd George, were dismayed at the time he spent on his personal correspondence during meetings over which he should have been presiding, lost in his private thoughts while grave wartime matters were being discussed.

Instead of giving his undivided attention to the war, Asquith was inventing nicknames for his colleagues to amuse Venetia: Seely was the "Arch-Colonel," John Simon was "The Impeccable," Beauchamp was "Sweetheart," the Irish leader Redmond was "The Leviathan," and Montagu, his closest associate, was "The Assyrian."

Born into a wealthy Orthodox Jewish family, Edwin Montagu was the eighth of ten children. Swarthy, with a large, ungainly body, he protected himself from disappointment behind a parapet of pessimism. He was fierce about trifles and defeatist about important matters. From 1906, he was Asquith's Parliamentary Secretary, and one of his duties was to relay political gossip, as in this item when Churchill was at the Board of Trade: the progress of the Port of London Bill "was rather hampered by the fact that Winston always insists at frequent intervals on each point on making a really Imperial speech worthy of the occasion if he were giving Home Rule to India."

In 1910, Montagu's loyalty to Asquith earned him the post of Under-Secretary for India, which he held until 1914, when he became Financial Secretary to the Treasury. In February 1915 he was given the minor Cabinet post of Chancellor of the Duchy of Lancaster. Montagu met Venetia at about the same time as Asquith, and his feelings for her went from loathing to fear to adoration. Like Asquith, he wrote her daily, and competed for her attention. In 1912, he proposed and was rejected, but his devotion was stubborn, even though he despaired of being "in the position of lavishing hopelessly affection where it was not wanted." Behind his back, Asquith and Venetia cruelly mocked Montagu, laughing at his attentions, and writing anti-Semitic doggerel about him, which referred to his house in Queen Anne's Gate as "the tents of Shem,"[224] such as this quatrain from Asquith:

> *Venetia, though a Christian child,*
> *Born of an Aryan stem,*
> *Frequents, too easily beguiled,*
> *The silken tents of Shem.*

Passion made Asquith reckless. He passed on Cabinet secrets to Venetia, never questioning the wisdom of communicating classified military information, such as the sinking of the *Audacious*, to a twenty-eight-year-old girl whose flirtatiousness was joked about by those who knew her. He also sent her interesting documents, such as the original of Churchill's resignation offer from Antwerp, to add, he said, to her collection of *mémoires pour servir.*[225]

Asquith postponed Cabinet decisions until he could talk them over with Venetia, hoping to keep his hold on her by bringing her into the decision-making process. "What do you think, my darling?" was a frequent refrain. What did she think of sending troops to the Dardanelles, or of Kitchener's New Armies, or of Winston's conduct at the Admiralty? She was treated in government matters like a consultant. If he could not have her as a mistress he would make her an accomplice, for she gave him the lifeblood of all that he did. As he repeated in his pleading, fervent letters, she was the soul of his life. Anyone who wanted to destroy him could do it by separating him from her.[226]

On April 26 he wrote her that to see her and be with her and hear her voice and feel that everything was unchanged had made a new creature of him. She was the best and richest of life-givers. A pleading tone had entered his letters. He sometimes worried that he bored her. He was desperate because she was due to leave for a military hospital in France on May 10 (not because of patriotism, she said, but because she hungered for the experience), but her departure was delayed because she was ill.[227]

Crushed by the emotional burden of Asquith's attachment, Venetia had sought comfort and understanding from Montagu, and decided to escape into marriage. On May 12 she told Asquith. He had known that one day she would marry; but Montagu, the object of their mockery, the outsider who was always kept at a distance . . . it was a shattering blow.

Having decided to marry, Venetia cut herself off from Asquith just when he needed her most. He had felt the need to share the cares of office, to confide his most personal impressions, and now that was gone. The most hellish thing about these hellish days, he wrote her on May 17, the day he agreed to the coalition, was that she whom he had gone to in every moment of trouble, from whom he had always come back solaced and healed and inspired, was not there in his hour of need. To his dying day, it would be the most bitter memory of his life.[228]

He saw her once again before her marriage on July 26. Night and day, he had only one prayer, that she would be truly and perfectly happy.

That a Prime Minister in wartime, on whom the survival of the nation largely depended, could be incapacitated at a critical moment because of his infatuation with a woman half his age sounds like something that might happen in an *opéra bouffe* country with an imaginary name like Ruritania. But it happened in Great Britain in 1915, and the principal victim of Asquith's pathetic loss of will was Churchill, who later wrote of the Prime Minister's letters to Venetia: "They were addressed to brighter eyes than peer through politicians' spectacles."[229]

Knowing nothing of Asquith's despair, or of his decision to form a coalition, Churchill went to the House of Commons on the afternoon of May 17 to deliver the speech that would save the Liberal government. There he saw Lloyd George, who said the coalition could not be delayed. Surprised, Churchill went to Asquith, who told him that he no longer wanted a debate. When Churchill gave him the names of his new board, the Prime Minister said:

"No, this will not do. I have decided to form a National Government by a coalition with the Unionists, and a very much larger reconstruction will be required. . . . What are we to do for you?"[230] Honed by Fisher and swung by Asquith, the axe had fallen.

Seeing that he was no longer wanted at the Admiralty, Churchill said that Balfour could succeed him with the least break in continuity. Asquith seemed pleased, and then asked Churchill whether he would take office in the new government or prefer a command in France. Before he could reply, Lloyd George came in and said, "Why do you not send him to the Colonial Office? There is great work to be done there." Churchill indignantly refused, saying he would rather go to France than be cut off from the conduct of the war. At that point an urgent telephone message was brought in calling Churchill back to the Admiralty. An intercepted German telegram made it seem certain that the German High Seas Fleet was entering the North Sea.[231] The great naval battle he had dreamed of was about to start, at the very moment when he had been dismissed. At least he would go out fighting. He remained at his desk until late at night arranging the dispositions of the ships.

As he worked, a formal note arrived from Asquith announcing the formation of a coalition government. Churchill at once replied that he would be glad to be offered a position, but that if he could not get a military department he would find employment in the field. Unable to resist the temptation of Cabinet-making, he told Asquith, who was thinking of replacing Kitchener, that Lloyd George would not do at the War Office. Balfour at the War Office with Lloyd George handling Munitions as well as the Exchequer would be a much sounder arrangement.[232]

Churchill then went to bed, thinking it had been quite a day. In the morning, he had prepared for a Parliamentary ordeal of the most searching character. In the afternoon there had been a political crisis fatal to himself. And in the evening he had supervised preparations for the supreme battle on the sea.[233]

But on the eighteenth the great battle that might have kept him in office fizzled out. The German fleet went back to its harbors, the British squadrons turned morosely away to resume their long-drawn watch, and Churchill's hour passed.

He began to think that he had been wrong in turning down the Colonial Office so abruptly, and now wrote Asquith that if it were offered, it would not be right to refuse. Above all he wanted to stay at the Admiralty. He suggested that Asquith dump Kitchener, replacing him with Balfour. He and Balfour could work with perfect smoothness.[234]

Knowing that Churchill was eager to discuss the situation, Asquith cynically observed, "which means the situation as it concerns Churchill personally—how far he is likely to be affected. The situation for Churchill has no other meaning but his own prospects."[235]

Churchill's prospects were dim. For the first time in years, the bargaining that attended the formation of a new government went on without him. So long at the center, he was now on the margin. How tragic, thought Margot Asquith, that the great Cabinet that had weathered crisis after crisis, from the Lords' veto to Home Rule, was all crumpled up like a scrap of paper! The breakup of colleagues was very tragic. It would never be the same again. She did not care much for the other side, admiring neither their brains nor their behavior. Bonar Law was a mixture of slimness and simplicity. Lansdowne had a maidenly mind. Austen Chamberlain had no greatness and was a bore. Curzon was a peacock. You could have the whole lot! If only Fisher had not wanted to be a pendant to Kitchener, they could have done without the aliens in their midst.[236]

Churchill began making his farewells, telling his brother and several others that he was leaving the Admiralty. In the high command at the Dardanelles the news was received with disbelief. If only Kitchener had enthused the public with the dramatic story of the landings, Ian Hamilton said, a change at the Admiralty would have been impossible. De Robeck said that no one could have wished for more loyal support. Roger Keyes was very upset and blamed everything on Fisher, who he was sure was maneuvering to replace Churchill.[237]

Others agreed that the Admiralty crisis was essentially a Fisher power play. Lewis Harcourt, the Secretary for the Colonies, wrote Lord Esher on May 18: "I think Jacky has triumphed."[238] Already preparing his return, Fisher on the same day sent Captain Crease the "instant orders" he intended to issue, with the warning "*Keep secret. TELL NO ONE.*" The first order was to move Ian Hamilton's army to Haifa for the conquest of Palestine.[239]

Determined to return to the Admiralty with the same broad power that Kitchener held at the War Office, Fisher drafted a six-point ultimatum for Asquith, which he first showed to Hankey on the morning of May 19. Among Fisher's terms were that he would not serve under Churchill or Balfour. He wanted an entirely new Admiralty Board. He would be in complete charge of the war at sea and have absolute authority for new construction. The First Lord would be a figurehead, occupying the same position as Kitchener's Under-Secretary, Harold Tennant, who represented him in Parliament.[240]

Hankey thought Fisher was madder than ever and told him his terms were impossible. No self-respecting minister would look at these demands for naval dictatorship. The ultimatum convinced Hankey that it would be a mistake for Fisher to go back to the Admiralty.[241]

When Fisher brought the paper to Asquith, the Prime Minister saw further proof of mental aberration. Either his mind was unhinged or his conduct was almost treacherous. Asquith reported on developments to Lord Stamfordham at 1 P.M. on May 19, for the King was on an inspection tour in Scotland.[242] George V was glad to hear about the coalition. It was the only way to get Churchill, whom he disliked intensely, out of the Admiralty. He was the real danger, for he was also intriguing with Sir John French against Kitchener.[243]

At the same time that Fisher was maneuvering for supreme power at the Admiralty, Churchill was doing his utmost to hang on. Hoping for Tory support, he recruited Balfour as his emissary and wrote Bonar Law that he rejoiced at the prospect of their becoming colleagues.[244] But Bonar Law had long distrusted Churchill and believed that his mind was unbalanced.

Trying to enlist support among his colleagues, Churchill went to see Grey and Lloyd George, and realized in the course of the conversation that they took it for granted that he would not remain as First Lord. Angrily turning on Lloyd George, he said, "You don't care what becomes of me. You don't care whether I am trampled under foot by my enemies. You don't care for my personal reputation. . . ."

"No," replied Lloyd George, "I don't care for my own at the present moment. The only thing I care about now is that we win in this war."[245]

Willing to try anything to stay in power, Churchill thought of luring Fisher back. On the evening of May 19, he sent George Lambert, a Civil Lord at the Admiralty, with a verbal message: Fisher could have any terms he liked, including a seat in the Cabinet, which would make him the equal of Kitchener, if he would stay on.

Churchill's offer reinforced Fisher's conviction that he was the indispensable man. He at once wrote Bonar Law a "Very SECRET and Private" letter: "This evening Winston sent Lambert . . . to *offer* me a seat in the Cabinet if I would return as his Sea Lord with him, Winston, as First Lord! I rejected the 30 pieces of silver to betray my country."[246]

That night, at a dinner of the secretaries, those gray men who worked behind the scenes to influence events, Maurice Hankey, Maurice Bonham Carter, and James Masterton-Smith agreed after a very long discussion that Fisher and Churchill both must go. The next morning, sounding out Admiralty opinion, Hankey learned that most senior officials favored Balfour as

First Lord. There was some anti-Churchill lobbying inside the Admiralty. The Second Sea Lord, Sir Frederick Hamilton, passed a message on to Asquith that in his view and that of the Third and Fourth Sea Lords, naval morale would collapse unless Churchill went. The only loyal Sea Lord was Sir Arthur Wilson, who had agreed to take Fisher's place, and who wrote Asquith on May 19 that he would not serve under any other First Lord.[247]

Churchill thought that was the greatest compliment he had ever been paid. He wrote Asquith on May 20 that all the Sea Lords were ready to serve under him.[248] But Asquith knew from Hamilton's message that the other three were not. Keeping Churchill at the Admiralty meant nothing but headaches, whereas it would not be difficult to find another First Lord and another First Sea Lord. No one was eager to have Wilson as First Sea Lord, since he was known as a poor administrator. It was Wilson who had said, when McKenna was First Lord, that the Navy could not transport troops across the Channel. Jellicoe wrote Fisher that the fleet did not want him. Major General Charles Callwell, Director of Military Operations and Intelligence at the War Office, thought Wilson was of quite inferior caliber, all right for knocking down Fuzzy Wuzzies with his fists (he had fought in a skirmish with Arabs during the Sudan campaign) or getting a cable around a bollard, but a poor strategist who sat mute at War Councils.[249]

Churchill alternated between thinking there was still hope and seeing his career ruined. It was in this latter mood that George Riddell found him at the Admiralty on May 20, looking very harassed.

"I am the victim of a political intrigue," Churchill said. "I am finished!"

"Not finished at forty, with your remarkable powers!" said Riddell.

"Yes. Finished in respect of all I care for—the waging of war; the defeat of the Germans. I have had a high place offered to me—a position which has been occupied by many distinguished men, and which carries with it a high salary. But that all goes for nothing. This is what I live for."[250]

Clemmie could not bear to see her husband so mistreated. She had shared the adventure of his rise to office, and helped him through his periods of dejection. Often offering political counsel, she was a partner in his fortunes. Knowing all the actors in the drama, she blamed Lloyd George and his Welsh trickiness. He was the Judas who had destroyed her husband by demanding a coalition. But Asquith had been Winston's patron, had brought him into the Cabinet when he became Prime Minister in 1908, and had always defended him against criticism. The Churchills and the Asquiths were an extended family, always together at Walmer Castle and The Wharf. Surely, Asquith would not be so disloyal. On May 20, Clemmie took the unusual step of writing Asquith that he must stand by Winston. If he threw him overboard, he would be committing an act of weakness. Winston might have faults, but he had the supreme quality, which very few of the present or future Cabinet had, and that was the deadliness to fight Germany. If he was sent to another post, he would no longer be fighting. If Asquith wasted such valuable war material, he would be doing an injury to the country.[251]

Asquith was amazed that one of his minister's wives presumed to dictate what conduct he should follow in Cabinet appointments. He could only assume that Clemmie had broken down under the strain, for hers was truly "the letter of a maniac."[252]

If Churchill sank, it would be with all guns blazing. On May 21, he tried again to enlist Bonar Law's support, arguing that he was the best qualified to stay on at the Admiralty.[253] But his relations with the Tory leader in past years had been strained. They had been opposed on almost every issue, and Churchill had not spared him in debate. In 1908, at the time of the Licensing Bill, Churchill had accused Bonar Law of misquoting him. In the fight for Home Rule, he accused him of seditious behavior. At the time of the Curragh mutiny, Bonar Law suspected that Churchill had tried to engineer a coup in Ulster. After Antwerp, he wrote that "it seems to me an utterly stupid business, and what makes it worse is that, I am told, the Belgians had decided not to defend Antwerp and that Churchill persuaded them to do so by the promise of sufficient assistance from this country." Now, in one stroke, Churchill wanted to wipe out years of distrust and resentment, but it was too late. Bonar Law showed Churchill's written appeal to Austen Chamberlain, who replied on May 21 that it was impossible for Churchill to remain at the Admiralty "first because he has not the confidence of *either* the Navy or the Country. Secondly because it demands a full enquiry by a Cabinet, and there is no Cabinet to conduct it and we cannot wait to appoint a 1st Lord till *after* a Cabinet has been formed . . ."[254]

Aside from the enduring Tory enmity, there were rumblings against Churchill within his own party. John Burns, the workingman minister who had resigned from the Cabinet at the outbreak of war, summed up the feeling of many Liberals when he wrote in his diary on May 24 that Winston was doomed to go. It was a great pity, for he was patriotic (not in Dr. Johnson's sense of the last refuge of the scoundrel), energetic, and at times inspired to great thoughts and noble expressions. But at heart he was dictatorial, and his temper was demoniacal (one had only to take note of his expression in the newspaper photographs as he emerged from the Admiralty). He alternated in his passions between bloodlusts against the foreigner and brainstorms against his rivals, which ended up devouring him. Burns saw him go with regret, for he was brave.[255] Alfred Emmott, who as Liberal candidate for Oldham had defeated Churchill in the by-election of 1899 when he was running as a Tory, had served as Under-Secretary of State for the Colonies, and now wrote Asquith, imploring him "for the sake of the Dominions" not to send Churchill there. It would be disastrous. The first result might be an office revolt. Churchill had neither the temperament nor the manners for the post.[256]

William Pringle, a Liberal backbencher, also wrote Asquith to say that a number of Liberals regarded Churchill's presence in the government as a public danger. Pringle and those he spoke for held him responsible for the present crisis, not only because of his differences with Lord Fisher but because he was involved in the intrigue that led to the article on the munitions shortage.[257]

There was no truth in this last charge, as Asquith well knew, but it circulated widely in the bewildered Liberal ranks, suddenly pressed into a shotgun wedding with the Tories.

Churchill had not gauged the depth of hostility among the Liberals and continued to send Asquith impassioned pleas. On the morning of May 21, he argued that the arrival of German submarines in the Mediterranean made it necessary for him to stay on the job. He was not clinging to office but to his task and his duty. He would stand or fall on the Dardanelles, but it must not be taken from his hands. Could not Asquith send for him so they could discuss matters?[258]

Past entreaty, under pressure from the Tories and within his own ranks, Asquith had to drop Churchill out of the sledge and wrote him on the twenty-first a letter that stopped further discussion: "You must take it as settled that you are not to remain at the Admiralty. . . . Everyone has to make sacrifices . . . I hope to retain your services as a member of the new Cabinet . . ."[259]

Churchill knew that his career as First Lord was over. With a stroke of the Prime Minister's pen, he was removed from the conduct of the Navy. He felt like a scapegoat, thrown to the wolves to appease the Tories. For thirty-four months of preparation and ten months of war he had borne the prime responsibility, the misfortunes, the toils, and the disappointments. But he could also claim these achievements—the mobilization of the fleet, its secret transfer to the North Sea, the safe transport of tens of thousands of men across the Channel, the sinking of von Spee's squadron off the Falklands, the hunting down of German ships in their own waters, and the uncontested supremacy of the seas. It was no mean record, even though for the moment it was over-shadowed by the Dardanelles.[260]

The question now was whether he would remain in the government. Reply-ing to Asquith, Churchill said he was ready to accept the lowest office, for he wanted to continue to serve in it in this time of war. Within hours, Asquith wrote that he knew Churchill would ply a stout and laboring oar, whatever seat in the boat was assigned to him.[261]

Another casualty of the *remaniement* was Haldane, whom the Tories did not want as Lord Chancellor. A vicious press campaign accused him of being pro-German because he had once said that Germany was his spiritual home. Groundless accusations were printed, among them that he was the illegitimate son of the Kaiser, held Krupp shares, and ate German herring. This incident, so uncharacteristic of the British sense of fair play, showed that wartime brings out the worst as well as the best in a people. Too proud to fight, or to write pleas in the Churchill manner, Haldane retired without a murmur. Asquith felt the grief and shame of sacrificing the friend of his youth—they had been young lawyers together, young Liberal MP's returned from Scottish seats, and had served together in three Cabinets—but, adopting perhaps a line he knew from Tacitus, *odi quem laeseris* (I hate whom I have wronged), failed to write him a single comforting word. Churchill, whose friendship with the Lord Chancellor was more recent and less binding, wrote Haldane despite his own distress that he was so short of credit that he could do very little for him, and hoped that he would take the will for the deed. He wanted to be asked to lunch soon to eat one of his suspect herrings.[262]

So short of credit was Churchill that Margot Asquith wondered whether the coalition about which he had gassed so much would contain him. There was no doubt that Asquith could make himself supremely popular with both parties by excluding him. Margot did not want that to happen, for there was something lovable in Winston and he was a real pal, but she would not be surprised if he wrecked the new government.[263]

Rebuffed by Asquith, Fisher was still intriguing to return to the Admiralty on the Tories' coattails, writing Bonar Law on May 22 that he was prepared to serve as First Sea Lord with no guarantees, under him or McKenna. If Sir Arthur Wilson was First Sea Lord it would bring down the British Empire.[264] But getting no encouragement from Bonar Law, and hearing on the same day that Balfour would be named First Lord, Fisher decided to leave for Scotland. Hankey felt that in his excited state, Fisher might do great harm by his indiscretions, and spent the morning urging him to leave at once and remove himself from journalistic influences. He should play the strong, silent man, like Kitchener, injured but mute. It was his one chance of getting back to the Admiralty. By the time Hankey had persuaded Fisher to go, it was twelve-thirty, and his train left at two. He then remembered that technically Fisher was still First Sea Lord, as his resignation had not been accepted. Promising to square matters with Asquith, he made sure Fisher caught his train and then went to see the Prime Minister, who was with the King.[265]

At Buckingham Palace, Asquith submitted his proposed Cabinet changes to George V. Several prominent Tories would be brought in, including Balfour at the Admiralty. Churchill had the lowest rung on the Cabinet ladder, Chancellor of the Duchy of Lancaster. Asquith explained that sometimes a man had to be kept not because of his fitness but because he was safer *in* than out of office.[266]

The King suggested that a Minister of Munitions be appointed. Asquith said Lloyd George would do it, for the budget was settled and he was not that busy at the Exchequer, and in three months he would have the whole matter on a proper working basis, after which there would not be enough work for a separate ministry. As one of Kitchener's staunchest supporters, the King hoped he would be relieved of all responsibilities with regard to munitions.[267]

It was nearly 2 P.M. when Asquith returned to 10 Downing Street and found Hankey waiting for him to settle the matter of Fisher's resignation. Flustered and irritable, Asquith said to Hankey's astonishment that Fisher ought to be shot for leaving his post. It took all of Hankey's tact to persuade the Prime Minister to let him send a wire approving Fisher's leave.[268]

As all this was going on, Churchill said goodbye to the Admiralty officials, many of whom had read the article in that morning's *Times* by Commander Charles Robinson, the naval correspondent. News of Churchill's departure had been received with a feeling of relief in the service, wrote Robinson. Although Churchill had introduced a "breezy atmosphere" into naval affairs, there had been "a sense of uneasiness lest those very qualities of his which might be of advantage to the State in other circumstances, should lead him into making some false step, which, in the case of the Fleet, upon which our all depends, would be irretrievable."[269]

Braving the widespread hostility, Asquith offered Churchill the Duchy of Lancaster, which was vacated by Edwin Montagu, during the weekend of May 22–23. As he had explained to the King, sometimes it was safer to have a man in the Cabinet than out of it. Churchill accepted what his cousin Sunny called a bone on which there was little meat. The fare was poor, but for the time it was wise to live on emergency rations.[270] He no longer had an important department to run, but he kept his seat on the War Council.

Waiting to be formally relieved of office on May 25, Churchill received an unexpected visitor at the Admiralty, the overburdened Titan whose disapprobation had been one of the disconcerting experiences of his youth. Much more recently they had differed to the point of mutual distrust, exchanging angry words in Cabinet meetings. Kitchener asked if it was settled that Churchill was leaving the Admiralty. Churchill said it was. Kitchener asked what he was going to do. Churchill said he had no idea, not wanting to admit that he had accepted a minor post. As he got up to leave, Kitchener turned and said in the almost majestic manner that was natural to him, "Well, there is one thing at any rate they cannot take from you. The Fleet was ready."[271] Coming from this seemingly cold and forbidding man, the tribute was one that Churchill never forgot.

While he counted his last days at the Admiralty, Asquith haggled with the stubborn Tory leadership. On May 25, he reported to Lord Stamfordham that the coalition was threatened by extortionate Tory demands. They wanted to make Sir Edward Carson Attorney General: the instigator of civil war in Ulster would become the government official responsible for law and order, which was a bit much. They also wanted to name Bonar Law, the champion of tariff reform, Chancellor of the Exchequer, which would make it seem as if the Liberals were surrendering on free trade. Nor could Asquith accept Bonar Law at the War Office, for with Balfour at the Admiralty, that would give the Tories both service departments. Bonar Law threatened to scuttle the coalition, and Asquith said he would make no further concessions.[272] That afternoon, after further talks, matters were settled. The Liberals had to swallow the hated Carson as Attorney General, while Bonar Law came in as Colonial Secretary. Among the Liberals, the only major changes aside from Churchill were that McKenna became Chancellor of the Exchequer and Lloyd George took the newly created post of Minister of Munitions, just as the King had proposed. Arthur Henderson became the first member of the Labour Party to become a Cabinet minister, as President of the Board of Education. The new Cabinet was made up of twelve Liberals, eight Conservatives, one Labour, and Kitchener.

Augustine Birrell, who remained as Secretary of State for Ireland, thought the coalition was a twopenny-halfpenny thing, a big, swollen, loose-fibered affair with a lot of unwarlike commonplace fellows called from all quarters.

Why the country should have any more confidence in it than in its predecessor he could not guess. The war was the thing, thought Birrell, and for all his faults, Churchill had already played a great part in it, and his day would come again.[273]

Thus did the ten-year reign of the Liberal Party, first under Campbell-Bannerman and then under Asquith, come to an end. The last purely Liberal Cabinet to govern England fell, and the first wartime coalition was born. Aside from bringing down Churchill, Fisher's resignation could be seen as a turning point in British history, for in the 1915 coalition were planted the seeds of Liberal decline and Tory renewal.

Churchill's last days at the Admiralty were a time of tragic events in the Dardanelles. On May 25, the battleship *Triumph* was torpedoed by a German submarine, with seventy-three killed. One of the petty officers was heard to say: "I don't so much mind about the old ship; she's served her time; but there go all my Turkish curios!"[274] On May 27—Balfour's first day on the job—the same submarine sank the battleship *Majestic*, at anchor off Cape Helles, with forty killed.

Fisher's worst fear was confirmed. German submarines had arrived in the Dardanelles, where so many British ships were either anchored or moving about at one knot in water as calm as a millpond. Ian Hamilton's heart sank at the news. If the Germans started sinking his supply ships, he would be in Queer Street in a very short time. What cruel sorrow there was in Churchill's fall, Hamilton thought. It was the old tragedy of the husbandman who brought a snake in from the cold and warmed it in his bosom. A blacker-hearted or more unscrupulous rogue had rarely wormed his way across the pages of British history than Jacky Fisher.[275]

Charles Hobhouse, who had been dismissed from the Cabinet, where he had served as Postmaster General, while Churchill hung on in the minor post Hobhouse had once occupied, thought that Churchill had gotten more than he deserved. He was always in a hurry to be conspicuous, turning out memos on international law, shipbuilding, blockade-running, labor problems, and other *disjecta membra*, by the basketful. Nervous, fretful, voluble, intolerably bumptious and conceited, he squandered the Cabinet's time with his orations, interspersed with tags of Latin and French that were a source of unfailing amusement and contempt to the Prime Minister.[276]

In the view of his friend, the Liberal journalist J. A. Spender, Churchill had been done in because his mind was governed by rhetoric. In his breathless chase after the picturesque, he left behind practicability and common sense. He could leap from one side of an argument to the other without the slightest sense of incongruity—it was the way his mind worked. His vision of a conquering army entering Constantinople, restoring the sea road to Russia, and smashing the eastern flank of the Central Powers had made him hot for the Dardanelles and caused him to overlook the formidable obstacles. He lived in a perpetual state of mental excitement, entertaining many vivid and jostling ideas all at once, and being brilliant about them all. Surely Churchill's was the most extraordinary career of his time, as meteoric in its rise as it was sudden in its fall. He had been continuously in office since December 1905, and now he was nothing, or next to nothing. Would he pick himself up, Spender wondered, or would he finally be wrecked by his instability?[277]

It was not Churchill who had proposed the Dardanelles operation. The poisoned chalice had been handed to him by Kitchener, only too glad to have the Navy lead the way. Churchill preferred a combined operation, but since the troops were unavailable, and since the admiral on the spot said he could force the strait, he adopted the plan with his usual energy, convincing his naval experts to go along, although Fisher, in the light of his long experience, was against a naval action. Kitchener at first withheld troops, and then sent them. In March, the Navy fought without the Army, and in April the Army fought without the Navy. But what if Admiral de Robeck had gotten through? In the view of General Liman von Sanders, the resourceful German commander in the Dardanelles, the glittering prizes that Churchill coveted would not have been won. The Sea of Marmara was festering with U-boats, and the coast was lined with shore batteries. Even if the British fleet had bombed Constantinople, the Turkish government had made dispositions to govern from the hinterland. There was no reason to expect that a naval bombardment would force the surrender of a major power backed by Germany. Without an occupation force, the fleet would have had to sail back out and force the strait again.[278] Seduced by the siren song of quick gains, in contrast to the bloody plodding on the western front, both Kitchener and Churchill promoted a naval action that defied common sense.

In Churchill's words, they were playing for vital gains with nonvital stakes. Begun as a limited liability operation, using old battleships and no troops, the Dardanelles mushroomed into a second front, engulfing 470,000 British troops, nearly ten times the original allocation, of whom 120,000 were killed, wounded, or missing. All that this mighty military and naval effort succeeded in doing was to hold down 300,000 Turkish troops. In terms of gains against costs, the Dardanelles turned out to be a calamitous display of procrastination and mismanagement.

Churchill saw the Dardanelles in terms of might-have-been. If only de Robeck had tried again, when the Turks were short of ammunition. If only the troops had been sent sooner. If only Hamilton had captured the heights. He did not have the authority to carry out the plan he had proposed. He was caught in the middle between Kitchener's demand for a naval action and Fisher's demand for troops. If only Fisher had been at the War Office and Kitchener had been at the Admiralty! Brought in against his will, Fisher chafed and fretted and finally resigned. A divided Admiralty Board in wartime proved to be a fatal handicap. As the Dardanelles Commission Report noted:

> Considering what Mr. Churchill knew of the opinions of Lord Fisher and Sir Arthur Wilson, and considering also the fact that the other experts at the Admiralty who had been consulted, although they assented to an attack on the outer forts of the Dardanelles and to progressive operations thereafter up the Straits as far as might be found practicable, had not done so with any great cordiality or enthusiasm, he ought not merely to have invited Lord Fisher and Sir Arthur Wilson to express their views freely to the Council, but further to have insisted on their doing so . . . Without in any way wishing to impugn his good faith, it seems clear that he was carried away by his sanguine temperament, and his firm belief in the success of the undertaking which he advocated. Although none of his expert advisers absolutely expressed dissent, all the evidence laid before us leads us to the conclusion that Mr. Churchill had obtained their support to a lesser extent than he himself imagined.[279]

To the Australians, who had been led to the slaughter from the other side of the globe, Churchill was the villain of the expedition. C. W. Bean, in the *Official History of Australia in the War of 1914–18*, concluded: "So, through Churchill's excess of imagination, a layman's ignorance of artillery, and the fatal power of a young enthusiasm to convince older and slower brains, the tragedy of Gallipoli was born."

After May 27, when he went to Buckingham Palace to receive the seal of the Duchy of Lancaster from the King's hands, the Dardanelles was no longer Churchill's responsibility. He had believed in the operation, and others had not. It would continue to be fought under Balfour and Kitchener.

He was so haunted by the Dardanelles that Clemmie thought he would die of grief. It had run on like a Greek tragedy, he thought, the early successes converting what had been launched only as an experiment into an undertaking from which it was impossible to recede. The awful delays of the Army had given the Germans time to teach the Turks to entrench. Fisher's growing anxiety when checks and losses occurred, and his increasing dislike of the whole business, had led to one of the most painful separations in Churchill's life.[280]

But in public, the "setting sun" minister did not display his wounds. On May 27, after attending his first Coalition Cabinet, he had lunch at the Admiralty with Clemmie and Cynthia Asquith, who had married the Prime Minister's son Herbert, known as "Beb." Beaming at his little harem, with Cynthia looking fashionable in a short black taffeta dress, he said they were a much nicer tableful than the Cabinet. Cynthia thought Churchill had genius and imagination, although his strengths were also his weaknesses. He would always be a source of danger, pining for despotism, seeing himself as Napoleon and inclined to be unconstitutional. Deprived of power, he was dignified and unbitter. Clemmie said she had known it would happen from the day Fisher was appointed, but Churchill said that if he had it to do over, he would appoint Fisher again, for he had done really great organizing work. Cynthia was impressed by his lack of vindictiveness. He seemed genuinely pleased that Balfour has succeeded him, and congratulated himself on being able to extract enjoyment from "the austerity of changing fortune."

Suddenly, as he discussed that morning's Cabinet, his spirits lifted, and he said with naïve delight: "There was I after ten years in the Cabinet, and five years in the most important office, still by ten years the youngest member."[281]

XI

DUCHY OF LANCASTER

T HE CHANCELLOR OF THE DUCHY OF LANCASTER was a minister without
portfolio. His actual duties were to manage the property held by the
King in his Duchy of Lancaster, which had never been surrendered to the
Treasury. This took about two hours of office work a week. The Chancellor
had no department to run, and his power was limited to the appointment of
county magistrates and other minor officials. Churchill promised to lay down
a strong flotilla of magistrates for the 1915 program.[1]

Traditionally, the Duchy was a way of bringing someone into the Cabinet
without giving him departmental authority. It was humiliating to take such a
lowly post, which had been given to party hacks like Charles Hobhouse and
protégés like Edwin Montagu, after holding high office. But Churchill accepted it because he retained his place on the War Council, in his old seat at
Kitchener's left. He saw himself as the guardian of the Dardanelles policy,
which he could watch over in the restricted council, bucking up the Liberals
and educating the Tories.[2]

Still, it was a terrible fall. The man who had moved fleets from ocean to
ocean was now in charge of appointing a Commission of the Peace to Bootle.
Actually, in order to devote himself to policy, he passed on the work of the
Duchy to the Lord Lieutenant of the County, Lord Shuttleworth, who announced that Churchill was the eighth Chancellor he had done business
with.[3]

The former host of Admiralty House and the yacht *Enchantress* was shorn
of the trappings and substance of power. His office off the Strand, removed

535

from the political hub of Whitehall and the House of Commons, did not even have a messenger. His salary was reduced from 4,500 to 2,000 pounds a year, and he moved into his absent brother's house at 41 Cromwell Road, across from the Natural History Museum, Clemmie and her three doubling up with Goonie and her two sons. Things improved when Churchill asked for more room[4] and was given offices at 19 Abingdon Street, across from the House of Lords, and when the Cabinet decided to pool its salaries, raising his to 4,360 pounds a year.

Far more than the trappings, he missed the departmental activity, the morning meetings with the Admiralty War Group, the stream of memos, the conferences with Asquith, the late-night meetings, the Questions in the House and the policy speeches, the flow of secret telegrams, the decision-making. Now, without his department as a power base, he had no leverage to influence the heads of other departments. All he had was the power of the word, but his voice had lost its timbre.

At forty he was a little young for the part, but he might have thought of Lear:

> "... so we'll live,
> And pray, and sing, and tell old tales, and laugh
> At gilded butterflies, and hear poor rogues
> Talk of court news; and we'll talk with them too,
> Who loses and who wins; who's in, who's out;
> And take upon's the mystery of things,
> As if we were God's spies ..."

Churchill felt friendless. Asquith had withdrawn his patronage, and Lloyd George accused him of acting from ambition only. Of the new men in the Cabinet, Bonar Law hated him and Edward Carson had called him "the Belfast butcher" at the time of the Curragh mutiny. He was held responsible for every Admiralty mistake, from the sinking of the three *Bacchantes* cruisers to the even heavier losses of the Dardanelles, and Asquith, who was weak and indolent and seeking self-preservation at all costs, would not let him release the documents that would have vindicated him.[5]

The hour was bitter, idleness was torture, and Churchill was repelled by the political game. He was faced with the problem of living through days of twenty-four hours each, and averting his mind from the business that had been his life. It was a horrible experience to remain in the midst of things, passionately conscious of his capacity for service, yet paralyzed. It was like being in a cataleptic trance, while all he valued was hazarded. His mind in its malaise turned more and more on service with his regiment, but he had to stay on because of the Dardanelles. The Cabinet was not developing any of the qualities required for war. With its array of suspicious Tory notables, progress was cumbersome, there were too many opinions on every great topic, and they labored to unsatisfactory compromises. Asquith's power was diluted, Kitchener was increasingly secretive, and Lloyd George concentrated on munitions.[6]

Those closest to Churchill, his wife, his mother, and his secretary, were frightened at the depth of his depression. Blaming Asquith, Clemmie said her one remaining ambition was to dance on his grave.[7] The whole thing made Jennie's blood boil. When you had had your hand at the helm for four years, it was stagnation to take a back place. Winston had been given the sack even though no fault had been found with his work at the Admiralty, whereas Kitchener, who had made gigantic mistakes at the War Office, was given the Order of the Garter.[8] To the faithful Eddie Marsh, who followed Churchill to the Duchy, the summer of 1915 was that melancholy time when public anxiety was interwoven with personal misery. To see Winston torn from his work was like watching Beethoven go deaf. When he left his Admiralty office, Eddie picked up a photograph of Jacky Fisher inscribed "Yours till Hell freezes," tore it into pieces, and dropped the pieces into a wastebasket.[9]

In every mail, voices from the past brought Churchill encouraging words, proving that he was far from friendless. None was so touching as the note from his chum of Aldershot and India days, Reggie Barnes, now a brigadier general with the 111st Brigade in Andover, who said that some people were damned ungrateful, and Fisher had not played the game. Was he going out to fight?[10] John Brabazon (Colonel "Bwab"), his 4th Hussars commander, now seventy-two and retired, wrote to say that it was not pleasant to be superseded by inferior men, but that Churchill would come out top dog yet, and as old as he was he hoped to live to see it.[11] His Harrow mathematics teacher and housemaster, Charles Mayo, reported that he had told the boys in his house that future Harrovians would be as proud to have Churchill as a schoolfellow as today's were proud to have Palmerston and Peel.[12] Admiral Limpus, whom Churchill had rebuked for his epistolary style, wrote to say farewell with a heavy heart—and this was one letter he would not redraft— Churchill was young and would be needed again.[13]

Although depressed, Churchill was not inactive. The lowest trees have tops, and he intended to use the Duchy of Lancaster as a lobby for the Dardanelles, in which he believed as fiercely as ever, firing off almost daily position papers and memos. His argument was that winning three or four miles in France or Flanders would yield no strategic results, whereas the same gain in Gallipoli would be decisive. The whole battle depended on the conquest of three or four miles of ground. Where else in all the theaters of war could such extraordinary results be found?[14]

For Ian Hamilton at Gallipoli, gains were not measured in miles but in yards. In all the world's history, this was the strangest military situation that had ever arisen. They held a four-mile front with the sea on each flank, and it took fierce fighting and heavy losses to win a few hundred yards of ground. From June 4 to 6 they had attacked the village of Krithia, halfway between the cliffs and the heights, but failed to take it. Losses in Churchill's beloved Royal Naval Division were so severe that two battalions were disbanded, its survivors absorbed into the remaining three. The 29th Division was also decimated. The stupid Turks, thought Hamilton, were good at trench work, where all they had to do was shoot at anything that came at them. Some senior officers could not take the constant shelling.[15] Brigadier General Walter Doran, commanding the 88th Brigade at Krithia, did not last twenty-four hours and had to be invalided home.

Jack, however, was doing fine, Hamilton reported. He had been nicknamed "Lady Constance" because he went about in short shorts and an open-necked shirt with the sleeves rolled up. There was no progress, but Hamilton was pleased with his own *bon mots*. When Kitchener told him to be patient for munitions, Hamilton replied that he would not cry for the moon but that Kitchener must not cry for the Crescent.[16]

The War Council, renamed the Dardanelles Committee, held its first meeting with the members of the new government on June 7 and agreed to send Hamilton three more divisions. Aside from Churchill the true believer, Asquith and Kitchener still supported the operation, and the Tory ministers for the moment went along.

Gallipoli had become an obsession, thought the war correspondent Ellis Ashmead-Bartlett, just back from the Dardanelles, who dined with Churchill and his mother on June 10. The whole dinner was taken up with a monologue on what might have been. The usually rosy-cheeked Churchill was pale and looked years older. He had no one but himself to blame for his misfortune, thought Ashmead-Bartlett; he had held one of the most important posts in the Cabinet and had only to curb his own impetuosity, but his nature rebelled at being an armchair strategist.[17]

Casting about for something to do, Churchill's eye lingered on the air service, which was divided into army and navy wings. At the Admiralty, he had argued in favor of this separation, but now, seeing himself as Air Lord, he wrote Asquith to suggest the formation of an Air Department that would incorporate the two wings. On June 10, Maurice Bonham Carter passed his memorandum on to Maurice Hankey with the comment: "It looks to me like a scheme for providing Winston with something to do, and though I would gladly see his engines suitably employed at first sight I cannot say that I like it. The military wing is a success largely because it has been developed and trained as a branch of the Army and with military objects strictly in view. The naval wing is a failure because it has not been designed for naval objects with the result that it has degenerated into a crowd of highly skilled, daring, but ill-disciplined privateered men." Hankey agreed that the change would be unpopular in both services, and nothing came of it.[18]

Churchill saw himself as an evangelist for the Dardanelles and was pleased when the committee on June 12 agreed that new attacks should be mounted. Kitchener promised to send more high-explosive shells to Hamilton, while Balfour said that the Navy was sending submarines into the Sea of Marmara to sink Turkish supply ships. The pessimism was past, Churchill thought, and everyone was determined to carry it through, *coûte que coûte* (whatever the cost). Asquith once again seemed favorably disposed to him, and the Tories in the Cabinet were very friendly.[19] In pressing for yet more troops, he had fought as hard as any of Hamilton's battalions. He bore the pangs of being deprived of direct means of action because he could see the value of his influence on general policy.

On June 30 Ian Hamilton reported that in two days of fighting, his troops had advanced one thousand yards and taken an important knoll west of Krithia. They were hammer and tongs at it day and night, bayoneting the Turks in desperate fighting. Some of the Royal Naval Division officers, however, were completely demoralized, and their low spirits were spreading to the men. But Hamilton thought they had enough kick in them for one more attack.[20]

With the pace of work slackened, Churchill had more time for his family, with whom he spent weekends at Hoe Farm, near Godalming, in Surrey, which he had rented for the summer. There he relaxed with his children and nephews, playing games like "gorillas"—crouching behind a hedge and springing out when a child appeared, his arms hanging at his sides, growling grr-grr.[21] The gardens gleamed with summer jewelry. It was a simple life of hot baths, cold champagne, new peas, and old brandy.[22] One day, as he watched Goonie sketching, she suggested that he try her son's watercolors. It was the start of a lifetime avocation. Painting was an absorbing activity, in which he had complete authority over the canvas. He did not need the consent of the War Council to mount an attack on a landscape. He had full discretion to conduct independent operations with his brushes. It was a sedative, thought Eddie Marsh, that brought ease to his frustrated spirit. Graduating from a child's watercolor set, at the end of June he bought his first easel, a mahogany palette, oil, turpentine, paints, and brushes.

On July 2 at Hoe Farm, a brush hung poised in his hand as his eye moved from the empty canvas to the sky, which was unquestionably blue, pale blue—there could be no doubt that blue paint mixed with white should be placed at the top of the canvas. Gingerly, he mixed a little pale-blue paint on the palette with a small brush, then dotted the canvas with a tiny speck. The man who had mobilized the fleet stood irresolute before two square feet of canvas. At that moment, Hazel Lavery, wife of the distinguished portraitist Sir John Lavery and a painter in her own right, arrived on the scene. "Painting!" she exclaimed. "But what are you hesitating about? Let me have a brush—the big one." On seeing Hazel's large fierce strokes, Churchill lost his inhibition, seized the brush, and went at the canvas with fury.[23] Here was a new form of conquest to be mastered.

Churchill wished he was leading a brigade against the Turks instead of bickering with his colleagues in the Cabinet, some of whom, like Edward Carson, were having misgivings. Goonie heard Winston thinking aloud and passed it on to Jack, who wrote his brother on July 3 that he was far more useful at home—Gallipoli was a poor show, with long periods of nothing to do but be shelled. Why did he not instead come out for three weeks to report on the situation to the Cabinet?[24] Churchill began to seriously consider this suggestion after an item he read in the newspapers on July 5 threw him into further depression.

The item announced that the First Lord of the Admiralty, Arthur Balfour, with the approval of the Prime Minister, had named Jacky Fisher as chairman of the Board of Inventions and Research, an Admiralty committee. After his resignation, Fisher was unrepentant. To those who said he had wrecked the government, he replied that it was better to wreck the government than the Navy. Stung by press charges that he was a deserter, he wrote Balfour on June 18 that he would serve in any capacity without questioning the Dardanelles policy. He was ready for work. He had been looking at the new vessels being built on the Tyne and the Clyde and yearned to be back in harness.[25] On June 26, Balfour offered him the Inventions committee, a backwater where he could do no harm, which Fisher promptly accepted.

Churchill was dismayed. The man whose resignation had done him in was being returned to Admiralty employment after less than two months. Asquith had fumed that he had deserted his post in wartime and should be shot. The country had been ten days without a First Sea Lord. It was Fisher's extraordinary action that had led to Churchill's removal, humiliating him before the whole world and depriving him of the fruit of his work. And now Churchill was at the Duchy of Lancaster and Fisher was back at the Admiralty. On July 6, he protested to Asquith, who said that Fisher had come to him and made his act of contrition, admitting to having had a mental breakdown, and there was no reason why he should not be employed.[26] Churchill also complained to Balfour, who pointed out that Churchill himself had often praised Fisher's originality of mind and great inventive gifts. But Churchill was through with praising Fisher and warned Balfour that he would divide the Admiralty, and that he was an old man, without the nerve to carry on war, not quite sane in moments of crisis, and perfectly unscrupulous.[27]

Fed up with his vacillating colleagues and the interminable discussions, Churchill turned his thoughts to a visit to the Dardanelles. Fresh news from Gallipoli arrived from his brother, from Ian Hamilton, and from acquaintances such as Kenneth Dundas, son of the 6th Viscount Melville and company commander in the 2nd Naval Brigade in the June attacks. Setting out with a flag of truce to talk to a Turkish officer, Dundas found the dead so thick on the ground that they had to stand on corpses. Whether he lived or died, he would not regret having come. Life was only worth living by contrasts. He was thirty-three and felt ten years younger. There was romance in the thought that on this very spot the Athenian general Miltiades had fought the Persians. When men were sent into battle by the thousands, a single life did not seem to count much. He saw himself as one of the warriors who had crossed "the rainbow bridge into Valhalla."[28] Dundas crossed into the home for slain heroes on August 7, when he was killed after the landing at Suvla Bay, but his account stirred Churchill's imagination.

In mid-July, when Kitchener asked him to go to the Dardanelles to study the conditions and prospects, Churchill welcomed the chance. Asquith and Balfour, who hoped that a trip to the front would consume some of his excess energy, gave their blessing, but the other Tories in the Cabinet were not informed. Kitchener suggested that Hankey go along as chaperon. Hankey consented, but it was awkward, for he knew that he was being sent as a check on Winston.[29]

On the morning of July 19, after the Cabinet meeting, Asquith, Kitchener, and Grey lingered to say goodbye. As they shook Churchill's hand and wished him good luck, Curzon, the Lord Privy Seal, returned to the Cabinet Room. Where was Churchill going? he asked. Upon being told, he gave his startled good wishes, but went off to alert his Conservative colleagues, who were against the trip, feeling that the government would be held responsible for Churchill's activities. Bonar Law told Asquith that it might lead to a crisis, and Churchill said that in the face of this serious division of opinion he would not go. Hankey went alone. Kitchener had a good laugh over the incident, admitting to Esher that he would not have been sorry to have gotten rid of Winston for a while.[30]

Churchill was bitterly disappointed. There was no clear policy, and yet they would not let him go and find out what had to be done. When he spoke up in the Dardanelles Committee, he was ignored. He wondered whether he would ever again control a fighting department. He told Cynthia Asquith that watching powerless the mismanagement of the Dardanelles was like being bound hand and foot and watching one's best girl being violated.[31]

Having received fresh troops, Hamilton planned an attack in full force, with 120,000 men, to seize the thousand-foot-high Sari Bair ridge, cutting off the Turkish Army at Cape Helles. On the eve of battle, he was still sure that where the great Achilles had once fought lay the Achilles' heel of the German Empire. On August 6, attacks were launched from the Cape Helles and Anzac beachheads while IX Corps landed at Suvla Bay, a few miles north of the Anzac position, in steel-plated launches. After five days of fighting, the ridge had not been reached. To Churchill, the long and varied annals of the British Army contained no more heartbreaking episode. At Suvla Bay, the landing was successful, but IX Corps did not pursue the advantage. A fresh British army corps was unable or unwilling to advance against a line of outposts. The beaches were covered with men, reminiscent of a bank holiday at Hampstead Heath, but instead of moving inland, they went swimming. Hamilton blamed the placid sixty-one-year-old corps commander, General Sir Frederick Stopford, who had retired in 1909 in ill health, been brought back in 1915 to train an army corps in England, and was commanding troops in battle for the first time. Two days after the start of the battle, neither Stopford nor his chief of staff, General Hamilton Reed, had gone ashore. They were content to watch the action from aboard their sloop, the *Jonquil*. Hamilton sent Stopford polite notes, inquiring when he planned to attack, from one gentleman to another. It did not do to hurt the feelings of a fellow general, his social equal.

The divisional generals, Frederick Hammersley and Bryan Mahon, were equally apathetic. There was clearly a crisis in leadership. Stopford and Hammersley were relieved of their commands by Kitchener, who did not care whether they were gentlemen or not, and Mahon resigned but was reinstated. By contrast, the Turks were led by the ruthless Mustafa Kemal, who personally shot stragglers with his revolver, and later became better known as Atatürk. Hankey, who arrived in time to witness the battle, tore his hair out at seeing such a glorious victory thrown away. Jack Churchill felt that the chance of a real coup was gone.[32] Asquith thought it was the worst disappointment of the war. In fact, August 6 was the last British attack in full force at Gallipoli. Hamilton's army never reached any of the original objectives set in the April 25 landing orders.

The Suvla Bay fiasco caused some soul-searching when the Dardanelles Committee met on August 19, with Kitchener absent in France. Why was it, Bonar Law wanted to know, that Ian Hamilton was always *nearly* winning?

Asquith said that Hamilton blamed two or three of his generals. It was not easy to see why he was still confident when he had lost twenty-three thousand men.

On the question of whether to send further reinforcements, the committee was divided. Churchill pressed for more troops, for Hamilton was contemplating another attack that would save the situation.

Bonar Law did not want any more troops sent out. He considered that another attack would be a useless sacrifice of life, and Edward Carson agreed.

Why, Churchill asked, were the losses incurred at Gallipoli felt so much more than the losses incurred in France?

Because, Carson responded, in France the losses were incurred in killing Germans.[33]

When the committee met again on August 20 with Kitchener returned, the Secretary of War had a major piece of news that affected Hamilton's army. He had agreed with Joffre on a joint offensive in the West. Because of this, it would not be possible to send out the divisional units Hamilton had asked for, but he would get lesser reinforcements.

Churchill expressed his regret at such a course, for the Germans were too strong, and the allies might throw away two hundred thousand or three hundred thousand lives and gain little ground.

Kitchener admitted there was a great deal of truth in what Churchill said, but unfortunately they had to make war as they must, not as they would like to. The fear of a separate Russian peace and signs of defeatism in the French Army had convinced Kitchener that an offensive was necessary, even if it had only a small chance of success. Once again, his hand was forced by his allies.[34]

Although he desperately needed more men to fight the war in the West and in Turkey, Kitchener was oddly hostile to conscription, perhaps from a sense of pride in the voluntary system that bore his name. In mid-August, under the chairmanship of the Secretary of State for India, Lord Crewe, a War Policy Committee was formed, with Churchill as one of its six members, to study the need for a draft. On August 18, the committee heard the views of Lloyd George, who said that the longer they delayed conscription, the nearer they would come to disaster.[35] Churchill had come to agree with this view. It was going to be a long war, and they must have an overall manpower strategy.

As Asquith knew only too well, conscription was a sensitive political issue. In all its history, England had never resorted to compulsory service. Not a single man had been conscripted in the long-fought Napoleonic Wars. For the first time, England was taking heavy losses in a European land war, and behind the word "conscription" lurked the touchy subject of who does the dying. The professional Army was being wiped out, as were thousands of upper-class volunteers. The Tories favored conscription so the lower classes could pay a bigger share of the butcher's bill, while the Liberals had traditionally been against it.

Kitchener kept denying that he needed conscripts, but his Director of Military Operations and Intelligence, Major General Callwell, knew he was not telling the truth. The "New Armies" were a mirage. Kitchener had bluffed the Cabinet so far, but sooner or later they would find out. On August 20, Callwell was asked to testify. He either had to betray his chief or lie, and chose the latter, assuring the committee that Kitchener's faith in voluntary service was justified. But he knew that he was not a good liar and that he could not fool people like Curzon and Churchill, who did their homework. If Northcliffe got hold of the facts there would be a worse crisis than over munitions.[36] But there was no Jacky Fisher at the War Office who dared to differ from his chief.

On August 24 Kitchener appeared before the Crewe committee full of assurances that men could always be obtained by a voluntary appeal. Churchill suggested that it would be better to start conscription now instead of waiting until the suffering of the country made it unpopular. With the hauteur of the professional soldier, contemptuous of politicians and their strategems, Kitchener replied that he did not feel competent to form an opinion on the subject.[37]

Reporting to Asquith on September 7, Lord Crewe said the committee could not reach a conclusion because the positions of Kitchener and Lloyd George were contradictory. Four of the committee's six members, however, including Churchill, submitted a dissenting memorandum urging conscription. But Asquith, feeling that the measure would be unpopular among the Liberal rank and file, took no action.[38]

In the meantime, two Conservative members of the Dardanelles Committee, Bonar Law and Edward Carson, had become declared opponents of the Gallipoli operations. When they proposed at the August 27 meeting that the public should be better informed, Churchill asked with sarcasm if it was suggested that the hoardings should be placarded with "Great Disaster!"

Bonar Law asked whether Ian Hamilton was going to continue his course of sacrificing men without a chance of success or whether he could be ordered to adopt a defensive position.

Testily, Kitchener replied that he would not be a party to such categoric orders; he would never issue instructions to attack if it was hopeless. The general on the spot *must* be trusted to judge.

Carson asked for a definite statement of policy—should they hold on or withdraw?

Sir Edward Grey was also beginning to have doubts. Hamilton had originally said that with so many troops he could break through. He had received the troops and not broken through. He should now be asked whether he could conquer the peninsula, how many men he would need, and how long it would take.

Asquith agreed with Carson's and Bonar Law's objections to "pouring water into a sieve." But for the time being, the only decision taken was to ask Hamilton to hold the ground he had gained.[39]

The Cabinet would not face the hard fact that Hamilton was unable to capture Gallipoli. He had been there four months and was still clinging to his beachheads. Carson was so appalled at the drift and indecisiveness that he wanted to resign. Cabinet meetings were haphazard and a waste of time. Nothing was properly or usefully decided.[40]

Churchill was equally discouraged, unable from the powerless base of the Duchy of Lancaster to make his views prevail. Encouraged by Sir John

French, and hoping to escape from a situation he increasingly disliked, he asked Asquith on September 10 if he could go to France and command a brigade as a major general. Although embarrassed by the request, Asquith did not object; but Kitchener did,[41] for even though a year earlier, at Antwerp, he had been prepared to promote Churchill to lieutenant general, he now felt that promoting him from major to major general would offend the Army, and he saw a French-Churchill tandem as a threat to his command.

Frustrated in all directions, Churchill was filled with scorn for Kitchener and Asquith. On September 14, he had dinner with two other Cabinet malcontents, Lloyd George and Lord Curzon. Lloyd George thought Kitchener was incompetent and that Asquith worried too much about small points—if you were buying a large mansion, he would come to you and say, "Have you thought that there is no accommodation for the cat?" Curzon said the Tories in the Cabinet were on the verge of open rebellion. They would demand conscription and the removal of Kitchener from the War Office. Lloyd George and Churchill agreed to throw in their lot with the Tory dissidents, for they could no longer be a party to the shameful mismanagement and slackness.[42]

Privately, Lloyd George worried about going against his party. The Liberals would hate him violently. Nor was he sure of Churchill, who might pretend to go along and withdraw at the last minute, hoping that Asquith would put him in Lloyd George's shoes at the Munitions Office. Churchill was the only man in the Cabinet with the power to do him harm, and he did not trust him when it came to a matter of personal interest.[43]

For that matter, Churchill did not trust Lloyd George, who had not held out the helping hand when he was scuttled. He agreed with Lord Rendel's remark, "There are no real friendships at the top." The day after the dinner, Churchill told him what was on his mind: "I have done you many a good turn. You might have said the word that would have kept me there." "But my dear Churchill," replied Lloyd George, "I have said all along that I did not think you ought to stay there, that the Dardanelles campaign was a great mistake, and that someone else ought to be put into your place." "Whatever you thought," Churchill insisted, "I always thought you would stand by me when it came to the point."[44]

Asquith must have gotten wind of the mutinous whispers, for on September 18 he told Balfour that Lloyd George and Churchill were the two most unpopular and distrusted men in the Liberal Party. He felt that if he announced himself a wholehearted convert to conscription, he would still have to face the hostility of some of the best and most powerful elements in the Liberal Party. The time was not ripe.[45]

His hopes of high command dashed, Churchill could not decide whether to stay in the government or leave for the front as a major. It was odious to him to remain watching sloth and folly with full knowledge and no occupation.[46] A letter from his brother-in-law, who was serving in the Dardanelles aboard the cruiser *Edgar*, did not improve his disposition. The fleet was absolutely idle, reported Bill Hozier, and there was a feeling of despair owing to their inactivity. Some senior officers held that another attempt could force the strait, make a junction with the Russian fleet, and raze Constantinople to the ground.[47]

When the Dardanelles Committee met on September 23, Lloyd George sided with Bonar Law in proposing that four divisions be diverted from Gallipoli to Salonika to help prevent an Austro-German attack on Serbia. Bitterly, Churchill charged that their real aim was to abandon the Dardanelles. They only wanted to throw up the sponge, and he would not be a party to such a plan. On the twenty-fourth, the committee met again and agreed that arrangements would be made for a winter campaign in Gallipoli. "I need hardly say there is no intention of abandoning Dardanelles," Kitchener telegraphed Hamilton.[48]

On September 30, the most damning report on Gallipoli to date was circulated on the official stationery of the Dardanelles Committee. Its author was the correspondent of the *Sydney Sun*, Keith Murdoch (father of press magnate Rupert Murdoch), who after a week at the front had written to the Australian Prime Minister, Andrew Fisher. At Lloyd George's suggestion, a copy of the letter went to Asquith, who passed it on to the committee, without first showing it to Kitchener, or checking its sometimes fanciful allegations. After the sanguine dispatches they had been getting from Hamilton, the Murdoch report was an eye-opener. The August battle had been "a costly and bloody fiasco," Murdoch wrote, "because, in addition to wretched staff work, the troops sent were inadequate and of most uneven quality. . . . Sedition is talked round every tin of bully beef on the peninsula," he went on. "You would refuse to believe that these men are really British soldiers . . . after the first day at Suvla an order had to be issued to officers to shoot without mercy any soldiers who lagged behind or loitered in an advance." There were grave dangers in holding Gallipoli in the winter, he said, and the leadership was selfish and complacent. "Undoubtedly, the essential and first step to restore the morale of the shaken forces is to recall [Hamilton] and his

547

Chief of Staff [Lieutenant General Sir W. P. Braithwaite], a man more cordially detested in our forces than Enver Pasha [the Turkish War Minister]," wrote Murdoch. "It is not for me to judge Hamilton, but it is plain that when an Army has completely lost faith in its General, and he has on numerous occasions proved his weakness, only one thing can be done."

Murdoch's report substantiated the views of the doves and was not comforting to the hawks. Ian Hamilton, who knew that Murdoch had been used as a conduit by the bibulous and pessimistic *Daily Telegraph* correspondent Ellis Ashmead-Bartlett, who had been fighting a losing battle with the censor, said the report was based on reckless scraps of hearsay, and was shocked that Asquith gave it credence.[49]

But Hamilton was the report's principal victim. There was talk of changing the command. Lord Curzon particularly believed that Hamilton must be recalled, for he had lost the confidence of his men. As Hamilton's spokesman in the Cabinet, Churchill argued that to worry and harass him and make him defend himself against the malicious charges of an irresponsible newspaperman would be cruel to him and dangerous to his men. But privately, even Churchill was concerned about Hamilton, and wrote his brother that one complaint, if true, should be put right—that the General was not seen enough by his troops on the mainland and remained a remote figure at his headquarters on the Greek island of Imbros.[50]

At the Dardanelles Committee on October 6, Hamilton's stock fell further. Edward Carson complained that two months had elapsed since the August failure, and yet they had no report—not a single line.

Kitchener asked if he wanted the whole story, and Carson replied that he did.

Kitchener said he had assembled a number of generals to consider all the reports, and their conclusion had been very critical of Ian Hamilton.

Lloyd George said he had heard that from a good many directions.[51]

From the moment Kitchener admitted that the War Office had lost confidence in him, Hamilton's days were numbered.

In early October, the situation in the Balkans began to look menacing. Bulgaria seemed about to join the Central Powers. A combined attack on Serbia by the Austro-Germans and the Bulgarians would give Germany overland communications to Constantinople, for Bulgaria had a common border with Turkey. Once the Germans were able to supply Gallipoli by train and road, the game would be up for the British.

It was in this context that the unthinkable word "evacuation" was uttered by Asquith in the Dardanelles Committee on October 7. It was a shameful ending to a gallant operation, but the details of evacuation must be thought out.

Lord Crewe remarked that evacuation would be a very difficult operation.

Edward Carson said they would have to leave behind their artillery.

Asquith added that they might have to leave behind their wounded.

Churchill commented on the effect it would have on Russia.

Asquith said they had to decide of two disasters which was the worse.[52]

On October 11, Britain's Balkan strategy collapsed when Bulgaria mobilized. The whole thrust of the Dardanelles operation had been to bring in the Balkans on the allied side by attacking the Turks. But with the Army and the Navy bogged down, the Balkan plum did not fall. Bulgaria joined the Central Powers. Greece, with a pro-German King and Queen, remained neutral, as did Rumania, surrounded by hostile powers on three sides. Churchill's dream of winning the war through the back door faded. It was disconcerting that Bulgaria, after an impartial survey of each side's chances, had decided that Germany would win.[53]

And yet at the October 11 Dardanelles Committee meeting, Churchill still spoke of a naval domination of the Sea of Marmara, and Kitchener insisted that the abandonment of Gallipoli would be the most disastrous event in the history of the Empire. They would lose about twenty-five thousand men and as many guns.

What were the British forces supposed to do now at Gallipoli, Carson asked angrily, hold on and prepare to resist the Bulgarians, the Germans, and the Turks?

Carson, Curzon, and Lloyd George wanted troops to be sent at once to Salonika to help Serbia. It would be a great disaster to withdraw from Gallipoli, but it would be even worse to abandon Serbia.

When someone asked how long it would take British troops to reach Salonika, Lloyd George complained that they had always been two or three weeks late for everything. When Asquith noted that the Germans, too, might be late, Lloyd George said that it so happened that the Germans were not often late.

Churchill tried to focus the discussion on three main points: Should they send an army to Salonika to help the Serbians? Should they send a force to Gallipoli? Should they abandon the whole proposition in Gallipoli?

Asquith said it was out of the question to abandon Gallipoli or to send troops to Serbia.[54]

It was Lloyd George's turn to feel frustrated. Churchill had pressured the vacillating Asquith into remaining at Gallipoli by reminding him that he too was implicated in the campaign, and if it was acknowledged as a failure, he would be blamed as well as Churchill. Lloyd George was sick of Churchill, who refused to admit the futility of the campaign and who prevented the Prime Minister from facing the facts.[55]

Crestfallen at the Cabinet's unwillingness to help Serbia, Carson resigned on October 12. No private business would have tolerated such delay and absence of policy. He was ashamed to see Parliament and the country misled and would be a party to it no longer. Carson told the House of Commons that "the Dardanelles operations hang like a millstone round our necks and have brought upon us the most vast disaster that has happened in the course of the war."[56]

Carson's resignation prodded the Dardanelles Committee into activity, and when it met on October 14, as Bulgarian troops were crossing into Serbia, Hamilton's recall was decided. Only Churchill spoke in the General's defense, reminding his colleagues of the appalling difficulties he had had to contend with. Hamilton had made great efforts, never failing to attempt what was asked of him, and Churchill hoped that his recall would be effected without casting a slur on him.[57]

Lieutenant General Charles Monro, who had commanded the Third Army in France, would replace Hamilton. Churchill asked for a man of greater stature and experience. He was privately worried that coming from France, Monro would be imbued with the western school of strategy—anything that killed Germans was right, anything that did not kill Germans was useless. He would have no faith in the Dardanelles and would preside over capitulation.[58] But Churchill's objections were in vain—Kitchener had picked Monro and that was that.

On October 16, Hamilton received orders to return to England and left the Dardanelles on the following day. He was given no further military command. Hamilton felt that Kitchener had caved in. This was no longer the old Kitchener of Khartoum and Pretoria. He had been abandoned! His casualties, killed in battle or ravaged by the dysentery dubbed "Bosphoritis," were not replaced, and he was not sent the munitions he asked for. Kitchener had asked him whether his men were dispirited. Small wonder if they were, with each unit at half-strength. The War Office had given up on him after the Murdoch report, which was nothing but tittle-tattle, and was now talking of evacuation. If it did that, it would make the Dardanelles into the bloodiest tragedy in the world.[59]

As Hamilton steamed homeward, the anti-Kitchener forces in the Cabinet were gathering strength. Balfour wrote Asquith that Kitchener "detests interference; he detests giving information; when information is squeezed out of him it is not always accurate; he has no notion of playing the game with all the cards on the table . . ."[60] If a Cabinet member asked for a statistic, Kitchener put off giving it, either because he did not want to divulge it or because he did not know it. When he was asked on October 10 whether the German armies invading Serbia had crossed the Danube, he said he had no news. But the War Office had known for a day that the Danube had been crossed. Carson, who would resign two days later, sent a note to Lloyd George across the Cabinet table: "K does not read the telegrams—& we don't see them—it's intolerable."[61]

But Asquith, believing Kitchener's position in the country to be unassailable, insisted on keeping him. He may have been a false idol, but he was still worshiped. They were allies in their resistance to conscription. Asquith appointed the Tory leader Lord Derby as Director of Recruiting and asked him to come up with an alternative plan, which he presented on October 15. Under the scheme, a halfway house between the voluntary and the compulsory, every man between eighteen and forty-one would pledge to volunteer when his "class" was called. Derby's plan served two purposes—it delayed conscription, and it protected Kitchener from those who wanted to oust him because he favored volunteers.

Faced with an anti-Kitchener mutiny, and still mourning the loss of Venetia Stanley, Asquith, who had always enjoyed amazing good health, fell seriously ill on October 19. Margot thought he was *absolutely done*. The doctor's diagnosis was that overwork and hot rooms had gripped his liver and spread bad blood through his body. He slept for thirty-six hours after the initial shock and was back in harness in November.[62]

Asquith was absent at the Dardanelles Committee meeting on October 21, when the feelings against Kitchener came into the open. Lord Crewe presided, and after the meeting, all the members except Kitchener remained behind. Balfour raised the issue of Kitchener's unsuitability as Secretary of State for War, and no one disputed his reasons. The prime necessity was a competent civilian, responsible to Parliament and sustained by a strong General Staff. None of Asquith's principal colleagues had any confidence in the War Office. In addition, there was a unanimous view that the present size of the Dardanelles Committee made it ineffective. Lord Crewe was asked to inform Asquith that a drastic change was necessary. There should be a very small committee of ministers in charge of the conduct of the war.[63]

It seemed to Asquith that the Cabinet had taken advantage of his illness to present him with an ultimatum. Complaining letters from colleagues disturbed his convalescence. Walter Long, the President of the Local Government Board, wrote that "I have had many representations from quiet loyal men who only want to help win the war . . . They say they do not know how things stand or what we are doing." Lord Robert Cecil, the Under-Secretary of State for Foreign Affairs, proposed a War Council of three. "I am perfectly certain," he said, "that unless some step of this kind can be taken, the Ministry will be turned out."[64] Churchill also wrote a letter saying that he would resign unless there was a change at the War Office, but he did not send it.

Asquith was not about to dismiss Kitchener, leaving the War Office open to his chief rival, Lloyd George. To silence the critics, he agreed to set up a small War Committee in the place of the cumbersome Dardanelles Committee. Balfour advised him not to include Curzon, whose manner Margot Asquith described as "an enameled self-assurance," or Winston, for "I think you would find that the internal friction developed by such a machine would seriously interfere with the external work which it was designed to perform." Recalling Kitchener and Churchill in the War Council before the coalition, Balfour said that both had "very strong personalities with very incompatible temperaments. They would not work with each other, and neither of them would have tolerated for a moment the independent examination by any member of the committee of the experts belonging to their own departments . . . I am convinced we never should possess it [responsibility] in a committee of six or eight of which Kitchener and Winston were members . . ."[65]

Asquith decided on a triumvirate consisting of himself and the heads of the two military departments. Deprived of a seat on the inner council that conducted war policy, Churchill's usefulness was at an end. He had only remained in the government to take part in the work of the War Council and did not wish to remain in a sinecure.

On October 29, he drafted his letter of resignation[66] but was put off from sending it by Asquith's decision to make a policy statement in Parliament on the Dardanelles, which Churchill could help him with.

On October 31, Lloyd George threatened to resign unless Kitchener was removed. With Lloyd George, Churchill, and the Tory ministers all after Kitchener's scalp, there would be a Cabinet crisis unless Asquith did something, but what? He thought of being his own Secretary of War, combining it with the premiership, as he had done when he had dismissed Jack Seely during the Curragh crisis. But when he suggested this approach to Bonar Law, the Tory leader said it was out of the question. Asquith was already criticized for dispersing his energies in party matters. It would not improve if he combined the two most important Cabinet posts.[67]

In the meantime, General Monro had reached the Dardanelles on October 28, landing at Gallipoli on the thirtieth. He spent six hours studying the situation with the local commanders, and on October 31 he sent a bleak report to Kitchener: "I am . . . of opinion that another attempt to carry the Turkish lines would not offer any hope of success . . . On purely military grounds . . . in consequence of the grave daily wastage of officers and men . . . and owing to lack of prospect of being able to draw the Turks from their entrenched positions, I recommend the evacuation of the peninsula."[68] On November 2, Monro urged that the evacuation not be delayed: "The longer the troops remain on the peninsula, the less efficient they will become."

It was just as Churchill had feared. Monro had no faith in the operation. His mind was made up on the ship going out. Indeed, his chief of staff, General Lyndon-Bell, had told Roger Keyes: "We made up our minds before we left England." Without going beyond the beaches, Monro was confident that he knew the conditions prevailing on the entire front. He came, he saw, he capitulated. Churchill's wrath focused on the General, the emblem of surrender, and he told Violet Asquith: "I should like him to starve, to starve without a pension in a suburban hovel facing a red brick wall."[69]

On November 2, Asquith made his statement to the House of Commons, defending the Dardanelles operation in general terms but making no use of the material that Churchill had provided. His most vexing problem was Kitchener, but Monro's report advising evacuation gave him a way out. At the Cabinet meeting on November 3, Asquith proposed that Kitchener go to Gallipoli and assess the situation. As he wrote Lloyd George, "We avoid by this method of procedure the immediate supersession of Kitchener as War Minister, while attaining the same result."[70] Lacking the courage to sack his Secretary of War, Asquith found a devious way to get rid of him for a month. Perfectly aware that he was being cast aside, Kitchener left on November 5, taking his seals of office with him.

The Dardanelles Committee held its last meeting on November 6, reaching no conclusions about Gallipoli. Since he would not be included in the new restricted War Committee, Churchill asked Asquith to make him governor-general and commander in chief in British East Africa. He had a scheme for attacking the Germans with armored cars. If he succeeded, the military objections to his holding a high post of command would disappear. Certain that the appointment would be hotly fought in the House of Commons, which would leap at anything that smacked of favoritism, Asquith said no.[71]

Kitchener's absence gave Asquith an excuse to set up the War Committee without him. On November 11, its five-man composition was announced: Asquith, Balfour, Lloyd George, Bonar Law, and Reginald McKenna. The three strongest advocates of the Dardanelles operation, Churchill, Kitchener, and Curzon, were excluded. This was a committee specially picked to preside over the evacuation of Gallipoli.

With no other duties left but the administration of the Duchy of Lancaster, Churchill resigned on the same day. He did not feel able to remain in well-paid inactivity. He was an officer, his regiment was in France, and he would place himself unreservedly at the disposal of the military authorities.[72]

For the first time in ten years, Churchill held no political office. He sat in the House of Commons as a private member. But he was sure he was doing the right thing. For month after weary month, he had watched folly, sloth, and indecision ruin large conceptions. Now, he would do his utmost to win his way in the Army, his old profession, where his heart was.[73]

On November 15, he made a personal statement in the House of Commons. He had not addressed the House for a long time, he noted, and did not expect to address them again for some time. But before leaving for France, he felt the need to reply to the criticism of his conduct at the Admiralty. This he did at some length, dealing with each of the principal episodes. Within the limits imposed by secrecy, it was a plausible exercise in self-justification. The only note of rancor came when he referred to Fisher.

> "I am not going to embark upon any reproaches this afternoon [he said rhetorically], but I must say that I did not receive from the First Sea Lord either the clear guidance before the event or the firm support after which I was entitled to expect. If he did not approve the operation, he should have spoken out in the War Council. War is a hard and brutal job, and there is no place in it for misgivings or reserves . . . If the First Sea Lord had not approved the operations, if he believed they were unlikely to take the course that was expected of them, if he thought they would lead to undue losses, it was his duty to refuse consent . . . That was the time for resignation."[74]

He did not want to go into the events following Fisher's resignation, which would afford "a fine theme for the Crokers and the Creeveys of our time."

(John Croker and Thomas Creevey were two minor nineteenth-century politicians whose private papers were published.) But he did want to assure the small powers of Europe that the allies would win: "Some of these small states are hypnotized by German military pomp and precision. They see the glitter, they see the episode; but what they do not see or realize is the capacity of the ancient and mighty nations against whom Germany is warring, to endure adversity, to put up with disappointment and mismanagement, to re-create and renew their strength, to toil on with boundless obstinacy through boundless suffering to the achievement of the greatest cause for which men have fought."[75]

In the debate that followed, Churchill received praise from an unexpected quarter. "I entered the Cabinet, to put it mildly, with no prejudice in favor of the right honorable Gentleman," said Bonar Law. "I have now been his colleague for five months. He has the defects of his qualities, and as his qualities are large the shadow which they throw is fairly large also, but I say deliberately, in my judgment, in mental power and vital force he is one of the foremost men in our country . . ."[76]

Not everyone felt as Bonar Law did. Some MP's were horrified by Churchill's reference to the Dardanelles as a "legitimate gamble." It seemed further proof that he was recklessly ambitious, willing to sacrifice the lives of soldiers and sailors in a risky operation that would enhance his reputation.

Others, like Lord Esher, felt that he had been unfair to Jacky Fisher. No one felt this more strongly than Fisher himself, who rose in the House of Lords to roar out a brief statement that might have been heard across the Channel. Astonished, for he had never spoken before, the peers barely had the presence of mind to murmur a few nervous "hear hears" as Fisher said: "I have been sixty-one years in the service of my country, and I leave my record in the hands of my countrymen. The Prime Minister said yesterday that Mr. Churchill had said one or two things which he had better not have said, and that he had necessarily and naturally left unsaid some things which will have to be said. I am content to wait. It is unfitting to make personal explanations affecting national interests when my country is in the midst of a great war." Then the old warrior crumpled up his sheet of paper, stuffed it into the side pocket of his reefer jacket, turned on his heel, and walked out, as if saying "be damned to you all."[77]

After giving his vindication speech in the House of Commons, Churchill decided to leave at once for France to join his regiment, the Oxfordshire Hussars, which was stationed near St. Omer, south of Calais. Messages of sympathy arrived in bundles from friends and strangers.

To Edward Grey, Churchill's going was a great wrench, adding to his hatred of the war—if he survived he would look back on it as a time of horrible memory.[78]

Lloyd George said it was a stupid blunder to let him go, for his special knowledge and gifts would be invaluable.[79] In his heart, Lloyd George was not unhappy to get rid of the only man in the Cabinet he considered dangerous. The twenty-seven-year-old Frances Stevenson, who was Lloyd George's secretary and mistress, while Mrs. Lloyd George occupied herself with the "Woolies for Soldiers" appeal, and who usually echoed her employer's opinions, felt that it must be a terrible experience for someone who had held so much power in his hands, but that he deserved it all the same.[80]

At Newbuildings, Wilfrid Blunt and two Liberal MP friends, Hilaire Belloc and Mark Napier, drank Winston's health and sang the French children's song that poked fun at the 1st Duke of Marlborough, *"Malbrouck s'en va-t'en guerre"* (Marlborough goes off to war). Blunt congratulated Churchill for breaking loose from his official bondage to the gang of incapables that had been making a fool of the British Empire.[81]

Violet Asquith asked if she could fill any lacuna in his equipment. What did he need? A luminous wristwatch? A muffler? A tinderlight?[82]

Claude Lowther, a wealthy Conservative MP who had gone to France with a battalion of Sussex men known as Lowther's Lambs, sent him a prismatic compass.[83]

Commodore Tyrwhitt, that magnificent sailor, the hero of Heligoland Bight, wished he were going with him, for there was nothing doing in his line. He had traversed the North Sea continuously and had sighted only one German naval ensign, that of a minelayer.[84]

Awaiting the order for evacuation in the Dardanelles, Roger Keyes thought that unless Churchill was killed in France, de Robeck and a few others would have an unpleasant time after the war. Keyes dreaded the postmortem and did not want to be mixed up in it, for Churchill held all the trumps.[85]

Recovering from his wounds, Josiah Wedgwood thought that the stupidest disaster of the war was that Churchill's daring genius and inventive brain should have been lost to the country through the jealousy of the Admiralty and the Tory critics.[86]

On November 16, Churchill gave a farewell lunch at 41 Cromwell Road. Picking their way past baggage and military impedimenta that were piled in the hall and stacked on the landings were Violet and Margot Asquith, Gwendeline Churchill, Eddie Marsh, and Nellie Hozier, who had been released almost immediately after her capture by the Germans while serving as a nurse in Belgium.

Clemmie was admirably calm and brave, and the others tried to "play up," but poor Eddie Marsh blinked back tears. He had been with Churchill for ten years, patiently enduring his moods and helping his ascent up the Cabinet ladder, accompanying his chief to darkest Africa, and to darkest England on his election campaigns. A frantic but rewarding decade was coming to an end. A place had been found for Eddie at No. 10, as extra private secretary in charge of Civil List Pensions, but he felt that in some mysterious way, Churchill's departure was symbolic of a disintegrating world. Confirming signals came from different directions, in the letter that D. H. Lawrence had sent him, saying, "I feel as if some hope were broken in my chest that has never been broken before," and in a note from Patrick Shaw-Stewart, a lieutenant commander in the Royal Naval Division at Gallipoli, who wrote: "I continue to believe that the luck of my generation must change. . . . Nowadays we who are alive have the sense of being old, old survivors."[87] Shaw-Stewart was killed in Flanders in December 1917.

Churchill was at his best, and he and Margot held sway over the table. The Prime Minister's waspish wife, who was convinced that Winston had conspired to bring down her beloved Henry, could not resist rubbing it in, and reminded him that he had always wanted a coalition.

Churchill replied that they should have sought one not in their hour of weakness but at a time of strength.

"If we had been full of strength," said Margot, "we should never have asked the second- and third-rate men that we've got from the other side today to come and help us," and she proceeded to list the shortcomings of the Tory ministers.

Somehow, Margot told Violet as they left Cromwell Road, the lunch had not been a great success. Violet agreed. It had been more like a wake.[88]

On the eve of Churchill's departure, the whole household was upside down in last-minute preparations, while the soldier-statesman buckled on his sword. Downstairs, the faithful and moist-eyed Eddie helped with the packing. Upstairs, Jennie was in a state of despair at her son's being relegated to the trenches. She had seen her share of wounded soldiers at the hospital where she worked, and she had known many of the dead and missing. It all seemed ominous. She knew Winston's need to be in the frontline fighting, and hoped he would be sensible and take the trenches in small doses after ten years of more or less sedentary life.[89]

On the morning of Thursday, November 18, James Masterton-Smith, who had been at the Admiralty since 1901, serving five First Lords, and often shaking his head at the excesses of the last one, thought of Churchill as he watched the shutters go up in his successor's office. Not even the high gods—whether they sat in Fleet Street or on Mount Olympus—could erase the record, and he now knew and understood that Winston had been the greatest First Lord that the old Admiralty had ever had, or was ever likely to have.[90]

At that moment, Churchill was on his way to France. In less than two weeks, he would be forty-one years old. He had hoped to be Prime Minister before he was forty, and now his life was a shambles. He might never hold office again. At least he had lasted longer than his father, who had resigned as Chancellor of the Exchequer at the age of thirty-seven, wrecking a brilliant career.

Like his father, he had failed. In 1890, when he had just turned forty-one, Randolph was completely discredited, having broken with his party over the Parnell Commission. A forged letter had implicated the Irish leader Parnell in the murder of a high civil servant in Dublin's Phoenix Park. A Parliamentary Commission of Inquiry was named, clearing Parnell, but broadening its scope to judge the whole recent course of Irish history.

Breaking party discipline, Randolph spoke out against the special tribunal on March 11, denouncing its "arbitrary and tyrannical character, used against individuals who are political opponents of the Government of the day—procedure such as Parliament has for generations and centuries struggled against and resisted . . ."

At one point he asked for a glass of water. Not a man moved. Thinking he had not been heard, he asked again. So bitter was party passion that this small courtesy was refused. Finally a young Conservative member from below the gangway went out for some, and when he returned, Randolph, taking the glass from his hand, said in an undertone: "I hope this will not compromise you with your party." Exhausted by his speech, and weakened by the terrible disease that would carry him off, Randolph ended with these pathetic words: "There was a time not very long ago, when my words had some weight with honorable gentlemen on this side of the House . . ." The next day, the Tory press denounced him as a traitor.[91]

The parallel was striking. Churchill too had been called a traitor when he had crossed the floor and had never been completely forgiven. The old rancors still surfaced whenever the Tories needed a convenient target. Like his father, he was discredited, unwanted by either party, repudiated by the men he had considered his friends. He had reached the topmost point, the head of a service department in wartime, and he had fallen from a great height, the Duchy of Lancaster breaking his fall. It was humiliating to accept such a contemptible sinecure, and now he did not even have that.

The summer before the Parnell Commission debate, when Winston was fourteen, his father had decided what to do with him. He was a shameful failure at school, who would never get into Oxford or Cambridge, who would never amount to anything. He was backward in everything except games with toy soldiers. That summer his father had asked him whether he wanted to go into the Army, the dunce's refuge. The toy soldiers had turned the current of his life.

Now, at the ebb of his forty years, crushed by his downfall, he conformed to his father's estimation. Randolph had said that he was only fit to be a soldier. Well then, he would vindicate his father's prophecy and return to the profession that had been chosen for someone who failed at everything else. The Army was a trade he had learned and practiced with distinction. Perhaps Jacky Fisher was right—he would only be happy fifty yards from a German trench. After all, he was the descendant of a great warrior with whom he identified so strongly that he sometimes began letters to Clemmie as the Duke of Marlborough had saluted his Duchess, with "my dearest soul."[92] Who could tell, perhaps in the fields of Flanders he would find his Blenheim.

There was another reason why Churchill wanted to take part in the war. Before he left, he had a talk with Violet, who was about to be married to her father's secretary, Maurice Bonham Carter. "In a fortnight you may be under fire in France," Violet said. "*Can* it be true?" She tried to visualize him huddled in a trench, up to his knees in mud under gray skies. Worse than any physical discomfort was the sudden exile from the heart of things. Would he endure it?

"Yes," Churchill replied, "and in a fortnight you will be married—that's just as strange and just as true."

"Don't forget you've got a star," Violet said.

"I shan't forget it—I may see rather more of it than I shall like during the coming months."[93]

That was it—Churchill had a star. Central to his being was the conviction that he had been put on earth for a special purpose. Whenever he had been under fire, he had been spared by providence. Men fell all about him, but he emerged unscathed. Surely there must be a reason. Now that he was in disgrace, he needed to confirm the magical state of invulnerability that he had come to believe in. He had to throw himself into a situation where it would be tested; he had to see if the magic still worked. If it did, it would be proof that a great destiny lay before him. If the fates abandoned him, he might as well die. Only in France would he find out.

That he was prepared to die came out in a letter "to be sent to Mrs. Churchill in the event of my death," which he had written in July, when he thought he was going to the Dardanelles. He did not want her to grieve too much, for death was only an incident, and not the most important. On the whole, he had been happy, especially since meeting his darling, who had taught him how noble a woman's heart could be. If there was a hereafter, he would be on the lookout for her. Randolph would carry the lamp. In the meantime, she should look forward, feel free, rejoice in life, cherish the children, and guard his memory.[94]

For that was the thing—there was already a memory to guard. Already, Churchill was a part of the history of his time. He and Lloyd George had been known as Alcibiades and Cleon, and as Aristotle said: "History is what Alcibiades did and suffered." If Clemmie ever opened the letter, Churchill at forty would be remembered for one of the most astonishing careers in British politics. His life had been like a fun-house ride, rising and dipping at stomach-churning speed, cursed with adversity, blessed with rewards.

Churchill had grown up as the family scapegoat, regularly reminded of his worthlessness by his father. By sheer force of will and character, he had withstood the tide of Randolph's strictures and formed an ambitious plan: he would be a politician, even though he had not inherited a safe family seat, as Randolph had inherited Woodstock, and even though he did not have the fortune required to finance unpaid membership in the House of Commons. Nor could he approach politics from the bar, as Asquith and F. E. Smith and other young men of modest background had done. He was a soldier, and would have to use the Army as a gangplank to Parliament. That is why he sought action, and medals, and fame, not from vanity, but because he was single-mindedly unfolding a methodical plan. Fame was necessary, without it he could not get elected. Again, once he was in Parliament, there was nothing haphazard about his rise. Every move was as carefully plotted as a navigator's chart. He did not marry until he was almost thirty-four and had a seat in the Cabinet, because he was too absorbed in his own advancement to disperse his energies in family obligations. Unlike most of us, whose lives are a jumbled amalgam of episodic aims, unrealized dreams, and overwhelming circumstance, Churchill's life was a vector, that line in mathematics that represents direction and magnitude.

Already, he was developing a mythic quality. Everyone agreed that he was larger than life, made up of bigger and more complicated elements than ordinary men. Churchill believed that what man has done, man can do, and a bit more. He was the director, writer, and star of his own serial, The Perils of Winston—see him charging with the Lancers, captured by the Boers, winning the polo tournament with his arm in a sling, challenging the Tory leadership and crossing the floor, introducing social legislation that improved the living conditions of millions of working people, and scaling the cliffs of power, his pickax leaving scars on the steep rock face in his unabashed pursuit of personal glory. His ascent had been too swift, his ambition too manifest.

This was not the way power was won in England. Ability was insufficient. One had to have patience, like Henry Asquith, who had toiled in the House of Commons for twenty-two years before reaching the highest office, or glide in effortlessly on the current of privilege, like Arthur Balfour. To some of his elders, and still more of his peers, Churchill was an upstart, a spoiled child, bumptious, bad-mannered and bad-tempered. He sulked and stormed, and had to be the center of attention. He was intolerably conceited, had no principles, and bullied those he worked with. In his lack of reticence, in his pushiness and drive, he was foreign to the characteristics of his class and nation. As Balfour was an upper-class Englishman, as Lloyd George was a Welshman of humble birth, as Asquith was a *grand bourgeois*, all fitting neatly into existing slots, Churchill was something as yet unheard of, a unique and peculiar semi-American hybrid.

There was one word used about Churchill that was not applied to any other English political figure of his time with the exception of Lloyd George, and that word was "genius"—like light, no one quite knew what it was, but they knew when it was present, and Churchill had it. It was agreed that he possessed great gifts, supreme intelligence, inspiring eloquence, a matchless capacity for work, but, as it was often said, he had the defects of his qualities. He was unbalanced, unstable, untrustworthy. Perhaps he had inherited some of his father's madness. He pursued personal rather than party or national goals, except when his own interests coincided with those of the party or the nation. This is how Churchill was seen by his contemporaries, not as a great man but as a flawed man, whose defects of character and judgment were as alarming as his gift of leadership was authentic.

He had many admirers, who followed the dizzying ups and downs of his career with intense loyalty, and already there were some "unconditional" Churchillians, like Eddie Marsh and Jack Seely. But the tragedy of Churchill's years in high office was that he could not win the trust of his closest colleagues.

Lloyd George, who had been his mentor and ally in the battles of the budget and the Lords' veto, and whom Churchill had rescued in the tainted Marconi affair, had come to believe that Churchill regarded the war as his personal playground. In Churchill's declared liking of the war, Lloyd George saw the capacity to exploit national disaster for personal ambition. He and Churchill remained friends, but Lloyd George sensed an unscrupulous side that made him keep a certain distance. Particularly in the Dardanelles operation, he felt that Churchill had refused to recognize a failure because he hoped it would bring him glory.

Kitchener never entirely overcame his early prejudice against the pushy young Lieutenant who got himself assigned to the Nile expedition and then described him unflatteringly in his book. Churchill was a busybody, always meddling in the affairs of other departments. Why did he go off to France to see Sir John French? What were they scheming behind his back? Why couldn't Churchill keep his nose out of army business? To Kitchener, who did everything by the book, Churchill was dangerously freewheeling.

Finally there was Asquith, who had been befriended by Churchill's father when he was a young politician, and who became Churchill's patron. It was Asquith who brought him into the 1908 government, and who promoted him to Home Secretary and First Lord. Having observed him over the years, Asquith now felt that Churchill's future was one of the most puzzling enigmas in politics.[95] There was a kind of monomania in Churchill. He could never get alongside the person he was talking to because he was always so much more interested in himself and his own preoccupations and topics than in anything his neighbor had to contribute, and his conversation, unless succumbing to orders or jokes made at his expense, was apt to degenerate into monologue. It was the same in Cabinet; in fact it did not matter whether his interlocutor was dreary and dry as dust or the most charming of women.[96] Asquith concluded that with all his wonderful gifts, Churchill would never get to the top in English politics. Though he spoke with the tongue of men and angels and spent laborious days and nights in administration, it was no good if he did not inspire trust.[97]

Asquith thought with harshness that this line of Coleridge suited Churchill: "A wild and dream-like trade of blood and guile . . ." Churchill was conscious of his burden in the death of men who had been sent into battle on his orders, and his departure for the front was a form of exorcism—at least he would subject himself to what he had subjected others. That August, the aging poet Wilfrid Blunt, still elegantly Byronic, had visited Hoe Farm and found Winston bitter over his political fortunes. Blunt thought he would have gone mad save for Clemmie. He was painting Nellie Hozier's portrait, which Blunt did his best to praise, saying it belonged to the Futurist school.[98]

Grown stout and thickset, Churchill was haunted by his responsibility for the loss of life at Gallipoli. With an odd little tragic gesture, he held out his hands and spread his paint-smeared fingers, saying: "There is more blood than paint upon these hands. All those thousands of men killed. We thought it would be a little job, and so it might have been if it had been begun in the right way. . . ."[99]

The equation of leadership in wartime was that men who did not know each other killed each other on the orders of men who knew each other and did not kill each other. Churchill had met the Kaiser on war maneuvers in Germany, exchanging polite chitchat, and Jacky Fisher knew his vis-à-vis, Admiral von Tirpitz. There was an obscene side of power. While their leaders sat in councils making decisions, breaking off for a good lunch with a fine wine, dining at their clubs in congenial company, perhaps visiting the front for a day to be photographed in a shell hole or a dugout, eating bully beef out of the tin, but returning that night to the warmth and comfort of their homes and families, tens of thousands of men lived through the alternating boredom and panic of warfare. A plan carelessly delayed, a little friction between the service departments, a minister absent because of a friend's wedding—these were small matters that caused men in the field to be killed. As a war leader, Churchill sometimes saw men not in terms of individual lives, but as "stuffing" to be thrown into battle, an abstract and nameless mass whose deaths could win a victory and bring him glory.

Yet at the same time the fate of individuals moved him deeply, and the whole point of the Dardanelles operation was to stop the slaughter in the West and bring the war to a rapid conclusion. If someday the killed-in-action, all those young men who had "fired to fame the life they owed to nature," were to rise and confront the living, if a vast army of the dead were to climb out of their shallow graves and march down the Horse Guards Parade in close formation to settle their accounts with the men in charge, Churchill would recognize many of them, and would weep as they passed.

There was his nephew Norman Leslie, killed at Armentières in October 1914 at the age of twenty-eight; and William Sheridan, who had married his cousin Clare Frewen, killed at Loos on September 25, 1915, five days after the birth of his son; and Lieutenant Colonel Gordon Wilson of the Royal Horse Guards, who had married his aunt, Lady Sarah Spencer-Churchill; and Major Hugh Dawnay of the 2d Life Guards, who had been at Omdurman with him; and Major Valentine Fleming, who had sent him such a stirring letter from the front; and Colonel Charles Bulkeley-Johnson, who had seen the Prussian Guards beg for mercy; and Gilbert Wildman-Lushington, who had taught him to fly; and Thomas Frankland, who had been captured with him in the armored train, killed in the Cape Helles landing on April 25, 1915; and John Milbanke, a friend from Harrow days, whom he had brought home for the holidays, Jennie finding him dull and stupid,[100] killed in action on Hill 70 in Gallipoli.

There were Lord Stamfordham's only son, John Neville Bigge; and Jack Seely's son Frank; and Lord Lansdowne's son, Lord Nairne; and Lord Rosebery's son, Neil Primrose; and Roland Garvin, the son of the editor of the *Observer*, James Garvin; and Hugo and Francis, the two sons of William Tyrrell, Sir Edward Grey's private secretary; and Maurice Hankey's two brothers, Hugh and Donald; and Lord Crewe's nephew, Arthur O'Neill; and the Duke of Westminster's brother, Hugh Grosvenor; and the Grenfell twins, Riversdale and Francis; and all the thousands who were not relatives and friends. How could he have known that death would undo so many?

The path to greatness was strewn with the bodies of the fallen, but as Churchill approached the shores of France, his ears straining for the sound of artillery, he was ready to pay "the well-known forfeit." He longed for action, for the decisiveness of military life, in contrast to the drift of the Cabinet. He did not know what was in store if he survived. Whatever it was, he would bring to it the granite patience of ambition, which outlasts suffering and shrugs off failure, which retires later than vice and rises earlier than virtue. The last line of the refrain that Wilfrid Blunt had sung while toasting Churchill was *"Dieu sait quand reviendra"*—"God knows when he will return."

Notes

Abbreviated Titles of Sources Frequently Cited

Winston S. Churchill by Randolph S. Churchill
Youth 1874–1900 (Houghton Mifflin, 1966): WSC 1.
Young Statesman 1901–1914 (Houghton Mifflin, 1967): WSC 2.

Winston S. Churchill by Martin Gilbert
The Challenge of War 1914–1916 (Houghton Mifflin, 1971): WSC 3.

Winston S. Churchill by Randolph S. Churchill
Companion Volume I, Part 1, 1874–1896 (Houghton Mifflin, 1967): CV 1.
Companion Volume I, Part 2, 1896–1900 (Houghton Mifflin, 1967): CV 2.
Companion Volume II, Part 1, 1901–1907 (Houghton Mifflin, 1969): CV 3.
Companion Volume II, Part 2, 1907–1911 (Houghton Mifflin, 1969): CV 4.
Companion Volume II, Part 3, 1911–1914 (Houghton Mifflin, 1969): CV 5.

Winston S. Churchill by Martin Gilbert
Companion Volume III, Part 1, July 1914–April 1915 (Houghton Mifflin, 1973): CV 6.
Companion Volume III, Part 2, May 1915–December 1916 (Houghton Mifflin, 1973): CV 7.

Public Record Office, Kew: PRO.
House of Lords Record Office: HL.
The British Library: BL.
Churchill College, Cambridge: CC.

I Childhood

1. CV 1, p. 2.
2. Ibid.
3. Ibid.
4. Ibid.
5. CV 1, p. 4.
6. CV 1, p. 5.
7. WSC 1, p. 16.
8. Mrs. George Cornwallis-West, *The Reminiscences of Lady Randolph Churchill* (New York, 1908).
9. Lord Rosebery, *Lord Randolph Churchill* (London, 1906).
10. Winston S. Churchill, *Lord Randolph Churchill* (London, undated).
11. Cornwallis-West, *The Reminiscences of Lady Randolph Churchill.*
12. Ibid.
13. Rosebery, *Lord Randolph Churchill.*
14. WSC 1, p. 17.
15. Peregrine Churchill and Julian Mitchell, *Jennie* (London, 1974).
16. Cornwallis-West, *The Reminiscences of Lady Randolph Churchill.*
17. CV 1, p. 12.
18. A. L. Rowse, *The Churchills* (New York, 1958).
19. Ibid.
20. CV 1, p. 12.
21. CV 1, p. 11.
22. CV 1, pp. 14 and 17; WSC 1, p. 18.
23. CV 1, p. 14.
24. Churchill and Mitchell, *Jennie.*
25. *Journals and Letters of Reginald, Viscount Esher* (London, 1934).
26. Churchill and Mitchell, *Jennie.*
27. WSC 1, p. 19.
28. CV 1, p. 19.
29. CV 1, p. 18.
30. Churchill, *Lord Randolph Churchill.*
31. Ralph Martin, *Jennie* (New York, 1969).
32. WSC 1, p. 35.
33. Winston S. Churchill, *My Early Life* (London, 1947).
34. WSC 1, p. 35.
35. WSC 1, p. 29.
36. Ibid.
37. Giles St. Aubyn, *Edward VII* (New York, 1979).
38. WSC 1, p. 31.
39. Churchill, *My Early Life.*
40. Ibid.
41. Ibid.
42. WSC 1, p. xxix.
43. Randolph Churchill papers, CC.
44. Ibid.
45. Lady Gwendolen Cecil, *Life of Robert, Marquis of Salisbury* (London, 1906).
46. CV 1, p. 78.
47. CV 1, p. 80.
48. Churchill, *My Early Life.*
49. CV 1, p. 90.
50. CV 1, p. 91.
51. WSC 1, p. 45.
52. Maurice Baring, *The Puppet Show of Memory* (London, 1922).
53. Virginia Woolf, *Roger Fry: A Biography* (New York, 1940).
54. Churchill, *My Early Life.*
55. CV 1, p. 95.
56. Churchill and Mitchell, *Jennie.*
57. Ibid.

58. Churchill, *My Early Life.*
59. Ibid.
60. CV 1, p. 106.
61. Randolph Churchill papers, CC.
62. CV 1, p. 106.
63. CV 1, p. 113.
64. Cecil, *Life of Robert, Marquis of Salisbury.*
65. Randolph Churchill papers, CC.
66. Ibid.
67. Cecil, *Life of Robert, Marquis of Salisbury.*
68. Randolph Churchill papers, CC.
69. CV 1, p. 114.
70. CV 1, p. 117.
71. Cecil, *Life of Robert, Marquis of Salisbury.*
72. CV 1, p. 127.
73. *The Diary of the Princess of Pless* (New York, 1929).
74. Randolph Churchill papers, CC.
75. CV 1, p. 124.
76. Randolph Churchill papers, CC.
77. Cecil, *Life of Robert, Marquis of Salisbury.*
78. Randolph Churchill papers, CC.
79. *The Letters of Queen Victoria,* Third Series (London, 1930).
80. Cecil, *Life of Robert, Marquis of Salisbury.*
81. Churchill, *Lord Randolph Churchill.*
82. Churchill and Mitchell, *Jennie.*
83. Margot Asquith, *An Autobiography* (New York, 1920).
84. Randolph Churchill papers, CC.
85. CV 1, p. 135.
86. CV 1, p. 154.
87. Randolph Churchill papers, CC.
88. Ibid.
89. CV 1, p. 143.
90. CV 1, pp. 143–144.
91. CV 1, pp. 157–158.
92. The stories that he was last in line because he had the lowest grades or be- cause he was the smallest are apocryphal.
93. Churchill, *My Early Life.*
94. Marthe Bibesco, *Winston S. Churchill* (London, 1938).
95. L. S. Amery, *My Political Life* (London, 1953).
96. CV 1, pp. 168–169.
97. CV 1, p. 174.
98. *Memoirs of the Prime Minister's Schooldays 1888–1892.* Collected by E. D. W. Chaplin (London, undated).
99. CV 1, p. 166.
100. Churchill, *My Early Life.*
101. CV 1, p. 194.
102. CV 1, p. 204.
103. CV 1, p. 207.
104. Churchill, *My Early Life.*
105. CV 1, p. 220.
106. Sir Felix Semon, *Autobiography* (London, 1926).
107. CV 1, p. 237.
108. Randolph Churchill papers, CC.
109. CV 1, p. 239.
110. CV 1, p. 290.
111. CV 1, p. 294.
112. CV 1, pp. 304, 305.
113. Churchill, *My Early Life.*
114. CV 1, p. 314.
115. CV 1, p. 328.
116. CV 1, p. 338.
117. Churchill, *My Early Life.*
118. CV 1, p. 355.
119. Churchill, *My Early Life.*
120. Randolph Churchill papers, CC.
121. CV 1, p. 371.
122. CV 1, p. 383.
123. CV 1, p. 407.
124. CV 1, p. 386.
125. CV 1, pp. 390–391.
126. CV 1, p. 394.
127. CV 1, p. 404.
128. WSC 1, p. 34.
129. Churchill and Mitchell, *Jennie.*
130. Churchill, *Lord Randolph Churchill.*

II Soldiering

1. WSC 1, p. 204.
2. CV 1, p. 414.
3. Churchill, *My Early Life.*
4. CV 1, p. 421.
5. CV 1, p. 424.
6. CV 1, p. 460.
7. Henry W. Lucy, *Sixty Years in the Wilderness* (New York, 1909).
8. Frank Harris, *My Life and Loves* (New York, 1963).
9. CV 1, p. 470.
10. CV 1, pp. 468–469.
11. CV 1, p. 474.
12. CV 1, p. 499.
13. CV 1, p. 515.
14. Churchill, *My Early Life.*
15. CV 1, pp. 513, 520, 523, 530, 532.
16. CV 1, pp. 534–535.
17. CV 1, p. 518.
18. CV 1, p. 519.
19. CV 1, p. 525.
20. CV 1, p. 540.
21. CV 1, p. 545.
22. Churchill, *My Early Life.*
23. Confidential source.
24. Shane Leslie, *Salutation to Five* (London, 1951).
25. WSC 1, p. 232.
26. David Scott Daniell, *The History of the Fourth Hussars* (Aldershot, 1959).
27. Ibid.
28. Ibid.
29. CV 1, p. 567.
30. CV 1, p. 629.
31. CV 1, p. 630.
32. CV 1, pp. 649–652.
33. CV 1, pp. 636–638.
34. CV 1, pp. 631–662.
35. CV 1, p. 625.
36. CV 1, p. 626.
37. CV 1, p. 628.
38. CV 1, p. 654.
39. CV 1, p. 578.
40. CV 1, p. 579.
41. CV 1, pp. 589–595.
42. CV 1, pp. 596–600.
43. CV 1, p. 618.
44. WSC 1, p. 266.
45. CV 1, p. 664.
46. CV 1, p. 664.
47. Churchill, *My Early Life.*
48. CV 2, p. 681.
49. CV 2, p. 680.
50. WSC 1, p. 283.
51. WSC 1, p. 284.
52. Andrew Boyle, *Trenchard* (New York, 1962).
53. WSC 1, p. 285–286.
54. CV 2, p. 697.
55. CV 2, p. 765.
56. Daniell, *The History of the Fourth Hussars.*
57. CV 2, pp. 771–772.
58. WSC 1, p. 333.
59. CV 2, pp. 777–781.
60. CV 2, p. 784.
61. CV 2, p. 792.
62. CV 2, p. 806.
63. WSC 1, p. 349.
64. CV 2, p. 823.
65. WSC 1, p. 367.
66. Ibid.
67. CV 2, p. 930.
68. CV 2, p. 858.
69. CV 2, pp. 868–870.
70. Sir Robert Baden-Powell, *Memories of India* (Philadelphia, undated).
71. Aylmer Haldane, *A Soldier's Saga* (London, 1948).
72. CV 2, p. 908.
73. WSC 1, p. 373.
74. CV 2, p. 929.
75. CV 2, p. 922.
76. CV 2, p. 949.
77. Churchill, *My Early Life.*

78. Ibid.
79. WSC 1, p. 380.
80. CV 2, p. 949.
81. CV 2, p. 957.
82. Ethel Smyth, *What Happened Next* (London, 1940).
83. Churchill, *My Early Life.*
84. Winston S. Churchill, *The River War* (London, 1899).
85. CV 2, p. 969.
86. WSC 1, p. 396.
87. Churchill, *The River War.*
88. W. S. Chalmers, *The Life and Letters of David Beatty* (London, 1951).
89. CV 2, pp. 976–983.

III Fame

1. Churchill, *My Early Life.*
2. WSC 1, p. 433.
3. WSC 1, p. 434.
4. WSC 1, p. 435.
5. Balfour papers, BM.
6. CV 2, p. 1046.
7. CV 2, p. 1043.
8. Churchill, *My Early Life.*
9. Ibid.
10. Milner papers, Bodleian, Oxford.
11. WSC 1, p. 439.
12. Thomas Pakenham, *The Boer War* (London, 1979).
13. WSC 1, p. 442.
14. CV 2, p. 1057.
15. J. B. Atkins, *Incidents and Reflections* (London, 1947).
16. CV 2, p. 1058.
17. Atkins, *Incidents and Reflections.*
18. Pakenham, *The Boer War.*
19. Aylmer Haldane, *A Soldier's Saga.*
20. L. S. Amery, *My Political Life.*
21. Pakenham, *The Boer War.*
22. Tommy Atkins was the hypothetical name on a specimen form given to British Army recruits. Thus soldiers became known as Tommy Atkins or Tom-

90. Cecil, *Life of Robert, Marquis of Salisbury.*
91. Churchill, *The River War.*
92. Ibid.
93. Churchill, *My Early Life.*
94. WSC 1, p. 406.
95. CV 2, p. 999.
96. CV 2, p. 1000.
97. Ibid.
98. CV 2, p. 988.
99. Sir Algernon West, *Private Diaries* (New York, 1922).
100. WSC 1, pp. 415–417.
101. WSC 1, p. 417.
102. CV 2, p. 1017.
103. CV 2, p. 1016.

mies, as sailors were known as Jack Tars.
23. CV 2, p. 1079.
24. Pakenham, *The Boer War.*
25. Haldane, *A Soldier's Saga.*
26. CV 2, p. 1075.
27. Milner papers, Bodleian, Oxford.
28. CV 2, p. 1086.
29. Haldane, *A Soldier's Saga.*
30. Ibid.
31. WSC 1, pp. 472–474.
32. Haldane, *A Soldier's Saga.*
33. CV 2, pp. 1106–1110.
34. CV 2, 1110–1115.
35. WSC 1, p. 488.
36. WSC 1, p. 489.
37. Churchill, *My Early Life.*
38. WSC 1, p. 494.
39. WSC 1, p. 495.
40. Pakenham, *The Boer War.*
41. CV 2, p. 1153.
42. CV 2, p. 1160.
43. Lloyd George papers, HL.
44. WSC 1, p. 509.
45. Pakenham, *The Boer War.*
46. CV 2, p. 1177.

IV Parliament

1. Martin, *Jennie.*
2. CV 2, p. 1188.
3. CV 2, p. 1190.
4. Milner papers, Bodleian, Oxford.
5. Balfour papers, BL.
6. WSC 1, p. 520.
7. Violet Bonham Carter, *Winston Churchill* (New York, 1965).
8. CV 3, p. xxix.
9. CV 2, pp. 1220–1221.
10. *The New York Times,* Dec. 16, 1900, p. 20.
11. *The Letters of Theodore Roosevelt* (Boston, 1951).
12. *Springfield Republican,* Dec. 16, 1900.
13. Churchill, *My Early Life.*
14. Winston S. Churchill, *Amid These Storms* (New York, 1932).
15. CV 2, p. 1224.
16. Milner papers, Bodleian, Oxford.
17. CV 2, pp. 1224–1225.
18. *Michigan Quarterly Review,* 5, no. 2 (1966).
19. CV 2, p. 1229.
20. Winston S. Churchill, *Great Contemporaries* (London, 1941).
21. CV 2, p. 1231.
22. *Hansard,* Feb. 18, 1901.
23. Ibid.
24. WSC 2, p. 6.
25. *Hansard,* Feb. 18, 1901.
26. Ibid.
27. Ibid.
28. Peter de Mendelssohn, *The Age of Churchill* (London, 1961).
29. CV 3, p. 104.
30. CV 3, p. 46.
31. Ibid.
32. *Hansard,* May 13, 1901.
33. *Hansard,* May 16, 1901.
34. CV 3, p. 93.
35. Frances Warwick, *Life's Ebb and Flow* (London, 1929).
36. CV 3, p. 102.
37. CV 3, p. 98.
38. CV 3, pp. 104–105.
39. Milner papers, Bodleian, Oxford.
40. Churchill, *Great Contemporaries.*
41. *Hansard,* Feb. 5, 1902.
42. Ibid.
43. *Hansard,* Apr. 24, 1902.
44. Churchill, *My Early Life.*
45. *Hansard,* July 10, 1902.
46. CV 3, p. 168.
47. CV 3, p. 183.
48. Balfour papers, BL.
49. *Hansard,* May 28, 1903.
50. Beatrice Webb, *Our Partnership* (London, 1948).
51. CV 3, p. 217.
52. Ibid.
53. *Hansard,* Aug. 11, 1903.
54. CV 3, pp. 217–219.
55. *Hansard,* Aug. 14, 1903.
56. CV 3, pp. 232 and 235.
57. CV 3, p. 242.
58. Margot Asquith, *An Autobiography.*
59. CV 3, p. 252.
60. Wilfrid Scawen Blunt, *My Diaries,* 2 vols. (London, 1919, 1921).
61. CV 3, p. 266.
62. CV 3, p. 269.
63. CV 3, pp. 267–268.
64. CV 3, p. 300.
65. Balfour papers, BL.
66. *Hansard,* Mar. 17, 1904.
67. CV 3, p. 311.
68. WSC 2, p. 76.
69. *Hansard,* Mar. 29, 1904.
70. Ibid.
71. CV 3, p. 333.
72. *Hansard,* Apr. 22, 1904.
73. CV 3, p. 339.

74. CV 3, p. 344.

75. WSC 2, p. 78.

76. CV 3, p. 346.

77. CV 3, p. 393.

78. CV 3, p. 358.

79. "How Churchill Influences and Persuades," by Leslie Hore-Belisha, in *Churchill by His Contemporaries* (London, 1953).

80. Mendelssohn, *The Age of Churchill.*

81. *Hansard,* June 20, 1904.

82. *Hansard,* July 4, 1904.

83. *Hansard,* Aug. 2, 1904.

84. Blunt, *My Diaries.*

85. CV 3, p. 386.

86. CV 3, p. 425.

87. *Hansard,* July 11, 1905.

88. *Hansard,* July 24, 1905.

89. CV 3, pp. 398–399.

90. CV 3, p. 400.

V   The Colonial Office

1. CV 3, p. 416.

2. CV 3, p. 417.

3. Ibid.

4. CV 3, p. 427.

5. Roger Fulford, *Votes for Women* (London, 1957).

6. Viscount Grey of Fallodon, *Twenty-Five Years* (New York, 1925).

7. WSC 2, p. 120. In Book I, Canto xxii of Byron's *Don Juan,* which Churchill had read, there occur the lines: *"But—oh! ye lords and ladies intellectual/Have they not henpecked you all?"*

8. Christopher Hassall, *Edward Marsh* (London, 1959).

9. CV 3, p. 466.

10. CV 3, p. 170.

11. CV 3, p. 487.

12. CV 3, p. 490.

13. CV 3, p. 488.

14. *The Letters of Theodore Roosevelt* (Boston, 1952).

15. Hassall, *Edward Marsh.*

16. J. A. Spender, *The Life of the Right Hon. Sir Henry Campbell-Bannerman, G.C.B.* (New York, 1924).

17. WSC 2, p. 114.

18. WSC 2, pp. 118–120.

19. H. A. Taylor, *Jix, Viscount Brentford* (London, 1933).

20. CV 3, p. 426.

21. Bonar Law papers, HL.

22. Ronald Hyam, *Elgin and Churchill at the Colonial Office* (New York, 1968).

23. Dilke papers, BM.

24. Austen Chamberlain, *Politics from Inside* (London, 1936).

25. Hyam, *Elgin and Churchill at the Colonial Office.*

26. Ibid.

27. Ibid.

28. Ibid.

29. Ibid.

30. *Hansard,* Feb. 22, 1906.

31. Ibid.

32. CV 3, p. 432.

33. WSC 2, p. 169.

34. *Hansard,* Feb. 28, 1906.

35. *Hansard,* Mar. 14, 1906.

36. WSC 2, p. 171.

37. *Hansard,* Mar. 21, 1906.

38. Ibid.

39. Ibid.

40. WSC 2, p. 180.

41. *Hansard,* Apr. 5, 1906.

42. Hyam, *Elgin and Churchill at the Colonial Office.*

43. Ibid.

44. Ibid.

45. *Hansard,* Apr. 2, 1906.

46. Ibid.

47. Hyam, *Elgin and Churchill at the Colonial Office.*
48. Ibid.
49. Burns papers, BL.
50. Hyam, *Elgin and Churchill at the Colonial Office.*
51. Bonham Carter, *Winston Churchill.*
52. CV 3, p. 571.
53. CV 3, p. 566.
54. WSC 2, p. 191.
55. Hyam, *Elgin and Churchill at the Colonial Office.*
56. Ibid.
57. *Hansard*, June 8, 1906.
58. Ibid.
59. *Hansard*, Nov. 15, 1906.
60. Ibid.
61. Hassall, *Edward Marsh.*
62. CV 3, p. 605.
63. Hyam, *Elgin and Churchill at the Colonial Office.*
64. Ibid.
65. Ibid.
66. Ibid.
67. Ibid.
68. CV 3, p. 656.
69. Sir Almeric FitzRoy, *Memoirs* (London, 1925).
70. Hassall, *Edward Marsh.*

71. WSC 2, p. 214.
72. Hassall, *Edward Marsh.*
73. CV 4, p. 677.
74. CV 4, p. 678.
75. Hyam, *Elgin and Churchill at the Colonial Office.*
76. Mendelssohn, *The Age of Churchill.*
77. H. H. Bell, *Glimpses of a Governor's Life* (London, undated).
78. *The Letters of Theodore Roosevelt* (Boston, 1952).
79. Hassall, *Edward Marsh.*
80. CV 4, pp. 731 and 738.
81. CV 4, p. 724.
82. CV 4, p. 735.
83. CV 4, p. 742.
84. Hyam, *Elgin and Churchill at the Colonial Office.*
85. Spender papers, BL.
86. WSC 2, p. 233.
87. Ibid.
88. Asquith papers, Bodleian, Oxford.
89. Ibid.
90. Hyam, *Elgin and Churchill at the Colonial Office.*
91. Ibid.
92. Ibid.
93. Ibid.

VI   Board of Trade

1. Hassall, *Edward Marsh.*
2. WSC 2, p. 242.
3. WSC 2, p. 243.
4. CV 4, p. 781.
5. Elizabeth Longford, *A Pilgrimage of Passion: The Life of Wilfred Scawen Blunt* (London, 1979).
6. Joan Haslip, *The Lonely Empress* (Cleveland, 1965).
7. Longford, *A Pilgrimage of Passion.*
8. Taylor, *Jix, Viscount Brentford.*

9. WSC 2, p. 247.
10. WSC 2, p. 249.
11. CV 4, p. 791.
12. CV 4, p. 787.
13. WSC 2, p. 255.
14. CV 4, p. 774.
15. Mendelssohn, *The Age of Churchill.*
16. Charles Hobhouse, *Inside Asquith's Cabinet* (London, 1977).
17. Keith Robbins, *Sir Edward Grey* (London, 1971).

18. Dudley Sommer, *Haldane of Cloan* (London, 1960).

19. Crewe papers, Cambridge University Library.

20. Lucy Masterman, *C. F. G. Masterman* (London, 1939).

21. Mendelssohn, *The Age of Churchill.*

22. Bonham Carter, *Winston Churchill.*

23. Lloyd George papers, HL.

24. Frank Owen, *Tempestuous Journey* (London, 1954).

25. *Hansard*, July 6, 1908.

26. Lord Beveridge, *Power and Influence* (New York, 1955).

27. Ibid.

28. *Journals and Letters of Reginald, Viscount Esher.*

29. Sommer, *Haldane of Cloan.*

30. Milner papers, Bodleian, Oxford.

31. Sommer, *Haldane of Cloan.*

32. Ibid.

33. *Journals and Letters of Reginald, Viscount Esher.*

34. WSC 2, pp. 493–496.

35. Owen, *Tempestuous Journey.*

36. Robbins, *Sir Edward Grey.*

37. CV 4, p. 836.

38. CV 4, p. 857.

39. CV 4, p. 800.

40. WSC 2, p. 260.

41. CV 4, p. 802.

42. Ibid.

43. CV 4, p. 808.

44. WSC 2, p. 264.

45. Longford, *A Pilgrimage of Passion.*

46. Owen, *Tempestuous Journey.*

47. Clare Sheridan, *Naked Truth* (New York, 1928).

48. Longford, *A Pilgrimage of Passion.*

49. Bonham Carter, *Winston Churchill.*

50. Webb, *Our Partnership.*

51. Arthur J. Marder, ed., *Fear God and Dread Nought, The Correspondence of Admiral of the Fleet Lord Fisher of Kilverstone* (London, 1956).

52. J. A. Fisher, *Memories* (New York, 1919).

53. Winston S. Churchill, *Great Contemporaries.*

54. Ibid.

55. Marder, *Fear God and Dread Nought.*

56. Owen, *Tempestuous Journey.*

57. Fisher papers, CC.

58. CV 4, p. 937.

59. CV 4, pp. 939–954.

60. Lloyd George papers, HL.

61. Masterman, *C. F. G. Masterman.*

62. *Journals and Letters of Reginald, Viscount Esher.*

63. Ibid.

64. Fisher papers, CC.

65. Asquith papers, Bodleian, Oxford.

66. Chamberlain, *Politics from Inside.*

67. Masterman, *C. F. G. Masterman.*

68. Asquith papers, Bodleian, Oxford.

69. Stephen McKenna, *Reginald McKenna* (London, 1948).

70. Winston S. Churchill, *The World Crisis* (New York, 1923).

71. Fisher papers, CC.

72. Ibid.

73. Asquith papers, Bodleian, Oxford.

74. Masterman, *C. F. G. Masterman.*

75. *Hansard*, May 18, 1909.

76. Masterman, *C. F. G. Masterman.*

77. Lloyd George papers, HL.

78. Owen, *Tempestuous Journey.*

79. Masterman, *C. F. G. Masterman.*

80. Ibid.

81. Sommer, *Haldane of Cloan.*

82. *Hansard*, Mar. 31, 1910.

83. Masterman, *C. F. G. Masterman.*

84. Bonham Carter, *Winston Churchill.*

85. CV 4, pp. 893–894.

86. CV 4, p. 908.

87. Masterman, *C. F. G. Masterman.*

88. Roy Jenkins, *Asquith* (London, 1964).
89. CV 4, p. 908.
90. CV 4, pp. 959–961.
91. CV 4, pp. 907–908.
92. CV 4, pp. 910–912.
93. Blunt, *My Diaries.*
94. Ibid.
95. Longford, *A Pilgrimage of Passion.*
96. Webb, *Our Partnership.*
97. Masterman, *C. F. G. Masterman.*
98. Gladstone papers, BL.
99. CV 4, pp. 912, 914, 915, 918.
100. *Journals and Letters of Reginald, Viscount Esher.*
101. Asquith papers, Bodleian, Oxford.
102. Hassall, *Edward Marsh.*
103. Ibid.
104. CV 4, p. 1134.
105. *Hansard,* Feb. 22, 1910.
106. CV 4, p. 1132.
107. CV 4, p. 1133.
108. Ibid.
109. CV 4, pp. 967–968.

VII Home Office

1. CV 4, p. 974.
2. Masterman, *C. F. G. Masterman.*
3. *Hansard,* Feb. 22, 1910.
4. Chamberlain, *Politics from Inside.*
5. Jenkins, *Asquith.*
6. St. Aubyn, *Edward VII.*
7. *Hansard,* Mar. 29, 1910.
8. St. Aubyn, *Edward VII.*
9. Blunt, *My Diaries.*
10. Margot Asquith, *An Autobiography.*
11. Jenkins, *Asquith.*
12. Gladstone papers, BM.
13. CV 4, p. 1142.
14. CV 4, pp. 1154–1155.
15. WSC 2, p. 374.
16. CV 4, p. 1158.
17. CV 4, pp. 1149–1150.
18. Bonham Carter, *Winston Churchill.*
19. Masterman, *C. F. G. Masterman.*
20. *Hansard,* June 22, 1910.
21. Christopher Addison, *Four and a Half Years* (London, 1934).
22. Blunt, *My Diaries.*
23. Masterman, *C. F. G. Masterman.*
24. Ibid.
25. CV 4, 1031.
26. WSC 2, pp. 330–331.
27. WSC 2, 331.
28. CV 4, p. 1028.
29. CV 4, p. 1027.
30. Hassall, *Edward Marsh.*
31. WSC 2, p. 333.
32. Robert Blake, *The Unknown Prime Minister* (London, 1955).
33. Ibid.
34. WSC 2, p. 334.
35. *Hansard,* July 12, 1910.
36. *Hansard,* July 20, 1910.
37. McKenna papers, CC.
38. Ibid.
39. Ibid.
40. CV 4, p. 1179.
41. Mendelssohn, *The Age of Churchill.*
42. CV 4, p. 1196.
43. CV 4, p. 1205.
44. General Sir Nevil Macready, *Annals of an Active Life* (London, 1924).
45. Ibid.
46. Ibid.
47. Fulford, *Votes for Women.*
48. CV 5, pp. 1457–1465.
49. CV 5, pp. 1466–1467.
50. Hassall, *Edward Marsh.*
51. Julian Symons, *Horatio Bottomley* (London, 1955).
52. Asquith papers, Bodleian, Oxford.
53. CV 4, pp. 1031–1032.

54. CV 4, pp. 1238–1244.
55. Clement Attlee, *As It Happened* (New York, 1954).
56. CV 4, pp. 1032–1033.
57. Hassall, *Edward Marsh*.
58. *Hansard*, June 26, 1911.
59. Masterman, *C. F. G. Masterman*.
60. Hassall, *Edward Marsh*.
61. *Hansard*, Feb. 23, 1911.
62. CV 4, p. 1037.
63. CV 4, pp. 1038–1039.
64. CV 4, p. 1040.
65. CV 4, p. 1046.
66. CV 4, p. 1047.
67. CV 4, p. 1053.
68. CV 4, p. 1069.
69. William Kent, *John Burns* (London, 1950).
70. *Hansard*, July 24, 1911.
71. CV 4, p. 1103.
72. CV 4, p. 1109.
73. CV 4, p. 1337.
74. CV 4, p. 1094.
75. CV 4, p. 1087.
76. WSC 2, p. 340.
77. CV 4, pp. 1087, 1090, 1099.
78. CV 4, p. 1099.
79. Lord Riddell, *More Pages from My Diary* (London, 1934).
80. Owen, *Tempestuous Journey*.
81. CV 4, p. 1100.
82. Cynthia Asquith, *Diaries* (New York, 1969).
83. CV 4, p. 1274.
84. *Hansard*, Aug. 22, 1911.
85. Masterman, *C. F. G. Masterman*.
86. Ibid.
87. *Hansard*, Aug. 22, 1911.
88. Ibid.
89. CV 4, p. 1271–1272.
90. FitzRoy, *Memoirs*.
91. Hassall, *Edward Marsh*.
92. Churchill, *The World Crisis*.
93. Ibid.
94. WSC 2, p. 504.
95. CV 4, pp. 1107–1108.
96. Asquith papers, Bodleian, Oxford.
97. C. E. Callwell, *Field-Marshal Sir Henry Wilson* (New York, 1927).
98. Michael Lawrence Dockrill, *Lloyd George, Twelve Essays* (New York, 1971).
99. Ibid.
100. Cabinet papers, CAB 38, PRO.
101. Ibid.
102. Sommer, *Haldane of Cloan*.
103. Ibid.
104. Jenkins, *Asquith*.
105. CV 4, pp. 1123–1124.
106. CV 4, p. 1124.
107. CV 4, p. 1125.
108. CV 4, pp. 1127–1128.
109. Bonham Carter, *Winston Churchill*.
110. Richard Burdon Haldane, *An Autobiography* (London, 1929).
111. Ibid.
112. Jenkins, *Asquith*.
113. Haldane, *An Autobiography*.
114. Ibid.
115. Bonham Carter, *Winston Churchill*.
116. Ibid.
117. Ibid.

VIII   The Admiralty in Peace

1. Churchill, *Lord Randolph Churchill*.
2. Riddell, *More Pages from My Diary*.
3. CV 4, p. 1303.
4. CV 5, pp. 1473–1476.
5. Riddell, *More Pages from My Diary*.
6. CV 4, p. 1298.
7. Fisher papers, CC.
8. Ibid.

9. Churchill, *The World Crisis.*
10. Fisher papers, CC.
11. Ibid.
12. Ibid.
13. Ibid.
14. Sommer, *Haldane of Cloan.*
15. CV 4, pp. 1314–1316.
16. CV 4, pp. 1346–1347.
17. Chalmers, *The Life and Letters of David Beatty.*
18. Fisher papers, CC.
19. Ibid.
20. Asquith papers, Bodleian, Oxford.
21. Richard Hough, *The Mountbattens* (New York, 1975).
22. Ibid.
23. CV 4, p. 1342.
24. Churchill, *The World Crisis.*
25. *Hansard*, Oct. 14, 1912.
26. Peter Gretton, *Winston Churchill and the Royal Navy* (New York, 1968).
27. CV 5, pp. 1874–1882.
28. WSC 2, p. 438.
29. CV 5, p. 1375.
30. CV 5, p. 1383.
31. CV 5, p. 1384.
32. CV 5, p. 1388.
33. Churchill, *The World Crisis.*
34. Blunt, *My Diaries.*
35. CV 5, p. 1408.
36. FitzRoy, *Memoirs.*
37. Jenkins, *Asquith.*
38. CV 5, p. 1592.
39. Riddell, *More Pages from My Diary.*
40. Ibid.
41. Hankey papers, CC.
42. Churchill, *The World Crisis.*
43. CV 5, p. 1543.
44. CV 5, p. 1495.
45. CV 5, pp. 1545–1546.
46. Fisher papers, CC.
47. Hough, *The Mountbattens.*
48. CV 5, p. 1547.
49. Chalmers, *The Life and Letters of David Beatty.*
50. Bonham Carter, *Winston Churchill.*
51. Fisher papers, CC.
52. Hassall, *Edward Marsh.*
53. Bonham Carter, *Winston Churchill.*
54. Hassall, *Edward Marsh.*
55. Bonham Carter, *Winston Churchill.*
56. Ibid.
57. CV 5, p. 1929.
58. Fisher papers, CC.
59. Ibid.
60. Hobhouse, *Inside Asquith's Cabinet.*
61. Frances Stevenson, *A Diary* (New York, 1971).
62. CID, July 11, 1912, CAB 38, PRO.
63. Ibid.
64. CV 5, p. 1619.
65. Hobhouse, *Inside Asquith's Cabinet.*
66. Gretton, *Winston Churchill and the Royal Navy.*
67. CV 5, pp. 1656–1657.
68. CV 5, p. 1653.
69. Callwell, *Field-Marshal Sir Henry Wilson.*
70. CV 5, pp. 1663–1664.
71. CV 5, p. 1675.
72. CV 5, p. 1678.
73. CV 5, p. 1679.
74. *Hansard*, Dec. 11, 1912.
75. CV 5, pp. 1684–1685.
76. Hobhouse, *Inside Asquith's Cabinet.*
77. CV 5, p. 1687.
78. Dudley De Chair, *The Sea Is Strong* (London, 1936).
79. CV 5, p. 1689.
80. *Hansard*, Dec. 20, 1912.
81. Ibid.
82. Ibid.
83. De Chair, *The Sea Is Strong.*
84. WSC 2, p. 621.

85. CV 5, p. 1664.
86. CV 5, p. 1665.
87. CV 5, p. 1669.
88. Ibid.
89. Ibid.
90. CV 5, pp. 1670–1671.
91. CV 5, p. 1760.
92. De Chair, *The Sea Is Strong*.
93. CV 5, pp. 1761–1762.
94. CV 5, p. 1763.
95. *Journals and Letters of Reginald, Viscount Esher*.
96. *Hansard*, Apr. 30, 1912.
97. WSC 2, p. 453.
98. *Hansard*, Oct. 10, 1912.
99. *Hansard*, Nov. 13, 1912.
100. Ibid.
101. *Hansard*, Nov. 14, 1912.
102. Ibid.
103. Cabinet papers, CAB 38, Dec. 6, 1912, PRO.
104. CAB 38, Jan. 7, 1913, PRO.
105. CAB 38, Jan. 3, 1913, PRO.
106. Ibid.
107. Mottistone papers, Nuffield College, Oxford.
108. Churchill, *The World Crisis*.
109. CV 5, p. 1704.
110. CV 5, pp. 1890–1917.
111. *Hansard*, Jan. 8, 1913.
112. *Hansard*, July 1, 1913.
113. CV 5, p. 1714.
114. CV 5, p. 1754.
115. Asquith to Venetia Stanley, Apr. 27, 1915.
116. Ibid., Mar. 7, 1915.
117. *Hansard*, Mar. 31, 1913.
118. Haldane, *An Autobiography*.
119. CV 5, p. 1740.
120. WSC 2, p. 535.
121. CV 5, pp. 1741–1745.
122. CV 5, p. 1746.
123. CV 5, p. 1745.
124. Jenkins, *Asquith*.
125. CV 5, p. 1739.
126. Hassall, *Edward Marsh*.
127. Ibid.
128. Ibid.
129. Ibid.
130. Bonham Carter, *Winston Churchill*.
131. CV 5, p. 1752.
132. Jenkins, *Asquith*.
133. Ibid.
134. CV 5, p. 1399.
135. CV 5, p. 1400.
136. Blake, *The Unknown Prime Minister*.
137. CV 5, p. 1781.
138. Balfour papers, BL.
139. Chamberlain, *Politics from Inside*.
140. Ibid.
141. Mary Soames, *Clementine Churchill* (New York, 1979).
142. Ibid.
143. CV 5, p. 1884.
144. WSC 2, p. 682.
145. CV 5, p. 1894.
146. CV 5, p. 1920.
147. CV 5, p. 1890.
148. CV 5, p. 1892.
149. CV 5, pp. 1891–1892.
150. CV 5, p. 1895.
151. CV 5, p. 1920.
152. Soames, *Clementine Churchill*.
153. CV 5, pp. 1921–1922.
154. CV 5, pp. 1801–1802.
155. Geoffrey Bennett, *Charlie B.* (London, 1968).
156. CV 5, p. 1796.
157. Ibid.
158. De Chair, *The Sea Is Strong*.
159. CV 5, p. 1797.
160. CV 5, p. 1798.
161. CV 5, pp. 1796–1798.
162. Hobhouse, *Inside Asquith's Cabinet*.
163. CV 5, p. 1825.
164. CV 5, p. 1833.
165. Ibid.

166. Ibid.
167. Hobhouse, *Inside Asquith's Cabinet.*
168. CV 5, pp. 1833–1834.
169. CV 5, pp. 1834–1835.
170. CV 5, p. 1837.
171. CV 5, p. 1838.
172. WSC 2, p. 636.
173. *The Political Diaries of C. P. Scott, 1911–1928* (London, 1970).
174. Owen, *Tempestuous Journey.*
175. CV 5, p. 1841.
176. CV 5, p. 1844.
177. CV 5, pp. 1842–1843.
178. Riddell, *More Pages from My Diary.*
179. Ibid.
180. Lloyd George papers, HL.
181. Jenkins, *Asquith.*
182. Hobhouse, *Inside Asquith's Cabinet.*
183. CV 5, p. 1859.
184. CV 5, p. 1860.
185. CV 5, p. 1861.
186. Churchill, *The World Crisis.*
187. CV 5, p. 1873.
188. WSC 2, p. 471.
189. WSC 2, p. 472.
190. Mottistone papers, Nuffield College, Oxford.
191. J. E. B. Seely, *Adventure* (New York, 1930).
192. Mottistone papers, Nuffield College, Oxford.
193. Asquith papers, Bodleian, Oxford.
194. Mottistone papers, Nuffield College, Oxford.
195. Ibid.
196. Callwell, *Field-Marshal Sir Henry Wilson.*
197. Asquith papers, Bodleian, Oxford.
198. *Hansard*, Mar. 25, 1914.
199. Ibid.
200. Ibid.
201. Jenkins, *Asquith.*

202. Mottistone papers, Nuffield College, Oxford.
203. CV 5, p. 1416.
204. *Hansard*, Mar. 30, 1914.
205. Mottistone papers, Nuffield College, Oxford.
206. WSC 2, p. 484.
207. Wemyss papers, CC.
208. *Hansard*, Apr. 28, 1914.
209. CV 5, pp. 1966–1973.
210. Fisher papers, CC.
211. Ibid.
212. *The Naval Memoirs of Roger Keyes* (New York, 1934).
213. Churchill, *The World Crisis.*
214. Ibid.
215. Ibid.
216. Jenkins, *Asquith.*
217. Churchill, *The World Crisis.*
218. Hough, *The Mountbattens.*
219. Churchill, *The World Crisis.*
220. Ibid.
221. Ibid.
222. Ibid.
223. CV 5, p. 1989.
224. CV 5, p. 1993.
225. CV 5, pp. 1996–1997.
226. Churchill, *The World Crisis.*
227. Ibid.
228. Hobhouse, *Inside Asquith's Cabinet.*
229. Viscount Simon, *Retrospect* (London, 1952).
230. Churchill, *The World Crisis.*
231. Ibid.
232. CV 5, p. 1998.
233. Crewe papers, Cambridge University Library.
234. Anthony Eden, *Another World, 1897–1917* (New York, 1977).
235. Viscount Grey of Fallodon, *Twenty-Five Years.*
236. Jenkins, *Asquith.*
237. Churchill, *The World Crisis.*
238. Ibid.

239. Viscount Grey of Fallodon, *Twenty-Five Years.*
240. Churchill, *The World Crisis.*
241. Bonham Carter, *Winston Churchill.*
242. Longford, *A Pilgrimage of Passion.*

243. Spender papers, BL.
244. Churchill, *The World Crisis.*
245. Ibid.
246. Stevenson, *A Diary.*
247. CV 5, p. 1999.

IX The Admiralty in War

1. CV 6, p. 23.
2. Fisher papers, CC.
3. CV 6, p. 9.
4. CV 6, p. 10.
5. CV 6, pp. 15–16.
6. CV 6, p. 16.
7. CV 6, p. 17.
8. Chalmers, *The Life and Letters of David Beatty.*
9. WSC 3, p. 15.
10. CV 6, p. 12.
11. CV 6, p. 17.
12. WSC 3, p. 29.
13. WSC 3, p. 30.
14. CV 6, p. 18.
15. Churchill, *The World Crisis.*
16. CV 6, p. 33.
17. Fisher papers, CC.
18. Churchill, *The World Crisis.*
19. CV 6, p. 467.
20. WSC 3, p. 38.
21. Cabinet papers, CAB 42, Aug. 5, 1914, PRO.
22. Philip Magnus, *Kitchener* (London, 1958).
23. Churchill, *The World Crisis.*
24. CV 6, p. 112.
25. Cabinet papers, CAB 42, Aug. 7, 1914, PRO.
26. Callwell, *Field-Marshal Sir Henry Wilson.*
27. CV 6, pp. 36–37.
28. Nicholas Moseley, *Julian Grenfell* (London, 1976).
29. Ibid.
30. Soames, *Clementine Churchill.*

31. CV 6, p. 34.
32. Soames, *Clementine Churchill.*
33. CV 6, p. 49.
34. Hobhouse, *Inside Asquith's Cabinet.*
35. Churchill, *The World Crisis.*
36. Ibid.
37. Ibid.
38. Douglas Jerrold, *The Royal Naval Division* (London, 1923).
39. WSC 3, p. 51.
40. WSC 3, p. 57.
41. Chalmers, *The Life and Letters of David Beatty.*
42. Churchill, *The World Crisis.*
43. Chalmers, *The Life and Letters of David Beatty.*
44. Ibid.
45. WSC 3, p. 59.
46. CV 6, pp. 66–70.
47. WSC 3, p. 60.
48. CV 6, p. 79.
49. CV 6, p. 106.
50. WSC 3, p. 72.
51. CV 6, pp. 81–82.
52. WSC 2, p. 683.
53. WSC 3, p. 74.
54. Churchill, *The World Crisis.*
55. CV 6, p. 123.
56. Churchill, *The World Crisis.*
57. Hobhouse, *Inside Asquith's Cabinet.*
58. CV 6, pp. 127–128.
59. Crewe papers, Cambridge University Library.
60. CV 6, p. 148.

61. WSC 3, p. 84.
62. CV 6, p. 128.
63. CV 6, p. 141.
64. WSC 3, p. 91.
65. Soames, *Clementine Churchill*.
66. CV 6, p. 143.
67. CV 6, p. 144.
68. Churchill, *The World Crisis*.
69. CV 6, p. 19.
70. CV 6, p. 46.
71. CV 6, p. 47.
72. CV 6, p. 99.
73. CV 6, p. 145.
74. CV 6, p. 150.
75. CV 6, p. 154.
76. Churchill, *The World Crisis*.
77. CV 6, p. 159.
78. CV 6, p. 161.
79. WSC 3, p. 110.
80. CV 6, p. 165.
81. Churchill, *The World Crisis*.
82. CV 6, p. 166.
83. Soames, *Clementine Churchill*.
84. CV 6, pp. 174–175.
85. Hassall, *Edward Marsh*.
86. WSC 3, p. 117.
87. CV 6, p. 173.
88. CV 6, pp. 177–178.
89. CV 6, pp. 179–180.
90. Hassall, *Edward Marsh*.
91. CV 6, p. 188.
92. Lloyd George papers, HL.
93. Chalmers, *The Life and Letters of David Beatty*.
94. Bonar Law papers, HL.
95. CV 6, p. 203.
96. CV 6, p. 219.
97. Cabinet papers, CAB 38, Oct. 7, 1914, PRO.
98. CAB 38, Oct. 21, 1914, PRO.
99. CV 6, p. 210.
100. Hobhouse, *Inside Asquith's Cabinet*.
101. CV 6, p. 220.
102. CV 6, p. 222.
103. CV 6, p. 241.
104. CV 6, p. 224.
105. CV 6, p. 223.
106. CV 6, p. 220.
107. CV 6, pp. 220–221.
108. CV 6, p. 224.
109. CV 6, pp. 231–232.
110. CV 6, p. 243.
111. Churchill, *The World Crisis*.
112. Ibid.
113. Ibid.
114. CV 6, p. 249.
115. Churchill, *The World Crisis*.
116. CV 6, p. 253.
117. Ibid.
118. Stevenson, *A Diary*.
119. Chalmers, *The Life and Letters of David Beatty*.
120. Fisher papers, CC.
121. CV 6, pp. 263–264.
122. CV 6, p. 276.
123. CV 6, p. 275.
124. *Hansard*, Nov. 26, 1914.
125. WSC 3, p. 175.
126. CV 6, p. 269.
127. CV 6, p. 247.
128. CV 6, pp. 277–279.
129. *Hansard*, Nov. 25, 1914.
130. *Hansard*, Nov. 27, 1914.
131. Churchill, *The World Crisis*.
132. CV 6, p. 283.
133. CV 6, p. 271.
134. CV 6, p. 290.
135. CV 6, p. 296.
136. CV 6, p. 299.
137. CV 6, p. 318.
138. Churchill, *The World Crisis*.
139. Ibid.
140. CV 6, p. 318.
141. CV 6, p. 302.
142. Fisher papers, CC.
143. CV 6, p. 307.
144. Churchill, *The World Crisis*.
145. Chalmers, *The Life and Letters of David Beatty*.

146. CV 6, pp. 320–321.
147. CV 6, p. 322.
148. CV 6, pp. 312–313.
149. CV 6, p. 313.
150. CV 6, pp. 313–314.
151. CV 6, p. 315.
152. Ibid.
153. CV 6, p. 335.

154. WSC 3, p. 167.
155. CV 6, p. 332.
156. CV 6, p. 374.
157. Ibid.
158. CV 6, p. 333.
159. Fisher papers, CC.
160. CV 6, p. 322.

X The Dardanelles

1. CV 6, p. 272.
2. CV 6, p. 273.
3. WSC 3, pp. 236–237.
4. Owen, *Tempestuous Journey*.
5. CV 6, p. 346.
6. Fisher papers, CC.
7. CV 6, pp. 359–360.
8. Kitchener papers, PRO.
9. CV 6, p. 361.
10. Cabinet papers, CAB 38, Nov. 25, 1914.
11. CV 6, p. 367.
12. CV 6, p. 371.
13. CV 6, p. 380.
14. CV 6, p. 381.
15. CV 6, pp. 391–396.
16. CV 6, p. 400.
17. CV 6, p. 405.
18. WSC 3, p. 221.
19. WSC 3, p. 222.
20. CV 6, pp. 406–407.
21. CV 6, pp. 407–411.
22. CV 6, p. 437.
23. WSC 3, p. 253.
24. WSC 3, p. 258.
25. CV 6, p. 427.
26. CV 6, p. 429.
27. Fisher papers, CC.
28. Churchill, *The World Crisis*.
29. CV 6, p. 431.
30. CV 6, p. 430.
31. Churchill, *The World Crisis*.
32. Ibid.
33. Chalmers, *The Life and Letters of David Beatty*.

34. Churchill, *The World Crisis*.
35. Fisher papers, CC.
36. CV 6, p. 451.
37. CV 6, p. 458.
38. WSC 3, p. 265.
39. CV 6, p. 462.
40. CV 6, p. 463.
41. CV 6, pp. 463–470.
42. Admiral Lord Fisher, *Memories* (London, 1919); and CV 6, p. 470.
43. Fisher papers, CC.
44. CV 6, pp. 463–470.
45. CV 6, p. 471.
46. CV 6, pp. 485–490.
47. CV 6, p. 495.
48. CV 6, p. 497.
49. Kitchener papers, PRO.
50. Cabinet papers, CAB 42, Feb. 9, 1915, PRO.
51. CV 6, p. 512.
52. CV 6, p. 513.
53. CV 6, pp. 506–512.
54. WSC 3, p. 288.
55. Cabinet papers, CAB 42, Feb. 16, 1915, PRO.
56. CV 6, p. 517.
57. Owen, *Tempestuous Journey*.
58. Hobhouse, *Inside Asquith's Cabinet*.
59. Ibid.
60. CV 6, pp. 517–518.
61. CV 6, p. 525.
62. CV 6, p. 521.
63. CV 6, p. 518.

64. CV 6, p. 522.
65. CV 6, p. 525.
66. CV 6, pp. 527–534.
67. CV 6, p. 521.
68. CV 6, pp. 527–528.
69. CV 6, p. 555.
70. WSC 3, p. 305–306.
71. WSC 3, p. 306.
72. Bonham Carter, *Winston Churchill*.
73. Jerrold, *The Royal Naval Division*.
74. CV 6, pp. 567–577.
75. Churchill, *The World Crisis*.
76. CV 6, p. 577.
77. Jenkins, *Asquith*.
78. Marder, *Fear God and Dread Nought*.
79. Bonham Carter, *Winston Churchill*.
80. CV 6, p. 604.
81. WSC 3, p. 318.
82. Churchill, *The World Crisis*.
83. CV 6, pp. 610–618.
84. Ibid.
85. Kitchener papers, PRO.
86. CV 6, p. 645.
87. CV 6, p. 644.
88. CV 6, p. 646.
89. CV 6, pp. 637–638.
90. CV 6, pp. 663–673.
91. Ibid.
92. Ibid.
93. WSC 3, p. 325.
94. Ian Hamilton, *Gallipoli Diary* (New York, 1920).
95. CV 6, pp. 676–677.
96. CV 6, p. 680.
97. CV 6, p. 677.
98. Kitchener papers, PRO.
99. CV 6, p. 696.
100. CV 6, p. 687.
101. CV 6, p. 695.
102. Ibid.
103. CV 6, pp. 690–691.
104. CV 6, p. 701.
105. CV 6, p. 703.
106. *The Naval Memoirs of Sir Roger Keyes*.
107. Kitchener papers, PRO.
108. Hamilton, *Gallipoli Diary*.
109. CV 6, p. 710.
110. Hamilton, *Gallipoli Diary*.
111. CV 6, p. 708.
112. *The Naval Memoirs of Sir Roger Keyes*.
113. Charles F. Horne and Walter F. Austin, *Source Records of the Great War*, Vol. III (New York, 1923).
114. Churchill, *The World Crisis*.
115. Fisher papers, CC.
116. Ibid.
117. CV 6, pp. 710–716.
118. Dardanelles Commission Report, PRO.
119. WSC 3, pp. 357–359.
120. CV 6, p. 719.
121. CV 6, p. 720.
122. CV 6, p. 709.
123. Hamilton, *Gallipoli Diary*.
124. CV 6, pp. 726–727.
125. CV 6, p. 727.
126. Churchill, *The World Crisis*.
127. CV 6, p. 726.
128. WSC 3, p. 367.
129. Churchill, *The World Crisis*.
130. CV 6, pp. 728–729.
131. CV 6, p. 740.
132. CV 6, p. 741.
133. Churchill, *The World Crisis*.
134. CV 6, p. 746.
135. CV 6, pp. 751–753.
136. CV 6, p. 755.
137. CV 6, p. 756.
138. Churchill, *The World Crisis*.
139. WSC 3, p. 361.
140. CV 6, p. 760.
141. CV 6, p. 763.
142. CV 6, p. 760.
143. CV 6, p. 764.
144. CV 6, p. 769.

145. CV 6, p. 765.
146. CV 6, p. 770.
147. Stevenson, *A Diary*.
148. CV 6, p. 769.
149. Lloyd George papers, HL.
150. CV 6, p. 773.
151. CV 6, p. 775.
152. CV 6, p. 778.
153. CV 6, p. 782.
154. CV 6, p. 791.
155. CV 6, p. 792.
156. CV 6, p. 794.
157. CV 6, p. 799.
158. Asquith papers, Bodleian, Oxford.
159. CV 6, p. 804.
160. CV 6, p. 801.
161. CV 6, p. 802.
162. Hamilton, *Gallipoli Diary*.
163. CV 6, p. 807.
164. CV 7, p. 841.
165. Hassall, *Edward Marsh*.
166. Ibid.
167. CV 6, p. 814.
168. Bonham Carter, *Churchill*.
169. Hamilton, *Gallipoli Diary*.
170. Jerrold, *The Royal Naval Division*.
171. Ibid.
172. CV 6, pp. 825–826.
173. CV 6, p. 820.
174. Hamilton, *Gallipoli Diary*.
175. CV 6, pp. 822–823.
176. CV 6, pp. 816–817.
177. WSC 3, p. 410.
178. CV 7, p. 848.
179. Hamilton, *Gallipoli Diary*.
180. CV 7, pp. 849–850.
181. WSC 3, p. 419.
182. CV 7, pp. 855–856.
183. CV 7, p. 858.
184. CV 7, p. 861.
185. CV 7, p. 862.
186. CV 7, p. 864.
187. Fisher papers, CC.
188. CV 7, p. 865.
189. Kitchener papers, PRO.
190. WSC 3, p. 423.
191. Ibid.
192. CV 7, p. 867.
193. CV 7, p. 864.
194. CV 7, p. 871.
195. CV 7, p. 873.
196. CV 7, p. 872.
197. CV 7, p. 873.
198. WSC 3, pp. 430–431.
199. CV 7, pp. 875–880.
200. Ibid.
201. Ibid.
202. CV 7, p. 883.
203. CV 7, pp. 884–885.
204. WSC 3, p. 435.
205. Ibid.
206. CV 7, p. 885.
207. WSC 3, pp. 436–437.
208. WSC 3, p. 437.
209. CV 7, p. 887.
210. CV 7, p. 888.
211. WSC 3, pp. 438–439.
212. Stevenson, *A Diary*.
213. CV 7, pp. 888–889.
214. CV 7, pp. 891–892.
215. CV 7, p. 891.
216. Fisher papers, CC.
217. CV 7, pp. 892–893.
218. CV 7, p. 894.
219. WSC 3, p. 444.
220. Churchill, *The World Crisis*.
221. Bonar Law papers, HL.
222. WSC 3, p. 446.
223. Confidential source.
224. Jenkins, *Asquith*; and S. D. Waley, *Edwin Montagu* (London, 1964).
225. Ibid.
226. Ibid.
227. Ibid.
228. WSC 3, p. 447.
229. Churchill, *Great Contemporaries*.
230. Churchill, *The World Crisis*.
231. Ibid.

232. CV 7, p. 898.
233. Churchill, *The World Crisis.*
234. CV 7, pp. 902–903.
235. WSC 3, p. 451.
236. CV 7, pp. 898–899.
237. CV 7, p. 905.
238. WSC 3, p. 452.
239. Ibid.
240. CV 7, p. 906.
241. CV 7, p. 914.
242. CV 7, p. 911.
243. Ibid.
244. CV 7, p. 908.
245. Stevenson, *A Diary.*
246. CV 7, p. 915.
247. WSC 3, p. 457.
248. CV 7, p. 920.
249. Fisher papers, CC.
250. WSC 3, p. 457.
251. CV 7, p. 921.
252. WSC 3, p. 459.
253. CV 7, p. 922.
254. CV 7, pp. 924–925.
255. CV 7, p. 941.
256. CV 7, p. 919.
257. Ibid.
258. CV 7, pp. 925–926.
259. CV 7, pp. 926–927.

260. Churchill, *The World Crisis.*
261. CV 7, p. 927.
262. CV 7, pp. 928–929.
263. WSC 3, p. 466.
264. CV 7, p. 931.
265. CV 7, p. 933.
266. CV 7, p. 930.
267. Ibid.
268. CV 7, p. 933.
269. WSC 3, pp. 467–468.
270. CV 7, p. 940.
271. Churchill, *The World Crisis.*
272. CV 7, pp. 943–944.
273. CV 7, pp. 940–941.
274. CV 7, pp. 952–954.
275. Ibid.
276. Hobhouse, *Inside Asquith's Cabinet.*
277. J. A. Spender, *Life, Journalism and Politics* (New York, undated).
278. V. W. Germains, *Gallipoli* (London, 1930).
279. Dardanelles Commission Report, PRO.
280. Churchill, *The World Crisis.*
281. C. Asquith, *Diaries* (New York, 1969).

XI Duchy of Lancaster

1. CV 7, p. 1017.
2. Churchill, *The World Crisis.*
3. CV 7, p. 973.
4. CV 7, p. 1033.
5. Thurso papers, CC.
6. Ibid.
7. WSC 3, p. 479.
8. CV 7, p. 1074.
9. Hassall, *Edward Marsh.*
10. CV 7, p. 987.
11. CV 7, p. 989.
12. CV 7, p. 993.
13. CV 7, pp. 994–995.
14. CV 7, p. 982.

15. Hamilton, *Gallipoli Diary.*
16. CV 7, p. 1032.
17. E. Ashmead-Bartlett, *The Uncensored Dardanelles* (London, 1928).
18. Asquith papers, Bodleian, Oxford.
19. CV 7, p. 1015.
20. CV 7, pp. 1064–1065.
21. John Spencer-Churchill, *A Churchill Canvas* (Boston, 1961).
22. CV 7, p. 1042.
23. WSC 3, pp. 502–503.
24. WSC 3, p. 505.
25. Fisher papers, CC.
26. CV 7, pp. 1081–1082.

27. CV 7, p. 1084.
28. CV 7, pp. 1086–1087.
29. CV 7, p. 1097.
30. CV 7, p. 1103.
31. C. Asquith, *Diaries.*
32. CV 7, pp. 1125–1130.
33. CV 7, pp. 1140–1144.
34. CV 7, pp. 1145–1149.
35. CV 7, p. 1138.
36. CV 7, p. 1156.
37. CV 7, p. 1155.
38. WSC 3, p. 529.
39. CV 7, pp. 1157–1162.
40. CV 7, pp. 1169–1170.
41. CV 7, p. 1171.
42. Stevenson, *A Diary.*
43. Ibid.
44. Ibid.
45. Jenkins, *Asquith.*
46. Thurso papers, CC.
47. CV 7, pp. 1182–1183.
48. WSC 3, p. 539.
49. Hamilton, *Gallipoli Diary.*
50. CV 7, pp. 1192–1193.
51. CV 7, pp. 1200–1201.
52. CV 7, pp. 1209–1210.
53. *Hansard,* Nov. 15, 1915.
54. WSC 3, pp. 549–550.
55. Stevenson, *A Diary.*
56. Bonham Carter, *Winston Churchill.*
57. CV 7, pp. 1217–1218.
58. Churchill, *The World Crisis.*
59. Hamilton, *Gallipoli Diary.*
60. Balfour papers, BL.
61. WSC 3, p. 557.
62. Jenkins, *Asquith.*
63. WSC 3, pp. 558–559.
64. Jenkins, *Asquith.*
65. Balfour papers, BL.
66. CV 7, p. 1244.
67. Bonar Law papers, HL.
68. CV 7, p. 1245.
69. Bonham Carter, *Winston Churchill.*
70. Lloyd George papers, HL.
71. WSC 3, p. 566.
72. CV 7, pp. 1249–1250.
73. CV 7, p. 1279.
74. *Hansard,* Nov. 15, 1915.
75. Ibid.
76. Ibid.
77. Marder, *Fear God and Dread Nought.*
78. CV 7, p. 1257.
79. CV 7, p. 1271.
80. Stevenson, *A Diary.*
81. CV 7, p. 1267.
82. CV 7, p. 1272.
83. CV 7, pp. 1268–1269.
84. CV 7, p. 1273.
85. *The Keyes Papers,* edited by Paul Halpern, Vol. I (London, 1980).
86. Josiah Wedgwood, *Memoirs of a Fighting Life* (London, 1941).
87. Hassall, *Edward Marsh.*
88. Bonham Carter, *Winston Churchill.*
89. Martin, *Jennie.*
90. CV 7, p. 1275.
91. Churchill, *Lord Randolph Churchill.*
92. CV 7, p. 1277.
93. Bonham Carter, *Winston Churchill.*
94. CV 7, p. 1097.
95. CV 6, p. 499.
96. CV 6, p. 484.
97. CV 6, p. 742.
98. Longford, *A Pilgrimage of Passion.*
99. Ibid.
100. WSC 1, p. 150.

Index

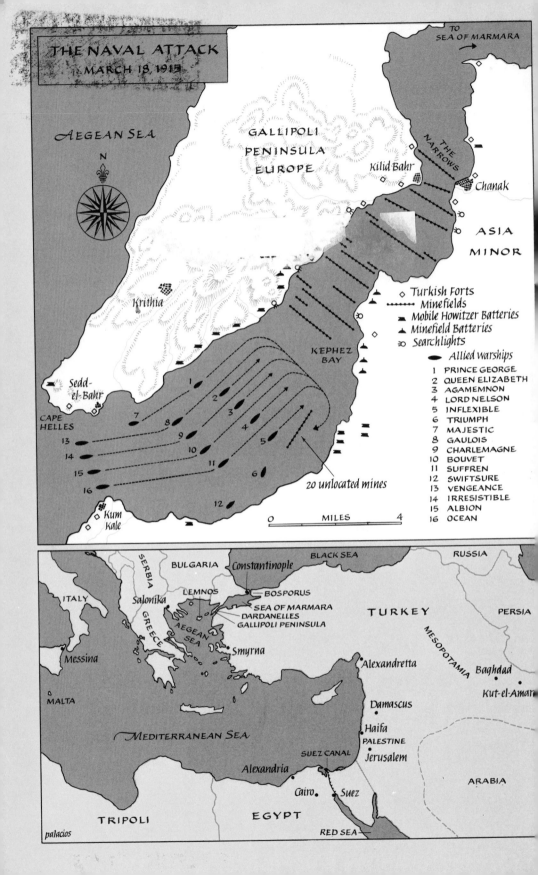

THE NAVAL ATTACK
MARCH 18, 1915

TO
SEA OF MARMARA

AEGEAN SEA

N

GALLIPOLI
PENINSULA
EUROPE

Kilid Bahr

THE NARROWS

Chanak

ASIA
MINOR

◇ Turkish Forts
•••• Minefields
⊶ Mobile Howitzer Batteries
▲ Minefield Batteries
ⴲ Searchlights
● Allied warships

Krithia

Sedd-
el-Bahr

CAPE
HELLES

KEPHEZ
BAY

7
1
2
3
4
5
6
8
9
10
11
12
13
14
15
16

20 unlocated mines

Kum
Kale

0   MILES   4

1 PRINCE GEORGE
2 QUEEN ELIZABETH
3 AGAMEMNON
4 LORD NELSON
5 INFLEXIBLE
6 TRIUMPH
7 MAJESTIC
8 GAULOIS
9 CHARLEMAGNE
10 BOUVET
11 SUFFREN
12 SWIFTSURE
13 VENGEANCE
14 IRRESISTIBLE
15 ALBION
16 OCEAN

BLACK SEA

RUSSIA

SERBIA

BULGARIA

Constantinople

ITALY

Salonika

LEMNOS

BOSPORUS

SEA OF MARMARA
DARDANELLES
GALLIPOLI PENINSULA

TURKEY

PERSIA

GREECE

AEGEAN
SEA

Smyrna

Messina

Alexandretta

MESOPOTAMIA

Baghdad

MALTA

Kut-el-Amara

Damascus

MEDITERRANEAN SEA

Haifa
PALESTINE
Jerusalem

ARABIA

SUEZ CANAL

Alexandria

Cairo

Suez

palacios

TRIPOLI

EGYPT

RED SEA